Ethics in Counseling and Psychotherapy

Standards, Research, and Emerging Issues

THIRD EDITION

Elizabeth Reynolds Welfel
Cleveland State University

Beth Carnes)
402-755-4394

THOMSON
———※———
BROOKS/COLE

Australia • Brazil • Canada • Mexico • Singapore • Spain • United Kingdom • United States

THOMSON

BROOKS/COLE

Ethics in Counseling and Psychotherapy: Standards, Research, and Emerging Issues, 3rd Edition
Elizabeth Reynolds Welfel

Publisher/Executive Editor, Counseling: Lisa Gebo
Acquisitions Editor, Counseling: Marquita Flemming
Assistant Editor: Monica Arvin
Editorial Assistant: Christine Northup
Technology Project Manager: Barry Connolly
Marketing Manager: Caroline Concilla
Marketing Assistant: Rebecca Weisman
Project Manager, Editorial Production: Adam Grafa
Creative Director: Rob Hugel

Art Director: Vernon Boes
Print Buyer: Doreen Suruki
Permissions Editor: Stephanie Lee
Production Service: Graphic World Publishing Services
Copy Editor: Graphic World Publishing Services
Cover Designer: Brenda Duke
Cover Printer: Coral Graphic Services, Inc.
Compositor: Graphic World Inc.
Printer: Thomson/West

Printed in the United States of America
2 3 4 5 6 7 09 08 07 06

For more information about our products, contact us at:
Thomson Learning Academic Resource Center
1-800-423-0563
For permission to use material from this text or product,
submit a request online at **http://www.thomsonrights.com**.
Any additional questions about permissions can be
submitted by e-mail to **thomsonrights@thomson.com**.

Thomson Higher Education
10 Davis Drive
Belmont, CA 94002-3098
USA

Library of Congress Control Number: 2005933934

ISBN 0-534-62833-8

Excerpts on pp. 273, 275, 278, 280, and 285 are reprinted by permission of the American School Counselor Association.

Appendix B and its excerpts throughout this text are Copyright 2002 by the American Psychological Association. Reproduced with permission.

Ethics in Counseling and Psychotherapy

Standards, Research, and Emerging Issues

To F.M.W.—33 years is not enough.

About the Author

Elizabeth Reynolds Welfel is professor and director of the doctoral programs in counseling at Cleveland State University. In 2004, Cleveland State awarded her the Distinguished Faculty Award for her teaching and research in professional ethics. She has also served on the counseling faculty at Boston College and was a teaching fellow at the University of Minnesota prior to receiving her doctorate there in 1979. In addition to this book, Dr. Welfel has co-authored *The Counseling Process* (with Lewis Patterson) and has co-edited *The Mental Health Desk Reference* (with Elliott Ingersoll). She has been publishing in the field of professional ethical issues in counseling for 25 years. Her special interests are the process of ethical decision making, the design of ethics education to promote responsible practice, and the ethical use of technology in counseling practice. Dr. Welfel's involvement in these topics began when she was a graduate student at the University of Minnesota, doing research on moral and intellectual development in adulthood. Her fascination with the process by which adults sort through moral and intellectual dilemmas in their lives eventually focused on the unique moral dilemmas that the counseling profession presents to its practitioners.

Ethics is in origin the art of recommending to others the sacrifices required for cooperation with oneself.

-Bertrand Russell

Contents

Preface

The goal of this book is to sensitize readers to a wide range of ethical issues in the practice of counseling and psychotherapy and to provide them with resources upon which they can rely to help them deal responsibly with such issues. The book uses the codes of ethics and guidelines of the major professional associations (American Counseling Association, American Psychological Association, and the American School Counselor Association) to familiarize readers with the fundamental standards for responsible practice, and also includes analysis of the writings of ethics scholars and citations of relevant research. Ethics codes alone do not answer many ethical questions practitioners face, but the writings of scholars and the relevant research can help them respond appropriately to complex and confusing ethical issues not directly discussed in the code. For example, Chapter 7 includes analysis of the ethical considerations in nonerotic touch in counseling and psychotherapy, Chapter 4 discusses the emerging challenges to confidentiality in electronic communications with clients and colleagues, and Chapter 11 discusses the ethical issues in coaching.

The book also presents a 10-stage model of ethical decision making and shows its application to a variety of ethical dilemmas. The aim of this model is to guide readers through complex dilemmas in a systematic way. Coping with ethical issues in practice can be an intense, emotional experience. The availability of a systematic model for analyzing ethical issues helps practitioners make decisions that are reasoned and client-centered even when they feel strong emotions. Numerous cases for discussion are also offered, many of which include extensive analysis using the codes and related literature. Cases for independent analysis are available both in the text and in the supplemental *Instructors Guide and Test Bank for Ethics in Counseling and Psychotherapy* (Wadsworth, 2006). The cases used in this book tend not to have simple answers. Instead, they are designed to present realistic, complex, and sometimes confusing scenarios that mirror situations that counselors may encounter.

Another major goal of the book is to devote comprehensive attention to major ethical issues that confront practitioners—such as confidentiality, informed consent, dual relationships, and competence to practice—and the ethical issues that practitioners experience in special settings. Thus, the book addresses the unique concerns of school counselors, community counselors, group and family counselors, researchers, and counselor educators. In addition, the content of the book includes material on emerging ethical issues in counseling and psychotherapy, such as ethics in electronic communications with clients and colleagues, managed mental health care, forensic practice, and consultation. Because sensitivity to multicultural issues is so crucial in responsible practice, that topic is interwoven throughout many chapters and is discussed in more depth in its own chapter.

Lastly, the book aims to help readers understand the philosophical and historical underpinnings of current ethical standards and to tie ethical standards to important legal rulings and statutes. Such knowledge is especially valuable in situations at the cutting edge of practice. I do not shy away from addressing controversies in the profession, and in these discussions I attempt to provide insight into each side of the argument. My approach to the text is not relativistic, however. The standards of the profession were not arbitrarily determined, and I show readers the reasoning and values underlying those standards.

The Intended Audience

The book has several potential audiences. Masters and doctoral students in counseling, counseling psychology, and psychotherapy are likely to be the primary audience, but the book will also be useful to professionals seeking to extend their knowledge about ethical decision making, to advanced undergraduate students, and to graduate students in related professions such as pastoral counseling and educational psychology. Consumers of psychotherapeutic services may also find its contents helpful in their search for a responsible professional. Its comprehensive approach to the subject matter and its inclusion of codes of ethics as appendices make it appropriate for use as the main text in professional ethics or professional issues courses. The book contains an extensive reference list and recommended readings for each chapter, so readers who want to explore the ethics scholarship in greater depth are directed to the proper resources.

The Structure of the Book

The book contains four parts. Part One provides a framework for understanding ethical decision making and gives readers a specific step-by-step method for resolving complex ethical questions. In this section, I describe the relationship of professional ethics in counseling to the broader discipline of ethics, integrate relevant literature from developmental psychology, and present a new model of ethical decision making. Part Two reviews the fundamental ethical issues for counselors and therapists, including the ethics of competence to practice, confidentiality, informed consent, multiple relationships, responsible assessment, and multiple-person therapies. It ends with an extended discussion of the ethical issues in counseling in a multicultural society. Ethical issues in special settings are the focus of Part Three. Its topics include the ethics of supervision, teaching, research, community practice, forensic activities, consultation, and school counseling. This portion of the book deals most extensively with the emerging ethical dilemmas in the profession, such as the ethical dimensions of managed care and therapy mandated by the courts. Part Four, the final section, deals with a topic often neglected—the ethical responsibilities of those who recognize that they have violated the ethical standards of their profession. Because self-monitoring and personal accountability are at the core of the profession's values, the book discusses the steps professionals can take to redress their own misconduct and to reduce the likelihood that mistakes will recur. In that way, it is unique among the professional ethics books currently published. That chapter also includes a review of the disciplinary actions against counselors and psychologists and an analysis of the patterns of violations. Each of the 15 chapters also includes a set of questions and cases for further discussion and a list of recommended readings.

The chapters are presented in a logical order, but readers who choose to follow a different sequence will not be at a disadvantage. Also, those who find particular chapters irrelevant to their purposes may omit that material without compromising their comprehension of other parts of the book.

Because I refer repeatedly to the current codes of ethics of the American Counseling Association and the American Psychological Association, I have omitted the dates of their publication in all but their first citations. Continuous use of the publication dates would serve no useful purpose. I do, however, place dates with any other version of the ethics codes that I mention in the book.

Acknowledgments

I wish to thank the many individuals who assisted me in this project. My students and colleagues at Cleveland State have encouraged me, offered valuable insights into the content, and often taken on extra work to free me to make a full commitment to this book. Carl Rak deserves special recognition for his support, as does Lew Patterson, without whose mentoring I might not have ever written the first edition of this book. My graduate assistants, Karen Wallis and Tia Piacquadio, have done yeoman service well beyond their official duties. The following reviewers offered perceptive and extensive feedback on the chapters: William Casile, Duquesne University; Paula R. Danzinger, William Paterson University of New Jersey; Dennis Engels, University of North Texas; Rex D. Filer, Adams State College; Maura Krushinski, Duquesne University; and Rita Sommers-Flanagan, University of Montana. Their careful attention to the manuscript has significantly improved the book.

The editorial staff at Brooks/Cole provided just the right combination of support and challenge for the project. I owe a special debt to Marquita Flemming, counseling editor; Adam Grafa, production editor; and Caroline Concilla, marketing editor, who were delightful to work with. I also thank Anne Williams for her attentive assistance with copyediting.

Most of all, I extend my thanks to my family—to my spouse, whose calm and thoughtful responses to my worries and frustrations with writing always helped me do better work, and to my son, whose compassion and commitment to ethical values far outstretch any level I can hope to attain.

Elizabeth Reynolds Welfel

PART ONE

A Framework for Understanding Professional Ethical Standards

Chapter 1

Introduction to Professional Ethics
A Psychology and Philosophy for Ethical Standards

Counselors, psychologists, social workers, and other therapists make some audacious claims. They assert that they are so uniquely skilled at helping people with their personal problems that they deserve to be licensed by the state and fairly paid for their services. Moreover, they claim that the state should prevent people without their training and credentials from offering the same services. Apparently, this argument has been quite convincing because currently all 50 states and 10 Canadian provinces license psychologists and social workers, 48 states (and the District of Columbia) license professional counselors for independent practice, and 47 states license professional marriage and family therapists. With this public endorsement of their special competence to help people in need, counselors, psychologists, and other psychotherapists offer hope to those confused, distressed, or traumatized. They advertise counseling and psychotherapy as processes wherein people can learn to think more clearly, act in more self-enhancing ways, cope with psychological disorders, and feel better.

To be responsible professionals, counselors' claims of skill in relieving people's pain must be based on scientific evidence of effectiveness to carry out those interventions to a good result for the client. Otherwise, counselors are little different than the "snake oil" salespeople who sold false cures to desperate, gullible people without sufficient education to understand the nature of their ailments or the absurdity of the claims they were hearing. Thankfully, mental health professionals can point to a large body of research that demonstrates the effectiveness of competent counseling and psychotherapy in both natural settings and research clinics (for example, see Lambert, 2003; Seligman, 1995; Sexton, Whiston, Bleuer, & Walz, 1997). That audacious claim of help for suffering, then, is based in fact, and well-trained professionals can deliver on their pledge.

In essence, then, professional ethics is about being confident one has the correct combination of attributes and skills to alleviate human distress as promised. Specifically, ethics encompasses four dimensions:

1. Having sufficient knowledge, skill, and judgment to use efficacious interventions
2. Respecting the human dignity and freedom of the client(s)
3. Using the power inherent in the counselor's role responsibly
4. Acting in ways that promote public confidence in the profession of counseling

Pared down to those four essentials, acting ethically sounds simple. The first necessary ingredient seems to be a quality education so that one is knowledgeable. Virtually all states require counselors and therapists to pass a licensing examination, have supervised work experience, and participate in continuing education experiences to prove their knowledge and skill. The other components of ethical practice are consideration of the client's needs and rights as the highest priority, avoidance of self-advancement at the cost of the client, and transaction of one's business in a way that peers and the public cannot disparage. In practice, however, determining the combination of factors that render counseling most effective, most respectful of clients, and most in keeping with the good reputation of the profession is much more complicated. Sometimes little is known about which interventions will really be helpful, and at other times, even interventions with demonstrable effectiveness fail with a given person. In our rapidly changing profession, keeping knowledge and skills current is a difficult task. If a counselor has neglected to keep up with the literature or lacks adequate training in a given area, can he or she still provide effective service? How current does one's knowledge need to be to do effective counseling? Because no one is infallible, even the most diligent and well-trained professional will on occasion act incompetently—how can the professional (and the public) cope with this recognition?

Similarly, when counselors honor the dignity of clients by giving them free choices about their lives, they sometimes make choices contrary to their own best interest. Naturally, when a client is considering a counterproductive choice, the counselor discusses it with the client and works to help the client see its negative potential. Sometimes this review of the impact of the choice changes the client's mind. At other times, the counselor's perspective has no effect. Is it preferable for the counselor to use his or her power to limit a client's freedom by preventing the client from making a choice that will probably be regretted later? Is that an abuse of power or an appropriate extension of counselor influence? How do cultural and social factors influence the determination of which choices are in a client's best interest and which are not?

Finally, sometimes the very actions that help individual clients are actions that the public does not understand and that cause ordinary citizens to view counselors with a skeptical eye. For example, in most situations counselors are legally and ethically bound to maintain the confidentiality of the disclosures of an accused criminal about a past crime (if that person is in an ongoing counseling relationship) unless the client releases them from their obligation or a court orders them to reveal this information. This refusal to betray the client's trust often dismays and frustrates the public. Does this loyalty to the client result in more or less public confidence in the profession? This, too, is not a simple matter. Thus, living one's professional life in accordance with these principles is more complicated than it seems. Fortunately, there are a number of resources to help counselors wrestle with these issues.

Literature from Developmental Psychology

The first resource is the abundant literature on morality and moral reasoning. This literature helps counselors understand professional ethics and ethical decision making as a subset of the broader category of morality and moral decision making. It places professional codes of conduct into a context of fair, decent, and responsible human behavior and provides a framework for explaining what has gone wrong in the ethical decision-making process when misconduct occurs. Unlike other resources that focus on the content a person should consider to deal with an ethical question, the literature from developmental psychology gives a framework for conceptualizing the internal process of ethical decision making. It gives a view of the psychology of ethics. From this information, counselors derive methods to improve the quality of their own ethical decision making and find better ways to teach ethics to students and practitioners.

Components of Moral Behavior

When a person faces a moral or ethical decision, what provokes him or her to behave morally or immorally? Counselors often raise this question when they hear of a courageous or outrageous act by another professional. Rest (1983, 1994) has provided a useful framework for understanding that process. First, he defines a moral action as any behavior that can affect the welfare of another. For instance, if a person observes someone breaking into a neighbor's home, what he or she does when watching this burglary is defined in moral terms because it affects the neighbor's well-being. (Of course, the robber's actions also have a moral dimension, for the same reason.) If the person engages in an action that may benefit the neighbor, such as calling the police or trying to scare the burglar away, then that action is moral. Clearly, any attempt to help may backfire and the police may not arrive or the robber may not respond, but an action need not be successful to be moral. What makes the action moral is that one makes a good-faith effort to help the neighbor. Conversely, if one did nothing, that action could not be labeled *moral* unless the individual were endangered in some way by this burglar. We are not required by morality to risk our own welfare for another. That's why we label as heroes people who risk their own safety to help others; they have gone beyond their moral duty to ensure another's well-being.

Rest identifies four components of moral behavior that must take place if a moral action is to result—that is, before anyone can engage in an act intended to benefit another. The first of these is called *moral sensitivity,* the process of recognizing the situation as one with implications for the welfare of another. In the situation just described, it's possible that a person could see this intruder trying to break the lock on the neighbor's front door and think about the burglar's expertise, or lack thereof, with the crowbar. In these thoughts, one might even criticize or applaud the burglar's approach while silently watching the spectacle unfold. Some people might just feel grateful that the burglar did not choose their own home. Such a reaction suggests no assumption of responsibility to intervene on behalf of the neighbor and exclusive concern with one's own welfare. If these responses occurred, Rest would say that the person lacks moral sensitivity.

Translated into professional ethics, moral sensitivity means realizing the implications of one's behaviors on clients, colleagues, and the public. If a counselor at a social gathering repeats a funny story about a client, that counselor probably did not consider the welfare of the client before he or she spoke. This person has missed the moral meaning of his or her action. The person did not need to have a malicious *intent* to act immorally. In fact, immoral actions frequently result from distraction from the moral implications of actions.

To illustrate in another way, consider the counselor's actions in the following case:

The Case of Mitchell and Maria

Mitchell decides not to explain the limits of confidentiality at the start of counseling because he considers that material bureaucratic and distracting from the client's real purpose for coming. He does not intend to harm his clients and actually intends to serve a good purpose by immediately focusing on the "issue at hand." One day at the beginning of a session, Maria tells Mitchell that she has suicidal thoughts, mistakenly assuming that *everything* she says to a counselor is confidential. In reality, if a counselor believes a client to be at significant risk for suicide, he or she is obligated by the ethics code and (and probably the law) *not* to keep this material confidential. Maria's status as a minor obligates the counselor to consider her parents' rights too. When Mitchell explains the limits of confidentiality to Maria after she has already blurted out her secret, she now feels alone and betrayed, outcomes that are clearly detrimental to her already compromised welfare. She feels her lack of knowledge about the parameters of confidentiality robbed her of the choice of whether or when to disclose this private material.

Thus, Mitchell's notion that explaining the limits of confidentiality to a client is merely "bureaucratic" shows his moral insensitivity and resulted in unethical behavior. Obviously, sharing suicidal thoughts with a counselor can ultimately benefit a client. Counselors have an ethical duty to encourage clients to express such thoughts. However, when the client does not understand the implications of this disclosure, feelings of betrayal occur and the suicidal impulse may escalate when trust is broken in this way. No such negative consequences ensue when the client discloses such information after building trust in a skillful and compassionate counselor and gaining some understanding of what may happen after such a revelation.

Rest's second component of moral behavior is *moral reasoning*. Moral reasoning is the process of thinking through the alternatives once a situation has been recognized as having moral dimensions. At first glance, moral reasoning sounds like a methodical, logical process, but it usually takes place rapidly and without great deliberation. It has an emotional as well as a cognitive aspect. When a person sees a burglar at a neighbor's door, one must act quickly so the process of thinking about what action(s) would benefit the neighbor is completed in seconds. Sometimes only one alternative comes to mind—call the police. At other times, the person weighs the merits of two or more alternatives such as going outside, calling another neighbor, or getting the gun kept for protection in the bedroom. Moral reasoning is the process of evaluating the choices and deciding which is best.

The research by Kohlberg (1984), Gilligan (1982), and others suggests that not all people reason about moral issues in the same way or with the same moral maturity. In fact, these researchers posit stage models of moral development based partly on biological maturity and partly on social experience. Some research suggests that counselors at higher stages of moral development make ethical decisions more in keeping with the standards of the profession (Bombara, 2002; Uthe-Burow, 2002; Welfel & Lipsitz, 1983), but other studies contradict this finding (Doromal & Creamer, 1988; Fox, 2003; Royer, 1985).

According to Rest, the third component of morality is *moral motivation*. Once a person has evaluated the options and determined which is most moral, then that person must decide whether to go forward. For example, a counselor may have observed a colleague whose behavior with clients is inappropriate. The colleague may be missing appointments, neglecting paperwork, and showing signs of intoxication at work. The counselor recognizes this as a moral dilemma because the welfare of clients and the counseling service are at stake. The ethics codes also identify this as her ethical responsibility (American Counseling Association [ACA], 2005, Section H.2.a; American Psychological Association [APA], 2002, Sections 1.04, 1.05). She has weighed the moral alternatives and has concluded that the best course of action is confronting the colleague and insisting that he modify his behavior with clients.

Essentially, at this point the counselor asks herself, "Will I *choose* to do that which I now *know* is the right thing to do?" If she answers affirmatively, the counselor is one step closer to a moral action, but if not, then no moral action will take place. At this point competing values may interfere. Professional ethical values are not the only values operating in a person, and values that compete with ethics may take priority. These other values may be admirable—such as the commitment to earning a salary sufficient to supporting one's dependent children or the commitment to protect a person from illness—or they may be contemptible. Self-interest is one such ignoble value. The counselor may realize that if the dysfunctional colleague deteriorates even further, he may leave the practice, resulting in more clients and more income for her. Or the counselor may value harmony in the workplace more than ethics and may decide not to risk conflict among the staff. In short, this is the point in the process where the power of the counselor's ethical values is tested against other values. If the ethical values take precedence, then the counselor decides to act responsibly. Research has found that when presented with hypothetical ethical situations, graduate students in psychology indicate that they *would* do what they know they *should* do approximately 50% of the time (Bernard & Jara, 1986). Research by Betan and Stanton (1999), Fox (2003), and McDivitt (2001) report similar percentages of students and practicing school counselors who would do less than they believe they ought to do. Betan and Stanton (1999) also found that emotions played a significant part in these students' decisions; those who were more anxious about taking action and less optimistic about its effectiveness were less likely to report an unethical colleague. Practicing psychologists do somewhat better. In a related study, Bernard, Murphy, and Little (1987) found that at least two-thirds of the psychologists chose the ethical value. Two other studies (Smith, McGuire, Abbott, & Blau, 1991; Wilkins, McGuire, Abbott, & Blau, 1990) reported a similar pattern. These statistics show how strong competing values can be and how they can operate both on intellectual and emotional processes.

Of course, ethical decision making is not always fully conscious. Counselors often experience cognitive dissonance when choosing not to carry out the most responsible choice. Because counselors like to view themselves as ethical, their dilemma becomes how to retain that positive self-evaluation if they are rejecting the ethical choice. To reduce their mental discomfort, they may redefine the problem. In the case of the intoxicated colleague, the counselor might reinterpret the behaviors she sees and hypothesize that the colleague is not really drunk or that the missed appointments are not as frequent as they seem. She may even convince herself that this colleague is taking medication that affects his behavior. Of course, that may be true, but when the counselor's goal is to extricate herself from the ethical responsibility, the hypothesis is not tested and the facts of the case are not explored. Instead, she rationalizes, and thus her definition of her ethical responsibility has changed and her motivation to act declines. With this distortion of the facts, the counselor gets to avoid painful confrontation with the colleague and still view herself as ethical. This kind of self-deception may be fairly common.

If the counselor works in an environment that places a high priority on professional ethics, the risk of self-deception is reduced. Counselors in supervisory positions facilitate responsible behaviors when they make it known to their subordinates that ethics truly matter and that employees will be rewarded and not punished for taking an ethical path. In business, such leadership is called "creating an ethical culture in the organization." The competing values have less pull then, and the person who pursues the ethical action is likely to be supported and not isolated. The research of Wilkins et al. (1990) also shows that mental health professionals deviate from the ethical value more frequently when the law or code of ethics governing an issue is not clear. If, however, work climate is hostile to ethical action, Vansandt's research (2002) suggests that organizational culture can suppress an individual's inclination to act ethically.

Social and political factors also affect a person's capacity to make an ethical choice. Social norms sometimes render ethical action more difficult. A college student may believe that he or she ought to intervene to assist a gay student who is being harassed but may decline to do so because of fear of social alienation. For the same reason, a citizen in a small, homogeneous community may support legislation he or she thinks is morally wrong for fear of social reprisals.

Cultural definitions of what is ethical also vary (Pedersen, 1995, 1997). The high priority given to individual autonomy in Western cultures is not universally endorsed by other societies. Thus, culture affects not just the values that compete with ethical values but the very definition of what is ethical to some extent. (A later chapter will discuss the dilemma of a client whose parents have arranged a marriage that he does not want but which his cultural and religious tradition makes it difficult for him to refuse.)

Moral character is the final component of the process in Rest's model. Betan and Stanton (1999) use the term *resoluteness* to refer to this aspect of moral behavior. One must actually carry out the moral action to its conclusion. Doing so typically requires virtues such as compassion, integrity, and moral courage. People who lack these characteristics may change their minds or withdraw before implementing the action or when encountering resistance. In the case described in the last section, the counselor may express her concerns about the colleague's behavior, but if she receives an angry response or a revelation about personal troubles, she may back down and not ask him to stop drinking at work. A moral action cannot take place if it is not implemented. Sometimes, persevering with the moral plan is uncomfortable and has personal costs. That's where integrity and character are critical. Keeping one's eyes on the goal and on the welfare of clients in spite of other pressures is often a difficult task. Again, working with other professionals who are committed to the ethical ideals of the profession eases the difficulty of implementing the moral action.

Codes of Ethics

The second resource for ethical decision making is the code of ethics of the professional association. These codes have a variety of names, but they all specify the rules of conduct and standards of care for members. These codes represent "both the highest and lowest standards of practice expected for the practitioner" (Levy, 1974, p. 267). Licensed professional counselors and school counselors rely on the *Code of Ethics and Standards of Practice* of the American Counseling Association (2005), psychologists rely on the *Ethical Principles of Psychologists and Code of Conduct* of the American Psychological Association (2002), and social workers rely on the *Code of Ethics* of the National Association of Social Workers (NASW, 1999). Because many mental health professionals are members of more than one professional association, they often can refer to two or more of these codes of ethics to guide them through ethical dilemmas. In addition, professional associations supplement the codes with casebooks (Nagy, 2005), commentary (Fisher, 2003; Knapp & VandeCreek, 2003), and guidelines for practice related to specific populations that have come to their attention. For example, APA has published ethical guidelines for providing services to culturally diverse populations (APA, 2003a) and older adults (APA, 2003b). Other organizations have similar specialized codes, and a sampling of these is contained in Appendix C.

These codes represent the official statements of the professions about what is expected of members, and all members are held accountable for actions that violate the code. When they accept membership in the professional association or a credential from a licensing agency, professionals are agreeing to abide by the stipulations of the code in their professional activities even if the values of the code contradict in some way the moral values that guide their personal lives. Each professional association has established an ethics committee and empowered it to enforce its code. (Most state associations also have ethics committees and standards, but they rely heavily on the national codes to determine their rules of conduct.) ACA first published its code of ethics in 1961 and has revised it five times since (most recently in 2005). APA produced its first code in 1953 and published revisions in 1959, 1981, 1992, and 2002.

The intent of the code is to guide the professional through the most common pitfalls in practice and to identify the ethical goals of the profession. Thus, codes of ethics define prescribed (required) activities of counselors, such as explaining the benefits and risks of counseling to clients, as well as prohibited activities, such as having a sexual relationship with a current client. Codes also define the conditions under which certain other behaviors are permissible. For example, the ACA and APA codes both elaborate on the circumstances under which a professional can accept barter rather than money for services (ACA,

2005, Section A.10.d; APA, 2002, Section 6.05). Moreover, codes include "aspirational statements" that clarify the fundamental ethical values of the profession. For example, ACA's code (2005) states in its Preamble, "Association members recognize diversity and embrace a cross-cultural approach in support of the worth, dignity, potential, and uniqueness of people within their social and cultural contexts" (p. 1). Codes of ethics are usually included in regulations governing the practice of counseling and psychotherapy in the states. Thus, a licensed professional is accountable not only to the professional association but also to the state licensing board. This means that acting unethically automatically violates the laws in a number of states. All members of a professional association are thereby obligated to be familiar with the published codes and guidelines and to act accordingly. Ignorance of the codes does not excuse problematic behavior. The professions assert that if practitioners are benefiting from their professional identity, they have a duty to know and respect ethical standards. Here is the wording on that point from the ACA *Code of Ethics* Section H.1.a (2005): "Lack of knowledge or misunderstanding of an ethical responsibility is not a defense against a charge of unethical conduct."

Advantages and Limitations of Codes of Ethics

For the individual practitioner, the major contribution of a code is the support it gives the professional faced with an ethical question. A prudent counselor always refers to the code because a review of the applicable standard often reveals the responsible action, and no further deliberation is necessary. No code of ethics provides a blueprint for resolving all ethical issues, but codes represent the best judgment of one's peers about common problems and shared professional values. The existence and enforcement of codes of ethics also demonstrate that counselors take seriously their responsibility to protect the public welfare, thus enhancing the reputation of the profession and minimizing the damage done by irresponsible practitioners. The lengthy process of obtaining input from members about new revisions of the code and educating them about those changes keeps the code in the limelight so that members are frequently reminded of its importance. The inclusion of statements of aspirational ethics also furnishes members with a definition of what their colleagues consider the ethical ideal.

Codes also have limitations. First, the members of a professional organization ordinarily work with diverse populations in a variety of settings and engage in different activities. This variability means that the code must be written broadly. Its application to any one setting is limited. Second, because the profession changes rapidly, with new forms of practice and new populations emerging constantly, parts of the codes are outdated as soon as they are published, despite the best efforts of their writers. Codes, therefore, do not uniformly address cutting-edge issues (Mabe & Rollin, 1986) such as Internet counseling or impact of human immunodeficiency virus (HIV) infection on professional practice, and counselors wrestling with such dilemmas must find other support. In addition, codes are developed within organizations that also have other values and priorities, so that the resulting documents sometimes represent what the board of directors can agree to, rather an ethical ideal. For example, the first 15 drafts of the 1992 APA code banned all sexual intimacies with former clients, but the version that the governing body approved (and that is still included in the current APA code) allowed sexual contact with former clients after 2 years under limited conditions. Gabbard (1994) regards this change as a result of compromise and self-interest rather than concern about the public welfare. The self-interest of professional associations also dilutes the clarity and strength of other statements in the codes. Ladd (1991) makes another important point about the limitations of a code of ethics—it can focus so much attention on the minor issues of the profession (such as the permissibility of barter) that it distracts professionals from the major questions (such as the ethical responsibility to promote social justice).

Most important to note, however, is that codes of ethics are not cookbooks for responsible behavior. To take the cookbook analogy further, codes fail to provide recipes for healthy ethical decision making, although they do offer two essential components of cookbooks—goals for good ethical nutrition and, as Handelsman has noted, lists of ethical poisons (Kuther, 2003). Largely because of the limitations already mentioned, they provide unequivocal guidance for only a few problems. For example, there is no doubt about the prohibition of a sexual relationship with a current client. The codes state that it is *never* appropriate. To quote section A.5.a of the ACA code, "Sexual or romantic counselor–client interactions or relationships with current clients, their romantic partners, or their family members are prohibited." For many other issues, however, the guidance is not so clear. The following situation illustrates the help a code typically provides:

The Case of Dr. Remmard and Ms. Harks

Ms. Harks serves on a civic committee with Dr. Remmard, a counseling psychologist, and approaches him for help with depressive feelings. She says that she feels comfortable with him now that she's gotten to know him on this committee and hears that Dr. R. has a good reputation in the community. May Dr. Remmard accept her into counseling while they are serving together on the committee?

The codes address this matter but do not make the decision clear cut. (Note that the term *multiple relationship* means having a second kind of relationship with a client in addition to the counselor–client relationship).

APA *Ethical Principles,* Section 3.05: Multiple Relationships

(a) A multiple relationship occurs when a psychologist is in a professional role with a person and (1) at the same time is in another role with the same person, (2) at the same time is in a relationship with a person closely associated with or related to the person with whom the psychologist has the professional relationship, or (3) promises to enter into another relationship in the future with the person or a person closely associated with or related to the person.

A psychologist refrains from entering into a multiple relationship if the multiple relationship could reasonably be expected to impair the psychologist's objectivity, competence, or effectiveness in performing his or her functions as a psychologist, or otherwise risks exploitation or harm to the person with whom the professional relationship exists.

The psychologist must interpret the relevant code and apply its provisions. The code does supply the questions the counselor must ask, such as, Is this a social or close personal relationship? Can I avoid it? If I cannot, how do I ascertain that I will be objective with a client whom I see periodically in another setting? The code even gives recommendations for responding to the last point. However, in the end, Dr. Remmard must sort out the ethical considerations and use his best judgment. The counselor must deliberate about the nature of the connection with this woman and the degree to which objectivity may be compromised and the client's best interests served. The client's access to other qualified counselors is also a factor to consider.

On other ethical issues, the code provides even less guidance. Consider a counselor who works primarily with children and adolescents. This professional needs support in determining how much material from counseling must be shared with parents and guardians and what the disclosure of that material means to the progress of the counseling relationship with the child. Here is what the ACA code includes on this topic:

ACA *Code of Ethics,* Section A.2.d: Inability to Give Consent
When counseling minors or persons unable to give voluntary consent, counselors seek the assent of clients to services, and include them in decision-making as appropriate. Counselors recognize the need to balance the ethical rights of clients to make choices, their capacity to give consent or assent to receive services, and parental or familial legal rights and responsibilities to protect these clients and make decisions on their behalf.

These statements are very general and say only that inclusion of parents or guardians is not prohibited and that the criterion for determining when to disclose is the broad principle of acting in the client's best interest. This approach provides relatively little help to a counselor struggling with an adolescent client who feels alienated from his family and wants the counselor to keep his violations of curfew and experimentation with alcohol secret from his parents. The APA code makes even less reference to this topic in Section 3.10.b: "For persons who are legally incapable of giving informed consent, psychologists nevertheless (1) provide an appropriate explanation, (2) seek the individual's assent, (3) consider such persons' preferences and best interests, and (4) obtain appropriate permission from a legally authorized person, if such substitute consent is permitted or required by law. When consent by a legally authorized person is not permitted or required by law, psychologists take reasonable steps to protect the individual's rights and welfare." Here, the burden of analyzing ethical issues falls squarely on the professional and requires careful reasoning to judge the best solution. The counselor must turn to other resources to guide this decision-making process.

In short, ethics codes do not always simplify ethical decision making and do not provide easy answers to complex questions. They serve instead as the critical starting point for developing independent judgment based on the shared wisdom of the profession. Counselors who ignore them do so at their own peril; counselors who view them as the prescription for all ethical issues are equally at risk.

Literature from Philosophy

The third resource for making responsible ethical judgments is the growing body of literature that ties professional ethics to philosophers' writings on ethics and explains the philosophical underpinnings of the ethics codes. This scholarship defines the ethical principles and theories that form the rationale for the specific statements in the codes. (See Freeman, 2000, for a detailed analysis of the relationship between philosophical principles and professional ethics.) In essence, these writings connect the standards for professional conduct to the wisdom of the ages and are of greatest use in coping with the most difficult and confusing ethical dilemmas. The philosophical literature also clarifies the values and virtues underlying the actions of responsible professionals and highlights that ethical practice always requires value judgments on the part of the professional. Some authors (for example, Freeman, 2000; Urofsky & Engels, 2003) make a strong argument for extensive integration of moral philosophy into the ethics education of counseling professionals. Consider the following situation:

The Case of Annette and Archie
Archie, a 17-year-old student, tells his high school counselor in a counseling session that the claim he made of sexual abuse by his stepfather is not true. He now says that he fabricated the story because he wanted his mother to end her relationship with his stepfather, who has punched her many times. Archie made the statements about abuse to his coach, who reported them to authorities. As his school counselor, Annette was then in-

formed of the report when she began individual counseling with Archie. They have had four sessions.

Should Annette maintain confidentiality if the client does not agree to release this information? The counselor here is in a true ethical dilemma because there are potentially harmful consequences no matter what she does. The welfare of the boy, his mother, and his stepfather are all at stake. Reference to the ethics codes does not resolve the question, although it does provide some relevant information. The codes stress the importance of confidentiality as a protection of the client's right to privacy and indicate an exception to that right when laws demand and in situations of clear and imminent danger to the client or others. The codes inform the counselor that the decision to violate confidentiality should not be taken lightly, and then they broadly define the exceptions. Does the law require disclosure? Consultation with an attorney may be necessary to answer that question. Is there a clear and imminent danger? There would be if the boy were talking of shooting the stepfather or committing suicide because he felt so hopeless. But is subjecting the stepfather to an investigation by children's services, and possibly causing the stepfather to leave the home, the same kind of danger? If criminal charges were brought against the stepfather and he faced incarceration, would that be clear and imminent danger? Is it Annette's responsibility to bring this information to the investigators from children's services, or is it their responsibility to ascertain the facts of the case? Is disclosing the confidential information ethical if it results in the boy terminating the counseling relationship at a time when he is in serious psychological distress and feels alienated from his family? Should the boy's age influence the counselor's decision?

In this situation, the counselor needs more information than the codes provide. An understanding of how philosophers conceptualize and prioritize ethical obligations can shed light on the problem and provide more structure to the decision-making process. (We will return to this case in the next chapter.) As Chapter 2 also describes in detail, the ethics codes spring from several ethical principles. By thinking through these ethical principles, counselors can better evaluate their options in such complex situations. For example, Kitchener (1984, 2000) suggests that five ethical principles underlie professional codes of conduct in human service and medical professions. These principles include respect for autonomy, beneficence (the obligation to do good), nonmaleficence (the avoidance of harm), fidelity to promises made, and justice. In confusing dilemmas, counselors should weigh the alternatives according to these broader ethical principles. Beauchamp and Childress (2001) and Cohen and Cohen (1999) add the principle of veracity, the obligation to be truthful in professional interactions, to this list.

Philosophers go on to describe another level of ethical reasoning that they term *ethical theories* (Freeman, 2000; Kitchener, 1984). Consideration of ethical theories is needed when the ethical principles do not resolve the problem. As noted earlier, the next chapter elaborates on both ethical principles and ethical theories in the context of professional practice.

Other philosophers offer an alternative way to think about ethics. They talk not about ethical principles or rules or about ethical problem solving; instead, they talk about an ethics of virtue. They are not interested so much in how professionals behave as in who they ought to be (May, 1984). This scholarship centers on the qualities professionals should develop and the habits of character they need to reach the profession's goals. Reference to such scholarship keeps the profession's attention not just on the rules of behavior and the criteria for applying those rules but also on the moral ideals of the profession (Cohen & Cohen, 1999; Jordan & Meara, 1990; Meara, Schmidt, & Day, 1996). The five virtues most commonly referred to in this literature are as follows: *integrity,* the capacity to act consistently on deeply held personal values; *prudence,* the ability to act with discernment and to restrain impulses to act in good faith; *trustworthiness,* the capacity to act and follow through on promises and commitments even in the face of difficulty; *compassion,* deep concern for another's welfare and sympathy with their pain; and *respectfulness,* an attitude that recognizes others' concerns and that commits the person to avoid actions that diminish another's rights or dignity.

Another major philosophical perspective on professional ethics comes from feminist theory (Hill, Glaser & Harden, 1998; Lerman & Porter, 1990; Nodding, 1984). This view emphasizes systemic variables such as the power of the participants within the system and the impact of race, class, and oppression as crucially important to the ethical decision-making process. Feminist theorists also advocate for attention to the uniqueness of each client and as much equality in decision making between client and professional as possible. An addition to the literature on philosophical influences on ethical standards comes from the writings of Cottone (2001), who advocates a social constructivist model of ethical decision making in which ethical choice is viewed as primarily a socially interactive process and not a process that is internal to the individual.

Research on Professional Ethics

Another important source of information is the professional literature that examines specific ethical issues in great detail, such as the limits of confidentiality with children and the ethical considerations in advertising counseling services. During the past 35 years, published materials on ethics have increased dramatically. These books and articles are particularly helpful for professionals trying to cope responsibly with new and emerging areas of practice where the codes of ethics are less likely to offer specific guidelines for ethical conduct. In controversial areas, such as sexual contact with former clients or the limits of confidentiality with clients who have HIV, these writings give practitioners a sense of the dimensions of the debate and the critical factors that influence experts' views on the issue. These resources are also free from the political and organizational pressures that often influence the development of ethics codes. They usually encourage professionals to practice in the most responsible way possible.

In the case of Archie, the boy who tells his counselor he lied about sexual abuse, this literature can assist the counselor in several ways. It more fully defines the meaning of "clear and imminent danger" from the code (for example, Swenson, 1997), clarifies the limits of confidentiality with adolescents (Gustafson & McNamara, 1987; Lawrence & Kurpius, 2000; Taylor & Adelman, 1998), and explores the potential effects of breaking confidentiality on the future of the counseling relationship (Baird & Rupert, 1987; Nowell & Spruill, 1993; Rokop, 2003). Used in conjunction with the codes and ethical principles, this literature offers the counselor an opportunity to consult with the most knowledgeable and experienced scholars in the profession on a given ethical issue.

The Scope of Unethical Practice

Ethics scholars have also researched the most common types of ethics offenses and the practitioner characteristics associated with them. Their findings warn counselors about red flag issues and the circumstances under which others have fallen short. Specifically, researchers have studied the pattern of complaints to licensing boards and professional associations, the nature of malpractice suits filed against counselors and psychologists, and the self-reports of professionals in national surveys. In addition, ethics committees publish annual accounts of their activities and the outcomes of the cases they handle (see, for example, APA Ethics Committee, 2004; Kocet & Freeman, 2005). Moreover, when APA and

ACA terminate members for unethical behavior, the committees send notice of the termination to all members with their dues statements. APA also publishes the names of all individuals found guilty of less serious offenses and the punishment imposed. Many state licensing boards are also posting all disciplinary actions taken against licensed mental health professionals in their states. California, for instance, provides both summary data on the recent history of disciplinary action at www.psychboard.ca.gov/enforce/stats.pdf and the specific rulings against psychologists disciplined in the last several years at www.psychboard.ca.gov/enforce/actions.html.

From all these data, several important findings emerge. First, although some variation occurs depending on the source of the data, the same problems appear across different studies—sexual misconduct, improper practices, and dual relationships. Ethics complaints about psychologists are related primarily to sexual misconduct and other dual relationships, insurance or fee problems, and inappropriate professional practice. Inappropriate practice means working in areas where one is not competent, violating confidentiality, or making fraudulent or misleading public statements (APA Ethics Committee, 2004). Complaints related to child custody evaluations have occurred more commonly in recent years. For example, in 1999, 10% of the complaints to APA dealt with child custody matters, and in 2003 16% of the 25 new cases opened related to child custody. Nearly 80% of complaints that came to APA in 2003 were forwarded by a state licensing board after the psychologist lost his or her license to practice in that state. In such a circumstance the APA Ethics Committee investigates and makes a separate ruling on the case.

The formal investigations opened by ACA's Ethics Committee also center on violations related to the counseling relationship, such as sexual misconduct (Hubert & Freeman, 2004; Kocet & Freeman, 2005). The pattern is somewhat different for informal inquiries brought to the committee. Of the 1236 informal inquiries brought forward in 2002 and 2003, nearly half (47%) of these involved issues of confidentiality. The second most frequent category included questions related to the counseling relationship (n = 305). An analysis of the complaints to NASW over an 11-year period shows the familiar pattern of a predominance of violations of dual relationship standards, both sexual and nonsexual (Strom-Gottfried, 1999, 2003). More than 56% of the cases brought against social workers fell into this category.

The total number of complaints filed each year is small when compared to the number of members of each organization. APA has 88,500 members but opened an average of 30 cases per year in the period between 1982 and 2003. ACA, with a membership of almost 60,000, received only 12 complaints against counselors between 2002 and 2003. That means that for APA, in a 23-year period, the number of active cases per member was 1 per 2950 members, or 0.0003% of the membership. Data from state licensing boards also suggest that very few mental health professionals are likely to have an ethics complaint filed against them. Van Horne (2004) reports that in 2001 only 1809 complaints to state boards were filed against psychologists, representing only 2% of those with licenses. In parallel fashion, Neukrug, Milliken, and Walden (2001) indicate that less than 1% of licensed counselors experienced an ethics claim to a state board. Most authors suggest that the actual number of ethical violations is much higher (Biaggio, Duffy, & Staffelbach, 1998; Pope & Vasquez, 1998) and that few are reported because clients do not know their rights or do not feel empowered enough to complain or colleagues knowledgeable about the infraction do not want to get involved.

Historically, malpractice insurers reported sexual misconduct as the major reason for claims against mental health professionals, but because policy language has been changed to exclude coverage for sexual misconduct, failure to prevent client suicide or other violent behavior has emerged as the most frequent and costly category of claim. Violations of standards related to nonsexual multiple relationships are the second most frequent category of claim. The experience of the ACA Insurance Trust shows that claims against counselors seeing families in the midst of divorce and custody conflicts are increasing (personal communication, Paul Nelson, January 4, 2001). Kirtland and Kirtland (2001) report a similar increase in complaints against psychologists to licensing boards.

State licensing boards for counselors (Neukrug, Milliken, & Walden, 2001) indicate that the most common complaint they receive is for an inappropriate dual relationships (Neukrug et al., 2001). Of all complaints, 24% fall into that category. Complaints about incompetent practice rank second, representing 17% of all complaints, and problems with misrepresentation of credentials in an application for a license or for practice without a license represented 8% of all complaints to state boards. Certification boards that oversee addiction counselors indicate that complaints about sexual misconduct are most frequent, with claims of impairment related to substance use and practicing without a certificate as the next most common types of complaints (St. Germaine, 1997). Pope and Vasquez (1998) report that 35% of complaints to state psychology boards involve sexual or dual relationships with clients and another 28.6% involve claims of unprofessional, unethical, or negligent practice.

The 20-year pattern of malpractice claims against social workers shows a significant proportion of claims in two areas: incorrect treatment (18.6% of all claims) and sexual misconduct (18.5% of all claims) (Reamer, 1995). The largest settlements were focused on sexual misconduct, accumulating 41% of the total money paid in claims. Following the pattern in psychology and counseling, only a small percentage of social workers have malpractice claims filed against them. There are 155,000 members of the NASW, but in the 20-year period ending in 1995 only 634 malpractice claims have been filed (Reamer, 1995).

Because ethics complaints and malpractice claims do not provide data about unreported ethical violations, researchers have surveyed mental health professionals about misconduct they have engaged in or observed. The most common intentional violation of ethical standards described in this research involves breaches of confidentiality. In one major study of psychologists (Pope, Tabachnick, & Keith-Spiegel, 1987), 8% of the sample indicated that they had discussed a client by name with a friend. In that study more than half admitted that they had also unintentionally violated confidentiality in other ways, but a smaller study 14 years later found that fewer professionals (40%) admitted unintentional violations of confidentiality (Tubbs & Pomerantz, 2001). This change represents a statistically significant change from the 1987 data but still shows an alarmingly high percentage of psychologists who have violated client privacy at least once.

Researchers have tried to determine which professionals are most vulnerable to misconduct. The goal is to find predictors of unethical behavior so that preventive strategies can be devised. However, studies that examine demographic characteristics of ethics violators have found only one significant correlate: Male therapists and educators are more likely to engage in sexual misconduct than are female therapists (Pope, 1994; Tabachnick, Keith-Spiegel, & Pope, 1991; Thoreson, Shaughnessy, Heppner, & Cook, 1993). In addition, those who engage in sexual misconduct are likely to have done so more than once. No other clear pattern links other forms of unethical practice to demographic or educational characteristics. Even professionals honored for their scholarly and professional accomplishments, elected to high office in professional associations, and appointed to ethics and licensing boards are not immune from convictions for unethical conduct (Pope & Vasquez, 1998).

What is the risk that an individual mental health professional will experience the threat of an ethics complaint to a licensing board or a malpractice suit? Montgomery, Cupit, and Wimberly (1999) report that 71.5% of the psychologists they surveyed reported that they knew a colleague who had a complaint filed against him or her to a state licensing board. A much smaller percentage (14.4%) had been threatened with a complaint by a client but only 39% of those had followed through with the filing of the complaint documents. Montgomery et al. also explored the respondents' experience with malpractice claims, with 38.7% of the sample indicating that they knew a colleague against whom a lawsuit had been filed but only 7.4% of them had personally experienced a threat of legal action against them. Slightly more than half of these threats (57.1%) resulted in the filing of a lawsuit. Others had no prior warning from their clients about the lawsuit. In all, 17 of 284 respondents in their sample had gone through a malpractice lawsuit and 21 psychologists had dealt with a licensing board complaint. These figures are slightly higher than data from professional associations and licensing boards, suggesting that professionals may hear threats from upset clients and worried colleagues more frequently than those threats are acted on.

Psychologists and counselors have been asked what kinds of ethical dilemmas they face in their work. The focus in this research is not on violations but on the ethical questions that arise in the ordinary course of events. They report that the most frequent dilemma concerns confidentiality and its limits. Specifically, Pope and Vetter (1992) found that 18% of their sample listed this topic more than any other. This finding is consistent with reports from the ACA Ethics Committee regarding questions they receive from members (Hubert & Freeman, 2004). A study of British psychotherapists reported a similar pattern of results, with 73% of the sample indicating that they had experienced an ethical dilemma during the past year, the majority of which related to confidentiality (Lindsay & Clarkson, 1999).

Unfortunately, a national survey of ethical practices of counselors has not yet been published (although a national survey of counselor beliefs about the ethics of a wide range of behaviors has been published; see Gibson and Pope, 1993). Only the most notorious of ethical violations, sexual misconduct, has been studied with a sample of counselors. Thoreson et al. (1993) reported that 1.7% of the male counselors responding admitted sexual misconduct with clients during a professional relationship. However, when sexual intimacies with supervisees and former clients were included, the prevalence rate increased to 17%. In a parallel study, Thoreson, Shaughnessy, and Frazier (1995) found that less than 1% of female counselors reported a sexual relationship with a current client or supervisee, but 4.6% reported engaging in a sexual relationship with a former client or supervisee after the professional relationship ended. Obviously, more research is needed to understand the other kinds of counselor misconduct and the types of ethical issues they face regularly.

The Impact of Unethical Practice

Thirty years ago scholars characterized counseling and therapy as a benign enterprise; at best it helped, and at worst, it had no effect. History has proved that notion wrong. Inadequate, incompetent, or inappropriate counseling and psychotherapy are demonstrably harmful to clients, often leaving them worse off than if they had done nothing at all about their problem (Lambert, 2003; Hubble, Duncan, & Miller, 1999).

Because it is the most prominent violation, much empirical evidence on the negative effects of specific violations is concentrated on sexual contact with clients. Clients of counselors who have sexually exploited them show significant negative effects (Bouhoutsos, Holroyd, Lerman, Forer, & Greenberg, 1983; Brown, 1988; Williams, 1992). Some have committed suicide or undergone hospitalization related to the therapist's actions, and most others suffer additional psychological distress in addition to their preexisting problem. Research demonstrates that these problems are not simply acute reactions that abate with time. Instead, they tend to be long-lasting and can become chronic. Bates and Brodsky (1989) present a detailed case example of the devastating effects of sexual abuse. Moreover, an experience with one exploitive counselor tends to make clients wary of all mental health professionals and reluctant to seek professional help for mounting problems. Pope (1990b) compares the effects of sexual exploitation by a therapist to the effects of rape or incest.

Unethical behavior causes harm in several ways. It has powerful harmful effects on clients and undermines the willingness of others who may benefit from counseling to seek professional help. Its legal ramifications are substantial: Some counselors end up in civil court in malpractice suits or in criminal court for libel, slander, or abuse (Crawford, 1994). The true frequency of violations is unknown, but it is probably a rare counselor who practices an entire career without a single minor ethical misstep. Ignorance of ethical standards or distraction from the ethical dimensions of practice is likely to cause harm more frequently than can be seen from ethics committee reports or licensing board sanctions. Some professionals appear to make a regular habit of such behavior (Pope et al., 1987).

Ethics and the Law

Ethics deals with the actions professionals ought to take in relation to each other, to those who seek their services, and to the public. Ethics codes are the standards adopted by national professional associations to govern the definitions of ethical behavior for their members and lay out the penalties for misbehavior. As noted, they also include comments about the profession's ethical ideals and central values. The most severe penalty a professional association can inflict is expulsion from membership.

In contrast, statutes that govern professional practice are enacted by state legislatures, and case law is handed down by the courts of each state. Moreover, laws vary from state to state, but codes apply to the whole membership of a national association. Even when all states have laws governing the same issue, such as child abuse, variations in the exact wording of the laws result in varying interpretations in different jurisdictions (Foreman & Bernet, 2000). Thus a behavior considered legal in one state may be illegal in another. Violations of the law carry much stiffer penalties than codes, of course, ranging from limitations placed on one's license, to practice and vulnerability to being sued, to criminal liability for the most egregious actions.

Ethical standards cover a wider range of behaviors than do laws and generally are written partly to inspire professionals to do their best. Professional ethics do not exist merely to present lawsuits; they exist at least partly to inspire professionals to act in ways that promote public confidence in the profession and enhance the dignity of all with whom they work (Bricklin, 2001). Laws deal only with the "do's and don'ts" of practice and tend to describe a threshold level of behavior for professionals. State regulations governing counseling or psychology and the codes of ethics generally show similar content. For instance, most state regulations indicate a duty to avoid discrimination, and codes contain similar wording. However, areas of conflict appear between the guidelines of the code and any given state's regulations. The ethics codes comment on this matter as follows:

APA *Ethical Principles,* Section 1.02: Conflicts Between Ethics and Law, Regulations, or Other Governing Legal Authority

If psychologists' ethical responsibilities conflict with law, psychologists make known their commitment to the Ethics Code and take steps to resolve the conflict in a responsible manner.

ACA *Code of Ethics,* Section H.1.b: Conflicts Between Ethics and Laws

If ethical responsibilities conflict with law, regulations, or other governing legal authority, counselors make known their commitment to the ACA Code of Ethics and take steps to resolve the conflict. If the conflict is irresolvable via such means, counselors may adhere to the requirements of law, regulations, or other governing legal authority.

Counselors, then, are encouraged by the professional association to abide by the laws governing their profession. Usually this guideline is easy to follow, but sometimes counselors believe that what is truly in their client's best interest conflicts with the law. For example, Pope and Bajt (1988) found that 57% of psychologists intentionally violated a law or rule because they believed compliance would injure more than help their clients. The failure to comply with the law can be merely a part of the self-deception that takes place when other values compete with ethics, but, on occasion, the practitioner may feel morally compelled to act according to a higher standard. Defying the law and/or code is an act of civil disobedience and is a serious matter. Counselors taking this path are still accountable to the state and the profession. One cannot claim immunity from laws and codes even if one considers an action to be a matter of conscience. Thus, any counselor entertaining such an option should consider it carefully and be willing to suffer the full penalty of the law if discovered.

One other reason that laws and ethics sometimes conflict is that they derive from different philosophical perspectives and different cultural world views (Rowley & MacDonald, 2001). According to these authors the law focuses on order, rationality, fact-finding, and stability while mental health professions focus on the subjective needs of the individual and place facts and the greater good in a secondary position if they are achieved at the expense of the individual. Counselors who understand these cultural differences are able to interact with the legal system and appreciate laws in a fuller way, although the essential conflict is not resolved even with this understanding.

Mental health professionals have expressed increasing concern about being disciplined by licensing boards or being sued by clients. Presentations at professional conferences on avoiding malpractice claims are well attended. Special seminars on legal issues in counseling and psychotherapy have attracted thousands of participants eager to learn the path to a lawsuit-free work life. The first online course ACA offered dealt with legal issues for counselors and ways to avoid malpractice claims. Although such knowledge is important, scholars repeatedly tell attendees that the single best way to avoid a malpractice suit or discipline by a licensing board is to know and follow the profession's code of conduct. Acting ethically offers counselors the best protection from legal problems. Consequently, in this book, the focus is on the ethical guidelines of the profession. Legal issues are certainly addressed, but starting with legal issues implies more self-interest than devotion to client welfare. By aiming higher to understand the contents of the code and the reasons for the guidelines therein, counselors and the general public gain both ethically and legally.

SUMMARY

Because counselors, psychologists, and other mental health professionals boldly claim to be professional helpers, they have a duty to fulfill their promise of help and to protect the public from unscrupulous professionals. Acting ethically means being as competent as professed, considering the client's welfare as predominant, using power responsibly, and conducting oneself so as to enhance the reputation of the profession. When faced with an ethical dilemma, a counselor has four primary resources. The first is the literature from developmental psychology, which provides a framework for understanding the components of moral behavior. The second is the code of ethics of the professional association, which includes the standards one's colleagues have set for the profession. Next is the philosophical literature, which helps counselors understand the ethical principles and theories that underlie professional codes of conduct. Finally, counselors can rely on books and articles by their colleagues who are experts in professional ethics. These scholars discuss ethical dimensions of emerging types of practice and debate the critical controversial ethics topics. These resources can guide the professional through many agonizing dilemmas. Ultimately, however, individual counselors must take responsibility for their own actions.

The documentation of unethical behavior shows that sexual contact with clients is a frequent violation for which counselors are brought to ethics committees and court. Other kinds of dual relationships that compromise objectivity also occur repeatedly. Incompetent practice, including violations of confidentiality, negligence in responses to suicidal clients, and inappropriate fees are also recurrent problems. There is little correlation between types of unethical practice and the characteristics of mental health professionals with one exception. Male therapists are more likely than female therapists to engage in sexual misconduct with clients, former clients, students, and supervisees.

Codes of ethics and laws related to counseling and psychotherapy overlap substantially, but some conflicts arise. Moreover, laws seek to eliminate problematic behaviors, whereas codes also define good and desirable behaviors. Sometimes practitioners disregard state laws because they feel compliance would harm their clients. Such civil disobedience should be carried out only after serious deliberation and comprehension of the possible conseuences. The best insurance for avoiding legal problems is knowledge of the codes of ethics and their underlying principles and acting in accordance with them.

DISCUSSION QUESTIONS

1. Only a tiny proportion of unethical practice is reported. Why do you think this occurs? Does this low level of reporting hurt or benefit the professions?
2. What competing values may be operating when professionals decide to do less than they know they ought to do?
3. The reports of practitioners about the ethical dilemmas they most commonly face in their work do not match the ethical violations reported to ethics boards or used in civil suits. What do you think accounts for this discrepancy?
4. One alternative to the general ethics codes currently published by the mental health professions is a lengthier document that addresses ethics for specific kinds of practice. Should the professions retain the current form of the codes or change to another format to make them more relevant to specific settings? What advantages or disadvantages would accompany such a change?

5. When ethics codes conflict with laws, the codes indicate that the professional may follow the law. Do you agree with that position? Why or why not?
6. How do you think the professions should deal with professionals who violate codes and laws because they have a different personal morality?
7. Have you ever known anyone who experienced an unethical action by a mental health professional? Was their response similar to those documented in the professional literature?
8. Based on what you have read, go back to the case of Annette and Archie and determine what you think Annette should do in this case. What do you notice about both your emotional and intellectual response to this case?

RECOMMENDED READINGS

American Psychological Association (APA) Committee on Professional Practice and Standards. (2001). Legal issues in the professional practice of psychology. *Professional Psychology: Research and Practice, 34,* 595–600.

Fisher, C. B. (2003). *Decoding the ethics code: A practical guide for psychologists.* Thousand Oaks, CA: Sage.

Freeman, S. J. (2000). *Ethics: An introduction to philosophy and practice.* Belmont, CA: Wadsworth.

Gibson, W. T., & Pope, K. S. (1993). The ethics of counseling: A national survey of certified counselors. *Journal of Counseling and Development, 71,* 330–336.

Pope, K. S., Tabachnick, B. G., & Keith-Spiegel, P. (1987). Ethics of practice: The beliefs and behaviors of psychologists as therapists. *American Psychologist, 42,* 993–1006.

Tjeltveit, A. C. (1999). *Ethics and values in psychotherapy.* New York: Routledge.

Chapter 2

A Model for Ethical Decision Making
Using Resources to Enhance Individual Judgment

The first chapter explored the importance of ethical standards in counseling and psychotherapy as the representation of the profession's common moral vision. That chapter also identified resources to guide professionals to responsible ethical decisions and described common ethical pitfalls. This chapter presents a systematic 10-step model of ethical decision making that incorporates intellectual, emotional, and sociocultural aspects of ethical choices. The most complex dilemmas require completing each step, but the more obvious questions can be dealt with in an abbreviated approach. Although the model focuses largely on the cognitive components of ethical choices, its steps are embedded in the view that a decision that is truly ethical can occur only when a professional possesses a personal commitment to the ethical values of the profession, integrates the social and cultural context from which the ethical question arises into the decision making, and is resolute enough to implement an ethical choice. The chapter begins by clarifying the varying forms of ethical reasoning that underlie ethical behavior.

Forms of Ethical Reasoning

Kitchener (1984, 2000) has suggested that there are two distinct forms of ethical reasoning: intuitive and critical-evaluative. The following sections define these terms and illustrate their roles in ethical decision making.

Intuitive Ethical Judgments

When people make moral or ethical judgments, they commonly do so at an intuitive level. Moral judgments tend to be fairly spontaneous and motivated by emotion or by a person's ordinary moral sense. According to Kitchener (2000) ordinary moral sense derives from past learning about being moral and a person's character. Rarely are the reasons for intuitive judgments in full conscious awareness or deliberately chosen. For example, when reporters interview people who risked their lives to save others, these heroes are notably inarticulate about what made them act so courageously. Many say that the thought of doing anything else never entered their minds. Others say they were not aware of any thoughts at all; they just acted. If pressed, they may refer to their upbringing or spiritual beliefs as a fundamental motivation for their behavior, but virtually no one provides a philosophical justification for his or her extraordinary behavior, even after the fact. To apply Rest's model of morality (1983, 1994), these heroes had immediate moral sensitivity, used good intuitive moral reasoning, had strong moral motivation, and were resolute in following through on their commitment to do what they sensed was right.

Needless to say, not all people have such admirable moral intuitions. Those who walk away from people in trouble also tend to be inarticulate about their motivation. The people who failed to respond to Kitty Genovese's cries for help in the famous 1954 case just said they did not want to get involved (Cunningham, 1984). Twenty-seven neighbors in her apartment building ignored her repeated screams and pleas for help. No one even picked up the phone to call the police. She was stabbed to death in the alley outside her apartment. Daily, the media records similar callousness to others' pain. In a more recent example, many soldiers who witnessed the abuse of detainees at the Abu Ghraib prison in Iraq failed to intervene or report the abuse to senior officers.

Moral insensitivity is not limited to the general citizenry or the military, however. The history of the helping professions offers ample testimony to the problematic nature of some professionals' ethical intuitions. For example, in the 1960s and 1970s some mental health professionals (for example, McCartney, 1966) argued that sexual intimacies with clients were desirable actions for therapists and that sex with clients constituted a legitimate *treatment* for some disorders. Similarly, in the mid nineteenth century a new medical diagnosis called *drapetomania* was coined by Samuel Cartwright, a Louisiana physician, and added to the psychiatric nomenclature. It meant running-away-from-home disease and was used to diagnose slaves who tried to run from their masters (Szasz, 1971). By this definition, any slave who chose freedom over enslavement was considered mentally ill. In these and other cases, professionals either lacked ethical sensitivity or rationalized an unethical act as ethical. Some of this lack of ethical sensitivity relates to cultural norms and political or social pressures at the time. Thus, relying on the uneven and unpredictable intuitions of some counselors to guide them to the responsible ethical choice has proved an unwise approach to protecting the public welfare. Consequently, our profession demands that we be able to *justify* our ethical decisions according to ethical principles and show how they fit with accepted standards for professional behavior. It is important to note that the view that intuition is insufficient in itself for making ethical decisions does not imply that it should be ignored. Ethical decision making should always take into account an individual's immediate ethical impulse along with contextual factors such as culture and interpersonal relationships (Betan & Stanton, 1999). What is likely to be problematic is a reliance on intuitive judgment to the exclusion of other approaches to judgment. Just as there are heroes in ordinary settings who rely on their moral intuition to make courageous decisions, so too are there times when the intuitions of mental health professionals are just as admirable. Unfortunately, those occurrences are insufficiently predictable to rely on.

Critical-Evaluative Ethical Judgments

To make adequate ethical decisions on a reliable basis, Kitchener (1984, 2000) recommends deliberately analyzing the ethical issue in a process that includes considering professional standards, examining the knowledge of ethics scholars, and engaging in intensive problem solving based on ethical principles. This analysis must also be grounded in a commitment to the moral vision and the virtues that the profession values (Cohen & Cohen, 1999; Hill, 2004; Meara, Schmidt, & Day, 1996). Otherwise, the process degenerates into an empty intellectual exercise.

Kitchener (1984) named this method the *critical-evaluative* level of justifying an ethical decision. When ethical issues are critically examined in this way, the public is less vulnerable to the idiosyncratic intuitions of a given professional. Preliminary evidence suggests that the use of ethical justification improves clinical decision making more than other pedagogies (Dinger, 1997). The following model of ethical decision making builds on the work of Kitchener (1984, 2000) and provides a step-by-step method of deliberating about ethical issues. Figure 2.1 graphically represents the model.

Step 1:	Develop ethical sensitivity.
Step 2:	Clarify facts and sociocultural context of the case.
Step 3:	Define the central issues and the available options.
Step 4:	Refer to professional standards and relevant laws/regulations.
Step 5:	Search ethics scholarship.
Step 6:	Apply ethical principles to the situation.
Step 7:	Consult with supervisor and respected colleagues.
Step 8:	Deliberate and decide.
Step 9:	Inform supervisor and implement and document actions.
Step 10:	Reflect on the experience.

Figure 2.1   A model for ethical decision making

A Model of Ethical Decision Making

At first glance, this model seems to suggest that ethical decision making is unavoidably time consuming and that at the first hint of an ethical issue a professional must immediately proceed through all steps of this elaborate process. A model that required so much time would be neither realistic nor practical. Counselors and therapists do not regularly have extended periods of time in which to deliberate about ethical problems; sometimes they must act immediately. For example, a school counselor who sees a teacher supplying correct answers to students during a standardized test must act quickly or the test results will be invalid. Similarly, when a therapist learns that an 11-year-old client is about to meet an adult she met on the Internet on a "date" there is little time for the therapist to deliberate about how to intervene because of the immediate risk to the child. Even when a professional need not make an instant decision, there is still pressure to act expeditiously. How do counselors apply the decision-making model in such situations? Quite simply, they comply by having done their ethics homework. Counselors must have a sufficient knowledge base to arrive at a decision based on more than intuition. Counselors advance the process by being well studied in the ethics codes. Prudent counselors keep a copy of the code within easy reach in their offices. Similarly, counselors who work in specific settings, such as addictions or school counseling, expedite decision making by keeping up with the ethics literature for their setting. Practitioners with this kind of preparation are more likely to act responsibly despite the time pressure. Experience in using a systematic process or model with hypothetical cases also hastens the process. (See Cottone and Claus [2000] for a review of this model and eight other systems for ethical decision making.)

There is a second benefit to this preparation and experience. Confronting an ethical dilemma is a highly stressful experience for a counselor. For example, Holland and Kilpatrick (1991) found that their sample of social workers experienced "a poignant sense of loneliness or isolation in their struggle with moral questions" (p. 140). Figuring out how to respond to the dilemma of a teenager who now asserts he was lying about prior disclosures of sexual abuse, for example, is both intellectually challenging and emotionally agonizing. The potential harm from a wrong choice is obvious, and counselors feel tremendous anxiety about their responsibility in such situations. Comprehension of ethics standards, familiarity with the literature, and background in sorting out other complicated dilemmas all help to keep the stress manageable and let the decision making proceed with a clearer head.

Step 1: Become Sensitive to the Moral Dimensions of Counseling

In this era of declining budgets, managed care pressures, and multiple role demands, mental health professionals have many crucial issues besides ethics to think about. Clients do not always come to counseling willingly, and their problems seem more complex than allowed for by time, budget, or insurance reimbursement. Much energy is expended to establish rapport with clients and help relieve their distress. Defining potential ethical dilemmas is often the last thing on a counselor's mind during a counseling session. Rest (1984) comments that graduate education often encourages this focus on the technical aspects of the profession and provides little encouragement to see its ethical dimensions. Research confirms that mental health professionals get caught up in the clinical aspects of their work and often disregard even well-publicized ethical problems. Lindsey (1985) and Volker (1983) found that more than one-third of the counselors and psychologists they studied failed to recognize ethical issues in taped simulations of counseling sessions. Instead, these professionals attended to the potential diagnosis of the client, the counselor's skills, and the types of interventions that would be appropriate with such a client. In fact, one-fourth of their samples failed to recognize the ethical issues even when prompted by the researcher in follow-up questions. Using the same measure, Podbelski and Weisgerber (1988) reported that 25% of counseling students failed to recognize the ethical issues. More recent studies show a similarly discouraging pattern of moral sensitivity among students and practitioners in social work and psychology (Fleck-Henderson, 1995; Flower, 1992; Somberg, 1997). Obviously, six studies do not constitute a definitive body of research, but they do suggest a vulnerability to ethical insensitivity that is important to examine. Combined with the documentation of unethical practices and erroneous beliefs of many professionals discussed in Chapter 1 (see, for example, Gibson & Pope, 1993; Neukrug, Milliken, & Walden, 2001; Pope et al., 1987; Reamer, 1995), these studies point to a substantial lack of ethical sensitivity among some practitioners.

How can a counselor whose personal moral vision and values are consistent with those of the profession work to improve ethical awareness? Ethics scholars have several recommendations. The best strategy is the development of a professional ethical identity through formal education in courses and involvement in a graduate program that provides a culture of commitment to the ethical values of the profession (Handelsman, Gottlieb, & Knapp, 2005). Enrollment in courses that deal with both professional standards and processes for moral decision making heightens the likelihood that counselors will be aware of the ethical dimensions of their practice (Dinger, 1997; Eberlein, 1987; Wilson & Ranft, 1993; Ziebert, Engels, Kern, & Durodoye, 1998). Educators obviously endorse this view; the number of ethics courses available during the past 30 years has increased dramatically (Hill, 2004a; Urofsky & Sowa, 2004; Vanek, 1990; Wilson & Ranft, 1993). When ethics courses include a pedagogy that transcends indoctrination into the rules of the profession and offers students the space to integrate professional values into their own belief system, they are more likely to be effective in promoting ethical sensitivity (Handelsman et al., 2005). After completing graduate school, counselors can foster ethical sensitivity through continuing education and dialogue with colleagues. At a more personal level, practicing clinicians need to take steps to avoid burnout and emotional exhaustion from their work because these factors appear to put professionals at risk for inadvertent violations of professional standards. Especially in complex cases, the perspectives of fellow professionals can counterbalance the counselor's sometimes one-sided view. In fact, consultation about ethical questions appears to be the preferred mode of seeking help when school counselors and community-based professionals are grappling with an ethical issue (Bombara, 2002; Cottone, Tarvydas, & House, 1994). Next, as noted, prior experience in dealing with ethical dilemmas seems to make a counselor more alert when a new ethical issue arises. Therefore, much ethics training focuses heavily on case analysis and class discussion.

Counselors also need insight into their own values and motivation for entering the mental health field. Ethical sensitivity assumes not only knowledge and background in professional ethics but also personal principles and philosophy consistent with the profession. A person motivated exclusively by narrow self-interest has little likelihood of achieving ethical sensitivity. Consistently doing the right thing demands altruistic motives and resoluteness in the face of obstacles to good conduct. As Jordan and Meara (1990) suggest, an ethical professional is first a person of virtue. People at the start of their careers ought to frankly assess their reasons for choosing this profession, and people in the midst of their careers should periodically conduct the same kind of self-analysis. Real compassion for human problems and an unwavering commitment to be of service are essential for ethical sensitivity. Experienced clinicians need to take care so that they avoid burnout and emotional exhaustion from their work as these factors diminish real empathy for clients and appear to put professionals at risk for inadvertent violations of professional standards. The ethical standards of the American Counseling Association (ACA; Section A.4.b) and American Psychological Association (APA; Principle A) both highlight the importance of not allowing personal values to compromise counselors' duties to clients.

Finally, a shift in one's mental set about ethics is needed. Because so much of what is presented about ethical violations deals with sensational cases, many new professionals mistakenly conclude that only those who are unscrupulous or naive act unethically. As Hill (2004b) notes, counselors often view ethics as a secondary, peripheral concern with rules and regulations when ethics is, in reality, the core of a professional's work life. A corollary misperception is that ethical dilemmas rarely occur, but if they do, they are immediately visible. All of these conclusions are mistaken. Instead, counselors need to recognize the commonness, complexity, and subtleties of ethical dilemmas. Without vigilance, even well-intentioned and fundamentally virtuous counselors can sometimes end up significantly harming clients. As a practical step to heighten ethical sensitivity, counselors need to establish a protocol for examining the ethical dimensions of every intake and ongoing session. The simple step of adding a question about potential ethical issues to the intake form or the outline for case notes may be sufficient to alert the counselor to issues he or she might otherwise miss.

Step 2: Identify the Relevant Facts and Stakeholders

Once a counselor knows that a situation with ethical dimensions exists, he or she needs to organize all relevant case information, including the cultural and social context in which the case emerges. Consider Archie's case from Chapter 1.

The Case of Archie and Annette

Archie, a 17-year-old student, tells his high school counselor in a counseling session that the claim he made of sexual abuse by his stepfather is not true. He now says that he fabricated the story because he wanted his mother to end her relationship with his stepfather, who has punched her many times. Archie made the statements about abuse to his coach, who reported them to authorities. As his guidance counselor, Annette was then informed of the report and began individual counseling with Archie. They have had four sessions.

Annette's initial task here is to ask herself if all relevant information about the particulars of the situation and its sociocultural context is available. Fact-finding is the foundation on which all subsequent reasoning is built. Neglect of relevant facts can lead a professional to a mistaken line of reasoning or unsatisfactory ethical outcome. In the case of Archie, here are some of the relevant facts Annette should attempt to learn:

- What are Archie's wishes about the confidentiality of the disclosure he has just made? Has he discussed his retraction of the charges with anyone else?
- What is Archie's current emotional health, and how much does he appear to need to see a counselor?
- What is his history of making responsible choices about other matters (i.e., what is his intellectual maturity level)?
- Has an investigation been initiated by children's services? If so, what is the current status of that investigation?
- What is the current status of Archie's relationship with his mother and stepfather? What can Archie reveal about their current level of distress?
- How strong is Archie's counseling relationship with Annette, and how much influence does she have on his thinking and behavior?
- Does Archie have siblings who are directly affected by this? Are there other relatives living in the home (e.g., a disabled grandparent) who are also affected by these events?
- What is known about Archie's cultural and social background and worldview that may be influential to the ethical options for this situation or his perception of the situation (Garcia, Cartwright, Winston, & Borzuchowska, 2003)?

A great deal of this information comes from the client or from the counselor's assessment of the client. In this case Annette is likely to obtain reasonably reliable responses from

Archie about most of these questions and can rely on her professional judgment and prior therapeutic contact with the client for additional data. In the event that important information is not available, the counselor should explore avenues to obtain that information without compromising client confidentiality. Another important aspect of the delineation of important facts is the identification of other stakeholders in the situation in addition to the client. A stakeholder is defined as a person or group of people who are likely to be helped or harmed by the counselor's actions (Garcia et al., 2003; Treppa, 1998). Whenever a counselor is working with a minor, parents or guardians are crucial stakeholders because they are ultimately responsible for the welfare of their child. The welfare of the other stakeholders cannot take priority over the welfare of the client, but the goal of the counselor is to consider options in which the welfare of all stakeholders can be protected if possible. The obvious stakeholders here are Archie's mother, stepfather, siblings, or other members of the household.

Step 3: Define the Central Issues in the Dilemma and the Available Options

Once the facts of the case and the relevant stakeholders are sufficiently clear, the counselor attempts to classify the fundamental ethical issues or the type of ethical problem involved. In this case the main issues deal with (a) the promotion of the welfare of the client when his best interest is not clear, (b) the degree of confidentiality a counselor owes a minor when the welfare of other family members is also at stake, and (c) the question of the counselor's legal obligation to communicate with child welfare professionals investigating the abuse claim if a client's subsequent counseling disclosures do not constitute claims of abuse. Some situations may present even more ethical issues. Defining the broad type of problem allows a counselor to use the ethics codes and the literature more effectively and access prior training on the topic. Because ethical questions do not arise in a vacuum, professionals should also think about the ways in which the context and setting in which the situation is embedded may affect the decision (Treppa, 1998). For example, Annette's role obligations as a school counselor should be a component of her organization of relevant information.

Next, the counselor needs to brainstorm the potential courses of action that come to mind—listing options without censorship. Evaluating and eliminating options comes later. This brainstorming is important to ensure that the counselor's analysis goes beyond the one or two choices that might emerge from his or her ordinary moral intuition. In this process, counselors should acknowledge which options are intuitively appealing and recognize the ways in which their personal moral values are influencing their professional decision making. Treppa (1998) advises that mental health professionals actively challenge their own assumptions and preferences to improve the openness to all reasonable alternatives. On a practical level, this may mean consciously evaluating how emotionally difficult each alternative may be to implement either because of competing values or personal moral philosophy. As Hill (2004b) recommends, a counselor facing an ethical dilemma is wise to ask, "What would this action say about me as a person as well as a counselor?"

In this case, Annette's alternatives are as follows:

- Tell no one and maintain confidentiality, letting the client decide what to do next.
- Inform Archie that she needs to break confidentiality to tell his parents, even if he is uncomfortable with this option.
- Call the investigator from children's services in the case, and tell him or her about Archie's disclosure, even if Archie is uncomfortable with this action.
- Encourage Archie to tell either his mother or the investigator himself but do not disclose without Archie's consent.

- Advise Archie that continued counseling is contingent on his disclosing this information himself or allowing her to do so.
- Wait 1 week and see if Archie maintains or withdraws his retraction or if he changes his request for confidentiality, and then decide about a breach of confidentiality.

Thus, at the end of Step 3 the counselor has broadly defined the type of ethical dilemma and listed potential responses available. Further reading and consultation may produce additional alternatives, of course, but at least a workable list now exists. In Archie's case, Annette also acknowledges that her moral intuition and ordinary moral values lead her to want to disclose this information to Archie's mother or the social worker investigating the case. She consciously decides to postpone immediate action on this intuition until she has studied the issue further (a demonstration of the virtue of prudence). Evaluating the merits of each alternative takes place through the next several steps in the process. Professionals who are unsure that they have developed an adequate list of alternatives may opt to consult with trusted colleagues at this point to ensure that they have not overlooked crucial information or options. Keeping a written record of the alternatives is obviously useful, as is documenting the reasoning process and actions taken throughout the steps.

Step 4: Refer to Professional Ethical Standards and Relevant Laws and Regulations

Once a counselor identifies an ethical issue and his or her options, the next step is to refer to the code of ethics to determine how it applies. As Chapter 1 discusses, the code indicates that confidentiality is important but is limited by laws, by Archie's status as a minor, and by situations of clear and imminent danger.

ACA *Code of Ethics,* Section B.1: Respecting Client Rights

B.1.b. Respect for Privacy. Counselors respects client rights to privacy. Counselors solicit private information from clients only when it is beneficial to the counseling process.

B.1.c. Respect for Confidentiality. Counselors do not share confidential information without client consent or without sound legal or ethical justification.

B.2.a. Danger and Legal Exceptions. The general requirement that counselors keep information confidential does not apply when disclosure is required to protect clients or identified others from serious and foreseeable harm when legal requirements demand that confidential information must be revealed. Counselors consult with other professionals when in doubt as to the validity of an exception. Additional considerations apply when addressing end-of-life issues.

B.5.a. Responsibility to Clients. When counseling minor clients or adult clients who lack the capacity to give voluntary, informed consent, counselors protect the confidentiality of information received in the counseling relationship as specified by federal and state laws, written policies, and applicable ethical standards.

The code provides Annette with relevant questions to ask, such as the following: Would revealing Archie's retraction be a warranted or unwarranted disclosure? Does this situation constitute serious and foreseeable harm and to whom? Is it appropriate in this situation to include the parents, and is it in Archie's best interest to do so? Ultimately, though, the code sets only the path for her thinking and does not give her resolution to the dilemma. Because she is working as a school counselor, Annette may also refer to the *Ethical Standards for School Counselors* (ASCA, 2004). This code's relevant provisions about confidentiality read as follows.

ASCA *Ethical Standards:* Confidentiality

A.2.f. The professional school counselor protects the confidentiality of information received in the counseling relationship as specified by federal and state laws, written policies and applicable ethical standards. Such information is only to be revealed to others with the informed consent of the student, consistent with the counselor's ethical obligation.

g. Recognizes his/her primary obligation for confidentiality is to the student but balances that obligation with an understanding of the legal and inherent rights of parents/guardians to be the guiding voice in their children's lives.

These statements echo the provisions of the ACA code, emphasizing both the primacy of her duty to the confidentiality of the student without denying the reality of responsibilities to a student's parents. This code also suggests that whatever she decides, she probably needs to keep Archie informed of the outcome and to seek his consent if possible. Ultimately, however, the ASCA Standards do not result in resolution and this counselor must move on to the next step of the decision-making model to determine what is most ethical.

Fortunately, for many other problems review of the code does provide a reliable answer. These cases are best conceived as ethical problems or questions rather than ethical dilemmas because they do not possess the complexity or the reality of competing ethical options. The following case illustrates an ethical problem that can be resolved at this stage.

The Case of Yolanda and Justine

Yolanda, a supervisor of counseling interns, has been supervising Justine, an exceptionally skilled and mature intern, for several months. In various friendly conversations during internship meetings, Yolanda has discovered that she and Justine share a number of mutual interests. Both play stringed instruments and ride horses in their free time. Yolanda wants to ask this intern to audition for the open cello seat in the community orchestra to which she belongs and to join her in horseback riding one weekend soon. She wonders if it would be ethical to offer Justine these invitations.

Yolanda shows ethical sensitivity insofar as she recognizes that the behavior she is entertaining has an ethical dimension (Step 1). Organizing the facts of this case is fairly simple because this dilemma came from Yolanda, not from an interaction with a client or colleague. Three facts are clear from Step 2. First, Justine is under her supervision and will be so until the end of the academic year. Second, Justine may need reference letters from Yolanda from time to time after this year. Third, Yolanda is unlikely to supervise this intern again or be in any other evaluative role with her. Yolanda then identifies the category of ethical issue involved. Yolanda thinks these outside contacts might represent an inappropriate relationship with her intern, a kind of dual relationship, and has identified three possible courses of action (Step 3). The first is to go ahead with the invitations. The second option is to withhold the invitations until Justine's internship is completed, and the last is to ask Justine to do just one of the two activities with her.

The fourth step in the process is for Yolanda to refer to the ethics code to weigh the merits of her options. The ACA code states the following.

ACA *Code of Ethics:* Relationship Boundaries with Supervisees

F.3.a. Relationship Boundaries with Supervisees. Counseling supervisors clearly define and maintain ethical, professional, personal, and social relationships with their supervisees. Counseling supervisors avoid nonprofessional relationships with supervisees. If supervisors must assume other professional roles (e.g., clinical and administrative supervisor, instructor) with supervisees, they work to minimize potential conflicts and explain to supervisees the expectations and responsibilities associated with each role. They do not engage in any form of non-professional interaction that may compromise the supervisory relationship.

This section of the code has no unmistakable directive but suggests that if Yolanda were to extend the invitations, she would be acting as though she were a colleague or casual acquaintance of Justine's rather than her supervisor. Thus Yolanda would be failing to acknowledge her power over the supervisee. On this basis, Yolanda also reasons that riding together would be the more problematic of the two situations because it would set up a personal relationship that blurs the boundaries in their supervisory relationship. Inviting this intern to audition for the orchestra is a less obvious violation because there is no guarantee that the supervisee would pass the audition, and no one-on-one relationship would necessarily follow if Justine were accepted. However, belonging to the same orchestra could be uncomfortable for Justine, and if the invitation to audition came from Yolanda, Justine might feel she had no choice but to agree and that refusing her supervisor's invitation could negatively affect her internship grade. If Justine learned of the orchestra opening in some other way and decided on her own to try out, there would be no inherent ethical problem with belonging to the same arts organization, provided Yolanda did not develop a separate personal relationship with her during internship. This section of the code also reminds Yolanda that discussing power differences between supervisees and supervisors is her responsibility. Therefore, she concludes that she should also initiate discussion of this topic in the next supervision meeting.

Because Yolanda is also an associate member of APA, she consults that ethics code and finds the following statement.

APA *Ethical Principles,* Section 3.05a: Multiple Relationships

A psychologist refrains from entering into a multiple relationship if the multiple relationship could be reasonably expected to impair the psychologist's objectivity, competence, or effectiveness in performing his or her functions as a psychologist, or otherwise risks exploitation or harm to the person with whom the professional relationship exists. Multiple relationships that would not reasonably be expected to cause impairment or risk exploitation or harm are not unethical.

Section 3.08

Psychologists do not exploit persons over whom they have supervisory, evaluative or other authority such as clients/patients, students, supervisees, research participants, and employees.

Here Yolanda finds a clearer statement of standards. She must not begin a friendship with an intern if it would affect her objectivity about supervision, interfere with her ability to supervise Justine or the other interns in the group, or otherwise take advantage of the supervisee.

Having reviewed both codes, Yolanda decides to refrain from inviting Justine to join her in either social activity because doing so makes it harder for her to objectively evaluate the student's work and it sends confusing messages to other interns. Moreover, Justine might misunderstand the invitations and may feel awkward in future supervision meetings. For these reasons Yolanda decides she will consider a social relationship with this (or any other) intern only after the supervision is completed and she no longer has an evaluative role in the intern's professional development. This point would most likely occur when the intern has graduated from the program.

This case illustrates how carefully interpreting the code of ethics and consulting related codes as necessary can help a counselor resolve an ethical problem. When a professional is so familiar with the codes that he or she can quickly locate the appropriate section, a decision can be made without delay. Then the counselor may skip Steps 5–7 of the model and can move directly to the last three steps as appropriate.

The codes of ACA, APA, and other mental health professions differ somewhat. This divergence is a particular problem to those belonging to more than one organization. For example, APA forbids all sexual contact with any former clients for at least 2 years after the termination of services (Section 10.07), whereas the 2005 ACA code (Section A.5.b) forbids sexual contact with former clients for at least 5 years after professional services have been completed. Counselors motivated by narrow self-interest might decide to review the codes to find the least demanding standard and follow that one. Such a rationale is shortsighted and ignores the aspirational parts of the codes. The wisest course is to abide by the strictest mandate.

Professionals also need to be aware of other official statements of ethics committees. From time to time ethics committees publish special guidelines to inform members about emerging ethical issues or to respond to an issue brought to the committee by many members. In 2001, for example, APA published *Guidelines for Test User Qualifications* (Turner, DeMers, Fox, & Reed) to address questions about the training and background that is essential for competent use of psychological tests. An extensive list of special guidelines and statements is included in Appendix C of this book. Reference to these resources ties the decision making of practitioners to that of their most knowledgeable colleagues.

Mental health professionals employed by agencies and institutions may also need to consult with employer policy manuals for statements regarding professional ethics. Manuals may provide additional guidance about confidentiality, informed consent, recordkeeping, and procedures for unethical conduct by co-workers (Hansen & Goldberg, 1999). Institutional policies do not take precedence over ethics codes or regulations, but they can provide additional guidance to clinicians in circumstances where the codes and regulations are ambiguous or nonspecific.

Finally, all codes direct counselors to act in accordance with existing laws. This means that the counselor needs to refer to relevant federal and state statutes and regulations governing an issue. Case law, the rulings of courts in cases that come to trial, may also apply. The laws in Yolanda's state may make no special reference to a social relationship between a supervisor and an intern. However, the state's regulations governing licensed counselors may specify that all should abide by the ACA code.

Archie and Annette revisited. Returning to the more difficult case of Archie and Annette, Annette's next task in ethical decision making is to explore whether any legal rulings or state or federal statutes are relevant to her actions. This is particularly important because the laws about confidentiality with minors differ from state to state. Moreover, even within the same state, statutes and court opinions about confidentiality with minors may be conflicting. Therefore Annette would be well advised to get information about her own state's laws. Of particular relevance are the laws related to reporting child abuse and to the legal status of minors to have secrets in therapy that are not disclosed to parents. In a number of other situations, both the law and the codes will not be definitive or will be mute on a subject. When that happens, the counselor should move to the fourth step in the process. If the legal requirements are inconsistent with provisions of a code of ethics, the clinician is freed from the obligation to honor the code. No professional association requires its members to violate laws to comply with their standards for conduct.

Step 5: Search the Relevant Ethics Literature

Step 5 involves consulting the professional literature exploring the thinking of other clinicians and scholars who have grappled with the same ethical issues. Researching this literature gives the counselor the perspectives of experts and helps the counselor become aware of previously unconsidered aspects of the situation. Reading what other professionals have written about complex ethical issues also has the added benefit of removing the emotional isolation involved in making a tough ethical decision. Unfortunately, some evidence suggests that the abundant literature on complex ethical issues is underused by professional counselors, although those with formal courses in ethics appear to refer to it more frequently (Bombara, 2002).

In the case of Archie, Annette can locate literature that suggests how to determine the circumstances under which a child's disclosures should be kept confidential (for example, see Glosoff & Pate, 2002; Gustafson & McNamara, 1987; Stone & Isaacs, 2003; Taylor & Adelman, 1998). This literature, which is less general than the ethics codes, suggests that the degree of confidentiality that must be maintained is related to the child's maturity (and gives criteria for maturity) and more fully defines the child's best interests (Koocher & Keith-Spiegel, 1990). It also underscores that Archie's request for confidentiality is not unusual—other researchers have found that confidentiality is one of the most salient issues for adolescents who seek counseling (Kaser-Boyd, Adelman, & Taylor, 1985) and that adolescents believe that their rights of confidentiality should be respected to virtually the same degree as adults (Collins & Knowles, 1995). From this literature, Annette concludes that Archie's age (17) is relevant and that his right to decide to keep disclosures private from his parents is greater than if he were several years younger. Other writers provide suggestions for dealing with parents to get them to waive their right to information and affirm the privacy of the interactions between counselor and client (for example, see Taylor & Adelman, 1989). Annette decides that immediately communicating his disclosure to parents or investigators would probably fail to acknowledge his age and maturity. Annette concludes that the options that involve breaking confidentiality immediately must be revised to allow disclosure after additional discussion with Archie. She is still unsure about whether her other options are ethical. The literature has reminded her about attending to Archie's feelings and has affirmed that her primary responsibility is to him, not his parents. However, she cannot disregard or minimize his parents' rights and their responsibility for Archie or the current suffering they are enduring because of Archie's revelation about abuse.

The literature on a wide variety of common ethical issues has mushroomed in the past 30 years. Especially valuable is the literature that puts individual ethical decision making in the context of a multicultural society. The following chapters introduce counselors to the extensive scholarship on issues such as confidentiality, informed consent, multiple relationships, diagnosis and testing, group and family counseling, and special ethical concerns for counselors employed in school and agencies. This body of work is a rich resource for counselors who tend to feel vulnerable and isolated in ethical decision making. When they are familiar with this literature, counselors can better justify their decision to superiors, clients or their relatives, or legal bodies and can trace their own reasoning to that of the experts. One can also argue that knowledge of this literature is a necessity, not a luxury, for a competent counselor, especially when dealing with an ethical issue that is common to a population or setting. To function without knowledge of this literature could be seen as acting incompetently, especially now that electronic communication makes published works so easily accessible.

Of course, review of the literature is no panacea for all ethical issues. It will not always be definitive and does not reduce the responsibility of the individual counselor for the choice taken. Many times counselors will need to deliberate further about the issue. They will then go to Step 6 in the process.

Step 6: Apply Fundamental Ethical Principles and Theories to the Situation

At this point the counselor applies the fundamental philosophical principles that underlie the codes to the situation. The professional literature narrows and clarifies the options, but it does not always point to a single path. By thinking in terms of basic ethical principles, counselors can bring "order and coherence" to the discussion of particular cases (Beauchamp & Childress, 1983, p. 1). In addition, by understanding ethical principles, counselors can better see the patterns among different cases and seemingly unconnected situations and better understand their own ethical intuitions. Building on the work of Beauchamp and Childress (1983) and Drane (1982), Kitchener (1984) has identified five primary ethical principles governing human service professions. None of these principles is absolutely binding. For example, counselors may commit a person to a hospital if that person is endangering himself or herself or others. Involuntary commitment violates autonomy but serves a greater good of protecting human life. Most philosophers describe ethical principles as *prima facie binding,* which means that they are binding in all situations except when in conflict with equal or greater duties (Beauchamp & Childress, 2001). Ethicists argue that principles must always be reckoned with: "Principles count even when they don't win" (Beauchamp & Childress, 2001, p. 47). In the next section, each principle is defined and applied to the case of Archie.

Respect for Autonomy. Respect for autonomy means respect for the inherent freedom and dignity of each person. In other words, because they are people with inherent dignity, all individuals should be free to make choices for themselves. This principle derives from philosopher Immanuel Kant's notion that people are ends in themselves and should not be treated only as a means to another end (Kant, 1785/1964). Implicit in autonomy is the concept that the person is responsible for himself or herself. To respect autonomy means that "a person's choices should not be constrained by others" (Beauchamp & Childress, 2001, p. 62). Paternalism, the opposite of autonomy, means acting as a parent to another and determining that person's best interest.

Respect for autonomy does have limits, of course. One's actions cannot interfere with the freedom of others, and autonomy must be based on an understanding of the meaning and implications of one's choices. The actions do not need to be rational in the sense that they need not seem sensible to others. A person is free to act foolishly, even in ways that harm himself or herself, if that person is capable of understanding the implications of the choice and if others are not hurt by those actions. Children, people who are profoundly mentally handicapped, or people in a psychotic state do not have autonomy of actions because they are (at least at the moment) unable to understand the implications of their choices for themselves or others. In these circumstances, others act paternalistically on behalf of the individual.

The right to privacy is coupled with freedom of choice as a part of respect for autonomy. A person should have the power to decide what information about himself or herself to share—a right to control what others know about his or her private life. As with autonomy, without privacy there is no dignity. In the United States a person's right to privacy is also guaranteed by its constitution.

The connection between respect for autonomy and the codes of ethics is obvious in nearly every section. The duties for counselors to obtain informed consent to counseling and to maintain confidentiality of disclosures made in session derive directly from this principle. Similarly, many aspects of research ethics and the ethics of diagnosis and testing relate to respect for autonomy. This principle also implies that people have the right to relinquish or suspend their own autonomy to achieve some other aim they see as beneficial. For instance, an adult may surrender autonomy by agreeing to a marriage arranged by parents because that practice is consistent with the adult's cultural and social beliefs.

Counselors trying to resolve an ethical dilemma use the principle of respect for autonomy by asking which of the alternatives under consideration is most consistent with this principle. In Archie's case, respect for autonomy is crucial. If he can be granted the same measure of autonomy as an adult, then the counselor must honor his wishes for confidentiality to the extent that those wishes do not substantially harm others. Immediately, two questions arise. Can he be granted the same measure of autonomy as an adult? How much harm does his action cause others? (The counselor at this point is probably wishing that Archie had waited until his next birthday to share this information with her.) Most children have limited competence, and as they mature, the limits on their competence decrease. The ethics literature explains the relationship between competence and maturity and suggests that an adolescent at age 17 probably is mature enough to act autonomously (for example, Gustafson & McNamara, 1987). It suggests that a counselor with a client so near adulthood should start by assuming maturity and autonomy, unless there is evidence to the contrary. Given her knowledge of Archie, Annette decides that he can be granted a nearly full measure of autonomy. Her analysis of the potential harm inflicted is another important consideration. An allegation of sexual abuse may affect his stepfather's work, his emotional stability, his marriage, his ability to parent his stepson, and perhaps his personal freedom. His mother may also suffer psychological distress and be affected by the harm her husband experiences.

If Archie is now telling the truth, then his refusal to admit his prior lie to anyone else violates the stepfather's rights. Of course, Archie may be lying *now*, feeling uncomfortable with his earlier revelation. Young people sometimes recant revelations of abuse because they fear the consequences. This later denial may be an effort to reduce the present distress. If so, disclosing his denial would clearly not be in his best interests. The stepfather might even be free to abuse him again. The process of applying the principle of respect for autonomy to this case reveals the importance of the particular facts of the case. The counselor's ethical analysis depends on the skill and quality of her assessment of the boy and his family. Her knowledge about the client is crucial in helping her evaluate which is the real lie and what the consequences of disclosure (or nondisclosure) are likely to be. The principle of respect for autonomy requires that Archie's wishes must figure prominently in Annette's decision and that if doubt exists about the harm to others, the client's right to make his own choice about what is revealed should weigh heavily in the counselor's decision.

Nonmaleficence.   The second ethical principle has its roots in medical ethics and is often associated with the Hippocratic oath, which physicians take. This oath admonishes physicians to heal the sick and never injure or harm them. This is derived from the principle called nonmaleficence and is often seen in its Latin form, *primum non nocere*. Its specific translation is "First, do no harm," and it has been called the most fundamental ethical principle for medical and human service professionals. This principle also includes avoiding preventable risks. Professionals have a duty to use only those interventions that they know are not likely to harm clients. This duty means that they must know and evaluate the risks of treatment for their clients and act accordingly. The duty to avoid harm also applies to the other roles of mental health professionals. For example, researchers are prohibited from conducting research that will hurt participants, educators may not use teaching methodologies that damage students, and consultants may not use interventions that harm the people they were hired to help. Professionals cannot always foresee all consequences of their services because unexpected events happen. The duty to nonmaleficence does not require omniscience, just knowledge and careful, prudent judgment.

The concept of avoiding harm must be put in a context because many aspects of counseling and psychotherapy can be uncomfortable and clients may temporarily feel worse before they feel better. A person trying to cope with a history of physical abuse in childhood may be more distraught after counseling sessions that examine the impact of those experiences on current functioning than he or she was at the start of the sessions. For a while, the person may have trouble sleeping, may cry often, and may be less productive at work. This would constitute harm if the intervention had no evidence of benefit in the long run or if the client had not consented to a treatment that included temporary negative effects. If a counselor is competent in the use of a treatment that is known to have positive effects, and has evaluated the effectiveness of this approach with this client, the counselor is complying with the principle of nonmaleficence. The professional's only additional duty is to monitor the client's progress to identify and respond to unanticipated negative effects of counseling.

Another aspect to the principle of nonmaleficence implies that doing nothing is preferable to engaging in an action that could be reasonably anticipated to cause harm. For example, a family physician untrained in cardiac surgery would never attempt a cardiac bypass operation—even if a patient needed it and refused to see another physician. The ethical rationale is clear. A family physician is likely to do great harm engaging in a procedure in which he or she is untrained. That harm is avoidable because other doctors with that training are available. Consequently, the only ethical stance is for the physician to refuse the patient's request. Except in the most extreme emergency, the risk of death from surgery by an untrained physician is greater than the risk of death by no treatment, or at least death is a more immediate risk with an unskilled surgeon. Similarly, mental health professionals cannot engage in actions that they know or should know are likely to do harm—even if they are asked to by clients or colleagues and even if it means counselors do nothing instead. The harm they would cause is probably not as visible and dramatic as in the medical example just given, but the psychological injury can be just as real. Nonmaleficence demands that clinicians untrained in powerful interventions do nothing rather than engage in procedures that are likely to do harm in inept hands.

The principle of nonmaleficence is the basis for the ethical standards concerning competence to practice, informed consent to counseling and research, dual relationships, and public statements. It also is the foundation for the sections of the code dealing with appropriate use of psychological tests and research methods with animals.

When we apply the principle of nonmaleficence to the case of Archie, we realize that we must consider the harm that can come from each alternative, beginning with the harm to Archie if Annette discloses the information without his consent. Because the counselor's primary duty is to the client, the analysis starts with Archie. Therefore the counselor must carefully weigh the young man's mental state, emotional stability, and tendency to impulsive or destructive behavior along with the effect disclosure would have on each of these facets of functioning. She also needs to acknowledge that revealing the confidence may cause Archie to drop out of counseling or at least lose trust in her and refuse to reveal any other personal information. She must consider the harm the loss of a trusting counseling relationship could cause her client. Then she should evaluate the harm that comes to Archie's family members from each of her options. In different ways both the mother and stepfather are harmed if the allegation goes forward but is not really true. Finally, the counselor needs to weigh the injury her client would suffer against the injuries his family members would suffer. If Archie is likely to experience minor, brief discomfort but his stepfather is likely to have a criminal conviction or his mother is likely to file for divorce, then that information should be part of Annette's deliberation. The principle of nonmaleficence asks counselors to use their power wisely so that the client, student, or research participant leaves the experience at least no worse off than he or she began.

Beneficence. The third ethical principle is beneficence, which is defined as the responsibility to do good. Because counselors advertise themselves as professional helpers, they have a duty to be of real help to those who enlist their services. Beneficence also includes a duty to help society in general and people who are potential clients. This duty is not imposed on all workers who sell their services to the public. People who manufacture shoelaces, copiers, or potato chips do not market themselves as helpers, and so ethically they have no obligation to help, only to produce the goods without causing harm to the public. Of course, it is *desirable* for such workers to help others. The distinction is that helping others is not a *duty* imposed by the nature of their work.

The principle of beneficence also underlies the provisions in the code requiring counselors to work within the limits of their competence and to promote the public welfare. Acting in an incompetent way means that the professional will not be able to give the help that has been promised (and paid for) and that a client has the right to expect.

Of course, not all professional service ends up benefiting the client. Sometimes counseling and therapy are ineffective, and, less often, they may inadvertently leave the client feeling worse. Moreover, counseling can help only those who agree to actively participate in the process. The ethical obligation of beneficence is not to a guaranteed positive outcome; rather, the obligation is to do one's best to be of help and to offer alternatives when treatment does not appear to be succeeding. When professionals consistently leave clients no better off at the end of service than at the beginning, they are violating the principle of beneficence.

Beneficence also requires clinicians to engage in professional activities that provide general benefit to the public. Thus, determining the benefits in each possible course of action is important in resolving an ethical dilemma. Beneficence asserts that it is insufficient for professionals simply to avoid injuring their clients. A counselor's interventions should be based on avoiding harm as a first requirement and on doing good as a second requirement.

Applied to Archie's case, beneficence means being committed to a resolution that not only avoids preventable harm to Archie but also leaves him better off after counseling. Moreover, beneficence means that Annette ought to evaluate what course of action could really help the whole family the most. She also must examine the impact of breaking confidentiality on her role as a secondary school counselor. If other students learn that she disclosed Archie's statements outside the counseling office, perhaps they would refrain from using the counseling service, even when they might benefit. In other words, she should seek a solution that increases her likelihood of continuing to help all those she serves. Again, her responsibility to do good for Archie takes precedence over other considerations, but all aspects of beneficence need to be explored.

Justice.   Justice is the obligation to act fairly. This principle calls for counselors and therapists to recognize the dignity of all people and avoid bias in professional action. This principle is best expressed in a statement attributed to Aristotle: "Justice means treating equals equally and unequals unequally, in proportion to their inequality" (cited in Kitchener, 1984). Justice means being fair and nondiscriminatory. When Oscar Wilde defined morality as "the attitude we adopt towards people we personally dislike," he was emphasizing the justice component of morality. The risk of violating this principle is greatest when one stereotypes a group. Counselors should not show bias on the basis of race, age, gender, culture, and any other variable irrelevant to the real matter at hand because doing so is inherently unfair.

Justice is more than avoiding prejudice, however. It also means offering additional services to those whose difference is relevant. For example, a psychology educator has an obligation to evaluate all students' performances using the same criteria. However, if one student has a hearing impairment, it would be unfair for the educator to treat that student exactly the same as the others. Instead, justice dictates that the student's hearing problem be recognized and adaptations to the teaching environment be made so that the student can understand what is being communicated. Once those adaptations are in place, however, fairness also demands that equal performance standards be used. It would be unethical for a faculty member to grade that student's work more leniently because of the impairment.

The principle of justice also obliges professionals to be sure their services are accessible to the public. For instance, it is unethical to deny those who are poor access to counseling and psychotherapy because they cannot pay or to deny care to people who do not speak English because their language is different. Justice does not require that counselors accept so many poor clients that they cannot support themselves or that they become multilingual, but it does require counselors to make accommodations so that factors that are really irrelevant to a person's ability to profit from therapy do not determine that person's access to therapy.

This principle is at the root of statements in the codes against discrimination and sexual harassment and in support of pro bono work and public service. It is also the foundation for the obligations to protect the public welfare and to actively combat discrimination whenever found.

Applying this principle to Archie's case suggests that Annette should deal with Archie as she would with any other adolescent client of hers, insofar as she should not let extraneous variables enter into her ethical reasoning. Archie's parents' position in the community, for example, should have no bearing on her actions because their social status is irrelevant. Similarly, if Annette dislikes the stepfather or sees parallels between Archie's mother and her own mother, justice demands that she give these personal feelings no weight in the decisions she makes about confidentiality with Archie. If Annette is unable to treat Archie and his family fairly, she should arrange for Archie to see a counselor who can.

Fidelity. The fifth ethical principle is fidelity, and it deals with faithfulness to promises made and to the truth. Fidelity is loyalty. Counselors must place clients' interests ahead of their own and be loyal to clients even when such loyalty is inconvenient or uncomfortable. Fidelity derives from the central role of trust between counselor and client. Trust becomes impossible if a counselor's words or actions are unreliable. In addition, fidelity is necessary because clients are vulnerable and the role of the counselor holds inherent power. Truthfulness is an essential aspect of fidelity in counseling and psychotherapy because the primary medium of the service is verbal communication. Clients expect to be able to believe what counselors say—the whole enterprise would likely crumble without trustworthy counselors. The emphasis is on avoiding deception and on building trust—but it is not about brutal honesty. Obviously, a professional who finds a client's style of communication boring or who disagrees with a client's political views has no obligation to share all these reactions with a client. Honesty must be tempered with consideration for the effects of such information on clients. Still, the *prima facie* duty is to truthfulness, unless overruled by another principle.

The principle of fidelity also implies loyalty to colleagues and the profession. It obliges us to do what we have agreed to do. Because counselors have a contract with their employers to give professional service in exchange for compensation, they should be loyal to that agreement as long as they are collecting a paycheck. Counselors have a similar contract with the profession. In exchange for the benefits of their professional status, they have agreed to act according to the rules of the profession and to respect other professionals. These agreements sometimes take the form of written contracts, but at other times they are informal or implied.

Fidelity is the principle underlying the statements in the codes regarding the structure of the counseling relationship and relationships with colleagues, employers, and professional associations. Fidelity is also the foundation for the caution about the use of deception in research designs. Counselors wrestling with an ethical dilemma need to ask themselves which of the courses of action under consideration is most faithful to the promises that have been made.

In Archie's case, fidelity demands that Annette remain loyal to Archie and to promises made to him. If promises have been made or implied to Archie's parents, then she also has a duty to be loyal to those promises. If the loyalties conflict, then her first obligation is to her client. Annette cannot desert her client, making excuses to refer him elsewhere just because the situation is now difficult for her. Fidelity means keeping commitments.

When Ethical Principles Conflict. Applying ethical principles to a particular dilemma can reveal internal conflicts between different principles. In Archie's case, different principles lead to incompatible conclusions. The principle of respect for autonomy emphasizes Archie's freedom and responsibility for his decision, whereas the principle of nonmaleficence uses harm to Archie and others as the measure of what is right. The principle of fidelity implies loyalty to the promise made to keep disclosures private, whereas the principle of beneficence suggests that disclosure may be best for the whole family.

How are these conflicting recommendations reconciled? As noted earlier, some philosophers argue that nonmaleficence is the most important ethical principle and that its requirements take priority over the claims of other ethical principles (Beauchamp & Childress, 2001). The central issue is the nature and intensity of harm to the client if disclosure is made without his or her consent. The principles of autonomy, beneficence, fidelity, and justice play secondary roles. The counselor's ultimate goal is to find a way to abide by all the ethical principles, but his or her first task is to ascertain as best as possible the probable injury to the client.

Returning to Archie, the crux of the issue then becomes whether Archie is telling the truth now or when he made the initial disclosure about abuse. If the client is acting out of fear or worry now and the abuse actually happened, then the harm from disclosing this current denial could be significant for the boy. If he was really fabricating the abuse in a misguided attempt to help his mother, then the harm to Archie from disclosure may be of a different nature and severity. In any case, Annette should consider the potential injury to Archie if he abandons counseling after she breaks confidentiality. Clearly, others are at risk for injury here. If the abuse never happened, then the parents are also being unnecessarily harmed.

The principle of nonmaleficence suggests that the counselor has a duty to be as sure as possible about what the real truth is. That probably means that Annette needs more discussion with Archie to get a better sense of his motivation for retracting his prior claim of abuse. Annette needs a fully informed judgment about what really happened to decide on the least harmful alternative. Caution in proceeding also fits with the other three principles. If the abuse did not occur, respect for autonomy, in conjunction with nonmaleficence, might lead Annette to help Archie disclose the lie himself, either to his family or to the investigator from children's services. By exploring the implications of his behavior with Archie, Annette may help Archie gain enough insight that he himself decides to undo the harm he has caused. Such an approach is consistent with the duty to beneficence. Helping Archie take responsibility for his actions helps him behave in a more mature and self-sufficient way—clearly a desirable outcome. Supporting Archie in communicating about the frustrations and fears that led him to lie might be an outcome that benefits the whole family and gets them intervention for the real domestic violence. Obviously, if Archie chose to disclose the fabrication himself, then Annette would not be breaking any promises to Archie or to his family.

Ethical Theories. There are even thornier dilemmas than the one Archie presents. For instance, a client whose medical condition is terminal and who is experiencing overwhelming pain may seriously consider suicide. Is suicide under such circumstances always wrong, or is there such a thing as rational suicide? Does the counselor have a duty to prevent suicide for this kind of client, too? This is an agonizing problem. In such situations, the principles conflict, and the harm seems equal no matter which alternative is chosen. Under those circumstances, counselors can turn to ethical theories that are broader than ethical principles. Ethical theories are at the very foundation of Western societies' beliefs about morality. Ethical theories represent the perspectives of great ethicists throughout history. A full discussion of ethical theories is beyond the scope of this book, but the following material gives a sense of the scholarly thinking. (See Freeman [2000] for a full discussion of this topic.)

In Western culture, several ethical theories have been proposed by philosophers. These theories are at the core of our religious, social, and political institutions. One is the moral law theory, which argues that there are universal moral values that must be absolutely followed. A similar theory is what Newton (1989) describes as biblical theory, encompassing absolute laws for human behavior expressed in the holy writings of the great religions of the world. In either case, the rules are treated as moral laws and are held to be universally binding. At the other end of the continuum is utilitarianism, a theory that defines morality in terms of the benefits an action provides for society. In the simplest terms, utilitarianism defines morality as the action that brings the greatest happiness to the greatest number. No action is inherently good or bad in utilitarianism; an action's effects on the happiness of the larger group determine its morality.

Ethical theories describe different assumptions about the central essence of moral behavior. For the most complex dilemmas, in which a counselor agonizes about the process and in which each alternative seems to have negative consequences, thinking about how he or she defines morality at the most basic level may help in resolving the dilemma. Counselors are well advised to consult with ethicists when analyzing the relationship between moral theory and the facts of a particular case.

Step 7: Consult with Colleagues About the Dilemma

An ethical dilemma can be intellectually overwhelming and emotional distressing for both the client and the counselor. Objective feedback from trusted colleagues can provide a wider view of the problem, a new focus on unconsidered facts, or additional relevant literature. Research by Cottone et al. (1994) suggests that consultation frequently results in reconsideration of an ethical decision. Consultation also offers comfort and reduces the moral and emotional isolation that counselors often feel. Colleagues do not often have easy answers, but they do have insight, experience, and compassion to share. Consultation with colleagues can take place at any point in the decision-making process and need not be limited to this step. For instance, one might seek input from a colleague about interpreting a confusing section of an ethics code or clarifying the relevant facts of the case. Research suggests that psychologists underutilize consultation to assist them with the dilemmas of practice, and this failure sometimes diminishes the quality of the care clients receive (Clayton & Bongar, 1994). In one study only 65% of licensed counselors indicated that they would consult with colleagues and supervisors about serious ethical issues related to interactions with managed care companies (Danzinger & Welfel, 2001). Counselors are more likely to use consultation with colleagues when they fear a malpractice suit (Wilbert

& Fulero, 1988). It is important to note that consultation at this step in the ethical decision-making process is essential but that consultation is an option at any point to assist the professional in sorting out the relevant considerations and options.

Whether a colleague can be approached with information that identifies a specific client depends on the consent to consultation a counselor has obtained from the client. Identifying information can be released to colleagues or supervisors with client consent or, in the absence of consent, with legal authority. Counselors who have not received such consent may discuss the case only in a way that protects the client's identity. Usually that means disguising not only the name but also other information that might make the client's identity obvious to other professionals.

When consulting with colleagues, counselors should describe the facts of the situation, their own understanding of the relevant ethical standards, their interpretation of how the ethics literature and ethical principles apply to the case, and their current assessment of which alternatives are most responsible. In other words, the counselor should summarize the decision-making process thus far and ask the colleague the following questions:

- What facts of the case seem most important to you in determining the ethical alternatives?
- What have I not considered? What do you think my blind spots may be here? What sociocultural considerations am I overlooking or misunderstanding?
- Is my interpretation of the ethics code accurate?
- What other parts of the code are applicable that I have not identified?
- What other books and articles do you know of that are relevant to my decision?
- Does my analysis of the ethical principles appear sound?
- Is my evaluation of the most responsible options consistent with your judgment?
- How would you resolve this dilemma? Why would you make that choice?

The number of colleagues one consults will vary with the nature of the dilemma and a counselor's prior experience, but some consultation is always advised. Of course, not all the feedback received will be useful. Some colleagues may even advise an unethical route, and conflicting advice is not uncommon. Even when the feedback is disappointing, the endeavor is worthwhile. The process of articulating one's dilemma and the steps one has taken to resolve it force a counselor to clarify his or her thinking and make fully conscious ideas that may have been at the periphery of awareness. Just as the process of self-disclosure helps clients see their problems more clearly, discussing ethical dilemmas with colleagues helps counselors gain a fuller vision of the issues. In fact, Duke (2004) found that when psychologists consulted with colleagues about ethical dilemmas, they felt more certain of their response, more satisfied with it, and better able to conceptualize the reasoning behind their choice.

If a mental health professional is under supervision to obtain a professional license or as part of a training experience, consultation with supervisors is mandatory. Discussion with one's supervisor should take place at the first opportunity, and the feedback from one's supervisor should be weighed more heavily than any from colleagues in making the final decision. In practice, supervisors usually advocate for the trainee, supporting him or her and providing practical advice. Of course, even those not yet licensed for independent practice are still obligated to act in accordance with the standards of the profession, so that any advice contradictory to the standards may not be followed, even if it originates with a supervisor. The supervisee is still accountable and may not claim that "a supervisor made me do it." More explanation about responding to such dilemmas in supervision follows in Chapter 13.

Consultation with colleagues can include discussion with members of professional ethics committees to get advice about the problem. National associations are accessible to members through a toll-free phone call. ACA's toll-free telephone number is (800) 347-6647 and APA's is (800) 374-2721. Many state organizations also have ethics committees who can discuss dilemmas with members. Moreover, state licensing boards usually provide access for licensed professionals seeking ethics advice. The role of these bodies is to help the professional understand the standard of care based on published codes and related documents. Because none of these committees will have the full facts of the case, they do not provide members with recommendations guaranteed to comply with their standards. Rather, they help members understand the professional standard of care as expressed in the codes and related publications and assist them in raising all the relevant questions. In other words, they do not take the responsibility for the decision, but they can offer considerable guidance about how other professionals have dealt with similar situations.

Step 8: Deliberate Independently and Decide

At this step the data collection process has ended and the private, individual process of sorting out the information begins in earnest. Through this personal deliberation, the counselor decides which alternative is most ethical and develops a plan for implementing that action. For example, in Archie's case Annette's deliberations might result in calling Archie back for another session later that same day to explore his new disclosure more fully to ascertain, to the degree possible, what the real events were. She decides that if Archie was fabricating the story of the abuse, the counseling must focus on helping him understand the implications of his action and how he can undo some of the damage already done. She will not threaten or coerce him into disclosing his lie, but she will engage in a respectful process of helping him face the meaning of his actions and take responsibility for making things right. She will maintain confidentiality for the immediate future. If Archie refuses to change his position after additional counseling, she will need to reconsider her decision. She may still honor the confidentiality but will want to go through the decision-making process again at that time. If Annette believes Archie is now lying for fear of the consequences of admitting abuse, she has a duty to maintain confidentiality but will work with him to find alternative ways to cope with his obvious distress.

Essential to this personal deliberation is an examination of the competing values that may make implementing the ethical choice more difficult. As noted in Chapter 1, competing values are other personal values that influence a person's behavior. All people have other values, and there is nothing inherently problematic about them. In themselves, many competing values have ethical merit. A professional's commitment to provide financial support for his or her family and to have a harmonious relationship with co-workers is a good value to have. These values become problematic only when they override a counselor's ability to choose the professional ethical value. What motivates individual counselors not to implement ethical choices differs somewhat in each case, but worry about negative consequences to self, concerns about lack of support from colleagues or supervisors, or fears that doing the right thing will complicate one's life are frequent competing values. When counselors become aware of the factors that pull them in another direction, they can devise a plan to counteract these pressures and increase the likelihood of acting responsibly.

Counselors should also acknowledge the costs of the ethical choices. Sometimes complying with ethical standards results in more work, pressure, and anxiety. For instance, Annette will need to schedule extra sessions with Archie to ascertain the truth, and if she maintains confidentiality, she risks angering the parents, investigators, and even school administrators. Acting ethically may sometimes mean defying supervisors or even risking one's employment or income. By frankly confronting these possible costs, the counselor may discover ethical ways to minimize or eliminate them or, at least, to protect himself or herself from an unexpected cost. In addition, the counselor can muster strength for uncomfortable consequences of the ethical choice.

Of course, not all choices are painful or difficult. Clinicians who believe they have come to an informed decision about the problem often feel a sense of professionalism and allegiance to the highest values of the profession. They take pride in their moral courage and gain confidence to face future problems. The ethical climate of the profession and the workplace also influences the feelings about implementing an ethical action. The past 30 years have spawned greater awareness of the major ethical issues in the profession, and counselors trained in recent years have more formal education in ethics (Welfel, 1992; Hill, 2004a). When a counselor knows colleagues are committed to ethical practice, the temptation of competing values decreases and support from those co-workers increases. Counselors gain the respect of their colleagues and also have the satisfaction of knowing that they are modeling ethical behavior for others in the workplace. Most important, they have the satisfaction of knowing that even under pressure, they considered the welfare of the client above their own needs.

Step 9: Inform Appropriate People and Implement the Decision

This step, Step 9, sounds deceptively simple but it may be more difficult to carry out the decision than it is to make it, even in a case as complicated as Archie's. In implementing the ethical choice, the counselor should remember to engage the supports outlined in the last step when resistance is encountered. One may benefit from another consultation with a trusted colleague or from rereading the codes or literature to help one shore up resolve to stick with the choice. Ethical courage has several sources. One's moral character is one piece of it; being aware of the consequences of failing to act and structuring the environment to minimize temptation are others. A fourth aspect is habit—people are more likely to act morally when faced with major issues if they have made a habit of acting responsibly in the less important matters.

When a professional is ready to carry out an ethical decision, he or she needs to inform supervisors. Supervisors have a legal and ethical right to hear the choice and the rationale for it. Then the counselor needs to communicate with other people. Who else may be relevant? Needless to say, the client is the first person to consider. If Annette decided to break confidentiality with Archie, then Archie should be told about her decision. He should also hear her rationale and be given time to discuss the issue with her. Informing the client is necessary because of the principle of autonomy, and it is mandatory unless a greater ethical good is at stake. For example, sometimes when clients are violent, counselors may break confidentiality to warn the intended victim. Under these circumstances, the client should be told only if the disclosure does not put the victim at greater risk for harm. If the client is a child, parents or guardians may need to be informed. In each case, only people who truly have claim to the information should get it. The client's right to privacy must still be honored to the fullest extent possible.

Formal documentation of one's decision in records, case notes, or other files is the final portion of this step. Written information about the choice taken and the rationale for that decision offers a mental health professional the best available protection from later challenges to that decision. Process notes ought to begin at Step 2 with the list of options to consider and then include the outcomes of each step of the decision-making process. Additional discussion of the ethics of documentation follows in Chapter 11.

Step 10: Reflect on the Actions Taken

Experience without reflection is wasted. Only when coupled with reflection can experience provide real insight. Such reflection gives counselors an opportunity to acknowledge the responsible way in which they acted and a chance to evaluate the flaws in their thinking and actions that should be avoided when the next dilemma comes along. Now that the pressure is at least temporarily reduced, the mind may be able to see what the emotions had clouded. Reflection also increases ethical sensitivity so that the next ethical issue that arises will be noticed more quickly and addressed more effectively. Specifically, at this step the counselor should ask himself or herself the following questions:

- Did I attend to the ethical dimensions of the situation as soon as they arose?
- Did I know enough about the ethics codes to use them effectively?
- What ethical literature do I need to keep in my personal library for easier access the next time it is needed?
- How effectively did I consult? What could I have improved?
- What else could I have done differently? How well did I identify the competing values and other pressures affecting my decision making? What could I have done better?
- What else could I have done differently?
- What am I proud of doing? How has this situation changed me as a counselor and a person?
- How can I use this experience to assist other counselors faced with similar problems?

This period of reflection begins after the decision is fully implemented and its consequences are known. Thus some delay may occur between the last two steps. Counselors must take care to engage in this step so that they gain the full benefit of the experience.

SUMMARY

When counselors make ethical decisions that affect others' lives, these decisions should not be intuitive; they should be made after careful deliberation about the ethical justification of various potential actions. A 10-step model for justifying ethical decisions begins with recognizing the ethical dimensions of the situation (Step 1) and moves to examining all the relevant facts (including the sociocultural context of the situation) and categorizing the type of ethical dilemma involved (Step 2). In Step 3 counselors define the central issues and options for action. In Step 4 counselors consult the codes of ethics of their profession and laws of their jurisdiction for applicable standards for practice. In Step 5 counselors examine the relevant ethics literature to learn the views of experts in applied ethics. Step 6 involves analyzing the five ethical principles that govern human service professions: respect for autonomy, nonmaleficence (avoiding harm), beneficence (doing good), justice or fairness, and fidelity to promises made. If analysis of these principles does not resolve the dilemma, a counselor may need to move to a deeper level of ethical justification—ethical theories. At Step 7 consultation with supervisors and re-

spected colleagues obtains alternative perspectives. In Step 8, once all the data are obtained, the counselor must deliberate and decide on his or her own. Deliberation entails acknowledging pressures and practicalities that may make implementing the decision more difficult. Step 9 involves informing supervisors and other relevant individuals, usually including the client, and then implementing the chosen action. The final step is a period for reflection on the experience that allows one to take pride in one's honest effort to act responsibly and to identify ways in which the process could be improved when the next similar dilemma occurs.

Not all ethical issues require progressing through all 10 steps. Some are resolved expeditiously. When ethics codes or laws are definitive, a counselor can move immediately to the final three steps of the model. In addition, although the process appears time consuming, it can be shortened by familiarity with the ethics codes and the relevant ethics literature and by ensuring ready access to a set of knowledgeable colleagues with whom to consult. Up-to-date ethics knowledge and prior experience with ethical problems also speeds up decision making.

DISCUSSION QUESTIONS

1. Do you agree with the view that nonmaleficence should be the primary ethical principle governing the human service professions? Why or why not?
2. Which aspect of the codes of ethics seem most definitive to you? Why?
3. How would you determine which colleagues to consult about an ethical problem?
4. How would you define your own implicit theory of morality? What fundamental assumptions do you make?
5. Do you agree with the way Annette and Yolanda resolved their ethical dilemmas? Why or why not?

CASE FOR DISCUSSION

Benita is a 54-year-old executive in an international company that manufactures athletic shoes. Before she became successful in business she was a Olympic-caliber runner, winning medals in two consecutive Olympics and other national and international titles. After retiring from competition she earned her Masters in Business Administration, joined the company, and quickly rose to the top of the organization. She is now a wealthy woman who donates much of her income to charity. In fact, she has set up a foundation that offers girls in poor countries opportunities to compete athletically. Eighteen years ago she adopted a child from Kenya and has been a good parent to that child who is now enrolled in college. Recently, Benita has been diagnosed with a Stage II melanoma, and her chances of survival for more than 3 years are about 30% with aggressive treatment. Benita has decided to forego treatment and has come to see a counselor to get advice about how to tell her family of her decision and get them connected to professional support as she becomes ill and dies. Benita is convinced that she does not wish treatment, that she has lived a full life, and that she does not want to sacrifice the quality of the time she has left for an uncertain prospect of cure. Your assessment shows no evidence of depression or other mental illness or cognitive deficit. Can you ethically agree to her request? Do you have an ethical obligation to do anything to get her to reconsider her decision about refusing a treatment with a reasonable chance of success? What do you think you ought to do if Benita tells you that she is considering suicide when she begins to get debilitated by her cancer?

RECOMMENDED READINGS

Beauchamp, T. L., & Childress, J. F. (2001). *Principles of biomedical ethics* (5th ed). Oxford, England: Oxford University Press.

Cottone, R. R., & Claus, R.E. (2000). Ethical decision making models: A review of the literature. *Journal of Counseling and Development, 78,* 275–283.

Freeman, S. J. (2000). *Ethics: An introduction to philosophy and practice.* Belmont, CA: Wadsworth.

Gibson, W. T., & Pope, K. S. (1993). The ethics of counseling: A national survey of certified counselors. *Journal of Counseling and Development, 71,* 330–336.

Jordan, A. E., & Meara, N. M. (1990). Ethics and the professional practice of psychologists: The role of virtues and principles. *Professional Psychology: Research and Practice, 21,* 107–114.

Kitchener, K. S. (1984). Intuition, critical evaluation and ethical principles: The foundation for ethical decisions in counseling psychology *The Counseling Psychologist, 12,* 43–55.

Pedersen, P. B. (2001). Cross cultural ethical guidelines. In J. B. Ponterotto, J. M. Casas, L. A. Suzuki, & C. M. Alexander (Eds.), *Handbook of multicultural counseling* (2nd ed) (pp. 34–50). Thousand Oaks, CA: Sage.

PART TWO

Major Ethical Issues for Counselors

Chapter 3

Competence to Practice
Building a Foundation for Doing Good and Avoiding Harm

Competence is in many respects the most obvious ethical obligation of the practitioner because incompetent practice greatly increases the likelihood of harm to a client and radically decreases the potential for helping. Nevertheless, professional competence defies easy definition; however, three major components capture the essence of its meaning. These components are *knowledge, skill,* and *diligence.* This chapter begins with an explanation of each term, then reviews the relevant statements in the ethics codes and offers guidelines for determining the limits of competence and for expanding areas of competency. It ends by analyzing the impact of counselor distress and impairment on competent functioning.

Components of Professional Competence

Knowledge

To be knowledgeable means being schooled in the history, theory, and research of one's field and cognizant of the limits of current understanding. Knowledge includes a body of information about theory and research in the field, the judgment to make an informed choice about what knowledge and interventions apply in a given situation, and a set of objective criteria for evaluating new theory and research (Spruill et al., 2004). The latter is especially important in counseling because theory and research are always evolving. In mental health professions, knowledge is first achieved by completing a credible graduate-degree program in a mental health discipline. The most direct measure of the quality of a training program is accreditation by the discipline because accredited degree programs have been judged to meet the discipline's standards for an adequate knowledge base. The American Counseling Association (ACA) (through its branch the Council for Accreditation of Counseling and Related Educational Programs), American Psychological Association (APA), American Association of Marriage and Family Therapy (AAMFT), and National Association of Social Workers (NASW) all set high standards for graduate programs that seek accreditation. For counseling, marriage and family therapy, and social work the entry-level degree is the master's, but psychologists have defined the entry-level degree as the doctorate. However, because knowledge is not static and research on human behavior is evolving, a graduate degree, even from an accredited program, is only a starting point for competence. Without continued study, a professional's knowledge base soon erodes. In fact, Dubin (1972) and Jensen (1979) suggest that approximately half of what a mental health professional learns in graduate school is obsolete within a decade of graduation. Unfortunately, research evidence suggests that many practitioners fail to stay current with the published literature (Morrow-Bradley & Elliott, 1986) and thereby hasten the erosion of their knowledge. For this reason, many state licensing boards have begun to mandate continuing education for their members. For example, 42 states require 20 or more hours of continuing education for psychologists every 2 years, although the number of hours required and the content of those hours vary significantly. Twenty-two states stipulate completion of 2–6 hours of continuing education in professional ethics for psychologists every biennium (APA, 2003). Whether the licensing boards' requirement for regular continuing education reverses clinicians' erosion of knowledge or the incidence of unethical practice terminates remains to be determined by research (Sharkin & Plageman, 2003), although evidence from the impact of continuing education on the performance of practitioners in other health care professions is encouraging (VandeCreek, Knapp, & Brace, 1990).

Skill

The second component of competence is skill, not just in practicing therapeutic procedures in the classroom but also in successfully applying interventions with actual clients. Norman (1985) and Overholser and Fine (1990) divide this component into two kinds of skills. *Clinical skill* is the counselor's appropriate use of basic interviewing skills, and *technical skill* concerns effective use of specific therapeutic interventions. Clinical skills include abilities such as the capacity to build a productive therapeutic alliance, to communicate effectively, and to sensitively explore uncomfortable aspects of a client's problem. Spruill et al. (2004) identify cultural competence, knowledge of ethical and legal guidelines, and the ability to think critically as additional foundational clinical skills. Technical skills are exemplified by the ability to conduct desensitization for a client with test anxiety or to administer an individual intelligence test. Implicit in the general concept of skill is the capacity of the professional to make judgments about which interventions are appropriate in which situations. These judgments should be informed by the current research on what works in counseling and psychotherapy under what circumstances (e.g., Barlow, 2004; Hill, 2004; Lambert, 2003; Wampold, 2001).

To help students develop clinical judgment and intervention skills, all mental health training programs require field experiences such as practica and internships as major parts of their degree requirements. Applying knowledge with a client is a higher-order process than comprehending that information, and no one is competent until he or she has mastered both. For example, graduate students usually learn about treating phobias in their classes, becoming familiar with both the theory and the research on phobia treatments. They may read transcripts of sessions, may view videotapes of model sessions, and may practice these approaches in role-plays with each other. Then students are evaluated on their grasp of the material. However, even students who pass such tests are not competent unless they can skillfully apply this knowledge to clients likely to benefit from such interventions. Because of the complexity of skill building in counseling and psychotherapy, many hours of closely supervised field experience are necessary to achieve success in applying counseling interventions. Additional supervised experience after the awarding of a degree is also typically required before states will license mental health professionals for independent practice. Many states require 2 years of full-time supervised work experience before granting a license to a master's level professional and 1 year of full-time supervised practice for doctoral level psychologists. For an excellent review of competency issues in psychology practice and training, see Rodolfa, Bent, Eisman, Nelson, Rehm, & Ritchie (2005).

The complexity of counseling and psychotherapy also means that no single professional will be skillful in all interventions, either at graduation or at any point in his or her career. The staggering range of human problems people experience, coupled with the diversity of counseling interventions, renders universal competence impossible. Counselors must limit their work to some subsample of problems and populations. Some focus on particular problems such as anxiety and depression or career indecision, whereas others focus on particular age groups, such as college students or older adults. Still others limit their practice to group or family counseling. Beware the professional who claims to do everything well: Either some of those skills are underdeveloped or that person is a fraud.

Diligence

Diligence, the third component of competence, is a consistent attentiveness to the client's needs that takes priority over other concerns. A diligent counselor gives deliberate care to appropriate assessment and intervention for a client's problem and maintains that care until counseling is completed. Diligence means that the professional is willing to work hard to help a client and is ready to refer the client elsewhere if the counselor feels unable to give competent help. This attentiveness is grounded in self-knowledge— only counselors who understand their strengths and limitations can be truly diligent. Evidence of a diligent attitude emerges in several ways. It is present in the thoroughness of counseling. A diligent counselor wants to be as sure as reasonably possible about the diagnosis and the treatment. (Note the words *reasonably* and *sure*; diligence does not require obsessive concern with detail.) Diligence is also present in the counselor's willingness to engage in additional reading and research about a client's diagnosis and treatment and to consult with colleagues. A diligent professional is interested in following up clients who complete counseling to check the long-term effectiveness of their interventions. Such information can help both the former client and future clients. In short, diligence means that one is willing to "go the extra mile" to help each client and to improve professional skills.

Thus competence takes much intellectual and emotional energy and is both a goal and a reality. The competence continuum runs from incompetent to exceptionally competent (Koocher, 1979). Spruill et al. (2004) used a similar model developed by Dreyfus to delineate five levels in the development of competence from novice to expert. A competent professional is always seeking to enhance current skills and knowledge, but his or her aim is not perfection. Instead, competence implies adequacy in skills and is at least partially measured in a comparative fashion. One is competent when one's knowledge and skills are as well developed as those of other professionals previously demonstrated to be competent in the specified area. In other words, one is deemed competent if, after education and supervised practice, one can carry out an intervention at least as well as supervisors or colleagues.

A comparative criterion has its perils, however—one might settle for being as incompetent as one's colleagues. A more valid and objective criterion for competence is one's effectiveness in helping clients, in developing plans for counseling, in implementing those plans, and in evaluating the outcomes of counseling (Spruill et al., 2004). Counseling that benefits the client and avoids unnecessary risk to him or her is the more fundamental measure of competence. Sometimes a third criterion exists—attainment of the standards established by a professional association for a particular type of practice. For example, the APA has produced specialty guidelines for providing services in clinical, counseling, school, and organizational psychology (1993b, 2003) that identify skills essential for competence with multicultural clients. Similarly, AAMFT has established criteria for competence in that discipline (Everett, 1990).

Competence as Performance, Not Capacity

Competence refers to a person's professional performance, not to abilities. One may have the *ability* to perform a task competently, but competence is judged in the *performance* of the task itself (Jensen, 1979). Many factors can interfere with a capable person's performance. These factors range from environmental circumstances (such as impossible work demands) to unpredictable events (such as a sudden illness in the middle of a session) to mental health problems in the therapist (such as depression or burnout). Ability is a prerequisite for competence, but it is not identical to it.

Competent performance probably also varies from client to client and day to day. No mental health professional performs at the identical level of skill and diligence with every client. Fatigue, distraction, and stress are just a few problems that can compromise competent performance. No clinician should expect completely uniform performance in all situations. A more realistic standard is a set threshold level, which is not crossed, for competent work with clients. This threshold level should be defined as adequate service that provides the client with the likelihood of benefit. If counselors give service less competent than that, they need to make diligent efforts to rectify the problems created by their actions. For instance, a counselor may invite a client back for another session without charge to compensate for a prior meeting, or he or she may consult a colleague or supervisor to deal with the stress that caused the lapse. (A later section of this chapter discusses service made persistently inadequate by impairment or distress.)

Professional Standards for Practice

All the major codes of ethics governing mental health professions contain statements about competence. Both the ACA and APA codes make lengthy comments on the topic, underscoring its importance. These standards derive from the ethical principles of beneficence and nonmaleficence, the duty to do good and to avoid harm. As mentioned in Chapter 1, genuine skill at helping people in distress is essential for professions that publicly proclaim their expertise in this area. Offering anything less constitutes dishonest advertising.

ACA *Code of Ethics,* Section C.2: Professional Competence

a. Boundaries of Competence. Counselors practice only within the boundaries of their competence, based on their education, training, supervised experience, state and national professional credentials, and appropriate professional experience. Counselors will gain knowledge, personal awareness, sensitivity, and skills pertinent to working with a diverse client population.

b. New Specialty Areas of Practice. Counselors practice in specialty areas new to them only after appropriate education, training, and supervised experience. While developing skills in new specialty areas, counselors take steps to ensure the competence of their work and to protect others from possible harm.

c. Qualified for Employment. Counselors accept employment only for positions for which they are qualified by education, training, supervised experience, state and national professional credentials, and appropriate professional experience. Counselors hire for professional counseling positions only individuals who are qualified and competent for those positions.

d. Monitor Effectiveness. Counselors continually monitor their effectiveness as professionals and take steps to improve when necessary. Counselors in private practice take reasonable steps to seek out peer supervision to evaluate their efficacy as counselors.

f. Continuing Education. Counselors recognize the need for continuing education to maintain a reasonable level of awareness of current scientific and professional information in their fields of activity. They take steps to maintain competence in the skills they use, are open to new procedures, and keep current with the diverse and/or special populations with whom they work.

APA *Ethical Principles,* Section 2.01: Boundaries of Competence

(a) Psychologists provide services, teach, and conduct research with populations and in areas only within the boundaries of their competence, based on their education, training, supervised experience, consultation, study, or professional experience.

(b) Where scientific or professional knowledge in the discipline of psychology establishes that an understanding of factors associated with age, gender, gender identity, race, ethnicity, culture, national origin, religion, sexual orientation, disability, language, or socioeconomic status is essential for effective implementation of their services or research, psychologists have or obtain the training, experience, consultation, or supervision necessary to ensure the competence of their services, or they make appropriate referrals, except as provided in Standard 2.02, Providing Services in Emergencies.

(c) Psychologists planning to provide services, teach, or conduct research involving populations, areas, techniques, or technologies new to them undertake relevant education, training, supervised experience, consultation, or study.

(d) When psychologists are asked to provide services to individuals for whom appropriate mental health services are not available and for which psychologists have not obtained the competence necessary, psychologists with closely related prior training or experience may provide such services in order to ensure that services are not denied if they make a reasonable effort to obtain the competence required by using relevant research, training, consultation, or study.

(e) In those emerging areas in which generally recognized standards for preparatory training do not yet exist, psychologists nevertheless take reasonable steps to ensure the competence of their work and to protect clients/patients, students, supervisees, research participants, organizational clients, and others from harm.

APA *Ethical Principles,* Section 2.03: Maintaining Competence

Psychologists undertake ongoing efforts to develop and maintain their competence.

Both codes acknowledge the impossibility of universal competence and emphasize the importance of working within the boundaries of one's knowledge and skill. They place the duty to monitor one's competence and make necessary improvement directly in the hands of the individual professional. Finally, the codes indicate that competence ordinarily results from formal education, supervised practice, and continuing education. They imply that informal, unstructured approaches to developing new competencies are likely to be insufficient. Professionals seeking to extend their competence to a new area should have a plan consistent with existing standards and committed to a comprehensive understanding of the new area. APA's code also attends to the difficult issue of establishing competence in new and emerging areas of practice for which widely accepted standards of competence do not yet exist. APA's guidance in such situations is not definitive, but the standard imposes a duty to do as much as reasonably possible to become competent and to protect clients and other consumers of such untested approaches. It is important to note that professionals need not exclude new or experimental procedures from their practice; instead, they should be cautious and prudent in their use to protect client welfare. If a treatment approach with demonstrated evidence of effectiveness for a given population or problem exists, the use of an unproven intervention is difficult to justify. (See APA's Policy Statement on Evidence-Based Practice in Psychology [2005a] for a description of the appropriate use of research to guide practice.)

The APA code clarifies the responsibility of professionals in situations where alternative service is not reasonably available. It advises professionals that if their competence is in an area closely related to the service the client needs, professionals may go forward with treatment provided that they make efforts to become competent through training, consultation, and supervision.

In a section new with the current code, APA also advises professionals about the ethics of competent service in emergency situations:

APA *Ethical Principles,* Section 2.02: Providing Services in Emergencies

In emergencies, when psychologists provide services to individuals for whom other mental health services are not available and for which psychologists have not obtained the necessary training, psychologists may provide such services in order to ensure that services are not denied. The services are discontinued as soon as the emergency has ended or appropriate services are available.

This standard frees professionals from undue concern about an ethics violation in circumstances in which they are attempting to respond compassionately to an emergency in the absence of immediately available referral sources. It also highlights the promotion of the welfare of the client as the highest priority—to deny treatment in a crisis for fear of violating competency standards would violate that most fundamental ethical principle of promoting the welfare of the client. At the same time, when professionals are providing emergency care outside the customary boundaries of their competence they must act as conservatively as possible to meet the client's needs and work diligently to obtain more competent care as soon as possible.

The Relationship Between Competence and Professional Credentials

Licenses and certificates are designed to protect the public from frauds and charlatans pretending to provide professional services. Procidano, Busch-Rossnagel, Reznikoff, & Geisinger (1995) capture the function of licenses well: "What the states license is the absence of deficiencies, rather than the presence of competencies" (p. 427). Certifying bodies review only the knowledge component of competence. They can weed out the least knowledgeable because they prevent people who lack appropriate graduate degrees from becoming licensed or certified. A graduate degree is, after all, the primary credential for professional competence; licenses and certificates are secondary (Koocher, 1979). Because clinicians usually need to pass a state examination to get a license, individuals who managed to receive a degree without learning much are not likely to pass that examination.

Credentialing bodies evaluate the skills component rather indirectly through the requirement that candidates for licensing amass a substantial number of hours of supervised experience in the field. These bodies tend not to measure diligence at all, except as they inquire about prior ethics violations or personal impairments that may compromise practice. When the other requirements are met, diligence is assumed. The continuing education requirements built into most mental health licenses aim to protect the public from practitioners whose knowledge and skills are obsolete. Unfortunately, in most cases these continuing education requirements are too minimal to serve the purpose. Finally, licensing boards usually require applicants to specify their areas of competence. This is also referred to as defining one's *scope of practice*. Many credentialing bodies also request this information at each subsequent renewal of the license. In a small way, this process forces practitioners to identify the boundaries of their competence and reminds them that the limits they specify are a matter of public record. Working outside those boundaries carries a risk to their license. Some states such as Ohio are also requiring licensees to describe their competencies in multicultural counseling and psychotherapy in an effort to ensure competent practice with diverse populations. (For more discussion of multicultural competencies, refer to Chapter 10.)

Professional organizations that branch off from the national associations have been formed to provide more stringent measures of competence and more direct assessment of therapeutic judgment and skills. One such organization is the American Board of

Professional Psychology. Practitioners may apply to this body to be certified as "diplomats" in their field. If applicants pass the rigorous review process for this status, they have demonstrated a well-recognized level of professional accomplishment. The National Board of Certified Counselors provides the same service for counselors. These certifications go a step beyond a professional license to practice, although they are also categorized as secondary credentials. However, even such status does not guarantee competence because of the inherent weaknesses in the procedures used to evaluate candidates. True measures of therapeutic effectiveness are difficult to find. Moreover, possessing such certificates does not imply future competence. Without continued effort to maintain knowledge and skill, competence still erodes, no matter how firmly established it has been at any prior point.

Woody (1997) points out that some "dubious and bogus" credentials have emerged in mental health partly because of increased competition in the marketplace for clients and reimbursement (p. 337). Practitioners "earn" these credentials when they pay the requisite fees and are often required to provide little additional verification of their training or qualifications. He goes on to suggest that such credentials offer little more than an ego boost to the individual paying for them and are dangerous insofar as they deceive the public about the expertise of the practitioner and place the professionalism of the occupation in jeopardy.

Challenges in Defining the Limits of Competence

How do counselors determine the areas in which they are competent, and how do they develop new areas of competence after completing graduate school? The codes give reasonable direction in this area in Sections C.2a and C.2b (ACA Code of Ethics, 2005) and APA Ethical Principles, Section 2.01c (2002). Before one can claim competence in any given procedure, population, or assessment tool, formal training is necessary. Formal training usually entails classroom learning, reading, and discussion with experts. The length and depth of the instruction depends on the complexity of the new competence, its potential to help or harm clients, and the prior background of the counselor. For example, a counselor well trained in play therapy with school-age children who wants to become competent in a new form of play therapy probably requires less classroom time than another child therapist unfamiliar with any play therapy methods. The latter person would require indepth instruction in the history, theory, and procedures of play therapy, along with supervised practice in established interventions, before he or she could advance to the new technique. Both would need supervised experience in the new technique, but the amount of supervised experience would differ with each practitioner; the criterion for success is the capacity to judge when the technique is appropriate and to apply the knowledge skillfully with a number of children. If the new play therapy technique has been demonstrated to be a powerful counseling intervention (one that can offer substantial help when used properly or cause substantial harm when used improperly), the standard for competence with the intervention should be set very high. This translates into longer and more intensive training and practice with the technique. It is important to remember that the requirements for competence are not different for those who are already competent in other forms of counseling. What may be different is the speed with which counselors can proceed through the requirements because of their history and background.

Some weekend workshops and brief seminars are advertised as training professionals in new interventions. Recently this author received a brochure for a 1-day seminar that claimed to teach a new therapy that treats all personality disorders, addictions, and repetitive criminal behaviors. The presenter was described as a trained psychologist with a private practice who is currently writing a book about his new therapy. No other information about the scientific basis for the intervention was provided, and the schedule for the seminar did not include time for assessing the skills of the attendees in this new therapy, although the presenter did offer to sell tapes and videos to interested professionals. Because workshops such as this one seldom offer time for reading, research, and supervised practice in the technique with actual clients, they are unlikely to produce counselors truly competent in the technique. When these interventions have the potential to be powerful therapeutic tools, lack of time for reading, reflection, and supervised practice can be particularly problematic. Only professionals who take extra time to read, reflect, and seek out competent supervision will develop real competence. (Presenters also have a responsibility to clarify the goals and limitations of their seminars along with the descriptions of the possible benefits of attendance.) Moreover, the definition of competence implies scientific value. In other words, one can really claim competence only for interventions that have provided scientific evidence of their effectiveness in helping clients. Independent research demonstrating the efficacy of the approach is the cornerstone of such evidence. Without such evidence of their therapeutic value, new interventions are considered experimental, and claiming competence in such situations is premature. Thus, when counselors are looking for continuing education to expand their competencies, they need to ascertain whether the proposed training (a) is based on scientific evidence, objectively obtained; (b) includes sufficient classroom time to absorb the new material; and (c) provides opportunities for supervised practice and recommendations for obtaining additional supervised experience. Sometimes direct inquiries to the workshop organizers are necessary to obtain this information. The wording of the APA code in the following sections supports this interpretation.

APA *Ethical Principles,* Section 2.04: Basis for Scientific and Professional Judgments

Psychologists' work is based on established scientific and professional knowledge of the discipline.

10.01 Informed Consent to Therapy

(b) When obtaining informed consent for treatment for which generally recognized techniques and procedures have not been established, psychologists inform their clients/patients of the developing nature of the treatment, the potential risks involved, alternative treatments that may be available, and the voluntary nature of their participation.

Limits of Competence with New Populations of Clients

The boundaries of competence extend not just to intervention strategies, such as play therapy or career counseling, but also to new populations and age groups. A person may be skilled in career counseling for one cultural group or age group but may be incompetent to use that intervention with other age groups or cultural groups. This happens because these contexts can affect the way the intervention is received and its effectiveness. Competent work with particular populations also assumes knowledge of the group and demonstrated skill in working with clients from that group. For example, a college counselor who begins working with middle school students but applies without modification the career counseling approaches he uses with university students is unlikely to help those children. He has failed to adapt his intervention to their developmental level, and he may thereby have inflicted unintended negative effects on the children.

Similarly, helping a Cambodian immigrant to the United States deal with depressed feelings may demand competencies different from those needed to treat a client who is depressed and was raised in the United States. In this situation, knowledge of the impact of culture and immigration status on the etiology and symptoms of depression is important. Counselors competent in treating depression in America have a duty to recognize the unique parameters of this case and to seek additional training or consultation to help the client or refer him to another counselor already competent with these issues.

The professional associations recognize the need for knowledge and skill in working with different populations in two major ways. First, APA has published special guidelines for conducting therapy with women (APA, Task Force, 1978) and for providing services to ethnic and culturally diverse populations (APA, 1993b, 2003). These documents are a resource for practitioners seeking to evaluate their competence with clients from these populations. Second, ACA has addressed the topic in its ethics code in Sections C.2.a and C.2.f cited earlier. In addition, ACA also publishes its criteria for competent service to diverse publications (Arrendondo et al., 1996).

Limits of Competence in Rural Environments

One challenge in identifying and working within the boundaries of competence arises from the geographic location of a given counseling practice. Professionals in urban and suburban settings tend to have many local referral sources accessible to clients to whom they do not feel competent to offer services, and they also tend to have easier access to face-to-face consultation and supervision (Helbok, 2003). Thus, urban and suburban practitioners have relatively little difficulty limiting their scope of practice and have the luxury of focusing on areas in which they have developed significant expertise. In contrast, practitioners in rural areas and small towns do not have many referral sources nearby. Seeing another professional frequently entails a real inconvenience for a client because it means traveling some distance. Sometimes the local mental health professional is the only available source of services. If he or she cannot provide counseling, clients may not seek further help and may try to cope on their own. Consequently, out of necessity professionals in rural areas usually practice as generalists. If they became highly specialized, they probably would not have enough clients to sustain their practices and they would need to turn away clients with problems outside their specialty who truly need mental health services.

The ethical challenge for rural counselors and psychotherapists is to provide competent service across a wide range of issues, age groups, and populations while acknowledging that they are not super counselors who can do everything (Hargrove, 1986; Schank, 1998). What criteria should rural counselors use when trying to decide whether a given client request is beyond the limits of their competence? The major determination evolves from the principle of nonmaleficence—avoiding harm to clients. Clients who are at risk for significant harm from an incompetent counseling intervention are better served by a referral, no matter how inconvenient. Second, counselors should evaluate the opportunity to do good and should compare the risk of harm to the opportunity to help. If the risk of harm is high and the chance to help is low, then one should refrain from intervention. If the risk of harm is low and the opportunity to benefit the client is significantly greater, then the intervention can be considered. Access to alternative service is an important variable for counselors to consider because there is a shortage of practitioners in rural areas. The U.S. Department of Health and Human Services has designated two-thirds of rural counties in the country as shortage areas (Benson, 2003). This deficit of service places an added responsibility on rural professionals to use inventive strategies to enhance their competence and gain access to appropriate supervision. Thankfully, the advent of the Internet and World Wide Web has provided easier access to a variety of educational resources for rural mental health professionals. (See Chapter 4 for a fuller discussion of the ethical issues in using computer technology for communication about particular clients.) Finally, rural practitioners should monitor client progress and aggressively intervene when the client seems not to be benefiting from counseling. If rural counselors see a pattern of client problems at the boundaries of their competence, they have a duty to gain additional education to become more competent in serving this community need. (Needless to say, informed consent takes on even greater importance when the intervention approaches the bound-aries of a counselor's competence. Clients should be informed about the level of their counselor's competence and give written consent to counseling.)

Additional Criteria for Evaluating Competence

Haas and Malouf (2005) recommend that mental health professionals ask themselves two other questions when they are unsure about their competence with a particular client. The first question is "Are you emotionally able to help the client?" (p. 28). They suggest that counselors ask themselves whether they can maintain objectivity in the situation. Perhaps the nature of the client's problem is too close to the clinician's own experience to avoid countertransference. To maintain objectivity, counselors need to have insight into their be-havior and have a professional support system available to double-check the accuracy of their own interpretations of the client. Even then, some client issues are strong triggers for some counselors, and those safeguards are insufficient. Referral is then the safest choice. The second question Haas and Malouf suggest is "Could you justify your decision to a group of your peers?" (2005, p. 30). They also refer to this as the "clean, well-lit room stan-dard," which means that any action that a counselor would feel comfortable describing in an open discussion with his or her peers is likely to be appropriate. Conversely, any coun-seling activity that a professional would like to hide or be ashamed to admit to peers is probably not a responsible action. This standard applies not only to questions of compe-tence to treat but also to other ethical issues in practice, especially boundary violations.

The Limits of Competence: Case Examples

Consider the following cases, both of which illustrate the challenges of defining the lim-its of one's competence as a counselor.

The Case of Mrs. Varos

A couple makes an appointment with Mrs. Varos, a licensed professional clinical coun-selor with 10 years of experience in private practice. This couple is requesting sex ther-apy, and the initial assessment suggests that they have accurately identified the major dif-ficulty in their relationship. In fact, the sexual dysfunction they describe is very common and is usually responsive to therapy. Mrs. Varos had no formal courses in sex therapy in graduate school, but she has read several books on the topic and attended a 2-day work-shop on the topic 9 months ago. Mrs. Varos also has a colleague with extensive training and experience in this area who is willing to supervise her for this case. In this situation, can Mrs. Varos consider herself competent to offer professional services to this couple?

The first step in determining whether Mrs. Varos should accept them as clients is to as-certain whether she has the requisite knowledge of sex therapy. Knowledge usually means formal education, which she lacks. However, if Mrs. Varos can demonstrate that her indepen-dent reading and the workshop she attended are equivalent to what others receive in formal courses, then it is conceivable that she could meet the knowledge requirement. The second issue is whether she has enough appropriate supervised experience in sex therapy to be skill-ful in its application. She has no such experience, which is a significant obstacle to demon-strating competence in sex therapy. If her experience as a professional counselor includes mar-riage and family therapy, and she is competent in this related field, she may not need extensive hours of supervised experience in sex therapy to become competent. However, her complete lack of such supervised experience probably renders her incompetent to serve as sex therapist to this couple at this time, although their problem usually responds to therapy. Her colleague's offer to supervise her work with this couple is an important factor to consider, but it does not appear sufficient to make her competent unless he was willing to provide close supervision and she was willing to do additional work to upgrade her knowledge. However, the availability of a colleague with expertise to help this couple actually constitutes an argument for referral. Why risk harming or simply not helping this couple when another professional with proven skill is easily accessible? The "clean, well-lit room" standard also leads to a recommendation for referral. Mrs. Varos probably would not be comfortable reporting to respected colleagues that she treated this couple without close supervision or additional knowledge.

One way in which Mrs. Varos could accept these clients would be for them to consent to treatment by her as a novice under supervision in sex therapy. If they understood the limits of Mrs. Varos' competence and the implications of supervision by another therapist, and they wanted to continue with her, then she could work with this couple. She would have the responsibility to fill gaps in her knowledge as soon as possible, to monitor their progress closely, and to use supervision wisely. The couple should also be informed of the identity of the colleague/supervisor in the event that they have questions about their counselor's effectiveness.

The Case of Dr. Marcello

Dr. Marcello is a licensed psychologist who has worked in a community mental health agency for 5 years. He specializes in family therapy, an area in which he has had considerable academic training and supervised experience. Dr. Marcello views himself as competent as a family therapist. Mr. and Mrs. Turner make an appointment to see him because they are concerned about their teenage son, who has been truant from school often and has been ignoring curfews and other family rules. The Turners are African-Americans and Dr. Marcello has little experience in counseling African-American families. He did have formal courses in multicultural issues in graduate school and has kept up with the literature in this area. His own cultural background does not match that of the Turners. In fact, the mental health center has very few African-American clients and no other staff member at the agency has such experience or ethnic background. Does Dr. Marcello's experience in family therapy make him competent to work with the Turners?

The case of Dr. Marcello is more complicated than the first case. There is no doubt of his competence in family therapy. His knowledge base on multicultural issues may also be adequate. The cultural difference between the therapist and the potential clients here, coupled with Dr. Marcello's lack of experience in family therapy with African-American families, is the central issue. Should his lack of experience with African-American families prevent him from accepting this family as clients? To resolve this question, several other questions must be addressed:

- To what degree does the literature suggest that family dynamics in African-American families differ significantly from those in other cultures?
- To what degree have the approaches to family therapy in which Dr. Marcello has been trained been shown to be effective for African-American families?
- What evidence exists that these approaches have harmed or failed to benefit African-American families?
- What is the attitude of this family to this psychologist, and what are their views about whether the cultural differences between them will inhibit effective therapy?
- Exactly how much prior experience has Dr. Marcello had with African-American families and individuals? Can he arrange for competent supervision/consultation for this case?
- Are there other competent professionals in the community to whom Dr. Marcello can refer this family?

By reviewing the requirements for competence, knowledge, experience, and diligence to resolve this dilemma, we can surmise that Dr. Marcello's knowledge is probably adequate, given his education and continued reading. His commitment to stay current in the literature on multicultural issues and his demonstrated competence as a family therapist also are positive signs of diligence and cultural sensitivity. His limited supervised experience is the problem, a problem complicated by the unavailability of an appropriately trained professional at his agency. At the very least, because of this deficit Dr. Marcello cannot proceed in a business-as-usual way. He has two ethical alternatives. He may refer the family to a competent professional at another agency, or he may make arrangements for supervision/consultation from a professional outside the agency and then obtain the Turners' consent to such supervision. In the latter case, the Turners would understand Dr. Marcello's strengths and weaknesses as their family therapist and would agree to the supervisor's involvement in the case.

Of course, referral to a professional competent in this area is not always practical. If obtaining a competent referral is problematic and the Turners are likely to benefit from intervention, the argument in favor of Dr. Marcello's taking on this case is significantly stronger. As in the case of Mrs. Varos, the family's progress must be carefully monitored so that any negative effects of counseling can be identified and counteracted. In the end, the central consideration is doing good for the clients and avoiding harm to them—both the harm that derives from incompetent practice and the harm that derives from failing to provide them with access to services likely to be beneficial.

Distress, Burnout, and Impairment Among Professionals

The jobs of counselors are inherently stressful. They repeatedly see the pain and destructiveness of people, and although they can usually offer help and hope to those in need, they have no magic wand to quickly cure suffering. The cumulative effects of witnessing so much human suffering can wear down even the most competent professionals. Counselors also have the increasingly burdensome responsibility of dealing with institutions and governmental agencies indifferent or hostile to counseling or with managed care providers whose demands for short-term counseling for lifelong problems frequently seem absurd and counterproductive. It is interesting that several studies suggest that clinicians with a greater proportion of managed care clients feel more work stress and are at greater risk for emotional exhaustion than those with fewer managed care clients (Rupert & Baird, 2004; Orr, 2000; Thompson, 1999). Practitioners are being asked to do more with less, and there is no end to that trend in sight. It's no wonder that in the face of these external pressures counselors often become emotionally exhausted by their work. In its most extreme form, this emotional exhaustion becomes burnout, a syndrome that significantly compromises the competent performance of mental health professionals. A true burnout syndrome consists of emotional exhaustion, the loss of a sense of accomplishment in one's work, and a depersonalization of those served (Maslach & Jackson, 1986). Glickhauf-Hughes and Mehlman (1996) contend that the very personality characteristics that dispose people to become good clinicians render them especially vulnerable to burnout. These characteristics include (a) parentification, a willingness to take responsibility for others when necessary; (b) perfectionism, extremely high standards for self; (c) imposter feelings, self-doubt, and the sense that the good opinion and praise of others is not merited; and (d) audience sensitivity, a high level of awareness of others' feelings and responsiveness to them. Research shows that burnout affects a small but significant number of mental health professionals (Ackerly, Burnell, Holder, & Kurdek, 1988; Fortener, 2000; Raquepaw & Miller, 1989), school counselors (Rovero, 2004), and school psychologists (Wylie, 2003). One study of psychologists also found about one-third admitting "episodes of emotional exhaustion and fatigue" (Mahoney, 1997). Jevne and Williams (1998) suggest that mental health professionals may be at the initial stages of burnout when the begin to feel *less* of everything—less valued, enthusiastic, competent, connected, idealistic, involved, energetic, and creative.

Counselors who work in crisis situations with those traumatized by violence, war, and natural disasters often experience a form of trauma themselves. They can suffer from the very symptoms of posttraumatic stress that they are treating, a phenomenon labeled in the literature as *compassion fatigue, vicarious traumatization,* or *secondary posttraumatic stress disorder* (Figley, 1995; McCann & Pearlman, 1990). Mental health support for those who help victims of crises such as the attacks on September 11, 2001 or the 2004 tsunami in Asia is being recognized as a necessary component of crisis intervention services. Not surprisingly, clinicians who see a high proportion of survivors of trauma or higher weekly caseloads tend to experience higher levels of symptoms themselves (Brady, Guy, Poelstra, & Brokaw, 1997; Trippany, Wilcoxon, & Satcher, 2003). According to VandeCreek and Jackson (2000), the primary manifestations of compassion fatigue are withdrawal and isolation from others, inappropriate emotionality, loss of pleasure, loss of boundaries with the client, and a sense of being overwhelmed or pressured. Some therapist beliefs seem especially predictive of burnout and vicarious traumatization, according to research by McLean, Wade, and Encel (2003). They found that therapists who feel a very high level of responsibility for their clients, who avoid strong emotions and rigidly adhere to a preferred clinical model, and who have strong allegiance to the stance of the therapist as agent of change have higher levels of these problems.

Of course, counselors and therapists have their share of stress in their personal lives, too. They juggle careers, family responsibilities, relationships, and civic duties simultaneously and sometimes get hit broadside by unexpected catastrophes. From time to time these stresses become overwhelming for all counselors. If the distress is temporary, the usual coping mechanisms of taking time off, restructuring responsibilities, or getting support from colleagues and loved ones usually prevent any lengthy compromise in competent performance (Coster & Schwebel, 1997). Occasionally, however, the stress becomes so unmanageable that the usual coping strategies are inadequate and job performance is impaired. According to Stadler (1990), "impaired counselors have lost the ability to transcend stressful events" (p. 178). Research has documented that this phenomenon is not uncommon. Pope et al. (1987) found that 62% of psychologists reported working when overwhelmed by stress, and most of these (85%) recognized that it was unethical to do so. In another study, Guy, Poelstra, and Stark (1989) found that more than one-third of their sample of mental health providers admitted giving substandard care while distressed, although only 5% of those thought the care was poor enough to be defined as incompetent. Psychologists have called such impairment a serious problem for the mental health professions (Laliotis & Grayson, 1985; Wood, Klein, Cross, Lammers, & Elliott, 1985). Findings from Gizara & Forrest (2004) suggest that psychology trainees also experience substantial levels of distress and impairment. Unfortunately, few data exist regarding the incidence of impairment in practicing licensed counselors (Stadler, Willing, Eberhage, & Ward, 1988).

Other researchers have reported that substance abuse problems occur frequently among psychologists and psychiatrists. Thoreson, Nathan, Skorina, and Kilburg (1983) estimated that approximately 6000 psychologists suffer from alcohol and drug abuse. In a more recent study, 9% of the psychologists sampled by Thoreson, Miller, and Krauskopf (1989) indicated that drinking was a problem for them. Substance abuse has been cited as the most frequent cause of impairment in physicians (Bissell & Haberman, 1984). In a rare study that included master's-level counselors along with other therapists, Deutsch (1985) found that 10% of her sample reported substance abuse difficulties.

Of course, mental health professionals are not immune to other psychological disorders. In fact, some studies show a higher rate of suicide among psychiatrists (Knutsen, 1977) and female psychologists (Roeske, 1986) than in the general population. The U.S. Occupational Health and Safety Administration reports that male psychologists have the highest rate of suicide of any professional group (Ukens, 1995). The rates of depression and other emotional problems do not appear different from rates in the general population, with about 10% of psychologists reporting depression (Thoreson et al., 1989) and about 15% of psychiatrists showing evidence of emotional problems (Herrington, 1979). The only study that showed a significantly higher report of depression among therapists than in the general population was that of Deutsch (1985), in which about half of the therapists reported difficulties with depression.

Another common cause of distress among practitioners is dissatisfaction with their intimate relationships (Deutsch, 1984; Sherman & Thelen, 1998). These researchers found this the most common problem cited by mental health professionals, and Guy et al. (1989) reported this difficulty as the second most frequent one identified by psychologists. Sherman and Thelen (1998) added major medical illness or injury, along with work issues such as malpractice claims by clients, demands of third party payers, and time pressures, to this list.

The codes of ethics comment directly on the phenomena of distress and impairment.

ACA *Code of Ethics,* Section C.2.g: Impairment

Counselors are alert to the signs of impairment from their own physical, mental, or emotional problems and refrain from offering or accepting professional services when such impairment is likely to harm a client or others. They seek assistance for problems that reach the level of professional impairment, and if necessary, they limit, suspend or terminate their professional responsibilities until such time it is determined that they may safely resume their work. Counselors assist colleagues or supervisees in recognizing their own professional impairment and provide consultation and assistance when warrented with colleagues or supervisees showing signs of impairment and intervene as appropriate to prevent imminent harm to clients.

APA *Ethical Principles,* Section 2.06: Personal Problems and Conflicts

(a) Psychologists refrain from initiating an activity when they know or should know that there is a substantial likelihood that their personal problems will prevent them from performing their work-related activities in a competent manner.

(b) When psychologists become aware of personal problems that may interfere with their performing work-related duties adequately, they take appropriate measures, such as obtaining professional consultation or assistance, and determine whether they should limit, suspend, or terminate their work-related duties.

These codes place the responsibility for avoiding incompetent practice on the individual professional. (This responsibility is discussed in greater detail in Chapter 15.) The professional has the duty to self-monitor and to take steps to amend or interrupt practice, if necessary, to prevent harm to clients. Both codes imply that professionals ought to seek counseling and psychotherapy as appropriate or to engage in other activities that will help the professional regain his or her prior level of professional functioning. The ethical principle underlying the comments in the codes is nonmaleficence.

Research shows that compliance with this standard is far from universal. Guy et al. (1989) found that 70% of their sample took steps to help themselves, including getting therapy, but Deutsch (1984) reported that the majority of therapists in her sample showed reluctance to seek therapy for personal problems. Results from Pope et al. (1987) also suggest that this duty is breached fairly often. Even more recent research reveals resistance to seeking help: Eliot and Guy (1993) reported that 50% of their sample with a substance abuse problem were unwilling to seek treatment.

Avoiding Harm to Clients from Burnout and Distress

In addition to monitoring their own emotional status and stress levels, counselors and therapists can take additional actions to prevent burnout, vicarious traumatization, and impairment (Baker, 2003; Brems, 2000; Norcross, 2000; Skovholt, 2001; Trippany, Kress, & Wilcoxon, 2004):

1. Recognize the risks and hazards of mental health practice and celebrate its rewards. In the face of external stresses such as managed care, budget cuts, and unsympathetic administrators, clinicians need to work in a cross-disciplinary way to fight changes that harm clients and to get support from colleagues who share their experiences. Isolation increases the risk of burnout. Conversely, practicing professionals consistently report that their profession is a significantly positive influence on their sense of well-being and mental health (Radeke & Mahoney, 2000). They feel wiser, more aware, and more able to enjoy life because of their profession. In the face of the stresses of the work, professionals need to maintain focus on the less tangible benefits it provides them. Stevanovic and Rupert (2004) have identified several "career sustaining behaviors" that focus on a balanced professional and personal life. These behaviors, such as finding time for relationships and generativity outside of work, appeared to increase career enjoyment and reduce the negative impact of work stress.

2. Set clear limits about how much help they can humanly give. Out of misguided good intentions, members of this profession sometimes take on more than they can handle. This tendency to overpromise and overcommit may be related to the personality characteristics that initially drew professionals to the work—a heightened capacity for empathy with people in need, a perfectionism about work tasks, and a sense of self-doubt that encourages one to keep doing more to be worthy of others' good judgments. However, if not kept in check the tendency to give until depleted leaves one exhausted and ill-equipped for competent work.

3. Take their own advice about self-care. All too often counselors fail to take time for themselves even as they admonish client after client about the importance of self-care. Brems (2000) divides self-care into two major components: professional self-care, including engaging in continuing education, consultation and supervision, networking, and stress management, and personal self-care, including maintaining healthy personal habits, paying attention to relationships, making opportunities for relaxation and centeredness, and practicing self-exploration and awareness. Baker (2003) and Skovholt (2001) provide excellent resources on self-care for clinicians.

4. Recognize their own vulnerability and seek help and support when overwhelmed. The combination of work stress and life's complexity often leads to emotional difficulties. Acknowledging these difficulties is a strength, not a weakness. A self-help network for psychologists has been available for more than two decades (Kilburg, Nathan, & Thoreson, 1986; Schwebel, Schoener, & Skorina, 1994), and 18 of 59 states and provinces operated a formal program for colleague assistance (Barnett & Hillard, 2001). It is interesting that this number declined from prior years, partly as a result of liability concerns and lack of volunteer support. Through the APA network psychologists can find colleagues who volunteer their time to help other psychologists with drug and alcohol problems, although utilization of such services is limited (Floyd, Myszka, & Orr, 1999). The state-level programs usually seek to rehabilitate impaired professionals who have been disciplined by the licensing board or who come to their attention through referrals from other professionals. Unfortunately, ACA has not been an active force in confronting the issue of impairment among counselors or providing resources for them (Stadler, 2001).

5. Consider counseling for their personal problems, even if they are not overwhelmed by them. Practicing clinicians ought to consider periodic returns to therapy, perhaps for just a

few sessions at a time, to explicitly assess their current functioning and redress any emerging problems before they risk professional competence. Surveys of therapists indicate that between two-thirds and three-fourths of clinicians have been in therapy either in training or subsequently. They consistently report that it was helpful to feel empathy for clients; respect client dignity, boundaries, and pacing; and gain the confidence to work at a deeper level (Marcan & Shapiro, 1998). In Great Britain and in some training programs in the United States, personal counseling is required (Marcan, Stiles, & Smith, 1999; Patrick, 1989).

6.   Prepare for symptoms of secondary posttraumatic stress and take full advantage of support services available to crisis workers if working regularly with clients in crisis. Professionals should be especially careful to avoid emotional isolation or social withdrawal from others.

Legal Ramifications of Incompetent Practice

Counselors who perform incompetently are potentially subject to legal action as well as discipline by their professional association or licensing board. Incompetent service is often negligent service, and counselors can be sued for negligence in civil court. Malpractice is often used synonymously with professional negligence, and it refers to a "negligent act committed by a professional that harms another" (Packman & Harris, 1998, p. 153). If the facts of the case merit a judgment against a mental health professional, damages can be awarded to the person(s) who has (have) brought the suit (the plaintiff). The thought of being sued frightens most counselors, and with some justification. Litigation against mental health professionals has increased in recent years. As Voltaire once wrote, "I was never ruined but twice: once when I lost a lawsuit and once when I won one." However, counselors should not be immobilized by such fears. They ought to take comfort in the relative infrequency of civil suits for practicing outside of the boundaries of one's competence.

Many responsible counselors who worry about lawsuits fail to understand the distinction between ordinary mistakes, to which every professional is sometimes vulnerable, and negligence, for which one can be held liable. Four criteria must be met for a court to rule in favor of the plaintiff in a negligence action. (For a fuller explanation of these concepts, see Bednar, Bednar, Lambert, and Waite, 1991, or Swenson, 1997.) The first criterion is that *the professional's duty to the client must be established*. To establish a duty to a client, a counselor needs to be in a professional relationship with that client. When a client enters into a professional relationship with a counselor, that client implicitly cedes to the counselor some control over his or her concerns, and the counselor's duty to the client is thus created. A counselor does not have a duty to the person sitting next to him or her on the bus or to a person encountered at a social event. Moreover, a counselor cannot be found negligent for any harm another person may inflict on other bus riders or partygoers. The next logical question is "How long does it take to establish a relationship so that a duty can be defined?" Courts have varied somewhat in their judgments, but in some jurisdictions as little as a single counseling session has been found sufficient.

The second criterion for negligence is that *the counselor must have breached a duty to the client*. Specifically, this means that the care the counselor provided fell below the accepted standard of care for the profession. The standard of care is defined as the quality of care that other competent professionals would provide in this kind of situation. The standard of care is *not* the best possible care—it is adequate care. Formerly, the standard of care was judged largely according to local standards, but since the onset of electronic communication and easy access to professional literature, the standard of care has become more nationally uniform. It is important to emphasize that this standard allows for mistakes and errors in judgment and the errors one makes constitute negligence only if they are errors that other professionals, acting competently, would be unlikely to make. For example, a mental health professional, exasperated with a client's frequent threats of suicide, suggests that a client "put up or shut up" about suicide. Later that day, after taking an overdose of sleeping pills, the client is rushed to the hospital. If a suit is brought against that counselor, the central issues would be whether the suggestion made by the counselor is an error and whether this error was one that other competent professionals would not make under the same circumstances. To answer these questions, the attorneys would look to the professional literature and the experts in suicide. If both evidence of error and substandard practice exist, then the counselor's behavior would have met the second criterion for negligence. However, the suit can be successful only if two additional criteria are met.

To meet the third criterion, *an injury or damage to the client must be established*. A counselor's mistake, no matter how wrongheaded or incompetent, is not legally meaningful unless some injury results. (By the way, this criterion need not apply for an ethics complaint to be upheld.) If the suicidal client just described ignored the counselor's advice and immediately sought assistance from another more competent professional, that client would have difficulty demonstrating injury. Even an irresponsible blunder does not result in legal liability in the absence of a negative effect on the client.

Finally, if injury or damage does happen to the client, *the harm must be caused by the therapist's mistake*. If the harm would have happened to the client regardless of the therapist's action, then negligence cannot be proved.

In short, the standard for liability for negligence is a rigorous one, and its very rigor should reassure counselors about the risks of frivolous or unjustified lawsuits. However, the best protection against lawsuits is, in accordance with the codes of ethics, practicing within the boundaries of one's competence. Civil suits for practice beyond the limits of one's competence are unlikely to decrease in the decade ahead.

SUMMARY

Competence has three primary components: knowledge, skill, and diligence. Competence means that one performs effective counseling techniques as well as other skilled professionals and according to accepted criteria. Competence is distinguished from perfection because universal competence is unattainable. Rather, competence should be thought of as spanning a continuum from incompetent to exceptionally competent. A counselor should always aim for higher levels of competence. Because of the evolving nature of knowledge and practice, competencies must be maintained through continuing education and consultation, or they will erode.

The ethics codes demand that to avoid harm to clients, professionals must practice within the limits of their competence. When seeking to develop new competencies or to determine whether a particular activity is within their existing skills, counselors must evaluate their level of formal training and supervised practice in the area. Both formal training and supervised practice are prerequisites for competence. Counselors who judge their skills inadequate for a client's needs should refer the client to a competent colleague. Counselors in rural areas have special concerns about the limits of competence because referral sources are scarce and the pressures on them to act as generalists are great. The central ethical issue is the capacity to assist the client and avoid risk of harm. Counselors need to take developmental and cultural issues into account when evaluating their competencies because no counseling intervention has been demonstrated effective across all ages or cultures.

At times the stress of this occupation becomes overwhelming. When this happens, competent performance is threatened and a formerly competent counselor may provide inadequate service. The codes place the responsibility for self-monitoring stress on the individual counselor, and they mandate that counselors limit or interrupt their practices if necessary to avoid harm to clients. Burnout caused by occupational stress and impairment caused by emotional, relationship, or substance abuse problems are the most common reasons for this kind of incompetent service.

When counselors practice outside the boundaries of their competence or provide incompetent service, they are at risk for a civil suit against them in addition to an ethics complaint. Lawsuits are still relatively uncommon, and no diligent counselor needs to worry excessively about this eventuality. Counselors need to understand that negligence is not identical with professional error and that a lawsuit against a counselor for negligence can be won only if (a) the counselor has a demonstrable professional relationship with the client, (b) the counselor made a mistake that showed substandard care, (c) the client suffered an injury, or (d) the injury was directly caused by the counselor's actions.

DISCUSSION QUESTIONS

1. There is debate in the mental health professions about the value of professional credentials such as licenses and certifications. Some argue such credentials do more to protect the professions than to protect the public. What is your view on this issue?

2. Some say that the standards for practicing within the limits of one's competence are unfair to rural practitioners, who must try to help an extraordinarily wide range of people if they are to have any practice at all. They contend that the standard has a bias in favor of urban and suburban practitioners. What do you think of this argument?

3. Managed care presents new dilemmas for mental health professionals, who see competence as a combination of knowledge, skill, and diligence. What do you see as the dilemmas in managed care (as they relate to competence)?

4. How well do the workshops and continuing education programs you have seen advertised meet the criteria set forth here for evidence of scientific value?

5. A number of people enter the mental health professions because of their own histories of recovery from emotional pain. They want to help others live full lives, as they have learned to do. How might this history affect their risk for impairment? Is such a history an advantage or a disadvantage in this regard?

CASE FOR DISCUSSION

Kim is a successful career counselor with more than 30 years of experience in the field. Her special interest is in helping "workaholics" learn to live more balanced lives without significantly compromising work performance. She developed an innovative counseling intervention for helping workaholics and has begun to offer seminars to teach other professionals her method. Enrollment in the 6-hour seminar costs $475. During the seminar she lectures on the approach, shows videos of the techniques with client-actors, and asks participants to role-play counseling sessions as practice. She also distributes a list of recommended readings and cautions participants about circumstances in which the procedure is contraindicated. After the question-and-answer period is completed, Kim wishes the audience success in their work with this population. One month later Kim sends a questionnaire to participants, seeking feedback about their experience with the treatment procedures. Are graduates of this seminar competent to implement the intervention technique Kim has designed? Is Kim acting ethically in structuring the seminar as she has done? If a dissatisfied client of one of Kim's students filed an ethics complaint against both Kim and the counselor who provided the service for incompetent and harmful treatment for her workaholic tendencies, would that claim have any merit?

RECOMMENDED READINGS

Baker, E. K. (2003). *Caring for ourselves: A therapist's guide to personal and professional well being.* Washington, DC: American Psychological Association.

Brems, C. (2000). The challenge of preventing burnout and assuring growth: Self-care. In C. Brems (Ed.), *Dealing with challenges in psychotherapy and counseling* (pp. 262–296). Pacific Grove, CA: Brooks/Cole.

Figley, C. R. (Ed.). (1995). *Compassion fatigue: Coping with secondary traumatic stress disorder in those who treat the traumatized.* New York: Brunner/Mazel.

Neufield, V., & Norman, G. (Eds.). (1985). *Assessing clinical competence.* New York: Springer.

Pines, A., & Aronson, E. (1988). *Career burnout: Causes and cures.* New York: Free Press.

Rodolfa, E., Bent, R., Eisman, E., Nelson, P., Rehm, L., & Ritchie, P. (2005). A cube model for competency development: Implications for psychology educators and regulators. *Professional Psychology: Research and Practice, 36,* 347–354.

Schwebel, M., Schoener, G., & Skorina, J. K. (1994). *Assisting impaired psychologists* (rev ed.). Washington, DC: American Psychological Association.

Skovholt, T. M. (2001). *The resilient practitioner: Burnout prevention and self care strategies for counselors, therapists, teachers and health professionals.* Boston: Allyn & Bacon.

Chapter 4

Confidentiality
Supporting the Client's Right to Privacy

This chapter discusses the scope of confidentiality; the distinction between its legal and ethical dimensions; the legal limits on confidentiality in counseling and psychotherapy; and the need to balance confidentiality against other ethical obligations, such as the professional's legitimate need to consult with colleagues. The next sections of the chapter deal with the special considerations regarding confidentiality when working with minors, clients with human immunodeficiency virus (HIV) spectrum disorders, and clients in group and family services. The final section analyzes emerging issues in confidentiality, including dilemmas in managed care and electronic communications between mental health professionals and the public.

"Can I tell you something in confidence?" is a question most people have been asked by friends and family. The questioner is seeking support or advice while keeping some control over private information. If the receiver of a secret promises confidentiality but fails to honor that promise, the other person feels betrayed and the relationship is ruptured or compromised.

There are parallels between this experience and the expectations clients have when they enter counseling or psychotherapy. Usually clients expect that the private material they reveal to a professional will not be shared without their consent. If clients discover that their trust has been misplaced, they feel betrayed and their capacity to trust mental health professionals diminishes. Clients, even in the best of circumstances, usually have conflicting feelings about revealing personal information to professionals. On the one hand, they feel they need support and direction, and on the other hand, they worry that they will be judged negatively for private thoughts and feelings about which they themselves feel uncomfortable. Thus, both clients and friends reveal secrets only when they believe the receiver is worthy of their confidence and will not berate them for their imperfections.

Of course, the confidentiality of the professional relationship differs in many respects from that of ordinary friendship. First, with few exceptions, every portion of the conversations between mental health professionals and their clients is confidential, no matter how mundane. Clients may mention that they dislike Chinese food, play the harmonica, or lift weights. This information is not especially private or embarrassing, and it is probably easily shared with acquaintances without any expectation of confidentiality. However, if that communication takes place within a counseling relationship, it must be kept confidential. Why is this so? As Bok (1989) suggests, by guarding the privacy of even inconsequential disclosures the professional is reassuring the client that more personal material will also be kept safe. After all, much of the material clients disclose is sensitive information to which no one else in their lives, not even their closest friends or partners, is privy. For example, a college student may admit that she has used cocaine to a counselor before she tells anyone else, or a professional dancer may reveal that he uses self-induced vomiting to control his weight, although he has hidden this information from all others.

The next distinction between confidences in friendships and in professional settings relates to clients' assumptions about the therapeutic process. Clients usually assume they can trust mental health professionals, so they omit the step of asking for reassurance of confidentiality. In fact, research suggests that most clients expect that *virtually everything* disclosed in counseling will be held in strict confidence (Miller & Thelen, 1986; VandeCreek, Miars, & Herzog, 1987). This frame of mind, coupled with the sensitive nature of the material revealed, heightens the sense of betrayal a client experiences if confidentiality is violated. Of course, not all clients assume clinicians are trustworthy, but most give them the benefit of the doubt. Unless the professional engages in an informed consent process about confidentiality and its limits, clients are likely to hold on to this misperception of the absolute nature of therapeutic privacy.

The fourth contrast deals with the difference in consequences for the violator of the confidence. If friends violate a confidence, their major risk is a rupture in the friendship. If a professional violates a confidence, that individual's reputation, job, and license may be at stake, and he or she may be vulnerable to civil action for malpractice or breach of contract.

The last major distinction is in the scope of confidentiality. Confidentiality in counseling and psychotherapy encompasses not only the words spoken between counselors and their clients but also all records related to those interactions and the identity of the clients. A counselor is obligated not to disclose even the names of clients without their permission. Scholars have named this form of confidentiality *contact confidentiality* (Ahia & Martin, 1993). Mental health professionals are expected to provide a therapeutic environment in which client words cannot be overheard, their records are kept secure from unauthorized people, and their presence at the counseling office is protected to the fullest extent possible.

Moreover, the ethical obligation to confidentiality extends past death, as is codified in the 2005 version of the American Counseling Association (ACA) Code (Section B.3.f). In other words, the death of a client does not release a counselor from his or her obligation to maintain confidentiality. (The American Psychological Association, or APA, code is silent on this issue except to indicate that psychologists should follow all laws relating to professional practice.) A notorious example of a violation of this imperative occurred after the murder of Nicole Brown Simpson (ex-wife of O. J. Simpson), when her therapist spoke with the press about matters her client had revealed to her in therapy. As a result of those unauthorized disclosures, the Board of Behavioral Science Examiners of California took disciplinary action against the social worker (Simpson case, 1994). Similarly, when the therapist who treated Anne Sexton, the acclaimed American poet who had died by her own hand some years before, released hundreds of tapes of her therapy sessions to Sexton's biographer, there was a public outcry, and many called it a betrayal of Sexton (Burke, 1995). The therapist broke no law because he complied with a statutory requirement to have a release from the deceased person's legal representative, but many professionals believe that the ethical obligation to confidentiality to the former client must sometimes take precedence over the rights of the next of kin. There is also the question of the ethics of retaining audiotapes of therapy sessions for many years after the termination of services (and long after the death of the client). Current advice recommends declining to release confidential records even to legal representatives in situations in which the professional has a reasonable basis on which to believe that release would be inconsistent with the deceased client's wishes or not in his or her best interest (Werth, Burke, & Bardash, 2002). Of course, should the professional receive a court order for such release, compliance is advisable.

In short, although confidentiality in counseling is built on the same foundation as confidentiality in social relationships, it holds unique obligations for the mental health professional. Driscoll (1992) calls the profession's duty to confidentiality a "sacred covenant." Research also supports the prominence of confidentiality in the ethical issues practitioners face. For example, when surveyed about the ethical dilemmas they encounter in the course of their work, psychologists from nine different countries across the world named dilemmas involving confidentiality most frequently (Pettifor, 2004; Pope & Vetter, 1992). Most of these dilemmas involved the management of confidentiality when clients appeared to endanger others, but others dealt with the relationship between confidentiality and child abuse reporting and with clients with HIV spectrum disorders. Two studies of college counselors revealed the same pattern, with a majority of all dilemmas cited by the samples relating to confidentiality (Hayman & Covert, 1986; Malley, Gallagher, & Brown, 1992). In recent years, confidentiality complaints were the fourth most common topic brought before psychology boards for investigation (Peterson, 1996) and the fifth most common for counseling boards (Neukrug et al., 2001), but they still represent a minority (approximately 5%) of such complaints.

Ethical Principles and Virtues Underlying Confidentiality

The importance of confidentiality derives primarily from the ethical principles of autonomy and fidelity and secondarily from the principles of beneficence and nonmaleficence. Respect for autonomy affirms that each person has the power to decide who may have access to private information. Newton (1989) argues that privacy is an essential component of individuality and selfhood. If the individual loses the power to decide who knows his or her secrets, then in many respects no true self remains. Violations of confidentiality are fundamentally disrespectful to the dignity of the person and constitute invasions of privacy. Confidentiality is also based on the principle of fidelity because counselors implicitly and explicitly promise not to disclose what clients reveal to them.

The principles of beneficence and nonmaleficence come into play because breaches of confidentiality leave clients feeling betrayed and thereby reduce or destroy their engagement in the counseling process. Clients cannot benefit from an enterprise in which they have lost faith. Violations of confidentiality can also place clients at psychological and physical risk. For example, clients whose disclosures about their sexual orientation are betrayed can be ostracized from their families, victimized by gay bashing, and discriminated against at work. In a less dramatic example, a client who hears an embarrassing anecdote he shared with a mental health professional repeated at a social gathering can feel stripped of dignity and may remove himself both from counseling and from a circle of friends important for his emotional stability. Moreover, violations of confidentiality undermine the public trust in the profession, diminishing the profession's capacity to help people who may benefit from counseling but who have come to distrust counselors. Bok (1989) refers to this as a threat to the utility of counseling.

From a virtues perspective, when professionals honor confidentiality they are demonstrating the virtues of integrity, trustworthiness, and respectfulness. Zealously guarding client privacy also indicates a true compassion for the courage it takes for clients to enter treatment and for the suffering that violations of trust cause all people. Honoring confidentiality requires integrity precisely because it can be difficult—the human tendency to want to share experiences does not bypass mental health professionals simply because they have a credential, nor does the desire to discuss important or difficult issues that arise at work end with entrance into this profession.

Codes of Ethics

The ethics codes of both ACA and APA refer extensively to confidentiality, emphasizing its place at the foundation of professional behavior. The codes discuss confidentiality as follows.

ACA *Code of Ethics:* Confidentiality, Privilege and Privacy

B.1.b. Respect for Privacy. Counselors respect client rights to privacy. Counselors solicit private information from clients only when it is beneficial to the counseling process.

B.1.c. Respect for Confidentiality. Counselors do not share confidential information without client consent, or without sound legal or ethical justification.

B.2.a. Danger and Legal Requirements. The general requirement that counselors keep information confidential does not apply when disclosure is required to prevent clear and imminent danger to the client or others or when legal requirements demand that confidential information must be revealed. Counselors consult with other professionals when in doubt as to the validity of an exception. Additional considerations apply when addressing end-of-life issues.

B.2.d. Minimal Disclosure. To the extent possible, clients are informed before confidential information is disclosed and are involved in the disclosure decision-making process. When circumstances require the disclosure of confidential information, only essential information is revealed.

B.1.d. Explanation of Limitations. At initiation and throughout the counseling process, counselors inform clients of the limitations of confidentiality and identify foreseeable situations in which confidentiality must be breached.

B.3.a. Subordinates. Counselors make every effort to ensure that privacy and confidentiality of clients are maintained by subordinates including: employees, supervisees, students, clerical assistants, and volunteers.

B.3.b. Treatment Teams. When client treatment involves a continued review by a treatment team, the client will be informed of the team's existence and composition, information being shared, and the purposes of sharing such information.

B.3.c. Confidential Settings. Counselors discuss confidential information only in settings in which they can reasonably ensure client privacy.

B.6.a: Confidentiality of Records. Counselors ensure that records are kept in a secure location and that only authorized persons have access to records.

B.6.b: Permission to Record or Observe. Counselors obtain permission from clients prior to recording sessions through electronic or other means.

B.6.c: Permission to Observe. Counselors obtain permission from clients prior to observing counseling sessions, reviewing session transcripts, or viewing recordings of sessions with supervisors, faculty, peers or others within the training environment.

B.8.b. Respect for Privacy in Consultation. Information obtained in a consulting relationship is discussed for professional purposes only with persons clearly concerned with the case. Written and oral reports present data germane to the purposes of the consultations, and every effort is made to protect client identity and avoid undue invasion of privacy.

APA *Ethical Principles* Sections 4.01–4.06

4.01 Maintaining Confidentiality Psychologists have a primary obligation and take reasonable precautions to protect confidential information obtained through or stored in any medium, recognizing that the extent and limits of confidentiality may be regulated by law or established by institutional rules or professional or scientific relationship.

4.02 Discussing the Limits of Confidentiality

(a) Psychologists discuss with persons (including, to the extent feasible, persons who are legally incapable of giving informed consent and their legal representatives) and organizations with whom they establish a scientific or professional relationship (1) the relevant limits of confidentiality and (2) the foreseeable uses of the information generated through their psychological activities. (b) Unless it is not feasible or is contraindicated, the discussion of confidentiality occurs at the outset of the relationship and thereafter as new circumstances may warrant. (c) Psychologists who offer services, products, or information via electronic transmission inform clients/patients of the risks to privacy and limits of confidentiality.

4.03 Recording

Before recording the voices or images of individuals to whom they provide services, psychologists obtain permission from all such persons or their legal representatives.

4.04 Minimizing Intrusions on Privacy

(a) Psychologists include in written and oral reports and consultations, only information germane to the purpose for which the communication is made.

(b) Psychologists discuss confidential information obtained in their work only for appropriate scientific or professional purposes and only with persons clearly concerned with such matters.

4.05 Disclosures

(a) Psychologists may disclose confidential information with the appropriate consent of the organizational client, the individual client/patient, or another legally authorized person on behalf of the client/patient unless prohibited by law.

(b) Psychologists disclose confidential information without the consent of the individual only as mandated by law, or where permitted by law for a valid purpose such as to (1) provide needed professional services; (2) obtain appropriate professional consultations; (3) protect the client/patient, psychologist, or others from harm; or (4) obtain payment for services from a client/patient, in which instance disclosure is limited to the minimum that is necessary to achieve the purpose.

4.06 Consultations

When consulting with colleagues, (1) psychologists do not disclose confidential information that reasonably could lead to the identification of a client/patient, research participant, or other person or organization with whom they have a confidential relationship unless they have obtained the prior consent of the person or organization or the disclosure cannot be avoided, and (2) they disclose information only to the extent necessary to achieve the purposes of the consultation.

Confidentiality and Communication with Other Mental Health Professionals

Both the APA and the ACA ethics codes allow counselors and psychologists to share some case information in order to consult with other professionals for guidance about a case. The presumption is that the other professionals understand the need for confidentiality and carry the same obligation to keep client disclosures private. Whenever possible, however, it is important to conduct the consultation without revealing client-identifying information. Such a procedure avoids unnecessary risk to the client's privacy, especially because inadvertent disclosures of client data are acknowledged to be a rather frequent occurrence among clinicians (Pope & Vetter, 1992). When working in treatment teams that routinely discuss all cases by name, the codes recommend that the client be informed that team discussions will occur and that he or she must give consent to that arrangement. (See ACA *Code of Ethics*, B.3.b, and APA *Ethical Principles*, 4.06.) Clients who feel confident that the treatment team is working in their best interest usually agree to this arrangement.

Consultation to maximize the helpfulness of counseling services must be distinguished from idle discussion of client material among co-workers. Professionals have a normal human impulse to share events from their workday with colleagues. Communicating such anecdotes can add a little humor to a stressful day or elicit peer support over a particular work stress. How do counselors ethically meet this need? The first consideration must be for the dignity and welfare of the client. The best standard for determining whether to share information with colleagues is whether one would make the comment in the client's presence. Almost always, the answer is no. First, the counselor probably does not have consent to release information that does not fit the criterion of professional consultation. Second, even if the identity of the particular client is not revealed, the client may feel humiliated by the disclosure and be less willing to disclose personal information in future sessions. Similarly, clients who share pain in the privacy of the counseling office expect that their privacy be guarded, not violated. Thus, embarrassing or painful information should be shared only within a formal consultation environment, and all sharing should respect the dignity of the individual. Counselors who are unsure of whether a particular situation fits that criterion should use a variation of Kant's universalization principle (Newton, 1989): If the roles were reversed, and the counselor were in the client's position, would the disclosure seem necessary and appropriate? If the answer is yes, the disclosure is probably acceptable.

As discussed in greater detail in Chapter 13, when a counselor is not yet licensed or is still in training, his or her supervisor also has access to confidential information from counseling. In fact, someone in training may not accept a client unless that client is willing to have the supervisor receive identifying information and know about the progress of counseling. Whenever a mental health professional is being supervised for training or licensing purposes, that training status must be disclosed to the client at the initiation of services. (See APA *Ethical Principles*, 10.01c, and ACA *Code of Ethics,* E.1.b.)

Counselors in school, military, and business settings are working in cultures that are unaccustomed to the level of confidentiality necessary in counseling (Lowman, 1998; Orme & Doerman, 2001; Tompkins & Mehring, 1993). For example, psychologists in the military indicate that dilemmas involving confidentiality of client disclosures are the second most common ethical conflicts they face (Orme & Doerman, 2001). Teachers, administrators, and other school personnel often share student information and expect counselors to do the same. Managers and senior officers are accustomed to discussing employee performance with human resource personnel or other supervisors and are unlikely to understand the reluctance of counselors to do likewise. In these environments counselors have a responsibility to educate their co-workers about their unique professional responsibilities and to resist the ever-present temptation to trade client confidentiality for a perception of being a team player.

When mental health professionals employ assistants to work in their offices, those assistants sometimes need access to client data to carry out their responsibilities. In some states, office assistants are frequently covered under privileged communication statutes, but regardless of their legal status, professionals are responsible for any breach of confidentiality by someone who works for them, as is expressed in B.3.a of the ACA *Code of Ethics* and indirectly in APA *Ethical Principles,* Section 2.05: Delegation of Work to Others. Privacy regulations promulgated under the Health Insurance Portability and Accountability Act (HIPAA) (Department of Health and Human Services, 2003) also stipulate that professionals are obligated to thoroughly train and monitor their employees' handling of client files and inform clients of the access that assistants may have to those files.

Confidentiality and Communication with Significant Others of the Professional

Counselors and therapists are part of families, either traditional or nontraditional, and have committed relationships with other adults. The norms of committed relationships suggest that adult partners share information about their daily lives with each other. This sharing helps the partners feel supported and revitalized for the next day, and it also is a symbol of closeness between them (Baker & Patterson, 1990). Similar communications occur in very close friendships. This relationship norm conflicts with the rules on professional confidentiality, however. Nowhere in those rules is an exception to confidentiality written for families or friends of counselors. Baker and Patterson (1990) suggest that this standard is routinely violated, that mental health professionals frequently share information about client sessions with their partners. Woody (1999) refers to sharing of private client information with friends and family members as "the Achilles heel of the profession" (p. 608). Evidence from Pope et al. (1987) and Dudley (1988) offers some support for this interpretation, and research by Boudreaux (2001) offers stronger evidence that clinicians share client information with significant others. Boudreaux reported that 96% of his national sample of psychologists shared client data with partners. Participants characterized a majority of these disclosures (70%) as anonymous at least sometimes. On a more encouraging note, participants indicated client names were rarely disclosed along with personal information. When queried about the reasons they discussed client issues with partners the psychologists indicated that they did so to reduce stress, help clients, and gain self-understanding. They believed that these disclosures benefited them but had a neutral effect on their relationship with their partners. The professionals who tended to withhold client information from partners did so to protect confidentiality, comply with regulations, and separate worklife from homelife. Woody (1999) points out that family and friends are under no obligation to protect private client information and in the event of divorce or other deterioration in the relationship that client information may even be used in vengeful ways that result in harm to both the clinician and the client.

Is there an alternative way to resolve this conflict between family loyalty and professional responsibilities? Yes. The best solution is to develop a regular supervision or consultation relationship with another professional to deal with emotional reactions to client cases. In that way, the professional gets the benefit needed to continue effective work without compromising confidentiality to a nonprofessional. Some practitioners also keep a private journal of their own feelings about counseling. This journal is not a record of counseling and does not include any identifying client information, but it is a reflection of the counselor's experience of their day-to-day worklife and can serve as an outlet for emotion. Next, professionals should explain to their partners the standards governing confidentiality and the ethical principles underlying this rule, and they should establish clear limits about the material that can be disclosed at home. An acceptable boundary allows a counselor to discuss broad outlines of problems he or she is experiencing at work. In this way, counselors can still feel connected to a partner by discussing important aspects of their work but not breach professional standards. This guideline means the following statement would be acceptable: "I'm saddened by news of a client's life-threatening illness that is adding further pain to an already difficult situation," but the following wording would be problematic, "I'm working with a 35-year-old woman who has two small children and is not responding to treatments for her HIV infection. She may have to leave her restaurant job, has no health insurance, and her ex-husband who is a lawyer often misses child support payments and is not committed to caring for their children." (Notice that the first option omits age, occupation, gender, and details of the client's individual experience of the problem. It does not even identify the medical problem specifically.) A partner or close friend who has been informed about the professional's obligations in advance will likely understand the counselor's stress or the sense of accomplishment and offer support without seeking further disclosure. In any case, the burden of maintaining confidentiality always rests with the professional.

Mental health professionals who have home offices; who use facsimile machines, home computers, or personal digital assistants (PDAs) to store client information or communicate with clients; or who bring client records home from work are vulnerable to inadvertent breaches of client confidentiality to family members. In these circumstances the onus for avoiding such breaches falls squarely with the professional. Both the ACA and APA codes are explicit about this professional duty to confidentiality when using technology.

ACA *Code of Ethics,* Section B.3.e: Transmitting Confidential Information

Counselors take precautions to ensure the confidentiality of information transmitted through the use of computers, electronic mail, facsimile machines, telephones, voicemail, answering machines, and other electronic or computer technology.

APA *Ethical Principles,* Section 4.04: Minimizing Intrusions on Privacy

(b) Psychologists discuss confidential information obtained in their work only for appropriate scientific or professional purposes and only with persons clearly concerned with such matters.

APA *Ethical Principles,* Section 4.01 Maintaining Confidentiality

(c) Psychologists who offer services, products, or information via electronic transmission inform clients/patients of the risks to privacy and limits of confidentiality.

Confidentiality and Privileged Communication

The terms *confidentiality* and *privileged communication* are frequently misunderstood by mental health professionals (Shuman & Foote, 1999). These terms are often used interchangeably, but there are important differences in their meanings. Confidentiality refers to the ethical duty to keep client identity and disclosures secret. It is a moral obligation rooted in the ethics code, the ethical principles, and the virtues that the profession attempts to foster. The legal term *privileged communication* refers to the client's right to prevent a court from demanding that a mental health professional reveal counseling material (Swenson, 1997) as part of evidence in a legal proceeding. Whereas the term *confidentiality* deals with the prevention of voluntary disclosure of inappropriate material by mental health professionals, the term *privilege* refers to the rules for preventing involuntary disclosures requested by parties in a legal action (Roback, Ochoa, Bloch, & Purdon, 1992). In other words, confidentiality binds the counselor not to reveal client material even if the counselor feels inclined to do so, and privilege protects client information from inappropriate disclosure pressed for by legal authorities, rather than entertained by the counselor. Privilege, formally termed testimonial privilege, is established by law. Because common law requires all citizens to testify when called by the court, exceptions must be established by statute (Knapp & VandeCreek, 1986). Federal courts may interpret privilege differently from state courts. In the course of identifying relevant evidence to prepare for a trial, attorneys go through a process they call *discovery* in which they seek out information to support their case. Materials obtained through discovery are usually available to both sides in any action coming before a court.

It is important to emphasize that the privilege is the client's, not the professional's; it is the client's right to refuse to reveal counseling or psychotherapy information to the court. Thus, a professional asserts privilege on behalf of a client and does not have the option to disclose privileged client information even if so inclined. The laws of all 50 states include some form of patient–psychotherapist privilege. The mental health disciplines whose clients can assert privilege vary considerably from state to state. Clients of psychiatrists and psychologists are routinely included; licensed social workers and counselors are also frequently named. Glosoff, Herlihy, and Spence (2000) found that licensed counselors were included in the privileged communication statutes of 44 states. In 16 states the clients of school counselors are also covered by privileged communication statutes, and privilege sometimes extends to paraprofessionals and office assistants of mental health professionals (Fischer & Sorenson, 1996).

Officers of the court can make demands for client information in three ways. First, they can issue a *subpoena,* a legal demand to appear to give testimony. Second, they can issue a *subpoena duces tecum,* a command to appear in court and bring along specific documents. Subpoenas are usually issued by a clerk of the court without review of the legal merits of the demand for information. Finally, a court can issue a *court order* for a mental health professional to provide either documents or testimony, or both. In contrast to a subpoena, a court order is issued by a judge who has evaluated the legal merits of the demand for information and has ruled that it is properly executed and consistent with current law. In states where privileged communication statutes have been passed, counselors, social workers, and psychologists may not disclose material *even if subpoenaed by an attorney* unless they have client authorization to release that information. However, this does not mean that mental health professionals may ignore subpoenas! Instead, with the assistance of their own attorneys, they should inform the court about their legal and ethical obligation to keep communication privileged, seek further guidance from a judge, and work toward limiting disclosure as much as legally permissible. To resolve the matter, the judge usually holds a hearing and then rules on the applicability of privilege in the case. A judge may also ask to view the disputed materials or speak with the professional about the contested testimony in his or her chambers. This is called an *in camera review,* and professionals may reveal confidential information to a judge for such a review because the purpose is to resolve whether the legal privilege holds in the case. Moreover, the judge is bound to protect the privacy of such information received in camera (Filaccio, 2005). If the judge rules that privilege is not applicable, he or she is likely to order the professional to comply with the attorney's request. In that event, the professional may testify, produce records from the counseling interaction, or both. Clinicians who relinquish records and testimony without first seeking a judge's ruling about privilege are at risk of violating ethical standards.

Huber and Baruth (1987) make an important point about subpoenas: "Subpoenas should be viewed as the formal commencement, not the conclusion, of any disclosure controversy" (p. 20). Mental health professionals practicing in states that grant privilege to their clients are also at risk of a civil legal action against them if they disclose therapeutic information to a court without first seeking client consent or asserting privilege. Professionals are ethically and legally protected, however, if a court refuses to acknowledge the client's right to confidentiality. The counselor's alternatives are to file an appeal of the ruling to a higher court or to endure the legal penalties imposed for refusing to testify or produce documents. Often this means being found in contempt of court. The Committee on Legal Issues of APA has published a document that mental health professionals may find useful in sorting out these legal requirements. It is entitled *Strategies for Private Practitioners Coping with Subpoenas or Compelled Testimony for Client Records or Test Data* (APA, 1996). The specific language in the ACA code is as follows.

ACA *Code of Ethics,* Section B.2.c: Court-Ordered Disclosure

When subpoenaed to release confidential or privileged information without a client's permission counselors obtain written, informed consent from the client or take steps to prohibit the disclosure or have it limited as narrowly as possible due to potential harm to the client or counseling relationship.

The concept of privilege derived from one-on-one conversations, such as those between priest and penitent and lawyer and client. Thus, when clients make disclosures to mental health professionals when others who are not co-participants in family or group therapy are present, their comments may not be viewed as privileged by a court because the client had no reasonable expectation of privacy. A case that came before the Michigan Court of Appeals is a good example of this interpretation of privilege (Galley & Walsh, 2002). The Michigan court held that students who disclosed information to a school counselor in the presence of other students and an administrative assistant were not protected by the privilege that usually covers school counselors in Michigan because it was not a confidential communication. The students had no reasonable expectation of privacy when they made the initial disclosure to this counselor.

The Limits of Confidentiality

Newton (1989) notes that our society is ambivalent about confidentiality. On the one hand, we value it and admire those who are loyal to their friends. Children ridicule tattle-tales, and nations reserve their most severe punishments for traitors. Most democracies have enacted laws to ensure that people can trust their lawyers with their confidences, their physicians with their illnesses, and their priests with their confessions. As indicated earlier, state laws also govern confidentiality between mental health professionals and their clients, requiring them to keep therapeutic disclosures private. It is important to note, however, that therapists and counselors are relative latecomers to this protection, and these laws are generally less complete and more weakly supported than for lawyers, physicians, or priests. This unwillingness to grant mental health professions the same degree of confidentiality as other professionals is a reflection of our society's ambivalence about confidentiality for clients of mental health.

These reactions emerge from the antisocial nature of confidentiality, according to Newton (1989), because confidentiality frequently acts in opposition to some other public interest. To return to an earlier example, although there is no public interest in a client's preferences for Chinese food or harmonica skills, there is a strong public interest in a client who tells a counselor about fantasies of violence against a boss. In the latter situation, the antisocial nature of confidentiality is clear because maintaining the confidence is in direct opposition to the society's desire to protect a citizen against harm. The stronger the likelihood this client will act on the fantasy, the greater is the public interest in disclosure. Prosecutors in criminal cases have also claimed a public interest in obtaining evidence from mental health professionals who have been seeing the accused person in counseling. Society's discomfort with confidentiality has led to increasing the limits on professional confidentiality. Some ethical and legal scholars argue that the ways in which the courts have eroded confidentiality are counterproductive to the client, the profession, and the public's need for access to the mental health system (for example, see Baumoel, 1992; Bollas & Sundelson, 1995). These scholars wonder if people will seek counseling if they are not assured of confidentiality. However, Shuman and Foote (1999) contend that there is no convincing evidence that any of the legal limits imposed on confidentiality in counseling have negatively affected clients' willingness to seek help. Clearly, more systematic study of this question is needed.

However, the public also has an interest in the continuation of professional confidentiality insofar as professionals can help those who have antisocial tendencies to change their behavior. If no confidentiality existed, people may be less willing to disclose such tendencies and feelings. In a study of commuters at Union Station in Washington, DC, Marsh (2003) found evidence to support that view. Her sample reported that they would be significantly less likely to disclose information that would put them at risk for involuntary commitment or criminal prosecution during therapy if their communications were not covered by state and federal privilege statutes. Without disclosure of antisocial tendencies, the counselor's opportunity to prevent such acts in the future is lost. For these reasons, the legal system and professional organizations have sought to limit exceptions to confidentiality. Both systems have affirmed the fundamental value of confidentiality even as exceptions and limitations are codified. The tension between the public interest in the content of counseling sessions and its acceptance of confidentiality as a client's right has not been resolved. Thus, counselors and psychologists should keep current with changes in statutes, case law, and ethical mandates.

Currently there are nine major types of exceptions to confidentiality in counseling, described as follows.

1. Client Request for Release of Information

The first limit to confidentiality is based on the client's autonomy. Because clients have control over personal information, any client who wishes material disclosed or releases information for communication elsewhere has the right to have that disclosure made. The ACA code addresses this provision in Section B.6.f. Unless exceptions to confidentiality exist, counselors obtain written permission from clients to disclose or transfer records to legitimate third parties. Steps are taken to ensure that receivers of counseling records are sensitive to their confidential nature." The APA *Ethical Principles* (4.05.) states, "Psychologists may also disclose confidential information with the appropriate consent of the patient or the individual or organizational client (or other legally authorized person on behalf of the patient or client), unless prohibited by law." Clients frequently waive their right to confidentiality when moving to a new community or when they are obtaining a consultation about a specific issue and wish the new clinician to see their records or speak with their former counselor. Similarly, sometimes clients want their physicians to have access to counseling records and waive their rights so that copies of their records can be sent to those professionals. Many people waive the right to confidentiality so insurers will cover the costs of their mental health services. (The impact of federal regulations from HIPAA, Public Law 104-191, and the Family Educational Rights and Privacy Act [FERPA] on client releases will be discussed fully in Chapters 11 and 12, respectively.) Professionals are also obligated to make arrangements so that the confidentiality of records is maintained when they end their practices because of their own incapacity from illness or injury (B.6.h of the ACA code and in 10.09 of the APA standards).

A release from a client does not give a counselor blanket approval to release confidential information to any party the client has named on a release form without communication to the client about the likely implications of such releases. If doubt exists about a negative impact on the client, the professional ought to discuss those potential negative outcomes with the client prior to release. If a client insists on a release to a party that the professional believes will not be in their best interest, the counselor should document that discussion in the client record and obtain a signed release of information. Before the advent of legislation that so thoroughly protects consumer access to client records, ethical standards insisted that counselors release client information only to qualified professionals. Such broad provisions have been eliminated because they are inconsistent with many state laws. The current wording is more consistent with most, but not all, state statutes. Ohio, for example, offers unlimited client and patient access to health records and provides legal remedies for patients to sue professionals who fail to comply with the law (Ohio Revised Code Section 3701.74, 2003). The ACA code mandates that clients give permission to release confidential information in Section B.6.f. It also addresses this issue when the client is a minor, allowing the counselor to seek authorization from an appropriate person but advising that the minor client be informed about the release.

ACA *Code of Ethics,* Section B.5.c: Release of Confidential Information

When counseling minor clients or adult clients who lack the capacity to give voluntary consent to release confidential information, counselors may seek permission from an appropriate third party to disclose information. In such instances, counselors inform clients consistent with their level of understanding and take culturally appropriate measures to safeguard client confidentiality.

The ACA code also requires that clients be allowed access to their own counseling records, unless such access would not be in their best interests. The mandate also derives from the principles of autonomy and beneficence.

ACA *Code of Ethics,* Section B.6.d: Client Access

Counselors provide reasonable access to records and copies of records when requested by competent clients. Counselors limit clients' access to their records, or portions of their records, only when there is compelling evidence that such access would cause harm to the client. Counselors document clients' requests and the rationale for withholding some or all of the record in the files of clients. In situations involving multiple clients, counselors provide individual clients with only those parts of records that related directly to them and do not include confidential information related to any other client.

e. Assistance with Records. When clients request access to their records, counselors provide assistance and consultation in interpreting counseling records.

The APA code specifies client consent to release confidential information in Section 4.05 and makes a more general comment on records, again focusing on the relationship between access and the best interests of the client in Section 6.01.

APA *Ethical Principles,* Section 6.01: Documentation of Professional and Scientific Work and Maintenance of Records

Psychologists create, and to the extent the records are under their control, maintain, disseminate, store, retain, and dispose of records and data relating to their professional and scientific work in order to (1) facilitate provision of services later by them or by other professionals, (2) allow for replication of research design and analyses, (3) meet institutional requirements, (4) ensure accuracy of billing and payments, and (5) ensure compliance with law.

As will be discussed in Chapter 11, this right to access means that counseling records should be written with the assumption that the client may be reading them.

Releases are not needed when a mental health professional has judged it necessary to begin involuntary commitment proceedings or when a mental health client has signed the HIPAA Notice of Privacy Practices document to allow for communications to other mental health professionals, to third party payors, or to staff involved in processing client records, appointments, and the like. Once the client has signed the Notice of Privacy Practices, clinicians are free to discuss relevant aspects of the client's history and treatment to professionals involved in the hospitalization and to share client records with them as appropriate. The crucial word here is relevant—even HIPAA does not free a mental health provider from their obligation to limit such disclosures to content that is essential to treatment and to restrict disclosures to individuals responsible for care, payment, and operations of the professional service.

2. Court Orders for Confidential Information

The second major limitation to confidentiality occurs when the courts demand access to records and counselor testimony. There are several circumstances under which this may occur and under which privileged communication statutes usually do not apply. Confidentiality is generally not protected when a counselor acts as an expert witness or as a consultant for the court to evaluate a person involved in a legal proceeding. Mental health professionals may be used to assess whether a person is mentally competent to stand trial, is a fit parent, was mentally ill at the time of a crime, or has suffered psychological distress subsequent to an injury or accident. Mental health professionals have been increasingly involved in such activities over the last several decades. The person being evaluated has either waived confidentiality or the court never recognized any such right in the first place. In these circumstances, the entire professional relationship is based on the assumption that information disclosed will be shared with the court.

Sometimes attorneys seek to obtain counseling records from mental health professionals who have a preexisting counseling relationship with someone accused of a crime or whose fitness as a custodial parent is being challenged. Attorneys have also sought this information in civil suits and in federal courts adjudicating civil rights cases. In criminal courts prosecutors often want to use, as evidence of guilt, the material the accused has revealed in counseling. In a significant federal case that came before the U.S. Supreme Court after conflicting holdings from lower courts (*Jaffee v. Redmond,* 1996), the family of a person killed by a police officer filed a wrongful death action and then sought counseling information from the licensed social worker who counseled the officer after the shooting. The state courts considered that information privileged, but no such privilege for social workers had been established in federal courts. The federal district court ruled that the social worker should testify (thereby refusing to recognize the privilege), but the federal appeals court overturned that ruling. In its response to the final appeal, the U. S. Supreme Court determined in an 8–1 vote that the privilege should be honored and the social worker could not be forced to testify about her client's disclosures. Professional mental health organizations were relieved that the Court took such a strong stance in favor of the value of confidentiality in psychotherapy. Whether a mental health professional has a legal right to refuse to give testimony in a particular court is not fully resolved, however. The Supreme Court ruling in *Jaffee v. Redmond* applies most directly to social workers, psychologists, and psychiatrists and does not address the privilege of other kinds of mental health professionals. Remley, Herlihy, and Herlihy (1997) contend that in the future federal courts will honor the privilege of clients of mental health counselors licensed to conduct psychotherapy in their states. Shuman and Foote (1999) point out that in the first 3 years since *Jaffee,* significant changes in case law or statutory law have not occurred. They note that most courts still use the relevance of the professional's testimony to the case at hand as the primary criterion for compelling testimony and that privilege considerations often "take a back seat" when the information the professional has to share is crucial to establishing the facts of the case (p. 481). Thus mental health professionals need to be informed about the regulations governing privileged communication in their states and how those regulations apply to their profession.

Shuman and Foote note that the effectiveness of an argument in favor of privilege has depended partially on the number of other disclosures of confidential information to third parties that the professional and/or client have made. These authors go on to suggest that even routine disclosures to third-party payors, referral sources, or consultations with colleagues may, in some circumstances, limit privilege. Clients' voluntary disclosures of psychotherapy content to other hospital patients have also compromised privilege. In situations in which the threat of court action is a substantial risk they recommend that clinicians use caution even when making disclosures for which the client has signed a release. Shuman and Foote also advise professionals to discuss with clients the implications of voluntary disclosures of psychotherapy content to other people.

3. Client Complaints and Litigation Against Mental Health Professionals

The third limit to confidentiality occurs when clients bring a legal action against their counselors (Swenson, 1997). If a client sues a counselor for negligence or breach of contract, by virtue of initiating a legal action the client is waiving the right to confidentiality. Therefore, the counselor may discuss the treatment in court without threat of legal or ethical sanction because all mental health professionals have a right to defend themselves against malpractice claims. Similarly, if a client files an ethics complaint against a mental health professional, the client must waive the right to confidentiality if the claim is to be pursued. Thus, when accused of misconduct one can respond with case information and counseling records to an ethics committee without worry about an unethical or illegal release of private information. The ethics committees and licensing boards routinely require a release of information from any individual making a complaint prior to contacting a licensee.

4. Other Client Litigation

The fourth limit comes into play when clients initiate against another party a civil legal action that includes claims of psychological harm or emotional distress (Association of Trial Lawyers of America, 2001; Shuman & Foote, 1999; Swenson, 1997). The claim of psychological injury makes any relevant counseling material potentially available to the court. Access to that information is important for a fair hearing of the complaint and can be made available if the defendant seeks it. If the client reasserts a right to confidentiality of that information, the case may not be able to go forward. For example, when someone alleges that her anxiety disorder originated from the car accident for which another driver was responsible (if the client connects the need for counseling to the accident), the counselor can release to the court information about the extent and etiology of the disorder. In either case, because the client is voluntarily revealing psychological information to pursue the claim, the client is waiving the right to have other relevant psychological information kept confidential. In essence, to build an adequate defense the person against whom the claim is being made has the right to all relevant data. It is important to note that confidentiality in such situations does not hold precisely because the client is voluntarily bringing legal or professional action against someone else and has the freedom not to go forward with these claims if he or she does not wish to do so. A defendant in a criminal case is not there voluntarily; hence the legal system more scrupulously guards his or her confidentiality.

5. Limitations Based on State and Federal Statutes

Some material has been excluded from professional confidentiality by statute. Every state has statutes mandating that counselors, psychologists, and other mental health professionals report child abuse and neglect to the proper authorities. The Federal Child Abuse Prevention and Treatment Act (1987) also requires such reporting. The details of the statutes vary somewhat by state, but the central message is consistent. Mental health professionals and educators who learn of child abuse or neglect are legally obligated to report this information to social service or police agencies, usually within 24 hours. The penalties for failing to report usually include criminal sanctions. The reporting of abuse and neglect takes precedence over any legal privilege or ethical obligation to confidentiality. The APA Committee on Professional Practice has published a helpful document on the legal and professional issues in child abuse (APA, 1995). This publication summarizes the professional's role in assessing, reporting, and intervening when abuse occurs and lists national resources available to assist mental health professionals in these processes.

The legislatures have reasoned that the public interest in protecting those who cannot protect themselves from abuse outweighs the obligation to confidentiality. However, even in mandated reporting situations, the law usually limits disclosure of confidential information to content relevant to the abuse or neglect. Other aspects of counseling disclosures that have no bearing on this matter can and should be kept confidential. Because the statutes vary from state to state, counselors must be aware of changes to and wording of statutes in their states.

Research shows that mandated reporting of child abuse occurs commonly in mental health practice; in 2002, for example, nearly 1.5 million mental health professionals and educators made reports about possible abuse or neglect (National Clearinghouse on Child Abuse and Neglect Information, 2002). According to Melton et al. (1995), 90% of child psychiatrists, 63% of clinical psychologists, and 70% of social workers have filed one or more reports of child abuse. Hermann (2002) reported that 89% of school counselors she sampled had reported child maltreatment to authorities. Only a few studies have examined the impact of a report on the therapeutic relationship, and they have found mixed results (Steinberg, 1994; Watson & Levine, 1989). The most negative result seems to occur when the client is reported as the perpetrator (Levine & Doueck, 1995).

Brosig and Kalichman (1992) also describe a substantial amount of noncompliance with the reporting law. Their analysis of the literature concludes that almost one third of clinicians have declined to report suspected child abuse. Research suggests professionals experience a conflict between the desire to keep the client involved in counseling and maintain confidentiality on one hand and recognition of legal mandates and potential harm to the child on the other. Kennel and Agresti (1995) contend that "many professionals appear to place child abuse on a continuum of severity that separates *suspected* abuse from *reportable* abuse" (p. 612). The vagueness of some states' reporting laws also contributes to this noncompliance (Melton et al., 1995). Those who sometimes decline to report seem to want to be sure about the existence of abuse, given the implications of a breach of confidentiality, but their hesitancy can cause them legal and ethical problems. Many statutes mandate reporting *suspicions* of abuse, not *incidences* of abuse. Thus the counselor bears the burden of determining if the suspicion is reasonable, although making this determination can be difficult. The ultimate criteria are avoiding harm to the child and protecting the child's best interests. For an excellent clarification of state laws on child abuse reporting see Foreman and Bernet (2000).

A number of other variables seem to influence this reluctance to report. When mental health professionals fail to report, they often believe that reporting will not be in their client's best interest (Kalichman, 1999) and view child protective services as ineffective (Levine et al., 1991). They worry that reporting will sever the counseling relationship or otherwise irreparably damage therapeutic progress (Haas, Malouf, & Mayerson, 1988). Qualitative research by Rokop (2003) offers possible avenues for reducing the damage. Rokop's findings suggest that the damage to the therapeutic relationship from a mandated report can be substantially reduced if the therapist has developed a strong working alliance with these clients, communicated clearly about the mandate to report, expressed empathy with the client's distress over the report, and offered support subsequent to reporting.

Some mental health professionals attribute their failure to report to a personal conviction that confidentiality in counseling is absolute and should not be violated even in cases of child abuse or neglect. In essence, they are engaging in civil disobedience and opposition to the ethical standards of the profession that encourage compliance with legal requirements. Such counselors should understand that they are at risk for ethical and legal sanctions against them. Moreover, if their failure to report results in greater harm to a child, they must bear moral and legal responsibility for that harm. In other words, refusing to report child abuse has serious and long-lasting consequences for all involved and should not be done lightly. Counselors who find themselves declining to report should examine their motivation and reasoning and seek out consultation with peers about this issue. Failing to report abuse may stem from counselor bias or counter transference rather than from moral values or concerns about client welfare. Counselors should apply the "well-lit room standard" and should ask themselves whether they would be proud to communicate such a decision to a group of professional peers and could expect that audience to respect their position. If not, failing to report is not really a matter of principles or civil disobedience; it is a matter of personal needs or lack of objectivity.

All states also have statutes related to elder abuse, and 45 of them mandate that mental health professionals report neglect or abuse of dependent elders by those responsible for their care (Welfel, Danzinger, & Santoro, 2000). In states that have such statutes, counselors are mandated to report elder abuse or neglect to human service agencies if clients disclose this information in counseling. As with child abuse, state legislatures have reasoned that the duty to protect a dependent elder from harm is stronger than the counselor's obligation to confidentiality. Because the wording of these statutes varies substantially by state, counselors need to be familiar with the law in states where they practice. (See Welfel et al. [2000] for a state-by-state analysis of legal requirements.)

6. Dangerous Clients and the Duty to Warn and Protect

Communications from clients who are dangerous to themselves or other people are generally not protected by the same level of confidentiality as other material. When the mental health professional judges a client to pose an immediate threat to others or to the client himself or herself, the ACA and APA ethics codes allow disclosure of confidential information. The wording in the codes follows.

ACA *Code of Ethics,* Section B.2.a: Danger and Legal Requirements

The general requirement that counselors keep information confidential does not apply when disclosure is required to protect clients or identified others from serious and foreseeable harm or when legal requirements demand that confidential information must be revealed. Counselors consult with other professionals when in doubt as to the validity of an exception. Additional considerations apply when addressing end-of-life issues.

APA *Ethical Principles,* Section 4.05(b): Disclosures

Psychologists disclose confidential information without the consent of the individual only as mandated by law, or where permitted by law for a valid purpose such as to (1) provide needed professional services; (2) obtain appropriate professional consultations; (3) protect the client/patient, psychologist, or others from harm; or (4) obtain payment for services from a client/patient, in which instance disclosure is limited to the minimum that is necessary to achieve the purpose.

The current codes are written to allow counselors and psychologists to breach confidentiality when they believe clients are dangerous, but courts in many states have tended to view this breach as an obligation, not an option, under some circumstances (Kachgian, & Felthous, 2004). The legal requirement to act to protect third parties from imminent danger stems from a 1974 California case in which the family of a woman sued her killer's psychologist (and the University of California) because he failed to tell the woman at risk about the client's threat to kill her. The rulings of the lower state courts on this now-famous *Tarasoff* case were appealed to the California Supreme Court, which ruled twice on the issue (*Tarasoff v. Regents of the University of California,* 1974, 1976). The result of these rulings imposed on mental health professionals a "duty to warn and protect" victims of clients who are violent. This duty soon came to be endorsed not just by California but by courts in at least 26 other states (Herbert, 2003). Soon after the *Tarasoff* ruling, professional associations revised their ethical standards to better reflect the legal position on this issue. Before the *Tarasoff* case, ethical guidelines advised *notifying* the authorities about dangerous clients, but they contained no recommendation to breach confidentiality otherwise. In essence, the ruling in *Tarasoff* means that if a counselor evaluates a person to be in imminent danger from the actions of a client, the counselor must now act to protect the intended victim from that danger. The court envisioned mental health professionals as having a duty to the public as well as a duty to their clients (Smith & Meyer, 1987). The court reasoned that if someone's life or health is at risk from a client, the benefit from a breach of confidentiality significantly outweighs the cost of that breach and should be undertaken. The court ruled that "the privilege ends where the public peril begins" (*Tarasoff*, 1976, p. 347). In 2005 the California Supreme Court extended the duty to protect to situations in which the disclosure of violent intent against a third party comes to the therapist from a family member of the client. (Goldstein vs. Ewing is the case. See Greer [2005] for a discussion of the facts of this case.) In the two related cases that came before the court the mental health professionals had tried to assert that because the client did not disclose violent threats directly to the professional the duty to protect could not be imposed. They tried to argue that disclosure of violence to the therapist from a family member was not sufficient to breach privilege, but the court rejected this argument. This extension of the situations in which a mental health professional has a duty to protect has already been included in other state laws relating to the limits of confidentiality with dangerous clients. Ohio is one such example (Ohio Revised Code, Section 2305.51, 1999).

Many mental health professionals refer to this obligation as *the duty to warn*. That designation is misleading because the crucial obligation identified by the courts is to use reasonable care to *protect* the one at risk (Givelber, Bowers, & Blitch, 1984). A breach of confidentiality to the victim is frequently a means to that end, but it is not an end in itself. Moreover, if a mental health professional deals with this duty by breaching confidentiality to an intended victim, the responsibility does not end with the action of warning the victim. If it did, a telephone conversation with an intended victim might go something like this:

Counselor: Are you Mr. X?

Mr. X: Yes.

Counselor: I am the counselor for Ms. Y, who has made a threat to kill you that I strongly believe she intends to carry out as soon as she can. I do not know of Ms. Y's whereabouts since she left my office 1 hour ago. The police have been informed as well. Ms. Y stated that she had access to a gun. I believe she was going to get that gun when she left my office. Do you understand what I have told you?

Mr. X: Yes, I understand.

Counselor: Goodbye, then.

Such a scenario is ludicrous. The counselor in this situation has technically warned the intended victim but has done little to protect the victim. The person receiving the phone call might disbelieve the counselor and do nothing to protect himself, he might be so traumatized from the stress of the news that he does not take steps to protect himself, or he might get angry and decide to get his own gun and kill Ms. Y first. And these are only the obvious possibilities. The point is that the California court's initial rulings did not limit the responsibility to warning, and they focused more on protection than on warning. In the *Tarasoff* case, warning the victim was viewed as a necessary part of protection because of the facts of that case, but the court did not see warning as essential in every situation. Put another way, the legal duty of the professional is to take steps to help protect the person from foreseeable harm from the client; warning the victim is a common way to discharge that duty, but it is not the only possible way to protect the third party in most jurisdictions (Quattrocchi & Schopp, 2005).

If the counselor does warn a victim, the counselor is expected to take reasonable steps to help that person get protection from the client. That assistance may take the form of assisting the person to connect with loved ones who can offer safety or obtaining police protection. A frequent way of protecting the victim is to restrain the freedom of the client so that access to the victim is not possible, an outcome usually achieved through hospitalization or involuntary commitment to a psychiatric unit. That option is not always available because most states require that a person be diagnosed as *both* mentally ill and dangerous in order to authorize involuntary commitment. People who are dangerous but not mentally ill often cannot be committed to a psychiatric unit. Another option is to intensify outpatient treatment to decrease the client's intent to harm. This option carries more risk because the freedom of the client is not restricted, but it also offers more protection to the privacy of the client. If intensifying outpatient treatment is the option chosen to protect the potential victim, the professional should take extra steps to ensure that this is the best alternative. Consultation with a knowledgeable colleague about the client's care is essential to making a responsible choice for this option.

If all this sounds as if counselors and therapists must put themselves in jeopardy to protect victims, that impression is wrong. Professionals are not expected to risk their personal safety; however, they are expected to intervene with the client and/or the victim to prevent the violence as fully as reasonable.

Subsequent court cases have clarified and extended the *Tarasoff* ruling to limit the duty to situations of *imminent* danger, usually interpreted to mean situations in which a threat of immediate action has been made or implied. If this threat is judged by the counselor as significant and likely to be carried out in the near future, the duty is imposed (Ahia & Martin, 1993; Anderson, 1996). The duty does not extend to every situation in which a client may express a violent feeling toward another person. When people are angry, they often use violent language to express their anger. Many people in the midst of divorce have threatened to do bodily harm to their partners, and many people have said they would rather commit suicide than get cancer or acquired immune deficiency syndrome (AIDS). Few clients who utter these words will carry out a homicide or suicide. The counselor must often sift through these angry and desperate words and identify those whose intent is truly violent.

As Truscott and Evans (2001) point out, when clinicians develop strong therapeutic bonds with their clients, they are more likely to have sufficient influence to diffuse violent impulses and reduce the risk of acting out. This process is called *risk assessment*. The literature indicates that although mental health professionals cannot predict dangerousness with a high degree of accuracy, their predictions are measurably better than chance (for example, see Bednar et al., 1991; Mossman, 1994; Otto, 1992), especially in the short term. If they err, they are more likely to overpredict violence. In other words, they tend to predict danger in cases where no violent action ends up occurring (Smith & Meyer, 1987). Despite the difficulties in reliably assessing future violence, the courts impose on mental health professionals the duty to act to protect victims in cases of foreseeable danger. For this reason, professionals are well advised to become familiar with the literature on risk management with dangerous clients and to become as skilled as possible in assessing the risk of violence. The assessment always includes a history of the client's violent behavior, the current social conditions that may exacerbate or diminish the likelihood for violence, and the client's current psychological functioning (Ahia & Martin, 1993). Monahan (1981) specifies access to a means for committing violence as a crucial part of evaluating social and environmental conditions. A client who has easy access to a gun is more dangerous than a client without such access, all other factors being equal. Borum and Reddy (2001) note six major topics for clinicians to evaluate:

1. The presence of attitudes that support or facilitate violence

2. The client's capacity or means to carry out violence
3. The crossing of a threshold toward violence such as purchasing a gun or breaking a law
4. The presence of an intent to carry out a violent action (in contrast to the idea of act-ing violently)
5. The responses of others to the client's plan
6. The degree of client compliance with professional recommendations to reduce risk

A methodic assessment of dangerousness is also important because of the emotion that having a violent client evokes in a counselor. Working with a client one thinks may cause serious injury is very stressful. Counselors can be overwhelmed by their sense of responsi-bility for the client's actions and may be concerned about their own safety under such cir-cumstances. If not balanced by a careful evaluation of the real risk, these fears and worries can compromise clear thinking and ethical action. For a more detailed discussion of risk management, see Costa and Altekruse (1994), Monahan (1993), and Otto (2000). Borum (1996) also describes standardized instruments that have been developed to enhance the accuracy of risk assessment.

Court rulings in California (Leong, Eth, & Silva, 1992) suggest another reason for care-ful risk assessment before breaching confidentiality. In at least three cases, once a warning was issued to a third party, psychotherapists were required to give court testimony that went well beyond the *Tarasoff* warning. This testimony was used in all three cases to help establish the guilt of the defendants (clients) in criminal trails. According to Meyers (1991), "There is no way to tell whether psychotherapists, following *Tarasoff,* have ever saved a po-tential victim from injury, but it is clear that at least two psychotherapists, ordered to tes-tify over objections and claims of privilege, helped prosecutors convict an ex-patient of first-degree murder and contributed to sentencing him to the penalty of death" (p. 27). It is too early to determine whether other state courts will follow California's lead in this matter, but these events offer mental health professionals another reason to be prudent and reasoned in their decision to warn third parties.

When attempting to determine the predictability of danger, a professional should con-sult with colleagues and possibly an attorney, both because of the risk of injury and be-cause the exception to confidentiality applies to imminent danger, not potential danger. In other words, breaching confidentiality without immediate danger can result in legal and ethical complaints against the counselor by the person whose privacy was not protected (Schultz, 1982). Although many states, such as California and Ohio, have offered mental health professionals protection from liability claims stemming from good-faith breaches of confidentiality under this duty, not every state has addressed this matter either in case law or statutory law (Glosoff et al., 2000).

When warning is appropriate, the courts have also clarified who should be told about violent clients. In most circumstances, law enforcement officers should be informed about the dangerous client, and the potential victims should be told of the client's violent intent. Counselors should disclose to the police only information relevant to the danger, not other counseling communications. Counselors should also warn victims the counselor can rea-sonably identify and those so close to the possible victim that they too are in danger. For example, a dependent child of a custodial parent who is the object of the threat also is seen by the legal system as a person the counselor has a duty to protect. Most state courts have rejected the notion that counselors and therapists have a duty to warn and protect in sit-uations in which clients make broad or vague threats or in situations in which the coun-selor has no information to identify the victim. In that situation, the professional's duty shifts somewhat. If the risk assessment leads to the conclusion that the client is truly dan-gerous, but the counselor has no way to identify a victim to prevent the injury, the coun-selor should consider initiating involuntary commitment proceedings against the client. (In a number of states, only psychiatrists and psychologists have the authority to initiate such proceedings on their own.) If a client is detained in a hospital setting as an emergency procedure, he or she endangers no one during the period of hospitalization.

The states vary in their interpretation of the duty to warn and protect, with approximately half the states requiring protection of third parties (Quattrocchi & Schopp, 2005). Some states have rejected the *Tarasoff* doctrine (Texas is most notable), and some others have extended it to include nonidentifiable victims (Bednar et al., 1991; Monahan, 1993; Quattrocchi & Schopp, 2005). In a few states, a *history* of violent action coupled with a reasonably identifiable victim may be enough to require a breach of confidentiality, even in the absence of any specific threat (Ahia & Martin, 1993). In other words, in those states an explicit *threat* of harm is not a necessary component for the duty to be imposed. These wide variations in state statutes are confusing and show that mental health professionals need to become informed about their own state's laws. Complicating matters even further is the rapid rate at which case law and statutory law on this subject change. For instance, Ohio law changed three times between 1991 and 1997.

One final note about the duty to warn and protect is in order. Courts interpret this duty to apply not only to situations in which a counselor knows about a dangerous person making an imminent threat but also to situations in which the counselor *should have known* about the danger. This means that if the counselor's ignorance about a danger stems from incompetent or negligent practice, or from a refusal to explore issues for fear of what the client might say, then that counselor has also violated this duty. The courts simply do not view incompetence or negligence as an adequate defense against a claim of failure to protect.

Given this history of legal challenges to the confidentiality of client communications, one may mistakenly conclude that confidentiality does not apply to violent clients. Such an interpretation is not only wrong, it is also inconsistent with court rulings that tend to support the need for confidentiality as a general principle in counseling and psychotherapy. Even in situations of imminent danger, confidentiality is not entirely eliminated. Any communications about the client must be limited to information relevant to the threat so as to help prevent harm to the victim. No relevant information to prevent the harm should be withheld, but no peripheral information unrelated to the threat should be disclosed.

Duty to Warn and Protect When a Client is Suicidal. When clients are at immediate risk of suicide, the primary obligation of the counselor is to protect the client from the self-destructive impulse. Whether there is a legal duty to breach confidentiality to inform significant others in the client's life is uncertain (Bongar, 2002). The legal and ethical responsibility to protect the client from harm is unequivocal, however. To achieve this goal, counselors have a number of options. They may intensify treatment; notify law enforcement authorities, significant others who can offer the client support and protection from the suicidal impulses, or both; or hospitalize the client. Counselors who choose to breach confidentiality should act prudently in communications with family members and should reveal only material necessary to help the client. In an ideal situation, such disclosures are made with the client's consent and involvement, so that they are not truly breaches of confidentiality but the result of a joint decision to act toward a therapeutic goal. If a counselor judges that the client would not be safe with significant others or that intensifying the current treatment would be insufficient, then hospitalization may be wise.

Careful risk assessment is important for the welfare of the counselor as well. Working with suicidal clients has been termed the most stressful aspect of clinical work (Deutsch, 1984; Hendin, Lipschitz, Maltsberger, Haas, & Wynecoop, 2000). Brems (2000), Bongar (2002), and Capuzzi (2004) are excellent sources of information on assessing suicidal risk. The special concerns in responding to suicide potential in adolescents are thoroughly discussed in Zimmerman and Asnis (1995). Gaining competency in suicide assessment is crucial because of the likelihood that mental health professionals will confront this issue frequently in their careers. Rogers, Gueulette, Abbey-Hines, Carney, and Werth (2001) reported that 71% of the counselors they sampled had experienced at least one client suicide attempt, and McAdams and Foster (2000) found that 20% of counseling psychology trainees had parallel experiences.

7. Clients Planning Future Crimes

According to Glosoff et al. (2000), when clients disclose that they are planning criminal action in the future, mental health professionals may be compelled to disclose those comments to investigating law enforcement officers in the 17 states in which privilege excludes this type of content. These states are Alaska, Arizona, District of Columbia, Idaho, Illinois, Indiana, Kansas, Louisiana, Massachusetts, Montana, New Mexico, Oklahoma, Oregon, South Carolina, South Dakota, Tennessee, and Washington. Examples of criminal activity to which this restriction might apply would be the selling of stolen goods, the purchase or sale of controlled substances, or involvement in schemes that defraud older adults of their money. Mental health professionals ought not to confuse this limit to privilege with the duty to warn and protect that applies when a third party is in imminent danger from a client. Even in those states listed, the restriction of privilege for planned criminal activity is limited to situations in which a client is under investigation by law enforcement officials and those officers seek information from the treating professional. In these states professionals who know about a criminal act being planned may be forced to provide information over their own objections and the objections of their clients. Needless to say, any counselors confronting such circumstances should research the particulars of their state law and consult with an attorney to determine the proper response to such requests.

8. Counseling Clients with HIV

Counseling people with HIV spectrum disorders raises a number of ethical issues. Of greatest concern for counselors are (a) the confidentiality of client disclosures, (b) the risk of discrimination against clients with HIV disorders if information about their health status is not protected, and (c) the welfare of third parties at risk for infection because of their contact with the client. The behaviors that place others at high risk are the sharing of needles during intravenous drug use and unprotected sexual contact. (Of course, not all forms of unprotected sexual contact carry exactly the same degree of risk, but unprotected sex is the category under which some very-high-risk behaviors fall.) The ethical dilemma for counselors lies in balancing their responsibility to the client with an HIV disorder and to people who that client places at risk for the infection. Given the restrictions on confidentiality when clients make threats of imminent homicide or suicide, scholars have vigorously debated whether the same ethical responsibility to warn and protect applies in this circumstance (for example, see Anderson & Barret, 2001; Harding, Gray, & Neal, 1993; Stanard & Hazler, 1995).

Only the ACA *Code of Ethics* makes special reference to the limits of confidentiality with people with life-threatening contagious diseases.

ACA *Code of Ethics*, Section B.2.b: Contagious, Life-Threatening Diseases

When clients disclose that they have a disease commonly known to be both communicable and life threatening, counselors may be justified in disclosing information to identifiable third parties, if they are known to be at demonstrable and high risk of contracting the disease. Prior to making a disclosure, counselors confirm that there is such a diagnosis and assess the intent of clients to inform the third parties about their disease or to engage in any behaviors that may be harmful to an identifiable third party.

The APA code does not specifically mention exceptions to confidentiality regarding contagious diseases, although in Section 4.05.b. it does indirectly address this issue when it allows psychologists to disclose confidential information without consent in order to protect someone from harm. However, in 1991 APA published a resolution on applying duty-to-warn issues to people with HIV disorders. In this document APA opposed the establishment of a legal duty-to-warn provision for clients who had HIV whose behavior increases the risk of transmitting the virus. As of this writing, except in the state of Utah (Glosoff et al., 2000) no legal duty to warn and protect people at risk for HIV exposure has been imposed on mental health professionals. The APA resolution goes on to describe the wording the association would find acceptable if such laws were written. These words closely parallel the contents of the ACA code:

> If, however, specific legislation is considered, then it should permit disclosure only when (a) the provider knows of an identifiable third party who the provider has a compelling reason to believe is at significant risk for infection; (b) the provider has a reasonable belief that the third party has no reason to suspect that he or she is at risk; and (c) the client/patient has been urged to inform the third party and has either refused or is considered unreliable in his/her willingness to notify the third party. (APA, 1991)

The welfare of the client cannot be ignored—even when a professional decides he or she must breach confidentiality to protect a person at risk. That action should be carried out with prior notice to the client that a disclosure is forthcoming, and it should be implemented in a way that minimizes the harm to the client. These documents show that hasty breaches of confidentiality based on emotion or intuition, rather than on careful assessment of the risks of disclosure to clients and third parties, are inherently problematic. This message is underscored by research suggesting that the ability of mental health professionals to make objective decisions about breaches of confidentiality in this circumstance is compromised by their attitudes toward homosexuality (McGuire, Nieri, Abbott, Sheridan, & Fisher, 1995). McGuire et al. found that psychotherapists who scored higher on a measure of homophobia were more likely to breach confidentiality in hypothetical cases than those who scored lower in homophobic attitudes. In their sample of mental health professionals Crawford, Humfleet, Ribordy, Ho, and Vickers (1991) also found evidence of prejudiced attitudes toward people with HIV disorders. Palma and Iannelli (2002) reported that counseling psychology students used different decision rules when deciding to breach confidentiality to warn unprotected sexual partners. Uninformed male partners of gay men were significantly less likely to be identified as parties to warn than uninformed female partners of heterosexual men. The pattern of findings that irrelevant variables affect clinicians' judgments about reporting is also supported in the work of Pais, Piercy, and Miller (1998), who surveyed practicing marriage and family counselors. Thus, the research demonstrates that mental health professionals from many disciplines need to be especially careful that any decision to warn a third party is based on a rational consideration of the facts and on a balanced assessment of the rights of the client and of the person at risk.

Studies by Kozlowski (2004) and Nichols (2003) highlight that decision making on breaching confidentiality to protect a third party at risk for HIV infection is a complicated and contentious issue for practitioners even when heterosexist bias is not a major factor. For example, Kozlowski (2004) reported that 25% of his sample of psychologists were unwilling to breach confidentiality even when given a scenario in which a client with an HIV disorder persistently refused to disclose his or her status to an at-risk partner. Based on this preliminary research, the permission that the codes offer for professionals to break confidentiality to protect an at-risk person does not appear to have resulted in any uniform response to this dilemma. On a more positive note, Kozlowsky and Nichols also report that professionals frequently consult with colleagues when they are confronted with this difficult issue.

One factor that may contribute to the lack of consensus in practitioner response is the reality that laws governing communication about a client's HIV status to third parties are varied and confusing. Most laws refer to physicians and health care providers, and their applicability to mental health professionals is either uncertain or untested. Even scholars who analyze the content of these laws come to contradictory conclusions about confidentiality related to HIV communications to counselors and therapists. (See Melchert and Patterson [1999] and Chenneville [2000] as examples of contradictory interpretations of state laws.) Some states mandate confidentiality; others permit disclosure in the event of risk to a third party, and, according to Chenneville (2000), a few require disclosure. In jurisdictions that mandate confidentiality, breaches of confidentiality could lead the client to bring a civil suit against the counselor. In states that permit disclosure to partners and other people at risk of infection, immunity from liability for professionals is often part of the law. Needless to say, in this uncertain and rapidly changing environment, mental health professionals need to obtain competent legal advice about the regulations that govern practice in their state and to regularly update their knowledge.

Another option to direct breach of confidentiality to a person at risk for HIV infection may be disclosure to a partner identification program. These programs exist to inform people at risk of their vulnerability to exposure to the HIV virus when clients are hesitant or unable to notify partners themselves. In some states submitting information to the partner notification program may substitute for an ethical or legal obligation to breach confidentiality (Chenneville, 2000). In 26 states, physicians and other health care professionals are required to make confidential notification of all who test positive for HIV to an appropriate public health department (Melchert & Patterson, 1999).

The emergence of new medications to treat the HIV virus (Farber & McDaniel, 1999; Kalichman, 1998; 2003) may have some bearing on the interpretation of the ACA code. Combination therapies with protease inhibitors can reduce the amount of the virus in patients' bodies to an almost undetectable level. Are individuals with undetectable levels of virus as contagious as those with higher levels? A definitive answer to that question is not yet known. Obviously, other advances in medical treatment will affect counselors' considerations about breaching confidentiality to warn others about their risk of contracting the virus. Similarly, evidence of the emergence of more virulent or treatment-resistant forms of the virus may also affect professionals' assessment of the risks and need to inform a person at risk.

9. Counseling Individuals at the End of their Lives

Clinicians who work with clients at the end of their lives may sometimes encounter clients whose pain and suffering lead them to consider hastening their own deaths. Professionals faced with this circumstance are facing one of the most complex and troubling ethical dilemmas in practice—are they obligated to intervene to prevent the client's actions in the same way they would be obligated to prevent a suicide for an individual at a different point in the lifespan? Does the proximity of a painful and difficult death of a competent person change in any way the clinician's duty to prevent suicide? Does the consideration of suicide in itself indicate the presence of a depressive disorder in a person nearing death from illness or injury? In other words, is there such a thing as *rational suicide?* If hastening the end of one's life can be rational in some circumstances, is it ethically acceptable for a mental health professional to assist or support the client in completing this action? What confidentiality obligations are imposed on a professional working with a client who has decided to hasten the end of life? The APA *Ethical Principles* do not directly address this topic, but the most recent version of the ACA code discusses it at length. In addition to the provisions that outline competency requirements for counselors who work with clients at the end of their lives, the code offers some guidance in Section A.9.c. regarding confidentiality of client disclosures related to the hastening of death.

ACA *Code of Ethics,* Section A.9: End-of-Life Care for Terminally Ill Clients

a. Quality of Care. Counselors strive to take measures that enable clients (1) to obtain high quality end-of-life care for their physical, emotional, social, and spiritual needs; (2) to exercise the highest degree of self-determination possible; (3) to be given every opportunity possible to engage in informed decision making regarding their end-of-life care; and (4) to receive complete and adequate assessment regarding their ability to make competent, rational decisions on their own behalf from a mental health professional who is experienced in end-of-life care practice.

b. Counselor Competence, Choice, and Referral. Recognizing the personal, moral, and competence issues related to end-of-life decisions, counselors may choose to work or not work with terminally ill clients who wish to explore their end-of-life options. Counselors provide appropriate referral information to ensure that clients receive the necessary help.

c. Confidentiality. Counselors who provide services to terminally ill individuals who are considering hastening their own deaths have the option of breaking or not breaking confidentiality, depending on applicable laws and the specific circumstances of the situation and after seeking consulation or supervision from appropriate professional and legal parties. *(See B.5.c., B.7.c.)*

This section clarifies that no counselor is mandated by the code to breach confidentiality if a client is considering hastening death if that person is near the end of life. Instead it advises professionals to make decisions on a case-by-case basis and to obtain consultation or supervision rather than attempt to deliberate in isolation. The ACA code allows counselors either to breach or maintain confidentiality depending on the particular client issues. It is important to note that other documents on end-of-life issues published by APA take a similar view—that no psychologist is mandated to breach confidentiality when a client is considering the hastening of death—but this position has not been integrated into the APA code (APA, 2001). In other words, the codes give permission (after critical evaluation of the case and consideration of relevant laws), but they do not mandate disclosure. The literature on this topic (for example, Werth & Gordon, 2002; Werth, Burke, & Bardash, 2002; APA Working Group on Assisted Suicide and End-of-Life Decisions, 2000) offers a list of issues for professionals to consider:

- The competence and capacity of the client to give an informed consent (i.e., to understand the meaning and implications of the decision to hasten death)
- The influence of comorbid psychological conditions, pain and suffering, overall quality of life, cultural factors, financial concerns, and fears of loss of autonomy
- The availability of a social support system for the client
- The possible influence of coercion to hasten the end of life—either direct or indirect pressures

In a situation in which a client is suffering from serious depression or in which the client's competence to give consent appears compromised by his or her medical condition, it seems clear that a mental health professional may break confidentiality to prevent that person from hastening death or take other measures to keep that person safe. It also appears clear that a professional may defer a decision about breaking confidentiality until an assessment of the factors previously listed is complete. The professional may maintain confidentiality if the individual appears to be making a decision that is rational, uncoerced, uncomplicated by psychological problems, and undertaken after all reasonable alternatives to improve quality of life have been explored. However, the public policy debate now under way about assisted suicide may lead states to pass legislation that requires mental health professionals to take a different stance, so clinicians must keep abreast of changes in state statutes and case law that may affect the legality of their actions. The following case exemplifies the dilemma of a professional working with a person who is planning to hasten her death.

The Case of Bernie. Bernie is a 54 year-old nurse who was diagnosed with early-onset Alzheimer's disease 2 years ago. Bernie is a widow who has three grown children and two grandchildren. Bernie has never sought counseling or mental health treatment and she herself describes her life as fulfilling and happy, though the pain of her husband's sudden death 5 years ago was difficult to endure. Even since the diagnosis she has not been immobilized by emotional distress, using the time to travel, spend time with her children and grandchildren, and engage in the activities she loves most. Now that her disease is progressing, Bernie has decided to hasten her own death. In her nursing career, she has seen the ravages of advanced Alzheimer's disease on both the patient and the family and wants especially to spare her children that pain. She consults a conselor to be sure that she is doing all she can to prepare herself and her children for her death and asks the counselor to keep her plan confidential.

Confidentiality with Special Populations

Much of the prior discussion assumes that counseling and psychotherapy are one-on-one activities with competent adult clients. When treatment varies from that framework, different considerations regarding the ethics of confidentiality emerge. The following will discuss the interpretation of confidentiality when counseling children, groups, families, and people with diminished capacity.

Children and Adolescents

A counselor working with minors is required to honor confidentiality in most of the same ways as with adults. No counselor may gossip about a minor client, nor may the counselor share client information with people other than parents or guardians without proper consent. The counseling records of a minor must be kept secure from unauthorized people, and the identity of minor clients should also be protected. The rationale for this position is the same as for adult confidentiality. Without it, client autonomy is diminished and the trusting counseling relationship is jeopardized. In short, respect for the client's dignity and welfare is not a concept limited to any age group. (Of course, the limits on confidentiality with adults described in the last section of this chapter also apply to minors.)

The distinction in applying confidentiality to young clients stems from their legal status as minors. Minors are not granted the same privacy rights as adults. In fact, until 1967 U.S. law did not recognize that minors were "persons" with any privacy rights in constitutional terms. In that year a U.S. Supreme Court ruling concluded, "neither the Fourteenth Amendment nor the Bill of Rights is for adults alone" (In re Gault, 1967, p. 28). Since 1967 some foothold has been gained to view children and adolescents as persons; however, minors are generally not allowed to have secrets from their parents or guardians (Koocher & Keith-Spiegel, 1990). Thus, in the absence of state or federal statutes to the contrary, parents have a legal right to information disclosed in counseling unless they give permission for it to be kept from them.

As mentioned in Chapter 2, the ethics codes give only broad-brush attention to confidentiality with children and adolescents. The ACA code states the following.

ACA *Code of Ethics*, Section B.5: Clients Lacking Capacity to Give Informed Consent

a. Responsibility to Clients. When counseling minor clients or adult clients who lack the capacity to give voluntary, informed consent, counselors protect the confidentiality of information received in the counseling relationship as specified by federal and state laws, written policies, and applicable ethical standards.

b. Responsibility to Parents and Legal Guardians. Counselors inform parents and legal guardians about the role of counselors and the confidential nature of the counseling relationship. Counselors are sensitive to the cultural diversity of families and respect the inherent rights and responsibilities of parents/guardians over the welfare of their children/charges according to law. Counselors work to establish, as appropriate, collaborative relationships with parents/guardians to serve clients.

The APA code is even less specific in Sections 4.01 and 4.02, simply stating that psychologists protect the confidentiality of information they obtain and that they discuss with clients or the person legally capable of giving informed consent the nature and limits of confidentiality. Thus, the codes leave to the judgment of the individual professional the burden of applying these broad ethical standards to particular client situations. Not surprisingly, then, research has shown that practitioners find the ambiguities surrounding confidentiality a significant complication in working with children and adolescents (Mannheim, et al., 2002; Sullivan, Ramirez, Rae, Razo, & George, 2002).

Fortunately, a number of ethics scholars have examined the issue of confidentiality in counseling minors and have suggested guidelines for determining how much confidentiality a child can be granted (Gustafson & McNamara, 1987; Rozovsky, 2000; Taylor and Adelman, 1989). A common thread is that the degree to which confidentiality can be honored is directly related to the age and maturity of the minor. The closer the young person is to the age of maturity, the greater the likelihood that he or she can be granted a fuller measure of confidentiality. This judgment is based on research that has found that adolescents age 15 or older seem capable of making judgments about counseling as competently as adults (Mann, Harmoni, & Power, 1989; Weithorn, 1983). In other words, they seem to understand the nature, risks, and benefits of counseling sufficiently to give informed consent (Gustafson & McNamara, 1987). In contrast, children younger than age 11 have not been able to show the necessary level of understanding to give informed consent. Moreover, younger children tend to be less assertive and to defer to authority rather than express their own wishes.

The capacity of children between ages 11 and 14 years to understand counseling varies according to their level of cognitive development, particularly their attainment of formal operations thinking (Weithorn, 1983). When children have attained this level of thinking, they can conceptualize abstract possibilities and reason hypothetically, capacities that seem crucial for effective participation in counseling. Thus, when working with youngsters in this age range, scholars suggest assessing the client's cognitive maturity to determine his or her capacity to participate independently in counseling. Of course, not all children older than age 15 have attained the level of formal operations. Thus a careful judgment about intellectual maturity is appropriate whenever counseling a minor. Arguing that cognitive maturity alone is not sufficient for judging a minor's capacity to understand and agree to treatment, Fundudis (2003) recommends taking into account four factors to determine a minor's competence:

1. Chronologic age (including developmental history and maturational progress)
2. Cognitive level (including language, memory, reasoning ability, and logic)
3. Emotional maturity (including temperament, stability of mood, attachment, educational adjustment, and attitudinal style)
4. Sociocultural factors such as family values and religious beliefs

The law has also defined four general exceptions to parental consent for counseling minors (Gustafson & McNamara, 1987). The first exception is for the mature minor, a minor capable of understanding treatment and its consequences. Minors nearing the age of majority are most likely to be ruled mature by a court. According to Rozovsky (2000), the courts also take the complexity and risks of the therapy into account when deciding on maturity. The second exception is for a minor who is "legally emancipated" from parents and guardians. These adolescents operate with independence in virtually all aspects of their daily lives. The criteria for emancipation vary from state to state and are applied in a case-by-case basis, but they generally include factors such as the minor's status as the head of a household, employment, service in the armed forces, or marriage (Rozovsky, 2000). The third exception is for emergencies. Any minor can be treated if immediate treatment is urgently needed. Parents should be informed about treatment as soon as possible after the emergency is resolved (Lawrence & Kurpius, 2000). Finally, parental consent can be waived by a court order.

A number of states have enacted legislation that allows minors to receive medical and psychological treatment without parental consent when the requirement for parental consent would interfere with a youngster's willingness to seek treatment. For example, teenagers may often seek care for substance abuse, pregnancy, sexually transmitted diseases, and contraception without parental knowledge or consent. Federal law also stipulates that minors receiving substance abuse evaluation or treatment services must consent before information can be released (Gudeman, 2003). Other states, such as Ohio, allow adolescents at age 14 or older to seek mental health services without parental consent for a limited number of sessions, after which parents must be informed or treatment must be ended. California affords the same rights to minors at 12 years or older, and the California Attorney General has clarified that the right to confidential care for minors prohibits school districts from informing parents they are releasing the student from school if the student is seeking services for which the minor has the right to receive without parental knowledge (Lockyer & Duncan, 2004).

Some authors suggest that focusing on ways to keep counseling information from parents and guardians is misguided. Instead, they maintain that because parents have so much power in their children's lives, they should be welcomed into the process rather than excluded from it (Taylor & Adelman, 1989; 2001). This belief is consistent with the language in the ACA code that advises counselors to work collaboratively with parents to best serve clients (B.5.b). These authors argue that at times, keeping information confidential from parents "can seriously hamper an intervener's efforts to help a client" (Taylor & Adelman, 1989, p. 80). Enlisting parents' cooperation as an initial phase in the counseling process encourages them to cooperate with treatment and provides an opportunity to educate them about the appropriateness of confidentiality with minors. They suggest a preliminary session in which parents are given information about the counseling process, are reassured that vital information that affects their child's well-being will be shared, and are instructed about the importance of trust and privacy for any person who enters counseling. After such an orientation, parents are more likely to give consent to counseling, and they are also more willing to support rather than sabotage the counselor's efforts and to respect their child's right to privacy in counseling sessions. Research by Nevas and Farber (2001) demonstrates that parents need not be viewed as adversaries or cynics to child therapy. Their research found that parents generally have very positive attitudes toward their children's experiences in therapy and that parents respect the skills of the child therapist and appreciate the work the therapist is doing with their child. It is not surprising that, if highly positive change is occurring in the child's symptoms, parents' attitudes toward the therapist are even more supportive.

Nevas and Farber (2001) describe several therapist actions that can foster continued positive attitudes of parents and children in therapy. They recommend that parents be explicitly informed that setbacks in progress are normal and that if a minor entered therapy with some ambivalence, a brief period in which the child acts in protest to therapy may ensue before services can be helpful. They also advise that ongoing communication with parents is essential, even if therapy is progressing satisfactorily, to keep therapy attendance steady if progress stalls at a later point. In regard to confidentiality, they recommend that parents directly communicate to their child that they understand the child's desire for confidentiality and that they will honor it as much as possible.

Of course, not all parents are willing to engage in such a process, and all too often a child's difficulties stem from the parents' problems. Adolescents caught in an alcoholic family may have parents who deny their substance abuse. Such parents often object to the teenagers' attempts to get counseling, but the adolescents still need a forum in which they can discuss their concerns and learn coping skills. Similarly, an adolescent struggling with sexual identity issues often may not be free to broach these matters with family. Some adolescents who do so are turned away from their homes and are also at risk for violence, even from family members, according to Hetrick and Martin (1987). In their study, 49% of adolescents who were gay and lesbian who sought services to help them deal with violence against them indicated that they were assaulted by family members.

In such situations, the counselor needs to weigh the legal rights of the parents or guardians against the child's emotional well-being and decide on a course of action that serves the child's best interests. The ultimate goal of the counselor should be to find a way to get the family involved because the best resolution to the youngster's difficulty may be family treatment. In the absence of family cooperation, promoting the welfare of the child and protecting him or her from harm always prevails. (For a discussion of confidentiality in school settings, see Chapter 12.)

Group and Family Counseling

The fundamental ethical responsibility to respect the client's right to confidentiality does not change in group or family counseling. The counselor must not disclose the identity of clients or information revealed in counseling to those who do not have a right to it. The presence of other people in the room when an individual client reveals personal information complicates confidentiality from both an ethical and legal perspective. First, as the codes indicate, the counselor cannot guarantee that the other people hearing these disclosures will also respect the client's privacy. Of course, the counselor emphasizes the importance of confidentiality in any multiple-client situation and asks all participants to honor confidentiality, but the counselor has no real power to enforce that request. Thus, all participants in group and family counseling need to understand this as another "limit" on confidentiality.

ACA *Code of Ethics,* Section B.4.a: Group Work

In group work, counselors clearly explain the importance and parameters of confidentiality for the specific group being entered.

ACA *Code of Ethics,* Section B.4.b: Couples and Family Counseling

In couples and family counseling, counselors clearly define who is considered "the client" and discuss expectations and limitations of confidentiality. Counselors seek agreement and document in writing such agreement among all involved parties concerning each individual's right to confidentiality and any obligation to preserve the confidentiality of information known.

APA *Ethical Principles,* Section 10.03: Group Therapy

When psychologists provide services to several persons in a group setting, they describe at the outset the roles and responsibilities of all parties and the limits of confidentiality.

APA *Ethical Principles,* Section 10.02: Therapy Involving Couples or Families

(a) When psychologists agree to provide services to several persons who have a relationship (such as spouses, significant others, or parents and children), they take reasonable steps to clarify at the outset (1) which of the individuals are clients/patients and (2) the relationship the psychologist will have with each person. This clarification includes the psychologist's role and the probable uses of the services provided or the information obtained.

(b) If it becomes apparent that psychologists may be called on to perform potentially conflicting roles (such as family therapist and then witness for one party in divorce proceedings), psychologists take reasonable steps to clarify and modify, or withdraw from, roles appropriately.

Second, whether information disclosed in group or family counseling can be regarded as privileged information in a courtroom is an open question. The privilege concept is based on one individual communicating privately to a lawyer, physician, or priest. When a person communicates information to a mental health professional in front of third parties, the claim that that information is privileged has not been universally honored in the legal system. This is called the *third-party rule*—any information disclosed in front of third parties is generally ruled by the courts not to be privileged (Swenson, 1997). Thus, clients in multiple-person counseling also need to understand the uncertainty of whether privilege really applies even in states that may grant the mental health professional privilege for individual counseling (Corey, Williams, & Moline, 1995). Some states, such as Minnesota, have privilege statutes protecting communications in group and family therapy, but most do not (DeKraai, Sales, & Hall, 1998; Myers, 1991). The codes of ethics of the Association for Specialists in Group Work (ASGW, 1989, 1998) and the American Association for Marriage and Family Therapy (AAMFT, 2001) extensively discuss confidentiality issues in multiple-person therapies and should be read thoroughly by all who conduct these therapies.

Confidentiality in a Multicultural Context

Confidentiality is based on the belief that the individual has the right of autonomy, the freedom to be make decisions for himself or herself, including, in this case, decisions about entering therapy and controlling the release of information about participation in therapy. Autonomy is an ethical principle with roots in Western philosophy—nowhere else on the planet is this principle given such an elevated status. In fact, in some cultural traditions, freedom to self-govern clearly takes second place to loyalty to family or deference to the wishes of elders, even with fully competent adults. The notion that family members can be excluded from information about a loved one's mental health is fundamentally inconsistent with some cultural values; it is just as incompatible in those cultures as the belief that a person who wants acceptance from the family can defy the wishes of elders to satisfy a personal desire or goal.

In such a context, confidentiality of communications in counseling can become complicated, as Meer and VandeCreek (2002) illustrate so well in their description of three cases of adult clients from South Asia receiving therapy in the United States. On learning that these adults were in treatment, their clients' families demanded complete disclosure about the content and progress of therapy. They also expressed great distrust of the therapist and high levels of hostility at the idea that a family member had discussed private family matters to a stranger in the first place. Complicating the matter even further was the reluctance of the clients to voice any disagreement with parents' demands, a behavior that violated cultural standards of respect. How can a professional comply with the ethical mandate to honor confidentiality in such a situation? One obvious way is to ask the client to sign a release of information; however, that is only a partial solution to the dilemma because the clients feel little freedom to assert themselves. The more ideal ethical response is to anticipate the complications of clients whose value systems are likely to differ from the value system underlying the profession's ethical principles and to discuss an approach to family communications at the initiation of service. Indeed, family treatment, if possible, may be the preferable mode of service in such a situation. (See *ACA Code of Ethics* section B.1.a for specific language on this issue.)

Emerging Challenges to Confidentiality: Managed Care and Technology

When counseling and psychotherapy originated nearly 100 years ago, the only people involved were clients and their counselors (Heppner, 1990; Whiteley, 1984). All services took place in a face-to-face meeting, and all financial aspects were handled directly by the individuals involved. Records were kept on paper if they were kept at all, and the counselor and the client were the ones who decided the length and nature of treatment. The advent of third-party reimbursement; computerization of records; and access to mental health professionals through media, telephone, and the Internet have revolutionized the counseling process and compounded confidentiality dilemmas. For example, when insurers began to reimburse people for mental health expenses, they sought information regarding the nature of the problem and its treatment. If they were to pay for services, insurers had a right to know that appropriate services were being rendered. Therefore clients signed a release so that their therapists could communicate with the insurers. When managed care came into being, the insurers' demands for information about diagnosis intensified and their involvement in recommending both the length and type of treatment expanded. Currently, managed care providers also claim the right to audit counseling records to ascertain that the reimbursement was properly used and to be deeply involved in monitoring the progress of treatment. Mental health professionals sometimes have to provide detailed information to justify additional sessions. Each of these demands compromises the privacy of the client. Not only does the gatekeeper at the managed care organization have extensive information on clients, but others in the managed care organization and the client's workplace may gain access to that material (Frager, 2000). It is not unusual for almost a dozen people to have private information if a client submits counseling costs for reimbursement by a managed care provider. Managed care companies have sometimes failed to prevent people who have no involvement in a case from accessing confidential mental health records of that case (Scarf, 1996). Of course, because clients and their employers pay for mental health insurance, they have every right to use it to offset costs. Many clients might not have access to mental health care without insurance help. Yet clients often fail to understand how deeply their privacy can be invaded in this process. Counselors have an obligation to help them understand the implications of using insurance on the confidentiality of counseling. For more discussion of the impact of managed care on counseling and therapy, see Chapter 11.

In light of the increased role of managed care in mental health and the computerization of client data, the U.S. Congress passed the Health Information Portability and Accountability Act in 1996 to safeguard client data communicated via electronic networks. This legislation is designed to protect patients receiving health care (including mental health services) from unwarranted disclosures of personal health information and to provide patients some level of control over release of that information. It also mandates that providers that handle health information follow privacy guidelines or be subject to liability claims from patients and even federal criminal prosecution in some situations. Both ACA and APA address this topic in their codes. In Section B.3.d the ACA *Code of Ethics* states, "Counselors disclose confidential information to third party payors only when clients have authorized such disclosure." In parallel fashion, the APA *Ethical Principles* specify in Section 10.01 that clients must give informed consent to the involvement of third-party payors in therapy.

The computerization of counseling records also can affect confidentiality. As Bongar (1988) points out, the computer's ability to store large amounts of data on small magnetic media make counseling records vulnerable to theft, duplication, or loss on a level unrivaled by old-fashioned paper records. Conceivably, a counselor's entire set of case records could be stored on one CD and thus easily stolen, lost, or ruined. In this era of the Internet and networks of computers, material stored on a counselor's hard drive may be equally vulnerable to loss. Counselors who use computers for client records must be alert to this potential for misuse and must make extra efforts to protect the client's confidentiality (Sampson, Kolodinsky, & Greeno, 1997). Research on psychologists' use of technology shows substantial reliance on computers (Rosen & Weil, 1996; Welfel & Bunce, 2003). In the Rosen and Weil study, for example, 52% reported storing client financial records on a computer and 15% reported keeping case notes on a computer. Another 11% administered psychological tests by computer, and 6% gave "direct client assistance" by computer (Rosen & Weil, 1996, p. 636). Welfel and Bunce (2003) found that 44% of the psychologists they surveyed had exchanged e-mails with current or prospective clients on at least one occasion and that one-fourth of those e-mail contacts included communication about therapeutic issues. The ACA language on this topic follows.

ACA *Code of Ethics,* Section B.3.e: Transmitting Confidential Information

Counselors take precautions to ensure the confidentiality of information transmitted through the use of computers, electronic mail, facsimile machines, telephones, voicemail, answering machines, and other electronic or computer technology.

APA makes a general statement of applicability of the provisions of its code to all electronic forms of communication in the Introduction and includes the following statement in Section 3.10 (c): "Psychologists who offer services, products, or information via electronic transmission inform clients/patients of the risks to privacy and limits of confidentiality."

Heinlen and Welfel (2001) recommend the following precautions for computerized client records:

- Avoid computers to which others have access if possible.
- Use an external hard drive, a floppy disk, CD, or similar hardware—not a hard drive—for the creation and storage of client records.
- Use code numbers or pseudonyms to identify files, CDs, and floppy disks.
- Maintain a paper file for each client that includes any code number or pseudonym used.
- Update virus protection compulsively, and create backup files that are stored separately from the original CDs or disks.
- Be cautious about computers that are networked, and take all appropriate steps to protect data from viewing by others in the network.

Pope and Vasquez (2005) make an even stronger recommendation, suggesting that professionals who use computers to create and store client records should use machines without Internet connection so that all chances of electronic snooping are eliminated. When using facsimile machines, caution should also be taken when transmitting client materials and client release forms. Fax machines may be located in an open, public space to which access is not restricted. Transmissions may occur when the receiving office is not open, so the documents may be unprotected for many hours. Consequently, a telephone contact before transmitting of the facsimile is prudent. The call can ensure that a qualified person is available to retrieve the confidential material. In parallel fashion, a follow-up call is desirable to ensure that all materials were received as transmitted. In addition, the cover sheet on the facsimile should include a clear and easily readable statement about the confidentiality of material on the following pages. Highly sensitive client records, such as data that reveal a client's HIV status or history of incest, may not be appropriate for facsimile transmission under any circumstances.

The Ethics of Internet Counseling and Therapy.

As the Internet and the World Wide Web have become major avenues for interpersonal communication, a small percentage of mental health professionals have begun to use this medium for communication with clients. Most who take advantage of it use it to advertise their office practices or to maintain contact with clients between sessions (Maheu, Allen, & Whitten, 2001; Welfel & Bunce, 2003), but some offer online counseling and therapy as an exclusive mode of treatment (Heinlen, Welfel, Richmond, & O'Donnell, 2003; Heinlen, Welfel, Richmond, & Rak, 2003). This use of the Internet and the Web for therapeutic purposes has attracted wide public and professional interest (for example, Bloom & Walz, 2000; Hsiung, 2002; Kraus, Zack, & Stricker, 2004; Maheu & Gordon, 2000) and has generated significant controversy. Some have argued that Internet counseling has the potential to reach people reluctant or unable to attend face-to-face sessions, that it may facilitate self-disclosure about embarrassing content, that it may have unique appeal to young people, and that it is a necessary convenience in a time-pressured culture (Childress, 1998; Grohol, 1999; Sampson, Kolodinsky, & Greeno, 1997). Others have cautioned that exclusively text-based communications do not provide clinicians with sufficient information to accurately diagnose or effectively treat the problems cyberclients present (Alleman, 2002; Childress, 1998; Ingram, 1998; Rabasca, 2000).

Accurate estimates of the number of Web-based providers are nearly impossible to obtain. A search using Google or one of the other search engines can yield more than 500,000 hits, but this number is deceiving because many of these sites offer services that do not constitute psychotherapy (such as credit counseling or spiritual guidance) or are more accurately defined as advertisements for traditional practices. One large-scale study that used common search engines to identify sites claiming to offer online counseling or psychotherapy for emotional or relationship issues found 136 Websites offering such services on the Web, usually for a fee (Heinlen, Welfel, Richmond & Rak, 2003). A parallel study that focused on doctoral level E-therapists who self-identified as psychologists located 50 psychotherapy Websites offered by this subset of professionals. Virtually nothing is known about the quality or competence of most Web counseling (Maheu & Gordon, 2000). The National Board of Certified Counselors (NBCC) (2001) and the ACA (1999) have both issued ethical standards for such practice.

Of particular concern are the risks of breaches of confidentiality. The use of encryption methods reduce but do not eliminate the possibility of unauthorized access to e-mail communications. A committed hacker can find ways around encryption. Another risk to confidentiality of e-mail communications arises from the paths they travel en route to their destinations. Most e-mail communications pass through a number of electronic channels before arriving at the final address, and copies of e-mails that are sent through major service providers (such as America Online) are kept for 1 year after transmission. Confidentiality is not guaranteed even when the e-mail arrives at its destination unless the passwords needed to open it are known only to the recipients. Any e-mail that comes into a workplace computer is the legal property of the employer, who may access it at will. Following is the language the ACA code uses to identify confidentiality obligations in technology applications.

ACA *Code of Ethics,* Section A.12: Technology Applications

g. Technology and Informed Consent. As part of the process of establishing informed consent, counselors do the following: (1) Address issues related to the difficulty of maintaining the confidentiality of electronically transmitted communications. (2) Inform clients of all colleagues, supervisors, and employees, such as Informational Technology (IT) administrators, who might have authorized or unauthorized access to electronic transmissions. (3) Urge clients to be aware of all authorized or unauthorized users including family members and fellow employees who have access to any technology clients may use in the counseling process. (4) Inform clients of pertinent legal rights and limitations governing the practice of a profession over state lines or international boundaries. (5) Use encrypted Web sites and e-mail communications to help ensure confidentiality when possible.

Unfortunately, preliminary evidence suggests that compliance with these standards is low. Heinlen, Welfel, Richmond, and Rak (2003) found that only 22% of the counselors in their sample indicated that they used any encryption method for client communications and only 27% of psychologists in the parallel study used encryption (Heinlen, Welfel, Richmond, & O'Donnell, 2003). Only 4% of the counselors made any mention about the preservation of e-mail communications. Although a majority of Websites offered potential clients reassurance about how seriously they took confidentiality, only 30% of counselors and 39% of psychologists discussed any of the limits of confidentiality such as the duty to warn and protect or the mandate for reporting child abuse. Especially troubling were the promises that confidentiality was absolute—these occurred in more than a few sites—and the statements that Internet counseling was more likely to be confidential than face-to-face counseling, an assertion for which no research evidence exists.

In light of the risks to confidentiality and the experimental nature of the medium, professionals entertaining the use of the Web as a means of clinical service need to be cautious about this venture. Careful attention to compliance with all ethics codes is crucial, and consultation with an attorney about the legal risks of Internet counseling is essential if clients are dissatisfied with services, if clients are harmed by them, or if their confidentiality is violated. Liability insurers should also be notified if such a professional activity is entertained.

SUMMARY

Confidentiality is the cornerstone of effective counseling and psychotherapy because it allows the client to freely share experiences without fear of unwarranted disclosure to others. The ethics codes devote considerable attention to this topic, emphasizing its importance and the situations in which counselors may have permission to communicate client disclosures to others. Confidentiality in counseling covers both the content of disclosures and contact with clients, so the identity of those who seek services is also kept secret from public knowledge. This ethical standard is rooted in the principles of respect for client autonomy and fidelity to promises made.

Confidentiality of counseling disclosures is often also protected by legal statutes. In many states, the clients of mental health professionals can prevent those counselors from testifying in court about material revealed in counseling. Such material is called *privileged communication.*

There are nine major exceptions to confidentiality in counseling:

1. A client's request for release of confidential information to himself or herself or to others
2. A court order for confidential information

3. An ethics complaint or lawsuit against a counselor
4. Other client litigation in which the client raises the issues of counseling treatment as part of the client's civil suit against another party
5. Limitations to confidentiality based on statutes, such as reporting child and elder abuse
6. Dangerous clients who are putting themselves or others at imminent risk for injury or death
7. Clients with intent to commit criminal acts in the future (in some states)
8. Clients with contagious life-threatening diseases, such as HIV disorders, whose behavior puts others at imminent risk of infection
9. Clients at the end of life who are considering hastening their deaths in some situations.

Confidentiality issues also arise when counselors work with children, families, and groups. With children and adolescents, the issue is the degree to which the child client can keep counseling disclosures secret from parents and guardians. The law tends to give minors few rights to privacy; the ethical guidelines tend to see confidentiality for minors increasing with age and maturity. Generally, the more mature the minor, the greater the measure of confidentiality that young person is given in counseling. When working with groups and families, counselors need to be aware that they cannot guarantee clients the same degree of privacy as in individual counseling. When clients reveal personal information in front of third parties, the counselor cannot prevent those third parties from breaching confidentiality. The counselor should contract with all participants to honor confidentiality as a condition for inclusion in the group or family counseling, but clients need to understand that these contracts are voluntary and counselors have little power to prevent other members from violating their promise if they decide to do so.

Confidentiality has also been threatened by several new developments. Managed care's persistent and extensive demands for sensitive client information, coupled with the uncertain protection of that data once released, are major concerns for professionals. The practice of ethics demands that clinicians use the full range of their influence to keep disclosures to managed care to the lowest limit possible and that they fully inform clients about the implications of their use of managed care for the confidentiality of their records. Second, the convenience and ease of electronic communications technology such as the facsimile machine and the Internet make them attractive vehicles for client communication. However, professionals must be fully cognizant of the risks of these technologies and take precautions to protect client data.

CASE FOR ANALYSIS USING THE 10-STEP MODEL

Using the decision-making model presented in Chapter 2, consider the following case.

Raymond is an 18-year-old college freshman living in a residence hall. He is the eldest of five children, and his parents live in a nearby state. Raymond is HIV positive as the result of an infected blood transfusion he received 6 years ago. He has been asymptomatic since then. No one, except his parents, knows of his HIV status. In fact, his parents have not even informed his younger siblings or either set of grandparents. He comes to see a college counselor because he is confused and worried. He has met a young woman and has dated her a few times. He wants to become sexually intimate with her, but he has not told her about his HIV status. Raymond is afraid that disclosure would end her interest in him or the interest of any young woman with whom he wants a serious relationship. He has some brochures about safer sex practices and believes if he did become intimate with this woman that he would use a condom and follow other guidelines for safer sex. He is currently resistant to the idea of disclosing his HIV status to anyone. After a lengthy counseling session, the counselor concludes that Raymond is likely to practice safe sex if he does become intimate with this woman. Moreover, intimacy is not imminent because he does not even see her again for a week. The counselor determines that there is no ethical basis for breaching confidentiality to this woman in the near future. Do you agree with that professional judgment?

Step 1: Develop Ethical Sensitivity.

- Do you agree that there is an ethical dilemma here? Why or why not?
- Whose welfare is affected by the actions of the counselor, and how?
- What was your immediate emotional and intellectual response to reading this case?
- How would you feel if you were in this counselor's position?

Step 2: Define Dilemma and Options.

■ Precisely how do you define the ethical dilemma(s) for Raymond's counselor?

■ What facts of the case cause you to define it in this way?

■ Are there any other facts you should be considering?

■ When you brainstorm about this case, what options can you identify?

Step 3: Refer to Codes.

■ What do the codes of ethics say about the dilemma and the options you have identified?

■ Do other documents from the professional associations speak directly to this dilemma? Describe.

■ Are there laws in your state that are relevant to this dilemma? Describe.

Step 4: Refer to Laws and Regulations.

■ Are there laws in your state that are relevant to this dilemma?

■ Is there case law or other regulation governing this situation?

Step 5: Review Ethics Scholarship.

■ What do scholars on this subject say about responsible resolutions of the dilemma?

■ If scholars disagree, which arguments seem most compelling, and why?

Step 6: Apply Ethical Principles.

■ What ethical principles underlie this dilemma?

■ Does consideration of the principles lead to a single response or to different responses? If different, which principle do you think should take priority? Why?

Step 7: Consult with Other Professionals.

■ What are the views of your supervisor and colleagues on ethical resolutions of this dilemma?

■ Do those views coincide with the recommendations of the codes, the scholars, and the ethical principles? In what ways do they differ?

Step 8: Deliberate and Decide.

■ Is your list of options still adequate? Should it be revised in any way? How?

■ Now that you have accumulated all this information and heard others' perspectives, what have you decided?

■ What is your rationale for that decision?

Step 9: Inform Supervisors.

■ How should you go about informing your supervisor, implementing the actions, and documenting your decision?

Step 10: Reflect on the Experience.

■ Now that you have been through this process, what has it meant to you?

■ What have you learned?

■ How will this experience change your response to similar ethical dilemmas?

■ Do you have any knowledge that you ought to share with colleagues? If so, how can you do that most effectively?

Resolutions of Raymond's Dilemma

First, the choice the counselor makes is clearly a matter of ethics because the welfare of several people is at stake. Raymond may be harmed if his HIV status is disclosed to a third party. He may withdraw from counseling, or he may suffer harm in the residence hall where he lives if that information becomes widely known, and it may be quickly communicated across the campus. After all, the third party to whom counseling information is disclosed has no legal or ethical obligation to keep that information secret. Raymond may drop out of college or feel the need to transfer elsewhere and lose credit for the term in the process. He may decide that his family's secretiveness about his health status is the best course and never reveal his HIV infection to anyone again, even to other sexual partners. Other students may assume that Raymond is gay and make him the victim of "gay bashing." Other negative consequences for Raymond are possible. He may even become suicidal or self-destructive. The disclosure of Raymond's HIV status at the college would also be painful for Raymond's family, whose capacity to cope with his illness seems already diminished.

In addition, the welfare of the young woman Raymond is dating is at stake. If they become sexually active, and if the couple fails to take appropriate precautions, the sexual contact puts her at some risk for being infected with the virus. Currently there is no known cure for HIV infection, although new therapies have substantially extended the life expectancy of people with HIV.

Given what's at stake here, the ethical dilemma can be defined as balancing Raymond's right to privacy and need for further counseling against the potential duty to warn and protect from HIV infection the young woman Raymond is dating.

The relevant facts of the case are that Raymond is an adult who is so concerned about how his HIV status will affect this emerging romantic relationship that he sought the assistance of a professional counselor. He is, at this point, resistant to revealing his medical condition to anyone else, but he is not unwilling to consider precautions that reduce the risk of transmitting the virus.

Several other facts are less clear. First, the counselor does not have independent confirmation of Raymond's HIV status. Although it is unlikely that the client would be purposely deceiving the counselor, it is possible he is delusional or does not really understand the medical information he received 6 years ago when he was only 12 years old. Moreover, it appears that his family has not talked much to him about his health, a circumstance that increases the possibility that Raymond may be misinformed about his medical status. A single session with Raymond may not be sufficient to judge his rationality, veracity, or sophistication of knowledge.

Second, the counselor has no verification that the young woman returns Raymond's affections, or that if she does, she is ready to advance the relationship to the level of sexual intimacy Raymond wants. Raymond's lack of dating experience makes such a misinterpretation of her interest even more likely than it might be for a college freshman with dating experience. Or her personal values may cause her to refrain from sexual intimacy until engaged or married.

Third, the counselor has no certain information about Raymond's commitment to using safer sex practices should he become sexually involved with this woman. He may or may not act responsibly. This fact is crucial because it has such important implications for the degree of danger to which the woman is exposed. Fourth, regardless of the use of safer sex practices, the exact risk of transmitting the virus in a single sexual encounter is unknown (Keeling, 1993). Many cases of repeated heterosexual intercourse have resulted in no transmission of the virus, but in some cases, transmission has occurred after a single contact. Fifth, the counselor has no knowledge of the woman's understanding of sexually transmitted diseases or her commitment to practices that minimize her risk of such infections. She may be fully prepared to insist on safe sex regardless of Raymond's inclinations on the matter. Sixth, the woman herself may be HIV positive. The rate of infection in heterosexual adolescents is increasing, and she may have already contracted the virus. This is a statistically unlikely scenario, but it is not impossible. Taken together, these uncertainties show how little this counselor really knows about the degree of risk Raymond represents to this particular young woman.

The counselor's options are as follows:

- To inform the young woman immediately even if Raymond does not agree to disclose immediately himself

- To keep the information confidential for the duration of counseling and to educate the client about safer sex practices
- To set disclosure of his HIV status to the woman as a counseling goal for Raymond
- To postpone a decision until the facts of the case are clearer

The ACA *Code of Ethics* allows disclosure of information about clients' life-threatening contagious diseases to third parties if certain requirements are met. The counselor must have confirming information about the disease, the third party must be at high risk of contracting the disease, and the client must be unwilling to disclose to the third party in the immediate future. It is important to note that the code *permits* such disclosure; the code does not mandate nor even recommend disclosure. The exact wording is "A counselor . . . may be justified in disclosing" (Section B.1.e). This wording means that the codes do not prescribe a certain behavior. Instead, they give permission for disclosing or for maintaining confidentiality. As in many other situations, then, the codes provide general guidelines, not specific mandates.

Applying these guidelines to this case, the first implication is that the counselor does not yet have confirmation that Raymond is HIV positive. Perhaps verification from Raymond's physician is needed. The counselor also cannot ascertain with any clarity the degree of infection risk to the young woman involved. In addition, the potential for any sexual contact is probably delayed for a week or more. Thus, the criterion of immediacy is not clearly met because the counselor could schedule additional sessions with the client in the intervening time period. From this analysis, it seems that the code does not endorse disclosure at this juncture, but future events may make it justifiable. The other professional documents on this topic also echo the message that counselors should carefully consider breaches of confidentiality in this situation and should avoid rushing to disclose because of the risk of harming the client.

The state laws on the issue of disclosure vary considerably. For example, states such as Massachusetts forbid any disclosure of HIV status to third parties (Chenneville, 2000), whereas other states allow such breaches. Thus, depending on the jurisdiction, one would respond in very different ways to this dilemma.

Scholars' views generally echo the arguments in the documents of the professional associations. They suggest weighing the implications of disclosure for the client as carefully as weighing the risk to the third party. The decision-making model of Melchert and Patterson (1999) is a representative example of this perspective. They also remind counselors that disclosure may rupture the counseling relationship and thereby eliminate the counselor's potential to help a client learn how to disclose HIV status or use safer sex practices. It is this argument that swayed the counselor in the case and that appears particularly compelling, given the young man's initial voluntary entry into counseling. After all, he could have continued developing the physical relationship with this young woman, never sought counseling, and never informed her of his medical condition. The counselor in this case has a valuable opportunity to help Raymond and to help prevent his ever infecting anyone with the virus.

The ethical principles underlying this dilemma relate to respecting the autonomy of this man and avoiding harm to him and those in contact with him. There is also the issue of fidelity to promises made, unless the counselor explicitly explained the limitations of confidentiality at the outset of counseling. The principle of nonmaleficence is most important to consider, especially the potential harm to the client and the woman. There is little doubt that disclosure without his consent will harm this young man, although his injuries are likely to be psychological rather than physical. Her potential injury is physical, but the psychological ramifications of exposure to HIV infection are also crucially important. Still, the probability of infection for her is lower than the risk of harm to him from disclosure. How should one balance an improbable but potentially fatal harm against a fairly certain (but not life-threatening) harm?

Given this information and the results of consultations with colleagues and supervisors, the revised list of options is as follows:

- Focus on safer sex practices and on getting Raymond to agree to a "no sex" contract for the immediate future. If the client agrees to these conditions, then no disclosure should be made at this juncture.
- Review with Raymond the limits of confidentiality again, and seek his permission to bring the young woman into a session to discuss the issue together. If he continues to refuse such an approach in the subsequent sessions as well, reveal the client's information to her.
- Decide that if Raymond commits to practicing safer sex, then the danger is so low that there really is no justification for a breach of confidentiality.

The option that seems most ethically sound at this point is the first one. Raymond needs counseling, is willing to participate now, and seems prepared to accept some responsibility for his behavior insofar as he seems positively disposed to practice safer sex. Moreover, the risk to the young woman is not imminent and the counselor has at least 1 week in which to work with the client before sexual contact is even possible. Given all this information, disclosure seems premature at this point. As events unfold, that decision may change, depending on Raymond's attitude and behavior and the degree of risk to the woman.

DISCUSSION QUESTIONS

1. Do you agree with the California court that "privilege should end where the public peril begins"? Why or why not?
2. Do you think that the fact that a child protection services agency is ineffective or overworked is a rationale for not reporting suspected child abuse? Why or why not?
3. Why do you think violations of confidentiality happen so frequently among practicing mental health professionals?
4. Do you think that "rational suicide" is possible? Should a duty to protect apply in this situation? Explain.
5. Some scholars are very concerned about the erosion of confidentiality in the courts and the managed care arena. How do you think counselors should approach the discussion of confidentiality with clients who want to submit claims to managed care companies or who may be facing court involvement?
6. Do you think children have the right to keep material confidential from their parents?

CASES FOR DISCUSSION

Freda is a licensed mental health professional in private practice. Freda's former client, Maximillian, was killed in a boating accident. Several weeks later Maximillian's wife, Dora, makes an appointment with Freda to find out more about what her husband had been discussing in counseling sessions. Dora's grief about the sudden loss of her husband is still quite strong, yet she also seems to be learning how to cope without him and how to handle that grief. Freda remembers that in his last session Max expressed how much he loved his wife and how fortunate he felt to have such a strong marriage. Freda discloses this information to Dora, judging that Max probably would have wanted it revealed and believing that, as his widow, Dora has a right to this information. Freda probably did not violate any law in telling Dora what Max talked about in counseling. Were her actions also consistent with the ethical standards of the profession? If the content of the sessions had been focused on Max's frustrations with his marriage, how would that affect your judgment about disclosing session content to Dora? What do you see as the ideal ethical solution here?

Abigail, a counselor in a community mental health agency, carries a caseload of clients with severe and persistent mental illness. To help her cope with the stress of such a demanding worklife, Abigail frequently discusses cases with her spouse, Martin, who is also a licensed counselor (although he works at another agency across town). In her conversations with him Abigail does not use clients' last names, but she does describe their problems and her therapeutic interventions in some detail. She is confident that this practice is ethical and that it has been useful to help her cope with the stresses of her work. She is convinced that she would be less effective as a therapist without them and that they have benefited her marriage as well. Abigail also believes these disclosures of client information are ethical because she uses no client names and because Martin is also a mental health professional who honors confidentiality and who understands its importance in therapy. Do you agree with Abigail's judgment that she is acting within the ethical boundaries of the profession?

RECOMMENDED READINGS

American Psychological Association, Committee on Legal Issues. (1996). Strategies for private practitioners coping with subpoenas or compelled testimony for client records or test data. *Professional Psychology: Research and Practice, 27,* 245–251.

American Psychological Association, Committee on Professional Practice and Standards. (1995). Twenty-four questions (and answers) about professional practice in the area of child abuse. *Professional Psychology: Research and Practice, 26,* 377–383.

Bongar, B. (2002). *The suicidal patient: Clinical and legal standards of care* (2nd ed). Washington, DC: American Psychological Association.

Foreman, T., & Bernet, W. (2000). A misunderstanding regarding the duty to report suspected child abuse. *Child Maltreatment, 5,* 190–196.

Gustafson, K. E., & McNamara, J. R. (1987). Confidentiality with minor clients: Issues and guidelines for therapists. *Professional Psychology: Research and Practice, 18,* 503–508.

Kalichman, S. C. (1999). *Mandated reporting of suspected child abuse: Ethics, law and policy.* (2nd ed.). Washington, DC: American Psychological Association.

Monahan, J. (1993). Limiting therapist exposure to *Tarasoff* liability: Guidelines for risk management. *American Psychologist, 48,* 242–250.

Remley, T. P., Jr., Herlihy, B., & Herlihy, S. B. (1997). The U.S. Supreme Court decision in *Jaffee v. Redmond:* Implications for counselors. *Journal of Counseling and Development, 75,* 213–218.

Shuman, D. W., & Foote, W. (1999). *Jaffee v. Redmond's* impact: Life after the Supreme Court's recognition of a psychotherapist-patient privilege. *Professional Psychology: Research and Practice, 30,* 479–487.

Truscott, D., Evans, J., & Mansell, S. (1995). Outpatient psychotherapy with dangerous clients: A model for clinical decision making. *Professional Psychology: Research and Practice, 26,* 484–490.

VandeCreek, L., & Knapp, S. (1993). *Tarasoff and beyond: Legal and clinical considerations in the treatment of life-endangering patients* (Rev. ed.). Sarasota, FL: Professional Resource Exchange.

Chapter 5

Informed Consent
Affirming the Client's Freedom of Choice

Counseling and psychotherapy clients purchase professional services (either directly or indirectly). Even when a client does not write a check to the provider, he or she pays for services through taxes, tuition, or health insurance fees. As consumers, all clients have ethical and legal rights to information about the nature and potential results of those services. Because most people have no other way to gain such "product information," counselors have an obligation to provide it. The need for information is heightened by the fact that the people's presuppositions about counseling and psychotherapy are often erroneous. For example, people may believe mental health professionals dispense advice or medication or that a single visit will be sufficient to relieve their distress. Also, counseling significantly affects the client's mental, emotional, and social functioning. Research shows that counseling and psychotherapy are effective interventions for many human problems (for example, see Lambert, 2003; Seligman, 1995; Sexton, Whiston, Bleuer, & Walz, 1997)—but the client still may experience negative as well as positive results. Even in successful counseling, clients often experience unsettling interruptions in normal patterns, feelings, and social relationships. They have a right to know and expect such occurrences. Finally, the most fundamental reason for providing information about counseling is that it shows respect for the client as a person with rights and responsibilities in a free society. A competent informed consent process shows that the professional is seeing the client as a person—not as a problem or diagnosis.

Informed consent has two central aspects. The first is *disclosure* of relevant information the client needs to make a reasoned decision about whether to start counseling. The second is *free consent,* which means that the decision to engage in an activity is made without coercion or undue pressure. Providing full information empowers the client to determine his or her level of involvement in counseling. Underlying the requirement of informed consent is a view of the client as an autonomous human being capable of directing his or her own life and of collaborating with a counselor to make necessary changes. The call for informed consent rests on a model of counseling and psychotherapy as a partnership in which mental health professionals use their expertise to help clients achieve their own goals. Clients, in turn, use their understanding of themselves and their personal circumstances to help the counselor identify useful interventions and to inform the counselor about their progress.

This chapter seeks to provide a well-rounded overview of informed consent, beginning with a history of how this practice developed. This chapter dispels several myths about informed consent in counseling. These myths include beliefs that informed consent has the following characteristics:

- It is dispensed in the initial counseling session by having a client sign some forms.
- It is restricted to discussion of the limits of confidentiality and little more.
- It is a distraction from the real business of counseling.
- It is undertaken primarily to protect the counselor from legal liability.
- It is quickly understood and easily retained by clients at the initiation of counseling.

This chapter also describes the stance of the ethics codes on informed consent and the ethical principles undergirding those guidelines, the research on practitioners' and clients' interpretations of informed consent, and the interplay between ethical and clinical considerations. In its later sections, the chapter also explores the application of informed consent with minors, in assessment, in emergencies, in court situations, and with adults with diminished mental capacity. Finally, it concludes with cases for analysis. (Informed consent in research is discussed in Chapter 14.)

The History of Informed Consent

The requirement of informed consent in mental health service evolved from medical case law. Although the first case can be traced to England in 1767 (Smith & Meyer, 1987), before the late twentieth century physicians had little legal or ethical obligation to explain medical procedures to their patients or to obtain their express consent. A paternalistic attitude that doctor knew best reigned supreme. This attitude sprang from a society in which consumer rights were an unknown concept and most citizens were poorly educated and ignorant about anatomy and physiology. Unfortunately, vestiges of such paternalism persist in the medical and human service professions. As Haas and Malouf (2005) point out, this attitude toward recipients of care is problematic for two major reasons. First, it prevents people from becoming actively involved in their own care. In a doctor-knows-best system, patients do not feel responsible for their own health and recovery. Second, it is vulnerable to abuse. Uninformed patients can be exploited more easily, and unethical practitioners can avoid accountability more readily.

The spark for change ignited when patients won medical malpractice suits showing that physicians harmed their patients by failing to communicate the nature and risks of medical treatment. Other factors also encouraged the trend away from paternalism. Outrageous violations of patient rights in Nazi Germany and in the infamous Tuskegee experiments in the United States were the most striking of these influences (Jones, 1981). (In the Tuskegee experiments, African-American men with syphilis were "studied" for 40 years, from 1932 to 1972, to observe the progression of the disease. These men were told they were going to receive free medical care in exchange for their cooperation in the project. However, they were never informed of their diagnosis, were required to undergo painful procedures, and for many years were denied the penicillin that could cure them. Many died unnecessarily from this cruel and inhumane treatment.)

By the 1970s case law had unequivocally established that patients had the right to knowledge that would equip them to make informed decisions about their own treatment. Because physicians were usually the ones who possessed the requisite knowledge, the courts ruled that physicians had an affirmative duty to provide such information. The court in *Canterbury v. Spence* (1972, p. 783) concluded that "The duty to disclose is more than a call to speak merely on the patient's request, or merely to answer the patient's questions; it is the duty to volunteer, if necessary, information a patient needs for an intelligent decision." In 1980 a California court expanded the physician's duty to include informed refusal. The term *informed refusal* means that physicians have an obligation to explain the medical consequences if patients refuse a treatment. This reasoning is based on the notion that ordinary citizens are not likely to have sufficient medical knowledge to accurately evaluate the implications of rejecting treatment. Because physicians do understand, they are bound to communicate that information as well (*Truman v. Thomas,* 1980).

The importance of providing the client with complete information about treatment emerged from a medical malpractice case, *Natanson v. Kline* (1960). The court in *Nathanson* specified that disclosure should include the nature of the illness, the treatment(s) available, their risks and the probability of their success, and alternatives to treatment and their risks. Another case from 1979, *Osheroff v. Chestnut Lodge* (Klerman, 1990), was also influential in clarifying the specific components of informed consent. This case involved the failure of a psychiatric facility to inform a patient of the option of medication and outpatient care as an alternative to hospitalization for depression. The case was ultimately settled out of court, but it became well known in the psychiatric community for demonstrating the importance of informing patients about alternative forms of care. These types of information are still major components of informed consent in medicine and mental health today. At least three states (Colorado, Ohio, and Washington) have passed laws mandating disclosure of relevant information to clients (Handelsman, 2001).

The mental health professions quickly applied these legal mandates to their work, and the ethics codes began to include requirements for practitioners to develop an informed consent process with their clients. The professions recognized the connection between these legal rulings and the client's inherent right to self-determination and endorsed the precedent in their codes of ethics. Although some have cautioned against applying medical methods of developing informed consent to the counseling process wholesale, without considering of the needs of the individual client (for example, see Pope & Vasquez, 1998), many scholars agree with the general trend.

Underlying Ethical Principles

The fundamental ethical principle underlying the precepts of informed consent is that of respect for autonomy. The client should not be treated paternalistically or have his or her freedom to choose usurped by a mental health professional, regardless of the professional's rationale in doing so. As mentioned, the effects of counseling rest on the client, who thus ought to have all the data needed to freely choose whether to proceed. This precept is also based on the principles of nonmaleficence and justice. When clients understand the procedures, risks, and potential benefits of counseling, they are probably somewhat insulated from unanticipated unpleasant consequences of counseling. For example, clients who are instructed about the emotional pain that can accompany exploration of family issues may better cope with that pain. Justice demands informed consent because justice implies treating other competent adults as equals. By developing informed consent with each client, counselors confirm that all people have the right to manage their own lives and have the potential to assist in their own care. Obviously, some people do not have that capacity, but justice requires that counselors assume competence until contrary information is available. Justice also means that counselors should treat clients as they themselves would wish to be treated. Any person embarking on counseling would want be fully informed about the process. A failure to honor that right implies that clients are being treated as unequal to or less human than the counselor. Nagy (2000) recommends that clinicians "consider telling [clients] what you would want a good friend to know ... if he or she were consulting a psychologist for the first time" (p. 89). Research also suggests that people want information about their prospective counselors (Hendrick, 1988) and that they may view professionals who provide information about informed consent as more expert and trustworthy (Wagner, Davis, & Handelsman, 1998; Walter & Handelsman, 1996).

Effective informed consent has also been demonstrated to have therapeutic benefits encouraging clients both to initiate counseling and to become more fully engaged in it (Beahrs & Gutheil, 2001).

Codes of Ethics on Informed Consent

The American Counseling Association (ACA) and American Psychological Association (APA) ethics codes contain similar standards for informed consent. The ACA code contains more detailed instructions about informed consent.

ACA *Code of Ethics,* Section A.2: Informed Consent in the Counseling Relationships
(See A.12.g., B.5., B.6.b., E.3., E.13.b., F.1.c., G.2.a.)

a. Informed Consent. Clients have the freedom to choose whether to enter into or remain in a counseling relationship and need adequate information about the counseling process and the counselor. Counselors have an obligation to review in writing and verbally with clients the rights and responsibilities of both the counselor and the client. Informed consent is an ongoing part of the counseling process, and counselors appropriately document discussions of informed consent throughout the counseling relationship.

b. Types of Information Needed. Counselors explicitly explain to clients the nature of all services provided. They inform clients about issues such as, but not limited to, the following: the purposes, goals, techniques, procedures, limitations, potential risks, and benefits of services; the counselor's qualifications, credentials, and relevant experience; continuation of services upon the incapacitation or death of a counselor; and other pertinent information. Counselors take steps to ensure that clients understand the implications of diagnosis, the intended use of tests and reports, fees, and billing arrangements. Clients have the right to confidentiality and to be provided with an explanation of its limitations (including how supervisors and/or treatment team professionals are involved); to obtain clear information about their records; to participate in the ongoing counseling plans; and to refuse any services or modality change and to be advised of the consequences of such refusal.

c. Developmental and Cultural Sensitivity. Counselors communicate information in ways that are both developmentally and culturally appropriate. Counselors use clear and understandable language when discussing issues related to informed consent. When clients have difficulty understanding the language used by counselors, they provide necessary services (e.g., arranging for a qualified interpreter or translator) to ensure comprehension by clients. In collaboration with clients, counselors consider cultural implications of informed consent procedures and, where possible, counselors adjust their practices accordingly.

d. Inability to Give Consent. When counseling minors or persons unable to give voluntary consent, counselors seek the assent of clients to services, and include them in decision making as appropriate. Counselors recognize the need to balance the ethical rights of clients to make choices, their capacity to give consent or assent to receive services, and parental or familial legal rights and responsibilities to protect these clients and make decisions on their behalf.

The APA code discusses the topic in several different sections, but most of the information relevant to counseling and psychotherapy is contained in Sections 3.10 and 10.01.

APA *Ethical Principles,* Section 3.10: Informed Consent

(a) When psychologists conduct research or provide assessment, therapy, counseling, or consulting services in person or via electronic transmission or other forms of communication, they obtain the informed consent of the individual or individuals using language that is reasonably understandable to that person or persons except when conducting such activities without consent is mandated by law or governmental regulation or as otherwise provided in this Ethics Code. (See also Standards 8.02, Informed Consent to Research; 9.03, Informed Consent in Assessments; and 10.01, Informed Consent to Therapy.)

(b) For persons who are legally incapable of giving informed consent, psychologists nevertheless (1) provide an appropriate explanation, (2) seek the individual's assent, (3) consider such persons' preferences and best interests, and (4) obtain appropriate permission from a legally authorized person, if such substitute consent is permitted or required by law. When consent by a legally authorized person is not permitted or required by law, psychologists take reasonable steps to protect the individual's rights and welfare.

(c) When psychological services are court ordered or otherwise mandated, psychologists inform the individual of the nature of the anticipated services, including whether the services are court ordered or mandated and any limits of confidentiality, before proceeding.

(d) Psychologists appropriately document written or oral consent, permission, and assent. (See also Standards 8.02, Informed Consent to Research; 9.03, Informed Consent in Assessments; and 10.01, Informed Consent to Therapy.)

APA *Ethical Principles,* Section 10.01 Informed Consent to Therapy

(a) When obtaining informed consent to therapy as required in Standard 3.10, Informed Consent, psychologists inform clients/patients as early as is feasible in the therapeutic relationship about the nature and anticipated course of therapy, fees, involvement of third parties, and limits of confidentiality and provide sufficient opportunity for the client/patient to ask questions and receive answers. (See also Standards 4.02, Discussing the Limits of Confidentiality, and 6.04, Fees and Financial Arrangements.)

(b) When obtaining informed consent for treatment for which generally recognized techniques and procedures have not been established, psychologists inform their clients/patients of the developing nature of the treatment, the potential risks involved, alternative treatments that may be available, and the voluntary nature of their participation. (See also Standards 2.01e, Boundaries of Competence, and 3.10, Informed Consent.)

(c) When the therapist is a trainee and the legal responsibility for the treatment provided resides with the supervisor, the client/patient, as part of the informed consent procedure, is informed that the therapist is in training and is being supervised and is given the name of the supervisor.

Taken together, these codes designate the following components to an ethical approach to informed consent, although the 2005 ACA standards present a fuller description of the components of informed consent. For each aspect, the code recommends a frank and clear communication of the following:

- Goals, techniques, procedures, limitations, risks, and benefits of counseling
- Ways in which diagnoses, tests, and written reports will be used
- Billing and fees
- Confidentiality rights and limitations
- Involvement of supervisors or additional mental health professionals
- Counselor's credentials and training status
- Client's access to records
- Client's right to choose the counselor and to be active in treatment planning
- Client's right to refuse counseling and the implications of that refusal
- Client's right to ask additional questions about counseling and to have questions answered in comprehensible language

Scholars further recommend that several other topics be added to this list. First, scholars suggest that many of the *logistics* of counseling be disclosed, not just the fees and billing procedures (Haas & Malouf, 2005). Clients should understand procedures for making and rescheduling appointments, for reaching the counselor in an emergency, and for handling interruptions in service such as counselor illness or vacation. If counselors have a standard length of appointment, such as the "50-minute hour," the client should be told about that practice. In addition, if counselors have an estimate of the number of sessions that may be necessary, that estimate should be shared. Third, for *insurance reimbursement*, clients who wish to submit the costs of service to insurers, and who thus must release records, need explicit information about the implications for the confidentiality of their counseling records. Because many managed care plans limit reimbursement to particular forms and lengths of treatment, clients should be told about these restrictions.

Hare-Mustin, Marecek, Kaplan, and Liss-Levinson (1979) advise that when discussing the benefits and risks of therapy, counselors should attend to the *indirect effects* of therapy—consequences that are secondary to the changes the client seeks and agrees to. For example, a client who seeks treatment for agoraphobia (fear of leaving familiar places) should understand that when his agoraphobia diminishes and he returns to his normal activities, this change may indirectly affect aspects of his life he did not expect to be affected. His aging parent may be uncomfortable with his son's absence from the home and may be angry or sad. Similarly, a spouse who is accustomed to always having her husband at home may have difficulty dealing with his mobility. Family members who prefer the client's old behavior may even sabotage the treatment. Of course, positive indirect effects of successful counseling are just as common. This client may experience new intimacy in his marriage or a less strained relationship with his parent, which he may not have anticipated. Counselors who know from experience and the professional literature that a therapeutic intervention is likely to affect additional aspects of a client's functioning need to tell the client as a part of the informed consent process.

Counselors should also disclose the *alternatives to counseling or psychotherapy* that may be available for the client's problems (Bednar et al., 1991; Bray, Shepherd, & Hays, 1985). The range of potential alternatives is wide; some examples include joining Alcoholics Anonymous for substance abuse problems, family or group therapy instead of individual counseling, psychotropic drugs for mental and emotional disorders, and self-help groups and books for less severe life stresses. Underlying this recommendation is the belief that a choice to enter counseling can be freely made only if the client knows the other options. It is important to note here that if counselors' professional judgment leads them to believe that counseling is the most desirable of the available alternatives, they can share that view with the client if the communication is noncoercive and objective. In addition, counselors are free to recommend any of the alternatives to treatment as adjuncts to counseling.

When psychologists are planning to *use an experimental or untested counseling technique* or procedure, clients need to be told and consent for treatment must explicitly include an understanding of the nature of the proposed intervention, the risks, and available alternatives (Section 10.01b). How does one determine which interventions fall into this category? The most basic criterion is the absence of research and clinical evidence of the technique's effectiveness. The APA *Ethical Principles* define experimental treatments as "treatment for which generally recognized techniques and procedures have not been established."

Finally, counselors should include in their informed consent procedures an indication of how the client can address *grievances* should any arise (Handelsman & Galvin, 1988). Some state licensing laws require similar disclosures about methods for filing ethics complaints. Ohio, for example, requires all counselors, marriage and family therapists, and social workers to post or give to clients copies of a disclosure statement, one part of which must include the address of the state licensing board in the event that a client has a grievance against a professional. Practitioners who work in agencies would be well advised to include internal agency grievance procedures as well as professional organization and licensing board procedures. The most practical way to communicate this information is in a form that the client may keep and refer to later.

Additional requirements for informed consent can be found in Section B.6.b and B.6.cs of the ACA code, which states, "Counselors obtain permission from clients prior to recording sessions through electronic or other means" and "Counselors obtain permission from clients prior to observing counseling sessions, reviewing counseling transcripts, or viewing recording of sessions." Section 4.03 of the APA code has the similar message, although it omits the requirement related to observation and adds a mandate to get permission before recording the image as well as the voice of a person receiving services.

APA *Ethical Principles,* Section 4.03: Recording

Before recording the voices or images of individuals to whom they provide services, psychologists obtain permission from all such persons or their legal representatives.

When counselors want to record sessions, they must disclose this intent to the client, explain the purposes of recording and the uses to which the recording will be put, and ask for the client's consent. A client who does not wish to be electronically recorded has the right to refuse. Similarly, a client should understand that he or she can withdraw consent to record at any time without penalty. If the counselor believes that electronic recording is essential for competent service, as may happen with an intern or novice, then the counselor must refer the client to a counselor who is competent to work without recording if the client so chooses. Some organizations, especially family counseling training centers, use a one-way mirror to observe trainees or have counseling rooms wired so that conversations can be heard by supervisors in an adjoining room. This arrangement is permissible only if the client freely consents to it.

In the current editions of the ethics codes both psychology and counseling specify that the provisions related to informed consent apply not only to face-to-face meetings but also to forms of service that involve electronic communications. Thus, when counselors or psychologists are providing Internet-based service, telephone consultation, or facsimile transmissions to their clients they need to abide by the informed consent standards.

It is important to differentiate between *informed consent* and *notice* (Jacob & Hartshorne, 1991). Notice means informing people involved about impending events, but it does not assume a prior agreement to those events. Informed consent, therefore, is quite distinct from the mere practice of telling people what will be happening to them in counseling or therapy. Notice alone is ethically insufficient. Similarly, professionals who attempt to deal with informed consent through a *blanket consent* form are not complying with ethical or legal standards. In other words, counselors who use a single, general verbal or written consent procedure that is nonspecific and all-purpose are vulnerable to charges that they failed to develop proper consent (Jacob & Hartshorne, 1991). The 2002 version of the APA *Ethical Principles* specifically requires psychologists to provide clients with sufficient opportunity to ask questions about professional services (and receive answers) in language they can understand.

Informed Consent and the Health Insurance Portability and Accountability Act

The U.S. Congress passed the legislation that created the Health Insurance Portability and Accountability Act (HIPAA) requirements in 1996, but regulations for the statute did not become effective for another 7 years. This legislation has two major components—the protection of personal health information that may be shared for treatment or payment purposes for health and mental health patients and the protection of the systems of electronic communication from unauthorized access. Technically, HIPAA requirements apply narrowly to electronic communication of personal client/patient information, but the wording in the legislation makes its provisions applicable to any professional who uses a fax or an email for any client. The legislation has two major goals—to give the patient/client control over release of personal health information while facilitating the most common types of communication about client/patient records without explicit permission for each and every release. In other words, HIPAA allows health care professionals to obtain a single signature on a Notice of Privacy Practices document to allow for transmission of information to obtain payment from third parties; to provide treatment; and to keep the ordinary operations of the practice, agency, or institution proceeding in an orderly fashion. Along with other requirements for protecting client/patient data, this federal law requires all community-based mental health professionals to have clients read and sign the Notice of Privacy Practices so that clients understand what information will be released without explicit consent and what recourse they have if personal health information is disclosed in ways that violate the law. If mental health professionals fail to follow the regulations outlined in HIPAA, the law explicitly allows for a client to bring a civil suit against the provider and allows for criminal prosecution for extreme and willful violations of HIPAA provisions.

It is important to note that compliance with HIPAA is not in itself sufficient to meet most of the ethical standards for informed consent. For example, nothing in HIPAA touches on benefits and limitations of service or alternatives to counseling or psychotherapy. Therefore, mental health professionals must supplement HIPAA procedures if they are to be compliant with other ethical (and legal) standards for informed consent.

Approaches to Informed Consent

Two primary methods are commonly used to obtain informed consent—a discussion of the issues with no written forms (except for the HIPAA privacy notice) or a discussion accompanied by additional documents, copies of which are given to the client. For the first time, the most recent revision of the ACA *Code of Ethics* specifies in Section A.2.a that informed consent should include both written and verbal components, whereas the APA code allows for either written or oral communication of informed consent (APA *Ethical Principles,* Section 3.10d). Research (Handelsman, Kemper, Kesson-Craig, McLain, & Johnsrud, 1986; Somberg, Stone, & Claiborn, 1993) suggests that a majority of psychotherapists rely exclusively on oral discussion of informed consent—thus practitioners who had not been using written consent materials prior to 2005 must begin to incorporate them into informed consent to comply with new ethical standards. According to the ACA code, Section A.2.a, informed consent is not completed when the initial discussion is over and the forms are signed; counselors need to have an ongoing discussion with clients about informed consent as necessitated by the services provided and to document in the client record each discussion of consent issues.

Verbal discussion has some advantages. It allows the professional to adapt the wording of the informed consent information to the unique needs of the individual and to humanize and personalize the process. In addition, a verbal format may encourage the client to ask questions and become more involved in the conversation. However, exclusive reliance on verbal discussion has drawbacks. Most important, clients can be overwhelmed with all that information and may forget or not absorb much of what they hear. Research suggests that forgetfulness is a significant problem even when written materials are used (for example, see Cassileth, Zupkis, Sutton-Smith, & March, 1980). The risk of forgetfulness increases with the level of distress the client is experiencing. The emotions that provoked a visit to a counselor may be so predominant that cognitive processing is compromised, but without a document to take home, clients have no way to review the information or to be sure that they really understood it. By the same token, the counselor who uses a verbal format must guess at how much the client understood and remembered or must quiz the client on his or her retention. Neither alternative is particularly appealing or professional. Also, much of the specific information most useful to the client, such as options for addressing a grievance or procedures for contacting the therapist in an emergency, is most vulnerable to forgetfulness. A final disadvantage is that this practice is at odds with the recommendations of legal scholars and ethics experts (and the ACA Ethics Code), who urge professionals not to rely exclusively on conversation to conduct informed consent. For example, Bennett, Bryant, VanderBos, and Greenwood (1990) contend that written documents are rapidly becoming the "community standard," and they caution professionals that failing to use them may have adverse consequences for them in any legal challenge or ethics complaint. It is important to emphasize, however, that written consent forms offer the professional no protection against legal claims if the forms are unreadable or the client was manipulated into signing them (Appelbaum, Lidz, & Meisel, 1987).

The written materials used in informed consent take various forms, but Zuckerman (2003) describes five distinct alternative formats. The first of these is the *client information brochure*. This document provides a detailed description of the benefits, risks, goals, and methods of therapy as well as information about its costs, length, and logistics. He emphasizes the importance of communicating the professional's views of the therapeutic process, including both theoretic orientation and types of services offered. This is usually a professionally designed document that extends for several pages. It serves as an invitation to counseling, as an implied contract between the parties, and as a communication about the standard of care the client has a right to expect (Woody, 1988).

The second format is the *question list* as a guide to discussion, which was first recommended by Handelsman and Galvin (1988) and updated in 2004 (Pomerantz & Handelsman, 2004). It provides a structure for the client to interview the professional about therapy and reinforces the power and active role the client has in an effective therapeutic relationship. Sample questions include the following:

- What is the name of your kind of therapy?
- How will I notice if I am getting better?
- How will I reach you in an emergency?
- If I do not pay my bill, what will you do?
- How would therapy be different if I chose to pay without using insurance?

The third format is a *declaration of client rights*. Bennett et al. (1990) provide a recommended model, and Zuckerman (2003) offers several examples. This form tends to be briefer and more formal than the others. There are also several models available on the Web, including the excellent version published by the Pennsylvania Department of Public Welfare at www.dpw.state.pa.us/Child/BehavHealthServChildren/ChildAdolescentGuidelines/003670809.htm.

A *psychotherapy or counseling contract* is the next option for written informed consent. In it, the rights and responsibilities of the participants are delineated. This structure may be especially useful with clients who are reluctant, but it must be supplemented with extensive discussion and must be signed by both parties. Finally, a *consent-to-treatment form* is an option that is best used when other formats seem too detailed for the particular counseling relationship being initiated, but its brevity means that it also needs extensive supplementation.

None of these forms must be used exclusively. In fact, Zuckerman and other scholars encourage professionals to use multiple formats with each client. All also urge that clients sign consent forms and keep copies of them and that professionals retain copies for the client file. The strengths of these forms are that they become a permanent part of the record and are available for consultation at a later date by both parties. If there is a grievance or misunderstanding about treatment, the forms can support the professional's claim that he or she explained that aspect of treatment in the consent process. Client forms can also speed up a time-consuming process. A verbal discussion of all the relevant aspects of consent might consume a good deal of the initial session, leaving inadequate time to hear the client's concerns. Finally, they can hold the attention of the client to the topic and reduce the amount of material that is missed or forgotten. Even the most clear-thinking and motivated client may tune out some of a lengthy verbal description.

The problems with the written materials lie primarily in their vulnerability to misuse. The most obvious disadvantage of such forms is the tendency for counselors to rely too heavily on them. Counselors can (and often do) erroneously assume that a document in the hands of a client substitutes for a discussion of the topic. When this happens, informed consent becomes pro forma and the client's rights are not really protected (Pope & Vasquez, 1998; Zuckerman, 2003). In some counseling settings, informed consent is (mis)handled by having a clerical staff member hand the document to a client and request a signature before an appointment. This approach violates both the spirit and the letter of the professional guidelines. The second major disadvantage is that the client may not have the necessary level of literacy. In fact, the research in mental health settings has found that the average informed consent form requires more than a 12th-grade reading ability (Handelsman et al., 1986; Handelsman & Martin, 1992). In fact, 63% of the forms used for informed consent in a study by Handelsman et al. (1995) were rated at the graduate school reading level, and the lowest rating was a 7th-grade reading level. Because the average reading level of a U.S. citizen is less than high school, (9th grade), the average client cannot understand the vast majority of such forms. Particularly troublesome is that the reading levels of counseling consent forms are significantly higher than those used in medicine (for example, see Feldman, Vanarthos, & Fleisher, 1994). In other words, our medical colleagues have made complex medical information more accessible to patients than we have made less complex information accessible to our clients. One practical suggestion from Handelsman (2001) to increase readability is to decrease the number of words per sentence and the number of syllables per word. Improving readability has also been made easier by the sophistication of word processing programs—most have readability formulas built into them.

The final significant problem is that these forms can distance the client from the counselor in the crucial early moments of counseling, when trust needs to develop. This situation occurs when counselors misunderstand informed consent and treat the documents as bureaucratic procedures to be rushed through and handled identically with every client. They see the process as an empty ritual (Pope & Vasquez, 1998) rather than as a process of collaboration and open invitation for the client to actively participate in therapy. Such a misuse of forms can give clients the message that their individual needs are being ignored, that the paperwork of counseling is more important than their concerns, and that the counselor does not care whether they really understand what they are being asked to sign. Forms that are written in a style suggesting they are meant to protect the organization from lawsuits, rather than to inform the client, also lend themselves to this negative interpretation. Pope and Vasquez remark, "Nothing blocks a patient's access to help with such cruel efficiency as a bungled attempt at informed consent" (1998, p. 126). As Beahrs and Gutheil (2001) note, unless informed consent procedures are carried out competently and sensitively, they can inadvertently replace a positive expectancy of help with a suggestion of a negative outcome.

A very small percentage of professionals (Somberg et al., 1993) rely on audiotapes or videotapes (or CDs or DVDs) to inform clients about counseling. These tapes may be sent home with a client to view at leisure, or they may be viewed in a private area in the counseling office. These approaches seem underused and have good potential. They may help clients absorb a great deal of information in an efficient and familiar format. A rapidly growing percentage of households have the equipment to play these devices. Moreover, clients are becoming accustomed to them as teaching tools as well as sources of entertainment. Many physicians use patient education tapes to help patients understand medical procedures, and home computer companies insert videotapes or DVDs into packing boxes to help consumers install their equipment. They can be replayed at will and are accessible regardless of the client's reading proficiency. They can even be made available in different languages and are a livelier and more human format than written materials. Tapes may reduce the client's anxiety because they can provide a preview of the counselor before sessions begin.

Undoubtedly, by this time some counselors have found ways to use audio and video capabilities on Web pages, e-mail, and fax machines to develop informed consent and get immediate information to prospective clients. However, problems may arise with electronic formats, too. They are subject to the same misuse as written materials if counselors substitute them for real dialogue about treatment, but they also have substantial potential to reduce clients' anxiety about counseling and increase their understanding of the treatment process.

Any method of developing informed consent requires a counselor who can communicate a lot of information in an efficient and interesting way so that the process doesn't become tedious and overwhelming. Debunking the myth that informed consent is completed at the initial session lets the client comfortably accept all this information. Informed consent is a process, not an event. The process must be substantially accomplished at the first contact, but it is not really finished until counseling ends. For instance, as treatment options emerge during the course of counseling, professionals need to get the client's consent to each new treatment. When conducted skillfully and respectfully, informed consent is not an obstacle to trust and therapeutic progress. Instead, it is a symbol of respect for the client's dignity and an invitation to actively collaborate with the counselor.

The Interplay of Ethical and Clinical Considerations

As with all other ethical dimensions of counseling, responsible development of informed consent requires good clinical judgment. Sound judgment about applying informed consent procedures is especially important when clients are in crisis or under very great stress. A client in crisis, for example, may be prepared to hear only about the nature and limits of confidentiality before discussing the crisis. A lengthy explanation of all aspects of informed consent could be counterproductive to a client whose mental health and well-being are at stake. (It is important to note, however, that the crisis may require postponing the full discussion, but it should not be eliminated.)

In rare circumstances, no time is available for informed consent. Consider the following situation:

The Case of Jerry
A 36-year-old man knocks on the counselor's door. When she opens it the man blurts out, "Please help me! I have a loaded shotgun in the trunk of my car outside and I think I'm going to kill myself." The man appears frightened, poorly groomed, sleep deprived, and desperate for help. The car is only 30 feet away, and the man still holds the keys in his hand. The counselor immediately invites the man inside and asks him to tell her more about his distress. Within 45 minutes the man has surrendered his car keys, agreed to be hospitalized, and wants to be saved from his own suicidal impulses. In another half-hour transportation to the hospital arrives and the man leaves in the ambulance. No informed consent procedure of any kind ever took place.

Was the clinician (the author) acting unethically by omitting discussion of informed consent? The answer is no if the counselor's professional judgment told her that to delay attention to the man's suicidal impulse would heighten his already high risk for self-destruction. Her primary obligation is to protect his best interests and his life. If she believed she would be putting him at jeopardy by diverting his attention to any other matter, and if other competent professionals in a similar situation would make the same judgment, then her decision was fully justified and fully ethical. Legal scholars may suggest that the man gave *apparent consent* insofar as his behavior implied agreement to talk with the counselor (Bray et al., 1985).

Judgment is also necessary in discussing the diagnosis, length of therapy, and potential benefits and risks. Learning that there is a psychiatric name for one's distress can be shocking sometimes, so the requirement to inform the client needs to be balanced against the discomfort it may cause. For example, parents who learn that their child is being diagnosed with attention deficit disorder may be highly distressed by this information. Similarly, adults who are told that their mood swings fit the diagnosis of manic depression may be overwhelmed with the news. Discomfort should be a signal to be tactful, compassionate, and cautious in disclosure and to consider a temporary delay in pursuing fully informed consent on this issue. Similarly, when providing information about the risks and benefits of counseling, mental health professionals need to take into account the client's need for hope of change and for optimism about the future as well as available research evidence about therapeutic success rates. Clients often enter counseling feeling fearful and pessimistic, and a counselor who is overinsistent about explaining risks and negative outcomes can cause a client to give up hope that counseling can help before the process even begins. Counselors must gauge clients' interpretation of this material and help them see both sides of the equation. The goal is to provide accurate information to maximize client understanding without dimming the client interest in or commitment to counseling.

Another clinical consideration about informed consent is that some information required in developing informed consent simply cannot be determined accurately in the first session. A valid diagnosis may take several sessions to develop, and reliable estimates of the length and intensity of treatment can seldom be reached at intake. Similarly, the techniques and procedures that may address the presenting problems sometimes do not become clear for several sessions, and even then they may change as counseling unfolds. The ethics codes acknowledge this reality and encourage the mental health professional to use professional judgment in determining how intensively and how frequently to discuss informed consent.

A final clinical consideration that interacts with the ethics of informed consent is that some clients tend to be reluctant to ask questions and unwilling to disagree with a counselor. Clients often view counselors as authorities and experts to whom an ordinary person tends to defer. Moreover, clients often hope their therapists approve of them and fear that they will be judged negatively. Thus, it is not surprising that clients may not ask about aspects of informed consent that they do not understand and may censor their inclinations to refuse an intervention the counselor is recommending. Counselors must be alert to nonverbal signs of confusion or resistance and must establish trust and acceptance so that real agreement to counseling can be secured. Settling for anything less undermines the chance of clinical success and compromises truly informed consent.

Applications to Special Populations

As with the issue of confidentiality, informed consent becomes more complex in counseling certain populations. Children and teenagers, people with impaired cognitive capacity, and involuntary participants are the most obvious such populations because they are legally and ethically incapable of giving consent. They do not have the capacity to fully understand the meaning and implications of their choices about counseling. The language in the APA standards is provided earlier in the chapter (Section 3.10.b) and the wording in the ACA code is as follows.

ACA *Code of Ethics*, Section A.2: Informed Consent in the Counseling Relationship

d. Inability to Give Consent. When counseling minors or persons unable to give voluntary consent, counselors seek the assent of clients to services, and include them in decision making as appropriate. Counselors recognize the need to balance the ethical rights of clients to make choices, their capacity to give consent or assent to recieve services, and parental or familial legal rights and responsibilities to protect these clients and make decisions on their behalf.

ACA *Code of Ethics*, Section B.5: Clients Lacking Capacity to Give Informed Consent

b. Responsibility to Parents and Legal Guardians. Counselors inform parents and legal guardians about the role of counselors and the confidential nature of the counseling relationship. Counselors are sensitive to cultural diversity among families and respect the inherent rights and responsibilities of parents/guardians over the welfare of their children/charges by virtue of their role and according to law. Counselors work to establish, as appropriate, collaborative relationships with parents/guardians to best serve clients.

c. Release of Confidential Information. When counseling minor clients or adult clients who lack the capacity to give voluntary consent to release confidential information, counselors may seek permission from an appropriate third party to disclose information. In such instances, counselors inform clients consistent with their level of understanding and take culturally appropriate measures to safeguard client confidentiality.

Minors

By law, minors usually cannot give informed consent for treatment; at least one parent or guardian must give consent instead. (See Chapter 12 for additional discussion of informed consent in school counseling.) When custody is shared after a divorce, consent of both parents is advisable. As discussed in Chapter 4, under some circumstances adolescents may be exempt from this law. For example, minors can receive treatment in an emergency without parental consent or if they are legally emancipated from family.

Ethical requirements are more flexible because the ethical standard for consent is based on the capacity of the client to understand the information presented and freely choose the course of action in response to that knowledge. The closer adolescents are to an age of maturity, the more likely they are to exhibit such comprehension and capacity to choose. Younger children are unlikely to have the cognitive maturity or ability to make a free choice. Given the interaction among these developmental factors, ethical guidelines, and legal requirements, most ethics scholars agree with the advice in the ACA and APA codes to obtain the *assent* of minors to counseling. As the adolescent matures, assent procedures should more closely approximate informed consent procedures. Assent to counseling means that counselors need to involve children in decisions about their own care and, to the greatest extent possible, obtain the child's agreement to engage in counseling (DeKraai et al., 1998; Koocher & Keith-Spiegel, 1990; Melton, 1981). The wording in the codes means that acquiring assent is not mandatory, although the good-faith effort to secure assent appears to be. However, scholars clearly argue that it is sound practice, with both clinical and ethical value. The ethical ideal embedded in this practice is the communication of respect for the inherent dignity of the person, regardless of age or circumstance. As a practical matter, children and adolescents who do not understand counseling, and whose commitment to the enterprise is unknown, are unlikely to be cooperative clients who can work toward therapeutic goals. Without assent, they have little ownership of the goals that have been established. The recommendation to seek the assent of the child does not exclude parents. Assent is a supplement, not a substitute, for parental consent. The goal of the codes here is to instruct counselors to honor the rights and preferences of both parties to the fullest extent possible. Ultimately the best interests of the child are the highest priority in circumstances where parental preferences and minor's interests conflict.

If a child refuses to give immediate assent, going forward with counseling anyway is not unethical, although its clinical value is questionable. In such a situation, a counselor would be well advised to work closely with the family to help them appreciate the importance of the child's willing involvement in counseling. In the meantime, the counselor should continue to attempt to build trust with the child so that assent can be gained as soon as possible. The ultimate criterion, of course, is the course of action most fitting with the best interests of the child. No professional should keep a child in counseling if therapy is not helping that child.

Research on counselor practices regarding consent with minors focuses primarily on adolescents and has found that a growing percentage of psychologists seek to secure an adolescent's agreement to participate in counseling (Beeman & Scott, 1991; Taylor, Adelman, & Kaser-Boyd, 1984). By 1991, 70% of child psychologists indicated that they regularly obtained the adolescent's agreement along with the parents' consent (Beeman & Scott, 1991).

People with Diminished Capacity

Generally, adults are assumed to be competent to consent until evidence exists to the contrary. At times counselors encounter clients with severe mental retardation, advanced dementia, or acute psychosis who are clearly not competent. Such clients are said to have "diminished capacity," meaning they can't currently comprehend events that affect them. Without comprehension, they cannot make an informed choice; others must make that choice for them. Usually a family member or a court-appointed guardian fills this role. Regardless of the specific person providing the substitute consent, the counselor must go through the consent procedure with the substitute as though he or she were the client. In addition, the counselor is responsible for giving the client as much involvement in the decision making as he or she can manage.

When a client's capacity to give consent is in question, a prudent practice is to give the client the benefit of the doubt and go forward to the greatest extent possible. In addition, counselors ought to consult with a colleague who is competent to objectively assess the client's capacity. The goal is to avoid treating clients paternalistically and to carefully evaluate the client's intellectual functioning. Taking away a client's freedom to choose is a serious step that should not be taken lightly. If the client's competence to consent is temporarily compromised (by intoxication or acute physical illness, for example), professionals should attempt to delay consent until the client's mental functioning is back to normal (Kitchener, 2000).

In Court-Mandated Counseling

Over the last 50 years, mental health professionals have become more involved with the courts (Stokes & Remley, 2001). Judges have learned of the value of counseling for citizens who come before them, and they frequently mandate counseling for people whose legal difficulties seem to stem from emotional, relationship, or substance abuse problems. Shearer (2003) has referred to court-mandated counseling as an ethical minefield, but others (for example, Rooney, 2001) are more optimistic about finding a way to conduct this treatment ethically. Usually defendants are given a choice between a criminal or civil penalty and counseling. Many defendants in juvenile and adult courts thus "choose" counseling. The histories and current predicaments of these people point to a strong need for intervention to help them cope with pain, learn alternative behaviors, and build healthier relationships. However, the circumstances under which they enter counseling raise questions about the degree to which their selection of counseling really represents a free choice. Consider the following questions:

- If jail is the only other alternative, is the selection of counseling really voluntary?
- If losing custody of children seems imminent, will a parent feel coerced into counseling?
- After a third or fourth arrest for driving under the influence, would anyone choose permanent loss of driving privileges over temporary loss of license and counseling? If not, is there really any choice?
- Can a client who opts for counseling over the alternatives in any of the preceding situations be considered a willing and motivated client ready to actively participate in the process?
- How does a counselor establish trust and measure therapeutic progress with a client who sees counseling as the "least worst" alternative?

These questions probe the contradiction between the usual definition of informed consent and its use in court settings. Ordinarily, informed consent is based on *capacity* (the ability to understand the information being presented), *comprehension* (the understanding of the specifics of the information), and *voluntariness* (a free, unforced choice). Voluntariness is at risk when the alternative is illusory and is an option no rational person would choose. This practice seems to fall within Warwick and Kelman's (1973) definition of manipulation: the "structuring of options in such a way that one is more likely to be selected than others while preserving the appearance of free choice" (p. 403). Thus, in this setting, the counselor has a dilemma: Should he or she accept the client regardless of the lack of voluntariness, or should the contradiction be pointed out immediately and the counseling delayed until the client is in a better position to decide his or her own fate?

There is no absolute rule for this situation. The ethics codes do not give extensive guidance, except for their general directive to promote the dignity and welfare of the client and to communicate with the mandated person about the professional's obligation to a third party. Once again, the counselor's judgment comes into play. The task is to weigh the deficiency in consent against the possible good that counseling might do for a particular person. In essence, one engages in a kind of risk–benefit analysis, asking oneself, Would counseling without free consent be likely to do harm? Would the failure to provide counseling, even under these compromised circumstances, be likely to cause more harm than providing it? Do I have the skills, compassion, and attitude to help the client overcome the distrust inherent in mandated counseling? The answers to these questions should guide the decision. In any case, the counselor needs to proceed through an informed consent process with such clients, disclose appropriate information about counseling, and make sure the client understands it. The ultimate objective of the mental health professional is to find a way to facilitate the court's interest in counseling services for citizens who require them without violating the rights and dignity of those citizens. Professionals should be encouraged by evidence that people can benefit from intervention even when they are mandated to participate and that they are often significantly better off than others in the same circumstance who are not involved in counseling (Keaton & Yamatani, 1993; Peters & Murrin, 2000). Some research also suggests that mandated clients are aware that they have serious mental health issues that need changing and that they agree with the directive to get service (Rooney, 2001). Consequently, counselors should not automatically assume that mandated clients are hostile to service or unwilling to participate. They are clearly at greater risk for feeling coerced and being unmotivated, but they are not hopeless cases. Rooney (2001) emphasizes the value of honest and direct communication during the informed consent process so that mandated clients are knowledgeable about the treatment and the implications of their participation in it.

The APA *Ethical Principles,* 3.10.c, specifies that when clients are legally mandated, the professional is responsible for informing them of the services to be provided, of the court order for services, and of the limits on confidentiality in this situation.

Informed Consent in Assessment

All counseling and psychotherapy includes some form of assessment, evaluation of client needs, or diagnosis of client problems—after all, a professional can treat only those concerns that have been identified. As will be described in greater detail in Chapter 9, the assessment process has been fraught with ethical problems for practitioners. Therefore, professional standards provide extensive description of the ethics of assessment, both in relation to informed consent and other aspects.

APA *Ethical Principles,* Section 9.03: Informed Consent in Assessments

(a) Psychologists obtain informed consent for assessments, evaluations, or diagnostic services, as described in Standard 3.10, Informed Consent, except when (1) testing is mandated by law or governmental regulations; (2) informed consent is implied because testing is conducted as a routine educational, institutional, or organizational activity (e.g., when participants voluntarily agree to assessment when applying for a job); or (3) one purpose of the testing is to evaluate decisional capacity. Informed consent includes an explanation of the nature and purpose of the assessment, fees, involvement of third parties, and limits of confidentiality and sufficient opportunity for the client/patient to ask questions and receive answers.

(b) Psychologists inform persons with questionable capacity to consent or for whom testing is mandated by law or governmental regulations about the nature and purpose of the proposed assessment services, using language that is reasonably understandable to the person being assessed.

(c) Psychologists using the services of an interpreter obtain informed consent from the client/patient to use that interpreter, ensure that confidentiality of test results and test security are maintained, and include in their recommendations, reports, and diagnostic or evaluative statements, including forensic testimony, discussion of any limitations on the data obtained.

ACA *Code of Ethics,* Section E.3: Informed Consent in Assessment

a. Explanation to Clients. Prior to assessment, counselors explain the nature and purposes of assessment and the specific use of results by potential recipients. The explanation will be given in the language of the client (or other legally authorized person on behalf of the client), unless an explicit exception has been agreed upon in advance. Counselors consider the client's personal or cultural context, the level of the client's understanding of the results, and the impact of the results on the client. *(See A.2., A.12.g., F.1.c.)*

b. Recipients of Results. Counselors consider the examinee's welfare, explicit understandings, and prior agreements in determining who receives the assessment results. Counselors include accurate and appropriate interpretations with any release of individual or group assessment results. *(See B.2.c., B.5.)*

Paralleling the ethical mandates for consent in counseling and therapy, these standards emphasize the right of the client to full information about the purposes and uses of assessments prior to their implementation. Unless a court or other legal body has ordered testing—for example, to determine a person's fitness to stand trial—the client also has the right to refuse testing or release of data to any other parties. These standards have their most obvious application when formal educational and psychological tests are used or when a formal diagnosis of an emotional or mental disorder is given, but they also apply whenever the counselor is making an evaluation of a client and placing that evaluation in a client record or communicating it to other parties. (A more detailed discussion of the ethics of assessment is contained in Chapter 9.)

Research Findings on Informed Consent

Research on informed consent in psychotherapy is both encouraging and discouraging. On the one hand, researchers have found that informed consent can benefit clients and therapists. Clients who have experienced a responsible informed consent process seem to view self-disclosure more positively and have more optimistic expectations for counseling outcome (Goodyear, Coleman, & Brunson, 1986). Also, some evidence suggests that adult clients view therapists who carefully develop informed consent as more trustworthy and expert than those who do not (Sullivan, Martin, & Handelsman, 1993). Similarly, parents of children appreciate informed consent information (Jensen, McNamara, & Gustafson, 1991) and expect that mental health professionals will provide that information to them.

On the other hand, research also suggests that compliance with informed consent mandates, both ethical and legal, is inconsistent. Moreover, some of the informed consent procedures in use seem to meet only the letter and not the spirit of the guidelines. In one study of the practices and attitudes of psychologists toward informed consent, Somberg et al. (1993) found that virtually no one in their small national sample dealt with the whole topic. A majority omitted several required components with most clients. Only 59.5% indicated that they discuss the limits of confidentiality with every client, and less than one-third of the sample discussed the risks of therapy, its length, or alternatives with every client. Moreover, 18% reported that they *never* discussed the risks of therapy with clients. The timing of informed consent discussions was also highly variable. Of those who discussed major components of informed consent, most tended to do so by the end of the first session. A disturbingly high percentage, however, indicated that they discussed informed consent matters only "as the issue arises" (Somberg et al., 1993, p. 156). That implies that these psychologists discuss duty-to-warn issues or mandated reporting of child abuse only when the client brings up the issue. Research on the consent practices of rehabilitation counselors reveals a similar problem—only 56% of those in this study discussed the limits of confidentiality relating to dangerousness at intake, and only 45% described limits relating to abuse and neglect of vulnerable persons at intake (Shaw, Chan, Lam, & McDougall, 2002). Waiting until the client discloses something that cannot be held confidential is like closing the proverbial barn door after the horse has escaped. Postponing informed consent in this way also violates the principle of fidelity. The point of the ethical mandates is that clients should understand the implications of such disclosures *before* they make them. Swenson (1997) describes the explanation of the limits of confidentiality as a "psychological Miranda warning" that clients must have in order to judge the consequences of their disclosures (p. 72). (A Miranda warning is the list of rights law enforcement personnel must disclose before questioning to a person accused of a crime.) Because in some circumstances courts can demand testimony from mental health professionals about clients, failing to develop properly informed consent can sometimes make clients incriminate themselves. Other researchers also have found the same variability and insufficiency in informed consent procedures and documents (for example, Claiborn, Berberoglu, Nerison, & Somberg, 1994; Croarkin, Berg, & Spira, 2003; Sherry, Teschendorf, Anderson, & Guzman, 1991; Talbert & Pipes, 1988). For instance, Claiborn et al. (1994) found that only 6% of the clients surveyed indicated that their therapists had given them information on the limits of confidentiality. In a study that compared psychiatrists with psychologists and social workers, Croarkin et al. (2003) found that psychologists had the highest level of endorsement of the importance of informed consent and psychiatrists had the lowest. Research on informed consent procedures with adolescent clients reveals better compliance with ethical guidelines. For example, Beeman and Scott (1991) found that 93% of the psychologists in their sample secured the informed consent of parents for treating their teenagers. As mentioned earlier, 70% also obtain the adolescent's agreement to participate.

Are professionals who are providing E-therapy, also called Internet counseling, doing a better job of compliance with informed consent? Unfortunately, no evidence supports that conclusion. In fact, research by Heinlen, Welfel, Richmond, and Rak (2003) and Heinlen, Welfel, Richmond, and O'Donnell (2003) suggests that more than half the professionals with online clinical services are largely noncompliant with informed consent provisions of the codes. Many consumers who are interested in online counseling or therapy must first pay for service before obtaining complete consent information, if they ever obtain it.

It is surprising that, according to Remley and Herlihy (2005), no malpractice cases have arisen from claims of negligent informed consent in outpatient psychotherapy or counseling despite evidence of inconsistent compliance with standards. Similarly, relatively few ethics complaints have dealt with this violation. Whether this low level of complaints will continue in an increasingly consumer-oriented and litigious society is an open question.

In summary, despite client interest in informed consent information and evidence that there may be both ethical and therapeutic value to communicating such information, the compliance of practitioners with this standard is incomplete at best and nonexistent at worst.

Cases for Discussion

The cases that follow illustrate the ethical dilemmas embedded in informed consent.

The Case of Dr. Doolittle

Dr. Doolittle is a counselor who works with adults rehabilitating from spinal cord injuries. His clients have all their intellectual capacities intact but are often paralyzed or have other mobility problems. The informed consent materials he uses make no reference to the risks or alternatives to counseling. He contends that his clients have experienced enough trauma and do not need to worry about the negative effects counseling may have. Their lives are already completely disrupted by their injuries, he reasons, and they have little to lose and everything to gain by counseling. He also believes there are no good alternatives to counseling for people with spinal cord injuries because they need emotional support, vocational counseling, and guidance in practical living issues. Is Dr. Doolittle justified in omitting these topics?

The Case of Ms. Berens

Ms. Berens is a high school counselor. One of her clients is a 15-year-old sophomore who has been truant from school for the last 9 weeks. Marianna has refused to attend school since she had a tonsillectomy. After her recovery from surgery, she told her mother she could not tolerate being in school. Now, she stays at home reading, watching television, and doing household chores. If Marianna does not return to school soon, legal action will be taken. Marianna is not a willing client in counseling. She has refused to assent to it, but her mother gave consent and insists that her daughter attend counseling anyway. She has agreed to schedule counseling in the last hour of the school day to make her daughter's presence in the school less difficult. Ms. Berens has outlined the aspects of informed consent with Marianna, and she believes the young woman understands the concepts. Marianna indicates that her problems are psychological and that she does not want to discuss her private life with a school counselor. How can Ms. Berens balance the girl's refusal to give assent against her mother's consent to counseling?

The Case of Dr. Marcello

Dr. Marcello is a skilled therapist with a full schedule of clients. To manage his busy schedule he delegates responsibility for informed consent procedures to his office assistant, Mr. Williams. New clients meet with Mr. Williams for 30 minutes prior to their first appointment to complete patient questionnaires, insurance forms, and informed consent documents. (They are mailed a patient information brochure in advance of the appointment.) Mr. Williams has no professional education in counseling, but he has been trained by Dr. Marcello to conduct these meetings. Mr. Williams is careful to follow the protocol established by his boss and is diligent about checking to ensure that patients understand the contents of the documents they sign. Using this approach, Dr. Marcello believes the counseling sessions are more focused and that his obligation to informed consent is substantially fulfilled, although he does recognize that additional issues related to informed consent may arise in the course of counseling. Is Dr. Marcello's practice consistent with current standards for informed consent?

The Case of Mr. Zimmer

Mr. Zimmer is a family therapist who has begun working with a 37-year-old father of two teenagers who has been convicted of drunk driving. As part of his sentence, the father has agreed to attend family sessions to work on the issues with his wife and children that are related to his recent abuse of alcohol. After the first few sessions Mr. Zimmer realizes that this father is "going through the motions" and is saying what he thinks he should say rather than what he feels. The client is aware that a summary of sessions is being provided to the judge and that the therapist may have to speak with the judge or appear in court about this client. Mr. Zimmer confronts the father in a family session, but the father denies holding back his real thoughts and feelings even after his wife states that she agrees with Mr. Zimmer that her husband is so concerned about this legal problem that he is not fully participating. Ultimately, Mr. Zimmer decides to tell the father that he will report to the judge what occurs in counseling and will respond truthfully if the judge asks whether the father fully participated in family treatment. All agree to this resolution. Is it ethical?

SUMMARY

Informed consent means that the client understands the counseling process and willingly agrees to it. Informed consent is required by the ethical codes and is based primarily in the ethical principle of respect for the client's human autonomy. Also, because counseling is a service that clients purchase and because that service has powerful effects on their lives, both during and after the process, clients have a right to understand its implications and to make a free choice about participating. The central ingredients in informed consent are understanding of the procedures, risks, benefits, and alternatives to counseling; the limits of confidentiality; the logistics of counseling; the counselor's qualifications; the use of counseling records and tests; and the indirect effects of counseling. In addition, clients have a right to know about any electronic recording, about

supervision of the counselor, or how to file grievances against their counselor. The need to discuss all aspects of informed consent as soon as feasible in the counseling process is superseded by considerations of the client's welfare. Particularly in a crisis, some aspects of informed consent may need to be deferred until the crisis is past.

In some situations, obtaining informed consent directly from the client is not always possible. Most notable among these are when the client is a minor or a person with diminished intellectual capacity. Scholars recommend securing the assent of a minor child to counseling, along with the informed consent of the parent or guardian. When a client does not seem to have the capacity to process information about informed consent to make a free choice about participating, then consent should be obtained from someone acting in the client's behalf. Usually that substitute is a family member or a person identified by the court.

Although some practitioners believe informed consent is a bureaucratic procedure to be dispensed with as soon as possible at the onset of counseling, both research evidence and ethics scholarship show that proper informed consent does not hinder, but potentially enhances, counseling. Moreover, developing informed consent is more appropriately thought of as a continuous process, not a finite procedure. This process symbolizes cooperation and collaboration between partners pursuing a common goal. The research highlights the need for greater attention to compliance with ethical guidelines by practitioners.

DISCUSSION QUESTIONS

1. What do you think accounts for the inconsistency in informed consent procedures used by practitioners?
2. Does a client have a right to be ignorant of risks of counseling if that person does not want to know? Explain.
3. What methods of structuring the review of informed consent information do you think are best? Why?
4. Can there ever be truly informed consent in court-mandated situations? If you think not, can a counselor ethically conduct such counseling? Explain.

5. In mental health settings, people with severe mental disorders, such as schizophrenia, have the legal right to refuse treatment, including medications. If their disorder is not in remission and it clouds their thinking, is their refusal really an informed refusal? How can their rights to control over their own body be balanced against their need for treatment?

RECOMMENDED READINGS

Bennett, B., Bryant, B., VanderBos, G., & Greenwood, A. (1990). *Professional liability and risk management.* Washington, DC: American Psychological Association.

DeKraai, M. B., Sales, B. D., & Hall, S. R. (1998). Informed consent, confidentiality, and duty to report laws in the conduct of child therapy. In R. J. Morris & T. R. Kratochwill (Eds.), *The practice of child therapy* (3rd ed., pp. 540–560). Boston: Allyn & Bacon.

Handelsman, M. M., & Galvin, M. D. (1988). Facilitating informed consent for outpatient psychotherapy: A suggested written format. *Professional Psychology: Research and Practice, 19,* 223–225.

Somberg, D. R., Stone, G. L., & Claiborn, C. D. (1993). Informed consent: Therapists' beliefs and practices. *Professional Psychology: Research and Practice, 24,* 153–159.

Weithorn, L. A. (1983). Involving children in decisions affecting their own welfare: Guidelines for professionals. In G. B. Melton, G. P. Koocher, & M. J. Saks (Eds.), *Children's competence to consent* (pp. 235–260). New York: Plenum.

Zuckerman, E. L. (2003). *The paper office: Forms, guidelines, resources* (3rd ed.). New York: Guilford.

Chapter 6

Sexual Misconduct
Violations of Power and Trust

There are two unmistakable facts about sexual contact with clients. First, all mental health professions expressly prohibit such contact during a therapeutic relationship. The wording of the codes is unequivocal.

ACA *Code of Ethics*, Section A.5.a: Roles and Relationships with Clients
Sexual or romantic counselor-client interactions or relationships with current clients, their romantic partners, or their family members are prohibited.

APA *Ethical Principles*, Section 10.05: Sexual Intimacies with Current Therapy Clients/Patients
Psychologists do not engage in sexual intimacies with current therapy patients/clients.

NASW *Code of Ethics*, Section 1.09a: Sexual Relationships
Social workers should under no circumstances engage in sexual activities or sexual contact with current clients, whether such contact is consensual or forced.

American Association for Marriage and Family Therapy (AAMFT) *Code of Ethics*, Section 1.4:
Sexual activity with clients is prohibited.

American Psychiatric Association *Principles of Medical Ethics*, Section 2.1:
Sexual activity with a current or former client is unethical.

The prohibition against sex with clients is grounded in empiric evidence of harm to clients, in philosophic argument, and in the theoretic foundations of counseling and psychotherapy.

In recent years the codes have also clearly prohibited sexual contact between counselors and therapists and the family members or romantic partners of current clients, as is noted in Section A.5.a of the American Counseling Association (ACA) Code mentioned previously and in the separate section of the American Psychological Association (APA) Ethical Principles and National Association of Social Workers (NASW) Codes cited on the next page. In parallel fashion psychologists are prohibited from initiating a professional relationship with prior sexual partners, although the ACA code is silent on this issue.

APA *Ethical Principles,* Section 10.06: Sexual Intimacies with Relatives or Significant Others of Current Therapy Clients/Patients

Psychologists do not engage in sexual intimacies with individuals they know to be close relatives, guardians, or significant others of current clients/patients. Psychologists do not terminate therapy to circumvent this standard.

APA *Ethical Principles,* Section 10.07: Therapy with Former Sexual Partners

Psychologists do not accept as therapy clients/patients persons with whom they have engaged in sexual intimacies.

NASW *Code of Ethics,* Section 1.09b: Sexual Relationships

Social workers should not engage in sexual activities or sexual contact with clients' relatives or other individuals with whom clients maintain a close personal relationship when there is a risk of exploitation or potential harm to the client. Sexual activity or sexual contact with clients' relatives or other individuals with whom clients maintain a personal relationship has the potential to be harmful to the client and may make it difficult for the social worker and client to maintain appropriate professional boundaries. Social workers—not their clients, their clients' relatives, or other individuals with whom the client maintains a personal relationship—assume the full burden for setting clear, appropriate, and culturally sensitive boundaries.

The second fact that emerges from the evidence is that sexual misconduct by mental health professionals has not been eradicated despite the prohibition. Moreover, violators are not confined to those who are poorly trained, mentally unstable, and at the margins of the professions; they have included leaders in their fields (see, for example, documentation by Noel & Watterson, 1992; Pope, 1990a). Pope (1990a) cites examples of therapists who were sexually exploitive who have served as presidents of state professional associations, chairs of state licensing and ethics committees, and faculty in prestigious universities.

This chapter examines the rationale behind the absolute proscription against sexual activity, the scope of the problem, and the characteristics correlated with sexual misconduct. The stance of the ethics codes on sexual contact with former therapy clients is described, along with the debate about its wisdom. The next focus is the ethics of sexual contact between counselors and those they teach, supervise, employ, or consult with. The chapter presents strategies to help counselors deal responsibly with their own sexual feelings that emerge during counseling and discusses the place of nonerotic touch in counseling. Finally, it reviews guidelines for counselors working with clients who have been sexually exploited by former therapists.

Rationale for the Prohibition

The reasons for the prohibition against sex with a client derive from the client's vulnerability to exploitation during counseling and the implications of that exploitation for the client, the counselor, and the reputation of the profession. Although it would be flattering to suggest that the professional associations have led the way in seeking to eradicate this problem, the truth is that the profession's history on this issue is blemished. In the 1960s and 1970s some mental health professionals argued that sex with clients could be therapeutically valuable (for example, see McCartney, 1966; Shepard, 1972), and scholars who tried to publish evidence of sexual misconduct had difficulty getting their research accepted in counseling and mental health journals (Dahlberg, 1970; Gechtman, 1989). For many years, until the landmark case of *Roy v. Hartogs* (1975), the courts were not interested in malpractice cases claiming sexual misconduct because the legal system accepted professionals' claims that the accusations arose from the sexual fantasies of women who were mentally unstable (Pope, 1994). The initial response of the therapist and police to Barbara Noel's claim that her psychiatrist sexually exploited her was, "You must be dreaming" (Noel & Watterson, 1992). However, the courage of many victims in pursuing claims despite the resistance, coupled with the perseverance of scholars researching this topic, has led all mental health professions to endorse the explicit ban on sexual contact with clients by all mental health professionals.

Factors That Affect Client Vulnerability to Exploitation

Research suggests that consumers of mental health services are sometimes ignorant about the ethics of sexual contact between therapists and clients. To complicate matters further, people usually enter counseling when their emotional distress is high, their interpersonal relationships are at risk, and their self-esteem is compromised. In this condition people are more vulnerable to harm from irresponsible professionals than they would otherwise be. Clients who suffer a traumatic event are also at some risk of being subjected to inappropriate professional behavior. The trauma they have just experienced affects their judgment and emotional vulnerability. In addition, scholars suggest that a history of emotional or sexual abuse, or both, may increase vulnerability to sexual exploitation by a therapist and heighten the damage inflicted (Pope, 1994). Kluft (1990) and Somer and Saadon (1999) found that the majority of clients who experienced sexual contact with their therapists had histories of childhood sexual trauma or incest. In all cases, the defense mechanisms of clients are weakened by stress, so they may have difficulty refusing the overtures of an unscrupulous professional, especially if the professional labels such activity "therapeutic"—an event that took place in 11% of the cases examined by Somer and Saadon.

Further complicating this vulnerability is the social stigma often associated with seeking mental health services. When belief in the stereotypes about people who see "shrinks" interacts with the self-doubt inherent in emotional distress, the possibility exists that clients will be overly deferential to a counselor's recommendation. In this context, clients may ignore their own intuitions about appropriate and inappropriate professional behavior. Carolyn Bates captures her feelings this way: "I remember walking into Dr. X's office feeling absolutely humiliated that I needed psychological help and at the same time, feeling out of control emotionally" (Bates & Brodsky, 1989, p. 21).

The status of counselor as "expert helper" also encourages the client to give the counselor the benefit of the doubt about what may be therapeutic. When she researched his background at the library, Barbara Noel remembers being impressed by the list of accomplishments of the psychiatrist to whom she had been referred (Noel & Watterson, 1992). Her skepticism about the wisdom of his recommended therapeutic approach was outweighed by her confidence in the judgment of such a renowned professional. Thus, a client may take at face value a professional's suggestions of an embrace at the end of a session or a dinner together after a session "to get a sense of your behavior in a social environment" and may not see these suggestions as overtures to start a social relationship. Even clients who wonder about the real meaning of such comments in other settings may resist making that interpretation about their counselor. Sometimes clients lack the assertiveness to refuse a professional's request, even if they recognize its inappropriateness. They may also worry about the effect of refusal on future treatment, wondering if the counselor will abandon or punish them if they fail to comply. Counselors intent on pursuing a sexual relationship have sometimes suggested that the client's resistance to sexual contact must stem from their emotional problems and suggest that physical contact would be a symbol of therapeutic progress. Carolyn Bates's therapist interpreted her denial of sexual interest in him as a sign of her problems relating to men in social settings (Bates & Brodsky, 1989). Clients may agree to the social or physical contact because they trust the professional to have a therapeutic intention, or they believe they have too much to lose if they fail to cooperate. Carolyn Bates describes the experience: "I could not doubt his interpretations of my resistance without doubting the doctor himself, and our entire therapeutic relationship. So I remained, unwilling to discount the trust I had spent 8 months building. I did not challenge him. I did not dare assert myself and state that I wasn't sexually attracted to him" (Bates & Brodsky, 1989, p. 32).

Sometimes clients may be somewhat responsive to the idea of a sexual relationship with a counselor, but this responsiveness is often rooted in the problems that caused them to seek counseling, in misunderstandings of the counseling process, or in the mistaken belief that the feelings they have toward the counselor are indications of true romantic love. Somer and Saadon (1999) found that 82% of the former clients they surveyed conceived of their sexual contacts with therapists as a romantic relationship at the time it was initiated. On rare occasions clients' misinterpretation of the professional relationship is so extreme or their sexual boundaries are so confused that they attempt to encourage a counselor to be sexually interested. People who have been sexually exploited before by others in power may believe that sexual favors are the price they must pay for emotional closeness and help with their distress. For other clients, the responsiveness stems from a misperception of the counselor's professional concern and unfamiliarity with the normal roles and behaviors associated with the counseling relationship. From the start of counseling, mental health professionals show concern through attentive listening, expressions of empathy, and attitudes of respect and warmth toward a client. Unless clients are informed about the nature of the counseling process, they may misinterpret these behaviors as expressions of personal interest and may be unaware that the counselor is not singling them out for special treatment. It is a small step from believing the counselor is treating one in a special way to speculating that the professional is interested in more than a professional relationship.

Two other factors sometimes lead clients to acquiesce to a sexual relationship at this point. First, in daily life most clients rarely experience such warm, attentive interest in their thoughts and feelings as they receive in counseling, and they are drawn toward people who provide such attention. Moreover, a client's past experience of such attention may have been limited to lovers or close friends. Frequently the counselor's behavior may represent exactly what the client has found desirable but often lacking in prior relationships. Thus the counselor may come to symbolize the kind of person the client is seeking for an intimate relationship. Second, the counselor's professional status adds further attractiveness to that fantasy because people are often flattered by the attention of a person they see as having high social status. None of these motivations is a solid foundation for a meaningful personal relationship, and it is the responsibility of the counselor to help the client understand the boundaries of the professional relationship. Consequently, if a counselor engages in sexual contact with a client who seems receptive to such contact, the counselor is still behaving irresponsibly. In terms of ethical principles, sexual contact is improper because it violates the autonomy of the client. The client's choice to enter into this sexual relationship is based at least in part on erroneous assumptions and dysfunctional experiences; hence, it is not an informed choice at all. For these reasons ethics committees, disciplinary boards, and courts have dismissed claims that clients consented to sexual relationships with their counselors. These bodies have consistently judged that the consent of the client in this situation is neither informed or freely given. Whatever the client's behavior, the professional may never use that client's apparent willingness as an excuse to violate the codes. No client behavior, however provocative, justifies a counselor's misconduct.

Professionals who endorse the concept of transference see an even deeper problem with sexual intimacies with clients. They envision the therapeutic relationship as a relationship in which the client transfers onto the therapist feelings from prior significant relationships that have not been resolved. Often this means the therapist is seen, at least on an unconscious level, as a parent figure, not just as another adult. Sexual contact with a client in such a framework takes on an incestuous character (Gabbard, 1989). Bates saw her relationship with Dr. X from this perspective: "I have no doubt that much of the trust and love I had for my father was directed toward Dr. X, for I perceived him as having both wisdom and an unconditional concern for my well-being" (Bates & Brodsky, 1989, p. 24). Even if the nature of the transference is not parental, sexual contact with a client is still inappropriate because any kind of transference means that the client is not really reacting to the counselor as a separate person but as a representation of someone significant from the past.

Still other dimensions of sexual contact make it inherently exploitive. For one thing, sexual contact is contradictory to the principle of beneficence, the responsibility of a professional to do good. Clients rarely understand that they are relinquishing the possibility of further therapeutic progress in exchange for a sexual relationship. Many continue to seek out the counselor's advice and insight about their problems, in hopes that they can make therapeutic gains while they are sexually involved with the therapist. However, researchers point out that meaningful therapeutic progress stops when sexual contact begins (Kitchener, 1988). The counselor has lost objectivity about the client and now has a personal interest in the client's present and future that inevitably affects professional functioning. For example, a counselor who is sexually involved with a client may refrain from making a necessary confrontation because of worry about interfering with a romantic evening later. At a deeper level, the counselor may no longer be inclined to facilitate client exploration of issues that threaten the future of their relationship. In parallel fashion, once a client begins having intimate contact with his or her counselor, the client tends to censor disclosures in counseling for fear of the counselor's reaction or the effect such comments may have on the personal relationship.

Sexual contact with clients also inflicts significant psychological damage on the client (Bouhoutsos et al., 1983; Brown, 1988; Pope, 1988). Sexual contact thereby constitutes a flagrant violation of the ethical principle of nonmaleficence, the duty of the counselor to avoid harming the client. Pope (1988) has postulated that the negative effects often form a pattern that he calls "the therapist–patient sex syndrome." He and others (for example, Gabbard, 1989) liken the psychological devastation of the syndrome to rape or incest and identify parallels to battered-spouse syndrome and posttraumatic stress disorder. The psychological damage may appear immediately, or it may remain latent for some time and then emerge, perhaps when the client is involved in a more appropriate intimate relationship. Specifically, Pope (1988, pp. 224–225) lists 10 features of this syndrome in clients:

1. Ambivalent feelings toward the therapist including rage, disgust, and fear on one hand and need for and worry about the therapist on the other
2. Guilt for their own behavior, although they bear no responsibility for the sexual contact
3. A sense of emptiness and isolation and an incapacity for other future deep connections with other people
4. Sexual confusion about their own sexual identity subsequent to the contact
5. Impaired ability to trust others, especially professionals, because of the betrayal they have experienced
6. Identity, boundary, and role confusion between the self and other significant people
7. Emotional lability in which the changeability of emotions is overwhelming to clients
8. Suppressed rage, which clients have difficulty acknowledging or dealing with because of the ambivalence toward the therapist and because of their own feelings of guilt
9. Increased suicidal risk from feelings of guilt and hopelessness
10. Cognitive dysfunction in the areas of concentration and attention because images from the trauma appear in the clients thoughts unpredictably

Pope is careful to caution that the syndrome is not experienced identically by all people. Others point out that there is no convincing empiric evidence to support this group of symptoms as a distinct psychological disorder (Bisbing, Jorgenson, & Sutherland, 1995). It is clear, however, that the mental health problems that victims of sexual exploitation incur are neither mild nor transitory and are widespread (Somer & Saadon, 1999; Stake & Oliver, 1991). Through survey research and case studies, researchers have documented suicides, hospitalizations, and prolonged psychological and interpersonal difficulties traceable to sexual contact with the therapist (Bates & Brodsky, 1989; Bouhoutsos et al., 1983; Feldman-Summers & Jones, 1984; Rutter, 1989; Sonne, Meyer, Borys, & Marshall, 1985). Pope and Vetter (1991) report that 11% of their sample needed psychiatric hospitalization and 14% attempted suicide. Another important negative effect is that clients feel reluctant to reenter therapy although their presenting difficulty has not been resolved and the problems spawned by the therapist misconduct need attention. Carolyn Bates's eloquent words capture this pain: "Within 2 months [of ending therapy] the combined effects of the sexual abuse and the unresolved problems that had originally prompted me to enter psychotherapy made life seem unbearable. I was burdened with an unending depression, and my thoughts progressed from occasional ideas about suicide to a studied contemplation of it" (Bates & Brodsky, 1989, p. 40). Family and friends of those who have been sexually exploited also suffer negative effects (Schoener, Milgrom, & Gonsiorek, 1989) and become secondary victims of the abuse. Similarly, colleagues of a professional found guilty of such behavior are significantly disturbed by the event, according to Regehr and Glancy (1995). Unfortunately, research suggests that violators fail to appreciate the harm they have done. Some try to rationalize their behavior (Herman, Gantrell, Olarte, Feldstein, & Localio, 1987) as having some positive effects for the client.

Counselors who engage in sexual misconduct usually do not limit their misconduct to the sexual arena. As Simon (1991, 1992) points out, sexual contact seldom arises suddenly. Instead, it usually occurs in a context of numerous ethical violations, such as omitting necessary treatments, including risky or counterproductive interventions, and diverting the sessions to focus on the therapist's problems. Besides their sexual contact with clients, the therapists cited by Bates and Brodsky (1989) and Noel and Watterson (1992) also engaged in many other practices that were unethical and substandard. Research continues to support this conclusion. Somer and Saadon (1999) and Lamb and Catanzaro (1998) also reported that other forms of boundary violations usually preceded sexual overtures, including inappropriate self-disclosures by the therapists, social contacts outside of sessions, unusually frequent physical contacts, and inappropriate discussions of the counselor–client relationship.

Some offending professionals often continue to charge the client for the sessions, even if sex was the only activity. This happened to 19% of the clients in the Somer and Saadon study. One psychologist who admitted having sex with his client argued that his continuing charges to the client were for the therapeutic minutes, not for the sexual minutes during their sessions (Bates & Brodsky, 1989). Because there is absolutely no evidence that sex can be therapeutically useful, or that clients or therapists can make such artificial separations between sex minutes and therapy minutes, charging for that time may be considered fraudulent. This practice also puts clients in the untenable position of either ignoring the billing or asking their therapists about why they are having to pay for physical intimacy. If bills are submitted to third-party payors, they too are being deceived about the counselor's activities.

Effects on the Counselor

The effects on the counselor judged guilty of the offense of sexual activity with a client are relatively minor compared to the harm caused to clients. Still, they are worth mentioning. First, because the professional taboo against sexual contact with clients has become quite strong, other therapists are likely to view this practice with serious concern (see, for example, Pope et al., 1987; Stake & Oliver, 1991). They probably have counseled clients who have been victimized by former therapists (Stake & Oliver, 1991; Wincze, Richards, Parsons, & Bailey, 1996), and they have watched the cost of their liability premiums increase, at least partly as a result of substantial cash awards to the victims in sexual exploitation cases (Reaves & Ogloff, 1996; Smith, 1996). In addition, they may have read news reports about the problem (for example, see Zane, 1990). The professions have also taken an active role in educating counselors about the implications of sexual misconduct. In the mid-1990s, for example, ACA sponsored many continuing education workshops on this issue. Those who violate this standard in such a climate risk loss of referrals from colleagues and vulnerability to complaints to ethics committees or licensing boards. Even colleagues who are reluctant to take active steps to report an irresponsible professional may stop referring clients to the offender and may end any collegial contact.

There are emotional and personal consequences to therapists as well. They tend to experience guilt and loss of self-esteem, and their personal relationships are disrupted (Bouhoutsos, 1985; Herman et al.,1987).

Statistics on the number of ethics complaints lodged annually suggest that many instances of sexual misconduct go undetected and that not all professional colleagues act with the level of professionalism just implied. Research suggests that only 5% of victims take formal action against the therapist (Bouhoutsos, 1984; Pope & Bouhoutsos, 1986). However, when a complaint alleging sexual misconduct does go forward, most adjudicating bodies tend to respond with careful consideration and penalize violators. Because the professional standard is so unequivocal, counselors do not have the option of finding a loophole or of claiming extenuating circumstances to justify their behavior. If the counselor is found guilty, the probability of disciplinary action is substantial, as is the risk of a malpractice suit with damages amounting to the hundreds of thousands of dollars (Reaves & Ogloff, 1996). Counselors employed by agencies may lose their jobs. Licenses are often suspended, or conditions are placed on future practice. Moreover, the professional liability insurers write policies to exclude or limit the amount they will cover for such claims, so that the burden of that huge payment falls largely on the individual. In 23 states criminal penalties for sexual misconduct have been added to the civil and professional liability (Advocate Web, 2005; Haspel, Jorgenson, Wincze, & Parsons, 1997). These states include Alabama, Arizona, California, Colorado, Connecticut, Delaware, Florida, Georgia, Iowa, Kansas, Maine, Michigan, Minnesota, Mississippi, New Hampshire, New Mexico, North Dakota, South Dakota, Texas, Utah, Washington, and Wisconsin. In all of them sexual misconduct is considered a felony. In 2002 Ohio became the 23rd state in this group; however, it limited criminal liability to situations in which the mental health professional suggests that the sexual contact has therapeutic value for the client, a restriction found in several other state statutes (Ohio Revised Code, Section 2907). Five states have determined that this is such an important public health issue that they have enacted reporting statutes that ask subsequent therapists to disclose client reports of sexual exploitation by prior therapists. Minnesota has gone so far as to mandate reporting even when clients object, but the other states (Wisconsin, Rhode Island, California, and Texas) allow either for anonymous reporting or for reporting only when the client consents (Haspel et al., 1997). This kind of legislation is controversial and restricts client confidentiality, but its existence highlights how seriously legislative and professional bodies have come to regard this problem. For a comparison of state statutes on regulations governing sexual misconduct for professional counselors specifically, see Avery and Gressard (2000).

Effects on the Reputation of the Profession

Data about the impact of sexual misconduct on the reputation of the profession are more difficult to obtain. Publicity about such misconduct probably makes people less likely to seek out counseling, and the profession cannot easily gather data about people who never become clients. Nevertheless, it is reasonable to assume some impact exists, especially in a culture that already exhibits such deeply rooted skepticism about the wisdom of seeking professional help for mental health problems. Worry about this problem can even affect those who are brave enough to begin counseling. Clients who have learned of sexual exploitation through the media or through experiences of friends and family may have difficulty trusting a counselor and may misunderstand legitimate inquiries into personal and sexual issues directly related to the presenting problem. Publicity about such unscrupulous behavior certainly does not simplify the task of convincing legislatures, government regulators, and insurers of the value of the professional services we provide.

Research on the Scope of the Problem

Who engages in sexual misconduct, and how frequently does it occur? This is the single most studied question in the area of ethical misconduct (Pope, 1994). Our knowledge about perpetrators comes largely from surveys of mental health professionals who have volunteered information about their sexual practices, along with data from ethics committees, licensing boards, and malpractice suits. A few studies have explored the reports of clients about sexual exploitation by former therapists (such as Brown, 1988; Kluft, 1990; Somer & Nachmani, 2005; Somer & Saadon, 1999; Wohlberg, 2000), and some case studies have been published (Bates & Brodsky, 1989; Noel & Watterson, 1992). None of these sources of knowledge is an ideal gauge of the true scope of the problem. Disciplinary committees and the courts deal only with the accused; those not yet accused are not counted. Similarly, national surveys obtain data only from those willing to complete and return them to researchers—usually less than half of those to whom the form is mailed. Are those who have violated the codes as willing to complete the surveys as those who have not? There is no way to judge. Moreover, given the professional taboo against sex with clients, it is not unreasonable to wonder if all those who report no history of misconduct are answering sincerely. Still other flaws in the research exist. Client reports of exploitation by former therapists tell us nothing about people who have been exploited but who have not sought counseling again. Case studies give us a sense of the depth of the injury to one client, but they do not address the breadth of the problem. For these reasons, it is important to evaluate with some caution research about the scope of the problem. At the same time, the evidence can lead to some tentative conclusions:

- The overwhelming majority of offenders are male, and the overwhelming majority of victims are female (Pope, 1994, 2000). Male therapists have shown from 1.5 to 9 times the frequency of sexual misconduct of female therapists. This trend holds true for Great Britain, Israel, Australia, and the United States (Bisbing et al., 1995; Garrett, 1998; Somer & Saadon, 1999; Somer & Nachmani, 2005; Wincze et al., 1996).
- Sexual contact is not limited to adult clients. Reported victims include girls as young as age 3 years and boys as young as age 7 years. The mean age for female minors is 13 years; for male minors it is age 12 years (Bajt & Pope, 1989).
- Therapists who violate this standard tend to be older than the clients they get involved with. The average age of psychiatrists was 43 years, and the average age of clients was 33 years (Gantrell, Herman, Olarte, Feldstein, & Localio, 1989). For psychologists, the mean age was 42 years, and the mean age of their clients was 30 years (Bouhoutsos et al., 1983). In the report of Somer and Saadon, therapists' ages ranged from 30 to 70 years, and clients' ages ranged from 19 to 46 years.
- The percentage of mental health professionals who admitted sexual misconduct with clients in the 1970s and 1980s varied from study to study, but the aggregate

average across all studies was 8.3% (Pope, 1988). Psychiatrists admitted this behavior more frequently than psychologists, and social workers had the lowest admitted rate (Pope, 1994). However, the admission rate does not necessarily correlate with the true incidence.

- Surveys conducted since the 1990s generally show smaller percentages, with studies of counselor misconduct showing rates ranging from 1.7% (Thoreson, Shaughnessy, Heppner, & Cook, 1993) to 0.7% (Thoreson, Shaughnessy, & Frazier, 1995). Nerison (1992) reported rates from 3% for sexual contact with a current therapist. Social work data show an average rate of 2% (Bernsen, Tabachnick, & Pope, 1994). One study of family therapists yielded zero admissions of sexual contact with clients (Nickell, Hecker, Ray, & Bercik, 1995). The change may represent a real decrease in incidence, a greater reluctance of professionals to admit such behavior even in anonymous surveys, an increased focus on mental health professionals other than psychiatrists or psychologists, or a combination of these factors.

- Therapist characteristics other than gender have not been reliable predictors of sexual dual relationships. Type of degree, experience, or theoretic orientation have not been consistently associated with this problem (Pope, 1994, 2000). Some evidence suggests that higher levels of education and higher levels of professional accomplishment are better predictors than more typical levels of professional achievement (Pope, 1990b), but neither of these variables is a strong predictor of sexual misconduct.

- Efforts to rehabilitate mental health professionals who have violated this standard have not shown much success (APA Insurance Trust, 1990; Pope, 1989). In fact, given the poor results of their research on this phenomenon, California licensing boards have concluded, "prospects for rehabilitation are minimal and it is doubtful that they [perpetrators] should be given the opportunity to ever practice psychotherapy again" (Callanan & O'Connor, 1988, p. 11, as cited in Pope, 1990b). Others are less pessimistic about rehabilitation, however (Gonsiorek, 1997; Schoener & Gonsiorek, 1988).

- Client reactions to sexual contact with therapists is negative, and the psychological effects are damaging even when the clients initially viewed the contact as romantic rather than exploitive (Somer & Nachmani, 2005).

Data on Sexual Attraction of Therapists to Clients

Sexual attraction to clients is an almost universal phenomenon among therapists, but most do not act on that attraction and work to handle their reactions in a responsible manner. Research shows that 80–90% of the psychologists sampled admitted at least one experience of sexual attraction to a client, but only a small percentage acted on those feelings (Blanchard & Lichtenberg, 1998; Giovazolias & Davis, 2001; Pope et al., 1987; Stake & Oliver, 1991). Data from social workers and family therapists reveal that sexual attraction to clients is a frequent occurrence in these professions also (Bernsen et al., 1994, Nickell et al., 1995).

Sexual Contact with Former Clients: A Controversial Issue

The incidence of therapist sex with former clients is very similar to the rate with current clients, although more recent studies do not necessarily report lower rates than earlier studies. In reports published between 1977 and 1998, the incidence has ranged from 3.9% to 11% (Akamatsu, 1988; Borys & Pope, 1989; Holroyd & Brodsky, 1977; Lamb et al., 1994;

Lamb & Catanzaro, 1998; Salisbury & Kinnier, 1996; Thoreson et al., 1995; Thoreson et al., 1993). In some cases the victims were "former clients" in name only. Somer and Saadon found that 33% of the offending professionals in their study ended therapy abruptly in order to begin a sexual relationship. Akamatsu (1988) reported a mean interval of 15.6 months between the end of therapy and the beginning of a sexual relationship. A majority of practitioners believe posttermination sexual relationships are unethical, but their disapproval of this practice is not as strong or unanimous as their condemnation of sex with current clients. Akamatsu found that 23% of his sample viewed this practice as "neither ethical or unethical" (1988, p. 455), and Lamb and his associates (1994) reported that the interval since termination affected psychologists' judgments of appropriateness. In other words, the longer the time elapsed since therapy, the fewer the number of respondents who condemned the practice. (When the time elapsed was a month or less, the practice was judged highly unethical.) In their survey of counselors, Salisbury and Kinnier (1996) indicated that one-third of their sample viewed sexual contact with former clients as acceptable, at least under some circumstances, whereas Gibson and Pope (1993) found that 23% of counselors rated this behavior as ethical.

Some of this lack of consensus on the ethics of sexual contact with former clients stems partly from the history of silence of the ethics codes on this issue. The codes of APA, NASW, and ACA were mute on the subject until the 1990s. Only the code of the American Psychiatric Association explicitly prohibits sexual contact with former clients (2001). The current standards are as follows.

ACA *Code of Ethics,* Section A.5.b: Former Clients

Sexual or romantic counselor–client interactions or relationships with former clients, their romantic partners, or their family members are prohibited for a period of 5 years following the last professional contact. Counselors, before engaging in sexual or romantic interactions or relationships with clients, their romantic partners, or client family members after 5 years following the last professional contact, demonstrate forethought and document (in written form) whether the interactions or relationship can be viewed as exploitive in some way and/or whether there is still potential to harm the former client; in cases of potential exploitation and/or harm, the counselor avoids entering such an interaction or relationship.

APA *Ethical Principles,* Section 4.07: Sexual Intimacies with Former Therapy Clients/Patients

(a) Psychologists do not engage in sexual intimacies with a former therapy patient or client for at least two years after cessation or termination of professional services.

(b) Psychologists do not engage in sexual intimacies with former clients/patients even after a two-year interval except in the most unusual circumstances. Psychologists who engage in such activity after the two years following cessation or termination of therapy and of having no sexual contact with the former client/patient bear the burden of demonstrating that there has been no exploitation, in light of all relevant factors, including (1) the amount of time that has passed since therapy terminated; (2) the nature, duration, and intensity of the therapy; (3) the circumstances of termination; (4) the client's/patient's personal history; (5) the client's/patient's current mental status; (6) the likelihood of adverse impact on the client/patient; and (7) any statements or actions made by the therapist during the course of therapy suggesting or inviting the possibility of a posttermination sexual or romantic relationship with the client/patient.

The wording of these sections is meant to convey the message that sexual contact is usually unethical even after the 2-year interval for psychologists and the 5-year interval for counselors. They imply that only extraordinary circumstances allow such a practice to be acceptable. In their commentary on the APA code, Canter et al. (1994) refer to this standard as an "almost never rule" (p. 98). The codes attempt to place a heavy burden of proof on the mental health professional to demonstrate that the situation with a former client is sufficiently extraordinary to qualify as an exception to the general rule. The professional bodies seem to want to allow for the circumstance in which the initial professional interaction between a client and a counselor was brief and uncomplicated by severe dysfunction, not deeply transferential, properly terminated, and entirely ethical while it endured.

The professions seem to be alluding to a scenario, for example, in which a client comes to a counselor to stop smoking, make a decision about a career change, or seek support during a normal grieving process. Strong emotional ties and deep transferences do not necessarily develop under such circumstances. The argument seems to be that if the professional relationship is truly terminated and the issues are effectively resolved, then the rights of consenting adults to determine the people with whom they associate should take precedence over what they judge to be a low risk of harm to the former client. The professional associations seem to have wanted to protect the professional who completes a counseling relationship in good faith from being forever barred from an intimate relationship with all former clients. The codes also suggest that any professional who entertains the idea of a sexual relationship with a client at any point before termination does not meet the criterion for the exception. The implication is that when professionals and former clients meet 2 years or more after therapy, their meeting must have been "accidental" and not anticipated by the therapist during their professional contact. In its 1995 standards ACA had also adopted the 2-year standard, but in the current code that group elected to extend that limit by 5 years, highlighting even more strongly the almost never nature of the rule.

The 2-year time period has also been recommended by Gonsiorek and Brown (1989) as the minimum interval before a sexual relationship with a former client. These authors have elaborated a set of rules for decision making about this matter that, when applied to the codes, make clearer the motive for the time limit in codes. Gonsiorek and Brown suggest that mental health professionals must differentiate between therapy in which transference is a central feature (Type A) and short-term therapy that gives limited opportunity for transference to become a major aspect of the interaction (Type B). These authors propose that sexual contact with Type A clients is never appropriate, regardless of the interval between the end of therapy and the subsequent contact. They also classify any therapy with severely disturbed clients as Type A, regardless of its duration. Posttermination contact with Type B clients is permitted only if the following conditions are met: (a) the initiation for the contact does not come from the therapist, (b) at least 2 years have elapsed since therapy, (c) no social contact has occurred in that 2-year interval, and (d) therapy was completely terminated and no recommendation for follow-up treatment was given. They suggest that if there is any doubt about whether a therapy falls into Type B, then it ought to be considered as Type A and be prohibited. Herlihy and Corey (1992, 1997) also refer to the length and type of counseling as factors that influence the ethics of a posttermination relationship. They contend that contact should be allowable if the counseling has been brief and not deeply personal.

The work of Gottlieb (1993) is also helpful in clarifying the professions' reasoning on this issue. Gottlieb identifies three aspects of the therapist–client interaction that should be considered in evaluating the ethics of dual relationships. The first is the *power* of the therapist, and Gottlieb argues that in traditional psychotherapy relationships, the power of the therapist is high. The second dimension is *duration* of the relationship. Duration is really a subset of power. The longer the relationship endures, the greater the power the mental health professional has over the client. The third dimension is *clarity of termination,* referring to the likelihood that the client will ever contact the professional for additional services at a future point. He suggests that the professional must assume that the "professional relationship continues as long as the consumer assumes that it does, regardless of the amount of time elapsed or the contact in the interim" (p. 44). The higher the relationship is positioned on the continuum of power, duration, and clarity of termination, the more clearly prohibited the sexual contact.

As mentioned in Chapter 1, this provision was not originally proposed by the APA Ethics Committee when it was developing drafts of the revised code. (Earlier drafts had included a blanket prohibition against sexual contact with former clients.) Nor was it included in the first 15 drafts of the 1992 revision, many of which were published for member comment (Gabbard, 1994). In fact, it was added in the final debate by the APA governing body on the request of delegates who had not been part of the code-writing process. Many scholars believe this policy runs counter to the public interest and the profession's reputation. Gabbard (1994, 2002) summarizes these scholars' disagreement with the policy:

- The two-year designation is arbitrary and not based on any empiric evidence that transference is resolved in any particular time period. The suggestion that 2 years is sufficient is speculative, not scientific, and the profession should not place former clients at risk based on speculation alone.
- Professionals do not have good measures of a successful resolution of transference. Moreover, it seems imprudent to leave the judgment of whether a transference has been successfully resolved in the hands of a counselor who is now entertaining a sexual relationship with a former client (Hartlaub, Martin, & Rhine, 1986). That professional has little objectivity about the issue at that point. As Gottlieb (1993) points out, only the client can determine that the professional relationship has ended.
- The suggestion that one's professional responsibilities to a client are completed within 2 years after termination conflicts with other professional standards. For example, client records must be maintained for significantly longer than 2 years, and confidentiality must be maintained in perpetuity. If asked to testify in a legal proceeding, mental health professionals have no 2-year limit on privilege. Thus, this standard conflicts with other guidelines that suggest that the professional relationship continues for substantially longer than 2 years.
- The unequal power relationship is never leveled off, and information obtained for therapeutic purposes can be misused in a later personal relationship. The counselor cannot simply "forget" all the information shared in counseling, and the client cannot ignore the unequal power levels that existed during their professional encounter. Moreover, if a former client later feels exploited by a therapist, he or she may be reluctant to file a complaint.
- Allowing posttermination relationships may change the nature of therapy. Patients who experience sexual feelings for a therapist may know that there is the possibility in the future that the therapist can have a sexual relationship with them. Clients with powerful attractions may resist delving into issues that must be explored for their recovery but that may interfere with acting on their attraction. In similar fashion, therapists may consciously or unconsciously shift the focus of therapy because of the potential, however distant, of after-therapy contact with the client.
- There is no evidence that sexual contact with clients after 2 or even 5 years of therapy is free of risk to clients. In fact, some research suggests that posttermination relationships can cause harm (Brown, 1988; Pope & Vetter, 1991). Clients have filed claims of psychological damage for relationships that began as long as 4 years after termination (Gottlieb, Sell, & Schoenfeld, 1988).

- The codes should not include an exception to the rule for a highly atypical case. The criteria set forth for a sexual relationship with a former client disallow all but the most unusual situation from consideration for sexual contact. The profession's interest in protecting the autonomy rights of the professional in this rare instance seem to be overriding its commitment to protect the public from harm by an unscrupulous professional using this loophole to serve his or her own needs. Given the evidence of significant harm to clients exploited by therapists, the profession should not give the impression that this atypical case happens more commonly than it really does.

What is the other side of the argument? One statement that can be made in defense of the standard is that it addresses a gap in the former codes. Prior to 1992, practitioners, ethics committees, and licensing boards had no guidance from the professions about how to address complaints against therapists who engaged in posttermination sexual relationships. Sell, Gottlieb, and Schoenfeld (1986) found that these bodies held widely divergent opinions about whether such relationships were ethical and about the appropriate length of time between therapy and the personal relationship. (At the same time, they point out that not a single psychologist charged with sexual exploitation was exonerated on the grounds that the disciplinary body believed an appropriate interval had elapsed since termination.) Thus this part of the code is an improvement over past codes, and it provides some guidance about how to evaluate the claims of therapists who tried to defend themselves against ethics' charges by arguing that the sexual activity began after therapy ended.

Canter et al. (1994) contend that this provision is more practical than the broader prohibition and easier to defend from constitutional challenges. They seem to be referring here to legal claims that such a rule would violate a professional's right of free association. They also state that this standard is easier than a blanket prohibition to defend "socially," but unfortunately, they do not explain what they mean by this term.

Finally, some forms of therapeutic contact do involve minimal transference and are better characterized as "consultations" than as counseling or psychotherapy. These consultations parallel what Gonsiorek and Brown (1989) refer to as Type B therapy. For example, a single parent may meet with a mental health professional about her child's night terrors and receive the needed information and reassurance in a single session. The professional relationship between this parent and the counselor is of a different character from the interaction between a counselor and a client who has multiple visits to help him cope with a child's substance abuse problem. If the client in the first case has no intention of contacting the counselor again for professional assistance and her life proceeds smoothly for the next 2 years, and she then wishes to initiate a personal relationship with the counselor, this standard allows the professional to respond if the situation meets the other criteria laid out in the codes.

The debate on this issue will continue. Research and the experience of ethics committees in dealing with claims from former clients will help illuminate which perspective is wiser. Counselors who consider such a relationship with a former client should be extraordinarily cautious about acting on the idea. Careful consideration of all the aspects mentioned in the code and consultation with trusted colleagues are essential to a truly ethical result in this situation.

It is important to note that individual state laws may differ from the ethics codes on this issue. For example, Florida views the therapist–client relationship as existing "in perpetuity" and thus allows clients to sue for damages regardless of time elapsed since termination (Lamb et al., 1994). A therapist in that state who uses the code to guide behavior may still be vulnerable to legal sanctions for sexual contact after termination. Thus, mental health professionals should understand the laws and regulations that may govern this issue in their states.

Consider the following case.

Manuel and Olga

Manuel, a 31-year-old librarian, sees Olga, a mental health counselor, for three sessions because he has been experiencing insomnia and loss of appetite. He is worried that he is depressed because his family has a history of depression. Both his brother and his mother have been diagnosed with major depression. Manuel is experiencing no other depressive symptoms, and although he is stressed by his work and his financial obligations to his aging parents, he describes his mood as positive and his life satisfactory. In the sessions, the counselor assesses Manuel's suitability for a depressive diagnosis and the quality of his coping skills and decides that no diagnosis of a mental or emotional disorder is warranted. Olga recommends that the client get a medical examination to rule out physiologic causes for his symptoms. Then she focuses attention in the second counseling session on bolstering Manuel's coping skills. In the third session, the client reports that he believes his coping skills have improved and he is now able to deal with stress better. He also discloses that his physician changed his high blood pressure medication so his sleep and appetite problems have eased considerably. After three sessions, counseling is terminated. The client expresses much relief that he does not have a depressive illness and seems very grateful for Olga's assistance. The file is put in the "closed cases" section.

For nearly 5 years, Manuel makes no effort to contact the counselor. At that point, they accidentally meet at an orchestra concert and have a wonderful conversation. Manuel has been promoted to director of his library, and he seems to be thriving. The next day he calls and asks Olga to dinner. The counselor is attracted to Manuel and would like to accept. Is it ethical for her to do so? Why or why not? (After you have analyzed the case and come to a decision, you may turn to the end of the chapter to read the author's analysis of the case.)

Sexual Contact in Educational, Consultation, and Employment Settings

The ACA and APA codes of ethics extend the prohibition of sexual intimacies with current clients to people in other kinds of professional relationships with counselors.

APA *Ethical Principles*, Section 1.19: Exploitive Relationships

(a) Psychologists do not exploit persons over whom they have supervisory, evaluative or other authority, such as students, supervisees, employees, research participants, and clients or patients.

(b) Psychologists do not engage in sexual relationships with students or supervisees in training over whom the psychologist has evaluative or direct authority, because such relationships are so likely to impair judgment or to be exploitive.

ACA *Code of Ethics*, Section F.3.b: Sexual Relationships

Sexual or romantic interactions or relationships with current supervisees are prohibited.

ACA *Code of Ethics*, Section F.3.c: Sexual Harassment

Counseling supervisors do not condone or subject supervisees to sexual harassment.

ACA *Code of Ethics*, Section F.10.a: Sexual or Romantic Relationships

Sexual or romantic interactions or relationships with current students are prohibited.

ACA *Code of Ethics*, Section C.6.d: Exploitation of Others

Counselors do not harmfully exploit others in their professional relationships.

The rationale for this prohibition parallels the rationale for excluding sex with clients—the power of the professional, the extended nature of the professional contact, and the frequent lack of clarity in termination. Supervisors and faculty determine whether a student will be allowed to graduate and practice his or her chosen profession. Graduate training in counseling and psychotherapy often lasts for several years, and new graduates rely on faculty and supervisors for references for a number of additional years. Employers have similar influence and determine whether their employees can succeed at their jobs. Participants in research projects rely on the good faith of researchers to interact with them appropriately. A person in any of these subordinate roles has significantly less power and may feel vulnerable to the potential misuse of the power of the superior. He or she worries about the risks of refusing an overture and usually becomes uncomfortable in the professional relationship thereafter, even if the person in power imposes no penalty for the refusal. An anonymous article entitled "Sexual Harassment" (1991) captures these strong feelings in the author's description of attempted sexual exploitation by a counseling faculty member. Even students and supervisees who agreed to a sexual relationship and believed they were making free and uncoerced choices about sexual contact with faculty and supervisors at the time later come to label those relationships as coercive and a hindrance to their professional development (Ahlstrand, Crumlin, Korinek, Lasky, & Kitchener, 2003; Barnett-Queen & Larrabee, 1998; Glaser & Thorpe, 1986; Lamb & Catanzaro, 1998; Lamb, Catanzaro & Morrman, 2003; Miller & Larrabee, 1995; Robinson & Reid, 1985). In other words, in retrospect they tend to view the relationship as one in which the faculty members took advantage of their higher status and power. Other students and supervisees who learn that one of their number is in a sexual relationship with a superior wonder whether they will receive fair consideration if they are competing with that person for professional rewards. When students or supervisees wish to end the sexual relationship before the superior does, they may be anxious about the implications of terminating the affair. Conversely, if superiors end the sexual contact before the termination of the professional contact, students may feel uncomfortable for the duration of their interaction.

Incidence of Violation of This Standard

Researchers have gathered data on this topic from two sources—from surveys of professionals who admit engaging in this practice and from surveys of mental health professionals who experienced sexual overtures from faculty or supervisors while they were in training. More psychologists have been canvassed on this issue than counselors, social workers, or psychiatrists, but some data are available about each profession. Most studies have found a higher rate of sexual contact with students than with clients. The prevalence rate for faculty–student sexual contact ranges from 0% for female counseling faculty describing their actions as professors (Thoreson et al., 1995) to 17% of female psychologists reporting on their own experiences during their student years (Glaser & Thorpe, 1986). The mean percentage for faculty–student sex across these studies is 8.8%. Fewer studies examined sexual contact between clinical supervisors and supervisees, but the range of finding is from 0.2% (Thoreson et al., 1995) to 4% (Pope, Levenson, & Schover, 1979) and the mean is 2.5%. Table 6.1 provides the specific findings for each study. Most of the contact has been reported to occur between male faculty in their 40s and female students in their late 20s and early 30s. In addition, the majority of relationships began while the supervisory relationship was in place. For example, Hammel et al. (1996) reported that 86% of the contacts in their study happened either during or prior to the professional relationship.

This literature also identifies a related problem. In the studies that asked mental health professionals about their experiences of sexual exploitation in graduate school, respondents described an even larger number of incidents in which faculty and/or supervisors made unwanted sexual advances. Unwanted sexual advances constitute sexual harassment. For example, Miller and Larrabee (1995) found that 18.7% of their sample of counselors experienced

Table 6.1   Rates of sexual contact between faculty, supervisors and students in the published literature

Researchers	Research Population	Rate for Faculty (%)	Rate for Supervisors (%)
Pope, Levenson & Schover, 1979	psychology educators	12	4
Robinson & Reid, 1985	psychologists' remembrances of training	13.6	NR
Glaser & Thorpe, 1986	female psychologist's remembrances	17	NR
Pope, Tabachnick, & Keith-Spiegel, 1987	psychologists	NR	3.3
Thoreson et. al., 1993	male counselors	1.7	2.5
Miller & Larrabee, 1995	female counselor educators' remembrances	6	2.5
Thoreson, et. al., 1995	female counselors	0	0.2
Hammel, Olkin, & Taube, 1996	psychologists' remembrances of training	11	
Lamb & Catanzaro, 1998	clinical and counseling psychologists	1.7	1.5
Barnett-Queen & Larraabee, 2000	counselors and social workers	.02 contact .07 advances made	
Caldwell, 2003	counselor educators' remembrances	1 male 9.8 female	NR
Lamb, Catanzaro, & Moorman, 2003	psychologists	3	
Ahlstand et al., 2003	psychologists' remembrances	10 harassment 6 contact for females 1 contact for males	

NR = not reported

unwanted sexual advances. Robinson and Reid (1985) and Glaser and Thorpe (1986) indicated even higher percentages for female psychology students—48% and 33%, respectively. The percentages of female students reporting sexual harassment by faculty or supervisors decreased slightly to 17.8% in two studies (Ahlstrand et al., 2003; Mintz, Rideout, & Bartells, 1994) and even more sharply (to .07%) in another study (Barnett-Queen & Larrabee, 2000). The codes of ethics also clearly forbid sexual harassment.

APA *Ethical Principles,* Section 3.02: Sexual Harassment

Psychologists do not engage in sexual harassment. Sexual harassment is sexual solicitation, physical advances, or verbal or nonverbal conduct that is sexual in nature, that occurs in connection with the psychologist's activities or roles as a psychologist, and that either (1) is unwelcome, is offensive, or creates a hostile workplace or educational environment, and the psychologist knows or is told this or (2) is sufficiently severe or intense to be abusive to a reasonable person in the context. Sexual harassment can consist of a single intense or severe act or of multiple persistent or pervasive acts.

The ACA code (Section C.6.a) uses very similar wording, save for the term *psychologist*. Its description of the behaviors that constitute sexual harassment come from the legal definition of the term.

Consider the following case.

Isabelle and Yoritomo

Isabelle, a graduate student in school counseling, enrolls in a course in substance abuse counseling as an elective. The course is taught by Yoritomo, an adjunct faculty member with an active private practice in the community. About 10 weeks into the semester,

Isabelle approaches Yoritomo after class, seeking additional readings on substance abuse educational programs for teenagers. They discuss the topic at length, and they meet a few times after that in Yoritomo's office to talk over the readings. When Isabelle is turning in her final examination, Yoritomo asks her to come to his office in a few minutes. At that time he suggests that they continue to meet to discuss this issue and get to know each other better. In an offhand way he suggests that perhaps they could have dinner together sometime. Isabelle hears in his comments an invitation to a dating relationship. If her assessment of the professor's interest is correct, did Yoritomo act unethically? (After you have analyzed the issue independently, turn to the case analysis at the end of the chapter.)

Distinguishing Between Sexual Feelings and Sexual Misconduct

As mentioned previously, research suggests that nearly all mental health professionals experience times when they have felt sexually attracted to a client and that they tend to feel guilty, confused, and anxious when this happens (Pope, Keith-Spiegel, & Tabachnick, 1986; Rodolfa et al., 1994; Stake & Oliver, 1991). Unfortunately, the literature also indicates that training programs give insufficient attention to this issue (Hamilton & Spruill, 1999; Pope & Tabachnick, 1993), although some modest improvements have been achieved over the last decade (Housman & Stake, 1998). Pope, Sonne, and Holroyd (1993) refer to it as "the topic that isn't there" (p. 23). Given the gravity of the problem of sexual misconduct by counselors and therapists, how should sexual attraction to clients or others under our professional authority be viewed? Is attraction an ethical violation in itself? Occasional counselor experiences of sexual arousal toward a client are normal and need not produce guilt or worry. They do not constitute misconduct. After all, counselors cannot leave their sexuality outside the consulting room door. Such feelings can be stirred by events in the counselor's personal life or by comments that the client makes. If counselors handle these feelings responsibly, they can work effectively in the future with that client. An experience of sexual arousal must be distinguished from sexualizing of the therapy relationship. A momentary feeling that is not acted on nor disclosed to the client, and that does not prevent the counselor from attending to the issues the client wishes to discuss, is not ethically problematic (Pope et al., 1993). Naturally, the counselor has a duty to self-monitor and carefully scrutinize the quality of his or her counseling in that session. If the arousal significantly compromises the competence of service, then the counselor should consider referring the client to another practitioner or, at a minimum, provide additional time to the client without charge to compensate for the inadequate service.

Sexual feelings that occur more frequently or that are more prolonged must be dealt with more carefully. To help resolve the sexual attraction, a counselor in this situation should consult a colleague or supervisor about what is occurring. In the Rodolfa et al. (1994) study, 60% of the sample took this action when attracted to a client. These psychologists reported that they used consultation to ensure that they were objective, that they were attending to the welfare of the client, and that they understood the motivation behind their attraction. If such consultation fails to keep the counselor's attention on the client's needs, a referral to another counselor is in order. Whenever sexual arousal is frequent or persistent, a counselor is well advised to seek therapy to understand the source of this feeling. In the meantime, the counselor should accept only those clients with whom sexual arousal is unlikely to occur. Again, Rodolfa's findings highlight the importance of this recommendation: Of the psychologists sampled, 43% believed that their sexual attraction to a client had negatively affected therapy.

Other research indicates that trainees can be reluctant to discuss sexual feelings with supervisors and that they frequently misinterpret sexual attraction to clients as unethical in its own right (Housman & Stake, 1998; Ladany et al., 1997). A positive supervisory relationship can facilitate such communication (Ladany et al., 1997), but even then some students' misconceptions about sexual contact with clients are not remedied.

Epstein and Simon (1990) have published an exploitation index that can help mental health professionals identify early signals that they may be at risk for engaging in exploitive activities with clients. One section of this index asks the following questions (p. 459):

- Do you find yourself comparing the gratifying qualities you observe in a patient with less gratifying qualities in your spouse or significant other?
- Do you feel that your patient's problem would be immeasurably helped if only he or she had a positive romantic involvement with you?
- Do you feel a sense of excitement or longing when you think of a patient or anticipate his or her visit?
- Do you take pleasure in romantic daydreams about a patient?
- When a patient has behaved seductively with you, do you experience this as a gratifying sign of your own sex appeal?
- Do you touch your patients? (Exclude handshakes.)
- Have you engaged in a personal relationship with a patient after treatment?

If sexual attraction prompts a counselor to seek consultation or therapy, or to refer a client to another counselor, that professional may wonder whether the attraction ought to be disclosed to the client. After all, the client may notice that something is different or may wonder about what motivated the recommendation to refer. The counselor in this situation must weigh the client's interest in disclosure against the potential for that information to cause harm or impede therapeutic progress. The nature of the transference, the client's distress, and the power of the professional make such a disclosure risky and potentially quite harmful. This revelation would probably draw attention away from the client's concerns and toward the counselor's problem. Only 5–10% of those who have experienced a sexual attraction have disclosed this feeling to the client, and most professionals refrained not only for personal reasons but also because they believed this type of therapist self-disclosure to be inherently unethical (Fisher, 2004). Pope et al. (1993) have published a very useful book to help counselors and therapists understand their sexual feelings and manage them appropriately in professional settings.

What should counselors who have experienced sexual feelings for a client do when that client discloses a sexual attraction to them? Generally, the literature cautions against revealing the feeling even if there is no intention to act on it (Pope et al., 1993) unless the revelation has a clear treatment rationale and would not risk harm to the client, but there are diverse opinions on this topic (for example, see Gorkin, 1987; Weiner, 1983). Almost 80% of psychologists and 83% of counselors view such a disclosure as unethical in itself (Gibson & Pope, 1993; Pope et al., 1987). Some research supports this position. Using an analogue study with taped, scripted counseling simulations, Goodyear and Shumate (1996) found that mental health professionals judged counselors who disclosed their sexual attraction to a client as less therapeutic and less expert than those who held their reactions to themselves. This negative evaluation occurred even though the counselor in the simulation made it clear that he or she would not act on the felt attraction. Goodyear and Shumate seem to capture the sentiment of most professionals when they state that client expressions of attraction ought to be handled as manifestations of the client's distress rather than true romantic interest (p. 614). Of course, refraining from such disclosures does not mean that a client's expression of attraction should be ignored; rather, it should be addressed as a possible representation of the problem that provoked them to enter counseling. Clients should also be told that such feelings happen to many clients in the course of an intense therapeutic relationship.

The Place of Nonerotic Touch in This Context

The issue of whether counselors should ever touch adult clients in counseling and therapy, even if the touch is meant to be nonerotic, has always been controversial (Durana, 1998). Nonerotic touch includes such things as a handshake; touch on the hand, arm, or shoulder; a hug; or other brief physical contact. In most cultures a kiss does not seem to fit in this category (Stake & Oliver, 1991). On one side of the issue are those who view touch as a forbidden behavior that interferes with therapeutic progress, confuses clients, and risks the generation of overtly sexual feelings in both parties (Menninger, 1958; Wolberg, 1967). Wolberg called physical contact "an absolute taboo" (1967, p. 606). This strong rejection of touch has been based on the concepts of transference and clear boundaries between the roles of client and therapist. Touching a client, some argue, can blur the boundaries and encourage the participants to view the relationship more as a personal than a professional contact (for example, Guntheil & Gabbard, 1993). Other therapists have taken the opposite view, believing that touch is valuable in engaging clients in the therapeutic process and promoting therapeutic change (for example, see Levy, 1973; Minter & Struve, 1998; Smith, Clance & Imes, 1998). These professionals point to the evidence that human touch is essential to development in children (for example, see Bowlby, 1951; Harlow, 1971) and to the common belief that a judicious use of touch may reassure or console a client in a way that verbal communication cannot. In fact, most therapists do have nonerotic physical contact with clients—handshakes and other socially stereotyped actions at least on occasion—and few evaluate that practice as unethical or untherapeutic (Nigro, 2004a; Pope et al., 1987; Stake & Oliver, 1991; Stenzel & Rupert, 2004). Unfortunately, the empiric evidence does little to clarify because some studies suffer from methodologic problems and others offer contradictory results. One frequent result is that the highest frequency of physical contact occurs between male professionals and female clients with the male professionals initiating the contact (Holub & Lee, 1990). This finding, coupled with the evidence of higher levels of sexual contact by male therapists, has led some writers to be concerned about a "slippery slope" phenomenon, in which nonerotic touch can be a first step toward sexual contact (Guntheil & Gabbard, 1993; Holroyd & Brodsky, 1980). Recent research, however, suggests that same-gender touch is more frequent than cross-gender touch except when the touch is an expression of the relationship (Stenzel & Rupert, 2004) In that study, male therapist–female client touch was more common. It is important to note that therapists who use touch are not more vulnerable to sexual misconduct than those who do not use touch (Pope, 1990b). Still, whenever professionals feel sexually attracted to their clients, they should at that time avoid even nonerotic touch (Kertay & Reviere, 1993).

What are the criteria for nonerotic contact with an adult client? The codes of ethics do not speak directly to this issue except insofar as they prohibit exploitive actions and behaviors that do not serve the best interests of the client. A definitive answer to this question awaits rigorous research on the subject, but several reasonable recommendations can be made. First, a counselor must be clear about his or her motivation to touch a client. Professionals who explain their approach to touch in counseling as a result of their personality, with comments such as "I'm just a touchy-feely sort of person," have not sufficiently examined their motivation or the need to modify personal habits to fill client needs and achieve therapeutic goals. In making such comments, counselors are implying that their own need to touch is more important than their clients' needs. Bacorn and Dixon (1984) hypothesized that counselors may sometimes touch clients to relieve their own anxiety in the face of the emotions clients express. Psychoanalytic therapists wonder if the urge to touch is based on unresolved personal issues or a need to be seen as an expert or loved person by the client. When counselors are feeling strong countertransference, they ought to be especially cautious about touch because those feelings may signal a risk of attending more to the counselors' personal needs than to the client's welfare. Strong countertransference feelings can blur professional boundaries even when touch does not occur, but touching may accelerate that process. Minter and Struve (1998) also suggest that touch should be avoided when the content of the session has focused on sexual matters, when a client has poor impulse control, and when the touch appears to function as a replacement for talk therapy. Other authors, such as Corey et al. (2002), suggest that counselors should avoid touch if the behavior is not congruent with their feelings or they feel uncomfortable with it. A disingenuous touch risks harming the trusting relationship, in their view. Of course, genuineness of feeling is not the only criterion that should be used. After all, counselors can be sincerely wrong or misguided in their feelings.

Counselors who find they have a pattern of differentially touching male and female clients must also examine their motivation for touching. A differential pattern based on gender alone has been called sexist (Holroyd & Brodsky, 1980) and may signal that the counselor is not as attuned as required to the client's needs. Alyn (1988) argued that even if touch is not interpreted in sexual terms by females touched by male therapists, its use by these men can contribute to feelings of disempowerment in female clients.

The decision about whether to touch an adult client must also be grounded in an understanding of cultural and social issues. Touching has highly variable meanings in different cultures, and it is easy for an uninformed counselor to violate cultural norms. For example, Orthodox Jews would see any touch by a person of the opposite gender as highly inappropriate. Among other cultural groups, kissing on both cheeks is as universal and nonerotic a greeting as a handshake. Any decision to touch a client must therefore take into account the client's cultural definitions of touch. Social psychology also teaches us that the privilege of touching is based on socioeconomic status. A higher-status person has greater freedom to touch than does a person of lower status. Thus, a counselor has more liberty to touch a client than a client has to touch a counselor. Similarly, a professor has greater privilege than a student. Consequently, touching without regard for its roots in the counselor's power can be an abuse of that power.

Geib (1982) hypothesizes about the factors associated with a positive interpretation of touching. Geib identifies five factors:

1. Clarity regarding touch, sexual feelings, and boundaries of therapy
2. Client control in initiating and sustaining contact
3. Congruence between the closeness in the relationship and the use of touch
4. Client belief that the touch is for his or her benefit rather than the therapist's
5. A match between the client's expectations for therapy and his or her experience of the therapist

In their research, Horton et al. (1995) also found that the strength of the therapeutic alliance is related to a positive interpretation of touch in therapy.

Client characteristics and experiences ought to weigh heavily in the decision about whether touch is therapeutically appropriate. Willison and Masson (1986) recommend avoiding touch if it creates discomfort in the client. Research shows that many clients have had prior experiences of sexual abuse and harassment, and these people may have difficulty with a therapist's use of touch. They may misinterpret it or be distracted from their therapeutic issues by it (Vasquez, 1988). Other clients dislike touch, either because of family history, individual experience, or the psychological issues that prompted them to enter counseling. For example, a client who has an obsessive-compulsive fear of germs may be overwhelmed by a counselor's touch. Physical contact early in counseling may even cause such a client to drop out rather than risk another touch. Even for clients whose backgrounds and experiences do not rule out touch, professionals must accurately assess their readiness for touch (Durana, 1998). Readiness is related, of course, to the strength of the therapeutic alliance. Kertay and Reviere (1993) recommend discussing with a client the role of nonerotic touch in counseling. As a general guideline, they suggest asking permission before physical contact occurs; however, Stenzel and Rupert (2004) found that few professionals discussed the contact prior to its occurrence. This recommendation seems especially prudent before the first time a counselor believes that physical contact may be therapeutic.

In short, all these factors should lead a mental health professional to be cautious about the use of touch. Some writers suggest completely abstaining from touch except for handshakes, but most recommend a judicious use of touch. Under the right circumstances, touch can be reassuring and therapeutically useful. In their study, Horton et al. (1995) found that clients were very positive about nonerotic touch and many viewed the physical contact as especially important in resolving their problems. One study does not lead to any definitive conclusions, of course, but wisely and prudently used, touch may be therapeutic. At the same time, it is wise for counselors to learn a whole repertoire of behaviors for demonstrating emotional connections with clients so that they can adapt their response to the needs of each client. If counselors decide to touch clients, the burden is on them to demonstrate that the touch served the needs of the client, not their own.

The topic of nonerotic touch is more complicated when providing counseling or psychotherapy for children because touch is normative in young children (McNeil-Haber, 2004). They initiate it for appropriate reasons and ways (such as showing pleasure with another's actions by hugging) and inappropriate reasons (such as showing anger by hitting). Indeed, the few studies that have been conducted show that nonerotic touch is common during child counseling (Cowen, Weissberg, & Lotyczewski, 1983; Rae & Worchel, 1991) with approximately 40% of the therapists in these studies indicating that they hug child clients frequently. At other times professionals must touch clients to keep them safe from injury or to prevent injury to themselves from hitting. Obviously, in those situations touching is entirely within ethical bounds—indeed the failure to hold a child's arm back before hitting another or striking at a pane of glass could be viewed as inherently unethical. When deciding whether touch is appropriate with children in less extreme circumstances, counselors must take into account the child's age and maturity, cultural background, diagnosis and history, parental preferences, and the capacity of the child to verbalize his or her needs and preferences. Some institutions and schools have instituted "no touch" policies that must also be considered. Restraint from touch and consultation are prudent approaches when in doubt. (For an excellent discussion of the ethical issues related to touching children, see McNeil-Haber, 2004.)

Providing Effective Subsequent Therapy for Victims

Research shows that between 22% and 65% of professionals will see at least one client who reports that former therapists sexually exploited him or her (Pope & Vetter, 1991; Stake & Oliver, 1991, Wincze et al., 1996). Effective treatment for such clients is difficult and requires expert and diligent treatment (Pope, 1994; Sonne, 1987). Therapists who seek to provide competent service to these clients should familiarize themselves with the growing body of literature on the topic, get qualified supervision, and be prepared to have an emotional reaction to the information the client is disclosing. Sonne and Pope (1991) caution therapists that when they first hear of this exploitation they may experience disbelief, denial, or minimization of the harm done. They may even be tempted to blame the victim or may experience sexual reactions to the material being revealed. Wohlberg (2000) reported that clients seeking therapy after sexual involvement with a prior therapist often feel revictimized by professionals who discount, minimize, blame, or react with inappropriate emotion. It is difficult to hear that one's colleagues in a helping profession have behaved in such destructive, self-serving ways. The kind of open, compassionate, empathic response a mental health professional would give in any other highly personal disclosure is essential here too. If a counselor doubts that he or she is competent to provide this service, then a referral is appropriate. The article published by the APA Committee on Women in Psychology (1989) and entitled "If Sex Enters into the Psychotherapy Relationship" is an important document to share with clients who reveal such a history. It is written for consumers to help them understand why the profession regards sexual contact as unethical and provides them with options to address their reactions, including ways to file a claim against the offender. If clients wish to pursue an ethics complaint against a former counselor, the current counselor is obliged to provide information about the process and to give the client the option to discuss, in subsequent sessions, feelings and reactions to pursuing a complaint. This document also has obvious use as part of an informed consent process for all clients. Both consumers and therapists support its value in that application (Thorn, Shealy, & Briggs, 1993). Wohlberg (1999) cautions professionals not to pressure clients into taking action against the offending therapist because clients who experience such demands feel interrogated and unsupported. Clients should also be informed about the Therapist Exploitation Link Line as another resource for support for them in their recovery (www.advocateweb.org/TELL/).

Cases Reexamined

The Case of Olga and Manuel

The first step in responding is to evaluate the facts of the situation as written. Manuel was not diagnosed with a mental or emotional disorder at the time of counseling, and the majority of his problems were attributable to medical rather than psychological issues. Three sessions were held in which the counselor first ruled out the existence of a depressive disorder and then focused attention on bolstering the client's coping skills for work stress and responsibilities for aging parents. By the third session the client reported improvement in coping skills, happiness that his other problems were relieved by changes in his medical treatment, and gratitude to the counselor for her assistance. Counseling terminated, the counselor reported the case as closed, and no contact occurred for 3 years. The initial meeting after those 5 years was accidental, at a community event, and the client, not the counselor, asked for the date. The client reports good functioning in the intervening period. The case description presents no information about the nature of the emotional ties or transference that occurred during the three sessions, nor does it indicate whether either party felt sexually attracted to the other while counseling was taking place.

When the standards in the ACA code are applied, the following conclusions seem valid:

- Nearly 5 years have elapsed since termination.
- Counseling was of short duration.
- Termination seemed to be desirable to both parties and appropriate insofar as the client did not again seek counseling from Olga or anyone else.
- The client did not suffer from significant psychological problems at the time of counseling and did not admit any current psychological issues in his accidental meeting with the counselor, although when he made the counseling appointment he was worried that he suffered from a serious mental illness.
- There is no evidence that the counselor initiated this personal contact with her former client.

Thus far, the contact seems to fit within the boundaries allowed by the rule. However, some important questions remain unanswered:

- What is the risk of an adverse impact of a dating relationship on the client?
- What was the nature of the emotional connection or transference between Manuel and Olga at the time of counseling?

- Did either party fantasize about a personal or sexual relationship while counseling was ongoing? If so, to what degree might this experience have affected the material disclosed by the client or the diagnosis assigned by the counselor?
- Does Olga practice in a state that has regulations that ban posttermination relationships under all circumstances?

In the absence of answers to these questions, one cannot conclude that this contact would be permissible. Moreover, even if these questions were resolved in the most positive way possible, a prudent counselor would agree to a social relationship only after clear and frank discussions of the possible problems that may arise in a posttermination relationship. The first such conversation should take place with a supervisor or trusted colleague who can more objectively evaluate Olga's motivation. If colleagues fail to agree that this contact fits the criteria, Olga would be wise to refuse the invitation, at least for some time. The counselor should also "consult" with experts in the field who have differing views about the advisability of posttermination contact by reading their writings and judging the merit of their arguments in her case. If colleagues conclude that the situation meets the criteria set forth in the code and Olga believes she has satisfactory responses to criticisms of this kind of contact, she should give herself a little more time to be clear about her decision. After all, there is no time limit to decision making in this case. (Given the possibility of a messy ending to a personal relationship in this circumstance, Olga may want to consult her attorney as well.)

If at that point she still wishes to go forward, her second discussion should be with Manuel before accepting or rejecting the invitation. At the end of that discussion, both the client and the counselor should understand that any future professional relationship between them would be completely ruled out. Even with this understanding, both should realize that their history will likely impose other complications on their personal relationship with which they will need to cope. Moreover, as the relationship continues, Olga should meet regularly with a colleague to discuss any issues that develop relative to her professional history with Manuel. Manuel may be well served by a referral to another mental health professional for the same kind of discussion if he wishes it.

This case highlights both the burden that is placed on a mental health professional when trying to decide what is ethical and the crucial importance of continuing to place the welfare of the client over one's personal needs or desires.

The Case of Isabelle and Yoritomo

A review of the facts of the situation reveals the following:

- An adjunct faculty member has asked a counseling student enrolled in his course to have dinner with him sometime.
- The invitation comes as the student is submitting her final examination and subsequent to several professional conversations related to the content of the course.
- The student's interest in pursuing a dating relationship with the instructor is unknown, as is her emotional reaction to his suggestion, but her interest in the subject matter he teaches is substantial.

The ACA ethics code prohibits sexual relationships with students, sexual harassment of students, and exploitive relationships with students. If Yoritomo was asking Isabelle for a date before completing his instructional control, then he was probably violating this standard. He had not yet graded that final exam, nor had he determined the course grade. Did he ask at this time because he knew (at least unconsciously) that he had more power and that Isabelle might be more agreeable to a dinner together while he was still her instructor? If so, that means he attempted to exploit his professional position to get what he wanted from this student. Even if he intended to keep the grading completely separate from her answer to his question, his objectivity in evaluating this student's work is also likely to be compromised. Is that fair to her or to the other students in the course?

From Isabelle's perspective, she may feel trapped, worrying about the implications of a refusal on her grade in the course. She also may have wished to continue her professional contacts with Yoritomo as she developed substance abuse programs in her school. She may wonder if the date is the "quid pro quo" for that continuing professional advice. If so, this behavior fits the definition of exploitation and sexual harassment. Similarly, she may have been considering asking him for a recommendation for doctoral programs if she did well on her final, an option that would be eliminated if she agreed to a date. She may also feel uncomfortable discussing a romantic relationship with a faculty member with friends who are also students in the program. In short, Isabelle is not in a position to make a free consent or refusal to his request.

Even if Yoritomo's intentions were entirely honorable, his request was unethical because he insensitively placed the student in an embarrassing and stressful position in which the lines between a professional and personal relationship were blurred. If he wanted to communicate to Isabelle a willingness to continue his assistance to her in her work at school, he had other options. He might have called her or sent her a note after course grades were submitted.

If Yoritomo had waited 1 month after the termination of the course to invite Isabelle to dinner, the ethics codes give less clear guidelines. They do not speak to the issue of post-termination sex with students. The judgment in this case is based on the likelihood that his evaluative role will continue in some way, so that Isabelle's freedom to consent or refuse is jeopardized. Full-time faculty are likely to continue in some sort of evaluative role, whether to teach other courses to the same students, to be involved in placement or scholarship decisions, or to decide whether students are admitted to advanced graduate study. Yoritomo's status as an adjunct faculty member makes it possible that he could have no further evaluative role with students after they finish his course. That may remove one aspect of the ethics problem. However, if Yoritomo uses his course as a way to fill his social calendar, then his intent is exploitive and waiting a short time until grades are submitted does not eliminate the ethics problem with dating former students. In this as in all cases, the welfare of the population served must be the first consideration.

DISCUSSION CASES

Benjamin, a clinical counselor in an outpatient unit of a general hospital, is about to meet a new client for an intake interview. He does not recognize the name of the person written on his calendar, but when he goes to the reception room to greet the new client, he sees a familiar face. Marcia is a woman he dated 20 years ago. Two years after their relationship ended Marcia married someone else and Benjamin started graduate school. Marcia has now been divorced for several years. She chose Benjamin for therapy for her depression because others recommended him and because she believed she could trust him with her problems. Benjamin tells Marcia that he is flattered that she still thinks so highly of him, but he must decline to accept her as a client. He goes on to explain that he does not believe he should provide counseling to someone with whom he once had a close relationship, even if it was many years ago. Marcia is upset by his refusal to see her and calls Benjamin's interpretation of ethics insensitive, legalistic, and uncaring. She storms out of his office, determined to try and cope with her problems on her own. Benjamin sends Marcia a letter in which he apologizes for upsetting her and tries to explain his views more fully. In that letter he also gives her the names of three other clinicians whom he recommends. Did Benjamin act ethically? How do you respond to Marcia's comment that his view is "legalistic"? At this stage is there anything else he ought to do about the situation?

SUMMARY

Sexual exploitation of clients by therapists is a blatantly unethical practice, as is sexual contact with students, employees, supervisees, research participants, and others for whom the professional has responsibility. Sexual contact with former clients is always prohibited for at least 2 years after the termination of therapy for psychologists and 5 years after therapy for counselors. Even after this time has elapsed sexual contact is permitted only in the most unusual circumstances. The codes do not directly address the issue of sexual contact after teaching or supervision responsibilities have ended, but in these cases professionals must demonstrate that the supervisory responsibilities have truly ceased. Moreover, they must be able to show that the sexual contact is nonexploitive.

Sexual misconduct by mental health professionals has been widely studied, and the results show clear evidence of sexual exploitation by professionals. Up to 12% of therapists have admitted sexual contact with current and former clients, and some have acknowledged multiple contacts. Because this research relies on the willingness of professionals and clients to disclose such events in therapy, the reliability of that figure is probably not high. In any case, surveys of mental health professionals have found that approximately half of those sampled have seen at least one client who reports an experience of sexual exploitation by a former therapist. A similar percentage of faculty and supervisors have admitted the same misconduct. The only demographic variables associated with this violation are gender and, to a lesser degree, age. Older male therapists and faculty are more likely to engage in this behavior than younger or female therapists. Victims, however, are more likely to be female and younger than the therapist. Children also have become victims of sexual exploitation by therapists. Research has shown that sexual misconduct inflicts serious and long-lasting psychological damage on victims. In fact, that damage has been compared to the effects of rape or incest.

Sexual misconduct needs to be distinguished from experiences of sexual arousal. A great majority of counselors report having been sexually attracted to a client on occasion. The experience of attraction is not unethical in itself as long as it is handled responsibly. The counselor has the duty to monitor his or her behavior so that the attraction does not distract the client from the therapeutic focus of the session and does not prevent the counselor from providing competent service. Consultation and supervision are also advised when an attraction occurs.

Given this context, it is not surprising that the use of nonerotic touch as a therapeutic approach is controversial. Some call it taboo, and others view it as appropriate if used wisely. All professionals regard nonerotic touch as inappropriate if it serves the counselor's needs over the clients' or is insensitive to cultural, social, or gender considerations.

DISCUSSION QUESTIONS

1. Given the contents of the codes of ethics, how would you evaluate the ethics of a sexual relationship between a child counselor and the parent of one of his or her clients? Would sexual contact several months after termination be considered ethical?

2. What is your analysis of the debate on the 2-year or 5-year rule for posttermination sexual contact with clients? Which approach seems more prudent? If you sat on the committee assigned to write the next revision of the code, what position would you take?

3. Professional associations seem caught between their commitment to protect the public from exploitive therapists and their obligation to promote the good image of the profession. Some criticize these organizations for being too passive about the dangers and too lenient with offenders, and others argue that so much attention to the problems of a small number of practitioners gives the misimpression that all members act exploitively. What do you think the proper role of the professional association is in dealing with a serious ethical problem such as sexual misconduct?

4. Do you think the codes of ethics ought to address sexual relationships with former students, supervisees, employees, or research participants? Why or why not?

RECOMMENDED READINGS

Anonymous. (1991). Sexual harassment: A female counseling student's experience. *Journal of Counseling and Development, 69,* 502–506.

Bartell, P. A., & Rubin, L. J. (1990). Dangerous liaisons: Sexual intimacies in supervision. *Professional Psychology: Research and Practice, 21,* 442–450.

Bates, C. M., & Brodsky, A. M. (1989). *Sex in the therapy hour: A case of professional incest.* New York: Guilford.

Gabbard, G. O. (Ed.). (1989). *Sexual exploitation in professional relationships.* Washington, DC: American Psychiatric Press.

Pope, K. S. (1994). *Sexual involvement with therapists: Patient assessment, subsequent therapy, forensics.* Washington, DC: American Psychological Association.

Pope, K. S., Sonne, J. L., & Holroyd, J. (1993). *Sexual feelings in psychotherapy: Explorations for therapists and therapists-in-training.* Washington, DC: American Psychological Association.

Vasquez, M. J. T. (1991). Sexual intimacies with clients after termination: Should a prohibition be explicit? *Ethics and Behavior, 1,* 45–61.

Chapter 7

Multiple Relationships and Boundary Issues
Risking Objectivity and Client Welfare

Consider whether the professionals acted ethically in the following situations:

Roberta, a physician and client of Dominique, a grief counselor, comes to the final session of their counseling relationship with a gift for Dominique. Roberta says she wants to show her counselor just how much she appreciates all the help and support she provided while the doctor was coping with the sudden death of her child in a car accident. The gift—a subscription to the next season of the most prominent theater company in the region—is valued at several hundred dollars. Dominique decides to accept the gift, although she usually refuses expensive gifts from her clients. Dominique has reasoned that for someone in Roberta's position, a gift of a few hundred dollars represents a token, such as a flower or paperback book may represent a token from a college student client.

Nicholas, a counselor for whom Marco acted as clinical supervisor during Nicholas's internship last semester, has just moved into the home across the street from his former supervisor. Marco did not know this was occurring until the moving van pulled up. Within days, the children from the two families became friends. Marco's wife suggests that he invite Nicholas and his family over for a "welcome to the neighborhood" barbecue. Marco agrees and volunteers to telephone the man himself to issue the invitation.

Li Qing, who has been going to counseling for shyness and social withdrawal, decides to take action to become more social, so she attends a church service one morning. Soon thereafter, she decides to join the congregation. Because her counselor, Roxanne, was out of town the weekends her client attended services, Li Qing does not know that Roxanne belongs to that church. When the client tells Roxanne that she has decided to join, the counselor discloses the coincidence of church membership and asks Li Qing to describe her feelings about it. The counselor decides to continue seeing the client, although they will be members of the same church.

Olive is a psychologist in private practice. Olive's husband is considering opening a fast-food restaurant. As they discuss the business opportunity, she learns that the regional representative from the fast-food chain is a former client who terminated therapy 8 months ago. The client had entered counseling for treatment of a major depression. If Olive's husband goes forward with this restaurant, he will have ongoing contact with this former client. Olive asks her husband to investigate other franchise opportunities, saying that her past professional connections with the representative could make the arrangement awkward for everyone. Reluctantly, her husband agrees.

Theodore is attending an open house at his child's elementary school. The child's teacher, Mr. Goodheart, approaches Theodore because he knows that Theodore is a licensed mental health counselor. The teacher asks if Theodore has room in his schedule for a good friend of his who is anxious and depressed. The counselor gives Mr. Goodheart his card and tells the teacher to have his friend call to arrange an appointment.

Wilma is a licensed clinical social worker. Wilma's former client operates a private college admissions advising service. This client works with high school students and their families to help them with the college application process and with securing financial aid. Wilma has twins who are beginning their senior year of high school. When the two accidentally meet one Saturday at the post office, Wilma wonders whether her former client could help her sort through the maze of college applications before her daughters. The next day Wilma telephones the former client and asks for an appointment for herself and the twins. In all, they have three meetings, for which Wilma pays the standard fee. At termination, Wilma and her daughters express satisfaction with the services they received.

Alberto is a psychologist who is married to a software engineer in a small company. Alberto's wife's boss at the software company requests that Alberto see in therapy the boss's 16-year-old son, who has been suffering from panic attacks. Alberto is well known in the community for his skill in counseling people with anxiety disorders. Alberto telephones his wife's boss and suggests that the family come in for a consultation the next day.

Gerhard, a stock broker and former client who terminated therapy with Nadine 3 years ago, calls Nadine to ask if she is interested in an investment opportunity. Nadine, a clinical counselor nearing retirement, does some research on the investment and learns that it is a legitimate opportunity and that the potential exists for a substantial return. Nadine also knows from her therapeutic contact with Gerhard that he is scrupulously honest and highly competent in his work. Nadine contacts him and suggests a meeting to discuss specifics. After several more meetings, she invests $10,000 in the business.

Each week Oscar, a family therapist, goes to the same bakery for bread. He establishes a friendly relationship with the young person behind the counter. On various occasions this bakery clerk has seen Oscar with his spouse, his children, and his parents. One day the clerk's name appears on Oscar's appointment calendar for a counseling session for relationship problems. The doctor learns from the secretary that when she made the appointment, this woman asked to see him in particular. Oscar is pleased that the person sought him out and looks forward to a productive professional relationship.

Robin is a counseling psychologist with a private practice. Jon, a therapist in town with whom Robin has been acquainted for 10 years, requests that Robin see him as a client. The two have served together on the ethics committee of the state psychological association. Jon's sister was killed in a terrorist bombing, and he believes he is now suffering from posttraumatic stress. He is adamant that he wants to see Robin and not another therapist because he trusts Robin's clinical judgment more than anyone else in the area. Robin schedules an initial appointment that afternoon.

What are your intuitions about the ethics of each situation? Do some seem more problematic than others? Do some seem acceptable with no clear ethical dimensions at all? Are some difficult to evaluate without more information? This chapter focuses on the issue of secondary relationships with those with whom we have a professional role (sexual relationships with current and former clients were discussed in Chapter 6). The chapter begins by defining terms and proceeds to review the ethical standards and the rationale for those standards, including research on practitioners' beliefs and practices about this topic. Next it presents a set of questions practitioners should ask themselves when considering whether to become involved in a secondary relationship with a current or former client. The chapter concludes by discussing the ethics of receiving gifts from clients, of managing secondary contacts with clients in rural settings, and of engaging in barter with clients—the practice of trading goods and services instead of money for counseling.

Definition of Terms

Whenever mental health professionals have other connections with a client in addition to the therapist–client relationship, a secondary relationship exists. For many years the term *dual relationship* was used to explain such overlapping connections, but that term has fallen out of favor and is no longer contained in current ethics codes, at least partly because of its lack of explanatory value (Cottone, 2005). The counseling and psychology professions now use either the term *counselor–client nonprofessional relationship* or the designation *multiple relationship* for such an occurrence. In each of the cases just described, some level of additional professional–client relationship has been established or has the potential to exist.

Two other terms appear frequently in the mental health lexicon: *boundary crossings* and *boundary violations.* Both are grounded in the notion that there should be a division, a boundary, between the professional and personal lives of counselor and client. This division fosters a more productive therapeutic process by increasing the likelihood that the professional has the objectivity needed to understand and treat the client's concerns and the client has sufficient trust in the good will and altruistic motives of the therapist to share personal information and work through uncomfortable issues (Gabbard, 1994; Sommers-Flanagan, Elliott, & Sommers-Flanagan, 1998). In other words, boundaries provide structure for the process, safety for the client, and the required emotional distance for effective therapeutic work (Gabbard, 1994; Sommers-Flanagan et al., 1998). According to Remley and Herlihy (2003), a *boundary crossing* is a departure from common practice with the intent to help a client and with some credible evidence that benefit is likely to result. Sommers-Flanagan et al. (1998) use the term *boundary extension* to describe the same phenomenon. They also underscore the importance of evidence of benefit to the client and the risk inherent in any such extension: "…the fact that a therapist believes a boundary extension is therapeutically justified or nonharmful to the client does not make it so" (p. 40). A *boundary violation* or *boundary break* is a departure from accepted practice that causes the client harm or is very likely to cause harm. Implicit in this definition is the notion that the harm probably could (and should) have been anticipated if the professional either had more altruistic intent or was more rigorous in analyzing the risks and merits of the action before it was undertaken. Boundary violations often occur when professionals are too compromised to function competently or too self-interested to attend to the effects of violations on clients. Boundary violations are never ethical.

Sonne (1994) clarifies that multiple relationships can be either concurrent with the professional relationship or consecutive. If consecutive, the therapeutic role may precede or follow the other role. Because counselors function in a variety of roles in their professional and personal lives, the possibility of a multiple relationship is always present. The following list shows examples of multiple relationships.

Concurrent	Consecutive
Professional and personal	Professional then personal
(researcher and friend)	(therapist, 1998–1999 and business partner, 2000–2001)
Professional and professional	Professional then professional
(supervisor and counselor)	(professor, 1996–1997, therapist, 1999–2000)
Multiple professional	Personal then professional
(employer, clinical supervisor, and clinician)	(friend since college—15 years—then marriage counselor in 16th year)

The debate about the conditions under which boundary crossings may be ethical has been one of the most energetic in the profession in recent years. Even ethics scholars who concur on the risks inherent in many kinds of multiple relationships do not advocate a universal ban on them and acknowledge the complexity of the issue (such as Glosoff, 1997; Herlihy & Corey, 1997; Kitchener, 1988; Younggren & Gottlieb, 2004). Others argue that the professional associations and licensing boards have encouraged an unproductive interpretation of ethical standards that at times has prevented professionals from crossing boundaries in ways likely to be helpful to clients (Campbell & Gordon, 2003; Lazarus & Zur, 2002; Moleski & Kiselica, 2005). All sources recognize that some multiple relationships result from accidental contacts and others are extremely difficult to avoid without denying clients access to services. Essentially, the major risk of concurrent or consecutive multiple relationships is that the existence of the nonprofessional relationship will compromise both the judgment of the professional and the response of the client to treatment. The relaxation of boundaries on one dimension also has the potential to loosen other boundaries along a "slippery slope" to unethical conduct. In fact, the majority of egregious boundary violations involving exploitation that have been addressed by licensing boards and ethics committees also include other boundary crossings, usually initiated prior to the serious violations. For example, a professional may precede hiring a current client to work for him or her with discussing office management practices during sessions. Indeed it is the crossing of the boundary to tap into the client's expertise in office management that leads the professional to seek to hire the client in the first place.

Kitchener (1988) and Jennings (1992) refer to the multiple-relationship problem as one of conflict in social roles and the often incompatible claims of each role on the professional. The greater the divergence between roles, the greater the risk of an unsatisfactory therapeutic outcome. Role differences entail different expectations for self, other, and the relationship, along with varying obligations for each party. Role differences exist along a continuum, and the risk of problems with role differences varies directly with the degree of disparity in expectations and obligations. For example, the role expectations and obligations of a spouse and a professor diverge significantly. A spouse is expected to support, assist, and be especially attentive to the partner's needs, but a professor is obliged to be objective and fair to all students, singling no one out for special treatment. Moreover, the professor's duty is to evaluate students and to give negative evaluations to those whose performance is substandard. Thus, the roles of spouse and professor are so highly contrasting that the risk of misconduct increases significantly if they are merged.

The case of Alberto and the boss's son at the beginning of the chapter is another good illustration of the concept of diverging role expectations and obligations. Examining each person's role in the scenario reveals that the roles Alberto is considering are highly incompatible. The term boundary violation applies to this scenario because Alberto's intent is not purely to benefit the client and because the risk of harm to the son is clear and predictable on the basis of a rational analysis of the facts of the situation. It would be extremely difficult for Alberto to put aside all his loyalty obligations to his spouse and attend only to the welfare of the client.

Other role expectations and obligations are more similar and involve less vulnerability to negative outcomes. Combining the roles of therapist and shopper in a supermarket in which a client works illustrates a situation with almost no potential for harm. There is no conflict between the role obligations of shopper and therapist, except in the extraordinary unlikely event that the client's knowledge of the therapist's purchasing habits and food choices poses a problem for the client's experience in therapy. Because this situation has a minimal risk of harm, the worker in the supermarket ought not to be denied the mental health service she seeks because of her outside contact with the therapist. Multiple relationships at the low end of the role difference continuum carry very little chance that they will harm either party. This is the primary reason that the professions have never banned all such overlapping relationships.

Three other factors weighed in to form the profession's position on this issue. First, in some forms of multiple relationships the consumer stands to benefit substantially from the contact. Returning to the case of Oscar at the beginning of the chapter, the bakery clerk's personal life may be significantly improved if she enters counseling with him. She may gain the strength to end an abusive relationship or learn how to achieve the emotional intimacy with her partner that she has been seeking. Second, avoiding all multiple relationships would place a great burden on mental health professionals and those with whom they associate. For example, in the second case in the chapter, a total prohibition of multiple relationships would be unworkable for Marco. Requiring him to move and uproot his family to avoid contact with Nicholas would be unthinkable, demanding him to ignore his new neighbor would be uncomfortable for the family (and the neighborhood), and asking Nicholas to relocate would be just as impossible. Third, repudiating all multiple relationships is inconsistent with the right to free association of citizens in a democratic society. Nicholas has a right to live where he chooses and to be as friendly with his neighbors as he sees fit. Also, although Marco's professional obligations take precedence over his right of free association with those with whom he has had a professional relationship, that right is not entirely eliminated when the professional contact is completed.

Still another circumstance that may make a boundary crossing more ethical is the cultural background of the client. Clients from non–Western collectivist cultures may be confused and offended by rigid boundaries that fail to flex in ways typical in the client's culture (Herlihy & Watson, 2003). For example, such a client may view a professional's refusal to accept a sibling as an additional individual client as a hurtful and rejecting event rather than the establishment of a therapeutic boundary aimed at maintaining professional objectivity. (See Ridley, Liddle, Hill, & Li [2001] for an excellent discussion of the role of culture in navigating multiple relationship issues.)

The current language in the standards of the American Counseling Association (ACA) and American Psychological Association (APA) attempts to take into account such complexity, but ultimately each applies a different standard for determining the conditions under which a multiple relationship may be acceptable.

ACA *Code of Ethics,* Section A.5: Roles and Relationships with Clients

c. Non-Professional Interactions or Relationships (Other Than Sexual or Romantic Interactions or Relationships). Counselor-client non-professional relationships with clients, former clients, their romantic partners, or their family members should be avoided, except when the interaction is potentially beneficial to the client.

d. Potentially Beneficial Interactions. When a counselor-client non-professional interaction with a client or former client may be potentially beneficial to the client or former client, the counselor must document in case records, prior to the interaction (when feasible), the rationale for such an interaction, the potential benefit, and anticipated consequences for the client or former client and other individuals significantly involved with the client or former client. Such interactions should be initiated with appropriate client consent. Where unintentional harm occurs to the client or former client, or to an individual significantly involved with the client or former client, due to the non-professional interaction, the counselor must show evidence of an attempt to remedy such harm. Examples of potentially beneficial interactions include, but are not limited to, attending a formal ceremony (e.g., a wedding/commitment ceremony or graduation); purchasing a service or product provided by a client or former client (excepting unrestricted bartering); hospital visits to an ill family member; or mutual membership in a professional association, organization, or community.

C.6.d. Exploitation of Others. Counselors do not harmfully exploit others in their professional relationships.

APA *Ethical Principles*

3.04 Psychologists take reasonable steps to avoid harming their clients/patients, students, supervisees, research participants, organizational clients, and others with whom they work, and to minimize harm where it is foreseeable and unavoidable.

3.05 Multiple Relationships

(a) A multiple relationship occurs when a psychologist is in a professional role with a person and (1) at the same time is in another role with the same person, (2) at the same time is in a relationship with a person closely associated with or related to the person with whom the psychologist has the professional relationship, or (3) promises to enter into another relationship in the future with the person or a person closely associated with or related to the person. A psychologist refrains from entering into a multiple relationship if the multiple relationship could reasonably be expected to impair the psychologist's objectivity, competence, or effectiveness in performing his or her functions as a psychologist, or otherwise risks exploitation or harm to the person with whom the professional relationship exists. Multiple relationships that would not reasonably be expected to cause impairment or risk exploitation or harm are not unethical.

(b) If a psychologist finds that, due to unforeseen factors, a potentially harmful multiple relationship has arisen, the psychologist takes reasonable steps to resolve it with due regard for the best interests of the affected person and maximal compliance with the Ethics Code.

3.08 Exploitative Relationships

Psychologists do not exploit persons over whom they have supervisory, evaluative, or other authority such as clients/patients, students, supervisees, research participants, and employees.

Note: The recommendation in the codes to be judicious about engaging in multiple relationships is not limited to the therapeutic setting. The care in the matter applies to the other professional roles counselors and psychologists take on—teacher, supervisor, consultant, researcher, or employer. The standards also clearly apply to individuals in close connection to the person in the professional relationship so that a client's partner, child, or close friend would also be subject to these provisions.

The language in the 2005 ACA code represents a major departure from the contents of the prior version (ACA, 1995). Instead of advising counselors to "make every effort to avoid multiple relationships with clients that could impair their judgment or increase the risk of harm to clients," the current code deletes reference to the risks to the counselor's judgment or objectivity and explicitly allows such relationships "when the interaction is potentially beneficial." The code advises professionals to avoid nonprofessional interactions when they cannot be demonstrated to be beneficial. The language goes on to explain that the rationale for the nonprofessional relationship, its potential benefit, and anticipated consequences must be documented in the client record prior to the initiation of the nonprofessional interaction. Unfortunately, no definition of the term *potential benefit* is included in the code, so its interpretation is uncertain. Many activities can be potentially beneficial, although the probability of benefit is low. (I can argue that it is potentially beneficial to me to buy a lottery ticket this afternoon and that statement would be true, but the probability of my gaining any benefit from that purchase in infinitesimal.) The language in the ACA code appears most helpful in situations in which the professional is entertaining a brief additional contact with a client such as attendance at a wedding or the concurrent service on a community board or activity with a current client. Those interactions and their likely consequences can be anticipated, discussed at length with the client in advance of their occurrence, and easily documented in the record. The language appears less helpful when a counselor is entertaining the acceptance of a person with whom the personal relationship is preexisting to the professional contact or the nonprofessional interaction may be lengthier or closer to the professional's personal life. For example, how does this section apply to the following situation?

The Case of Brendan and the Cabinetmaker

Brendan, a mental health counselor in a community agency, is seeing an unemployed cabinetmaker for mild depression and relationship problems at the same time that the professional is planning the remodeling of his kitchen. The client needs work and is highly qualified in his occupation. Brendan wonders whether he can ask this ongoing client to build the cabinets for his new kitchen using fair market pricing. The counselor knows the income would be beneficial for the client and the client is likely to be happy to accept the job, which should be completed in 3–6 months. He is also willing to document the arrangement in the record and obtain written consent from the client. Brendan is unsure whether such an arrangement is acceptable and refers to the ACA code for assistance.

The ACA code directs the counselor in this case to (a) provide a rationale for the boundary crossing, (b) identify the potential benefit to the client, and (c) clarify the anticipated consequences both for the client and those in close connection to the client. In this case, the rationale is that the action would provide employment that the client needs and its benefit would be the income earned from the job. The anticipated consequences would be ongoing contact with the counselor and presence in the counselor's home for 3–6 months, the possibility of more referrals from neighbors of the counselor who admire the client's work (assuming the client is able to produce cabinets of his usual quality), and some relief of financial stress on the client's family. Other possible consequences include an injury on the job for the client, a misunderstanding about some aspect of the cabinet construction or placement (not unusual in remodeling work), an increase in the client's knowledge of the counselor's personal life, a deterioration in the client's mental health that interferes with the completion of the project, and a blurring of boundaries so that the counselor or client seeks to discuss therapeutic issues with the counselor while working at the house or remodeling issues during counseling sessions. The code then demands that Brendan document each of these consequences in the record. Unfortunately, this section of the code does not offer guidance to help him evaluate whether any of those consequences make the secondary contact more or less ethical except perhaps to the extent that they may prevent the intended benefit to the client.

This section of the ACA code does not address the fact that this situation clearly also benefits Brendan. Does that make it unethical? In section C.6.d the code admonishes the counselor not to exploit the client, but because the client really wants the work and is being paid a fair market price for his services, the arrangement does not appear to be exploitive. If the counselor obtains written informed consent from the client and identifies a plan for remedying any unintended harm, the risk of exploitation is minimized even further. How should a counselor proceed in the event that a boundary crossing also benefits him or her? How does the counselor weigh the potential benefits against the possible harm? How should the counselor assess the effect of the additional contact on his or her objectivity in this counseling relationship? Is 3–6 months sufficiently time-limited to qualify as an exception? Because the ACA code is silent on these issues the counselor must go beyond its provisions to get the answer to these important questions.

Sonne's (1994) advice to be risk preventive when it comes to multiple relationships is applicable. The risks of complications to the objectivity of the counselor during treatment, the response of the client during the time that he is both client and contractor, and the possibility of problems in the counselor's satisfaction with the timing or quality of the installation of the cabinets make this relationship potentially risky. It is a multiple relationship that this author would avoid, especially because it is avoidable unless the client is the only cabinetmaker in the region. (Even then the multiple relationship is avoidable because there is no urgency to the kitchen remodeling; it can wait until the client is no longer in need of professional services.) The counselor can also help the client find other less risky ways to assist the client in earning income. For instance, with the client's permission he could offer the client's business card to a friend or neighbor doing home remodeling and brainstorm with the client about other marketing possibilities. In any event, prior to initiating a nonprofessional contact with a client the professional should consult with knowledgeable, objective colleagues, as noted in Section C.2.e of the ACA code, which reads, "Counselors take reasonable steps to consult with other counselors or related professionals when they have questions regarding their ethical obligations or professional practice." Without consultation the boundary crossing violates this requirement that the professional seek out other counselors' opinions about the ethics of the matter.

Two additional cases related to this provision of the ACA code are presented in the following for your consideration. Each in its own way illustrates the difficulty in applying this standard and the more fundamental complexity of boundary crossings for mental health professionals.

The Case of Mary Angela

Mary Angela, a counselor with a private practice, notices a man sitting in her waiting room. She finds this man attractive, and the book he is reading on the history of the American civil rights movement is one that she too is interested in. She learns that this man has accompanied her last client to the office. At the end of the next session Mary Angela asks the client about him; the client reveals that he is an old friend of her husband's from college who was widowed last year. He accompanied her to the office last week because her car had broken down that morning. The client volunteers to arrange a meeting between the man and therapist by bringing him to the office. The counselor wonders whether she can agree to this arrangement and looks to the ACA code for guidance.

The Case of Barney Johannes

A young adult client has been seeing Dr. Barney Johannes, a career counselor, for assistance in deciding on a career path after completing an undergraduate degree in psychology. As a result of counseling the client decides to seek a graduate degree in mental health counseling and applies to several accredited programs. This client graduated with honors and has high scores on admissions examinations. Dr. Johannes is also a faculty member at the same university to which the client is applying. Because the young man is so talented Dr. Johannes encourages him to apply to the university at which he teaches and volunteers to be his advisor and help him obtain financial aid. Ultimately the young man is accepted, awarded an assistantship, and enters that program. Both the counselor and this client are happy with the outcome, but a colleague of the counselor expresses concern that the counselor crossed a boundary inappropriately when he so actively advocated for this candidate over others. Dr. Johannes immediately reads the ACA code to determine whether there is merit to the colleague's concern.

The 2002 APA code also discourages multiple relationships, indicating that psychologists should "refrain from" such relationships if negative outcomes might reasonably be predicted. However, it places more emphasis on the impact of the multiple relationship on the psychologist in determining the ethics of the secondary contact. The standards require psychologists to evaluate whether the combination of roles being considered jeopardizes their professional judgment, the welfare of the client, or their capacity to function competently. The APA code notes that multiple relationships not likely to cause impairment to the psychologist's judgment or harm to the client are not unethical. Still, neither code provides a blueprint for practice, so the burden of assessing the ethics of any given prospective multiple relationship falls largely on the individual practitioner. Moreover, neither code directly addresses the issue of consecutive multiple relationships when the professional relationship precedes the personal (i.e., when counselors have ongoing social relations with former clients), except for the provisions about avoiding exploitation.

Underlying Dynamics in Multiple Relationships

Ethics scholars have identified three underlying dynamics of the therapeutic relationship that can help practitioners evaluate the risk of any potential boundary crossing: The professional has a fiduciary relationship to honor promises to the client, to be sensitive to their power over the client, and to be aware of the client's emotional vulnerability during treatment. These dynamics affect the potential for client benefit in such relationships.

The Fiduciary Obligation

Sonne (1994) focuses on the first dynamic, the *fiduciary relationship* between a mental health professional and client. The term *fiduciary relationship* derives from legal sources and means that the counselor's primary obligation is to promote the client's well-being. A counselor who fails in this responsibility is violating the most fundamental covenant with the client. Multiple relationships imply that the counselor is vulnerable to other interests that compete with promoting the welfare of the client and thus usually are contradictory to the fiduciary responsibility. Using the case of Alberto again, he may have difficulty placing the well-being of the adolescent client above the wishes of the client's father, who is the boss of Alberto's wife. Or Alberto may wish so much to impress the boss with his therapeutic skill that the therapy becomes more of a display of Alberto's therapeutic talents than a treatment of the boy's panic attacks. In a particularly problematic scenario, Alberto's concern about his wife's future employment may cause him to neglect to report to authorities the father's physical abuse of the boy. In all three instances, the counselor is neglecting his fiduciary responsibility.

Simon (1992) describes this dynamic a little differently. He asserts that counselors have a *duty to abstinence* from gratifying self-interests in therapy. This duty means that the only acceptable profit from therapy is the fee paid and the satisfaction received from a client's therapeutic gains. This obligation to abstain is incompatible with many multiple relationships. The duty to abstinence is very difficult to uphold when the temptations to serve self-interests are as strong as they are for Alberto if he takes on the son of his wife's boss as a client. More is at stake for Alberto than the income from the therapeutic time or the client's welfare. One could even wonder whether Alberto is accepting this case with the specific goal of enhancing his wife's career. The duty to abstinence is also relevant to the case of Brendan and the cabinetmaker insofar as the counselor is gratifying his need to simplify the search for a qualified cabinetmaker likely to do competent work in his home.

The fiduciary obligation to the client is also connected to another responsibility cited by Simon (1992)—the *duty to neutrality.* He postulates that a therapist is ethically bound to enhance the client's autonomy and independence. Simon also asserts that because autonomy and independence are so fundamental to achieving the client's therapeutic objectives, a counselor should have no other agenda. If Alberto is committed to his wife and her welfare, he has little neutrality about this adolescent client. He may even attempt to interfere with this adolescent's appropriate developmental separation from parents if that separation displeases the parents. Another way to frame the duty to neutrality is to describe it as a duty to objectivity and disinterest in any particular aspect of the client's life other than attaining therapeutic aims. Disinterest and objectivity should not be confused with a cold or uncaring attitude (Pope & Vasquez, 1998); rather they are highly compatible with a warm, empathic approach.

Note that Alberto is at risk for violating his fiduciary duty to this client even if he enters the relationship intending to honor that obligation. For this multiple relationship to be problematic, he need not be self-interested or callous about his client. The intensity of his connection to his wife and the ramifications to them both if counseling does not proceed as the boss intends make objectivity and exclusive devotion to the client's goals extremely difficult. In fact, counselors with good intentions to help people who need therapy are often especially vulnerable to boundary crossings that become boundary violations because they underestimate the limits their other role places on them and overestimate their capacity for objectivity in the face of strong personal interests. In other words, they do not recognize the conflict of interest inherent in the situation.

The Client's Emotional Involvement in Counseling

The second dynamic that makes multiple relationships risky is the client's *emotional involvement with the therapist.* The therapist becomes an important person in the life of the client, at least during their professional contact. Research shows that a substantial part of what makes counseling therapeutic is the human relationship between the people involved (for example, see Lambert, 2003; Hubble, Duncan, & Miller, 1999; Sexton & Whiston, 1994). Client trust, confidence in the therapist's expertise, clarity about the rules and boundaries of the relationship, and mutuality of expectations are all crucial features of successful therapy. When a counselor has another role in a client's life, the client's emotional reaction is confused. Trust may be endangered, the rules for interaction may be obscured, and expectations may diverge. Exposure to the therapist's foibles in other settings may erode the client's confidence. In addition, sharing a very painful or embarrassing secret may be more difficult for a client who has multiple contacts with a counselor. For fear of repercussions, a business executive may avoid disclosing her experiences of mania to a counselor who has invested in that business. The executive may feel she would be jeopardizing the company's future if she disclosed.

In a more practical vein, multiple roles may make the client unsure about when therapy begins and ends and what kinds of conversation are appropriate in which setting. A client who is also a neighbor may feel uncertain about when to bring up particular topics with the counselor or may feel that *every* contact with the counselor is appropriate for therapeutic dialogue. In the latter situation, a client could develop feelings of dependence and a counselor could develop feelings of resentment. It is possible in some circumstances to work out a mutual understanding of what topics are appropriate for counseling and which are not prior to the initiation of the nonprofessional contact. For instance, a counselor who serves on the community's board of United Way with a client can discuss with the client the parameters of their out-of-session contact and is likely to be able to work out a mutually agreeable arrangement.

Theoretic orientation also plays a role in deciding whether nonprofessional contacts are advisable. Therapists who view transference as a central feature of counseling are particularly troubled by this dynamic. They contend that a client cannot work through a transference with a counselor who plays another role in his or her life. Research shows that psychoanalytic therapists tend to view nonerotic multiple relationships as significantly less ethical than their cognitive or humanistic counterparts (Baer & Murdock, 1995).

The Power Imbalance

The third dynamic, the *power differential* between counselor and client, was discussed at length as an important factor in sexual exploitation (Chapter 6). This imbalance may make clients acquiesce to the therapist's wishes even when doing so is at odds with their own desires. This can happen not only in session but also in the second relationship. A supervisee who is also a supervisor's client may defer any disagreement with the therapist/supervisor because the risk of negative fallout is so great. Clients can also fear emotional abandonment (Sonne, 1994) if they offend the therapist in his or her other role. If clients refuse the therapist/friend's social invitation, they may wonder if the therapist will retaliate by missing a session or even terminating therapy. The client's autonomy is jeopardized by the secondary relationship (Kitchener, 1988).

The power difference also contributes to what has been called *role slippage* (Smith & Fitzpatrick, 1995). Role slippage means that the more powerful therapist may loosen the boundaries between the therapeutic relationship and the other relationship. A therapist might end a session with a conversation about a committee issue with a client who also serves on that body. Then, the therapist may suggest that they go out for a cup of coffee after a committee meeting to follow up on an unresolved issue. In this conversation, the therapist may disclose other information about himself to which the client does not know how to respond. Finally, the therapist may take even more time for the committee agenda in later sessions. Under these circumstances, a client may feel reluctant to divert the discussion to more relevant matters. After counselors disclose extensive information about their personal lives, clients may even come to see themselves as caretakers for the counselor (Smith & Fitzpatrick, 1995). Eventually, both the client and the counselor lose sight of the boundaries between the professional and personal relationships, and the focus on the client's therapeutic goal becomes secondary.

Still another aspect of boundary crossings is troublesome: The confidentiality of counseling may be endangered. The chances that a counselor may inadvertently reveal information disclosed in counseling are increased by the outside contact. In the situation described in the last paragraph, the counselor might accidentally repeat to another committee member something the client said within session. Keeping track of what was said in which setting is burdensome. Intentional violations of confidentiality are also more likely when a counselor's self-interest in a multiple relationship has not been met. The scenario of Wilma (the therapist who consulted a former client about her children's college applications) could easily lead to an intentional violation of confidentiality if Wilma were dissatisfied with the advice her former client gave her children. In anger she might disclose to her family something about the former client's reasons for seeking therapy.

The Views of Ethics Scholars

Given the potential for problems, many ethics scholars take a stronger stance than the codes do against boundary crossings, especially those in which one role is therapeutic. Kitchener (1988) and Sonne (1994) argue that mental health professionals cannot accurately predict the degree to which their capacity to practice competently will be compromised or the harm that may come to a client as their relationship progresses. In light of this reality, they contend that most multiple relationships represent "undue risks" that should not be undertaken. Pope and Vasquez (1998) assert that mental health professionals who engage in many kinds of nonsexual multiple relationships are frequently justifying their behavior with reasons that do not stand the test of logic or true commitment to the client's well-being. Using Simon's terms (1991, 1992), close examination of these counselors' motives sometimes reveals that they are acting without neutrality or abstinence. These practitioners seem to underestimate the conflict of interest or to overestimate their own skill. Simon also argues that a multiple relationship places the therapist at significant risk for other boundary violations, in a slippery slope analogy. A therapist who takes on a former business partner as a client may then accept investment advice from another current client, suggest a business relationship with a supervisee, and so forth. When business relationships with clients become common and acceptable, the extension to social and romantic relationships is rather natural. Clear boundaries help the counselor stay focused on the client's welfare and help avert many other problems as well. Essentially, these writers are basing their arguments on the principle of nonmaleficence. Because preventing harm is such an important professional value and because that harm cannot always be foreseen, prudence and devotion to the client's welfare demand that counselors should regularly avoid multiple relationships.

Other scholars take a more liberal stand (for example, see Cottone, 2005; Ebert, 1997; Herlihy & Corey, 1997; Lazarus & Zur, 2002; Moleski & Kiselica, 2005), suggesting that the ethics of multiple relationships need to be examined on a case-by-case basis and need to give more weight to potential client benefits. They contend that counselors can make reasonable assessments when they know about the facts of a particular situation. These scholars also view a rigid posture against multiple relationships as impractical because mental health professionals live in communities and are bound to have contacts with people who may at some point be clients. They also point out the importance of the principle of beneficence and argue that prohibiting multiple relationships may diminish the counselor's opportunity to do good. Finally, they appropriately stress the role of community and cultural variables in determining whether a multiple relationship is ethical. For instance, if at an agency with many Chinese immigrants only one counselor speaks Chinese, that counselor's special skill should be taken into account. That counselor may be well advised to establish somewhat looser boundaries with those Chinese clients because of the unique capacity to do good. Community variables also play a crucial role in a rural practitioner's decision making (see the fuller discussion later in this chapter). Ebert (1997) argues that the language in the APA code makes the association's stance on multiple relationships unenforceable and counterproductive. Lazarus and Zur (2002) contend that the current view of multiple relationships causes professionals to act with too much professional distance and results in less than ideal service to clients. Their views are not widely supported, but they do highlight the need to keep the focus in this debate on promoting the welfare of the client and not on protecting the professional from legal action or ethics complaints.

All scholars seem to agree on at least one point. Regardless of the stance a professional takes on any given multiple relationship, if he or she observes a pattern of involvement in multiple relationships that is more frequent than colleagues working in similar communities, that person should step back and reevaluate the dynamics underlying the behavior. Along with that reassessment should come careful supervision and consultation to unearth the underlying dynamics of the practice.

Questions to Consider in Decision Making

Based on the codes, the literature, and the ethical standards, the following questions present important issues to address in determining whether a particular relationship is ethical:

- Are the role expectations and obligations so divergent as to be incompatible?
- Is promoting the client's welfare the exclusive motivation of the counselor in initiating the professional relationship?
- Can the professional attain the same degree of objectivity about this person and competent practice as is achieved in other professional relationships?
- Is misuse of the professional's power a plausible occurrence?
- Is this multiple relationship a low-risk and high-benefit situation for the other person?
- Is the professional reasonably certain that the multiple relationship will not negatively affect the client's emotional involvement in counseling or capacity to achieve the therapeutic goal?
- Is the multiple relationship unavoidable? Have all other options really been considered?
- If a counselor is embarking on a boundary crossing, has a fully informed consent procedure been undertaken so that the client understands the situation, including its risks and the special arrangements that may be necessary?
- Have both parties evaluated the changes that may result in their other relationships because of the professional contact they are now considering, and are they both comfortable with these changes?
- If the decision were presented to the counselor's respected colleagues (using the "clear-light-of-day" standard), is it likely that they would support the decision to go forward with this multiple relationship?
- Is the counselor willing to document the nonprofessional contact in case notes?
- Has the counselor made provision for continuing consultation and/or supervision to monitor the risks and benefits to the client as the relationship develops?
- Have the client and counselor developed an alternative plan in the event that the relationship does not unfold as they expect so that harm can be remedied?
- Is the counselor committed to diligently following up, so that if problems from the multiple relationship arise after the professional contact has ended, the counselor will be able to provide assistance?

The length of this list of questions demonstrates the exceptional care a counselor must take when considering initiating a boundary crossing.

When the nonsexual multiple relationship under consideration involves a former client, Anderson and Kitchener (1998) present a model of ethical decision making for postcounseling relationships. As part of that model, they recommend the following considerations as well:

- Was the relationship explicitly terminated, were the termination issues successfully processed, and is the length of time since termination sufficient to allow both client and counselor to engage in new behaviors with each other?
- Can the confidentiality of disclosures from counseling be maintained in the postcounseling relationship, and is there a clear arrangement between parties for doing so?
- Does the client understand that by entering into this postcounseling relationship he or she may be relinquishing the opportunity to reenter a counseling relationship with this professional? Does the client understand the other possible ramifications?

- How serious were the former client's problems at the time he or she was receiving services, how strong was the transference, and how successfully were they resolved by the end of treatment? Have the problems resurfaced, or is the client emotionally stable and self-sufficient? Anderson and Kitchener (1998) recommend avoidance of all posttherapy contacts when the client's problems were severe or characterological (p. 94).
- If this postcounseling relationship is avoidable, what is the professional's motivation for entering into it and how seriously have the ramifications for the client been analyzed?

Research Findings: Practitioners' and Consumers' Views

The research on practitioners' attitudes toward nonsexual multiple relationships is not as abundant as the literature on their views about sexual contact, but there is sufficient evidence to draw some reasonable conclusions. First, significant diversity appears in practitioners' opinion about the ethics of this practice. Some call it unquestionably unethical, but others show considerable tolerance for such multiple commitments. For example, in one study 26% of psychologists labeled accepting a client's invitation to a party as unquestionably unethical, whereas 17.5% viewed the same practice as ethical under many circumstances (Pope et al., 1987). Responses to a related question in a study of Canadian counselors showed that 23% indicated that it may be ethical to invite a client to a party or social event (Nigro, 2004a), whereas 77% responded that such an action is never ethical. Second, most studies reveal a greater tolerance for nonsexual multiple relationships than for sexual ones (Lamb, Catanzaro, & Moorman, 2003; Nigro, 2004a). More professionals view some kinds of nonsexual contacts as ethical, and even when viewing them as unethical, they do not see them as such egregious violations as sexual misconduct. For example, four different surveys found that many therapists viewed the practice of becoming friends with a former client as ethical at least sometimes. The percentages endorsing this view ranged from 44% (Borys & Pope, 1989) to 59% (Gibson & Pope, 1993) to 70% (Salisbury & Kinnier, 1996) to 83% (Nigro, 2004a). Moreover, 26% of those surveyed by Borys and Pope admitted to engaging in this practice at least once. Pope et al. (1987) found that a much larger percentage admitted to this practice, a full two-thirds (67%) of their sample. Practitioners responding to surveys have also admitted engaging in several other kinds of multiple relationships. These include the following (Anderson & Kitchener, 1996; Borys & Pope, 1989; Pope et al., 1987; Lamb et al., 1994; Lamb & Catanzaro, 1998; Nigro, 2004b):

- Accepting friends as clients
- Providing therapy to an employee
- Employing a client
- Going into business with current and former clients
- Providing therapy to students and/or supervisees
- Allowing a client to enroll in a course taught by the therapist
- Inviting clients to a party
- Selling goods to a client

The specific percentage acknowledging such activities varies from survey to survey, as does the form of the question asked, but each of the surveys that found at least 2% of those responding endorsed these behaviors. The most common multiple relationship reported was providing therapy to a student or supervisee (29%, Pope et al., 1987) and the least frequent was going into business with a current client (2%, Pope et al., 1987).

Some of the behaviors just listed are clearly prohibited by the ethics codes (such as providing therapy to a supervisee—ACA, 2005, Section F.5.c), but most others fit the category of avoidance unless client benefit is demonstrable. The available evidence does not reveal whether these activities met the criteria established by the codes or fell short of them. Nor does it reveal the outcomes of these relationships for the consumers or therapists involved, unfortunately. These data suggest that mental health professionals may not be acting as cautiously as they should when faced with a prospective multiple relationship. To use a colloquial phrase—one need not be a rocket scientist to realize that providing therapy for a friend or employee has a high probability of clouding one's objectivity, impairing one's judgment, or impeding the progress of therapy—each of which harms the client.

Client and consumer attitudes toward multiple relationships are also ambivalent. Claiborn, Berberoglo, Nerison, and Somberg (1994) found that former psychotherapy clients expressed more reluctance about multiple relationship situations than about confidentiality or informed consent issues. Pulakos (1994) reported contradictory findings, with her small sample seeking more reaction from their therapists when they encountered their therapists outside of sessions. In a qualitative study of clients who become friends with their therapists during or after therapy, Gibb (2005) reported that clients who experienced negative outcomes from the multiple relationship also rated the harm they suffered as "devastating," and even those who did not regret establishing the friendship reported many negative reactions such as pain, confusion, awkwardness, and loss. Even this small and preliminary body of research underscores the need for professionals to use caution in entertaining multiple relationships and to consult extensively with clients and colleagues before their initiation and to maintain those lines of communication during the nonprofessional contact.

Accepting Gifts from Clients

Clients sometimes bring presents to their counselors. The urge to give gifts can be motivated by a number of different factors. Some clients are driven by a belief that gifts may gain them special status in their counselors' eyes or otherwise help maintain good service. For others, the action is connected to the very problems that sparked their decision to enter counseling. For instance, clients with low self-esteem may perceive gifts as the path to keep the counselor interested in them because they believe themselves to have little intrinsic value. A few clients may even attempt to use gifts as bribes for a positive report or a special favor. Still others wish to bestow a token of their appreciation for the gift that counseling has been to them or to ease the sadness of termination by leaving something from them with their counselor as they depart. Consequently, the ethics of accepting a gift from a client depends substantially on the circumstances under which it was offered. (It also depends on the attitude of and impact on its recipient.) The language in the current ACA Code captures the cultural and clinical issues in accepting gifts from clients.

ACA *Codes of Ethics,* Section A.10.e: Receiving Gifts

Counselors understand the challenges of accepting gifts from clients and recognize that in some cultures, small gifts are a token of respect and showing gratitude. When determining whether or not to accept a gift from clients, counselors take into account the therapeutic relationship, the monetary value of the gift, a client's motivation for giving the gift, and the counselor's motivation for wanting or declining the gift.

The APA code does not explicitly mention this topic, but its standards prohibiting exploitation and involvement in conflicts of interest indirectly address this issue.

When gifts are a "quid pro quo" for better or special service, or are a manifestation of the client's dysfunction, the professional probably should not accept them. Taking them implies, in the first case, that the counselor can be manipulated (and thus undermines trust and devotion to promoting client welfare) and in the second case, it suggests that the counselor agrees with the client's distorted self-assessment or view of relationships (and thereby inhibits therapeutic progress). However, when a present represents a token of appreciation for a successful therapeutic experience or a common cultural ritual (such as sharing holiday cookies in December), it may be ethical to receive it. Specifically, accepting a gift is more likely to be ethical if *all* the following criteria are met:

- It promotes rather than endangers the client's welfare.
- It does not compromise the therapist's objectivity or capacity to provide competent service in the future.
- It is a token of appreciation consistent with the client's cultural norms and with a small monetary value.
- It is a rare event in counseling rather than recurrent practice.

The definition of what is expensive varies from person to person and from decade to decade. Research seems to indicate some consistency in the way mental health professionals define a "token gift." Practicing psychologists, social workers, and counselors seem to believe that a value of approximately no more than $20 is the limit for what is ethical (Borys & Pope, 1989; Gibson & Pope, 1993; Nigro, 2004a). When clients want to bestow more elaborate gifts on their therapists, that desire may be "grist for the therapeutic mill" that the two parties should discuss in session. When a client seems insistent on giving a valuable gift as a symbol of the tremendously positive impact that counseling has had on his or her life, a compromise can sometimes be reached by having the client make an anonymous contribution to a charity in the name of the agency. The latter option seems prudent to consider only at the point of a successful termination and only after a full airing of the impact of the gift on the professional relationship and on the profession if the gift becomes known. An expensive present should not be accepted by an individual counselor because it poses such a high risk of reducing the counselor's objectivity. To expect counselors to be totally unaffected by an elaborate gift is to deny their humanity. It is for this reason the counselor described in the opening section of this chapter should not accept Roberta's gift of a theater subscription. Although a few hundred dollars represents little more than a token to this client, it probably carries more meaning to Dominique. The counselor would be unlikely to be able to work objectively with Roberta in the future because of the past largesse. Moreover, if another wealthy client came her way after Roberta, the counselor might be distracted by thoughts about the possibility of other such presents at termination. Instead of taking the tickets, Dominique could suggest that Roberta donate the tickets to a charity or to a school for the arts as an incentive for drama students. The counselor should simultaneously express to the client that the therapeutic change in her client is all the reward she needs and should make sure that before she leaves, Roberta fully understands Dominique's rationale for refusing the gift.

Even token gifts, such as a homemade loaf of bread or flowers from a client's garden, should not become a recurrent event. If it does, the practice ought to be discussed in the session. Perhaps the client brings presents because it is the only way she knows to express emotional connection. If so, helping the client learn alternative ways to express closeness can become an explicit therapeutic goal. A recurrent gift is also a distraction for the counselor. A counselor might start to look forward to that loaf of fresh bread each week and then be disappointed when the client did not produce one. Such a motivation to see a client is inconsistent with the principle of neutrality and objectivity.

Counselors who are tempted to conclude that the simplest path is to refuse all client gifts without exception should be cautious in taking such a stance. In some cultural groups, gifts are important interpersonal rituals. For these clients, an absolute refusal of all gifts might be counterproductive. Similarly, for clients who wish to present a small token at successful termination of an intense counseling relationship, the refusal to graciously receive a small present may interrupt a positive resolution of the relationship, especially if the client had no warning that gift giving might be inappropriate.

Herlihy and Corey (1997) recommend that the issue of gift giving be included in a professional disclosure statement or brought up during the informed consent process early in counseling so that no one ends up embarrassed, confused, or angry over an inappropriate present. They go on to suggest that a policy be written to discourage the practice. With such a policy clients will then understand both the counselor's interpretation of the practice and the rationale underlying it long before they are likely to want to bring the counselor a present. Moreover, if the counselor's policy to dissuade clients from gift giving conflicts with the client's cultural tradition, the two can then discuss this discrepancy at an early stage. In short, clarifying policy at an early stage can prevent later misunderstandings. If Roberta had known that Dominique might not accept her gift, she might have saved herself both the cost of the tickets and the distress of their refusal at what was otherwise a very positive final counseling session.

However, discussing gift giving early in therapy may present problems. Adding one more item to the already long list of topics to discuss early in the informed consent process may make that process even more burdensome. The client may misinterpret the policy and assume that token gifts *ought* to be given. In some cultural contexts in which gifts are an important aspect of interpersonal relationships, this policy would be vulnerable to misinterpretation. Thus, counselors ought to consider all the implications of such a policy before mandating it for all clients.

Multiple Relationships and Rural or Small Community Practice

Mental health practitioners who work in large metropolitan areas can rather easily avoid many forms of multiple relationships. The pool of potential clients from whom they can build their practices is large, so there is little economic incentive to engage in a multiple relationship. They can work in a different part of the city from their home to prevent contacts with clients, students, or supervisees in civic, religious, or social settings. In addition, urban practitioners have many referral sources for people they ought not to take on as clients and they can be confident that the clients they decline to accept will still receive competent professional service. Urban counselors also have the benefit of the relative anonymity of the large city. Few people in the community know or care about their occupation. If they accidentally meet their clients in other settings, neither party has to worry that a brief conversation would reveal to the community their professional contact.

In contrast, rural counselors have dramatically different experiences because of both the demographics of their communities and their cultural norms. Their pool of potential clients is smaller; their referral sources are more limited; and the chances of preexisting, concurrent, or subsequent connections with clients are significantly greater. A smaller population base from which to draw clients can mean that turning away clients may be a financial hardship for counselors. Competent referral sources are often distant and inaccessible by public transportation, so clients' access to mental health care is more restricted when local practitioners decline to see them. Unless rural counselors refrain from joining any social, religious, or civic organizations and commute long distances to the workplace, they cannot easily avoid additional contacts with clients (Campbell & Gordon, 2003; Schank & Skovholt, 1997). Pearson and Piazza (1997) refer to these as *circumstantial multiple relationships.* Moreover, in a small community many people know the counselor's occupation and are acquainted with the people with whom the counselor may interact. As Jennings (1992) points out, "Life in the city is characterized by anonymity; whereas life in rural areas is characterized by an unusual degree of openness—one's behavior, and the behavior of one's family are not only open to public scrutiny, but become favorite topics of community discussion" (p. 94). Thus the avoidance of multiple relationships is more complex for rural practitioners. Rural counselors often get requests to work with people with whom.they are acquainted or with whom they have seen at community, religious, or social functions. Even if the counselor is unfamiliar with a particular person, he or she may know a family member and may be privy to information about the client from those other people (Gates & Speare, 1990; Hargrove, 1982). Sobel (1992) points out that multiple-relationship complications arise when the secretary or others who work for the counselor have connections with prospective clients. Rural practitioners also know that when professional contact ends, they are likely to have at least intermittent contact with the client afterward. Their children may have the same teacher, they may both volunteer for the United Way drive, or they may bump into each other waiting at the dentist's office. Because they drive the same streets all the time, they may even be involved in the same traffic accident at some point.

Research by Horst (1989) supports these claims. In her study of psychologists from urban and rural communities in Minnesota, she found significantly more overlapping relationships between rural practitioners and their clients. Rural psychologists had more out-of-session contact and experienced more after-termination contact. Most of the out-of-session contact was through involvement in joint large organizations or in accidental meetings in stores or other community settings. Rural practitioners were not significantly more likely to engage in multiple relationships that carried with them high risks of complications, however. For example, Horst found no difference between the rates at which urban and rural psychologists indicated they had accepted friends or employees as clients.

Public perception of multiple relationships also differs in rural places. People in cities expect that the professionals who serve them will be strangers; they seem to prefer that arrangement. Rural dwellers tend to take the opposite stance because they are so accustomed to interacting with familiar people and feel strong community ties. Thus they may be more likely to seek out a familiar counselor rather than a stranger (Helbok, 2003). The challenge for the rural practitioners, then, is to serve the mental health needs of the community without causing undue harm to clients with whom they have at least peripheral connections. In spite of stereotypes of idyllic rural life, research shows that residents of rural America experience the same levels of trauma, anxiety, and depression as their urban counterparts and are at greater risk for poverty and health problems (Roberts, Battaglia, & Epstein, 1999).

Of course, one must be careful not to characterize the contrasts among urban, suburban, and rural settings too extremely. Sometimes clients in suburbs and cities choose a particular therapist because he or she is part of a "shared community" with a client, participating in the same civic organization, social action group, or ethnic or cultural minority (Adelman & Barrett, 1990). Mental health professionals in the military and university counseling centers and those who work with individuals with particular issues or experiences such as people who are deaf or clients who are gay, lesbian, bisexual, or transgender also experience many of the same problems with multiple relationships in communities with limited access to alternative services (Bleiberg & Baron, 2004; Guttman, 2005; Johnson, Ralph, & Johnson, 2005; Kessler & Waehler, 2005). Consequently, practitioners in these settings can be as familiar with the dilemma of overlapping connections as their rural counterparts. Kessler and Waehler (2005) present a case study of the ethical and clinical dilemmas a professional faced and worked to resolve when treating a client from a shared community. Still, counselors in larger population areas tend to have more referral sources and more opportunities for consultation and supervision than those in small towns.

Along with the case of the bakery clerk presented in the opening section of this chapter, the following examples of ethical dilemmas derive from the author's brief experience as the only psychologist in a community of 8000 people. In each instance, the author had to assess whether the problems that might accrue from the multiple relationship or circumstantial contact might reasonably harm clients or otherwise prevent them from benefiting from therapy. At that time the nearest referral sources were at least 30 miles away and inaccessible by public transportation.

- A woman who seeks counseling because of grief over her father's death works in the same office as the psychologist's husband. The husband is not the direct supervisor, but he is chief executive officer of the organization.
- A woman referred to the psychologist by her family physician for treatment of a panic disorder is the mother-in-law of the psychologist's neighbor. The psychologist sees this neighbor regularly, although they are acquaintances rather than friends. The woman does not drive a car.
- The psychologist is asked to give a deposition in a custody matter and finds when she goes to the hearing that the attorney doing the deposing is the estranged husband of a current client.
- The children of the psychologist and of her client attend the same day care center. In fact, on the day of the client's weekly appointment, both people drive directly from her office to pick up their children at day care. It is the only day care center in town, and the client's work schedule does not permit changing the time of her counseling appointment.
- The accountant with whom the psychologist has done business is referred to her for counseling after his hospitalization for a brief psychotic episode.

Jennings (1992) provides other vivid examples of recurring multiple-relationship problems in rural areas. In one case, he was involved in a court case to give expert testimony and discovered when he entered the courtroom that the judge and three of the jurors had been clients in his private practice. In a second case, his teenage son had asked a girl to the prom whose parents were in therapy with Jennings. The boy, of course, had no knowledge of his father's connection to the family. All these cases highlight the close interconnections of people's lives in rural communities. They also illustrate the kind of harm an unscrupulous counselor might inflict on clients. Participants in other research studies identify similar problems in rural practice (for example, see Schank and Skovholt, 1997).

Jennings (1992) and Hargrove (1986) have argued that the professions have not paid enough attention to the special concerns of rural practitioners and that ethical standards derive too heavily from an urban culture. The most recent versions of the codes show more responsiveness to this criticism with the clear statement that some kinds of multiple relationships are not unethical. Jennings offers additional guidelines to help the rural counselor act ethically. The first is to reject the notion that multiple relationships are avoidable in a rural setting. The price of rejecting all such contacts would be eliminating mental health services for many consumers. Traveling long distances to referral sources that the client is likely to distrust as "strangers" is not a viable option for most people. The decision about whether to accept a client must be made with the issue of accessibility of alternative services prominently in mind. Jennings recommends that those who work in rural settings make a real commitment to the fundamental ethical values of the profession and develop a generous capacity for tolerating ambiguity in their relationships. In his judgment, a mental health professional who is unequipped for such tolerance would be better suited to an urban climate. Research by Lear (1997) reveals that rural psychologists also tend to use the degree of emotional vulnerability of the client as additional consideration in their decision to enter or refuse a multiple relationship. Coyle (1999) recommends that the professional hypothesize about the "worst case scenario," and Campbell and Gordon (2003) advise consultation with colleagues prior to engaging in the professional relationship. Both activities can assist the professional in making an objective decision and changing any variables in his or her control to minimize the potential for a negative outcome.

Jennings also emphasizes the value of using extensive informed consent procedures when embarking on a therapeutic relationship with a client one knows from another interaction. Both parties should understand what the other expects when they meet in another setting. This aspect is especially important given the public awareness of the counselor's position. By merely addressing a person by name in the supermarket, a counselor could be perceived as signaling to other shoppers that the person is in counseling. Craig (quoted in Sleek, 1994) asserts that "When someone is parked in front of a psychologist's office, everybody in town knows it" (p. 27). Jennings also implies that ingenuity is an important asset for rural counselors in designing interventions to meet needs without putting clients at risk. His next recommendation is to use multiple relationship issues as "grist for the therapeutic mill." The client's feelings after encountering the therapist at a social function should be openly discussed, as should the client's interest in aspects of the therapist's life that are known in the community.

When the prospective multiple relationship is closer or more intense, Jennings suggests that "the psychological intervention is limited in direct proportion to the intensity of the interpersonal relationship" (p. 100). In other words, Jennings view is that the rural mental health professional ought to offer only brief, less intense services to those with stronger business, social, or community ties to the counselor and to reserve long-term counseling for people with whom outside connections are nonexistent or peripheral. A school psychologist in a rural community, for example, might go forward with an evaluation of a learning disorder in her physician's child, but he or she would arrange for a referral for ongoing counseling services to help the child and the family cope with the disorder. Effant (quoted in Sleek, 1994) takes a different view of the problem of such multiple relationships, cautioning professionals about unanticipated complications. "Too many psychologists in smaller communities think they can handle multiple relationships, and that their clients can, too. It always complicates the relationship. The psychologist needs to be very humble about how different the process of therapy is going to be because of it" (p. 27).

In short, the rural practitioner should be especially sensitive to the ethics of multiple relationships. Jennings calls this a more demanding standard than applies to urban professionals. Counselors need to continually balance the obligation to serve the public's mental health needs against the risk of harm and should seek out consultation to ensure that the difficult judgments necessitated by the environment are well founded.

The Ethics of Barter

The current professional codes allow bartering under some circumstances.

APA *Ethical Principles,* Section 6.05: Barter with Clients/Patients

Barter is the acceptance of goods, services, or other non-monetary remuneration from clients/patients in return for psychological services. Psychologists may barter only if (1) it is not clinically contraindicated, and (2) the resulting arrangement is not exploitative.

ACA *Ethics Code,* Section A.10.d: Bartering

Counselors may barter only if the relationship is not exploitive or harmful and does not place the counselor in an unfair advantage, if such arrangements are an accepted practice among professionals in the community. Counselors consider the cultural implications of bartering and discuss relevant concerns with clients and document such agreements in a clear written contract.

The language here limits bartering because without restrictions, the practice can be exploitive. The professional contact is jeopardized in many of the same ways as a multiple relationship. The client's power to complain about working conditions or address problems in the service arrangement is limited. If the client voices discontent with the barter, will he or she then worry that the counselor will end counseling? In addition, the emotional connections between the people get confused. For clients with some kinds of emotional problems, this confusion can stop or reverse therapeutic gains. For this reason, the APA code specifies the absence of clinical contraindications as one precondition for bartering to be allowed. Moreover, the progress of therapy may be endangered if the counselor's neutrality is compromised by his or her investment in the service the client is providing. For instance, if a client is trading carpentry services for therapy and begins to recover from his depression before the counselor's deck is completed, the counselor may be tempted to prolong counseling to meet her own needs or simply fail to recognize the client's progress because it conflicts with her own agenda. The client may delay or hasten work on the deck, depending on his evaluation of therapeutic progress. Conversely, professional judgment may be impaired if the client has a major setback after the deck is completed. The counselor may provide less diligent care if no remuneration is possible or may be inclined to terminate therapy sooner than appropriate. One final problem is the difference in cost between the services. The services clients usually can provide have a lower monetary value than counseling, so that when counseling is lengthy, the client may become like an indentured servant to the therapist, working long hours to pay off the accumulated debt (Kitchener & Harding, 1990; Keith-Spiegel & Koocher, 1998).

Bartering goods is somewhat less complicated because a market value for a good can be independently established, but even such arrangements can be exploitive. A client trading a piece of sculpture for sessions may believe the art has been undervalued and then feel cheated and resentful. Or the counselor may get salmonella poisoning from farm eggs bartered for treatment and feel poorly served by the arrangement. One final reason makes this practice risky. The legal recourse usually available to parties dissatisfied with a business transaction is not easily available to either client or counselor. A counselor who brought a client to small claims court would be violating confidentiality, and a client taking the same action would be risking disclosure of counseling information.

The issues just presented seem to lead to the conclusion that barter is simply not worth the trouble it can cause for both counselor and client. That generalization is mostly true. However, there are two important reasons not to eliminate the possibility of bartering altogether. Barter can have value in making professional services accessible to those whose financial resources are limited. Some people refuse to accept free services and see them as an affront to their dignity, but they are willing to offer a barter arrangement. For clients who reject the argument that they have already paid for "free" services through their taxes, barter may be an important option (Canter et al., 1994). Others (Pope & Vasquez, 1998) argue that therapists should be careful about the frequency with which they claim that pro bono arrangements are not feasible as an alternative to barter, cautioning that self-interest and lack of ingenuity may be the real motivations for accepting barter in some situations. Second, in rural communities and some cultural groups barter is a common practice and refusing to engage in it would run counter to cultural norms and restrict access to care (Canter et al., 1994; Helbok, 2003), as noted in the ACA code on this matter.

Sonne (1994) presents a divergent view, arguing that there is little evidence that barter is a common practice. Sleek (1994) echoes this view, suggesting that its prevalence has faded considerably even in rural environments in recent years. Fewer than 10% of psychologists have accepted goods or services for payment more than rarely in their practice (Borys & Pope, 1989; Pope et al., 1987). Sonne also points out the contradiction between the code and some state regulations. California (California Department of Consumer Affairs, 1997) prohibits all forms of bartering in therapy, and some malpractice insurers exclude claims arising from a bartering arrangement (Sonne, 1994). She contends that these bodies are judging the problems more realistically. In any case, professionals who are considering barter with a client should assess not only their compliance with the code but also the stance of their state licensing board and their liability insurer.

As with any other ethical issue, a practitioner should consult with other professionals and carefully scrutinize one's own motivation before proceeding with a bartering arrangement. One should also scrupulously document that process, the informed consent procedures, and the progress of therapy. Although only the counseling code requires a written contract for bartering, using such a document would be prudent for other mental health professionals. That document should include the details of the barter and an alternative to the barter should either party become dissatisfied with the agreement at a later point. The designation of a mediator for any disputes should also be included in that document.

It is interesting that counselors and psychologists seem divided on the issue of whether barter can be ethical. Research shows that psychologists tend to view the practice as rarely ethical (for example, see Baer & Murdock, 1995), but counselors view it more positively. In fact, Gibson and Pope (1993) found that slightly more than half (53%) the counselors they surveyed rated barter for services ethically acceptable and 63% viewed bartering goods as ethical. Canadian counselors hold similar views; Nigro (2004a) found that 61% rated bartering as ethical at least sometimes.

Cases Reexamined

Two of the cases from the opening section of the chapter are now analyzed using the codes and related literature.

Roxanne and Li Qing

In this case, the client, Li Qing, innocently began attending the same church that her counselor, Roxanne, frequents. When her counselor discovered the coincidence, she disclosed her membership to the client and initiated a discussion of the issue in a counseling session.

Because Li Qing is a current client, the remarks in the codes clearly apply. Roxanne has a responsibility to avoid exploiting the client's trust and misusing her influence or otherwise risking harm to the client. Now Roxanne must decide whether their attendance at the same church is likely to result in any of those negative outcomes. Too little information is given to determine whether bringing the topic up for discussion in session is a wise idea. Its wisdom depends largely on the client's emotional stability and particular problems, about which the case description doesn't give enough information. It also depends on the capacity of the counselor to respond in an appropriate way immediately after being surprised by this revelation. After all, there is no urgency to deal with this topic at this juncture. As long as the counselor can hold another session before the next church service, or refrain from church attendance until she analyzes the problem and decides whether to discuss it with her client, the topic can be postponed.

Several other factors should be considered before the counselor makes a judgment about the appropriateness of continued mutual participation in the church. The size and sense of community in the congregation is important. In a large congregation with multiple services, the two people could arrange not to attend functions simultaneously. A small congregation with one weekly service and strong sense of community would present more complications for both parties. In the latter circumstance, one option for the counselor would be to temporarily suspend her churchgoing until counseling with this client was terminated. Another alternative would be to attend services at a different church for the same period. One alternative seems clearly unethical—to ask the client to choose another church. Li Qing's choice of this congregation seemed to be driven by her therapeutic goals and made without knowledge of the counselor's affiliation. Suggesting that the client select another church might impede future progress and be especially difficult for a shy client.

If, in the end, both parties decided that this multiple connection is appropriate and workable, they would need to follow the code to be sure the client's best interests were protected,

including the practical management of times when they met at church function
multiple relationship is not judged problematic, Roxanne should avoid extens
contact with her client at church. For example, she ought not to co-chair a com
her client or spend every social hour after church in conversation with Li Qing
actions at church should be cordial, brief, and not too frequent, at least for the ?
the professional relationship. To answer questions from other church members who wonder
how they became acquainted, they also should prepare a response that does not include di-
vulging their professional relationship. These arrangements should be documented, and
Roxanne should obtain ongoing case supervision to ensure the continuation of objective,
competent care. The therapist has a responsibility to make a judgment about the advisability
of this multiple relationship independent of her client's current expressions about the matter. The client may not foresee the potential problems, may have motives for desiring personal contact that would be counterproductive to real change, or may simply be mouthing
words she believes the counselor wants to hear. The client's expressed feelings should be taken
into account, of course, but they should not be the only factor considered. The burden to
analyze all the considerations falls on the shoulders of the counselor, not the client.

Theodore and the Teacher's Request

Theodore, the parent of an elementary school child, is approached by his son's teacher (Mr.
Goodheart) to provide counseling for a depressed friend of his. Theodore responds by giving
the teacher his business card and suggesting he tell her friend to call to set up an appointment.

Does Theodore's connection through this prospective client's friend make this a multiple
relationship to be avoided? Because the case deals with a prospective client, it undoubtedly
falls within the purview of the codes. The crucial issue is whether his connection to the
teacher will impair his judgment, impede the progress of therapy, or affect the client's capacity to relate to Theodore or to otherwise benefit from therapy. There is relatively little chance
that this distant a connection will cause such problems, but more information is needed to
make a definitive judgment. At a minimum, Theodore ought to have asked Mr. Goodheart
some questions about his relationship with this person and about his understanding of the
rules of confidentiality should the friend accept a referral. The nature of the connection between the prospective client and the teacher is not clearly stated. The term *friend* has a wide
range of meanings. This man could be someone the teacher is simply acquainted with, or it
could be his life partner. The latter circumstance would make the multiple relationship more
problematic because Mr. Goodheart would have a very big stake in the progress and outcome of counseling and may even need to be involved in joint counseling sessions to resolve
relationship difficulties. In that case, the multiple-relationship risks become much more likely.
Even if the connection between the teacher and his friend is less intense, the counselor would
have an obligation to clarify to all parties involved the boundaries between contacts and to
reassure the client about the confidentiality of counseling material.

Next a responsible resolution of this case also requires more information about the
child and the family's frequency of contact with the teacher. If Theodore's son is an ordinary child whose parents need not be closely involved with his school, that circumstance
would argue for the choice Theodore made, but if the child's characteristics require the
family to have intense, frequent, or contentious contact with school personnel, that would
argue for a more cautious approach. In the latter circumstance, Theodore would be advised
to go forward with the referral only if the relationship between the teacher and the
prospective client is not especially close.

Finally, because of the potential complications, the prospective client may be reluctant to
enter counseling with a person his friend knows or may simply wish to see a different counselor. Perhaps he knows he would wish to discuss counseling sessions with Mr. Goodheart but
would hesitate if he chose Theodore as his counselor, or perhaps he would rather see a female

counselor or someone who is older. In other words, because Theodore cannot anticipate the client's preferences and because his ultimate commitment should be to the client's welfare rather than his own financial gain, Theodore's ideal action would be to give the teacher one or two other names of competent professionals, even if he also provides his own card.

SUMMARY

Effective, beneficial counseling and psychotherapy depend on the therapist's ability to provide objectivity and single-minded commitment to the client's welfare. It also depends on the client's ability to trust the professional. Implicit in that trust is confidence in the counselor's selfless interest in the client and a sense of emotional closeness to the professional. When a professional has an additional personal or professional relationship with a client, objectivity, selfless commitment to the client, and client trust are all endangered to some degree. In other words, when a practitioner is both friend and researcher or therapist and teacher, the professional is putting himself or herself in a conflict-of-interest situation. Both parties in the professional relationship may be hampered in reaching their therapeutic goals by the existence and demands of the other relationship. Having more than one relationship with a person with whom there is or has been a professional relationship is called a *multiple relationship* or *nonprofessional interaction*. The terms *boundary crossing* and *boundary violation* are also used, the former to designate multiple relationships at low risk for harm to clients and the latter to identify high-risk relationships.

The ethical difficulties of multiple relationships are most apparent in therapeutic relationships, but they are often inappropriate in other forms of professional contact as well. Nonsexual multiple relationships with clients seem to occur more frequently than sexual relationships, according to researchers. The professions' ethics codes do not universally endorse multiple relationships, but their provisions have become less restrictive in recent years and thereby place a greater burden on the professional to use good ethical judgment. The criterion on which they base this judgment is the counselor's duty to promote the client's welfare without undue risk of harm. Multiple connections with clients can impair counselor objectivity, interfere with therapeutic progress, and affect the client's emotional connection to the counselor. They also can intensify the power difference between counselor and client and can result in exploitation of clients. Multiple relationships have these effects partly because the obligations and expectations from different roles are often inherently incompatible. The more divergent the obligations of two roles, the more likely the multiple relationship will be unethical.

Because not all multiple relationships can be avoided, especially in rural settings, counselors need to examine carefully whether to start a particular multiple relationship. Clients' access to alternative competent care ought to be considered, along with cultural variables and the potential for an individual to benefit from counseling despite the multiple connection. Generally, however, the goal of the mental health professional should be to prevent risk (Sonne, 1994). High-risk relationships should not be initiated even if they have the potential to do good. If the relationship cannot be avoided, the counselor should discuss the implications and risks of the situation with the client and then carefully document both that discussion and the subsequent progress of counseling. The counselor should seek expert supervision and develop an alternative plan in the event of unforeseen complications. If counselors find themselves frequently engaging in multiple relationships, they need to examine their motivation and become more creative in finding alternative access to care for the clients involved.

Bartering—trading goods or services instead of money for counseling—is also a practice discouraged by the ethics codes, but it is not forbidden. A professional who is entertaining a bartering relationship with a mental health client should read the professions' codes carefully and should consult his or her state laws and regulations. Some states forbid the practice, and some professional liability insurers exclude claims resulting from a bartering arrangement.

CASES FOR DISCUSSION

Portia is a counselor educator with a small private practice. A professor in the history department at the same university calls Portia's practice to ask if she could schedule a counseling appointment. Portia knows this woman from campus and from serving together on the faculty senate. Portia suggests that the history professor make an appointment with her partner instead. Despite receiving an explanation of the reasons why Portia would prefer to have the prospective client see her partner instead, the historian is angered by the action and refuses to make an appointment. Did Portia act appropriately, or was she too legalistic in her interpretation of the multiple relationship provisions of the code?

Six months after Deborah, a counselor, successfully terminated counseling with a musician client she treated for social anxiety, this client sends her a ticket to the orchestra's next performance, indicating that he remembers Deborah is fond of the pieces the orchestra will be playing that night. Deborah attends and approaches the musician after the concert to thank him for the ticket. He asks Deborah to attend a postperformance party with him and his wife. Deborah agrees. Within a few months the three become friends who frequently attend music events together. In establishing a social relationship with a client 6 months after therapy, did Deborah violate the multiple relationship provision of the ACA code? Did she violate any other provision? What do you see as the ethical risks and benefits, if any, of Deborah's actions?

DISCUSSION QUESTIONS

1. Why do you think the codes of ethics are silent on the issue of nonsexual multiple relationships with former clients? Do you think they should take a stand on this topic, and if so, what position do you think best?
2. Research shows a great diversity in professionals' opinions about the ethics of nonsexual multiple relationships, in contrast to their views of sexual contact with clients. What do you think accounts for this diversity? Do you think it is healthy?
3. Do you agree with the standards written into the codes of ethics about nonsexual multiple relationships? Would you recommend stronger or more lenient wording? Why?
4. Friends, social acquaintances, and business associates frequently ask counselors to accept them as clients. Sometimes counselors do, taking the view that their preexisting knowledge of the client can facilitate therapeutic progress. They believe that in such rela-

tionships, trust occurs more easily and insight happens more quickly. Is their position justifiable? How would you respond to a colleague who made such an argument?
5. Should bartering of services be distinguished from bartering for goods in the ethics codes? Is this a real distinction or a semantic one? What would you describe as an ideal standard on this issue?
6. What stance do you think you will take on accepting gifts from clients? Do you agree that this topic should be included in informed consent? How would you feel if your counselor initiated this kind of discussion at that point in the process?
7. Given the literature on accepting gifts from clients, how would you evaluate the ethics of counselor gifts to clients, for example, at termination?
8. How would you evaluate the behavior of the other mental health professionals mentioned in the opening section of this chapter but not reviewed yet?

RECOMMENDED READINGS

Anderson, S. K., & Kitchener, K. S. (1996). Nonromantic, nonsexual posttherapy relationships between psychologists and former clients: An exploratory study of critical incidents. *Professional Psychology: Research and Practice, 27,* 59–66.

Borys, D. S., & Pope, K. S. (1989). Multiple relationships between therapist and client: A national study of psychologists, psychiatrists and social workers. *Professional Psychology: Research and Practice, 20,* 283–293.

Helbok, C. M. (2003). The practice of psychology in rural communities: Potential ethical dilemmas. *Ethics and Behavior, 13,* 367–384.

Herlihy, B., & Corey, G. (1997). *Boundary issues in counseling.* Alexandria, VA: American Counseling Association.

Herlihy, B., & Watson, Z. E. (2003). Ethical issues and multicultural competence in counseling. In F. D. Harper & J. McFadden (Eds.), *Culture and counseling: New approaches* (pp. 363–378). Needham Heights, MA: Allyn & Bacon.

Simon, R. I. (1992). Treatment of boundary violations: Clinical, ethical and legal considerations. *Bulletin of the American Academy of Psychiatry and the Law, 20,* 269–288.

Chapter 8

Group and Family Counseling
Unique Ethical Responsibilities

The fundamental ethical values and standards that guide individual counseling and psychotherapy are also at the core of group and family interventions. However, four features distinguish the ethical practice of group and family counseling. First, the client is encouraged to disclose personal information not only to a professional but also to other participants who are not mental health professionals. Under these circumstances, admitting personal secrets feels (and is) riskier. The others to whom this personal information is revealed may not respond sympathetically, may be judgmental, or may use that information in ways that are counterproductive to the client. Because only the professional can be held accountable for misusing personal disclosures, a client must rely on the good intentions of other members of the group to act responsibly. Both a high level of trust of others and a strong expectation of benefit from such disclosures are required for active participation in a group. In family therapy, the audience to whom a client discloses personal information is obviously quite familiar, but that familiarity does not necessarily reduce the risk for the participant. Indeed, family members have more opportunity to misuse that information than do strangers in a group.

Second, the dynamics of therapeutic change are different in multiple-person therapies. In individual counseling, the relationship between the two parties, coupled with the interventions used, results in therapeutic change. In group and family treatment, effectiveness is based largely on the interdependence that develops among all participants (Lakin, 1994; Yalom, 1995). Therapeutic change stems from the help and support group members give each other as much as from the activities of the group leader (Gladding, 2002; Morran, Stockton, & Bond, 1991). Usually, feedback from peers in a group has significant impact on members (Corey & Corey, 2003; Klontz, 2004). Given this facet of therapy, group and family therapists have a duty to help clients develop an interdependence that empowers rather than weakens them. The skills and ethical sensitivities necessary for this task differ substantially from those required by individual counseling.

Third, a group leader has less control over events that take place during or between sessions. The professional cannot always predict how participants will respond to other members, nor can he or she even be aware of all the interactions among members. The dynamics of this phenomenon are especially visible in family therapy where clients have continuous contact with each other, but they are no less real in group therapy. For example, group members may continue a discussion initiated in a session over coffee afterward or may telephone each other between sessions. Paradoxically, though, this lessening of control does not necessarily result in less power for the counselor. Clients in group therapy can also become excessively dependent on the leader if that counselor manipulates group process to foster such dependency. Family members may fall into the practice of deferring even minor decisions until the counseling session and may use the words and actions of the therapist as the sole influence in arriving at a decision.

Finally, research shows that group and family counseling are powerful interventions, with the capacity for greater good or greater harm than many forms of individual counseling (for example, see Lambert, 2003; Yalom, 1995). Kottler (1994) maintains that the emotional intensity of group therapy in itself makes group treatment more powerful. Moreover, groups and families lend themselves to interventions that may be inherently riskier (Lakin, 1994) than the approaches that dominate individual work. Because interpersonal issues can be resistant to traditional approaches, group and family therapists sometimes seek out innovative interventions to break through blocks to therapeutic gains. This drive to provide therapeutic benefit to these clients is well intentioned, but it must be balanced against the inherent risk in newer, riskier, and less proven techniques. In such situations, the principle of nonmaleficence should take precedence over beneficence.

This chapter examines the implications of these distinct features of group and family counseling on the ethics of practice. It also explores the applicability of the concepts discussed in previous chapters—competence, informed consent, confidentiality, and dual relationships—to multiple-person therapies. Finally, the chapter ends with a brief discussion of the legal issues affecting these modalities.

Group Counseling and Psychotherapy

The American Psychological Association (APA) *Ethical Principles* makes relatively brief references to group counseling and psychotherapy, whereas the American Counseling Association (ACA) code refers to three responsibilities. The first specific requirement for group leaders is to screen prospective members for compatibility with the group, the second is to avoid harm, and the third deals with confidentiality.

ACA *Code of Ethics,* Section A.8: Group Work

a. Screening. Counselors screen prospective group counseling/therapy participants. To the extent possible, counselors select members whose needs and goals are compatible with goals of the group, who will not impede the group process, and whose well-being will not be jeopardized by the group experience.

b. Protecting Clients. In a group setting, counselors take reasonable precautions to protect clients from physical, emotional, or psychological trauma.

B.4.a. Group Work. In group work, counselors clearly explain the importance and parameters of confidentiality for the specific group being entered.

APA *Ethical Principles,* Section 10.03: Group Therapy

When psychologists provide services to several persons in a group setting, they describe at the outset the roles and responsibilities of all parties and the limits of confidentiality.

Ethics scholars have criticized the codes' failure to attend to the many other distinctive features of groups (for example, see Lakin, 1994), but there are other sources of guidance for the practitioner beyond these codes. First, there are three useful documents published by the Association for Specialists in Group Work, (ASGW), a division of ACA. The first identifies a series of "best practices" for group leaders (ASGW, 1998a). (See Appendix C for information to access this code on the Web.) The precepts presented in this document provide extensive advice about specific procedures group counselors should use from the orientation and screening stage of a group to termination and follow-up. It also describes the practitioner's obligations regarding continuing education, referral of clients to other services, and the counselor's responsibility regarding the reporting of unethical behavior. ASGW has also produced *Professional Standards for Training Group Workers* (2000) and *Principles for Diversity-Competent Group Workers* (1998b). Both documents describe in detail the specific skills and knowledge base required for competent group leadership. Many years earlier, APA published standards for therapists of growth groups in 1973, but that document is still useful to those who lead such groups today.

The second type of resource is the body of literature by ethics scholars that comments on how the codes view group treatment (for example, see Corey, Williams, & Moline, 1995; Forrester-Miller, 2002; Klontz, 2004; Williams, 1996), gives in-depth analysis of particular ethical concepts (for example, Davis, 1980), and elaborates on the application of group ethics to certain kinds of groups (for example, see Aubrey & Dougher, 1990; Merta & Sisson, 1991; Ritchie & Huss, 2000). This growing body of research and theory offers the practitioner thoughtful analysis of some of the most complex issues in group work. Taken together, these resources compensate for the omissions in the codes and guide the practitioner to a solid understanding of his or her ethical duties in group settings.

Competence and Group Counseling

Obviously, competent group counseling requires knowledge of group theory, process, and research; successful supervised experience in leading groups; and a diligent attitude toward the work. Competent group leadership is not an automatic consequence of expertise in individual counseling. Effective leadership of a therapeutic group demands a background in this particular modality because of the power of the experience, the vulnerability of the client to harm from both the leader and other participants, and the potential for negative outcomes. The *Professional Standards for the Training of Group Workers* (ASGW, 2000) thoroughly delineates the knowledge base and skills essential for group leadership. It also identifies the special capacities required by the various kinds of therapeutic groups, ranging from task-oriented and psychoeducational groups to long-term psychotherapy groups. ASGW training standards identify the following as the major components of group competence:

- Comprehension of the major kinds of groups and the criteria to be used in assigning clients to membership in each
- Knowledge of the fundamentals of group dynamics and the therapeutic aspects of a group
- Understanding of how the personal characteristics of group leaders affect the group and how professional ethics apply to group situations
- Familiarity with the research on group process and outcome
- Comprehension of group stages and the roles members take on
- Knowledge of the circumstances that make groups beneficial or contraindicated for clients and the criteria for recruiting and screening potential members
- Mastery of current definitions of group work, its purposes, and four major forms
- Appreciation of the role of evaluation in group process

It proceeds to elaborate details of essential skills and minimum levels of supervised experience. The message of these standards is that brief and cursory exposure to group theory and practice is insufficient for competent practice.

Unfortunately, many counselors and therapists fail to monitor their own competence as group leaders. Lakin (1994) decries the casual attitude of many professionals toward the complexities of group process. He labels involvement in group leadership without appropriate competence a serious ethical violation and argues that a group counselor needs a comprehensive understanding of the role of group cohesion in fostering therapeutic progress. Helping the members develop enough cohesion to be beneficial without transforming group cohesion into pressure to conform is a difficult task. Inadequately trained professionals either fail to foster enough cohesion or overemphasize it and make the group suffocating for some members. Lakin cites other unique aspects of groups, such as the encouragement of emotional expression or the formation of subgroups and scapegoating, which also require a skilled therapist with good judgment. Otherwise, genuine emotional expression becomes false emotionality pressured by the group and has little therapeutic value.

Corey and Corey (2003) stress that no blanket group competence exists for all types of groups. A person qualified to lead a substance abuse group may not be competent to lead a long-term psychotherapy group or an assertiveness group. Counselors must always evaluate the match between the type of group under consideration and their prior training and experience.

The literature also suggests that not all clients can benefit from groups. In fact, some can be harmed by participation (Yalom, 1995). Counselors need the knowledge to identify such people and direct them to other types of counseling or to other kinds of groups. They must also be able to judge when a group is not helping a member and must take effective action to remedy the problem or refer the client to another source of assistance.

Finally, mental health professionals who lead groups are obligated to update their skills and knowledge lest they lose the competence they have established. The ASGW standards mandate participation in professional development activities, echoing the standards presented in the ACA and APA codes. The recent emergence of modalities such as Internet-based self-help groups (Humphreys, Winzelberg, & Klaw, 2000) highlights the importance of continuing education.

Another competency requirement is for group leaders to attend to the aftereffects of a group meeting or a group experience. Klontz (2004) points out that in groups that encourage emotional expression, the transition from group to participants' ordinary lives may be difficult. He recommends that group leaders assist clients in aftercare by providing specific instructions for the transition, including recommendations for communication with family and friends outside the group about the group experience without compromising confidentiality or threatening or confusing loved ones.

Informed Consent in Group Counseling

Because group counseling involves risks and responsibilities beyond those typically experienced in individual counseling, informed consent is crucially important. The informed consent process for groups begins with orienting the client to counseling before the beginning of the group sessions; that also involves screening prospective group members. As with individual counseling, developing informed consent in groups should include describing the goals, techniques, procedures, limitations, risks, and benefits of the group. Counselors should make a special effort to ensure that prospective clients understand the roles of the therapist and other group members as well as their personal responsibilities in group. Clients also need to know the characteristics of a typical group session and the expectations of members in those sessions. If the group is one in which emotional expression will be encouraged, clients should be told of this emphasis. Group sessions can be intense, and that intensity can be exhilarating, exhausting, or both. Clients who are prepared to expect an intense experience may make better choices about participation and they may better tolerate and learn from that climate.

Corey and Corey (2003) list risks specific to group counseling that should be explained to prospective group members:

- Scapegoating
- Group pressure to disclose private material
- Discomfort with confrontation or inappropriate use of this approach in the group
- Negative effects (even temporary) in the client's lives stemming from the group experience

Some groups that use physical techniques have injured clients. Any group that involves such techniques must also disclose this potential risk.

The practical matters regarding fees, times and locations of meetings, duration of the group, and so forth should be addressed. If insurance is to be billed for group sessions, all aspects of informed consent relevant to third-party payors as described in Chapter 5 should be reviewed. If a co-leader is participating, explaining the co-leader's role and qualifications to clients is an obvious aspect of a fully informed consent. The client ought to be given an opportunity to meet the co-leader before the group to ask him or her questions. In addition, clients should understand how co-leaders will communicate with each other about group members.

Because group cohesion is such an important feature of an effective group (Yalom, 1995), clients should also appreciate the degree of commitment asked of them when they join a group. Group members need to understand that their regular attendance and active involvement are necessary for the group's success. The delicate issue of dropping out of the group should be openly discussed. This is a delicate issue because all clients have the right to refuse to continue counseling if they wish, but most group leaders want members to maintain participation at least until an individual has reached his or her goals for the group experience (Corey & Corey, 2003; Yalom, 1995). Part of what makes a group beneficial is its power to help clients work through difficult emotions and persevere with commitments to others. When people drop out prematurely, they rob themselves of the opportunity for important personal learning and they diminish group cohesiveness and effectiveness for other members. Most leaders, therefore, ask members to attend at least one final session to explain their decision to terminate to the other members (Corey et al., 1995). The goals of that session are to help the member reach some degree of closure to the group process, to limit the damage to group cohesiveness, and to improve the chances that the group will continue to have therapeutic power for remaining members. Its not-so-hidden agenda is to encourage the person to change his or her mind and remain in the group (Kottler, 1982). When group leaders endorse this view about the importance of a "proper" termination process, they must disclose it to prospective clients and explain its rationale. With that knowledge, clients are then empowered to accept or reject the conditions of membership the leader has set forth. The legal concept of informed refusal (the right to reject offered services without penalty) also operates in groups. No group leader can ethically or legally mandate participation if an individual wishes to withdraw. Thus the goal of this portion of informed consent is to enlighten without biasing and to encourage without pressuring. When dealing with culturally diverse groups, leaders bear the burden to take into account the role of cultural diversity in the client's reaction to both the group process and the policy on dropping out (ASGW, 1998b).

Confidentiality and Privilege in Group Counseling

The counselor's duty to maintain the confidentiality of client communications is unchanged in group counseling. However, the fact that nearly all of what is disclosed is communicated before other group members complicates both the ethics of confidentiality and the legal interpretation of privilege. As already discussed, other group members cannot be held accountable if they violate confidentiality. Group members who keep confidences do so out of a personal moral standard, a commitment to the group process, some fear of group censure, or a combination of these factors.

Although group counselors cannot guarantee confidentiality, they are still obligated to do their utmost to encourage it. That responsibility entails thoroughly explaining the role of confidentiality to each prospective group member, describing the specifics of its operations, and asking for a commitment to honor confidentiality at all times in the group. The ACA standard (B.4.a) on group confidentiality is presented at the beginning of this chapter.

Most group scholars also recommend that leaders remind group members about confidentiality both at the first group session and periodically throughout the group process (ASGW, 1998a; Corey & Corey, 2003). Those intermittent reminders should be given immediately after particularly intense or risky sessions. Corey et al. (1995) emphasize that the issue of inadvertent disclosures should be addressed along with deliberate infractions because even well-intentioned members may be vulnerable to accidental violations. Pepper (2003) advises group leaders to be clear about whether complete confidentiality is required or whether members can discuss general issues and feelings aroused by the group, an issue that sometimes confuses group members.

A practical approach to ensuring that members have the skills and judgment to avoid both kinds of disclosures involves role-playing situations that tempt members to violate confidentiality. In this simulation, one person might take the role of a friend who asks the group member about the identities of other group members and another person role-plays a response. Group members themselves might develop scenarios they think could happen in their lives and act them out in group. Ideally, such simulations would take place fairly early in the group process and would give individual members confidence in their own abilities to honor confidentiality and in other members' commitment to secrecy. Group counselors may also opt to develop orientation videos that highlight confidentiality and show simulations of members coping with temptations to break confidentiality.

Some group counselors use contracts for confidentiality that members must sign to become part of the group. These written contracts clarify expectations and symbolize the importance of confidentiality to the therapeutic process. They are a visible representation of the value the leaders place on this facet of group behavior. The use of confidentiality contracts is supported by some ethics scholars (such as Arthur & Swanson, 1993; Corey et al., 1995), but preliminary research suggests that most practitioners do not favor them (Roback et al., 1992). These researchers found only 23% of group therapists in their survey actually used them. Bernstein and Hartsell (1998) point out that these contracts have symbolic rather than legal value and that no litigation related to group members' breach of confidentiality has ever occurred.

The limits of confidentiality that apply to individual counseling, elaborated in Chapter 4, are all transferable to group settings. The duty to protect, to report child and elder abuse and neglect, to respond to a court order for confidential information, and to answer charges of unethical or illegal behavior made by clients all hold for group counseling. Therefore, all prospective members need to be informed about these limits to confidentiality so that they freely choose what information to disclose to whom. Special care should be taken in explaining that the counselor's duty to confidentiality does not extend to other members of the group. Counselors need to help clients understand the risks they are undertaking as well as the potential benefits of the group experience.

Unfortunately, there is a paucity of published research on compliance with this standard. One published study that attended to this question found only 32% of group therapists who explicitly discussed the risks of disclosure of private information by other group members (Roback et al., 1992). A second study (Appelbaum & Greer, 1993) also reported that a significant proportion of group therapists fail to discuss the limits of confidentiality with their clients. What accounts for this reluctance? No empirically based answer can be given yet, but Roback and colleagues (1992) hypothesize that group leaders are concerned that such information would discourage people from entering groups or from revealing personal material during sessions. However well intentioned the motivation for such a stance, it is inconsistent with existing ethical standards. Disregard of this standard could also spell legal trouble. Roback et al. point out that consciously deciding not to discuss the limits to confidentiality could be interpreted as deliberately misrepresenting the risks of the process, for which a group counselor could be held liable in the courts.

There is still another reason for informing clients about this limit. When violations or breaches of confidentiality do occur, the group often experiences at least a temporary setback in cohesion and productivity (Roback et al., 1992). In addition, after such a breach some members permanently retreat from active involvement in group process. These negative outcomes argue strongly both for an emphasis on prevention by completely and explicitly discussing this issue with prospective group members and for a backup plan for recovery from such harm if prevention fails.

Legal considerations also argue for comprehensively discussing confidentiality. The degree to which privilege applies in group counseling varies considerably by state. Generally, state courts have held that any statement made in front of third parties is not covered by privilege (Paradise & Kirby, 1990; Swenson, 1997). In such jurisdictions, a group leader has no defense against disclosing client information to a court. In still other states, including California, Illinois, Kentucky, and Minnesota, a special kind of privilege for communications in group therapy has been established (Parker, Clevenger, & Sherman, 1997). Because of the changing nature of state statutes, professionals are well advised to stay current with laws in their state.

Of course, privilege usually applies only to the licensed professional in the session. There is rarely any privilege for other group members who heard the same information as the counselor, so they can be mandated to testify even if the mental health professional cannot. Explaining this reality to prospective members is essential. Failure to do so conflicts with their right to make autonomous decisions about activities that affect them. Lest clients become overly concerned about some legal risks, it is important to balance this explanation of risk against the low probability that it will occur. Clients need not be unduly frightened about a very-low-probability event. Court cases involving group counseling or therapy are relatively rare (Paradise & Kirby, 1990), and few counselors or participants have actually had to testify against a group member. That should not foster complacency, but if history is any guide, the level of that risk is very small.

The Ethics of Group Counseling with Minors and in the Schools

Many scholars view group counseling as a useful and practical intervention for children and adolescents in school and nonschool settings (for example, Gladding, 2002; Greenberg, 2003; Riester, 2002), although rigorous research on the effectiveness of group work is still in its infancy (Shechtman, 2002). When professionals provide ongoing group counseling for young people they face additional challenges to confidentiality. First, group leaders must consider how much information about children's disclosures in group can or must be shared with parents. Unless operating under a statute or court ruling that grants an adolescent a right to confidentiality of disclosures in counseling, parents usually have the right to information about their children's comments in counseling sessions. Of course, parents have the right to knowledge only of their own child's disclosures and not those of other participants. Therefore, group leaders are well advised to obtain parental consent to group counseling at the initiation of a group and to seek parental waivers to their right to know everything their child communicates so as to encourage the child's trust and openness to the group experience. (See Chapter 4 for additional discussion of minors and parental rights.)

In addition, group leaders must be sensitive to the developmental issues that may affect a young person's capacity to understand and maintain the confidentiality of disclosures made within the group. Young people may experience pressure from nonparticipating peers to discuss what has happened in group and may have limited skill in resisting such pressure (Ritchie & Huss, 2000). Therefore counselors have a duty to be diligent in screening potential group members to assess their capacity to honor confidentiality, to learn communication skills to resist peer pressure to breach confidentiality, and to respond empathically to peer comments in group. When groups are conducted in schools, they can be a valuable tool to help promote student development and academic success (Riester, 2002; Shechtman, 2002). However, whenever group members are part of a closed system (such as a school) where they have ongoing out-of-group contact with other group participants and where nonparticipants may be aware of which students are leaving classes to attend group sessions, the task of maintaining confidentiality is quite demanding for the counselor. To succeed in this task, not only should school counselors screen prospective members carefully, they should also orient students to expectations and regularly monitor compliance. Group leaders should also have a plan for responding should confidentiality be breached during an ongoing group experience.

Some evidence also suggests that inattention to group composition can negatively affect group effectiveness and even cause harm to children. For example, Dishion, McCord, and Poulin (1999) found that groups that included only aggressive children and adolescents actually increased the risk of aggressive behavior in participants. The comments and actions of the more aggressive and delinquent youth in the groups actually taught the less aggressive youth new ways to act out. Other evidence indicates that group leaders must be especially careful about the use of their confrontation and negative feedback with youth members and about the structure of the feedback from peers because harmful effects have been noted (Shechtman & Yanuv, 2001). These authors advise reliance on acceptance, empathy, and support as therapeutic approaches with a substantially greater likelihood of positive effects. The ASCA *Ethical Standards for School Counselors* (2004) notes these responsibilities in Section A.6.

The Ethics of Multiple Relationships in Group Counseling

The prohibition against sexual contact with clients obviously extends to group counseling, as does the standard of avoiding other forms of multiple relationships. Although the dynamics of therapeutic change differ in groups, the therapist's power is not significantly reduced. Social, personal, business, or other connections with current clients can compromise the leader's professional judgment and objectivity and can affect the client's emotional response to the group. In addition, multiple relationships with group members can diminish group cohesion when other members suspect that one of their own has a special relationship with the leader. Such contacts can also engender more hostility toward the leader and distract the group from productive activities.

The Ethics of Concurrent Individual and Group Counseling

According to Taylor and Gazda (1991) and Lakin (1994), the practice of seeing the same clients in both group and individual counseling, or of gathering one's individual clients together into a group, happens rather frequently. A client may also start out in group and then be seen individually, while the group continues. Professional codes do not address this behavior except in ACA *Code of Ethics*, Section A.5.e.. Lakin (1994) reports that most practitioners see no ethical problems with it. However, Lakin (1994) has identified several important potential difficulties with concurrent individual and group counseling:

- Risks to confidentiality and privilege because of communications between co-leaders or difficulty remembering which disclosures were shared in which setting
- Interference with the client's emotional relationship with the counselor and with transference, including "sibling rivalry" among group members and an increased risk of countertransference from the leader
- The creation of an overpowerful therapist and an overdependent client, resulting in a higher probability of misuse of therapeutic power
- The financial gain for referring to oneself that blinds a counselor to the client's real needs (Fisher, 2003; Lakin, 1994; Taylor & Gazda, 1991)

Taylor and Gazda identify several ways to minimize these risks, the most central of which are informed consent to concurrent treatment, careful monitoring of the professional's power and the client's dependence, and scrupulous attention to the client's well-being. Supervision and consultation also seem crucial. Regardless of the precautions taken, the dangers of this practice should be acknowledged and prudent counselors would be well advised to consider it "as a last resort." If individual therapy is needed for a group member, a referral elsewhere should be considered. Similarly, when therapists are entertaining the idea of gathering their clients together into a group, especially an open-ended therapeutic group, those professionals ought to examine their motivation, get supervision or consultation, and be prepared to accept responsibility for problems that develop.

The Ethics of Involuntary Group Participation

Both the ASGW *Best Practices* document (1998a) and ethics scholars discuss the complicated ethics related to involuntary group participation. Courts, treatment facilities, and other agencies often mandate participation in a group. The person involved theoretically has a choice, but the alternative is so unappealing that the person sees no other realistic course of action. A neglectful parent may be required to attend a parenting group as a condition of maintaining custody of his or her children or a person arrested for driving while intoxicated can "choose" between an alcohol education group or a criminal record. A person who enters a hospital for treatment of bipolar disorder (manic depression) may learn that participation in daily group therapy sessions is a condition of treatment. Without the group involvement, the person cannot receive the individual counseling or medication management that he or she really seeks. In each instance the person agrees to group participation as the least worst alternative. The fundamental questions underlying this practice, as noted in Chapter 5, are whether informed consent is really possible in the absence of a completely free consent and whether it is ethical for mental health professionals to make such demands on clients. Neither the major codes nor the ASGW documents address this basic issue for group counseling, implying (but not explicitly stating) that the benefit the person and the society can receive from the group outweighs the temporary loss of autonomy about this decision.

Corey and Corey (2003) also describe the practical dimensions of involuntary participation—the potential for the therapeutic work of the group to be advanced is severely limited if individuals do not have at least a basic level of commitment to the group. Involuntary clients who feel tricked and manipulated into group membership are unlikely to profit from the experience. Thus most writers on the subject highlight the importance of dealing with the clients' feelings about involuntary participation both in screening sessions and early in the life of the group. They should be allowed to express their frustration about the loss of autonomy and their fears or reservations about the group. Corey et al. (1995) suggest that the chance to openly discuss these feelings may reduce resistance and increase cooperation.

Developing informed consent is especially important with involuntary clients. If a client's activity in the group is to be reported to a court or public agency, the client should understand that fact and the implications of his or her behavior in the group for subsequent actions by those agencies. To return to the example of the parent who joins a group as a condition of retaining custody of his children, if the counselor must report to the child protective agency that the man has been silent and uninvolved in group sessions, the man should be informed of that fact. If the counselor knows from experience that such a report is likely to reduce the chances that the client will keep his children, the counselor should also tell the client that.

In short, the central message in acting consistently with the ethical values of the profession while accepting nonvoluntary clients into groups is that the counselor must zealously guard the client's remaining rights and work energetically to help the client make a free choice for participation. If that is not possible, at least the counselor should aim for fully informed consent about the ramifications of the client's reaction to the mandate. If a counselor believes that mandated group counseling is unlikely to benefit the client and may bring harm, the counselor then has an obligation to communicate that professional judgment to the parties demanding participation and to work toward an alternative therapeutic placement satisfactory to all involved.

Ethical Issues in Multicultural Groups

Few groups are truly homogeneous. Most include people of different religions, cultural background, ethnicities, gender, physical capabilities, sexual orientation, and age. Sometimes the diagnostic label they·share is all they have in common. Heterogeneous groups make group cohesion more difficult to achieve and make the leader's skill even more crucial to its accomplishment. Ironically, in diverse groups sometimes there is greater pressure for cohesion, and counselors must be alert to pressures for cohesion that are insensitive to cultural values (Corey et al., 1995). Similarly, counselors need to recognize how their own cultural backgrounds affect their values and their approach to building a cohesive group. APA's *Guidelines on Multicultural Education, Training, Research, Practice, and Organizational Change for Psychologists* (2003a) and ASGW's *Principles for Diversity-Competent Group Workers* (1998b) are especially useful resources for the mental health professional who seeks to develop these skills.

Leader sensitivity to diversity issues also increases the likelihood that members will be treated fairly. Fairness implies that there is no conscious or unconscious discrimination against members because of differences. For example, a client whose cultural background discourages intense emotional expression or direct confrontation must be given flexibility in responding to the tasks of the group and must not be ridiculed or labeled as dysfunctional because of this cultural background. Because cultural differences are not always apparent to others, counselors must work to protect the rights of all clients to dignified and fair treatment in the group. If leaders see other members scapegoating one participant because of cultural issues or otherwise behaving in insensitive ways, the counselor has a responsibility to intervene to stop that behavior. Leaders whose own behavior models respect for each client go a long way toward achieving the goal of sensitivity. In addition to sensitive attitudes and knowledge of cultural differences, group counselors are obliged to learn strategies for leading multicultural groups that increase the likelihood of success. Researchers such as DeLucia et al. (1992), Johnson et al. (1995), and Merta (1995) discuss such strategies.

Family and Couples Counseling

Because family and couples counseling is a separate discipline that demands significant expertise to practice effectively the first tenet of ethical family and couples counseling is sufficient training and supervised experience in the field to be competent (Gladding, Remley, & Huber, 2000). Counselors without training and supervision in this area would be well advised to remedy those deficiencies before involvement in this specialty to eliminate risks of ethical charges or malpractice claims for working beyond the boundaries of their competence (Gladding et al, 2000). Forty-seven states license professionals to conduct marriage and family therapy, and the professional associations, the American Association for Marriage and Family Therapy (AAMFT) and the International Association for Marriage and Family Counseling (IAMFC), have developed standards for graduate training and practice in the discipline.

Case Illustrations of Special Issues

The following scenarios represent fairly typical occurrences in the work of the family counselor. The pages that follow examine the ethical issues embedded in each.

Scenario 1. One participant in couples counseling telephones and asks for an individual appointment to share some information he thinks the counselor should know but that he wishes to keep secret from his partner.

Scenario 2. A wife calls for an appointment for family counseling because of family conflict over a teenager's rebellious behavior, but she cautions that her husband refuses to attend counseling, although he has agreed to the attendance of the other four members of the family.

Scenario 3. A couple asks for marriage counseling to save their marriage at all costs to each partner personally. They say their individual happiness and emotional well-being are secondary to staying married. They have six children.

Scenario 4. A couple whose child was killed in a car accident 18 months ago recently separated. They begin couples counseling to see if there is any hope for their relationship. After a number of sessions, the counselor concludes that continuing the relationship would probably be destructive for one partner, but ending the relationship would probably be destructive for the other.

Scenario 5. After six individual therapy sessions, a client asks to begin couples therapy because she has realized that the crux of her problem is relational. Her partner is willing, and the counselor agrees with her assessment about the need to attend to relationship issues at this point. She asks to have concurrent individual and couples counseling.

Scenario 6. A family with two parents and three children is experiencing significant conflict. The wife/mother started a business 1 year ago. It has been quite successful, and the demands on her time are extensive. Her efforts to get some household chores reassigned to her partner or teenage children have not been successful. Two weeks ago, she got so upset that she went "on strike" from those chores. The whole family is now angry at her and frustrated with the chaos that has developed at home. The husband/father has requested the appointment "to get this mess straightened out and get back to normal."

Scenario 7. A lesbian couple makes an appointment with a heterosexual counselor. The partners are considering adopting a child and wish to discuss the implications of their decision on their relationship and the child. Their motivation is to ensure that the transition to parenthood goes as smoothly as possible for all members of the family.

Scenario 8. A family counselor recommends that the parents of a 10-year-old boy who has refused to leave the house even to attend school should not continue to press the child to do any of the feared activities. In fact, the counselor suggests that if the boy shows any interest in those activities, the parents should not encourage that interest but should remain entirely neutral. The counselor's message to the boy is that he seems to need this time at home and should not worry too much about his behavior. In fact, he probably should not force himself to do things he does not feel ready for. The counselor's rationale for this recommendation is grounded in the literature on paradoxical approaches in family therapy. In the 3 weeks since that recommendation was implemented, the boy has not attended school or left his parents' side at any time. So far, the child has shown no signs of interest in school or other activities. The parents have complied with the therapist's directions.

Scenario 9. A minister refers a couple from his church to family counseling because of domestic violence. The man has shoved, kicked, and pushed the woman around on numerous occasions during their 10-year marriage. The most recent occurrence took place 5 days ago. The woman approached the minister because she is worried about the effects of the violence on the children. The minister reveals that the man was defensive when queried about the violence and tended to place a good part of the blame on his wife but was willing to attend counseling.

Analysis of the Scenarios

Scenario 1: Confidentiality of Disclosures to Family Counselors in Individual Contacts. The ethical standards of the ACA and the American Association of Marriage and Family Therapy directly address this question. See Appendix C for the Website that contains the complete AAMFT code.

ACA *Code of Ethics,* Section A.7.: Multiple Clients

When a counselor agrees to provide counseling services to two or more persons who have a relationship, the counselor clarifies at the outset which person or persons are clients and the nature of the relationships the counselor will have with each involved person. If it becomes apparent that the counselor may be called upon to perform potentially conflicting roles, the counselor will clarify, adjust, or withdraw from roles appropriately. *(See A.8.a., B.4.)*

B.4.b. Couples and Family Counseling.

In couples and family counseling, counselors clearly define who is considered "the client" and discuss expectations and limitations of confidentiality. Counselors seek agreement and document in writing such agreement among all involved parties having capacity to give consent concerning each individual's right to confidentiality and any obligation to preserve the confidentiality of information known.

AAMFT *Code of Ethics* (2001), Section. 2.2

Marriage and family therapists do not disclose client confidences except by written authorization or waiver, or where mandated or permitted by law. Verbal authorization will not be sufficient except in emergency situations, unless prohibited by law. When providing couple, family or group treatment, the therapist does not disclose information outside the treatment context without a written authorization from each individual competent to execute a waiver. In the context of couple, family or group treat-ment, the therapist may not reveal any individual's confidences to others in the client unit without the prior written permission of that individual.

In contrast, the APA code is rather vague.

APA *Ethical Principles,* Section 10.02: Therapy Involving Couples or Families
(a) When psychologists agree to provide services to several persons who have a relationship (such as spouses, significant others, or parents and children), they take reasonable steps to clarify at the outset (1) which of the individuals are clients/patients and (2) the relationship the psychologist will have with each person. This clarification includes the psychologist's role and the probable uses of the services provided or the information obtained.

The APA standard recommends that psychologists be clear about their roles and their use of information, but this section does not explicitly discuss the disclosure of material divulged by one family member in an individual session to the other family members in therapy. However, Section 4.02 of the APA code on confidentiality appears to support the view that individual communications are confidential unless the client waives confiden-tiality or some other legal duty is imposed. In her commentary on the code, Fisher (2003) interprets the code to mean that disclosures to psychologists in individual contacts may not be revealed in group or family sessions without permission of the client.

When these codes are applied to the first scenario, the ACA and AAMFT standards indicate that if the counselor hears the "secret" from the individual family member in a one-to-one conversation, the counselor is obligated to keep that information confi-dential, even from other family members, unless the client waives that right. Needless to say, in this situation the family counselor has no duty to hear the secret communi-cation in the first place and should decide how to respond to this client's request on the basis of clinical considerations and an assessment of what would be in the best in-terests of the family.

It is important to note that the codes do *not* indicate that it is unethical to conduct concurrent individual and family counseling. Heitler (2001) presents several recommen-dations for ethical resolutions of the risks of dual treatment. If a counselor chooses to do so, however, a heavy burden to maintain the confidentiality of individual communications falls to the professional. Whatever the course of action taken, ethics scholars in family ther-apy advise a comprehensive approach to informed consent on issues of confidentiality (for example, Lakin, 1994; Smith, 1999) and privilege (Swenson, 1997). Heitler (2001) presents other recommendations for ethical resolution of the risks of dual treatment that stem from dual roles and potential financial conflict of interest.

Scenario 2: The Problem of Nonattending Family Members. Many theories of family therapy are rooted in the view that real improvement in the functioning of family mem-bers is fundamentally tied to the treatment of the whole family system (see, for example, Becvar & Becvar, 1996), and research evidence suggests that for some relational problems, this claim has validity (Patten, Barnett, & Houlihan, 1991). According to this view, mean-ingful change in a dysfunctional family system requires the participation of all family members. If one member refuses to engage in therapy, systemic change becomes extremely difficult to achieve (Minuchin, 1974; Napier & Whitaker, 1978). For these reasons, some family therapists experience the nonattendance of one family member as both a clinical and an ethical dilemma. The codes of ethics are silent on this subject, but practitioners still wonder—should the members who want counseling be served, or should counseling be postponed until the reluctant member changes his or her view? How actively should the counselor work to involve the nonengaging person?

Scholars in family therapy have suggested a wide range of answers to these questions, but the recommendations of Teisman (1980); Wilcoxin and Fennel (1983); and Miller, Scott, and Searight (1990) are especially useful. All suggest efforts to remove the obstacles to the nonattender's participation without coercing involvement or interfering with that person's autonomy rights. The suggestions are as follows:

- Taping a session with the other family members for the nonparticipating individual to review, with the goal of helping that person gain more knowledge of the process. (Consent of the other family members to taping is required, of course.) If misperceptions or fears are at the core of the refusal, this procedure might be effective (Teisman, 1980).
- Writing a letter to the nonattending person, explaining the family therapy process and describing the changes that may take place in the rest of the family as a consequence of counseling based on the research evidence. The letter acts as an invitation to reconsider the refusal, both as a gesture to help others in the family and as a way of promoting his or her own interests. When a signed copy of this letter is returned, the therapist proceeds with family therapy even if the document is not persuasive to the nonattender (Wilcoxin & Fennell, 1983; Miller et al., 1990).
- Offering a single individual session with the nonattender to help that person understand the concerns and allay fears and misperceptions of counseling (Teisman, 1980).
- Referring other family members for individual therapy until the whole unit is available (Wilcoxin & Fennel, 1983).

The goal of each of these methods is to inform, demystify, and open the family counseling process to the reluctant person. Any of these methods can be misused to coerce participation, and such action would be clearly unethical. The counselor must approach this person with respect for his or her rights and with recognition that the resistance to therapy may serve an important function both for that individual and for the family. Whittinghill (2002) echoes this view in his discussion of the role of family counseling in substance abuse treatment and also suggests that the definition of family should not be limited to blood relations—coworkers, friends, or community members may also function as family for some individuals. Inviting such people into counseling may serve the same purpose for some clients as the inclusion of family members serves for others. Broadening the definition of family also makes this service more inclusive of diverse cultural traditions of kinship.

Scenarios 3 and 4: Conflicts Between Individual and Family Welfare.

Because the stigma of divorce has faded, counselors hear pleas to save a marriage at all costs less frequently than they probably did 20 years ago. Yet the words are still voiced often enough to be of concern to ethics scholars and practitioners in this field. This request asks the counselor to overlook the pain and dysfunction that maintaining the relationship causes the partners and focus exclusively on continuing the marriage. Sometimes this desire is grounded in religious convictions. At other times it occurs because of fears of change, worries about the children, or a dysfunctional mutual dependency. At still other times, the narrow focus on continuing the marriage is the agenda of a counselor who equates divorce with treatment failure (Margolin, 1982). In Scenario 4, the situation is somewhat different—the relationship is helping one partner and harming the other. Nevertheless, the ethical issue of how to respond to negative effects on the individuals involved is at the center of both cases.

Scholars in marriage and family counseling point out that the ideal interests of individuals are likely to conflict somewhat with the best interests of the family (Margolin, 1982; Patten et al., 1991). Promoting individual and family development simultaneously is not always possible. Still, coping with minor compromises in individual functioning for the good of the family is a different order of problem from that presented in these scenarios. The first section of the AAMFT code states the following.

AAMFT *Code of Ethics,* Preamble to Section 1

Marriage and family therapists advance the welfare of families and individuals. They respect the rights of those seeking their services, and make reasonable efforts to ensure that their services are used appropriately.

This section enjoins professionals to aim for increased well-being of all involved in therapy, despite the practical problems and minor deviations already noted. Engaging in family counseling to save or prolong a marriage that is inherently harmful to at least one participant (Scenario 3) does not appear to be an appropriate use of the service. That is not to suggest, however, that it is the role of the counselor to advise the couples to divorce. The AAMFT code is explicit on that point.

AAMFT *Code of Ethics,* Section 1.8

Marriage and family therapists respect the rights of clients to make decisions and help them to understand the consequences of those decisions. Therapists clearly advise clients that they have the responsibility to make decisions regarding relationships such as cohabitation, marriage, divorce, separation, reconciliation, custody, and visitation.

Ethics scholars in family counseling generally concur on this point (for example, see Gurman, 1985). When caught in such dilemmas, counselors should carefully assess the degree of harm they believe will ensue from continuing the relationship. If it represents a serious and continuing harm for either member, counselors should discontinue work on that goal. Instead, counselors should frankly discuss their reservations with both members. No counselor should participate in an activity that seriously compromises a person's mental health even if that person wishes the activity to continue. The principle of nonmaleficence always take precedence over other considerations.

Scenario 5: The Ethics of Consecutive Individual and Family Counseling. Consecutive individual and family counseling is not unethical as long as several conditions are met. First, the counselor has judged that such a sequence would be beneficial to the client and has the competence to engage in both activities. Second, an appropriate informed consent procedure has been conducted so that the client understands the different risks, benefits, procedures, and confidentiality issues of relationship counseling, especially the professional obligation to keep confidential information shared during individual counseling. Finally, a similarly careful informed consent procedure has been undertaken with the partner as well. As counseling progresses, the counselor must be alert for any issues that may arise because of the different histories of contact with the counselor. The partner needs time to develop the same level of trust as the original client, and the counselor should make a special effort to get a sound independent assessment of the partner's functioning in the relationship. Communications from the original client about the partner are not likely to convey a fully accurate picture of that person. In addition, the counselor should be alert for signs that either partner views the counselor as "taking sides" or for negative feelings the original client may develop in "sharing" the counselor with the partner.

Scenarios 6 and 7: The Influence of the Counselor's Beliefs and Values About Gender Role Socialization and Sexual Orientation on Diagnosis and Treatment. No counseling process is value free. Family counselors have definitions of good and poor functioning, healthy and unhealthy communication, and normal and abnormal ways of relating. In fact, without these definitions, no therapeutic work could take place. As long as one distinguishes between desirable and undesirable change, one is invoking values. Sometimes family therapists have beliefs about healthy families that are too rigid and narrow and that fail to allow for individual differences (Melito, 2003). Research by APA (APA, Task Force, 1975) has shown, for example, that mental health professionals tend to view behaviors that are nontraditional for women as less acceptable than traditional behavior. For example, they tend to assume that women will be better adjusted if they remain married than if they do not and that a woman's extramarital affair is more serious than a man's. Guterman (1991) and Sekaran (1986) also suggest that counselors are frequently less sensitive to the demands of a woman's career than to those of her partner's. In other words, evidence suggests that family counselors have not been immune to the effects of gender bias and that in the way they work with families they have sometimes attempted to perpetuate existing norms (Lewis & Mellman, 1999). Some scholars have argued that family therapists have a responsibility to change sexist patterns in their clients (and themselves, of course) (Hare-Mustin, 1980), but others caution against a campaign to change client beliefs to those the therapist endorses (for example, see Wendorf & Wendorf, 1985).

The goal of the responsible counselor in dealing with family issues related to gender roles is to respect the client's autonomy on the matter as much as possible and to identify the ways in which the family's conceptualization of gender roles may be related to their dysfunction. In Scenario 6, the family therapist will need to help the family members communicate and renegotiate their mutual expectations. There are two pitfalls to be avoided— blaming the husband and children for not respecting the woman's right to change her responsibilities in the family and assuming that the woman really should be taking responsibility for her household chores just because she's "the wife." The therapist should help the family develop a response to the changing family circumstances that respects each member's human rights and recognizes each person's responsibilities to the family. Counselors should consult the *Principles Concerning Counseling/Psychotherapy with Women* (Fitzgerald & Nutt, 1986) for a fuller discussion of these issues.

Counselor values clearly come into play in Scenario 7 as well. The codes of ethics of ACA, APA, and AAMFT all explicitly prohibit discrimination on the basis of sexual orientation:

ACA *Code of Ethics,* Section C.5: Nondiscrimination

Counselors do not condone or engage in discrimination based on age, culture, disability, ethnicity, race, religion/spirituality, gender, gender identity, sexual orientation, marital status/partnership, language preference, socioeconomic status, or any basis proscribed by law. Counselors do not discriminate against clients, students, employees, supervisees, or research participants in a manner that has a negative impact on these persons.

APA *Ethical Principles,* Section 1.10: Nondiscrimination

In their work-related activities, psychologists do not engage in unfair discrimination based on age, gender, race, ethnicity, national origin, religion, sexual orientation, disability, socioeconomic status, or any basis proscribed by law.

AAMFT *Code of Ethics,* Section 1.1

Marriage and family therapists provide professional assistance to persons without discrimination on the basis of race, age, ethnicity, socioeconomic status, disability, gender, health status, religion, national origin, or sexual orientation.

Thus, family counselors should be prepared to respond to the request of this couple for preparenting counseling, as they would for any other couple. The decision to accept them as clients should be based on clinical considerations without regard to their sexual orientation. If the counselor had competence in the area and had knowledge about the literature relevant to this particular couple's concerns (for example, see Fitzgerald, 1999; Ritter & Terndrup, 2002; Rohrbaugh, 1992; Scrivner, 1997), the couple should not be turned away simply because they are not heterosexual. If the counselor's personal beliefs about homosexuality prevent the counselor from providing objective professional service, then the counselor is responsible for locating competent referral sources for this couple. A counselor who accepted this couple with the intention of "getting them to change their minds" because the counselor thinks lesbians should not be parents would be violating the codes and the fundamental values of autonomy and respect for human dignity at the core of the values of counseling professions. (See Janson & Steigerwald, 2002; Janson, 2002.)

Scenario 8: The Ethics of Risky Interventions.   In this situation, the therapist is using a variation of a paradoxical technique: It seems both illogical and inconsistent with the obvious therapeutic goals of the family, yet it may be used for therapeutic gain. The therapist is seeking to dissipate the energy from the client's resistance to change and to remove the secondary gains the boy may be receiving for his school refusal. Therapists sometimes apply this technique when more traditional approaches seem unlikely to produce immediate results. Lakin (1994) points out that there is a deceptive element to its use because the therapist does not really want the child to be housebound, nor does he wish to eliminate the parents' concern for their son. He needs to persuade the family that such behaviors are desirable, but he does not fully disclose to them that it matters little to the therapist whether the family complies with the recommendation. In a paradoxical approach, the theory is to set up a "win–win" situation in which some therapeutic gain is made regardless of the family's reaction to the intervention. If the family complies, the boy's behavior loses its attention-gaining value for the child and the boy's energy to resist his parents' wishes may be reduced. If the boy does not comply with the suggestion to stay home and the parents react favorably to the child, the family still "wins" because they have achieved what they sought.

The use of such techniques has sparked a fierce debate in the professional literature. Some scholars have questioned their effectiveness (for example, see Sexton, Montgomery, Goff, & Nugent, 1993), their ethics (for example, see M. C. Henderson, 1987; Ridley & Tan, 1986), and their implications for the reputation of the profession (for example, Lakin, 1994). Stevens-Smith and Hughes (1993) also warn that the use of paradoxical techniques may foster an unhealthy dependence on the counselor. Others have defended their value, contending that they are important tools to systemic change (see Ghadban, 1995; Haley, 1976; Wendorf & Wendorf, 1985). Practitioners themselves seem divided in their view of their ethics and therapeutic value (Sexton & Montgomery, 1994). The most provocative elements of the approach are its deceptiveness, its manipulative quality, and its risk of negative outcomes. Lakin (1994) asserts that the dishonesty in this intervention contradicts the forthright communication that counselors seek to help clients develop. Haley (1976) referred to such methods as "benevolent lies," but others question whether such deceptions can ever be truly benevolent. Problems also arise with the significant risk of misuse by incompetent or overzealous professionals. Moreover, such interventions are inconsistent with informed consent and autonomy. Clients cannot consent to be the object of a therapeutic deception, however well intentioned.

This scenario also underscores the risk of paradoxical approaches; they may be ineffective or even harmful. In this case, no apparent progress has been made for several weeks and the boy has not developed the kind of impatience with his confined existence that the therapist hoped for. The parents may be waiting patiently for change or may be starting to question the competence of the therapist. People frequently stop counseling prematurely, and if the parents get discouraged enough they may even drop out of counseling and seek other methods to help their son. Even if they do continue in counseling, perhaps the ineffectiveness of this method will reduce their compliance with future interventions because their confidence in the expertness of the counselor may be shaken.

When counselors use paradoxical approaches, they are deciding, at least temporarily, not to use other approaches. If a counselor chooses this nontraditional intervention over a method with more evidence of efficacy, then he or she may be violating the client's right to the best possible service at the lowest possible risk. Nontraditional approaches with limited evidence of effectiveness are justifiable only when more proven approaches are unsuccessful or unworkable.

For all these reasons, paradoxical techniques should be used with caution. They are a method of last resort, at least until the evidence of therapeutic value is more convincing. In addition, if a paradoxical intervention is used, it may be wise to "debrief" clients after the intervention, just as one debriefs participants in research projects that involve deception. For additional recommendations about responsible use of such approaches, consult Hampton & Hulgus (1993), Sexton et al. (1993), and Solovey and Duncan (1992).

Of course, paradoxical techniques are not the only powerful interventions used in family counseling. Family sculpting, a procedure in which the relations between members are acted out by creating live sculptures of the people in a session, can also have powerful—and sometimes unpredictable—effects (Lakin, 1994). Family counselors have a responsibility to carefully consider the ramifications of these and any other interventions that evoke strong emotions or uncover feelings long held secret. Consultation with colleagues about the wisdom of using the method with a particular family, along with diligent monitoring of the intervention's effects on each participant, is well advised.

Scenario 9: The Ethics of Family or Relationship Counseling Concurrent with Domestic Violence. Effective family therapy requires that participants feel free to share their ideas and feelings in session and to enact behavior change between sessions. Honest, direct communication between family members is the cornerstone of this modality. When one family member is being abused by another, the foundation for successful therapy is gone. Fearing the consequences, the victim cannot openly express thoughts or feelings or attempt behavior change without risk of revictimization. In addition, one defense that victimizers frequently use—that the other partner provoked the abuse—is not really challenged when the problem is framed as a family issue. In such a context, it is harder to get abusers to take responsibility for their actions. Thus, many scholars recommend avoiding family therapy while there is ongoing abuse (for example, see Houskamp, 1994). In this view, family counselors should see partners individually so each can explore his or her own needs. Joint sessions can be initiated after the abuser takes responsibility for the abuse and begins to rehabilitate and the victim begins to feel some power and control. Because families that are experiencing domestic violence do not often freely disclose it, counselors should stay alert for signs of abuse in the assessment and screening phase of family counseling. Other writers argue that joint therapy can be conducted when there is a recent history of domestic violence as long as the professional is competent and takes special steps to monitor family dynamics and keep the victim safe (O'Leary, 2002; Stith, Rosen, & McCollum, 2003; Vetere & Cooper, 2001).

Legal Issues in Family Counseling

The most common legal issues for professionals working with families relate to divorce and custody. Many couples who have attempted couples counseling decide to divorce, so it is not surprising that the professionals who have worked with them get drawn into the legal battles. For instance, one partner's attorney may attempt to get the counselor to testify about the other partner's mental health and stability or about what happened during treatment. Obviously, the ethical duty to confidentiality applies here as in other forms of counseling, and some states may even protect communications in family counseling as privileged. Nevertheless, family therapists are advised to be explicit during informed consent about confidentiality and privilege. They should explain to clients, preferably in writing (Stevens-Smith & Hughes, 1993), that they regard the family unit as the client, not any individual members. They should elaborate further the implications of that view for any future legal actions. Needless to say, family counselors should consult with their attorneys about such requests for information or testimony about clients whenever they occur.

Divorcing couples in custody disagreements sometimes attempt to get the professional to take one side or the other in those battles. On other occasions, well-intentioned (but misguided) professionals providing individual services to one partner are willing to become involved in the court proceedings to advocate on behalf of the client. Professionals should use extreme caution under such circumstances. Evaluations of child custody arrangements require special competencies that many professionals have not developed, and even if the professional has such competencies, an independent evaluator better serves the purpose. The psychological evaluation of the children and the fitness of the parents often significantly influence the court's decision. In addition, the role of influencing the court's decision about child custody is a very different role from that of therapist for the couple. When a mental health professional who has been working with one partner testifies in court about his or her professional interactions with the client and professional judgments about the mental health of that individual client, the professional is acting as a *fact witness,* not as an *expert witness* conducting an objective evaluation of both parents (APA Committee on Professional Practice and Standards, 2003). A professional who is acting as an expert witness is usually employed by the court to evaluate the parents and has had no prior contact with either person. A fact witness has been a therapist for one or both parties and because of the nature of that prior contact may not give an especially clear or objective view of the child's best interests or the parenting skills of the adults because objective assessment for a legal proceeding was never the cause of the counselor's involvement with the family. Consequently, counselors are well advised to discuss the counselor's role when initiating couple's or family treatment whenever there is a reasonable possibility that the relationship will terminate. The ACA and APA codes use virtually identical wording in stating their standards for group and family services, with the responsibility of the professional to clarify roles and obtain proper consent. (See Section A.7 of the ACA code and Section 10.02 cited earlier in the chapter.)

The AAMFT code goes farther, explicitly prohibiting the treating professional from also serving as the custody evaluator.

AAMFT *Code of Ethics,* Section 3.14

To avoid a conflict of interests, marriage and family therapists who treat minors or adults involved in custody or visitation actions may not also perform forensic evaluations for custody, residence, or visitation of the minor. The marriage and family therapist who treats the minor may provide the court or mental health professional performing the evaluation with information about the minor from the marriage and family therapist's perspective as a treating marriage and family therapist, so long as the marriage and family therapist does not violate confidentiality.

Increasingly, courts are also using counselors, family therapists, and psychologists to act as expert witnesses and to assist in divorce mediation and child custody evaluations.

The obligation of the professional who provides such services is to give competent, honest, objective advice to the court and to ensure that all people being evaluated understand that the counselor is assisting the court and is not in a therapeutic relationship with the client.

Recent years have seen an increase in the number of ethics complaints against mental health professionals serving in these roles (Kirtland & Kirtland, 2001; Ohio Board of Psychology, 2003), and much negative press has been written about counselors and therapists who act as "hired guns" for attorneys. Professional associations have published guidelines to help professionals act ethically in such activities (see APA, 1994), and ethics scholars have written widely on the subject (for example, Benjamin, Andrew, & Gollan, 2003; Woody, 2000). Professionals asked to act in these roles should become familiar with this literature in order to make responsible decisions. Some of the most helpful materials are listed in the recommended readings at the end of this chapter.

SUMMARY

Group and family counseling entails special ethical and legal challenges for counselors. These challenges include the competent use of therapist power in modalities that have significant potential for good or harm depending on the counselor's professionalism and the wise management of confidentiality issues in a setting where client disclosures cannot be guaranteed privacy. The emotional intensity of the setting, the powerful interventions commonly used, and the pressure for group cohesion can all have negative effects on clients if the counselor does not manage these aspects of therapy skillfully and sensitively. Confidentiality is complicated because other clients may reveal material discussed in session, and not all courts recognize privilege for professionals when other people also hear client communications. These additional risks and benefits make a careful and thorough informed consent process even more imperative in group and family therapy than in individual therapy.

Counselor values and biases significantly influence group and family therapy. Counselors therefore need to recognize how their personal values may interfere with productive counseling and base their work on the principles of respect for human dignity and individual differences. Personal beliefs about what constitutes a family, about gender roles, and about sexual orientation play especially central roles in family counseling. Counselors using group and family therapy should consult the standards of the ASGW (1998a) and the AAMFT (2001) for additional guidance on ethical practice in these modalities.

CASE FOR DISCUSSION

A person who was a part of an online support group revealed in an electronic message to other members that he had murdered his daughter. Among those who received the communication were several psychologists. Some of the psychologist members elected not to disclose this information to legal authorities, but other members did report the admission. Eventually, the man was convicted of this crime. (This is based on a real occurrence.) Imagine that an ethics complaint came forward on one of the psychologists who did not disclose the comment to the police. Do you think this person acted unethically? On what basis? If you think there was an ethics violation, what discipline do you think would be appropriate for this infraction? What about the ethics of any psychologists who would break confidentiality for this reason?

Jeffrey and Joanne are co-leading a 10-session group for people recovering from divorce. Both are divorced professionals who are competent and experienced group counselors. At the start of the group they ask all members to sign an agreement that they will not get romantically involved with one another while the group is in progress. All members agree and have complied. Over the course of the first 5 weeks of the group, the co-leaders work closely together. They begin to develop a mutual attraction and start to date by week 6 of the group. They do not reveal their personal relationship to any group members.

Are their actions in violation of the codes of ethics or are their personal lives entirely separate from their professional activities?

Martin's parents are insisting that he attend family therapy with them although he strongly opposes the idea. Martin is a 13-year-old boy who lives with his father and stepmother. Martin is angry because his father began a relationship with a woman who is now his stepmother before he divorced his mother. Martin has been told that if he does not attend family therapy sessions he will lose weekend privileges. Because Martin enjoys his weekend social activities he feels as though he has no choice other than to accompany the rest of the family to therapy. In the sessions Martin says little and seems to spend much of the time daydreaming. The therapist's efforts to get Martin to become more involved have met with little success. Nevertheless, the therapist encourages the parents to bring all the children to family sessions. Are the actions of the therapist justifiable? What other information would be helpful to you in making this decision? Would your answer differ if Martin were 17 years old instead of 13?

DISCUSSION QUESTIONS

1. Research has shown that many practitioners choose not to use confidentiality contracts in group counseling. What do you see as the advantages and disadvantages of such a choice?

2. What do you see as the dangers and values of the methods that have been recommended to encourage nonparticipating family members to attend counseling?

3. Should a counselor conduct individual and couples counseling simultaneously with the same clients? Why or why not?

4. Many counselors regularly seek out co-leaders for their groups because of the therapeutic value of dual leadership. Does co-leadership also have ethical value? In what way?

5. If a member drops out of a group and is unwilling to attend even one more session to obtain "closure," should a leader try to persuade that member to change his or her mind? How far can the leader go in doing so before violating ethical standards?

6. Sometimes families have problems because members have differing ideas about social role expectations. For example, a man may believe that his wife should take care of the home, whereas she believes that responsibility is shared. How can a family counselor ethically assist a family with such a conflict?

RECOMMENDED READINGS

American Psychological Association, Committee on Professional Practice and Standards. (1994). Guidelines for child custody evaluations in divorce proceedings. *American Psychologist, 49,* 677–680.

Association for Specialists in Group Work. (1998a). *Best Practice Guidelines.* Retrieved May 26, 2005, from http://www.asgw.org/best.htm

Association for Specialists in Group Work. (1998b). *Principles for Diversity-Competent Group Workers.* Retrieved May 25, 2005, from http://www.asgw.org/diversity.htm

Association for Specialists in Group Work. (2000). *Professional Standards for the Training of Group Workers.* Retrieved May 25, 2005, from http://www.asgw.org/training_standards.htm

Benjamin, G., Andrew, H., & Gollan, J. K. (2003). *Family evaluation in custody litigation: Reducing risks of ethical infractions and malpractice.* Washington, DC: American Psychological Association.

Corey, G., Williams, G. T., & Moline, M. E. (1995). Ethical and legal issues in group counseling. *Ethics and Behavior, 5,* 161–183.

Dishion, T. J., McCord, J., & Poulin, F. (1999). When interventions harm: Peer groups and problem behavior. *American Psychologist, 54,* 755–764.

Gladding, S. T., Remley, T. P., Jr., & Huber, C. H. (2000). *Ethical, legal, and professional issues in the practice of marriage and family therapy* (3rd ed). Englewood Cliffs, NJ: Prentice Hall.

Swenson, L. C. (1997). *Psychology and law for the helping professions* (2nd ed.). Pacific Grove, CA: Brooks/Cole.

Woody, R.H. (2000). *Child custody: Practice standards, ethical issues, and legal safeguards for mental health professionals.* Sarasota, FL: Professional Resource Exchange.

Chapter 9

The Ethics of Assessment
Using Fair Procedures in Responsible Ways

Clients seek the professional help of counselors and therapists with two major goals in mind—to gain a better understanding of themselves and their problems and to find solutions to those troubles. The procedures that professionals use to achieve the first goal are collectively called *assessment*. A wide variety of assessment procedures has been developed, ranging from clinical interviews to standardized tests, behavioral observations, mental status exams, information from significant others, and analysis of case records. Ideally, assessment is a collaborative process between counselor and client(s), although the specific language usually derives from the expertise of the professional. Competent assessments include judgments about client prognosis, strengths, and social supports along with determinations of the scope and severity of problems (Ridley, Li, & Hill, 1998). Assessments can be expressed in a variety of ways, depending primarily on the clinician's theoretical orientation and use of formal classification systems for emotional difficulties. The more accurate the assessment of the problems, the more likely that they will be successfully resolved. Assessment is not limited to individual and group counseling and psychotherapy. For example, consultants assess the strengths and weaknesses of organizations, forensic psychologists assess a defendant's competence to stand trial, and educational psychologists assess the characteristics of effective learning environments. Whatever the setting, accurate, fair, and responsible assessment is the cornerstone of successful intervention.

Two aspects of assessment are especially vulnerable to abuse—the use of diagnostic categories to describe client problems and the use of psychological and educational tests. This chapter attends to the ethics of diagnosis and testing, elaborating on relevant comments in the American Counseling Association (ACA) and American Psychological Association (APA) codes, the views of ethics scholars, and related research evidence. The chapter also considers guidelines for ethical assessment in a multicultural society and the responsible use of technology in diagnosis and testing. Finally, the use of psychological tests in employment settings is reviewed. (The ethics of high-stakes educational testing is discussed in Chapter 12.)

The Ethics of Diagnosis

To *diagnose* means to define in professional terms the nature, limits, and intensity of a problem a client brings to counseling (Welfel & Patterson, 2004). The professional terms used to designate problems are derived from scholarly research and practice and are found in classification systems such as the *Diagnostic and Statistical Manual-IV-Text Revision* (DSM-IV-TR; American Psychiatric Association, 2000). However, the term *diagnosis* encompasses more than the medical model expressed in the DSM. Diagnosis refers to any organized system for defining client problems in common use by mental health professionals. For example, family therapists sometimes diagnose family system problems using typologies different from the DSM, but they are still classification systems because other family therapists give the same problems the same names (Kaslow, 1996; Sporakowski, Prouty, & Habben, 2001). In addition, career counselors often rely on their own terminology for evaluating career problems that is distinct from DSM or other psychodiagnostic categories (for example, Hardin & Leong, 2004). Whatever the classification system, diagnostic names provide a shared language for professionals and can guide them to appropriate interventions. Using common classification systems also makes the findings of researchers accessible to practitioners and allows counselors to better apply research advances to help clients.

Because of its association with naming and specifying problems, diagnosis has been pejoratively called "labeling" by some professionals, a term that implies that diagnosis is inherently dehumanizing and harmful (Hohenshil, 1996). Other writers caution against allowing diagnosis to distract from the human needs of the individual (Gergen, Hoffman, & Anderson, 1996; Gladding, 2003). Even counselors who acknowledge the value of diagnosis are somewhat ambivalent about its application (Hohenshil, 1996) or about the use of the DSM as the classification system of choice (Ivey & Ivey, 1998). When diagnosis is incompetently done or the diagnostic system lacks evidence of validity, such characterizations are not far from the mark. The history of mental health is replete with examples that show harmful effects when diagnosis is misused, but evidence also shows that when appropriately conducted, diagnosis serves a valid and beneficial function for clients. Section E.5.c. of the ACA *Code of Ethics* acknowledges the influence of both history and social prejudice on diagnosis. In fact, effective, ethical treatment *demands* careful definition of problems. One cannot treat what one has not identified. The relationship between diagnosis and treatment is like that of a map for a road trip. One is more likely to reach the destination by following a map than by intuitively selecting roads to see where they lead. The diagnosis is a map, a picture of the terrain that leads to a goal (destination), and a plan for reaching that goal (a sequence of roads to be taken). Nevertheless, it is important to acknowledge both the debate on the validity of diagnosis as currently practiced and the evidence that mental health professionals have sometimes misused the diagnostic processes (for example, see Pope & Vasquez, 1998; Valliant, 1984; Wakefield, 1992). Practitioners who are philosophically opposed to the term *diagnosis* are free to substitute another term. Central here is the recognition of the value of carefully assessed client strengths, weaknesses, and problem areas, not the acceptance of any particular word used to describe that process.

A Rationale for Emphasizing Ethics in Diagnosis

Ethics should govern the diagnostic process for many reasons. The most important is that diagnosing is one of the most far-reaching and influential activities in which a professional engages (Behnke, 2004). Applying a diagnostic name to clients' problems can powerfully affect many aspects of their functioning—self-esteem, career opportunities, eligibility for insurance, vulnerability to rejection and ridicule by others, and educational placement. Some kinds of diagnoses also influence whether licenses to practice an occupation will be granted, whether the state will allow a person the right to drive a car or purchase a firearm, or whether a court will allow an adult to adopt a child. For instance, people who have been diagnosed as chemically dependent are often required by law to reveal that diagnosis when they apply for a driver's license. A history of a DSM diagnosis of a psychological disorder can also limit a person's eligibility for health insurance.

Second, diagnosis has ethical dimensions because it is an inherently imperfect process. Although behavioral science has advanced substantially over the last century, our knowledge of psychological processes is still limited and our capacity to reliably assess the functioning of a given individual is also restricted. Practical problems with the implementation of diagnostic systems form one part of the difficulty. In the real world, neither clients nor third-party payors are usually willing to engage in truly thorough assessment. (The increasing pressure of insurers and managed care companies for "instant" diagnosis is in itself an ethical dilemma; it is addressed in greater detail in Chapter 11.) The imperfections in the diagnostic process are not solely the result of client or insurance impatience, however. Counselors and other mental health professionals have often made procedural and judgment errors (for example, Hill & Ridley, 2001; Rabinowitz & Efron, 1997; Smith & Dumont, 2000). McLaughlin (2002) refers to these as *human information processing errors.* Errors based on the timing and vividness of symptoms are especially common here. For example, the human tendency to seek quick answers to dilemmas flaws the diagnostic process (Anastasi, 1992), as does the inclination to emphasize information received early in the interview over data gathered later, called a *primacy effect* (Meehl, 1960). Especially vivid symptoms may be given more importance in the diagnosis than they deserve, with other important symptoms given less salience simply because they are less vivid (Spengler, 2000). In addition, research suggests that clinicians tend to use only the subset of the diagnostic criteria with which they are most familiar in arriving at a diagnosis, thereby drawing an erroneous conclusion (Rubinson, Asnis, Harkavy, & Friedman, 1988). Unfortunately, some evidence suggests that client payment method exerts undue influence over the diagnosis in subtle ways that professionals seem unaware of. Kielbasa, Pomerantz, Krohn, and Sullivan (2004) reported that psychologists were significantly more likely to use a DSM diagnosis when payment came through managed care than when clients paid out-of-pocket even when presented with identical descriptions of client symptoms. When evaluating symptoms of anxiety, psychologists in that study were 10 times more likely to apply a DSM diagnosis to managed care clients than self-pay clients.

The diagnostic systems currently used are also far from ideal. The research evidence supporting the categories is uneven, and the categories themselves are often overlapping, inconsistent, and vulnerable to gender, racial, and social class bias (Brodie, 2004; Campbell, 1999; Comer, 1996; Maddux, & Winstead, 2005). There are unresolved philosophical debates about what constitutes a dysfunction (Wakefield, 1992). These imperfections place a heavy burden on the practitioner trying to use the diagnostic system in a responsible way. Even well-trained professionals do not always arrive at the same diagnosis for identical symptoms using the DSM, partly because of the overlapping categories (for example, see Kirk & Kutchins, 1992; Kutchins & Kirk, 1997).

Third, the mere existence of diagnostic identifiers means that mental health professionals may be biased in favor of using them, even when a diagnosis is unjustified. Two classic studies illustrate this tendency. One was conducted by Langer and Abelson (1974), who found that therapists were more likely to diagnose as psychologically disturbed people identified as patients than people labeled as job applicants. The other study, even more famous, is that of Rosenhan (1973), in which pseudopatients got themselves admitted to mental hospitals by stating that they had been hearing voices. Once admitted, they displayed no other symptoms and denied any recurrence of the voices. In fact, they were instructed to behave as normally as possible from admission forward. No pseudopatient was ever identified as normal by the staff despite some lengthy hospital stays, and all had psychiatric diagnoses on their charts at discharge, although some charts were marked "in remission." (Ironically, the regular patients often questioned the pseudopatients about the legitimacy of their problems, but the staff never voiced such concerns.) Although others have severely critiqued Rosenhan's research (for example, Spitzer, 1975), the point is that whatever its flaws, Rosenhan's study demonstrates the tendency of mental health professionals to skew the information they receive to fit preexisting categories. This inclination to pathologize normal behavior can also be seen in less dramatic ways when counselors mistake normal feelings of bereavement for depression or label ordinary adolescent rebellion as conduct disorder. The counselor's first responsibility in assessment is to evaluate available evidence objectively, without presupposing that if a person is in the client role he or she must have a diagnosable disorder.

Fourth, in societies where stigma attaches to mental and emotional disorders, assigning an official diagnostic name to the client's pain can have powerful psychological effects in itself. Clients may feel ashamed or embarrassed or resist such a designation, and their coping skills may be tested. Clients may become despondent and erroneously conclude that they are beyond help, or they may even act out in inappropriate or self-destructive ways. However, clients may also have a powerful positive reaction to the designation, at least at first. Some may be relieved that there is a name for the confusing pattern of thoughts, feelings, and behaviors that they have been experiencing. Instead of engendering hopelessness, the name for their previously overwhelming problem encourages them to believe that they can be helped. Regardless of the specific reaction, however, its power means that counselors must act responsibly in communicating their assessments and help clients deal productively with them.

Fifth, as Matarazzo (1986) points out, the process of arriving at the diagnosis, of prodding the client for details of his or her experience, is in many ways an invasion of privacy no less severe than a physical examination by a physician or an audit by the Internal Revenue Service. Whenever a professional invades the privacy of another, certain conditions should exist: good reason for the invasion, potential for benefit, competent engagement in the activity itself, and the client's consent.

Counselors and therapists often lose sight of the threat that diagnosis represents to clients. Raimy (1975) suggests that people who voluntarily enter counseling have two underlying worries in addition to their presenting problems. First, they fear that professionals will confirm their worst fear—that they are truly crazy. Second, clients mistakenly believe that the problems they have are so unique and unintelligible that no one can understand or help them. The latter belief means that clients expect to be misunderstood and to remain isolated. Coming to a clear definition of the problem evokes the first deepseated fear: Clients think the diagnosis will confirm and make even more real their belief that they are crazy. Clients' second underlying worry sometimes results in a resistance to diagnosis, a resistance to believe that others have indeed had similar problems. Eventually, a skilled and compassionate professional can help a client revise such assumptions, but in the meantime the counselor needs to be sensitive to the invasion and threat that diagnosis and testing represent.

Sixth, knowledge of diagnostic language can lead to casual diagnosis, the application of diagnostic terms to people with whom one does not have a professional relationship. For example, counselors and therapists may be tempted to use their diagnostic skills to interpret the behaviors of politicians, disfavored colleagues, troublesome students, or others in their personal lives. (On one occasion a graduate student reported to me that a college instructor in a psychology class had wondered aloud to the class whether this student suffered from attention deficit disorder because she seemed distracted during lecture and then added insult to injury by suggesting that this student go to the counseling center to get an evaluation.) Those who do so damage the reputation of the profession and lead people who are considering professional help to wonder whether counselors will judge them in the same cavalier way. When mental health professionals engage in casual diagnosis, they encourage the misimpression that diagnosis is simple, magical, or dehumanizing. Television shows that include celebrity doctors with unspecified professional credentials may also lead the public to the same erroneous conclusion about diagnosis. The APA code is the most explicit on this point and on the need for the use of valid determinants of diagnosis:

APA *Ethical Principles*, Section 9.01: Bases for Assessments

(a) Psychologists base the opinions contained in their recommendations, reports, and diagnostic or evaluative statements, including forensic testimony, on information and techniques sufficient to substantiate their findings.

(b) Psychologists provide opinions of the psychological characteristics of individuals only after they have conducted an examination of the individuals adequate to support their statements or conclusions. When, despite reasonable efforts, such an examination is not practical, psychologists document the efforts they made and the result of those efforts, clarify the probable impact of their limited information on the reliability and validity of their opinions, and appropriately limit the nature and extent of their conclusions or recommendations.

(c) When psychologists conduct a record review or provide consultation or supervision and an individual examination is not warranted or necessary for the opinion, psychologists explain this and the sources of information on which they based their conclusions and recommendations.

The need for Section 9.01b first became apparent in the 1960s when Barry Goldwater was a candidate for the U.S. Presidency. At that time there were a number of mental health professionals who publicly questioned his mental stability and fitness for office but who had never interviewed or evaluated the candidate. Their willingness to make such bold statements in the absence of any direct professional contact led the American Psychiatric Association to initiate what came to be termed as "the Goldwater rule," which prohibits diagnosis in the absence of an examination (Slovenko, 2000). In a partial reversal of the standard in the 1992 version of the code, Section 9.01c of the current APA code does allow for assessment via review of records—that is, without a face-to-face evaluation—as long as the psychologist clarifies that the assessment is based on analysis of records rather than direct interaction with the clients and the professional explains the reasons the face-to-face evaluation is difficult to obtain or unnecessary in the particular circumstance (Behnke, 2005). A review of records to assess a client's needs is an activity quite distinct from casual diagnosis as long as it is based on the evidence provided and is prudent in the conclusions drawn in the absence of a more customary face-to-face assessment.

Still another misuse of diagnosis is to use it as a means to enhance insurance reimbursement for services rather than an accurate statement of client problems. Pope et al. (1987) found that 35% of their sample admitted to conscious use of this practice at least sometimes. Of these, 3.5% reported that they did so very often. When Tubbs and Pomerantz (2001) repeated this study 14 years later they found that 40% of psychologists admitted deliberately altering a diagnosis to meet insurance criteria, with 3.3% acknowledging that they engaged in this behavior very often. Research into diagnostic practices of mental health counselors reveals a similar pattern, with 44% of clinical counselors admitting that they had changed a diagnosis to obtain insurance reimbursement at least once (Danzinger & Welfel, 2001). Such a practice is not only inconsistent with ethical standards, it is illegal and would likely be called insurance fraud in most situations. Peterson (1996) notes that inappropriately using a diagnostic category to obtain insurance reimbursement is the most common type of financial misconduct to come before ethics committees, licensing boards, and the courts. Section 6.06 of the APA standards and Section C.6.b of the ACA standards clearly identify such practices as unethical. Such misdiagnosis is especially troubling when clients are prescribed psychotropic medications that are unnecessary and potentially harmful (Gray-Little & Kaplan, 1998).

Diagnosis can also be used to harm or discredit people who are already objects of discrimination and disfavor in the society. As Szasz (1971) noted, diagnosis can serve as a form of social control. He gives the example of labeling slaves who ran away from slaveholders as mentally disordered with a diagnosis of *drapetomania*. Another problem with diagnosis is evident in the tendency for members of minorities to receive more severe diagnoses than their majority counterparts for the same symptoms. For example, African-Americans and Latinos are more likely to receive diagnoses of schizophrenia than their European-American counterparts (for example, see Garb, 1997; Manderscheid & Barrett, 1991; National Institute of Mental Health, 1980; Pavkov, Lewis, & Lyons, 1989). At other times, emotionally disordered behavior is underdiagnosed, perhaps because deviancy is viewed as more normal or more frequent in diverse groups (see Gray-Little & Kaplan, 1998). In schools, ethical and legal challenges have been raised to many forms of educational and psychological testing, using evidence that such measures tend to discriminate against African-American and Hispanic children (Suzuki & Kugler, 2001; Walsh & Betz, 1995).

The now famous research by Broverman and her colleagues (Broverman, Broverman, Clarkson, Rosencrantz, & Vogel, 1970) first highlighted how professionals show gender bias in their professional judgments. They found that mental health professionals used discrepant definitions of a healthy male and a healthy female, but the same professionals used nearly identical adjectives to describe healthy males and healthy adults. Using this logic, a female adult could not be judged both a healthy adult and a healthy woman. Their research sparked a number of other studies that found similar conclusions. Even recent studies have shown that gender bias still affects some counselors' judgments (Danzinger & Welfel, 2000). Gender bias in assessment does not affect females alone, however. A study by Robertson and Fitzgerald (1990) illustrates bias against males. These authors found that counselors diagnosed males in nontraditional roles as more disturbed than males whose behavior aligned more closely with gender expectations. Other scholars suggest that the behaviors that are labeled as *disorders* or *dysfunctions* reflect the prejudices of society. Kaplan (1983) challenges the profession to explain why behaviors commonly found in women in Western society are labeled as pathological when parallel behaviors in men are not. She questions why the official nosology for psychiatric disorders identifies nonassertiveness and loyalty to loved ones even when they are cruel as dysfunctional but fails to categorize difficulty expressing feelings, resistance to emotional closeness, and aggressiveness in interpersonal relationship as disorders. The former characteristics are more common among women, and the latter are more common among men. A final example is equally disturbing. Despite the fact that homosexuality has not been identified as a mental disorder since 1973, a national survey of psychologists (Pope et al., 1987) found that 5.3% of the respondents believed that treating homosexuality *per se* as pathological was *unquestionably ethical.* When counselors were asked to respond to the same item, 14% of them made the same endorsement (Gibson & Pope, 1993). More recent research shows a reduction in misdiagnosis of clients who are homosexual (for example, Keffala & Stone, 1999; Stokes, 1999) but not an elimination of the problem. Taken together, these findings demonstrate the vulnerability of misuse of diagnosis for people from oppressed and marginalized groups.

This research also shows that defining a behavior as functional or dysfunctional does not take place in a social or cultural vacuum. As Maracek (1993) notes, all definitions of abnormal behavior are rooted in a culture's conception of what an ideal life is. Behaviors that appear bizarre in one society are viewed as normal and desirable in another. The variability in bereavement responses across cultures illustrates this fact. In some cultures, uncensored emotionality is encouraged and seen as completely normal, whereas in other cultures it is regarded as extreme and dysfunctional. Similarly, what one culture calls "appropriate assertiveness" another may label "disrespectful arrogance." Thus, counselors who fail to take into account the social and cultural context of current definitions of health and disorder may erroneously designate a normal behavior as pathologic. Marsalla and Kaplan (2002) propose that assessment of client problems should include *culturalogical interviewing,* a procedure that systematically explores the clients' life context and perceptions of health and abnormality. For an excellent review of the issues in the use of the DSM–IV–TR with culturally diverse populations, see Kress, Eriksen, Rayle, and Ford (2005) and Lopez and Guarnaccia (2005).

Finally, a diagnosis can become a "self-fulfilling prophecy" for a client. For instance, a person with an erroneous diagnosis of major depression may begin to interpret his or her normal variations in mood as problematic and may overreact to them. Others may begin to treat that person differently. In time, the focus on low mood can change behavior and thinking, and that person's ordinary adjustment problems may grow into the depressive disorder it has been labeled. A child erroneously diagnosed with an attention deficit may stop attempts to concentrate on school work because he believes that he is not capable of focus, given the diagnosis.

In summary, diagnosis is a powerful tool that counselors must learn to use responsibly so that it helps rather than harms the client. Its misuse stems from a variety of causes, but underlying them all is insensitivity to the implications of diagnosis, insufficient skill with diagnosis, or ignorance of the scientific and practical limitations of current diagnostic systems. For all these reasons the ACA stipulates the following.

ACA *Code of Ethics,* Section E.5: Proper Diagnosis of Mental Disorders

a. Proper Diagnosis. Counselors take special care to provide proper diagnosis of mental disorders. Assessment techniques (including personal interview) used to determine client care (e.g., locus of treatment, type of treatment, or recommended follow-up) are carefully selected and appropriately used.

b. Cultural Sensitivity. Counselors recognize that culture affects the manner in which clients' problems are defined. Clients' socioeconomic and cultural experiences are considered when diagnosing mental disorders.

The Ethics of Testing

The central ethical obligations in testing can be divided into (a) responsibilities of those who construct, market, and score psychological or educational tests, and (b) the responsibilities of professionals who use tests with clients. Not only do the ACA and APA codes of ethics include extensive comment on these issues, but other guidelines and statements are also available for counselors and therapists, including the following:

- *Standards for Educational and Psychological Tests* (American Educational Research Association [AERA], APA, & National Council on Measurement in Education [NCME], 1999), the outcome of a joint effort of AERA, APA, and NCME
- *Code of Fair Testing Practices in Education* (1988), issued by the Joint Committee on Testing Practices
- *Guidelines for Psychological Evaluation in Child Protection Matters* (1999), published by the American Psychological Association
- *Statement on the Use of Secure Psychological Tests in the Education of Graduate and Undergraduate Psychology Students* (2005b), American Psychological Association

Taken together, these documents give clear direction for responsible test construction and use. Familiarity with the terminology used in these standards facilitates their interpretation. A *test developer* is the person or organization that constructs and publishes a test. A *test user* is the professional who has decided to administer and/or interpret a test to a given population. A *test taker* or *examinee* is the person who will actually be completing the measure. We will first review the standards for test developers.

Ethics for Test Developers

The fundamental ethical directives for test developers are (a) to prepare instruments with substantial evidence to support their validity and reliability, with appropriate test norms, and with a clear and complete test manual, and (b) to keep the welfare of the consumer as a higher priority than profit. According to this standard, an acceptable test manual elaborates research evidence, describes appropriate applications, and honestly conveys strengths and weaknesses of the test. In addition, test manuals should describe the appropriateness of the test for groups of different racial, ethnic, and linguistic backgrounds. Current standards also encourage developers to provide data that help users to avoid common misinterpretations of results. Tests suited only for research should be clearly distinguished from those with clinical and educational applications. Professionals interested in developing a test for counseling or educational application should consult the *Standards for Educational and Psychological Tests* (AERA, APA, & NCME, 1999) for a full description of the ethical duties related to test construction.

In their marketing activities, producers must truthfully represent the test and restrict sales to professionals who can show they are qualified users. In other words, their drive to profit must be superseded by their commitment to the welfare of the test's intended audience. Most test developers require that users disclose their degrees, licenses, graduate courses, and training in psychological testing. Graduate students seeking to use tests in theses and dissertation research must provide similar information about the qualifications of the responsible supervisor. The research by Eyde, Moreland, and Robertson (1988) and the availability of many psychological tests on the Web to anyone with a credit card (Erard, 2004) suggest that compliance with these standards is far from universal, but professionals' obligation to limit their use of tests to those in which they have received training stands, regardless.

The ACA and APA codes delineate the following standards for test developers.

APA *Ethical Principles,* Section 9.05: Test Construction

Psychologists who develop tests and other assessment techniques use appropriate psychometric procedures and current scientific or professional knowledge for test design, standardization, validation, reduction or elimination of bias, and recommendations for use.

ACA *Code of Ethics,* Section E.12: Assessment Construction

Counselors use established scientific procedures, relevant standards, and current professional knowledge for assessment design in the development, publication, and utilization of educational and psychological assessment techniques.

Ethics for Test Users

Those who administer tests have two sets of people to whom they have ethical obligations: test developers and test takers. Our discussion begins with a description of the former. Because virtually all tests are copyrighted and dependent on the unfamiliarity of test takers with the items, test users have a duty to protect the security of a test from theft and unwarranted uses. This obligation means that test users must keep testing materials in their possession and refrain from copying or otherwise disseminating test items in inappropriate ways. Test developers have made a substantial investment in developing a valid and reliable measure. Thus they have a right to fair profit from that creation and a right to exert some control over the ways in which that material is disseminated.

This standard means that the practice of sending a standardized test home with clients is incompatible with the duty to protect test security unless it is designed for self-administration.

It is surprising that many professionals seem unaware of this prohibition. Pope et al. (1987) reported that 24.3% of the psychologists they sampled sent tests such as the Minnesota Multiphasic Personality Inventory (MMPI) home with clients to be completed. Counselors seem equally ignorant. In a later study 26% of counselors also failed to see the ethical problem in sending a test home with a client (Gibson & Pope, 1993). As soon as clients leave the office with a test, the professional has lost control of it and has no guarantee that it will be properly used or returned to them. Sending a test home with a client is unsatisfactory for clinical reasons as well. In this circumstance the counselor has no knowledge of the conditions under which the client took the test. The client may have failed to follow instructions, violated time constraints, or consulted with others about test items. In fact, counselors cannot even be certain that the test results they receive are those of the client. Perhaps a roommate or family member answered the questions, or perhaps responding to the items became a group project, with extensive discussion of the appropriate responses. If any of these events occur, the entire enterprise has become useless and counterproductive. Consequently, counselors should be resourceful about finding ways to get clients to complete instruments under controlled conditions. If necessary, they should postpone testing until such arrangements can be made. Scientific accuracy also demands that the test be administered under conditions as close as possible to the conditions established at the standardization of the test so that results can be compared to the norm group scores. The ACA code is explicit on this point.

ACA *Code of Ethics,* Section E.7: Conditions of Assessment Administration

a. Administration Conditions. Counselors administer assessments under the same conditions that were established in their standardization. When assessments are not administered under standard conditions, as may be necessary to accommodate clients with disabilities, or when unusual behavior or irregularities occur during the administration, those conditions are noted in interpretation, and the results may be designated as invalid or of questionable validity.

b. Technological Administration. Counselors ensure that administration programs function properly and provide clients with accurate results when technological or other electronic methods are used for assessment administration.

c. Unsupervised Assessments. Unless the assessment instrument is designed, intended, and validated for self-administration and/or scoring, counselors do not permit inadequately supervised use.

d. Disclosure of Favorable Conditions. Prior to administration of assessments, conditions that produce most favorable assessment results are made known to the examinee.

Sometimes practitioners entertain the possibility of modifying existing instruments to serve their purposes, or they consider appropriating existing items from other measures into their own assessments without the knowledge of the test developers. Because tests are copyrighted, it is both unethical and illegal for mental health professionals to attempt to use test items to develop their own tests or otherwise plagiarize existing measures. Test publishers may seek legal redress, and the practice violates a counselor's obligation to respect the rights of professional colleagues. The reliability and validity of the resulting homemade tests are also unknown, rendering its scores meaningless. Such instruments seem to have proliferated on the Web in recent years along with promises and claims that the Website providers do not often substantiate with objective research evidence (Buchanan, 2002; Kier & Molinari, 2004; Naglieri et al., 2004). This use of technology appears inconsistent with ethical standards and is generally misleading to the public. Both the ACA and APA standards address the problem of unscientifically developed measures and improper use and modification of copyrighted instruments.

ACA *Code of Ethics,* Section E.10: Assessment Security

Counselors maintain the integrity and security of tests and other assessment techniques consistent with legal and contractual obligations. Counselors do not appropriate, reproduce, or modify published assessments or parts thereof without acknowledgment and permission from the publisher.

APA *Ethical Principles,* Section 9.11: Maintaining Test Security

The term *test materials* refers to manuals, instruments, protocols, and test questions or stimuli and does not include *test data* as defined in Standard 9.04, Release of Test Data. Psychologists make reasonable efforts to maintain the integrity and security of test materials and other assessment techniques consistent with law and contractual obligations, and in a manner that permits adherence to this Ethics Code.

Test Security and Client Rights: Conflicting Legal Obligations

Changes in state and federal regulations have substantially changed the contents of the ethics codes in recent years regarding test security as it pertains to client rights to access to their counseling and psychotherapy records. For any professionals subject to Health Insurance Portability and Accountability Act (HIPAA) regulation (a category that includes virtually all who provide mental health services) those regulations require that clients be allowed to view their treatment records, including test results that are part of the personal record (HIPAA Privacy Rule, U.S. Department of Health and Human Services [DHHS], 2003). In parallel fashion some state legislatures have enacted open-records legislation that also affirms a client's right to access to all information about them in a medical or mental health record. Ohio, for example, passed a wide-reaching statute in 2003 that confers the rights of clients to view their records and also prohibits all mental health professionals except physicians from refusing access even if they have sound reason to believe access would be harmful to a client (Ohio Revised Code Section 3701.74). Such statutes also provide clients with the right to seek copies of their records; however, clients can be charged for the costs of copying. The conflict between this legislation, the copyright laws, and the language in the 1992 and 1995 versions of the APA and ACA ethical standards that demanded release of test data only to qualified professionals is apparent. Consider the following situations.

The Case of Margaret and Dr. DeJulio

Margaret, a 19-year-old community college student who has been having difficult completing her nursing courses, was evaluated by Dr. DeJulio, a psychologist, to attempt to determine her capacity to complete college-level work. As part of the assessment the psychologist administered the Wechsler Adult Intelligence Scale (WAIS-III, Wechsler, 1999). Soon after the assessment was completed Margaret formally requested copies of all information in her mental health record, including test findings. This request troubled Dr. DeJulio because the standard WAIS-III protocol sheet on which any test taker's responses are recorded also includes actual test items that appear to be covered by test security and copyright provisions. It seemed to the psychologist that to follow HIPAA and state law about client access to records meant that he could not comply with copyright laws or honor the test publisher's right to test security.

David and Ms. Richley

When David, a 32-year-old supermarket manager and new father, began to experience stress in coping with parenthood and a demanding job he sought counseling from Ms. Richley, a predoctoral intern in counseling psychology. As part of the assessment of his difficulties, the counselor administered an MMPI-2 (Butcher, Dahlstrom, Graham, Tellegen, & Kaemmer, 1989) to David. His responses showed mild elevations on scales 2 and 4, and both David and Ms. Richley found the test findings useful in his care. After 6 weeks of treatment, counseling was terminated by mutual agreement. Several weeks later Ms. Richley received a request from David for a copy of his complete record, a request that was quickly honored. She provided him with all notes and forms related to his treatment, the MMPI report, the bubble sheet for his MMPI responses, and the profile sheet on which his scores were plotted. Approximately 1 week later David called to seek a copy of the test booklet with the items. When Ms. Richley explained to David that she was not at liberty to release the test items, David said that he believed he was entitled to that information under Ohio's open records law. The counselor replied that she would explore the issue and get back to him as soon as she had an answer.

In response to such dilemmas, ethics committees of the professional associations have devoted much attention to strategies to address this conflict and provide professionals with better guidance. Ultimately, these questions may require legal resolution in the courts or legislatures, but the professional associations have offered the following standards and recommendations for professionals caught in similar situations. APA has taken the lead in this matter and has helped professionals by clarifying what constitutes test data that are part of the client's record and what is assessment information that belongs exclusively to the publisher (test materials).

APA *Ethical Principles,* Section 9.04: Release of Test Data

(a) The term *test data* refers to raw and scaled scores, client/patient responses to test questions or stimuli, and psychologists' notes and recordings concerning client/patient statements and behavior during an examination. Those portions of test materials that include client/patient responses are included in the definition of *test data*. Pursuant to a client/patient release, psychologists provide test data to the client/patient or other persons identified in the release. Psychologists may refrain from releasing test data to protect a client/patient or others from substantial harm or misuse or misrepresentation of the data or the test, recognizing that in many instances release of confidential information under these circumstances is regulated by law.

(b) In the absence of a client/patient release, psychologists provide test data only as required by law or court order.

Based on these provisions, Ms. Richley concludes that she is correct in refraining from providing David with the booklet with the MMPI items because that is *test material* that contains no client data. According to Behnke (2003), it is not subject to release because it contains no information that is unique to a particular client. Providing the booklet of items to a client would be violating the professional's obligations to test security. The situation Dr. DeJulio faces is more complex because the protocol sheet that includes the individual client's answers also contains WAIS-III items. Under HIPAA and the language in the code, that protocol sheet appears to fit the definition of *test data,* but giving it to the client seems inconsistent with copyright laws and with the agreement he signed with the test publisher when he purchased the instrument. Therefore, the ideal solution would be to speak with the client to determine whether she would be amenable to a summary of the protocol that omitted the copyrighted items or to a redacted version of the protocol that blacked out the test items but retained all of Dr. DeJulio's notations about her responses (Behnke, 2003; Fisher, 2003; Erard, 2004). If the client were to insist on the entire protocol as it exists in the record, Dr. DeJulio would be well advised to speak with an attorney about the conflict between copyright law and HIPAA. It is important to note, however, that both HIPAA and the APA standard allow a psychologist to withhold test data when release is likely to be a threat to the safety of the client or otherwise cause substantial harm to him or her (Behnke, 2003).

The 2005 ACA *Code of Ethics* retains language similar to the last version of the code and cannot be applicable to any counselors who must comply with HIPAA regulations or other state statutes.

ACA *Code of Ethics,* Section E.4.b: Release of Raw Data to Qualified Professionals

Counselors release data (e.g., protocols, counseling or interview notes, and questionnaires) in which the client is identified only with the consent of the client or the client's legal representative. Such data are released only to persons recognized by counselors as competent to interpret the data.

Of course, both the ACA *Code of Ethics* and the APA *Ethical Principles* allow professionals to follow the law in situations in which their ethical standards contradict provisions of the law or regulations.

ACA *Code of Ethics,* Section H.1.b: Conflicts Between Ethics and Laws

If ethical responsibilities conflict with law, regulations, or other governing legal authority, counselors make known their commitment to the ACA *Code of Ethics* and take steps to resolve the conflict. If the conflict cannot be resolved by such means, counselors may adhere to the requirements of law, regulations, or other governing legal authority.

APA *Ethical Principles,* Section 1.02: Conflicts Between Ethics and Law, Regulations, or Other Governing Legal Authority

If psychologists' ethical responsibilities conflict with law, regulations, or other governing legal authority, psychologists make known their commitment to the Ethics Code and take steps to resolve the conflict. If the conflict is unresolvable via such means, psychologists may adhere to the requirements of the law, regulations, or other governing legal authority.

Obligations to Test Takers

The ethical responsibilities of mental health professionals to the people to whom they administer tests are extensive and deserve detailed discussion. The first duty is *competence.* Weiner (1989) has remarked, "It is possible in psychodiagnostic work to be competent without being ethical, it is not possible to be ethical without being competent" (p. 829). Testing procedures are deceptively simple to the untrained person. At first glance the interpretation of personality inventories, achievement test scores, or other measures appears straightforward and uncomplicated. However, the process of choosing the right test for the intended purpose and audience requires sound professional judgment and extensive training to understand test manuals and research data (Cates, 1999). Similarly, proper test administration is crucial to a meaningful outcome and requires more than the ability to follow test instructions; it also demands knowledge of how to adapt the testing conditions to unique client circumstances without jeopardizing the validity of the results. For instance, mental health professionals should know how to modify, without invalidating the results, the administration of an individual intelligence test to a person who stutters and should then know how to account for this modification in a report of results. Finally, interpreting scores and communicating those findings to clients are often the most demanding tasks of all. The ethics codes and scholarly writings (for example, Anastasi, 1992; Pope, 1992) devote extensive attention to this topic.

What are the determinants of competence in these tasks? They are as follows:

- Formal study of the particular measures, including careful review of research, test manuals, and other related materials
- A background in statistics and measurement sufficient to understand the reliability, validity, norms, and descriptive data provided by the test publishers
- A knowledge of the strengths and limitations of the test and its proper applications with diverse populations
- A period of supervised experience in its use, including interpretation of the results to clients, after which a competent supervisor judges the counselor to be competent also

The length of time for developing such competencies varies depending on the background of the professional and the particular instrument. Instruction in complex personality tests such as the MMPI-2 (Butcher, Dahlstrom, Graham, Tellegen, & Kaemmer, 1989) or the Rorschach (Rorschach, 1951) requires significant study over many months. In our training program, for example, graduate students must have courses in statistics, educational measurement, psychopathology, and psychological testing before registering for the MMPI course. After successfully completing the MMPI course, they enroll in a 16-week internship in which they must administer, score, and interpret the instrument to appropriate clients and then write the test reports. Only after all these educational challenges are met are students deemed ready to use that test in practice. Even then, they are instructed that they should find additional supervision in testing until they are licensed. Of course, not all tests require this kind of protracted study, but each requires a similarly systematic approach to developing competence. Walsh and Betz (1995) suggest that the greater the likelihood that a test can be misused, the more stringent the criteria for competency should be.

Possessing a particular graduate degree is not in itself proof of competence. Nor does competence in the use of one test or one group of tests imply competence in any other test. Competence must always be determined on the basis of the particular training and experience of a given individual with a graduate degree in a mental health field. Historically, psychology programs have offered stronger training in testing (and most testing is conducted by psychologists [Frauenhoffer, Ross, Gfeller, Searight, & Piotrowski, 1998]), but not all psychologists have graduated from programs with strong training in testing. Similarly, counseling curricula have tended to be less thorough in this area, but particular programs may be exceptionally comprehensive in this domain. The judgment about competence then is always determined on the basis of the individual's experience and background with a particular measure. Smith and Dumont (1995) report findings that suggest that some professionals are not as diligent as they ought to be about the boundaries of their testing competence. The psychologists in their study readily offered interpretations of a poorly validated test with which they had little experience or training.

Professional standards mandate that practitioners act responsibly themselves, and they also intervene when tests and assessment procedures are used by those who are not qualified to use them. (See the APA *Ethical Principles,* Section 2.06.) This mandate stems from the risk of misuse and harm to clients. The APA standard also states that psychologists should not take any action that promotes the use of assessment procedures by incompetent individuals.

In some states there have been legal challenges to the use of psychological tests by nonpsychologists, and some of the legal issues are not resolved (Marino, 1995). In Ohio, however, the state attorney general ruled against the position that only psychologists could use procedures labeled as psychological (Montgomery, 1996), thereby supporting the rights of other competent mental health professionals to administer tests. In any case, at this time, the ethical standard is competence, not type of license. Needless to say, counselors should follow legal developments in their states to ascertain the legal standard that affects them. Professional associations have been actively involved in this controversy. APA formed a Task Force on Test User Qualifications, partly out of concern about incompetent test use. The final document they produced, *Assessment of Test User Qualifications* (Turner, DeMers, Fox, & Reed, 2001), identifies minimum competencies for proper test usage and takes the position that test competence is behaviorally based and not defined by a license or credential. When a movement began to restrict psychological testing only to licensed psychologists, another professional group, the Fair Access Coalition on Testing (FACT), was formed to challenge that position (www.fairaccess.org). The latter group also contends that skill in testing does not automatically derive from a particular professional credential.

In addition to competence, Anastasi and Urbana (1997) describe a second important aspect of the ethics of testing. They posit that tests should meet a standard of *relevance* to the needs of a particular client. Testing for its own sake, or because of an institutional mandate, is inappropriate. As long as tests cause clients stress, invade privacy, and are subject to misuse by unskilled people, the criterion of relevance must be met. Tests used for research may be used only with explicit informed consent to that use.

A third important ethical mandate for test users is *multiple criteria for decision making*. This means that tests never serve as the sole criterion on which clinical or educational decisions are based. Anastasi (1992) calls this the "hazard of a single score" (1992, p. 611). Tests are limited in their predictive ability, and the occasions in which they present invalid or unreliable results are not always apparent to the test user. Thus, all decisions that will affect a client's future must be founded on multiple criteria. For example, depression should never be diagnosed on the basis of an elevated test score. Counselors must find independent corroborating evidence to make such a diagnosis. That evidence should come from personal interviews, behavioral manifestations, reports from significant others, and so on. Ibrahim and Arrendondo (1986) cogently state this obligation, arguing that competent assessment should be "multisource, multilevel, and multimethod" (p. 350). In parallel fashion, no academic placement for a child should be completed on the basis of test scores alone. The likelihood of error and harm to the client from reliance on test data alone is simply too great.

Finally, professionals should understand their responsibilities when asked to make inferences on the basis of test results. In other words, they have a duty to acknowledge the limitations of tests in making inferences about behaviors not directly assessed by the test. A counselor or therapist may wish to know whether a score can help predict future violence or suicide risk. Whenever asked to make such inferences, professionals recognize that they cannot be as confident of their judgments as they may be of their description of current functioning based on test results. Predicting future behavior is especially difficult. For example, a therapist can be more certain that an elevation on a depression scale indicates current dysphoria than that the elevation is an indicator of future mood. Thus, the comments of counselors related to such inferences must not go beyond the available evidence and must include material that acknowledges the limitations of tests (Weiner, 1989).

APA has published a set of case studies of ethical issues in using tests that can help counselors examine the application of these ethical standards to specific situations (Eyde et al., 1993). Readers who plan to conduct testing as part of their professional practice are urged to consult this and the other resources listed in the recommended readings for further guidance.

Client Rights in Testing

Ethical standards delineate a number of rights for clients and accompanying responsibilities for professionals to ensure that client rights are protected. Foremost among these is the right to *informed choice* about tests. Clients should be informed about the purposes, tasks, uses, and implications of the proposed testing, including any risks and benefits that may result. If testing data will be used in any decision making, clients should know that. For example, if an MMPI-2 will be used to help determine a client's eligibility for a special treatment program, that should be disclosed. Similarly, if an educational test will have a role in deciding the appropriateness of special services, that information should be communicated to the child and the parents. Clients have a right to have their questions about a test answered, although test items and other data that might compromise test security or the validity of results should be excepted from this general guideline. If copies of test reports are to be kept in a client's file, that should be explained as well. Needless to say, clients should also understand that they have the right to refuse testing or to withdraw their consent at any time. The specific wording of the ACA code is as follows.

ACA *Code of Ethics*, Section E.3: Informed Consent in Assessment

a. Explanation to Clients. Prior to assessment, counselors explain the nature and purposes of assessment and the specific use of results by potential recipients. The explanation will be given in the language of the client (or other legally authorized person on behalf of the client), unless an explicit exception has been agreed upon in advance. Counselors consider the client's personal or cultural context, the level of the client's understanding of the results, and the impact of the results on the client.

The APA code discusses informed consent for assessment in the following way.

APA *Ethical Principles*, Section 9.03: Informed Consent for Assessment

(a) Psychologists obtain informed consent for assessments, evaluations, or diagnostic services, as described in Standard 3.10, Informed Consent, except when (1) testing is mandated by law or governmental regulations; (2) informed consent is implied because testing is conducted as a routine educational, institutional, or organizational activity (e.g., when participants voluntarily agree to assessment when applying for a job); or (3) one purpose of the testing is to evaluate decisional capacity. Informed consent includes an explanation of the nature and purpose of the assessment, fees, involvement of third parties, and limits of confidentiality and sufficient opportunity for the client/patient to ask questions and receive answers.

(b) Psychologists inform persons with questionable capacity to consent or for whom testing is mandated by law or governmental regulations about the nature and purpose of the proposed assessment services, using language that is reasonably understandable to the person being assessed.

(c) Psychologists using the services of an interpreter obtain informed consent from the client/patient to use that interpreter, ensure that confidentiality of test results and test security are maintained, and include in their recommendations, reports, and diagnostic or evaluative statements, including forensic testimony, discussion of any limitations on the data obtained.

The ACA code highlights another aspect for informed consent. Section E.7.d states, "Prior to test administration, conditions that produce most favorable test results are made known to the examinee." For example, if research suggests that sufficient rest and a positive test-taking attitude are likely to improve performance on an achievement test, clients should be told about the influence of these factors before the testing.

The second client right is to *feedback* about the results of the testing. For many years, feedback was regarded as optional, left to the discretion of the professional. As recently as 1983 Berndt found that only a minority of clinicians were enthusiastic about providing feedback and some believed it unwise to share such data. Others in his study favored a limited amount of feedback, with some stating that they shared only positive results. The consumer rights movement was one important factor in changing that view, but there are still sites where this right is not honored. The current standard is clear, however—unless a person waives his or her right to feedback before testing or if a law prevents it, the professional is bound to provide an interpretation of the results. The codes state the following.

APA *Ethical Principles*, Section 9.10: Explaining Assessment Results

Regardless of whether the scoring and interpretation are done by psychologists, by employees or assistants, or by automated or other outside services, psychologists take reasonable steps to ensure that explanations of results are given to the individual or designated representative unless the nature of the relationship precludes provision of an explanation of results (such as in some organizational consulting, preemployment or security screenings, and forensic evaluations) and this fact has been clearly explained to the person being assessed in advance.

ACA *Code of Ethics*, Section E.1.b b: Client Welfare

Counselors do not misuse assessment results and interpretations and take reasonable steps to prevent others from misusing the information these techniques provide. They respect the client's right to know the results, the interpretations made, and the bases for their conclusions and recommendations.

Direct communication with the client about results has been mandated for several reasons. First, tests are fallible and clients ought to have an opportunity to respond to erroneous or misleading conclusions. The opportunity to correct such errors is especially important if test data will influence decisions made about the client's future. Discussion of results also assists the counselor in evaluating the reliability and validity of findings and in accurately interpreting subtle or confusing findings from the test. For instance, a moderate elevation on the L (lie) scale of the MMPI may mean that the test taker was attempting to create a good impression in a very unsophisticated way, or it may mean that the person has had an unusually strict religious upbringing. A discussion with a client about historical or current life circumstances can help the counselor determine the more accurate interpretation of such scales and state with greater confidence the meaning of test scores.

Clients are also owed feedback. As Matarazzo (1986) notes, testing is not always easy for a client. The process often increases anxiety, pushes clients to focus on uncomfortable aspects of their experience, and is often tedious and intellectually demanding. Counselors, who usually thrive in academic settings and testing situations, tend to overlook the onerous connotation of the task for clients whose academic experiences may have been less rewarding. For some clients, the effort expended just to read the words on the page is substantial. Even for clients who are at home with the intellectual aspects of testing, there are still costs. For example, a person suffering from depression or anxiety must work hard just to focus enough to answer the questions and stay on task. In short, clients are making a considerable investment when they agree to testing, and clear, accurate feedback in language they can understand is a fair return for that investment.

A final reason for conducting a feedback session is that there is research evidence that it has therapeutic value. For example, in one study (Finn & Tonsager, 1997) clients who received feedback on their MMPI–2 results experienced significant reductions in symptoms and distress. They also reported no negative consequences from the feedback; instead, they were overwhelmingly positive about the experience. This finding is consistent with the views of other scholars that feedback benefits client–counselor rapport, client cooperation, and good feelings about tests and about mental health professionals (for example, see Dorr, 1981; Finn & Butcher, 1991; Fischer, 1986; Newman & Greenway, 1997).

Why then, aren't counselors enthusiastic about giving feedback? Pope (1992) identifies three reasons for their reluctance: (a) because they find giving bad news uncomfortable, (b) because they find it difficult to translate technical jargon into language clients can understand, and (c) because test results do not contain the kind of clear and unambiguous findings the client has hoped for (p. 268). Although all of these reasons are understandable, none is an excuse for avoiding feedback. When experiencing such reactions, counselors should seek out supervision about how to proceed skillfully and responsibly. If such reactions recur, a counselor's competence in using the test is probably less than adequate because competence in testing necessarily includes the capacity to explain negative findings sensitively, to translate jargon easily, and to discuss the limitations of tests openly.

The professional standards are rather vague in describing precisely what is meant by feedback. Does it mean sharing every descriptor associated with every scale? Does it require both verbal and written feedback? Can it be limited to a few sentences of general comments? How can the obligation to feedback be balanced against the publisher's right to security for the test? The general guideline that seems most prudent is to provide as full a description as time, interest, and test security allow, omitting or postponing review of results that the counselor judges would be harmful to the client's current well-being. It is important to note that the codes do not require feedback under all circumstances. If a counselor chooses to omit discussion of particular aspects of a test, the counselor's decision must be based on an objective consideration of the client's welfare, not on a wish to avoid an uncomfortable undertaking. Such a judgment should stand up to the "clean well-lit room standard" and be periodically reviewed so that if a client's state of mind changed to be receptive to those findings, the counselor would be in a position to disclose them.

When presenting feedback to clients, counselors are obliged to remind clients about the fallibility of tests and to present results in the form of hypotheses rather than conclusions. The test does not contain "absolute truths" about them; rather, it offers hypotheses that may be helpful in understanding their behavior and in suggesting treatment strategies. Counselors should prepare carefully for feedback sessions, be alert to the ways people can misunderstand scores, and take extra care to be precise in their descriptions (Pope, 1992). Each feedback session should include a focus on the client's experience during the test and on his or her goals for the session. The importance of plain, clear language understandable to the client is crucial—jargon does not communicate, nor does it advance client trust in the counselor's expertise. Even when counselors meet this criterion, they can err in another way—overwhelming the client with lengthy descriptions that cannot be absorbed in one session. This error occurs when trying to "cover the test" rather than to enlighten the client about its findings. When this occurs counselors end up talking at length, giving the client little opportunity to respond, and generally defeating the purpose of feedback—that is, to work collaboratively with the client to determine the meaning and impact of the test results for future sessions.

The professional's responsibility to provide feedback in language the client can understand has been highlighted in the codes recently. The *Standards for Educational and Psychological Tests* (AERA, APA, & NCME, 1999) define an appropriate explanation of results clearly: "...should describe in simple language what the test covers, what scores mean, the precision of the scores, common misinterpretations of the test scores, and how test scores will be used" (Standard 5.10, p. 65).

Statutes and case law may affect the provision of feedback in some states and some settings. For example, when courts mandate psychological testing to determine a person's competency to stand trial there may be no legal obligation at all to provide the client with information about test results (APA, Committee on Psychological Testing and Assessment, 1996). The court may even prohibit feedback. In that circumstance, the counselor may follow legal rulings without worry about ethical penalties. If possible and permissible within that setting, however, counselors should seek to give some information to test takers, in recognition of their basic human rights.

Sometimes test results provide information that must be acted on (Pope, 1992). For example, a test may suggest a high probability of suicide or a substance abuse problem in a 12 year old. In such an event, a counselor's duty to protect is evoked, at least insofar as the counselor must explore whether the test finding is accurate. If additional investigation reveals that the test result is supported by other information, the counselor should act to prevent the likely harm.

When mental health professionals are employed as consultants and evaluators for organizations, they often have no direct relationship with the test takers. An organization may use tests to screen inappropriate job candidates, or a court may seek to gather data to make a custody determination. In such instances, test takers may be asked to waive their right to receive test results. A mental health professional may honor such a waiver, provided the person agreed to it *prior to the testing* and was given appropriate information for an informed consent.

The length of feedback sessions will vary from client to client and from test to test. Practical concerns about the pressures imposed by managed care and brief therapy have a place in the discussion. However, the central determinants to the decision about how much time should be devoted to this task should be as follows:

- The client's satisfaction that he or she understands the meaning and implications of the test results
- The counselor's assessment that the feedback has been sufficient to clarify any confusions in the test findings or elucidate any subtle results
- Their mutual agreement about the ways in which test results should influence future treatment planning
- The implications of the release of these findings to others if the client agreed to the release prior to the testing

The process of providing clients with feedback about test results should be documented in the case record, along with the client's comments about the feedback and any aspects of the testing that need additional follow-up.

Clients also have the right to protection against another form of misuse of test results—the inappropriate use of outdated or obsolete test findings. This standard stems from the fact that tests sample behavior in a single time period (Anastasi, 1992), which cannot have perpetual validity. Both codes unambiguously refer to this topic.

ACA *Code of Ethics,* Section E.11: Obsolete Tests and Outdated Test Results

Counselors do not use data or results from assessments that are obsolete or outdated for the current purpose. Counselors make every effort to prevent the misuse of obsolete measures and assessment data by others.

APA *Ethical Principles,* Section 9.08: Obsolete Tests and Outdated Test Results

(a) Psychologists do not base their assessment or intervention decisions or recommendations on data or test results that are outdated for the current purpose.

(b) Psychologists do not base such decisions or recommendations on tests and measures that are obsolete and not useful for the current purpose.

The point at which tests become outdated or obsolete varies with the individual measure, the construct being assessed, and the person being evaluated. Depressed mood, for example, may be highly changeable and scores of that construct may be outdated rapidly, but measures of extroversion or spatial relations may be stable for an extended period. Judgments about this issue must be made on an individual basis according to the state of the science of measuring the relevant construct. Any test used to predict a future behavior, such as performance in graduate courses, becomes obsolete as soon as actual performance is known. In other words, standardized test scores are a much less reliable predictor of probability of successful completion of graduate school than a person's grades in their first year of graduate study. These provisions also apply to the assessments that professionals sometimes receive from outside sources such as school systems, courts, or other organizations.

Responsible Use of Test Interpretation Services and Computer-Based Testing

Counselors and therapists often contract with computer-based scoring and interpretation services for the psychological tests they administer to clients. Practitioners view these services as timesavers that relieve them of the onerous task of scoring complex instruments. In one study by McMinn, Ellens, and Soref (1999) 85% of psychologists indicated that they use computer-based services to score psychological tests. Use of scoring services is ethical and probably a wise decision because it avoids the scoring errors to which hand-scoring is prone. Along with the scores, these services frequently furnish a typed interpretation of the results; it is the use of these interpretations that is controversial. Several important conditions must be met before the use of computerized test interpretations is ethically justified.

First, the computerized interpretations must be based on criteria that have been subject to validation, and these results should be made available to subscribers to the service. Matarazzo (1986) has criticized the scoring criteria used by the services because they have not presented documentation that the criteria are supported by scientific evidence, nor have the criteria been offered for objective review by independent scholars. This omission is particularly important because the reports are packaged to appear so professional, complete, and carefully crafted that they seem scientific. Anastasi terms this "the hazard of illusory precision" (1992, p. 611). Second, according to Matarazzo, these interpretive reports do not generate multiple interpretations of results, although for some combinations of scores multiple interpretations are indeed possible. Other criticisms have been made about computerized reports. Bersoff and Hofer (1991) contend that such reports fail to be individualized and cannot take into account the unique characteristics of the test taker. In addition, they argue that these reports are "bland, impersonal, and nonspecific" (p. 243). Garb (2000) contends that the validity of some interpretive packages is highly questionable and that use of the packages may produce reports that have differential validity for different ethnic groups.

The most crucial danger of interpretive services is that counselors and therapists not otherwise competent to interpret tests will use these interpretations in their work and present these results to clients. *Standards for Educational and Psychological Tests* (AERA, APA, & NCME, 1999) condemn this practice. Computerized test interpretations should only be used in conjunction with professional judgment. A national survey of psychologists found that practitioners voiced concern about unqualified people using these interpretations as one of the primary ethical issues facing them in assessment (Pope & Vetter, 1992). The responsibility of the test user to ascertain the meaning of results for each client does not diminish just because an organization that appears credible (but has no firsthand knowledge of the client) has written a report. The only responsible way to use such material is as a "second opinion." These materials should serve as aids to accurate assessment of test results, not as substitutes for clinician deficiencies. Professionals who would not be judged competent to interpret an instrument in the absence of such a report must not use these reports. Bersoff and Hofer (1991) and Snyder (2000) point out that if there are legal challenges to the use of computer scoring and interpretations, both the test user and the organization that provides that service are likely to be listed as defendants. Test users who are unable to demonstrate their independent competence in that test would be particularly vulnerable to a malpractice claim.

The final risk of computerized test interpretation is that even professionals skilled enough to interpret test results will overly rely on the computer reports or will fail to be as diligent as necessary in their interpretation of scores. McMinn and his associates reported that a small percentage of psychologists (6%) used the computer interpretation as a substitute for their own interpretation at least rarely, but a larger percentage (56%) "cut and pasted" segments from the computer report into their own summary of test findings at least rarely. The McMinn study does not provide sufficient information to determine whether the professionals who cut and pasted violated any ethical guidelines in so doing. However, the procedure can be ethical only if the professional has a sound clinical rationale for selecting the designated segments in each case and if appropriate acknowledgment of the source of the statements is made in the professional's report. (For an excellent review of the ethical issues in computerized assessment, see Schulenberg & Yutrzenka, 2004.)

The ACA code speaks primarily to the duties of those who develop scoring and interpretation services. The APA code offers a similar statement but also discusses more fully the obligations of users of these services.

ACA *Code of Ethics,* Section E.9: Scoring and Interpretation of Assessments

c. Assessment Services. Counselors who provide assessment scoring and interpretation services to support the assessment process confirm the validity of such interpretations. They accurately describe the purpose, norms, validity, reliability, and applications of the procedures and any special qualifications applicable to their use. The public offering of an automated test interpretations service is considered a professional-to-professional consultation. The formal responsibility of the consultant is to the consultee, but the ultimate and overriding responsibility is to the client.

APA *Ethical Principles,* Section 9.06: Interpreting Assessment Results

When interpreting assessment results, including automated interpretations, psychologists take into account the purpose of the assessment as well as the various test factors, test-taking abilities, and other characteristics of the person being assessed, such as situational, personal, linguistic, and cultural differences that might affect psychologists' judgments or reduce the accuracy of their interpretations. They indicate any significant limitations of their interpretations.

9.09 Test Scoring and Interpretation Services

(a) Psychologists who offer assessment or scoring services to other professionals accurately describe the purpose, norms, validity, reliability, and applications of the procedures and any special qualifications applicable to their use.

(b) Psychologists select scoring and interpretation services (including automated services) on the basis of evidence of the validity of the program and procedures as well as on other appropriate considerations.

(c) Psychologists retain responsibility for the appropriate application, interpretation, and use of assessment instruments, whether they score and interpret such tests themselves or use automated or other services.

Multicultural Issues in Psychological Testing

The codes of ethics exhort mental health professionals to be alert to the ways in which gender, age, race, ethnicity, national origin, religion, sexual orientation, disability, language, or socioeconomic status may affect the appropriate administration or interpretation of assessment tools (APA *Ethical Principles,* Section 9.06). The ACA code attends both to the ethics of selecting tests for culturally diverse populations and to their appropriate administration and interpretation.

ACA *Code of Ethics,* Section E.6: Test Selection

Counselors are cautious when selecting tests for culturally diverse populations to avoid inappropriateness of testing that may be outside of socialized behavioral or cognitive patterns.

ACA *Code of Ethics,* Section E.8: Multicultural Issues/Diversity in Assessment

Counselors use with caution assessment techniques that were normed on populations other than that of the client. Counselors recognize the effects of age, color, culture, disability, ethnic group, gender, race, language preference, religion, spirituality, sexual orientation, and socioeconomic status on test administration and interpretation, and place test results in proper perspective with other relevant factors.

These standards, the *Guidelines on Multicultural Training, Research, Practice, and Organizational Change for Psychologists* (APA, 2003), and the scholarship on multiculturalism underscore the importance of three particular issues. First, because there is no such thing as a culture-free test (Anastasi & Urbana, 1997; Walsh & Betz, 1995) or a completely unbiased professional (Roysircar, 2005), professionals must select assessment instruments and interpret them in light of the client's cultural background. This position is echoed by Constantine and Sue (2005), who elaborate extensively on the meaning of competent multicultural assessment. These authors contend that counselors need *knowledge* of how potential bias may affect the interpretation of test results and *skill* in using measures for the benefit of diverse clients. (See Chapter 10 for more discussion of these competencies.)

One important consideration in this area is the availability of normative data for the client's population. When tests do not have norms for particular cultural groups, alternative measures should be sought. If no alternatives exist, those results should be interpreted with great caution. For example, a mental health agency should not use the original MMPI for personality assessment with Latino or Asian-American clients if the MMPI-2 can be substituted because the newer measure has included members of those populations in its norm group. The counselor's responsibility does not end with the use of the newer test, however. It extends to becoming familiar with subsequent research on scores of those populations on the test because such research can be crucial to accurate interpretation of a particular score or ambiguous finding.

Second, test users should also carefully examine tests for content bias (Roysircar, 2005; Walsh & Betz, 1995). Content bias occurs when the items in a test are differentially familiar to different cultural groups. Test items that ask respondents about deciduous trees may be impossible for Native Americans from the desert Southwest to respond to because they have few such trees in their environment. Similarly, urban dwellers may be unable to give meaningful responses to items that require knowledge of rural or suburban settings. Sensitivity to the impact of such items on the conclusions drawn from a test is crucial to avoid misinterpretation of the results. A desire to eliminate content bias in items has been a factor in the revision of several well-known personality inventories (such as the MMPI-2). Content bias has been the focus of much debate in the literature on tests of cognitive abilities with culturally diverse populations. Scholars have presented cogent arguments that lower scores from diverse groups on such measures are at least partially caused by content bias (Lonner & Ibrahim, 1996).

Third, because of counselors' duty to avoid discrimination and to intervene whenever possible to stop it, counselors should be alert to the ways their test reports are used with culturally diverse clients. The best known legal case involving discrimination on the basis of test results was *Larry P. v. Riles* in California (1979). In that case the court found that school officials had misdiagnosed a student and misused intelligence test results in a way that resulted in significant, perhaps permanent, harm to that child. This case acted as the impetus for reexamination of the testing practices with minority students in California and other states. That case is a blatant example of the problem, but there are many other less dramatic violations of client rights. Too often test reports are superficially understood and then used in a discriminatory fashion. School officials who expect Mexican-American students to have lower scores on achievement tests may be less likely to carefully interpret such test results and to account for the impact of culture and linguistic variables. They may overinterpret slight differences favoring European-American students, when an accurate analysis of the findings might reveal no meaningful difference in performance by ethnic group. In this situation, if many of the Mexican-American students spoke English as a second language, their almost equal scores to the European-American students might realistically be viewed as indicators of higher achievement potential, given their comparative language disadvantage. Counselors must work energetically both to develop the competence to see the influence of such factors and to communicate appropriate ways to interpret tests to other professionals. One especially helpful guide to competent and responsible assessment for diverse populations is *The Handbook of Multicultural Assessment,* written by Suzuki, Ponterotto, and Meller (2001). In essence, the standards and literature on this issue point to the importance of counselors' personal commitment to nondiscrimination and appreciation of cultural differences. The counselor must be alert to both intended and unintended discrimination because both have a negative impact on clients. In this context, the virtue of commitment to social justice and fair treatment for all takes on special importance.

Tests in Employment Settings

Psychological tests have found increasing use in employment settings over the last 30 years (Hogan, Hogan, & Roberts, 1996). They have been used primarily to assist in hiring and promotion (Arthur, Woehr, & Graziano, 2001). Intelligence tests, measures of verbal and mathematic reasoning, vocational aptitude batteries, and personality inventories are most commonly chosen. One trend is the use of "integrity tests" aimed at predicting a job applicant's honesty and attitudes toward theft (Camera & Schneider, 1994). When any tests are used in employment settings, there are several ethical issues to be dealt with:

- Has performance on the instrument been demonstrated by scientific evidence to be related to the job performance it ought to predict? Legal rulings have also emphasized that the standard for acceptability of such testing is a demonstrated relationship to the variables of interest in the employment setting.
- Has the publisher of the test followed ethical guidelines and avoided placing profit before client welfare?
- Do the people who select, administer, score, and interpret the results have the necessary competencies for those tasks, and do they work to restrain misuse by unqualified individuals?
- Do those who are asked to take such tests understand their rights, and are their dignity and confidentiality appropriately honored?
- Do the tests avoid discrimination against people for reasons unrelated to job performance? Are there no significant differences in rejection rates for different racial and ethnic groups (Cronbach, 1984)?
- Have the limitations and reservations about the test been acknowledged and taken into account in interpreting results?

- Are test results used in conjunction with other information so that they are not the sole criterion on which any decision is based? Does the test provide more accurate information than alternative selection procedures (Cronbach, 1984)?
- Does state law allow the kind of testing under consideration? For example, Massachusetts prohibits integrity testing for job applicants (Camera & Schneider, 1994). Integrity testing involves the use of psychological tests to assess honesty in work behavior.

If all these questions can be answered affirmatively, the use of testing in such environments is more likely to be consistent with current ethical standards.

Laws That Affect Testing

Counselors who use tests should be aware of several federal laws that affect their work. The implications of such laws are especially widespread in educational and employment settings.

- Family Educational Rights and Privacy Act of 1974, or FERPA (the Buckley Amendment). This law protects the rights of parents and guardians to view their child's academic records and to control who else may have access to them.
- The Education for All Handicapped Children Act (Public Law 94-142). This law was enacted to guarantee the rights of children with disabilities to an equal education and specifies that parents' or guardians' consent is required prior to testing their child. It also mandates a fully informed parental consent to testing and access of parents to test protocols when testing is completed. The law requires that tests be in the child's language and be appropriate for the intended use.
- Public Law 101-336 (the Americans with Disabilities Act of 1990). This legislation protects the rights of people with disabilities and mandates that testing be appropriate for the individual, that it not be used to discriminate in employment options for people with disabilities, and that reasonable accommodations be made in testing for such people.

Cases for Discussion

The Case of Lee

Lee, a 14-year-old 8th-grade student, is being considered for placement in advanced classes in high school. Lee's parents immigrated to the United States from Korea 5 years ago, and the whole family recently became U.S. citizens. Lee learned English quickly after his arrival in the United States, but he had no exposure to English in Korea. His test scores in mathematics and verbal reasoning place him at the 86th percentile for 8th-graders in his district. The district uses a cutoff score of the 90th percentile to assign students to advanced classes. Lee has earned As in both math and English classes. His teachers believe Lee is appropriate for advanced placement, but the guidance counselor is concerned about his test score. The counselor suggests a compromise: Enroll Lee in the advanced mathematics class only. She cites two reasons for the suggestion: the evidence that Asian-American students tend as a group to excel in math and the fact that Lee learned English only 5 years ago. Is her suggestion consistent with the ethical guidelines for counselors?

The Case of Miranda

After several counseling sessions that included some psychological testing, Miranda's counselor, Mr. Edwards, believes that this client's problems fit the criteria for two different diagnostic categories. For one of these categories Miranda's insurance company will reimburse services, but for the other she is likely to be denied such payment. Because Miranda is motivated for counseling and is experiencing real emotional discomfort from her problems, Mr. Edwards is leaning toward using the diagnosis that is acceptable to the insurance company. He reasons that because he can justify either diagnosis, he is acting in accordance with ethical standards. Do you agree?

Analysis of the Cases

A number of ethical considerations arise in the case of Lee. The central ethical principles involved are justice and beneficence, the obligation to treat this student fairly and to help him progress academically. The provisions in the codes raise a number of questions to be resolved:

1. Are there norms for Asian-American students or for English-as-a-second-language students for the achievement test that was used? If not, was appropriate caution used in interpreting Lee's results?
2. Is the counselor interpreting the percentile score appropriately, taking into account the psychometric evidence on the test? In particular, does she understand how the standard error of measurement affects the meaning of the 86th percentile in comparison to the 90th percentile?
3. Was the test appropriate in other ways for Lee? What level of content or selection bias was present in the items that might have distorted the young man's true score?
4. Is the counselor using the test score appropriately—as one factor among several criteria for placement? Has the counselor considered that for students whose native tongue is not English, Lee's score may actually show greater potential than an English speaker's score just a few points higher?
5. To what degree does the counselor's compromise represent a stereotype about Asian students and a failure to see Lee as an individual? Is the counselor unintentionally racist in this instance?
6. What evidence is there to support her assumption that 5 years' experience with English is insufficient for placement in advanced classes or that the test is a better predictor of high school success than are middle school grades or teacher recommendation?
7. To what degree have the school personnel involved Lee and his parents in the decision making? Have they honored the family members' rights to autonomy?
8. Will more harm come to Lee if he attempts the advanced classes and does not succeed or if he is denied the opportunity to enroll in them? Conversely, which option has the potential to provide the most benefit to Lee?

Without answers to these questions, it is difficult to come to a definitive judgment on the ethics of the counselor, but the brief evidence presented is enough to instill doubt that the counselor is in compliance with the letter or the spirit of the codes. At the least, she seems unequal to the challenge of properly interpreting test scores and insufficiently in awe of the power she wields to help or harm.

The case of Miranda deals with the counselor's effort to meet a true need for counseling that Mr. Edwards sees in Miranda without depriving her of insurance reimbursement for those services. He seems motivated by an interest in doing good for this individual. In this case, too, however, more information is needed before his behavior can be deemed ethical. Specifically, one should resolve the following questions:

1. Is his analysis that the two diagnostic categories are equally valid for this client supported by objective evidence? Would competent colleagues be likely to arrive at a similar conclusion?

2. Has he taken into account how cultural variables may influence the appropriate diagnostic category for Miranda?

3. To what degree does Mr. Edwards's interest in insurance reimbursement reflect a true commitment to the welfare of the client rather than an interest in reliable payment for his services?

4. What implications would the use of the reimbursable diagnosis have for the client, other than payment for counseling? Does this diagnosis indicate a more severe mental illness? Would the use of such a category have negative impact on the client's life?

5. To what degree is the client informed and involved in the decision-making process about the appropriate diagnostic category? Does she understand the implications of submitting for reimbursement? Because the effects all fall on Miranda, is she being given the freedom to make the final decision about this issue?

If Mr. Edwards's conclusion is supported by evidence and by competent colleagues, is freely chosen by a fully informed client, and is not motivated by self-interest or a desire to trick the insurer, then he has probably not violated an ethical standard. However, providing adequate answers to all those conditions may be more difficult than it first appears.

SUMMARY

The ethical standards applicable to assessment activities are based on the significant power the professional wields in this role. The imperfections in diagnostic systems and testing instruments, coupled with their vulnerability to misinterpretation by unqualified people, also add to their power. Counselors and therapists, however, cannot avoid the task of assessing client problems on the grounds that assessment tools can be misused. Without a clear definition of the client's issues, the professional's ability to provide effective treatment is significantly impaired. Thus, counselors must proceed carefully and diligently in assessment activities, mindful of the rights and responsibilities of all involved.

When engaged in diagnosis, practitioners must be careful to act competently, without discrimination or unintentional racism, and give clients clear information about the meaning and implications of the diagnosis. They should fully recognize the strengths and weaknesses of current diagnostic systems and the impact of such identifiers on clients.

Similarly, when using psychological or educational tests, counselors should have extensive skill and training to use the findings in suitable ways with a given individual. They must possess the knowledge and skill to discriminate between valid and invalid findings and to take into account the cultural and social background of the test taker. They must not encourage those unqualified for the activity to engage in it, nor should they use outdated test results in their work. In most instances, clients have a right to feedback about the test. The exact nature of that feedback is not prescribed by the code, but it must convey as accurate and full a picture of the results as circumstances allow. The history of the mental health professions is replete with examples of practitioners misinterpreting test results with diverse and oppressed populations, so counselors must be especially vigilant not to repeat those violations and to stay current with the literature on multicultural aspects of assessment. When tests are used in employment settings, their scores must be correlated with job characteristics and test takers must understand their rights in such a situation. Counselors would also be well advised to know how the laws in their jurisdictions affect the assessment process because state laws vary and change rapidly.

Not only are professionals bound to protect the rights of clients, they also have a responsibility to honor the rights of test producers, acting in ways that recognize their legal rights to ownership of and fair profit from test materials. Therefore, counselors must guard against violations of test security, must not plagiarize test materials, and must seek the option to use such materials only when qualified to do so, if possible. In turn, test producers are obligated to provide scientific evidence of the reliability and validity of their tests and other related materials in test manuals. They should assist counselors in the responsible use of assessment tools as much as possible.

ADDITIONAL CASES FOR DISCUSSION

Mittie counsels many adults who she diagnoses with attention deficit disorder. Mittie has searched for a standardized test to facilitate diagnosis of these clients, but she has not identified one that she finds suitable for adults. Consequently, Mittie has begun to extract items from other tests and combine them into a homemade instrument that she produces on her personal computer. Mittie does not think she is violating any copyright laws or ethical directives because she limits the use of her instruments to her own clients, does not charge a fee for the testing, does not use it as her only criterion in making the diagnosis, and does not allow other therapists access to it. Are the steps Mittie has taken sufficient to make her conduct consistent with her ethical and legal responsibilities?

Andrea is a skilled clinical counselor in private practice who is well respected by her colleagues for her expertise in treating women with depressive and anxiety disorders. As part of their intake into counseling she asks clients to take a battery of three tests—a measure of depression or anxiety, a personality inventory, and a measure of coping skills. Clients complete the tests in her office, but after scoring Andrea either mails or emails them a copy of the report of her finding prior to the next session. She finds this procedure to facilitate discussion in their face-to-face meeting because clients almost always read the report with great care. She does not use this procedure if the results suggest high risk of suicide or other dangerous acts; she calls clients in for a review in person in these cases. Because she screens out high-risk reports prior to sending them to clients she believes she is acting responsibly and sees no ethical problem with her action. Do you agree?

DISCUSSION QUESTIONS

1. Do you think the flaws in the current diagnostic system used in mental health make it impossible to use it responsibly? Why or why not? If not, how would you improve the diagnostic system?
2. Do you believe the benefits of employment testing outweigh its liabilities? Why or why not?
3. Research shows that some professionals do not give clients negative feedback from testing; they report only positive results. What do you think about the ethics of this practice?
4. Currently test producers are asked by professional associations to market their tests only to qualified users. Is that a fair request in a free-enterprise system? What would happen if that restriction did not exist?
5. Some have argued that testing should not be used at all in educational settings with culturally diverse students. They have contended that the risk of test results being misused is so great with this population that they should never be a part of educational decision making. What's your analysis of this argument?

RECOMMENDED READINGS

American Psychological Association. (2005). Statement on the use of secure psychological tests in the education of graduate and undergraduate psychology students. Retrieved August 1, 2005, from http://www.apa.org/science/securetests.html

American Psychological Association. (1999). Guidelines for psychological evaluations in child protection matters. *American Psychologist, 54,* 586–593.

Anastasi, A. (1992). What counselors should know about the use and interpretation of psychological tests. *Journal of Counseling and Development, 70,* 610–615.

Camera, W. J., & Schneider, D. L. (1994). Integrity tests: Facts and unresolved issues. *American Psychologist, 49,* 112–119.

Constantine, M. G., & Sue, D. W. (Eds.), (2005). *Strategies for building multicultural competence in mental health and educational settings.* New York: Wiley.

Eyde, L. D., Robertson, G. J., Krug, S. E., Moreland, K. L., Robertson, A. G., Shewan, C. M., Harrison, P. L., Porch, B. E., & Hammer, A. L. (1993). *Responsible test use: Case studies for assessing human behavior.* Washington, DC: American Psychological Association.

Harper, F. D., & J. McFadden, J. (Eds.), (2002). *Culture and counseling: New approaches.* Needham Heights, MA: Allyn & Bacon.

Naglieri, J. A., Drasgow, F., Schmit, M., Handler, L., Prifitera, A., Margolis, A., & Velasquez, R. (2004). Psychological testing on the Internet: New problems, old issues. *American Psychologist, 59,* 150–162.

Suzuki, L. A., Ponterotto, J. G., & Meller, P. J. (2001). *Handbook of multicultural assessment* (2nd ed.). San Francisco: Jossey-Bass.

Chapter 10

Ethical Counseling in a Multicultural Society
The Promise of Justice

American society has always been culturally diverse, but for many years mental health professions largely ignored the impact of that diversity on their work. Wrenn (1962, 1985) aptly described counseling as "culturally encapsulated." In recent years, however, the topic of cultural diversity has moved from the periphery of their consideration toward the center. Attention to multicultural issues has become so intense that some have called this movement psychology's "fourth force" (Pedersen, 1991a). Many scholars contend that the issue has not yet achieved the prominence it deserves (for example, see Pedersen, Draguns, Lonner, & Trimble, 1996; Sue & Sue, 2003), and the ultimate goal of full awareness and multicultural skill is far from achieved (Constantine & Sue, 2005), but the progress that has been made is undeniable.

Several factors account for this shift. Demographic changes are the most obvious cause. Racial and ethnic groups once referred to as minorities now comprise a larger percentage of the population and the labor force than ever. Projections are that within the next 50 years, those who have been minorities will become a numeric majority in the United States (Sue, 1995). In many urban communities, that transformation has already occurred (Sue & Sue, 2003). According to the U.S. Census Bureau, nearly 40% of the population consists of people of color (Jones & Smith, 2001) and one of every seven Americans is now of Hispanic origin (Bernstein, 2005). Populations of that size garner attention, not only for their magnitude but for their expanding political and social power. Second, in the latter half of the twentieth century, the legal system has provided increasing recognition of the rights of diverse groups through federal statutes such as the Civil Rights Act of 1964 and the Americans with Disabilities Act of 1990 (Public Law 101-336). Not all efforts to increase minority rights were successful (note the failure of the Equal Rights Amendment), but the momentum was clearly in this direction. Third, as professional education became more available to groups previously denied access, the professions themselves included more members of diverse populations. These professionals, along with other scholars, have actively fostered consideration of multicultural issues. They have also pushed the profession toward a fuller acknowledgment of its own history of failures in treating culturally diverse groups and of the harm that racist and ethnocentric attitudes can cause others (for example, see Ridley, 1995; Sue & Sue, 2003). In addition, scholarship in cross-cultural psychology has blossomed in this period, providing a rich conceptual base for that agenda (for example, Neville & Mobley, 2001). Finally, the reemergence of interest in professional ethics over the last two decades has also played a small role, placing the profession's fundamental ethical principles and virtues at the forefront of professional concern. Attention to multicultural issues is a natural outgrowth of discussions of respect for autonomy, fairness, and the obligation to do good for others. At its core, professional ethics is about commitment to reducing the suffering of other people (Fowers & Richardson, 1996). One cannot honor that commitment without working to eliminate racism, oppression, and stereotyping, which cause much suffering in modern society.

In this context, it is not surprising that the ethical implications of the multicultural society have been extensively discussed. The most recent versions of the ethics codes of the American Counseling Association (ACA) and American Psychological Association (APA) show an unprecedented concern for this topic. Moreover, the associations have published additional guidelines to enhance responsible practice with diverse clients. This chapter reviews those materials, discusses the relevant scholarly literature, and examines emerging aspects of professional ethics in a multicultural society not yet addressed by the codes. Its central theme is that ethics requires counselors to break free from cultural encapsulation and develop a set of competencies and commitments for productive work with diverse populations. Achieving this goal for all professionals is crucial if the ethical ideals of the profession are to be met, especially because the history of the profession is marred with incidents of ignorance, insensitivity, and ethnocentric bias.

The Language of Multicultural Counseling

A set of definitions of terms used in this chapter is a necessary preamble to the discussion:

- *Culture* is the "set of shared meanings that make social life possible" (Fowers & Richardson, 1996, p. 610). It is defined as "the belief systems and value orientations that influence customs, norms, practices, and social interactions, including psychological processes (language, care taking practices, media, educational systems) and organizations" (APA, 2003b, p. 8). Culture is dynamic, not static and has also been described as a worldview (APA, 2003b).
- *Culturally diverse clients* are clients from any group that has suffered discrimination and oppression.
- *Multicultural counseling* is any counseling situation in which the cultures of the client and the counselor differ. In some writings the terms *cross-cultural* or *transcultural counseling* are used.
- *Ethnicity* is a shared identity derived from shared ancestry, nationality, religion, and race (Lum, 1992). People are not limited to one ethic identity—some individuals have multiple ethnic identities (APA, 2003b).
- *Multiculturalism* is a "social-intellectual movement that promotes the value of diversity as a core principle and insists that all cultural groups be treated with respect and as equals" (Fowers & Richardson, 1996, p. 609).
- *Culture-centered* is a term APA has adopted to encourage psychologists to use a cultural lens in professional behavior—that is, to recognize that "all individuals are influenced by different contexts, including the historical, ecological, sociopolitical, and disciplinary" (APA, 2003b, p. 11).
- A *minority group* is a group that has suffered discrimination or has been oppressed. It is usually smaller in size as well as power than a majority cultural group, but it need not be small to be considered a minority. Minority status is primarily a function of access to power and history of oppression. Women, although they are a numeric majority of the population, are considered a minority group because of the discrimination they have suffered. This term is used less commonly in the current multicultural literature.

The Context of the Current Ethical Standards

To fully appreciate the ethical standards for counselors in a multicultural society, one must acknowledge not only that there are many cultural traditions beyond one's own but also that not all cultural groups have equal power in our society. Many have been subject to oppression and discrimination, and the prejudicial attitudes and behaviors that allowed such violations of human dignity to occur are far from extinct. Furthermore, counselors and therapists need to recognize that they themselves are not immune from the prejudicial attitudes that characterize Western society and that they can inadvertently perpetuate oppression and discrimination even if they abhor prejudice and want to practice sensitively (Sue, Ivey, & Pedersen, 1996). Professionals internalize society's biases just as other citizens do, and these biases frequently play themselves out in subtle or unconscious ways. For example, if a professional locates a practice so as to be inaccessible to public transportation, he or she is probably not deliberately discriminating or consciously choosing to deny access to particular segments of the population. Nevertheless, the effect is still discriminatory insofar as it denies access to people without their own cars—a group likely to contain a greater proportion of diverse clients. The implicit message is that counseling is meant to serve people with resources and that those without private transportation do not even figure into the equation when deciding on a suitable location for the practice. When confronted about this problem the person would be likely to respond, "I just didn't think about that." Or, to cite a different example, a school counselor might accept without challenge a Latina's request to drop out of a physics class because it's too demanding, when that same counselor might actively encourage a European-American boy to persevere or help him get tutoring to succeed in the course. The counselor need not have a conscious belief that Latinas are less intelligent or less deserving; he or she may just have lower expectations for Latino people (or for girls), without ever being aware that that assumption is operating. That belief has been absorbed from the negative messages and stereotyping in the culture. Recent literature on the differential treatment of boys and girls in American classrooms provides still another vivid example of unconsciously prejudicial behavior (Bailey, 1996). Ridley (1995) refers to such acts as "unintentional" racism or sexism. The harm such acts causes is no less real because it is unintended, however. For that reason, much of the effort in promoting effective and responsible service for diverse populations has focused on helping counselors become aware of such hidden beliefs and attitudes so that fairer judgments can be made.

Of course, unintentional bias is not the only form of bias counselors and therapists may exhibit. Sometimes professionals consciously endorse prejudiced beliefs and attitudes. As was mentioned in Chapter 9, as late as 1993 14% of counselors still equated homosexuality with psychopathology, although the professions had definitively asserted 20 years before that homosexuality was not a psychological disorder (Gibson & Pope, 1993). Endorsing of such beliefs and attitudes directly contradicts the provisions of the ethics codes of every major mental health association.

The Codes of Ethics on Multicultural Counseling

The 2005 ACA code speaks to the topic of multicultural counseling in the first paragraph of its preamble and in every major section. Sue (1995) notes this placement as an important symbol of the centrality of this issue to ethical practice. The section reads as follows.

ACA *Code of Ethics*, Preamble

The American Counseling Association is an educational, scientific, and professional organization whose members work in a variety of settings and serve in multiple capacities. ACA members are dedicated to the enhancement of human development throughout the lifespan. Association members recognize diversity and embrace a cross-cultural approach in support of the worth, dignity, potential, and uniqueness of people within their social and cultural contexts.

A similar statement appears in the Aspirational Introduction to the section of the code on the counseling relationship.

ACA *Code of Ethics,* Section A: The Counseling Relationship

Introduction: Counselors encourage client growth and development in ways that foster the interest and welfare of clients and promote formation of healthy relationships. Counselors actively attempt to understand the diverse cultural backgrounds of the clients they serve. Counselors also explore their own cultural identities and how these affect their values and beliefs about the counseling process.

In addition, the 2005 ACA code contains another 17 references to diversity issues, divided among nearly all sections of the code.

The 2002 revision of the APA *Ethical Principles* also includes numerous references to diversity issues, including a statement in its introductory General Principles.

APA *Ethical Principles,* Principle E: Respect for People's Rights and Dignity

Psychologists respect the dignity and worth of all people, and the rights of individuals to privacy, confidentiality, and self-determination. Psychologists are aware that special safeguards may be necessary to protect the rights and welfare of persons or communities whose vulnerabilities impair autonomous decision making. Psychologists are aware of and respect cultural, individual, and role differences, including those based on age, gender, gender identity, race, ethnicity, culture, national origin, religion, sexual orientation, disability, language, and socioeconomic status and consider these factors when working with members of such groups. Psychologists try to eliminate the effect on their work of biases based on those factors, and they do not knowingly participate in or condone activities of others based upon such prejudices.

The other sections of the codes that refer to cultural issues deal with the promotion of client welfare, competence to practice with diverse populations, avoidance of discriminatory behavior, fairness in assessment, and training and research issues.

Promoting Client Welfare

The sections of the ACA code that concern the promotion of client welfare identify responsibility to nondiscrimination (Section C.5), call members to respectful appreciation of cultural differences in implementing consent and confidentiality procedures (Section B.1.a), caution professionals against imposing personal values on clients in a diverse society (Section A.4.b), and encourage counselors to appreciate the cultural dimensions of gift giving (A.10.e). In a section new to this revision of the code, the profession exhorts members to be sensitive to the role of client support networks in a client's life and to involve support networks as appropriate in the counseling process (Section A.1.d). These sections highlight the degree to which counseling cannot be separated from personal values and beliefs and are grounded in the recognition that the power of the counselor can easily be misused. This language also reminds professionals that this occupation is one of service to others, not self-service. When counselors operate in a biased or monocultural way, they are serving their own needs, not those of their clients.

The content of the APA *Ethical Principles* echoes these messages with sections mandating nondiscrimination (Section 3.01) in the provision of psychological services along with a prohibition of harassment, sexual or otherwise (Sections 3.02 and 3.03). This code uses the terminology of cultural and cultural diversity much less frequently than the counseling code, but its message is identical—that psychologists must show sensitivity to the contextual factors that operate in a client's life and worldview and in their own lives.

Competence with Multicultural Populations

As discussed in Chapter 3, competence to practice means a professional has the knowledge, skill, and diligence required for the tasks he or she undertakes. There are two references to multicultural competence in the ACA code. The first is in the section explaining the boundaries of one's competence, and it states, "Counselors practice only within the boundaries of their competence, based on their education, training, supervised experience, state and national professional credentials, and appropriate professional experience. Counselors will gain knowledge, personal awareness, sensitivity, and skills pertinent to working with a diverse client population" (ACA, *Code of Ethics*, Section C.2.a). The second reference mandates that working professionals "keep current with the diverse and/or special populations with whom they work" (ACA, *Code of Ethics*, Section C.2.f).

The APA code addresses the topic as follows.

APA *Ethical Principles*, Section 2.01 b: Boundaries of Competence

Where scientific or professional knowledge in the discipline of psychology establishes that an understanding of factors associated with age, gender, gender identity, race, ethnicity, culture, national origin, religion, sexual orientation, disability, language, or socioeconomic status is essential for effective implementation of their services or research, psychologists have or obtain the training, experience, consultation, or supervision necessary to ensure the competence of their services, or they make appropriate referrals, except as provided in Standard 2.02, Providing Services in Emergencies.

Sue and Sue (2003) defined three primary dimensions of multicultural competency. These dimensions are (a) self-awareness so that one's values, biases, personal beliefs, and assumptions about human nature are known; (b) understanding without negative judgments of the worldviews and assumptions of culturally diverse clients; and (c) skill in using and developing counseling interventions appropriate with diverse clients. Other authors have organized the necessary multicultural competencies as appropriate beliefs and attitudes, cultural knowledge, and practical skills. Toporek and Reza (2001) emphasize that the institutional context of the professional plays an important role in multicultural competence, and Sue et al. (1998) offer an extensive discussion of approaches to institutional development to promote more culturally sensitive counseling. The Association for Multicultural Counseling and Development and the Association for Counselor Education and Supervision have joined together to produce competency guidelines for practitioners and mental health educators entitled *Multicultural Counseling Competencies and Standards* (Arrendondo et al., 1996). The ACA guidelines identify four major components of competency. The first is awareness of the influence of one's own cultural heritage on one's experiences, attitudes, values, and behaviors and the ways in which that culture limits or enhances effectiveness with diverse clients. Next comes being comfortable with cultural differences and with clients from diverse cultures and developing an attitude that values and appreciates cultural difference rather than disparages or tolerates it. Honesty with self about negative emotional reactions and preconceived notions about other cultures, recognition of the harmful effects such reactions can have on clients, and commitment to work on changing such attitudes is the third competency. Finally, they identify respect and appreciation for culturally different beliefs and attitudes as the last component. This can be accomplished, for example, by honoring natural community support networks and valuing bilingualism. (For an excellent discussion of the limitations of the current model of multicultural competencies in counseling, see Ridley, Baker, and Hill [2001].)

The document also details a knowledge base for counselors that includes a strong foundation of self-knowledge and a solid background in the particular cultures from which one's clients will be drawn:

- Comprehension of how one's own culture affects one's definition of normality–abnormality and the process of counseling
- Understanding of the implications of racism, oppression, and stereotyping on a personal and a professional level, including acknowledgment of one's own racist attitudes
- Familiarity with the literature on social impact on others, with special attention to the effect of one's communication style on diverse clients
- Appreciation of the cultural heritage of diverse clients with whom one is working and the impact that cultural identity development may have on clients
- Sensitivity to the ways in which culture may affect specific client attributes such as personality development, career choice, help-seeking behavior, manifestation of psychological distress, and so on
- Comprehension of the influence of social and political factors on clients who are culturally diverse, with appreciation of the harm that racism can inflict on individual functioning
- Knowledge of the aspects of traditional counseling that may clash with a particular client's culture, including assessment tools and intervention strategies
- Appreciation of institutional barriers that impede access to counseling for many clients who are culturally diverse
- Familiarity with cultural norms and practices regarding family structure and understanding of how the cultural group uses family and community resources to help people in distress
- Appreciation of the ongoing problems of discrimination and oppression that may have particular impact on culturally diverse clients in a given community

Finally, the document elaborates on a number of skills or activities that counselors should acquire to be effective multicultural counselors (the theme of this section is active engagement in activities that enhance skills):

- Pursuit of activities that enhance understanding of one's own culture and limit the degree to which the prejudiced attitudes of the culture affect one's behavior along with active involvement in activities that expand knowledge of cultural groups that is both intellectual and experiential
- Versatility in verbal and nonverbal helping responses and judgment about when to use each appropriately
- Skill in helping clients intervene effectively with institutional barriers to their goals and capacity to use community resources, such as traditional healers, when appropriate
- Bilingualism, or at least a willingness to appreciate the client's desire to use a first language in counseling and make an appropriate referral
- Expertise in the responsible use of assessment tools with diverse populations (Lonner & Ibrahim, 1996)
- Active involvement in activities meant to reduce prejudice and enhance cross-cultural knowledge in the community
- Skill in educating diverse clients to the counseling process in ways that make sense to them

APA's *Guidelines for Providers of Psychological Services to Ethnic, Linguistic and Culturally Diverse Populations* (1993b) echo the same themes, with somewhat greater emphasis on the impact of bias on diagnosis and assessment. This document also provides examples that help flesh out the concepts embedded in both sets of guidelines, such as the "healthy paranoia" of oppressed groups, to illustrate the ways diagnosis must take cultural factors into account if it is to be accurate. All too often that suspicion is treated as pathologic when it is indeed functional to the environment of that client.

Vera and Speight (2003) have proposed that professionals will not achieve multicultural competency unless they become active agents for change toward social justice, and they suggest that professionals should become advocates for individual clients and for social change that aims at eliminating institutional racism and related oppression. They argue that working person-by person to alleviate the effects of oppression is not sufficient for a profession truly committed to social justice and that broader action is essential. Helms (2003) cites the work of Brabeck, Walsh, Kinney, and Comilang (1997) in public schools as an example of the type of activity that has systemic influence.

Several objective measures to help counselors assess their level of multicultural competency has been developed. One test with evidence of reliability and validity is the *Multicultural Counseling Inventory* constructed by Sodowsky, Taffe, Gutlin, and Wise (1994). These instruments examine the skills, knowledge, and attitudes of counselors toward multicultural populations. Counselors who are unsure about their current competency might find one of these measures useful and should consult Ponterotto, Gretchen, and Chauhan (2001); Pope-Davis & Coleman (1998); or Suzuki and Kugler (2001) for a review of the literature on these instruments. Some of these instruments are appropriate for research, and some are appropriate for self-assessment.

Research on the multicultural competencies of counselors has shown some promising results, although it is clearly in the early stages of development. Zayas, Torres, Malcolm, and DesRosiers (1996) found that mental health practitioners endorsed the same components of culturally sensitive counseling as the scholars named in the literature. Manese, Wu, and Nepomuceno (2001) reported in a 10-year study that intensive multicultural training was an effective way to increase competencies during internship. Finally, Holcomb-McCoy and Myers (1999) indicated that professional counselors perceive themselves as culturally competent and rate their graduate training in this area positively. Using a longitudinal research design Tori and Ducker (2004) published encouraging findings of their intensive program to enhance multicultural competency in a professional psychology program.

A Critique of the Current Ethics Codes

Critics of the ethics codes note that the ethical principles that underlie its tenets are not universally endorsed by all cultures (for example, Herlihy & Watson, 2003; Pedersen, 1995; 1997). The emphasis on respect for the autonomy of the individual that girds the entire social and political structure in Western societies is much less dominant in some Eastern cultures. Instead, those cultures give primacy to the health and well-being of the group or the family. In another example, Herlihy and Watson (2003) suggest that the rigid boundaries the codes have imposed for professional–client relationships in the name of objectivity and non-exploitation of clients do not often serve clients from culturally diverse backgrounds. In these and other ways, the codes, the critics say, have abrogated their responsibility to acknowledge this diversity in ethical values and have failed to help practitioners deal responsibly with cultural conflicts in fundamental ethical values.

This debate highlights some of the thorniest ethical dilemmas that counselors confront in their work. Consider the following case.

The Case of Daniel

Daniel is a 23-year-old Orthodox Jew whose family has arranged a marriage for him, which is an accepted practice in his community. His reaction to this marriage has caused him so much distress that the rabbi recommended counseling. In session Daniel reveals that he is ambivalent about the marriage. On the one hand, he wants to follow the tenets of his religion, which places such strong emphasis on the importance of marriage for a Jewish man, but on the other, he knows he feels nothing for the woman his family has chosen. Daniel says he wants to marry eventually, but he feels completely unready now.

He feels trapped. To violate his parents' choice would be inconsistent with the expectations of his religion and would risk his family's goodwill and his community's acceptance, but he feels strongly unsuited to this woman at this time. He asks his counselor to help him find a way to be more accepting of his parents' and community's choice for him.

How should one respond when the situation of the client seems to compromise his or her personal freedom and dignity yet is condoned or encouraged by his or her culture? Here, Daniel seems caught between strong religious and cultural values that he generally endorses and his own hesitance about this particular value. (See the material at the end of the chapter for an analysis of this case.) What are the counselor's ethical choices here? In other examples, what is the ethical response when a client's culture refuses to allow girls to attend school or condones a kind of indentured servitude of some classes that is not far removed from slavery? Is there a point at which respect for the cultural tradition of the client gives way to universal human values? If so, who makes the decision about which values are universal? Does that come from the individual counselor or from somewhere else? LaFromboise, Foster, and James (1996) wrestle with these questions, suggesting that professionals must avoid both ethical absolutism (a rigid, dogmatic adherence to a particular set of ethical values) and ethical relativism (an equal acceptance of all ethical values). Instead, they recommend a middle position that allows for diversity in values but is not so relativistic as to deny the existence of any universal human principles. The themes by Fischer, Jome, and Atkinson (1998) echo this view as they discuss multicultural counseling as a "universal healing process that takes place in a culturally sensitive context" (p. 525). They remind professionals to attend to the common factors that make therapeutic work effective: a strong therapeutic relationship, a shared worldview, a client with expectations of positive results from counseling, and a set of interventions that both people accept as healing.

Cautions About a Multicultural Perspective

There are two extremes to be avoided in a multicultural perspective. One extreme is obvious from the preceding discussion—that is, the failure to take culture into account in the therapeutic process and to understand the interaction between individual characteristics, cultural norms, values and practices, and societal and global forces. The second extreme to be avoided is the failure to acknowledge intracultural variations and individual differences. Within the African-American community, for example, are many subcultures, and it is mistaken to assume a level of uniformity in culture that simply does not exist. Not all people from the same cultural group are identical, even if they share a subculture. Their individual beliefs, values, practices, and assumptions may vary substantially from those that typify their culture in general. Cultural groups overlap, too. A man may have an Asian mother, an African-American father, and a Latina stepmother, and he may be gay. In this situation, many cultures have contributed to his development and current functioning, and it would be inappropriate to single out any one group as "his culture." Pedersen (1991b) makes the point that each interpersonal encounter is a multicultural encounter. Ridley and his colleagues (Ridley, 1995; Ridley, Hill, Thompson, & Ormerod, 2001) advocate an *idiographic perspective* that recognizes that every individual is a blend of many social identities and that this blend is crucial in assessing and treating client issues effectively.

Cultural traditions, then, must be seen as hypothetic influences on individuals until evidence shows that they are operative. In other words, a balance is to be achieved that gives cultural variables their appropriate consideration without either overemphasizing or ignoring their influence on human behavior. Counselors who find themselves thinking thoughts such as "She's Native American, so she must feel . . ." or "He's Latino so he must think . . ." are falling victim to the very racist behavior they may be trying to avoid. Additionally, culture must be understood as a complex and dynamic force, not a static one

(LaRoche & Maxie, 2003). Counselors need to explore the changing meanings of culture with their clients and avoid static interpretations.

Scholars on this topic also note that the need for attention to issues of cultural diversity is not limited to European-American counselors. They are not the only cultural group that has internalized racist messages from the society, and they are not the only professionals who will encounter clients whose cultural background differs from their own. Any cultural group can stereotype or assume that its cultural tradition is the best or the only way to organize social reality. Of course, European-American counselors, as the majority in the professions and as the beneficiaries of the current social structure, have an especially strong obligation to develop and maintain multicultural sensitivity. A commitment to multicultural sensitivity and competence is a necessity for all counselors, however.

Cases for Discussion and Analysis

Consider the following questions for each case:

- How important is the client's cultural context in assessing the client's issues and determining treatment options?
- What is your emotional reaction to the problem the client presents?
- How do you think your personal values and cultural background would affect your capacity to counsel these clients?
- What multicultural competencies do you think are necessary to provide effective counseling in each of these cases?

The Case of Roberta

Roberta has come to counseling with her aunt, Mary Begay. Roberta is a Navajo who lives on the reservation with her father, stepmother, and four stepbrothers. She has been detached from the family and is acting in ways very atypical for Roberta. They are all worried about her, especially her aunt. Ms. Begay tells of a recent episode that she calls "moth madness," and Roberta acknowledges that this occurred. The counselor wonders if Roberta has developed an insect phobia and questions her extensively about her fears. Her responses do not point to a phobia, and the counselor is unsure of how counseling ought to proceed, but the client is willing to return to counseling again to explore the matter further. The counselor tentatively diagnoses an adjustment disorder but is unsure of the cause of Roberta's distress.

The Case of Mervin

Mervin is a 17-year-old African-American teenager who was found living on the streets and sent to counseling by the courts. He is now in a foster home. His mother and father died recently of complications from acquired immune deficiency syndrome (AIDS). His father was a hemophiliac who infected his mother with the virus before he was diagnosed. Mervin does not establish eye contact easily with his European-American counselor and has trouble sitting still for a whole session. The boy says that he wants to be left alone to finish high school, get a job, and get enough money to live on his own. He resists discussing his feelings about his parents' deaths or his current situation. He seems skeptical about the counselor's intentions and seems to have concluded that counseling is something to be patiently endured until the counselor gets tired of it.

The Case of Calvin

Calvin is a 20-year-old architecture student who comes to counseling because of procrastination. Calvin is of Korean ancestry, and his father is a scientist. As the counseling session progresses, Calvin's problem becomes clearer. He procrastinates because he has little interest in architecture. He loves to sculpt and has taken several electives in art. His behavior and affect reveal that sculpture is his true interest, but Calvin turns away suggestions that he may want to consider another major besides architecture. Instead of talking about his own interests, he discusses the long line of scientists in his family and his need to choose a profession with at least some relation to science. He asks the counselor to focus on the procrastination problem because he cannot really consider other majors.

The Case of Daniel (Repeated)

Daniel is a 23-year-old Orthodox Jew whose family has arranged a marriage for him, which is an accepted practice in his community. His reaction to this marriage has caused him so much distress that the rabbi recommended counseling. In session Daniel reveals that he is ambivalent about the marriage. On the one hand, he wants to follow the tenets of his religion, which places such strong emphasis on the importance of marriage for a Jewish man, but on the other, he knows he feels nothing for the woman his family has chosen. Daniel says he wants to marry eventually, but he feels completely unready now. He feels trapped. To violate his parents' choice would be inconsistent with the expectations of his religion and would risk his family's goodwill and his community's acceptance, but he feels strongly unsuited to this woman at this time. He asks his counselor to help him find a way to be more accepting of his parents' and community's choice for him.

Analysis of the Cases

In each of these cases, understanding the client's culture is a crucial component of ethical and effective counseling. Daniel, for example, lives in a religious community whose values, traditions, beliefs, and goals probably define almost every aspect of his life. He is part of a group that has been victimized by discrimination and oppression and that prefers minimal interaction with other cultures. His problem stems from a clash between personal wishes and cultural norms. Similarly, Roberta comes from a community that has suffered discrimination and oppression and has learned to be careful in interactions with non-Indians. The cultural norms of her tribe have probably defined her values and beliefs. She may view counseling as a last resort, and she may be skeptical about its capacity to help. The specific problem she mentions, "moth madness," is specific to her culture and is not part of most formal diagnostic systems used in counseling, so it is not meaningful outside the client's culture unless others have been taught its definition. Next, Mervin may have learned not to trust white people easily and to be uncomfortable with other people involving themselves in his personal affairs. Finally, Calvin has placed his family's expectations for his profession above his personal desires, a frequent choice in Asian-American culture (Sue & Sue, 2003) but one that conflicts with the dominant U.S. cultural values of individual freedom of choice and action.

Thus, culture is a major influence on the development and definition of the problems these people are experiencing and has an impact on the selection of an appropriate treatment strategy. A counselor who is unfamiliar with the Navajo concept of moth madness will have little sense of what Roberta is experiencing, and without asking questions and consulting with others, the counselor likely will misdiagnose and mistreat this girl. (In Navajo culture moth madness is a seizurelike experience that usually follows incestuous dreams or thoughts.) Similarly, a counselor who frames Daniel's or Calvin's problem as depression and anxiety stemming from a lack of assertiveness or a failure to appropriately separate from family may create greater pain and will have little success in selecting an intervention that alleviates their pain. Mervin might be misunderstood as hostile, unfeeling, or unable to form close social bonds if his counselor fails to take the cultural context of his behaviors into account. Under such circumstances, his real difficulties are unlikely to be remedied.

Each of these cases probably stirs an emotional reaction in those who imagine themselves in that counselor's position. The view that one's family has the right to choose one's marriage partner is a perspective that few in Western society hold, that most disagree with strongly, and that seems contradictory to the central concept of individual freedom. It probably evokes confusion, anger, and suspicion in counselors from Western cultures. At an intuitive level, many counselors probably believe that Daniel's lack of choice is morally wrong. Roberta's counselor may react with puzzlement and discomfort, or she may approach her with benevolent condescension for her use of such quaint language. The implication in the case description, that the counselor failed to ask the client the meaning of moth madness, suggests a discomfort with such a strange wording or a naive assumption that it is equated with an insect phobia. Such behavior epitomizes what Wrenn (1962) termed "cultural encapsulation."

Mervin's counselor may react to his behavior and attitude with frustration and may misinterpret the client's response as showing a personal dislike of the counselor. The counselor might assume that Mervin's parents were infected with the human immunodeficiency virus (HIV) virus through intravenous drug use because of a stereotype about heterosexual African-Americans who are infected with HIV. Mervin may have experienced this reaction previously from those who did not know his family.

Finally, in the case of Calvin some of the same emotions may emerge. Some counselors may feel angry with the cultural value that minimizes the importance of individual career choice. They may even disbelieve the family influence as a primary factor and wonder if Calvin has some deeper psychological problem that prevents him from doing what he wants. In this instance, too, some counselors may believe that the family is morally wrong to impose a career choice on a young adult. In any of these cases, a counselor can also feel the urge to rescue the client and show him or her a different way of understanding self and relating to family and others.

Multicultural Counseling Competencies

The competencies essential to avoid the many pitfalls just described include an *attitude of openness* toward other cultural views of the world. Understanding the influence of one's cultural heritage on one's own development, values, beliefs, and social behaviors is a prerequisite for this attitude. If one sees the roots of one's behaviors in culture, one is less likely to assume their universal truth or generalizability. In Daniel's case, a counselor would need a willingness to understand the history and function of the arranged marriage tradition in that culture and to identify its origins in a different philosophy of individual freedom. He or she should also be familiar with the implications of the choices Daniel is considering for his social, occupational, and individual functioning. If the counselor is likely drawn to encouraging the client to refuse the marriage at this point, he or she should understand that such a path may carry with it enormous costs for Daniel and may therefore not be in his best interests. That open mind is a prerequisite for helping a client sort out available alternatives and come to a free, self-made choice. Without it, the counselor has a hidden agenda of pushing the client toward a particular action. In the end, it is the client who must live with the consequences of the decision, not the counselor.

Second, a counselor must have *knowledge of the specific culture*. This is especially obvious in the case of Roberta. Ignorance of common cultural phenomena seem to be causing the counselor to badly misdiagnose the problem. Knowledge of the culture is also crucial when clients are torn between following the path typical of their culture and breaking off in a different direction. Knowledge would prevent Calvin's counselor from minimizing his parents' role in career decision making or underestimating the difficulty of violating that expectation.

Third, a counselor must be *competent in involving other support people* from the culture. Knowing when and how to engage the rabbi in Daniel's decision making (assuming, of course, that Daniel agrees) could be a crucial factor in resolving the dilemma. In Roberta's case, the counselor did not seem to understand the aunt's role or availability as a resource, nor did she seem to know to contact a healer from the tribe who might shed light on the situation. In these scenarios, all clients spoke English, but if they did not, this competency also implies the capacity to use the client's language, select a competent interpreter, or refer appropriately. Counselors should know how to seek out support for themselves, through consultation with peers and supervisors, to become better informed about the client's culture.

Fourth, the counselor needs to *modify interventions* or use interventions designed for cross-cultural counseling. Standard approaches to decision making or problem solving do not sufficiently account for the cultural aspects of situations such as Mervin's or Calvin's. Counselors must be skilled enough to adapt them or to use alternative approaches developed for cross-cultural counseling. For example, if Daniel decides to express his feelings about the marriage to his parents, the counselor must be competent in adapting traditional methods for effective interpersonal communication or assertive self-statements to this cultural context. The work of Pedersen (for example, see 2000) and the book edited by Ponterotto, Casas, Suzuki, and Alexander (2001) are important resources in developing such competencies.

Counselors must also *develop a tolerance for ambiguity and divergent views of right and wrong.* When counseling clients such as Daniel, Calvin, or Mervin, counselors need the ability to accept that others do not have the same philosophy, worldview, or system of morality. They must be able to tolerate the discomfort that watching a young person enter into an arranged marriage is likely to provoke. In parallel fashion, they must learn to accept Mervin's choice not to participate fully in counseling, if that is his decision. In essence, this competency springs from the principle of respect for autonomy. If clients freely elect a path and have considered its alternatives, counselors have a duty to respect that choice—provided, of course, it is not a serious risk to the client or others.

Additional Cases for Discussion

Jeremy is a clinical counselor from a Hopi tribe. He spent his developing years partly on a reservation and partly in a small town. He had no access to mental health services until college. After a college counselor helped him to pull his life together he decided to go to graduate school and become a counselor himself. When he opened his practice Jeremy knew that he wanted to provide services to people in rural areas who were probably not getting their mental health needs met. He also hoped to be of service to American Indians. To achieve this goal Jeremy decided to develop an Internet-based counseling service in addition to his regular practice. On this Website Jeremy offers clients email exchanges with him for very low fees. Some of the clients who use this Website are depressed, others are anxious, and still others are dealing with substance abuse issues. Many are just lonely. Currently he has contact with approximately 30 people each week who use his Website. Several of them are American Indians and Canadian First Nations peoples who live in small towns or rural areas. Jeremy feels grateful that he has accomplished his goal of helping rural and American Indian people cope better with their problems. Discuss the ethical risks and merits of Jeremy's actions. If he came to you for advice about his Web counseling practice, what would you advise him?

Tyrone is an African-American counselor who has devoted his life to improving the civil rights of his race. He has pictures of several African-American civil rights leaders in his counseling office, including Martin Luther King, Malcolm X, and Medgar Evers. He has recently added the picture of a highly controversial African-American man to his collection. This man has written comments and has been widely quoted in the media saying things that many interpret as anti-Semitic. The director of the agency has asked Tyrone to remove the latest picture because she believes it may offend some clients. Tyrone has refused, and the director is trying to get him to change his mind about the picture. In the meantime, the director orders the intake workers not to schedule any Jewish clients with Tyrone. Was it ethical for Tyrone to bring a picture of this controversial man into his office? Should he have agreed to remove it? Were the director's actions in response ethical? What do you see as the ideal ethical solution to this conflict?

SUMMARY

American society has never been culturally homogeneous, but recent and projected changes in population demographics will render it truly heterogeneous. In fact, by early in the twenty-first century, ethnic groups that have long been labeled *minorities* will collectively outnumber the rest of the population. These changes mean that counselors will need skills, beliefs, and attitudes that equip them for providing effective service to clients who are culturally diverse. The current versions of the codes of ethics place substantial emphasis on multicultural issues. Commitment to principles of equality and justice has never been more important. Along with the desire to be fair and accessible, one must have specific competencies in multicultural counseling to achieve that goal. These competencies include self-awareness that encompasses understanding of one's own cultural heritage and the impact of racism and discrimination on self and others. They also include knowledge about other cultures and the impact of culture on human behavior, with special emphasis on cultural effects on expressions of distress and dysfunction and on responses to counseling. Finally, competent counselors in a multicultural society will also possess skills in transcultural counseling techniques and in adapting other counseling interventions to meet the needs of a diverse clientele.

In the course of their work with diverse populations, counselors will confront dilemmas that are exceptionally difficult to resolve because some of them involve conflicts about deep personal values and beliefs. When this happens, counselors should act cautiously, seek consultation from those more knowledgeable about the client's culture, and refer to the abundant literature on responsible multicultural counseling and therapy.

DISCUSSION QUESTIONS

1. Do you believe the competencies outlined in this chapter are sufficient to equip counselors to work with clients from different backgrounds? Are there other competencies you think should be added to this list? Explain.
2. Racism, sexism, and other forms of stereotyping are certainly not extinguished. Sometimes they even seem to be getting worse. What is the responsibility of a counselor in the face of such eruptions of prejudice?
3. Some scholars suggest that all counseling should be seen as cross-cultural. Does this view make sense to you? Why or why not?
4. Language barriers have been one important reason that diverse populations have had less access to counseling. Should competency in a second language be added as a requirement of professional training to address this problem? Is using an interpreter a good solution to this deficiency?
5. Racist counselors still practice, and otherwise well-intentioned counselors still act in racist ways sometimes. How do you think a counselor should react when he or she encounters racist behaviors in colleagues?
6. Do Asian, African-American, and Latino counselors need to be as vigilant about self-monitoring for unconscious racism as European-American counselors do? Why or why not?

RECOMMENDED READINGS

American Psychological Association. (2003b). Guidelines on multicultural education, training, research, practice, and organizational change for psychologists. *American Psychologist, 58,* 377–402.

Arrendondo, P., Toporek, R., Brown, S. P., Jones, J., Locke, D., Sanchez, J., & Stadler, H. (1996). Operationalization of the multicultural counseling competencies. *Journal of Multicultural Counseling and Development, 24,* 42–78.

Constantine, M. G., & Sue, D. W. (Eds.). (2005). *Strategies for building multicultural competence in mental health and educational settings.* New York: Wiley.

LaRoche, M. J., & Maxie, A. (2003). Ten considerations in addressing cultural differences in psychotherapy. *Professional Psychology: Research and Practice, 34,* 180–186.

Pedersen, P. B. (2000). *A handbook for developing multicultural awareness* (3rd ed.). Alexandria, VA: American Counseling Association.

Pedersen, P. B., Draguns, J. G., Lonner, W. J., & Trimble, J. E. (1996). *Counseling across cultures* (4th ed.). Thousand Oaks, CA: Sage.

Ponterotto, J. G., Casas, J. M., Suzuki, L. A., & Alexander, C. M. (Eds.). (2001). *Handbook of multicultural counseling* (2nd ed). Thousand Oaks, CA: Sage.

Ridley, C. R. (1995). *Overcoming unintentional racism in counseling: A practitioner's guide to intentional intervention.* Thousand Oaks, CA: Sage.

PART THREE

Ethical Issues in Special Settings

Chapter 11

Ethics in Community, Consulting, and Forensic Settings
Avoiding Conflicts of Interest

In the early history of mental health work, most practitioners were employed by large institutions—schools, hospitals, colleges, or government agencies. The advent of licensing for mental health professionals resulted in a whole host of new employment opportunities, including the option to "hang out a shingle" and practice independently. Even more options came with the enactment of federal and state community mental health legislation in the 1960s. Forty years after these changes, a minority of counselors, psychologists, and social workers work for large institutions. Most are employed by public mental health agencies or group practices, or they function in solo practices. Even professionals who are employed by schools or hospitals now often operate part-time private practices. In addition to the ethical issues already enumerated in the previous chapters, there are also special ethical concerns for those who work in community and private practice settings. This chapter addresses those special issues, focusing on ethical standards for client contacts, relationships with other professionals, obligations to third parties (such as insurers), and ethical considerations in consultation and forensic activities.

Responsibilities to Clients

Community-based counselors and psychotherapists have six major types of responsibilities to clients. These responsibilities are not unique to community and private practice, but are more salient for practitioners in these settings.

Advertising Services and Soliciting Clients

All community-based practices depend on a steady flow of clients and "billable hours" to survive. Thus, professionals in the community are motivated to market their services to those who may benefit from them or to market themselves to the health insurers in order to be included on the list of providers eligible for reimbursement under their plans. For many years, advertising of mental health services was severely curtailed by ethical standards—limited to brief, descriptive entries in telephone and service directories. To advertise counseling services in a manner similar to other consumer products was judged unseemly and risky to the consumer. In the late 1980s the Federal Trade Commission (FTC) challenged the legality of such restrictions and caused a dramatic change in the professions' standards for advertising. (For a fascinating account of the confrontation between the FTC, with its emphasis on free speech and free trade, and the American Psychological Association [APA], with its emphasis on protection of the public and the reputation of the profession, see Koocher, 1994a). Currently the U.S. guidelines for advertising allow for almost unlimited freedom in advertising. In fact, they expressly prohibit only two activities—deceptive practices and direct in-person solicitations—and restrict only one—the use of testimonials. The wording in the APA document is illustrative.

APA Ethical Principles, Section 5.01: Avoidance of False or Deceptive Statements

(a) Public statements include but are not limited to paid or unpaid advertising, product endorsements, grant applications, licensing applications, other credentialing applications, brochures, printed matter, directory listings, personal résumés or curricula vitae, or comments for use in media such as print or electronic transmission, statements in legal proceedings, lectures and public oral presentations, and published materials. Psychologists do not knowingly make public statements that are false, deceptive, or fraudulent concerning their research, practice, or other work activities or those of persons or organizations with which they are affiliated.

(b) Psychologists do not make false, deceptive, or fraudulent statements concerning (1) their training, experience, or competence; (2) their academic degrees; (3) their credentials; (4) their institutional or association affiliations; (5) their services; (6) the scientific or clinical basis for, or results or degree of success of, their services; (7) their fees; or (8) their publications or research findings.

(c) Psychologists claim degrees as credentials for their health services only if those degrees (1) were earned from a regionally accredited educational institution or (2) were the basis for psychology licensure by the state in which they practice.

5.02 Statements by Others

(a) Psychologists who engage others to create or place public statements that promote their professional practice, products, or activities retain professional responsibility for such statements.

(b) Psychologists do not compensate employees of press, radio, television, or other communication media in return for publicity in a news item.

(c) A paid advertisement relating to psychologists' activities must be identified or clearly recognizable as such.

(c) Psychologists claim degrees as credentials for their health services only if those degrees (1) were earned from a regionally accredited educational institution or (2) were the basis for psychology licensure by the state in which they practice.

APA *Ethical Principles,* Section 5.04: Media Presentations

When psychologists provide public advice or comment via print, internet, or other electronic transmission, they take precautions to ensure that statements (1) are based on their professional knowledge, training, or experience in accord with appropriate psychological literature and practice; (2) are otherwise consistent with this Ethics Code; and (3) do not indicate that a professional relationship has been established with the recipient.

5.05 Testimonials

Psychologists do not solicit testimonials from current therapy clients/patients or other persons who because of their particular circumstances are vulnerable to undue influence.

5.06 In-Person Solicitation

Psychologists do not engage, directly or through agents, in uninvited in-person solicitation of business from actual or potential therapy clients/patients or other persons who because of their particular circumstances are vulnerable to undue influence. However, this prohibition does not preclude (1) attempting to implement appropriate collateral contacts for the purpose of benefiting an already engaged therapy client/patient or (2) providing disaster or community outreach services.

From these statements, it is clear that professionals are free to market their services in any way that avoids exploiting current or former clients or deceiving potential clients. Professionals may even solicit testimonials from former clients, as long as those clients are not vulnerable to undue influence, although this is a practice not recommended by most ethics scholars (for example, see Koocher, 1994b). The dangers inherent in such freedoms are clear, and the duty to maintain the boundaries between legitimate marketing and misleading advertising falls squarely on the shoulders of the individual professional. Practitioners considering advertising should ask themselves the following questions:

- Is the description of the service fair, honest, and as comprehensive as possible?
- Are my credentials and training presented accurately?
- Does the advertisement help the public obtain services and bring credit to the profession?
- If a testimonial from a former client is included, was it received from someone not under undue influence from me, and have I developed a plan for helping the person deal with any unintended consequences from his or her involvement in the testimonial?
- Do I have assurance that any former client offering a testimonial is unlikely to need my services again at any point in the foreseeable future?
- Would my peers agree that the advertisement complies with professional standards?
- Have I done all I can to guarantee that others involved in the advertising will abide by the ethical standards for advertising?

In advice to Canadian psychologists, Shead and Dobson (2004) caution against three types of advertising that they suggest are inconsistent with the ethical values of the profession, although none is prohibited by the standards: claims of unique abilities, claims of comparative desirability of one's own service over other comparable professional services, and appeals to client fears and anxieties as the reason to seek out service. They argue that these practices offer no real assistance to consumers seeking competent care and actually undermine public confidence in the profession.

Sturdivant (1993) points out that advertising of professional services can be a way to do good and do well. She argues that marketing can act as an educational tool that acquaints the public with resources they would not otherwise learn about. She refers to research by the Ohio Psychological Association showing that consumers respond positively to marketing information about counseling and psychotherapy and that marketing results in increased respect for the profession. Nevertheless, counselors must carefully evaluate whether advertisements and other marketing efforts meet applicable standards.

Here is the language in the American Counseling Association (ACA) Code on advertising.

ACA *Code of Ethics,* Section C.3: Advertising and Soliciting Clients

a. Accurate Advertising. When advertising or otherwise representing their services to the public, counselors identify their credentials in an accurate manner that is not false, misleading, deceptive, or fraudulent.

b. Testimonials. Counselors who use testimonials do not solicit them from current clients or other persons who, because of their particular circumstances, may be vulnerable to undue influence.

c. Statements by Others. Counselors make reasonable efforts to ensure that statements made by others about them or the profession of counseling are accurate.

d. Recruiting Through Employment. Counselors do not use their places of employment or institutional affiliation to recruit or gain clients, supervisees, or consultees for their private practices.

e. Products and Training Advertisements. Counselors who develop products related to their profession or conduct workshops or training events ensure that the advertisements concerning these products or events are accurate and disclose adequate information for consumers to make informed choices.

f. Promoting to Those Served. Counselors do not use counseling, teaching, training, or supervisory relationships to promote their products or training events in a manner that is deceptive or would exert undue influence on individuals who may be vulnerable. However, counselor educators may adopt textbooks they have authored for instructional purposes.

C.6.c. Media Presentations. When counselors provide advice or comment by means of public lectures, demonstrations, radio or television programs, prerecorded tapes, technology-based applications, printed articles, mailed material, or other media, they take reasonable precautions to ensure that (1) the statements are based on appropriate professional counseling literature and practice; (2) the statements are otherwise consistent with the ACA *Code of Ethics;* and (3) the recipients of the information are not encouraged to infer that a professional counseling relationship has been established.

The ACA standards overlap substantially with the APA code, but they omit some of the language on involvement with the media, a less frequent event for counselors, and add a more specific statement prohibiting the use of an employer to solicit clients for outside professional activities.

Consider the following case.

Shaun's Creative Strategies

Shaun has recently become licensed as a mental health counselor, but he has nearly 20 years of experience in mental health and is well recognized in his community for his expertise in treating clients with posttraumatic stress. He has opened a practice and has begun advertising his services in telephone directories and on his personal Website. He has been listed in the referral resource of his state counseling association. In addition, in his advertisements Shaun offers a "free initial consultation." So far more than a dozen clients have taken up that offer and all have decided to continue in counseling with Shaun.

Has Shaun violated any portion of the ACA code in the way he has marketed his practice? As long as the information he presents in the directories and Website is accurate and not misleading to potential clients, he is probably in compliance in those areas. The use of a free initial consultation is potentially problematic, however. Zuckerman (2003) urges practitioners to avoid this practice because clients may feel committed after the first hour and may have difficulty declining further treatment. He also suggests that this practice may be seen as taking advantage of clients and perhaps be viewed as what the code refers to as "undue influence."

Increasing numbers of professionals such as Shaun are now taking advantage of the marketing potential of the World Wide Web and Internet, using Websites to advertise their local practices. Such Websites usually include information about the educational background and license(s) of the professional, the types of services offered, and the logistics of scheduling appointments. They also aim at allaying prospective clients' fears and misapprehensions about counseling and psychotherapy by explaining some basic aspects of confidentiality and informed consent. They sometimes include pictures of the practitioners so that people can put faces with the names they see on the screen and options for email contact to ask additional questions of the professional prior to scheduling an appointment. All of these features are designed to make counseling more accessible and less uncomfortable. Because no systematic research has been conducted into the impact of such marketing on prospective clients, no judgments can be made about their effectiveness at this time, but on the surface, they appear to be a useful tool for reaching people in need.

Mental health professionals who offer Web counseling (also called E-therapy) without face-to-face contact also include extensive advertising of their services on their Websites. Some of the advertising claims appear reasonable, given the dearth of published research on the effectiveness of this medium. The following is an example of an advertising claim from a Website obtained in two studies from 2003 (Heinlen, Welfel, Richmond, & O'Donnell, 2003; Heinlen, Welfel, Richmond, & Rak, 2003) that is derived from the providers' past experience in offering the service: "Thus far most who have decided to try it report that virtual therapy is very helpful. About 1 in 10 finds usually in the first couple of exchanges that virtual therapy is inappropriate for their needs." Other professionals make much broader claims, none of which has yet been substantiated by research. Examples include, "We have arrived at the ultimate solution for your concerns…There is no problem too big or too small," or, "We know you'll be satisfied." And still others make statements that they cannot honor, such as, "By using this service you maintain complete anonymity and privacy." There is no such thing as complete anonymity and privacy on the Web. Any communication routed though a major server such as America Online or Netscape can be traced, and those servers ordinarily have policies that they retain copies of *all* email sent through them for 1 year. Moreover, if a client reveals child abuse or an imminent intent to harm self or others, the professional is legally and ethically obligated to report that danger to authorities. In short our research has found that some Web counselors do not understand the limitations of electronic communications, do not provide prospective clients with balanced statements about the potential benefits and risks of Web counseling, and generally appear to violate professional standards for advertising. Some professionals also use Web counseling sites to extensively market the books, audiotapes, and other products they have published (Heinlen, Welfel, Richmond, & O'Donnell, 2003; Heinlen, Welfel, Richmond, & Rak, 2003). One site, for example, includes box references to such products interspersed with information on services, fees, and confidentiality matters. Reading the claims and promises included on such Websites raises questions about whether self-promotion has taken priority over protection of the public welfare.

Public Statements and Other Interactions with the Media

As is evident from the APA and ACA codes cited earlier, counselors and therapists also come into the public eye by making statements about news events, discussing their research and writings, and giving interviews over print and broadcast media. For example, when a national news organization wishes to do a story on a psychological disorder (such as agoraphobia or attention deficit disorder), reporters often seek out experts in the field. Similarly, when analyzing the aftermath of a disaster, reporters often ask mental health professionals to comment on its psychological and social repercussions. The APA standards expressly allow professionals to describe professional services available in disaster situations; such a practice is not considered improper solicitation. Conducted ethically, such interactions educate the public and bring credit to the profession. However, professional standards are sometimes violated. The most common violations are failing to present one's credentials accurately, making claims not supported by evidence, drawing conclusions based on intuition or a cursory review of the situation, and attempting to do therapy rather than education. The following are case examples of some of these violations:

Dr. Doppert and the Television Talk Show
Dr. Doppert, a well-known marriage and family counselor, has agreed to participate in a local television talk show on the subject of how couples recover from an episode of infidelity. The format is for two such couples to appear before a live audience to describe their experiences. At the end of the show, Dr. Doppert is to come on stage and spend 5 minutes with each couple to "help them heal" from the wounds of infidelity. When the show is taped, the therapist takes the assigned part and works with each couple before a live audience with the cameras running. Aside from introductions and watching the earlier portion of the show, she has had no contact with the couples. Because the segment ran behind

schedule, the counselor had 3 minutes on the air to help each couple express their feelings about infidelity. At the end of taping she said good-bye to each couple and gave them her business card. Dr. Doppert was not paid for the time, but her book and practice were both mentioned when she was introduced to the audience.

Dr. Berwinger and the Book Tour

Dr. Berwinger has written a book challenging conventional understanding of obsessive-compulsive disorder, suggesting that it is largely caused by improper diet. His conclusions are based on his therapeutic practice treating clients with this disorder. He has conducted no formal research studies and provides only anecdotal evidence for his claims. When asked for specifics, Dr. Berwinger reluctantly reveals that he has treated 12 clients successfully with this method. In the introduction to the book, four of those clients offer testimonials to the value of the approach, and one tours with him to promote the book. Moreover, Dr. Berwinger does not dispute the public announcements that refer to him as a psychologist, although he is actually a licensed mental health counselor. (Please note that the hypothesis about the etiology of obsessive-compulsive disorder presented in this scenario has *no basis in fact* and was created solely for this case.)

Mertice Mentrison

Ms. Mentrison has a PhD in American history and a master's degree in counseling. Nevertheless, all the public announcements about her work as a substance abuse counselor use the title "Doctor."

All of these mental health professionals are violating the ethical standards listed earlier. Dr. Doppert's practice of intervening therapeutically with talk show guests violates the standard of providing care only within a professional relationship [ACA, Section C.6.c (3)]. It also violates stipulations about informed consent, confidentiality, and not risking harm to clients. Through her participation, she is also giving the television audience a false impression of the therapy process and of acceptable practices for marriage and family therapists. In addition, she is placing the chance to promote her book and practice ahead of the rights or needs of the couples on the show. Given the standards for public announcements, Dr. Doppert's only ethical role in the show would be to provide information to the audience about the kinds of psychological and relationship difficulties that research shows commonly occur after infidelity. She should not in any way give the impression that she is providing a therapeutic service to the couples in a few minutes on television. She also should make efforts to ensure that the host or others do not communicate that she is appearing for the purpose of providing counseling in any form to the individual couples. DeTrude (2001) cautions professionals against thinking they can exert this level of control in a live talk show. The pressure of the host and audience to break down boundaries may be overwhelming, compromising both the dignity of the client and the professionalism of the counselor.

Dr. Berwinger's claims about his new treatment for obsessive-compulsive disorder violate Section 2.04 of the APA code because they are misleading and do not give any scientific basis for his conclusions. They also seem to be motivated more by his desire to sell books than by any commitment to science or good treatment for this disorder. From the information provided, it is difficult to determine whether the testimonials he includes violate the standard of "undue influence," although the fact that a former client accompanies him on the book tour is worrisome. His conduct also contradicts the standard about misrepresenting his credentials because he is not actively trying to keep others from characterizing him as a psychologist. His misconduct represents a flagrant disregard for client welfare, scientific findings, and impact on former clients. This counselor is discrediting the profession and encouraging people who may have a serious emotional disorder to seek an unproved treatment, thus delaying their access to treatments that may truly help them.

Ms. Mentrison is disregarding the ACA code (Section C.4.d), which proscribes use of the title "Doctor" unless a person's degree is in counseling or a closely related field. Because historians have no training in counseling, psychology, or human development as part of their doctoral programs, there is no justification for using that title. Ms. Mentrison is attempting to deceive the public into believing she has a credential she does not possess. For comprehensive guidance about ways to avoid these pitfalls and interact responsibly with the media, Schwartz (1999) is an excellent resource.

Sometimes counselors and psychologists are asked to give public testimony about matters before the legislature or to comment about social problems. Their expertise can be valuable in helping governmental bodies devise socially beneficial legislation and policy and in advancing quality mental health care for citizens. Professionals who seek to undertake this activity in an effective and ethical manner should read Sorensen, Masson, Clark and Morin (1998), who provide a useful guide for professionals asked to provide testimony or advice about public policy issues.

Payment Issues

The amount of money a counselor or therapist in private practice earns depends on the number of sessions conducted for payment. Even Freud himself was well aware of this issue, complaining frequently about his money problems (Freud, 1954). The more sessions for which the practitioner is paid, the larger his or her paycheck (except, perhaps in managed care situations where practitioners are rewarded for minimizing the number of sessions provided to each client). Thus, the primary ethical issue for those in private practice is coping with the conflict of interest inherent in these arrangements. Consider the following situations.

Ms. Amberside's Wedding

Ms. Amberside, a mental health counselor in private practice, is planning an expensive wedding trip to the Caribbean, for which she is saving money. Mr. Klepper has been in her care for some time for treatment of panic disorder. He met his treatment goals 2 months ago but remains in therapy because he is reluctant to terminate. He says he enjoys his weekly session and worries that the panic attacks will recur if he ends therapy. Mr. Klepper writes a check for therapy each week and never misses a payment. Ms. Amberside decides that her client should be able to terminate when he is ready and that he is doing no one harm by extending his time in therapy beyond necessity.

Dr. Wrankley's Contract with the Court

Dr. Wrankley is seeing a client who has been mandated for counseling by the court. The court reimburses the therapist for these sessions at his full rate. This woman agrees to the arrangement because she sees it as her "least worst option," but she reluctantly attends counseling and spends most of her sessions in rather superficial discussion of her problems. She resists Dr. Wrankley's efforts to focus on deeper therapeutic issues and is making minimal progress. Dr. Wrankley recently established his practice and is struggling to meet expenses. Because he needs the income from the court, he allows the client to continue her current pattern in sessions. His reports to the court focus on her dependable attendance and describe the small changes she has made thus far and deemphasize her resistance to therapy. He does not lie to the court, but his correspondence less than completely reveals his true professional judgment about the client's therapeutic progress to date.

Both Dr. Wrankley and Ms. Amberside are engaging in what Cummings (1995) has called *unconscious fiscal convenience,* overlooking important therapeutic dimensions of counseling because attending them would conflict with the practitioner's financial self-interest. Such professionals are not maliciously exploiting their clients, but they do fail to see that the underlying motivation for their therapeutic decisions stems from their need for the money these clients provide. Thus both are acting unethically. Ms. Amberside should instead be helping Mr. Klepper cope with the stress of termination and develop alternative environmental supports. Similarly, Dr. Wrankley ought to stop colluding with his client to deceive the court and should begin to encourage his client's more active involvement in therapy. Moreover, he should immediately provide more complete reports of her therapeutic progress to the court, informing his client of this action before he does so.

Another aspect of unconscious fiscal convenience is the common belief that paying for psychotherapy is therapeutic. In this view clients who do not make a financial commitment to counseling are less invested in it and work less hard. Science does not support this interpretation. In fact, research has found no clear relationship between payment and outcome (Drexler, 1996; Pope, 1988).

To avoid such ethical lapses, professionals in private practice ought to engage in regular peer consultation and supervision about the financial management of their cases. Making the criteria for therapeutic decision making known to trusted colleagues is, in effect, using the "clean, well-lit room" standard (Haas & Malouf, 2005). This procedure acknowledges the difficulty in viewing clients objectively when one's financial well-being is at stake and provides an potentially effective method to prevent significant abuses.

Even professionals who are motivated by altruism and are insightful about the conflict-of-interest potential in private practice are often uncomfortable discussing money matters with their clients. They want to hurry past the financial details and focus on therapeutic issues. Although such an attitude is understandable, it is also fraught with risks. Clients who are unclear about the costs of counseling are not giving truly informed consent. Under these circumstances, clients may be more likely not to comply with payment conditions or may feel anger or resentment toward the counselor. According to the ACA code, Section A.2.b, clients must be informed about the financial aspects of therapy as part of informed consent. The code goes on to specify other responsibilities in relation to fee setting. The language in the APA standards is similar.

ACA *Code of Ethics,* Section A.10: Fees and Bartering

a. Accepting Fees from Agency Clients. Counselors refuse a private fee or other remuneration for rendering services to persons who are entitled to such services through the counselor's employing agency or institution. The policies of a particular agency may make explicit provisions for agency clients to receive counseling services from members of its staff in private practice. In such instances, the clients must be informed of other options open to them should they seek private counseling services.

b. Establishing Fees. In establishing fees for professional counseling services, counselors consider the financial status of clients and locality. In the event that the established fee structure is inappropriate for a client, counselors assist clients in attempting to find comparable services of acceptable cost.

APA *Ethical Principles,* Section 6.03: Withholding Records for Nonpayment

Psychologists may not withhold records under their control that are requested and needed for a client's/patient's emergency treatment solely because payment has not been received.

6.04 Fees and Financial Arrangements

(a) As early as is feasible in a professional or scientific relationship, psychologists and recipients of psychological services reach an agreement specifying compensation and billing arrangements.

(b) Psychologists' fee practices are consistent with law.

(c) Psychologists do not misrepresent their fees.

(d) If limitations to services can be anticipated because of limitations in financing, this is discussed with the recipient of services as early as is feasible.

(e) If the recipient of services does not pay for services as agreed, and if psychologists intend to use collection agencies or legal measures to collect the fees, psychologists first inform the person that such measures will be taken and provide that person an opportunity to make prompt payment.

As the last sentence of this section of the APA standards suggests, informed consent about payment issues is especially important if clients fail to honor their financial obligations. In that situation, sometimes professionals must decide whether to contract with collection agencies or pursue legal action to get paid. Because such methods compromise confidentiality, clients must fully understand the implications of nonpayment. It is interesting that almost 4% of the legal claims filed against psychologists involved counter suits over collection of fees (Peterson, 1996). Of course, professionals are not obligated to employ collection agencies to obtain delinquent payments, but they are not prevented from doing so, provided the client had prior warning that such methods might result from nonpayment. Even if a client has consented to collection or other legal means to recover payment, a prudent professional is well advised to remind the client of that agreement before taking that step, so the client has the option to provide payment and avoid such actions. As a matter of fact, the APA code includes that stipulation. Knapp and VandeCreek (1993) provide other recommendations for responsible use of collection services, including oversight of the means by which these services attempt to collect payment. Section A.10.c of the ACA code expresses the same view about response to client nonpayment.

When clients are delinquent in paying, professionals wonder whether it is ethical to withhold copies of their records from subsequent therapists until payment is rendered. As Section 6.03 of the APA code states, psychologists may withhold records for nonpayment if the situation is not emergent. If a client needs the records for emergency care, the psychologist must provide them. The ACA code does not directly address the issue.

In this era of managed care and inequality of mental health benefits with health care benefits, professionals are often aware that insurance benefits may not be sufficient to cover the full cost of the recommended course of counseling or psychotherapy. The APA standard 6.04d requires psychologists to disclose and discuss this situation with clients as soon as they recognize it and to assist clients in deciding what course of action they wish to take. As discussed in Chapter 5, clients should be empowered through informed consent to make payment issues themselves.

The ACA, APA, and American Association for Marriage and Family Therapy (AAMFT) codes encourage professionals to provide some services on a pro bono basis—that is, without fee—as a way of keeping in focus one's commitment to public welfare. Research suggests that many psychologists follow this guideline (Knapp, Bowers, & Metzler, 1992). All codes also note that in establishing fees, professionals ought to consider client's financial circumstances. Many professionals use a sliding scale, adjusting the fee to a client's level of income. Lien (1993) has questioned the ethical value of the sliding scale, but this practice is generally viewed as a responsible way to make services available to people with low incomes. Bernstein and Hartsell (1998) caution professionals about the legal ramifications of using a sliding scale or otherwise varying fees for individual circumstances. They note that all states have laws that prohibit health care providers from charging higher fees to those who have insurance than to those without coverage. Some states even have criminal penalties for violating this statute. They also advise against waiving the co-payment amount for a client with insurance, for the same reasons. A sliding scale arrangement is still possible, but it must be devised to comply with individual state laws and must always be used in a uniform way with full disclosure to prospective clients and insurers.

Interruption or Termination of Services

In personal relationships, adults can discontinue a personal relationship whenever they wish. Counselors and therapists, however, have no such freedom once they have embarked on a professional relationship with a client. A failure to continue needed services without cause or appropriate referral is usually termed *abandonment* and is prohibited by the codes.

ACA *Code of Ethics,* Section A.11: Termination and Referral

a. Abandonment Prohibited. Counselors do not abandon or neglect clients in counseling. Counselors assist in making appropriate arrangements for the continuation of treatment, when necessary, during interruptions such as vacations, illness, and following termination.

b. Inability to Assist Clients. If counselors determine an inability to be of professional assistance to clients, they avoid entering or terminating counseling relationships. Counselors are knowledgeable about culturally and clinically appropriate referral resources and suggest these alternatives. If clients decline the suggested referrals, counselors should discontinue the relationship.

c. Appropriate Termination. Counselors terminate a counseling relationship when it becomes reasonably apparent that the client no longer needs assistance, is not likely to benefit, or is being harmed by continued counseling. Counselors may terminate counseling when in jeopardy of harm by the client, or another person with whom the client has a relationship, or when clients do not pay fees as agreed upon. Counselors provide pretermination counseling and recommend other service providers when necessary.

d. Appropriate Transfer of Services. When counselors transfer or refer clients to other practitioners, they ensure that appropriate clinical and administrative processes are completed and open communication is maintained with both clients and practitioners.

This standard is rooted in the profession's devotion to client welfare and to the protection of its reputation. Counselors who stopped counseling on a whim or out of dislike for clients diminish public confidence in the profession and damage the clients involved. Of course, sometimes counselors must terminate service in the middle of counseling because they obtain new employment, retire, or get sick. In such circumstances, counselors must help clients find appropriate referrals and do all they reasonably can to smooth the transition to the new counselor. A similar approach is advised if a client fails to pay for counseling as agreed. The counselor may refer the client to alternative services but must facilitate the transition. If other services are not immediately available, counselors may not abandon clients in need because of nonpayment of fees. When interruptions in service are foreseeable (such as an elective surgery scheduled in advance), professionals ought to plan for them by refraining from accepting new clients and referring current clients to other mental health professionals.

In its 2002 revision of the *Ethical Principles,* APA changed its broad wording of the prohibition against abandonment and replaced it with language that allows for termination of services based on professional judgment, appropriate planning prior to termination, or risk of harm to the therapist from the client or person connected to the client.

APA *Ethical Principles,* Section 10.10: Terminating Therapy

(a) Psychologists terminate therapy when it becomes reasonably clear that the client/patient no longer needs the service, is not likely to benefit, or is being harmed by continued service.

(b) Psychologists may terminate therapy when threatened or otherwise endangered by the client/patient or another person with whom the client/patient has a relationship.

(c) Except where precluded by the actions of clients/patients or third-party payors, prior to termination psychologists provide pretermination counseling and suggest alternative service providers as appropriate.

Counselors and psychologists in a sole practice must also make provisions for another professional to handle their caseloads in the event of their sudden death or disability. (See

ACA Section A.11.a.) Those in larger agencies should see that policies and procedures for referral in this circumstance are in place at their agency. Because clients become attached to specific counselors and are often in the midst of emotional stress and disruption, professionals have a special duty to take all reasonable steps to ensure that clients will be well served in their absence. Bram's (1995) review of the literature in psychology suggests that this standard is frequently violated when therapists underestimate their clients' needs for interim service in their absence. Counselors who had been disabled for several months tended to minimize the impact of their disability on clients and to make only haphazard arrangements for referral in the interval. The APA standards address interruptions as follows.

APA *Ethical Principles,* Section 10.09: Interruption of Therapy

When entering into employment or contractual relationships, psychologists make reasonable efforts to provide for orderly and appropriate resolution of responsibility for client/patient care in the event that the employment or contractual relationship ends, with paramount consideration given to the welfare of the client/patient.

Pope and Vasquez (1998) have identified several issues to be addressed if a professional is incapacitated for a lengthy period:

- Who will provide both ongoing treatment and crisis intervention for clients?
- Who will notify clients about the therapist's absence?
- How can clients and others obtain information about the therapist's course of recovery?
- How will the therapist's records be handled, and who will have access to them?

These authors also caution practitioners in private practice to carefully think through a "worst-case scenario" to help protect the welfare of clients from negative effects of an interruption of service. A planned, proactive approach to such eventualities is an ideal strategy.

Records

Counselors and psychologists are obliged to keep records of counseling and psychotherapy, both to benefit clients and to help other professionals provide effective service. Good records encourage a professional to be reflective and prepared for therapeutic contacts. Records can also help researchers study therapeutic processes and outcomes. This obligation is codified in the ethical standards and further supported by state and federal statutes and case law.

The ACA code contains the following statement on the subject.

ACA *Code of Ethics,* Section A.1.b: Records

Counselors maintain records necessary for rendering professional services to their clients and as required by laws, regulations, or agency or institution procedures. Counselors include sufficient and timely documentation in their client records to facilitate the delivery and continuity of needed services. Counselors take reasonable steps to ensure that documentation in records accurately reflects client progress and services provided. If errors are made in client records, counselors take steps to properly note the correction of such errors according to agency or institutional policies.

B.6.g. Storage and Disposal After Termination. Counselors store records following termination of services to ensure reasonable future access, maintain records in accordance with state and federal statutes governing records, and dispose of client records and other sensitive materials in a manner that protects client confidentiality. When records are of an artistic nature, counselors obtain client (or guardian) consent with regards to handling of such records or documents.

The APA code uses similar wording in Sections 6.01 and 6.02. Moreover, APA has issued *Record Keeping Guidelines* (1993c), providing detailed information about the content, construction, and retention of mental health records. Although some professionals disdain such guidelines as an intrusion of bureaucracy into therapeutic work, most scholars find the current standards valuable for maintaining quality care and for protecting professionals whose work is challenged by disciplinary boards, lawsuits, or third-party payors (Barnett, 1994; Soisson, VandeCreek, & Knapp, 1987). According to Moline, Williams, and Austin (1998) properly kept records can work in favor of mental health professionals during malpractice litigation. The APA guidelines for records specify the content that ought to be included:

- Information relevant to the nature, delivery, progress, or results of services
- Identifying data, dates and types of services, fees, assessment and testing data, plans for intervention, consultations, summaries, and any release of information obtained
- Data in sufficient detail for subsequent mental health professionals to plan adequately for future care

Piazza and Baruth (1990) recommend that six categories of information be included in counseling records: identifying information; assessment information; treatment plans; case notes; termination summary; and other data such as consent forms, copies of correspondence, and releases. Adding to this list, Moline et al. (1998) suggest inclusion of medication history, a component also listed in Health Insurance Portability and Accountability Act (HIPAA) definitions of information to be included in health records.

APA *Ethical Principles,* Section 6.01: Documentation of Professional and Scientific Work and Maintenance of Records

Psychologists create, and to the extent the records are under their control, maintain, disseminate, store, retain, and dispose of records and data relating to their professional and scientific work in order to (1) facilitate provision of services later by them or by other professionals, (2) allow for replication of research design and analyses, (3) meet institutional requirements, (4) ensure accuracy of billing and payments, and (5) ensure compliance with law.

6.02 Maintenance, Dissemination, and Disposal of Confidential Records of Professional and Scientific Work

(a) Psychologists maintain confidentiality in creating, storing, accessing, transferring, and disposing of records under their control, whether these are written, automated, or in any other medium. (See also Standards 4.01, Maintaining Confidentiality, and 6.01, Documentation of Professional and Scientific Work and Maintenance of Records.)

(b) If confidential information concerning recipients of psychological services is entered into databases or systems of records available to persons whose access has not been consented to by the recipient, psychologists use coding or other techniques to avoid the inclusion of personal identifiers.

(c) Psychologists make plans in advance to facilitate the appropriate transfer and to protect the confidentiality of records and data in the event of psychologists' withdrawal from positions or practice.

Oversight of Other Staff Professionals are legally and ethically responsible both for maintaining the confidentiality of the records and for overseeing other staff who have contact with records. Those who work in large agencies or practices must educate support personnel about confidentiality issues and guard against careless procedures for handling client records. Nonclinical personnel should read only those data from client files needed for billing and related purposes. It is important to note that this guideline applies to all workers at agencies and practices without clinical licenses. Administrative directors with business degrees have no more right to access therapy notes than do typists or receptionists. Moreover, clinicians have no right to read the records of other practitioners without a legitimate professional reason. HIPAA regulations clarify the duties of professionals to effectively train and monitor employees to protect the privacy of client and patient records and specify that professionals can be held liable for failures to properly train and supervise employees in confidentiality protections.

Forms of Records Records may be maintained in more than one medium (written document, computer data, taped material), but the professional is responsible for the confidentiality of records regardless of the medium. Professionals who store client data on computer hard drives or external storage devices must be especially attuned to the security of those files and must prevent others from accessing confidential material. (See Chapter 4 for a full discussion of the confidentiality risks to client data stored on computers.)

Many agencies stipulate that client records (written or computer based) may never leave the building without a signed release from the client. Such a policy helps prevent inadvertently compromising confidentiality. Cars, briefcases, and laptop computers get stolen all too frequently.

Retention of Records Some states and provinces have laws that mandate that therapeutic records be retained for a specified length of time. HIPAA also has regulations governing record retention, mandating that all health care records be maintained for a period of 6 years. In the event of a client's death, records must be kept for at least 2 years after the date of the death. If a state law specifies that records should be maintained for longer than 6 years, that law should be followed. Whenever the provisions of HIPAA and state statutes conflict, whichever provision is stricter takes precedence. Mental health records of minors should be kept until they reach the age of majority, according to many agency policies.

Disposal of Records Because some information stored in client records can become outdated and invalid, the ethics codes stipulate that professionals attend to the time-limited validity of some material in client records and that they alert others who may seek such records to the existence of outdated data. (The results from standardized tests are one example of material in a client's record that may become outdated.) When any portion of a record is disposed of, professionals should shred all documents before placing them in trash containers or recycling bins.

Value of Records for the Professional Obviously, the primary goals in keeping records of therapeutic contacts are to provide high-quality service for clients and to maintain continuity of service if different caregivers are involved. A secondary purpose is to document that good care was provided, if questions about that care are raised in court or in disciplinary hearings. Appelbaum and Gutheil (1991) have referred to documentation and consultation as the "twin pillars of liability protection" (p. 201). Regardless of one's personal feelings about the merits of detailed records, this level of recordkeeping is rapidly becoming a "legal standard of care" for counseling and psychotherapy. In fact, the failure to keep adequate records has been used as evidence of poor care in court proceedings (Soisson et al., 1987). Some therapists have lost their licenses because they failed to keep appropriate records (Anderson, 1996). The courts, too, tend to conclude that if there is no record of good care, there is no good care (Soisson et al., 1987).

A good record also protects a therapist in high-risk situations, such as a threat of suicide or injury to others. In that circumstance, scholars recommend documenting not only the ultimate judgment reached but also a review of the factors evaluated to reach that judgment and of sources consulted in the process. Zuckerman (2003) also suggests that therapists quote the client's answers to risk-assessment questions. Professionals who detail such information in the record are less likely to be judged negligent in court, even if their decision turned out to be wrong (Peterson, 1996; Soisson et al., 1987).

Ownership of Records   Records of mental health care are considered in most jurisdictions to be the property of the professional, but clients usually have access to copies of those records and control their dissemination (Soisson et al., 1987). Anderson (1996) explains this concept succinctly: "You own the records, but your clients own the information contained in them" (p. 94). Consequently, mental health professionals ought to write notes that they would be willing to have the client read. Emotional statements, summary judgments, and personal opinions have no place in the record. Some scholars suggest that counselors write records collaboratively with clients to increase their involvement in the process, reduce their concern about what the records may contain, and reduce the risk of a malpractice claim (Anderson, 1996; Mitchell, 1991). Once again, however, because the legal requirements for recordkeeping vary from state to state, all mental health professionals should stay abreast of laws in their states related to this issue.

Ethics of Dual Records   Some counselors and therapists keep dual records. One set is the official record of services, and the other is their personal notes on the case. The latter allows the counselor to sort through feelings and reactions to the counseling process. Legal opinion on this practice is divided. Anderson (1996) points out that so far, only official notes have been successfully obtained for court proceedings and disciplinary hearings. Thus, she contends that there is no justification at this time to advise professionals who engage in this practice to change it. However, she advises that personal notes ought to always be anonymous, secure, and devoted primarily to the counselor's issues with the case, rather than the client's. Bernstein and Hartsell (1998) take the opposite approach, asserting that from a legal perspective "a therapist can maintain only one set of records. Private records or personal notations are usually subject to subpoena" (p. 7).

HIPAA and Psychotherapy Notes   When the federal government was writing the legislation for HIPAA, they included provisions that allowed for sharing of complete client records between providers and others involved in the health care and payment for services without separate client consents for each such contact as long as the client signed a copy of the Notice of Privacy Practices. This wording meant that third-party payors could not be refused access to complete client records if they wished to view them. Ultimately, the professional associations negotiated a compromise to such open records, with an exception to such access for *psychotherapy notes.* What is a psychotherapy note? Essentially, a psychotherapy record refers to what are usually called *process notes*—comments that express the professional's impressions of a client or analyze the nature of a conversation between a client and a professional (Holloway, 2003). Psychotherapy notes can be excluded from release without explicit client authorization as long as they are kept physically separate from the official client record. The following information can never be considered a psychotherapy note: "medication prescription and monitoring, counseling session start and stop times, the modalities and frequencies of treatment furnished, results of clinical tests, and any summary of the following items: diagnosis, functional status, the treatment plan, symptoms, prognosis, and progress to date" (HIPAA Section 164.501). It is important to note that many counselors and therapists do not habitually keep psychotherapy notes and are not required to do so by any ethical or legal standard, so this exclusion probably has more symbolic than real protection of client privacy from third-party payors.

Involuntary Commitment

Counselors in community agencies or private practice sometimes see clients who are unable to meet their basic human needs and to keep themselves safe because they are experiencing severe psychiatric dysfunction. In this mental state a person may refuse to agree to hospitalization because of delusions, hallucinations, or both. In such situations counselors and therapists sometimes ask the courts to place the person in a protected environment until stabilized. If such placement happens without the person's consent, it is called *involuntary commitment* to a psychiatric unit or hospital (Swenson, 1997). Needless to say, deciding to take away someone's freedom, even temporarily, is a serious matter that has both legal and ethical dimensions. History is replete with examples of people who were sent to mental institutions because they held deviant or unconventional beliefs and behaviors but who were not truly mentally ill. In the United States in the 1950s, for example, one of every 300 people was held involuntarily in a mental hospital (Stone, 1978). More recently, there has been public outcry about the placement of religious minorities in mental hospitals in China (Eckholm, 2001).

Currently, all states have elaborate procedures to ensure that the rights of the person are not violated any more than necessary and that the hospitalization is truly unavoidable. The specific criteria vary from state to state, but the general standard for such placement is to find "the least restrictive environment possible" while still protecting the safety of the individual (Swenson, 1997). Usually a preliminary hearing is conducted so that a judge can determine whether the action is legally warranted. Counselors and therapists involved in involuntary commitment decisions must be trained to assess mental and emotional disorders, familiar with applicable laws and regulations, and respectful of the dignity of the person involved. Counselors may breach confidentiality and ignore informed consent only as necessary to transfer the person to a safe environment. An involuntary commitment procedure is not a license to throw aside all usual protections of client rights and privacy. For example, if police are called to transport a client to a hospital, the officers should be given only that information they need to safely complete the transportation. The fundamental criteria to guide counselors' decision making are respect for their clients' inherent worth and dignity and promotion of their welfare.

Counselors deciding whether a given individual requires commitment are often facing complex and contradictory situations. As mentioned in Chapter 4, determining dangerousness is difficult. Sometimes even the best efforts of mental health professionals cannot guarantee the safety of clients and their families, but practitioners owe competent and diligent care to all involved. Counselors dealing with such complex situations can gather enough relevant information, carefully assess dangerousness according to accepted criteria, and work to identify the least restrictive environment possible that will protect both the client and others at risk (Bednar, Bednar, Lambert, & Waite, 1991). In the current funding environment, substantial obstacles often hinder committing even those who meet every professional criterion for hospitalization. The problems of hospitalizing a person without insurance can be daunting. If the person to be involuntarily hospitalized is a minor, parental consent may be all that is required, although in some states a court hearing is also mandated (Ellis, 1996). Throughout this frustrating and confusing process, counselors should maintain a steadfast commitment to the client's welfare and to an outcome that benefits the client, compromises his or her rights as little as possible, and also helps protect others at risk.

Responsibilities to Colleagues

Counselors and therapists have obligations to conduct their interactions with other professionals in a way that honors their dignity, brings credit to their own profession, and avoids exploiting clients.

Cooperation and Respect

The generous federal funding that sparked the community mental health movement in the 1960s has long since disappeared, and now agencies are rivals in the battle for limited resources. Private practitioners now compete with agencies and with each other for the limited numbers of voluntary clients. Most seek to become *preferred providers* for managed care networks to gain access to insured clients (Danzinger & Welfel, 2001). In such an environment, professionals may feel tempted to forget their shared purpose of public service and to attend instead to the race for funds and clients. Disciplinary differences in models of training and epistemological assumptions about mental health and mental illness may also lead to tension among professions (Berg, 1986; Glosoff, 2001). The directives in the codes caution professionals against oppositional attitudes toward peers and encourage them instead to actively collaborate with other mental health professionals. Such a perspective benefits the public and also serves the long-term interest of the professions, enhancing both access and quality of services. Professionals who take a short-term perspective or who center their energies on this month's billable hours may feel tempted to accept without question clients already receiving service elsewhere, or they may even try to lure clients away from other practitioners. Keith-Spiegel and Koocher (1998) label the latter practice "pirating." The codes strongly recommend against such practices.

ACA *Code of Ethics,* Section A.3: Clients Served by Others
When counselors learn that their clients are in a professional relationship with another mental health professional, they request release from clients to inform the other professionals and strive to establish positive and collaborative professional relationships.

APA *Ethical Principles,* Section 3.09: Cooperation with Other Professionals
When indicated and professionally appropriate, psychologists cooperate with other professionals in order to serve their clients/patients effectively and appropriately.

10.04 Providing Therapy to Those Served by Others

In deciding whether to offer or provide services to those already receiving mental health services elsewhere, psychologists carefully consider the treatment issues and the potential client's/patient's welfare. Psychologists discuss these issues with the client/patient or another legally authorized person on behalf of the client/patient in order to minimize the risk of confusion and conflict, consult with the other service providers when appropriate, and proceed with caution and sensitivity to the therapeutic issues.

Of course, if clients are dissatisfied with their therapists or strongly believe that supplemental care is needed, counselors must respect their rights to seek other care. As consumers, clients are free to choose as long as the professional does not judge the change in caregivers to be harmful to the welfare of the client. When two or more mental health caregivers are involved simultaneously in the care of a client, frequent communication among them is desirable, provided the client agrees to such contacts (Glosoff, 2001). If a client is not willing to allow such communications, then the professional must make an independent judgment about whether good care can be provided within that restriction. If a professional concludes that such a restriction represents a potentially harmful situation for the client, he or she should disclose that conclusion to the client; attempt to renegotiate the arrangement; or, if the renegotiation is not successful, ask the client to see the other professional exclusively. Of course, termination and referral should not be done abruptly and should try not to cause the client additional distress. In essence, where supplemental or alternative counseling appears contrary to clients' therapeutic needs, counselors must balance their obligations not to abandon clients against their duty to avoid harm to those clients. Supervision and consultation are important resources to help counselors sort through such issues.

A second important aspect of cooperation and respect among colleagues relates to the interactions among the different mental health professions. Disagreements about what services individual professions are competent to provide have erupted during the recent history of psychiatry, psychology, counseling, and social work. Professionals schooled in one discipline may view differing training models with suspicion and tend to limit referrals and professional contacts to those with the same degree. Depending on one's perspective, this tendency to disdain related professions may be rooted in financial self-interest or in legitimate concern about the quality of services available to the public. The codes address this issue as follows.

APA *Ethical Principles,* Principle B: Fidelity and Responsibility

Psychologists establish relationships of trust with those with whom they work. Psychologists consult with, refer to, or cooperate with other professionals and institutions to the extent needed to serve the best interests of those with whom they work.

The ACA code is even more specific on this issue.

ACA *Code of Ethics,* Section D: Introduction

Professional counselors recognize that the quality of their interactions with colleagues can influence the quality of services provided to clients. They work to become knowledgeable about colleagues within and outside the field of counseling. Counselors develop positive working relationships and systems of communication with colleagues to enhance services to clients.

D.1. Relationships with Colleagues, Employers, and Employees

a. Different Approaches. Counselors are respectful of approaches to counseling services that differ from their own. Counselors are respectful of the practices of other professional groups with which they work.

b. Forming Relationships. Counselors work to develop and strengthen interdisciplinary relations with colleagues from other disciplines to best serve clients.

Thus, behaviors that disparage the competence of other professions, that suggest to clients that other professions are less worthy than one's own, and that are based more on self-interest than on public need are unseemly and contradict the values and standards expressed in professional codes. When, in the current competitive climate, practitioners experience frustrations with other professionals they must guard against expressing those feelings to clients or colleagues they may influence. Counselors and therapists should aim at finding ways to work together to counteract some of the social and political realities that limit or deny citizens access to quality mental health care. In fact, according to Johnson, Stewart, Brabeck, Huber, and Rubin (2004), respectful and competent interprofessional collaboration is becoming a "best practice standard" in psychology.

Fee Splitting

The term *fee splitting* refers to the practice of paying a fee to someone who provides referrals or receiving a fee from a professional to whom one sends referrals. In colloquial terms, fee splitting is a kind of "kickback." The codes of ethics of all mental health professions prohibit such arrangements unless the fee can be traced to a specific service provided. A fee for a referral in the absence of a service is unethical. (See, for example, Section 6.07 of the APA code.) The rationale for this prohibition is the risk to client welfare inherent in fee splitting. If counselors personally gain from a referral, they are vulnerable to making referral decisions based on their own gain rather than on the best interest of clients. Many other professions, such as law and medicine, carry similar wording in their codes of ethics. Unfortunately, some counselors seem unaware of this prohibition. Gibson and Pope (1993) found that 8% of their sample endorsed this activity as ethical.

The prohibition of fee splitting raises questions about several rather common practices in private practice. Sometimes one professional whose name is on a practice (for example, Dr. Enterprising and Associates) receives a percentage of the income of the other professionals in the practice for each client they see. The associates are not employees of Dr. Enterprising, but they subcontract with her for space, support services, and the like. In light of the code, ethics scholars have expressed concern about this practice (Haas & Malouf, 2005; Koocher, 1994b; Peterson, 1996). In their analysis of the APA code, Canter et al. (1994) suggest that such fees are acceptable if the professional to whom the fee is paid offers some services to the referring professional. For example, if Dr. Stern uses office space, secretarial services, and utilities in Dr. Enterprising's practice, Dr. Stern may pay a fee to Dr. Enterprising for referrals he receives from her. The fee should be reasonable, in light of the expenses Dr. Enterprising undertakes for the work of Dr. Stern. Moreover, the nature of the financial arrangement between Dr. Enterprising and Dr. Stern should be disclosed to the clients involved. Keeping such arrangements hidden from clients or those who pay for services is inappropriate. However, if the two professionals had completely separate practices and Stern paid his counterpart for referrals, that arrangement would violate the code because Dr. Enterprising would be providing no service to the client directly or indirectly. It is important to note that many states have laws prohibiting fee splitting and other forms of kickbacks (Fisher, 2003).

Questions have also been raised about the ethics of participating in provider networks or referral services. The consensus of current opinion is that professionals may ethically participate in health maintenance organizations, preferred provider organizations, or referral services, such as those often operated by state or local psychological associations, if it meets two conditions. First, the relationship is disclosed to clients and does not violate the client's best interests, and second, the fee paid is justified based on services or expenses involved (Koocher, 1994b; Fisher, 2003). Peterson (1996) suggests that open communication with clients about these issues also reduces the risk of the appearance of a conflict of interest.

As competition to provide services increases and third-party payors figure ever more prominently in access to care, professionals need to be sensitive to the ethical dimensions of the financial agreements they reach with insurers and other providers. They must ensure that all decisions about client care are based on the needs of clients irrespective of the financial implications for themselves. Professionals should always be completely open about fees and billing procedures and should inform clients about the costs of services as soon as information becomes available. Some regulations are even more specific—Ohio, for example, requires mental health professionals to notify clients about fees no later than the end of the second session.

Responsibilities to Third Parties

The era is rapidly ending in which the interactions between a counselor and a client concerned no one other than the parties involved. Clients who are ordered into counseling as a result of a legal proceeding or as a condition of continued employment or who elect to use insurance to pay for services all have third parties deeply interested (and often knowledgeable about) the content and progress of therapy. This section discusses the counselor's ethical responsibilities to these third parties.

Mandated and Nonvoluntary Counseling and Therapy

American courts are increasingly mandating that people enter counseling and therapy as a condition of their sentence. Teens who shoplift, belong to gangs, run away, or engage in drug violations are frequently mandated to get counseling. College students who act disruptively may be pushed into counseling (Amada, 1993). Adults who drive drunk, have neglected or abused their children, or been found guilty of stalking often "choose" counseling over jail or loss of rights. Similarly, children with learning disabilities or with aggressive behavior patterns may be sent to counseling by the courts or parents. Licensing boards often add counseling to their rehabilitation procedures for professionals found guilty of misconduct. As mentioned in Chapter 5, there are important concerns about informed consent to counseling under such circumstances. First, the counselor and mandated person must be clear about who the client is and to whom the counselor owes allegiance. If an outside body has dictated the goals of counseling, then the counselor must make an independent judgment about the appropriateness of those goals for this individual. The involvement of a third party in the decision to enter counseling does not diminish one's responsibility to do good and avoid harm. If counselors believe that clients will be unable to profit from the type of counseling recommended by the courts, they must communicate their concerns to the mandating party. Counselors should also present alternatives to the mandated treatment, if any are available.

Clients need to understand that they have some choice about participating, although the alternative to counseling is not especially appealing. In addition, clients need to understand the limits of confidentiality. If counselors are to submit regular reports to a board or court, clients must comprehend the nature of the reports and the possible consequences of such reports. Next, not all counselors are competent to work with mandated clients. Competency in this realm requires knowledge, experience, and skill (Rooney, 2001). Finally, counselors must avoid the temptation of viewing mandated clients as "second-class" clients because they are involuntary. They ought to be accorded the same level of respect as any person who engages voluntarily in the process. Here is the wording from the codes on this issue.

ACA *Code of Ethics,* Section C.6.b: Reports to Third Parties

Counselors are accurate, honest, and unbiased in reporting their professional activities and judgments to appropriate third parties including courts, health insurance companies, those who are the recipients of evaluation reports, and others.

APA *Ethical Principles,* Section 3.07: Third-Party Requests for Services

When psychologists agree to provide services to a person or entity at the request of a third party, psychologists attempt to clarify at the outset of the service the nature of the relationship with all individuals or organizations involved. This clarification includes the role of the psychologist (e.g., therapist, consultant, diagnostician, or expert witness), an identification of who is the client, the probable uses of the services provided or the information obtained, and the fact that there may be limits to confidentiality.

Interactions with Insurers, Managed Care Providers, and Other Payors

Some of the most agonizing ethical dilemmas for those practicing in community settings have arisen because of interactions with outside payors. On the one hand, the availability of reimbursement for mental health care has dramatically increased access to care. On the other hand, it has diminished both the freedom of mental health professionals to treat clients independent of outside concerns and the privacy of clients. Moreover, the limits set on the type or duration of care eligible for reimbursement have prompted many mental health professionals to view access to quality care, particularly under managed care, as a sham. Its severest critics refer to managed mental health care (also referred to as behavioral health care plans) as the rape of psychotherapy (Fox, 1995) or as invisible rationing (Miller, 1996). Even calmer voices note that it has caused "an upheaval in the practice community" (Acuff et al., 1999, p. 563) and that most professionals find it a negative influence on their work (for example, Danzinger & Welfel, 2001; Neill, 2001; Phelps, Eisman, & Kohut, 1998). Practitioners also view managed care as a challenge to compliance with professional ethics (Corcoran & Gottlief, 2000; Glosoff, Garcia, Herlihy, & Remley, 1999; Murphy, DeBernardo, & Shoemaker, 1998). Decisions about reimbursement for care are made by people who have no contact with the client and who sometimes use criteria that over-simplify research findings or have no known scientific validity. When clients are denied re-imbursement for care that the counselors believe is essential, the professionals are placed in a difficult position. They then must provide care at lower cost, or without reimbursement, or ask clients to pay out-of-pocket. Moreover, insurers allow people to be reimbursed for services only when the professionals involved in the case meet their standards. Often, that means being listed on a network of preferred providers. Professionals who do not wish to contract with the insurer in that way are effectively prevented from working with clients insured by that company. The criteria for getting listed are variable. Some professionals with sterling credentials and proven records are denied, whereas others whose skills are un-proved are accepted. Danzinger and Welfel (2001) found that nearly half (48%) the men-tal health counselors they surveyed had difficulty getting accepted on managed care pan-els. Even if accepted, professionals can be removed from such lists whenever the insurers wish and usually have little recourse. Fear of being terminated as an approved provider places decision making about clients' needs under a shadow of worry about reprisals for recommending expensive or prolonged care.

Clients, too, face tough decisions—to see an insurer-approved professional and get help in paying for therapy, postpone service, or fund counseling themselves. Once in counseling, if they want to challenge the limits reimbursers place on the length or type of therapy, they must be willing to surrender some privacy because the typical channels of complaint are through their employers. To help consumers and professionals deal with these problems, the professional associations of 17 mental health disciplines, in-cluding counseling, psychology, psychiatry, social work, and family therapy, have pro-duced a *Mental Health Patient's Bill of Rights* (1997). Its ultimate goal is to protect clients from substandard care. Community practitioners should make copies available to all their managed care clients.

Regardless of the dissatisfaction of the professional community with managed care, there are no signs that this model of payment will disappear in the near future. Kiesler (2000) re-ports that 88% of U.S. citizens with private insurance are currently enrolled in managed care programs of some form. How can counselors and therapists cope with this form of reim-bursement and still abide by standards for care set by their professions, licensing boards, and often by law? The following is a primer for ethical survival in this context. Readers are urged to consult the sources listed in the Recommended Readings for a fuller discussion of these issues. I begin with a clearer definition and brief history of managed care.

Definition, History, and Data on Managed Care   Managed mental health care involves ef-forts by companies to control the costs of services and prevent payment for services that are ineffective, unnecessary, or counterproductive. It seeks to achieve this goal by regularly reviewing use of services, contracting with limited numbers of practitioners who agree to set fees for service, and preauthorizing care (Corcoran & Winslade, 1994, Frager, 2000). It originated as a response to the escalating costs of health care and was superimposed on outpatient mental health care, a small piece of the overall cost of health care in the United States (Iglehart, 1996). The costs of some segments of mental health care were growing rapidly, such as substance abuse treatment and inpatient adolescent treatment (MacCluskie & Ingersoll, 2000), but most costs for outpatient psychotherapy were not increasing at the same high rate as other forms of health care (Iglehart, 1996). Critics charge that the current mode of operation of most managed care companies stems primarily from profit motives and not from any overriding commitment to efficient, quality care except where quality may be profitable (for example, see Miller, 1995, 1996; Wrich, 1995). Others recognize that the old fee-for-service model of payment was not without its ethical challenges and abuses (MacCluskie & Ingersoll, 2000; Welfel, 2001). There is no doubt, however, that managed care has dramatically reduced expenditures for mental health care. Spending on mental health declined 54% between 1988 and 1997 and has decreased more than any other segment of the health care industry (McCarthy, 1998).

There are several variants of managed health care companies—health maintenance organizations, preferred provider organizations, and point-of-service plans. Almost all forms limit the numbers of outpatient sessions allowed annually and restrict access to inpatient care. A review of research on psychologists' experiences with managed care indicates, as noted, that they view the impact of managed care negatively and have experienced many episodes when necessary care was denied or delayed (Miller, 1996; Phelps et al., 1998). A few studies that have compared the outcomes of clients with depression in traditional fee-for-service arrangements with client outcomes in managed care found that managed care clients were more frequently underdiagnosed and had significantly worse outcomes (Rogers, Wells, Meredith, Sturm, & Burman, 1993; Wells, Hays, Burman, Rogers, Greenfield, & Ware, 1989).

Special Ethical Concerns in Managed Care When professionals are considering signing a contract with a managed care company, they need answers to each of the following questions before they agree to participate:

- Does the financial arrangement with the company let the practitioner make independent professional judgments based on the client's needs and goals (Haas & Cummings, 1991)? Does it minimize conflict-of-interest issues?

- Are the people who are conducting the preauthorization of care and the periodic review of services trained professionals capable of understanding diagnostic and treatment issues and able to use protocols for care responsibly? Are those protocols derived from scientific evidence? If so, what is that evidence?

- Are resources available to meet special client needs and take into consideration unique variables that may affect an individual's need for services? What resources are available? How well does the organization avoid a "one size (brief) fits all" approach to therapy?

- How well does the system respond to the needs of culturally diverse populations (Newman & Bricklin, 1991)?

- To what degree does the process of preauthorization of care and utilization review intrude into client privacy (Haas & Cummings, 1991)? Is this intrusion excessive?

- Are there reasonable protections of confidential therapeutic information in place within the managed care organization (MCO)? Is access limited to those who have a professional role, and do those professionals appreciate their obligations to protect client privacy (Scarf, 1996)?

- How accurate is advertising for enrollment in the plan? Are enrollees clearly informed about the limits of mental health benefits?

- Does the managed care plan respond positively, or at least neutrally, to professionals who take a comprehensive approach to informed consent, including explaining the limits of confidentiality, payment issues, and the like related to their use of the managed care plan for reimbursement of services?

- To what degree does the plan recognize that professionals have a duty to disclose the potential impact of managed care on treatment as well as the possibility that reimbursement for care may be terminated before treatment goals are reached (APA *Ethical Principles,* Section 6.04; Appelbaum, 1993)? Does it allow professionals to disclose the nature of their contractual obligations to the company?
- Does the MCO give a fair hearing to requests for exceptions to standard care based on individual client needs, and does it refrain from punishing professionals who make such requests?

Mental health professionals should also be advised that the standards of care used to make judgments about malpractice claims do not vary because of the limits of insurance or managed care policies (Appelbaum, 1993). Counselors cannot base decisions about mental health care on insurance or other financial considerations; they should focus decisions more narrowly on the welfare of the clients. Similarly, there is some suggestion in the law that mental health professionals need to act assertively when insurers deny coverage for treatment that they believe is necessary. Appelbaum (1993) refers to this standard as *the duty to appeal adverse decisions* and recommends that counselors and therapists act as advocates on their clients' behalf when care has been refused. Appelbaum also points out that the ethical and legal standards about abandonment and interruption of services are not suspended in managed care settings. Clients, of course, may elect not to continue treatment after reimbursement ends, but the choice should be in their hands and they should understand the implications of ending treatment prematurely.

In sum, practitioners must guard against shifting the responsibility for adequate client care to the managed care company. They must guide decisions by the principle of competent diagnosis and treatment and must energetically work toward that goal regardless of the funding source for services provided. Counselors and therapists should not relinquish all their power to insurers.

Evidence of Ethics Violations in Dealing with Third-Party Payors Professionals who feel frustrated by the power third-party payors exert over their clients' access to mental health care and their own access to income may use more severe diagnoses than warranted (called upcoding) so as to receive additional time in therapy or to otherwise change diagnoses to meet reimbursement criteria. In fact, between 1990 and 1993, 15% of the ethics claims filed with the APA Ethics Committee dealt with this form of misrepresentation (Peterson, 1996). Similarly, most of those responding to Pope, Tabachnick, and Keith-Spiegel (1987) reported that they had altered an insurance diagnosis to meet reimbursement criteria. As mentioned already, if there is no objective, clinically justifiable reason for a change in diagnosis, this practice violates ethical standards (ACA, *Ethics Code,* Section E.5.a; APA, *Ethical Principles,* Section 6.06). It is also fraudulent and subject to legal penalties. Remley and Herlihy (2005) point out that any misrepresentation to an insurer regarding the facts of services that is designed to increase the likelihood of payment is considered fraud. If fraud is discovered, mental health professionals can be subject to civil suits to recover costs; prosecutors may file criminal charges too because fraud is a crime. Unfortunately, counselors do not seem aware of the implications of changing diagnoses to gain additional reimbursement (Mayfield, 1996, as cited in Remley & Herlihy, 2005). Other unethical practices that have been documented in research studies include the following:

- Tailoring treatment to the parameters acceptable for MCO reimbursement even when the professional believes that alternative treatment protocols were preferable
- Failing to disclose to clients the full extent of information that will be communicated to MCO personnel for fear of losing clients

- Complying with "gag orders" imposed by the MCO that limit the information clients receive about treatment alternatives (such gag orders are usually also illegal)
- Implementing counseling interventions in which the professional has little training or supervision because they are defined as the acceptable protocol by the MCO
- Terminating treatment when reimbursement ends without a referral to a more affordable service even when continued counseling is needed

Emerging Issues in Interactions with Third-Party Payors Because of the frustrations and controversies related to managed mental health care some professionals are eschewing participation and are seeking alternative methods of providing quality, cost-effective services (Bittner, Bialek, Nathiel, Ringwald, & Tupper, 1999). Others are challenging the actions of behavioral health plans in court with some success (Nessman & Hendron, 2000), and still others have suggested that mental health professionals employed by managed care should be held accountable for actions inconsistent with the codes of ethics (Sank, 1997). Current federal law that protects MCOs against liability for injured patients denied reimbursement has been vigorously challenged, and efforts to change it are likely to continue, but the outcome of this matter is still unclear (Appelbaum, 1998). What remains clear, however, is that professionals who give substandard care or who fail to provide needed continuing care when insurance benefits are exhausted are at risk for malpractice claims and that defenses based on reimbursement issues alone have been insufficient to deflect such claims.

Also, much public concern has developed over the vast amounts of personal information insurers have accumulated and about their progress in establishing computer data networks so that they can share information more efficiently (Jeffords, 1999). As a result, new federal rules for the protection of the security of computer systems that include health records have been put forth (HIPAA, 2003). Other legislative actions may be forthcoming to further protect the privacy of medical information, so professionals should keep abreast of these developments.

The Ethics of Consultation and Coaching

Counselors in community agencies often act as consultants, either to other individual professionals or to organizations and groups (Dougherty, 1990). This development was sparked by the Community Mental Health Act of 1963 (Brown, Pryzwansky, & Schulte, 1991). Organizational consultation with executives is sometimes referred to as *executive coaching* (Kilburg, 2000; Stern, 2004). Graduate training in consultation and coaching is uneven (Newman, 1993), and the ethics codes have generally given this activity insufficient attention (Robinson & Gross, 1985). The APA code limits its specific comments to issues relating to situations in which a professional is consulting with another professional about an individual therapy, research, or training situation. The 2005 ACA code mentions this form of consultation in B.6.a, but neither code provides comprehensive ethical guidelines for consultants or broadly addresses organizational consulting. Fortunately, scholars have written extensively on the ethics of consultation, and such publications are a valuable resource. Newman (1993), for example, identifies four crucial ethical issues in consultation: (a) the relationships between the people involved, including the confidentiality of information disclosed; (b) the influence of the consultant's values on the process; (c) the competence of professionals who consult; and (d) the selection and implementation of interventions. What follows is a brief review of each ethical dimension. To this list, add consideration of the ethics of financial matters. Those interested in an in-depth analysis of this topic should refer to Newman (1993), Dougherty (1990), or Lowman (1998).

Consultation Relationships

Consultation relationships are triadic rather than dyadic (Brown et al., 1991) and include the consultant, the consultee, and the consultee's client system. However, the client system does not hire the consultant, shape the consultant's responsibilities, or sometimes even know a consultation is under way. Yet, ultimately, consultants influence the client system and are responsible for their effects on that system. Mental health professionals who are not attuned to the implications of their work on these rather invisible participants can violate their rights and impair the ways the system affects them. For example, the director of a large mental health agency may contract with a consultant to help increase the staff's productivity and generate more revenue for the agency. The impact of the consultant's work will be felt not only by the staff but also by the clients the agency serves. In some ways, both staff and consumers are part of the client system, although they had no voice in deciding whether to hire a consultant or in setting the initial goals for the arrangement. Yet both groups may experience the greatest impact of any recommendations implemented after the consultation. Newman (1993) cautions consultants to stay aware of all three participant groups in consultation, to be sensitive to the effects of their work on all parties, and to avoid situations in which their work may be used to the detriment of the client system. A wise consultant seeks to involve all parties in designing a consultation agreement at the earliest possible stage. Such involvement shows respect for client rights, and it also improves the chances of the project's success and helps identify related goals or problems. By including all parties, the consultant may learn, for example, that a given problem is a bookkeeping or reimbursement matter rather than a client contact issue.

Newman (1993) also points out that managing confidentiality and informed consent is more complicated in consultation situations, especially when the consultation is aimed at organizational change. How should a consultant handle one-on-one disclosures from employees? Are they confidential? Consultants need to be clear about their purpose and relationship with each employee with whom they interact and to forewarn any person when material cannot be kept confidential. A consultant hired to help smooth the merger of two mental health agencies should very directly tell the clients if he or she believes that keeping individual confidences may conflict with achieving broader institutional goals. In other words, the limits of confidentiality should be clearly spelled out to all involved. What is less complicated, of course, is the consultant's obligations to keep information related to the organization or people involved confidential from those who have no right to that information. Such disclosures are simply wrong.

As discussed in Chapter 5, informed consent refers to the free and educated choices people make about matters that affect them. In organizations, senior executives often make decisions about hiring consultants and their assignments. Employees and clients have less involvement and less power, and as a result employees who disagree with the process or goals of consultation may be reluctant to voice reservations for fear of losing status or other repercussions. Consultants need to be sensitive to the hierarchical nature of organizations and work skillfully with all parties to approach informed consent as closely as possible. Counselors can educate executives, for example, about the value of not coercing employees, and they can respect employees and encourage them to relinquish unwarranted caution.

Finally, consultants must also be alert to dual-relationship issues. Not only must they avoid sexually exploiting people they serve, but they must also be sensitive to nonsexual dual relationships that may compromise their objectivity. Consultants often work intensively with a few individuals in an organization. Such intensive contact can lead to inappropriate blending of roles. Consultant and friend, or consultant and business partner, are two such contacts that probably present ethical problems. When a consultant develops a personal relationship with one partner in consultation, he or she is vulnerable to ignoring the interests of the other partner. Moreover, when one is a business partner of a psychologist in a group practice and simultaneously a consultant on productivity, it is easy to lose track of the needs and rights of the clients and the other employees.

Values and Consultation

The values of the consultant are important in two respects (Newman, 1993). First, because consultants cannot be value free, they must become aware of the ways in which their values influence consultation process and outcome. Such awareness will help the professional avoid unconsciously imposing personal values in unproductive ways. Second, consultants should be prepared to respond to conflicting values in their work. Conflicts are not inherently destructive, but they can be harmful if ignored or improperly handled. For example, the consultant who is committed to collaboration to address problems may have significant conflict with directors who believe in a more authoritative and centralized approach to management, unless both parties can openly discuss and resolve the issue.

Consultation with the Military in a Post-September 11th World

The United States Department of Defense has hired psychologists and psychiatrists as consultants practically since the beginning of the profession. Psychologists developed psychological tests to help the military develop measures to assess combat fatigue as early as the 1920s. During the wars in Iraq and Afghanistan the Department of Defense employed psychologists to assist them in developing effective ways to interrogate detainees held in connection with that war. When several media reports surfaced that indicated that these mental health professionals had been involved in advising interrogators on how to "use detainees fears and longings to increase distress" (for example, Lewis, 2005), the president of APA formed a task force to analyze the ethics of such consultation. This group issued a report cautioning its members about the ethical dangers of such consultation (APA, 2005). In part it stated, "Psychologists who serve in the role of supporting an interrogation do not use health care related information to the detriment of an individual's safety and well-being." The report did not conclude that such activities were inherently unethical but that professionals who serve in such roles have a responsibility to recognize the delicate balance of ethical considerations inherent in the consultation. They also advise psychologists that they have a duty to report any torture or cruel or inhumane treatment to appropriate authorities.

Competence for Consultation

Many mental health professionals provide consultation in the middle and late stages of their careers, but relatively few have formal academic training in consultation. Scholars decry this situation, both because of the risk to clients and because of lost opportunities for good outcomes (for example, see Crego, 1985; Lowman, 1998). Practitioners seem to make the same mistake in thinking about competence to do consultation that they make in thinking about competence to supervise—they embrace the myth that clinical skills are sufficient. However, there is a body of knowledge related to consultation to be learned, a set of skills that need to be practiced under supervision, and a capacity for judgment that is acquired with experience (for example, see Dougherty, 1990). Lowman (1985) notes that most counselors and therapists would be appalled if people without any counseling training presented themselves as counselors, yet counselors sometimes offer themselves as consultants without having been trained to consult. The tendency to misjudge the knowledge required for consulting does not release any professional from the obligation to work within the boundaries of competence.

Finally, competence to consult in one setting does not imply competence in all consultation settings or activities. A professional competent to provide case consultations may not be the best resource for organization issues. Similarly, personal problems or preexisting relationships may compromise competence to be effective with a given client. The obligation to evaluate competence and to ensure that it is maintained always lies with the individual professional. Those who represent themselves as skilled consultants must be prepared to demonstrate the sources of their knowledge and be ready to take responsibility for harm their interventions cause.

Ethical Issues in Intervention for Consultants

Because of the triadic relationships among consultant, consultee, and client system in mental health, consultants should keep the effects of their interventions on clients in the forefront of their thinking. Moreover, they need to be alert for ways in which others might misuse their findings, and they must work to prevent such misuse. Executives who seem to want to use a consultant report to dismiss older employees, for example, must be energetically dissuaded from such action. If persuasion fails, consultants should withdraw from the project. In other words, consultants cannot shift to others the responsibility for the ways those others use their recommendations.

Consultants sometimes advocate interventions without sufficient forethought. Even well-designed interventions that are likely to do good may also carry some negative consequences. Counselors cannot ignore negative impacts because the cost–benefit ratio is positive. Instead, they must be cognizant of the power they exert and seek to prevent or minimize those side effects as much as possible.

Finally, consultants should base interventions and recommendations on empirical findings to the highest degree possible (Newman, 1993). They should distinguish experimental or untested recommendations from those well supported by prior research. Empirical data cannot always provide direct guidance for every consulting situation in cookbook fashion, but such data can act as a foundation for effective interventions (Newman, 1993; Newman, Robinson-Kurpius, & Fuqua, 2002).

Fees for Consulting

Why do many professionals become involved in consultation at some point during their careers? This involvement stems partly from the challenge of the activity; partly from the status inherent in it; and partly from the financial gain to be had, especially in organizational consulting. A well-reputed consultant can earn a handsome living. If one is competent, conscientious, and committed to the public good, that reimbursement is well deserved and not an ethical issue. However, at times the opportunity for significant income may cloud a professional's judgment. Such a person may accept consulting contracts without true competence, for the financial gain, or may ignore findings and interventions inconsistent with the hopes and expectations of whoever is writing the checks. In the latter situation, consultation becomes telling the executives what they want to hear and is a sham from which no one is likely to benefit, even the executives. This is a true conflict of interest and is obviously inconsistent with ethical standards. For example, a consultant who encourages a board of directors to replace its director and then maneuvers herself into the director's position is flagrantly violating ethical principles.

Records of Consultation

Just as records of counseling and psychotherapy improve service to clients and help protect professionals against claims of negligence or misconduct, records of consulting also increase the likelihood of effective service. Consultants should have written contracts setting out the relationship, fees, goals, and practical aspects of the consultation. Issues of confidentiality and informed consent should be addressed in such contracts, along with any unique elements of the consultation. Similarly, consultants should keep progress notes and document any areas of concern or disagreement with special care. A copy of all reports to the consultee should be retained, along with copies of correspondence and telephone contacts. Consultants should protect the confidentiality of these records in the same way counseling records are protected.

The Ethics of Forensic Activities

The term "forensic mental health work" refers to those professional activities of a psychologist, counselor, or social worker that involve, primarily, courts of law. These include, but are not limited to, the following:

- Conducting child custody evaluations for a divorce court
- Acting as an expert witness in a legal case
- Serving as consultant to attorneys on jury selection or other aspects of trials
- Assessing a defendant's competence to stand trial
- Providing psychological information about a convicted person to the court prior to the penalty phase of a trial

In each situation the court or an agent of the court employs or mandates the mental health professional to provide professional advice relevant to court business in civil or criminal cases. The ethics of forensic activities have received increasing attention in the literature over the last decade for several reasons. First, the courts are seeking such advice more often (Haas, 1993). Second, the roles and loyalties of professionals who participate in forensic work are often confusing and conflicting (Bersoff & Koeppl, 1993; Stokes & Remley, 2001). The demands, cultures, and norms of the courtroom and the community counseling center are very different (Hess, 1998; Melton, 1994), and to act ethically counselors and psychotherapists need knowledge of these differences (Anderton, Staulcup, & Grisso, 1980; Weikel & Hughes, 1993). Third, the professional sometimes has significant power in this role. A judge, for example, may rely heavily on a psychological evaluation of parents in making child custody decisions or in competency hearings for elderly people. And numerous ethics complaints to licensing boards stem from parents' dissatisfaction with professionals' evaluations (Kirkland & Kirkland, 2001). Finally, the ethics of forensics has earned a prominent place partly through dishonor. The existence, even in small numbers, of "hired guns" and experts who will argue for any side that pays them for testimony has placed a cloud of suspicion over the matter (Huber, 1991; Pope & Vetter, 1992). Some critics have nothing but disdain for expert testimony. Szasz (1973) referred to testimony by psychiatrists as "Mendacity masquerading as medicine." Sampson (1993) describes a mental health expert witness as "someone who wasn't there when it happened but who for a fee will gladly imagine what it must have been like" (p. 69). However, there is nothing inherently unethical in providing professional services to a court. In fact, when conducted with allegiance to high ethical standards, such activities can bring credit to the profession and can improve the likelihood that the court will make a fair and reasoned evaluation of the questions before it.

Psychologists and psychiatrists have had more involvement in these roles than other professionals, but counselors and social workers are increasingly present in the courtroom (Bersoff, 1995; Foster, 1996). Child welfare cases may even include a larger proportion of counselors and social workers than psychologists. Thus, questions about the ethics of forensics are the proper domain of all mental health professionals.

The central ethical questions to consider when engaging in such activities derive from the writings of ethics scholars (for example, Stahl, 1994, 1999), published specialty guidelines (APA, 1994; Committee on Ethical Guidelines for Forensic Psychologists, 1991), and the ethics codes. (Psychologists should note that the 2002 revision of the APA *Ethical Principles* deleted the specific sections on forensic activities that had been included in the last version of the code. Instead, references to forensic activities are integrated with other professional activities in appropriate sections of that code.) Those who seek a complete discussion on the ethics of forensic practice may see the recommended readings at the end of this chapter. The central questions follow.

Competence for Forensic Activities

1. Do I have the requisite knowledge about the issue before the court and about the law as it applies to my involvement? Is that knowledge current? Do I have enough time to perform the task competently?
2. Can I ensure that I will not be pressured to violate the boundaries of my competence?
3. Can I operate so that my personal values and beliefs do not compromise my capacity to provide good service?
4. Can I competently supervise my staff so that they too act within the boundaries of their competence?
5. Do I know and have access to all relevant codes and professional guidelines relevant to forensic work?
6. Do I have knowledgeable colleagues with whom I may consult if that becomes advisable?
7. Am I prepared to make available to the court the scientific data that support my conclusions or recommendations?
8. If an emergency arises, can I provide necessary care, assuming I am competent to provide it?

Informed Consent for Forensic Activities

1. Do all parties involved understand my role, my competence and its limits, the fees, duration, and other practical matters related to the activity?
2. Is there a written informed consent form for clients to sign and a written contract with court personnel?
3. Have I reviewed informed consent issues with clients myself and not relegated that duty to others? Do clients understand how evaluative data will be used and how my role differs from the role of a therapist?
4. Have I respected the civil rights of all involved?

Dual Relationships and Forensic Activities

1. Have I avoided or minimized potential conflicts of interest or declined to participate if the conflict cannot be resolved? Have I made the court aware of any potential conflicts?
2. Have I avoided situations of undue influence, dual relationships, and exploitation of clients?

3. Have I declined to act as an evaluator or expert witness for people who have been my clients (Greenberg & Shuman, 1997)? Conversely, have I declined to accept as clients individuals for whom I served as court evaluator?

Confidentiality

1. Do the parties involved understand confidentiality and its limits? Do clients know that court-mandated evaluations will be shared with the court, for example?
2. Are the records I keep secure?
3. Do I maintain confidentiality of any disclosures not relevant to the business of the court, unless otherwise released?

Fees

1. Are my fees fair?
2. Have I refused any contingency-based form of payment—that is, any payment based on the outcome of a case?

Communications

1. Have I ensured (as much as possible) that reports, testimony, and the like generated from my services are communicated honestly and without deception?
2. Have I acted to correct any misrepresentations of my work?
3. Do I advertise my services in a way that honestly and fairly represents my competencies?
4. Do I understand the implications of my role, especially as expert witness, for the reputation of the profession, and am I committed to acting in ways that bring credit to the profession?

Child Custody Evaluations

1. Do I have the specialized competence required to conduct such evaluations (APA, 1994; Stahl, 1994, 1999)?
2. Do I keep the best interests of the child in the forefront of my considerations and know how to deal with the ambiguity inherent in that criterion (Oberlander, 1995)?
3. Do I interview all involved and fairly assess multiple sources of data in making my evaluation?
4. Do I know how to deal responsibly with children's preferences for one parent (Oberlander, 1995)?
5. Do I refrain from agreeing to conduct such an evaluation if I have a preexisting relationship with any party or any other connection that may compromise my objectivity and effectiveness?

In light of these questions, consider the following cases.

The Social Worker's Evaluation

A clinical social worker is asked to make a child custody assessment in a divorce action. He interviews both children and the father in person. The mother needed emergency surgery and could not keep her scheduled interview. The interview was postponed 1 day, and the social worker went to the mother's hospital room for the interview. The mother was in pain and still somewhat groggy from the medication and anesthesia. The social worker submitted her report and recommendations based on these interviews and other available data.

The Psychologist and the Pregnant Defendant

A psychologist is asked to evaluate the competence to stand trial of a woman who is charged with killing her twin infant sons as they slept in their cribs. The woman's mental health records show a history of paranoid schizophrenia, and she was noncompliant with medications for several weeks prior to the violence. The psychologist is in her third month of pregnancy with twins herself, and she finds herself repulsed and frightened by this woman's actions. She believes she cannot deal with this case at this time and declines to participate, referring the case to a colleague.

The Psychologist and Jury Selection

A social psychologist has become a sought-after consultant to defense lawyers regarding jury selection. He uses his considerable expertise in human social behavior to help defense lawyers obtain sympathetic jurors. He keeps records of his effectiveness, and those records show that his advice generally results in impaneling juries more sympathetic to the defendant.

The mental health professional who recognizes the impact of her personal situation on her capacity to provide objective, professional service is acting in compliance with the professional standards and is making a judgment consistent with the best interests of the client. The social worker who uses unreliable information on which to base a custody evaluation is violating guidelines, however. A bedside interview while a person is still under the influence of anesthesia and pain medication is an insufficient basis for making generalizations about that person's fitness as a parent. In this situation, other pressures seem to have overtaken responsible judgment and promotion of the client's welfare. Moreover, the error is serious because the stakes are so high in this case.

A judgment about the ethics of the social psychologist's behavior needs more careful consideration. The U.S. system of jurisprudence is built on the right of a person to a zealous defense against any charges against him or her. The expertise of the social psychologist can be appropriately used to help defendants obtain jurors who are not likely to be biased against the person on trial and who will otherwise attempt to keep an open mind about the legal proceedings. His work is more likely to be within the ethical boundaries of the profession if his judgment about what constitutes a "sympathetic jury" is based on scientific evidence, not on personal whim or other idiosyncratic criteria. Similarly, if his judgments rely on stereotypes alone—for example, a European-American defendant should have a European-American jury—they deviate from the ethical standards of the profession and fail to bring credit to it.

SUMMARY

Counselors in community and private practice settings must wrestle with conflict-of-interest dilemmas. They must balance their own need for and right to a fair profit from their work against clients' rights to services and their roles as professional helpers. In addition, outside parties, especially those who provide payment for professional services, often affect the relationship between counselor and client. There are six central ethical mandates for community counselors. The first is to recruit clients with fair, complete, and honest descriptions of their capabilities and credentials and to avoid direct solicitation of potential clients. Second, the fees charged for services ought to be

fair, clearly communicated, and sensitive to the financial status of the client. Professionals have a right to a fair income, but they are not allowed to place their own financial gain ahead of the welfare of clients. Third, if service must be interrupted, mental health professionals ought to have in place mechanisms for alternate care so that clients' therapeutic progress will be minimally disrupted by the interruption. Fourth, records of services ought to be up-to-date, accurate, and confidential so that competent service can be provided and privacy can be protected. Those records should be maintained for sufficient time for follow-up care to be provided and disposed of in ways that guarantee client privacy. Fifth, if outside sources mandate therapy, the professional gives primary allegiance to the client, with due respect for the rights of the third parties and informed consent for all involved. Sixth, if clients need to be hospitalized against their wishes, the procedures used should be respectful to clients and minimally restrict their freedom.

Relationships with colleagues in the community are built on respect, honesty, and fairness. Turf wars, private judgments about competencies, and disagreements among professional disciplines ought not to be carried into the consulting room. Financial arrangements between colleagues should be open to client inspection and free from any hint of fee splitting or other forms of kickbacks.

When dealing with outside payors for counseling and psychotherapy, counselors must advocate for their clients for needed services and for limited intrusion into their clients' rights to privacy. Moreover, they must assess appropriate diagnosis and treatment separately from insurance and financial considerations. The frustrations with insurers that mental health professionals commonly experience do not excuse any misrepresentations in diagnosis and treatment to those payors.

Finally, when consulting or engaging in forensic activities, mental health professionals need to recognize that those specialties require professionals to have focused training and experience before they can assert competency. The tenets of good science, informed consent, confidentiality of records and disclosures, avoidance of dual relationships and exploitation, and sensitivity to individual differences and cultural background apply as strongly to these undertakings as they do to therapy relationships.

CASES FOR DISCUSSION

Jordan's community sponsors a picnic each summer to honor the founding of the city. Local merchants rent booths at the picnic to display their products or services. Many give away pencils, mugs, and bumper stickers to advertise their services. Jordan, a licensed counseling psychologist, rented a booth and put a banner on it that says, "The doctor is in." She also dresses up to resemble the cartoon character who made that statement famous. In addition, Jordan gives away free copies of popular self-help books to anyone who schedules an appointment with her. One of the other mental health professionals in the community who sees her booth contacts the licensing board and files an ethics complaint against her for unprofessional behavior. Based on what you know, do you think there is reason for the licensing board to conduct an investigation here? Why or why not? If Jordan had mentioned her plan for the booth to you prior to the community picnic, what would you have advised her to do?

AnnMarie is employed in a large private practice. In addition to the ongoing supervision she receives from the clinical counselor who supervises her, she meets biweekly with the psychiatrist who established the practice for additional consultation. A few months after she starts working there, AnnMarie learns that the psychiatrist is billing clients for services that he did not provide. For example, when AnnMarie mentions a client's name in her meetings with him, he writes it down and charges that client for case consultation time. When AnnMarie gets advice and supervision from the psychiatrist, she believes such a charge is justified, but usually the psychiatrist, gives no guidance at all. AnnMarie resigns from the practice as soon as she learns about the way the psychiatrist bills for that time. Before she leaves, she tells her clients to check the bills they receive to ensure that there are not mistakes or irregularities. She tells no one else at the practice the real reason for her departure, but she knows she cannot participate in any billing practice that is unfair. Has AnnMarie done enough to be considered an ethical professional in this situation? Why? If you think she should have done more, what exactly should that be?

Don is a family therapist in a public agency that serves economically disadvantaged children and their families. His position requires him to make home visits to observe children in their normal family interactions and to intervene to help the parents respond appropriately to their children's needs and behaviors. In this role he believes he gains tremendous insight into the families he serves and that he forms strong and productive therapeutic bonds with them. There are times, however, when providing services in the client's home raises ethical questions for him. When other people visit the home during the session, sometimes parents continue talking with him as though no one else is there. Even if the client assures him that they can talk freely in front of this visitor, Don is unsure whether to respond therapeutically or not. At other times he observes behaviors that are illegal, such as another member of the household "playing the numbers" or smoking a joint. He wonders about his ethical and legal responsibilities in such situations. What advice would you offer him?

DISCUSSION QUESTIONS

1. As mental health professionals feel increasing competitive pressures for limited financial resources, how can they better manage the competition between disciplines and avoid some of the disagreements that have plagued mental health professions in recent decades?

2. Do you agree that fee splitting is wrong? Does the distinction between fee splitting between individual professionals and participation in "provider networks" or referral services seem meaningful to you? Why or why not?

3. Some mental health professionals have welcomed the changes in advertising ethics spurred by the Federal Trade Commission, but others have decried those changes. How do you view the current standards for advertising and soliciting clients, especially the freedom to use testimonials?

4. Many have challenged the current standards for recordkeeping as bureaucratic and designed primarily to protect the mental health professional. Do you agree with this view?

5. Some mental health professionals have refused to deal with insurers and managed care companies, asking their clients to handle that paperwork. They argue that their role is to provide clients with information relevant to their treatment and diagnosis and then to empower clients to deal with their insurers. Discuss the merits and deficiencies in this approach to managed care.

6. In an era in which funding for counseling and therapy services is limited, activities such as consulting and forensic work seem especially enticing to underpaid mental health professionals. Should there be a special credentialing process or other gatekeeping mechanism to ensure that only competent professionals offer their services in these arenas? If so, what would you recommend?

RECOMMENDED READINGS

American Psychological Association. (1993). *Record keeping guidelines.* Washington, DC: Author.

American Psychological Association. (1994). Guidelines for child custody evaluations in divorce proceedings. *American Psychologist, 49,* 677–680.

Appelbaum, P. S. (1993). Legal liability in managed care. *American Psychologist, 48,* 251–257.

Committee on Ethical Guidelines for Forensic Psychologists. (1991). Specialty guidelines for forensic psychologists. *Law and Human Behavior, 15,* 655–665.

Haas, L. J., & Cummings, N. A. (1991). Managed outpatient mental health plans: Clinical, ethical and practical guidelines for participation. *Professional Psychology: Research and Practice, 22,* 45–51.

Hess, A. K., & Weiner, I. B. (1999). *Handbook of Forensic Psychology.* New York: Wiley.

Knapp, S., & VandeCreek, L. (1993). Legal and ethical issues in billing patients and collecting fees. *Psychotherapy: Theory, Research, Practice and Training, 30,* 25–31.

Moline, M. E., Williams, G. T., & Austin, K. M. (1998). *Documenting psychotherapy: Essentials for mental health practitioners.* Thousand Oaks, CA: Sage.

Newman, J. L. (1993). Ethical issues in consultation. *Journal of Counseling and Development, 72,* 148–156.

Piazza, N. J., & Baruth, N. E. (1990). Client record guidelines. *Journal of Counseling and Development, 68,* 313–316.

Schwartz, L. L. (Ed). (1999). *Psychologists and the media: A second look.* Washington, DC: American Psychological Association.

Stahl, P. M. (1994). *Conducting child custody evaluations: A comprehensive guide.* Thousand Oaks, CA: Sage.

Stahl, P. M. (1999). *Complex issues in child custody evaluations.* Thousand Oaks, CA: Sage.

Wrightsman, L. S. (2000). *Forensic Psychology.* Belmont, CA: Wadsworth.

Chapter 12

The Counselor in the Schools
Applying Professional Standards to the Educational Culture

Many of the ethical issues school counselors face are not unique to their setting. Consent and confidentiality issues are complicated whenever working with minors. All professionals who are part of large, public organizations deal with accountability to the public and delicate relationships with administrators. Both community and school counselors must respond sensitively and competently with culturally diverse clients (Hobson & Kanitz, 1996; Pedersen & Carey, 2003). However, several issues are unique: (a) the conflict between the open communication norms among educators and the confidentiality norm of the counseling profession, (b) the obligation to assist students experiencing personal and social difficulties and the frequent resistance of parents and communities to counseling for those problems, (c) the ethics of peer counseling and peer mediation with minors, (d) the conflicting state and federal laws about parental rights to educational information about their children, (e) the obligations of school counselors with students who are suicidal, (f) the complications of group counseling in schools, and (g) the ethical challenges in postsecondary planning. The other reality that complicates the job of the school counselor is the large number of students in their caseloads. According to the American Counseling Association's (ACA) Office of Public Policy (2005), the average student caseload in the United States is an incredible 478 students per school counselor.

The ethical standards that guide this chapter's discussion of these issues are the ACA *Code of Ethics* (2005) and the *Ethical Standards* of the American School Counselor Association (ASCA) (2004). The former document is enforceable for all members of ACA, and the latter is enforceable for all members of ASCA. Both bodies adjudicate complaints.

Clash of Cultures: Open vs. Closed Communication Systems

Many school counselors begin their careers as teachers. As teachers they appreciate the value of open communication with other school personnel about the students in their classes and know that effective teaching depends on adequate knowledge about psychosocial factors that affect student learning. A teacher who is concerned about a student's health or cleanliness, for example, would not hesitate to discuss those concerns with the school nurse. In fact, a failure to consult with other educators would be seen as shirking a responsibility of good teaching. Such consultation serves social purposes as well—it becomes an outlet for adult-to-adult conversation in a workday that is dominated by adult-to-child communications and helps maintain the web of social connections between the adults in a building

(Ferris & Linville, 1985). The counseling culture is significantly different. Counselors are taught that client communication is confidential and that disclosure is allowed only with client knowledge and permission or with the best interests of the child in mind. Counselors are not permitted to use specific client matters as a means of fostering adult-to-adult conversation. This clash of cultures makes the transition from the role of teacher to counselor more difficult for novices, and it also complicates the work of the experienced school counselor. Teachers and administrators expect them to communicate openly about students and see that expectation as grounded in concern for the best interests of students. When counselors are not forthcoming about matters disclosed by students, other educators can be confused and even offended. Educators who misunderstand counselors' reticence may come to view counselors as less than "team players" and may feel reluctant to refer students for counseling. The institutional pressures on counselors to conform to school norms can be substantial (Schulte & Cochrane, 1995). Research by Hermann (2002) supports this view; in her research 51% of school counselors reported that they had felt pressure to reveal confidential student information during the preceding 12 months and 19% had been asked to turn over student records of counseling.

School counselors often feel caught between these two cultures. On the one hand, they want acceptance, respect, cooperation, and referrals from other school personnel, all of which seem to depend on open communication, and on the other hand, they want to honor the confidentiality of student disclosures. At first glance, the two desires seem mutually exclusive, but there are responsible ways to resolve the conflict. Consider the following situations:

The Case of Reggie

Reggie is a fifth-grade student whose behavior has deteriorated over the last 2 months. He used to be an involved, conscientious student who wanted to learn. Now he seems to spend most of his time in class with his head on his desk or his gaze out the window. He is not submitting homework and is failing. After consulting with other teachers, the math teacher, Mr. Kearns, learns that Reggie behaves this way in all classes, and he refers the student to the school counselor, Dr. Jeffers. After a few counseling sessions and an explanation of confidentiality to Reggie and his mother, the child begins to reveal information about his personal life. His mother was recently diagnosed as human immunodeficiency virus (HIV) positive. Simultaneously, he learned that his mother had abused intravenous drugs until she became pregnant with him. Reggie feels sad, angry, and betrayed. Both Reggie and his mother do not want her illness or other matters about their personal lives disclosed to anyone else at school. Mr. Kearns has felt frustrated by the counselor's lack of response to his questions about Reggie and has asked the principal for a meeting among all educational personnel involved with Reggie to discuss the child's deteriorating behavior. Dr. Jeffers is asked to attend. The teacher and principal are truly concerned for Reggie's well-being and want the counselor to help them help this student.

The Case of Gloria

The lunchtime conversation in the teacher's room focuses on a sophomore named Gloria, whose mother was shot while robbing a bank several years ago. The mother is incarcerated, and the father has been emotionally unstable since the robbery. The father frequently comes to school dressed in his pajamas and accuses staff of trying to poison his daughter. The father has refused psychological treatment. Gloria has become painfully shy and often skips school for days after her father's visits there. Today's lunchroom conversation is recounting the father's most recent visit, and the emotions expressed around the table are a mixture of sympathy for the girl and shock at the wild accusations and outrageous behavior of her father. The counselor takes a seat at the table and is asked what she thinks about all this.

Case Analysis

In Reggie's case, the ethical standards are clear. If both Reggie and his mother are adamant about keeping counseling disclosures confidential, the counselor must abide by their wishes. None of the exceptions to confidentiality apply here; there is no child abuse or neglect, no imminent danger to Reggie or threat to another, no court order, and no parental permission or request to disclose. The ASCA code uses the following language.

ASCA *Ethical Standards,* Section A.1: Responsibilities to Students

The professional school counselor:

a. Has a primary obligation to the student, who is to be treated with respect as a unique individual.

A.2. Confidentiality The professional school counselor:

a. Informs students of the purposes, goals, techniques and rules of procedure under which they may receive counseling at or before the time when the counseling relationship is entered. Disclosure notice includes the limits of confidentiality such as the possible necessity for consulting with other professionals, privileged communication, and legal or authoritative restraints. The meaning and limits of confidentiality are defined in developmentally appropriate terms to students.

b. Keeps information confidential unless disclosure is required to prevent clear and imminent danger to the student or others or when legal requirements demand that confidential information be revealed. Counselors will consult with appropriate professionals when in doubt as to the validity of an exception.

f. Protects the confidentiality of information received in the counseling relationship as specified by federal and state laws, written policies and applicable ethical standards. Such information is only to be revealed to others with the informed consent of the student, consistent with the counselor's ethical obligation.

g. Recognizes his/her primary obligation for confidentiality is to the student but balances that obligation with an understanding of the legal and inherent rights of parents/guardians to be the guiding voice in their children's lives.

B.2. Parents/Guardians and Confidentiality

The professional school counselor:

a. Informs parents/guardians of the counselor's role with emphasis on the confidential nature of the counseling relationship between the counselor and student.

b. Recognizes that working with minors in a school setting may require counselors to collaborate with students' parents/guardians.

c. Provides parents/guardians with accurate, comprehensive and relevant information in an objective and caring manner, as is appropriate and consistent with ethical responsibilities to the student.

d. Makes reasonable efforts to honor the wishes of parents/guardians concerning information regarding the student, and in cases of divorce or separation exercises a good-faith effort to keep both parents informed with regard to critical information with the exception of a court order.

C.2. Sharing Information with Other Professionals

The professional school counselor:

a. Promotes awareness and adherence to appropriate guidelines regarding confidentiality, the distinction between public and private information and staff consultation.

b. Provides professional personnel with accurate, objective, concise and meaningful data necessary to adequately evaluate, counsel and assist the student.

c. If a student is receiving services from another counselor or other mental health professional, the counselor, with student and/or parent/guardian consent, will inform the other professional and develop clear agreements to avoid confusion and conflict for the student.

d. Is knowledgeable about release of information and parental rights in sharing information.

Is the counselor's only choice to alienate colleagues and remain silent in the meeting? Fortunately, there are other options at this point. The counselor can discuss with Reggie and his mother the teacher's concern about the child's academic performance; give his mother information about the forthcoming meeting; seek guidance about exactly what information, if any, the counselor may reveal in that meeting; and ask permission from the principal to invite Reggie's mother, Reggie, or both of them to the meeting. (The counselor may also wish to refer the family for family counseling and support in dealing with the difficult problem facing them. Such support may further assist Reggie to cope better with his mother's illness and history.) Before any conference about the student, the counselor ought to meet privately with the teacher and the principal to explain the confidentiality requirements and the limits they place on free and full discussion of counseling sessions. Description of any state and federal laws that seem relevant would also help other educators understand the dilemma posed by their request for counseling information.

The counselor can avoid a great deal of the aggravation in such situations by educating faculty, administrators, and school board members about the roles and responsibilities of school counselors before a problem erupts (Glosoff & Pate, 2002; Tompkins & Mehring, 1993; Watson, 1990). A straightforward staff education program would reassure colleagues that the goal of the counselor is to help teachers help students but that the legal and ethical parameters under which counselors work means that they must disclose student revelations carefully, if at all. Ferris and Linville (1985) and Cooney (1985) advise written policies on confidentiality and written referral procedures that have school board approval. In addition, Tompkins and Mehring (1993) recommend that communication about confidentiality obligations begin at the time a professional is interviewing for a position. By initiating such a discussion, a counselor can get a clearer sense of the knowledge and receptivity of other educational personnel to confidentiality of counseling disclosures.

In the second case, the lunchroom discussion about the sophomore's troubles and her father's unusual behavior seems more social than professional. Lunchroom discussions are not structured professional interactions clearly planned to benefit students. They can often deteriorate into gossip (Watson, 1990). Moreover, some teachers in the room may have no interaction with Gloria and, therefore, have no need or right to know anything about her. For the counselor to participate in any discussion of the people involved would demean those individuals and would not bring credit to the counselor or to the profession. Therefore, the counselor should avoid comment on this topic even if Gloria was not a student in her assigned caseload. The refusal to discuss this issue need not be expressed in a morally superior or self-righteous way. When such dramatic events occur, it is natural for people to wish to talk about them later. For counselors, especially, that natural human desire must be superseded by their professional obligations. As with the last scenario, educating teachers to the unique responsibilities of counselors might have alleviated the pressure the counselor felt to participate. Perhaps, though, the only truly safe way to avoid such discussions is to refrain from sitting in the lunchroom or teacher's lounge when such events are likely to become the focus of conversation. Counselors should know that participation in such gossip may have legal as well as ethical consequences. Under such circumstances, all school personnel are vulnerable to claims of defamation of character if the conversation is not motivated to assist the student's educational progress (Alexander & Alexander, 2005; Fischer & Sorenson, 1996; McCarthy & Sorenson, 1993).

School counselors need not think of other educators in an adversarial way, however. When students and parents are informed about the potential value of sharing information with relevant teachers and administrators and when they have control over the material that is revealed, they often agree to such releases. In the first case, Reggie and his mother may want to tell school officials something, and the counselor can help them articulate the kind of communication that would feel comfortable for them. For example, they may want to tell teachers that a member of Reggie's family is ill with a chronic disease and Reggie is quite distracted and worried about that. Counselors must balance the value such disclosures would have for the child's education against the risk of other people incidentally or intentionally violating guidelines for the proper use of that information. The counselor can help all parties define the clients' views of appropriate and inappropriate uses of the disclosures and thus help reduce the risk of violating the clients' wishes. The ASCA standards speak to this point.

ASCA *Ethical Standards,* Section C.2: Sharing Information with Other Professionals

The professional school counselor:

a. Promotes awareness and adherence to appropriate guidelines regarding confidentiality, the distinction between public and private information and staff consultation.

b. Provides professional personnel with accurate, objective, concise and meaningful data necessary to adequately evaluate, counsel and assist the student.

c. If a student is receiving services from another counselor or other mental health professional, the counselor, with student and/or parent/guardian consent, will inform the other professional and develop clear agreements to avoid confusion and conflict for the student.

d. Is knowledgeable about release of information and parental rights in sharing information.

Research on the compliance of school counselors with these directives is limited. Two studies by Wagner (1978, 1981) suggest that approximately one-fourth of the counselors sampled admitted engaging in informal communications with others about clients. Most who engaged in this practice did not view it as ethical, however. Such frequent participation in a practice they acknowledged as unethical suggests that the open communication culture of the school powerfully influences counselor behavior.

Davis and Ritchie (1993) advise school counselors to inform administrators about any counselor activity that is likely to have legal repercussions for the school. If, for instance, a counselor decides to call an ambulance to bring a student in the midst of a psychotic episode to a psychiatric emergency room without parental consent (because the parents could not be reached), he or she should tell the principal about the action and its rationale—that is, the parents' unavailability and the safety risk to the student. This situation has potential legal ramifications because the parents may claim that the action violated their right to consent and damaged the reputation of the family. At the same time, Davis and Ritchie caution counselors to use prudent judgment about such consultations, resisting the temptation to break confidentiality for any activity that has any potential for legal complications. However, in situations in which legal action is a significant possibility, administrators should be informed. After all, administrators will be in a better position to help and defend the school counseling program if they are aware of the situation.

Determining whether a disclosure from a student ought to be kept confidential or should be disclosed to parents or school authorities is one of the most difficult issues facing school counselors and school psychologists (Jacob & Hartshorne, 2003; Mitchell, Disque, & Robertson, 2002). Mitchell et al. (2003) note that school counselors "may feel as if they are walking a tightrope between being a professional helper and being an informant to parents" (p. 156). Jacob-Timm (1999) reported it to be the third most prominent ethical dilemma of school psychologists, and research by Humphreys (2000) elicited the same concerns from school psychologists. In a well-designed study of the factors that affect decisions about confidentiality among Florida school counselors, Isaacs and Stone (1999) found that counselors used the age of the student, level of the school, and dangerousness of the client situation as the primary criteria to decide whether to breach confidentiality. School counselors in that sample indicated that they would be likely to breach confidentiality under the following circumstances:

- Impending suicide with a firearm (97.6%) or information about possible suicide pact (88%)
- Retaliation for victimization (94.2%)
- Use of crack cocaine (83.7%)
- Sexual intercourse with multiple partners when HIV positive (80.7%)
- Imminent armed robbery plan (79.5%)
- Indications of depression (76.9%)
- Abortion (69.1%)
- Marijuana use (68.7%)

These percentages differ in some respects when the data are examined by level of school. Secondary school counselors are more likely to maintain confidentiality about sexuality and drug use than are elementary counselors. For example, 82.2% of the elementary counselors would breach confidentiality if a student confided that he or she was smoking marijuana, but only 43.8% of high school counselors and 41.7% of middle school counselors would do so. However, the responses of the entire sample are fairly consistent in regard to issues of dangerousness to self or others.

Anecdotal and research evidence suggests that students are deeply concerned about confidentiality. A 12-year-old once wrote to Dear Abby asking what to do about her frightening and persistent suicidal thoughts, mentioning that she could not tell her parents because they would react negatively and could not disclose to the school counselor because the counselor will inform the parents. Formal research suggests this middle school student does not represent an isolated case. In three studies of the attitudes of high school students toward confidentiality the overwhelming majority of students viewed it as important to their willingness to discuss their concerns with school counselors (Collins & Knowles, 1995; Helms, 2003; Lindsey & Kalafat, 1998). For example, Helms (2003) found that students were refusing professional assistance because they believed that counselors would tell parents everything they said, that counselors would gossip about them, or that counselors would judge them negatively or berate them. In contrast to the feelings of the 12-year-old correspondent to Dear Abby, most students generally appear to acknowledge the need to contact parents in situations of imminent danger but recognize few other reasons as sufficient justification to disclose their confidences to parents (Collins & Knowles, 1995).

The ASCA Ethics Committee has produced two useful documents for school counselors to support them in their quest to manage confidentiality responsibly. The first is entitled *Sharing Information with the Principal* (1999) and guides the school counselor to effective and ineffective strategies to meeting the demands of administrators and needs of students. The second document, *Developing an Informed Consent Brochure for Secondary Students,* was published in 1996, and it identifies the necessary components of consent with high school students. These documents also have value as tools to educate other school officials about the school counseling role and function.

Privilege for School Counselors

In this litigious era courts are increasingly likely to ask school counselors to provide evidence about their work with parents or students (James & DeVaney, 1995). They may subpoena a counselor to testify in a custody hearing for a child with whom the counselor has had extensive contact or ask a counselor to produce a client's counseling records. If counselors violate confidentiality and reveal information that ought to have been kept private, they themselves can be brought to court to defend against charges of malpractice or defamation of character (Fischer & Sorenson, 1996). For these reasons school counselors need to become aware of the laws about privileged communication in their states. Fischer and Sorenson (1996) identify 18 states where the clients of school counselors can assert at least limited privilege in state courts. These states include Alabama, Arkansas, Idaho, Indiana, Iowa, Kansas, Maine, Michigan, Missouri, Montana, Nevada, North Carolina, North Dakota, Ohio, Oregon, Pennsylvania, South Dakota, and Virginia. In other states, no statutory privileges are established for school counselors. The 1996 U.S. Supreme Court decision in *Jaffee v. Redmond* may spur further extensions of privilege (Remley, Herlihy, & Herlihy, 1997), so school counselors should stay alert for legal changes that affect confidentiality. Counselors who practice in states with privilege for clients of school counselors have a responsibility to educate other school personnel about the meaning and implications of that privilege for their work.

Parental and Community Values That Diverge from Professional Values

Kaplan (1996) describes the challenges that some parent groups and political organizations are bringing to school counseling. Their aim is to give parents increased control over the school-based activities of their children. Some groups oppose the involvement of school counselors with children in any personal, social, or career development activity unless parents give their express consent. In this view, counselors ought to restrict their work with children to activities such as schedule planning, educational testing, and educational problem-solving. According to Kaplan (1996), some of these groups want counselors and other educators to refrain from teaching decision-making skills or using programs designed to foster self-esteem and self-confidence in children. Some groups believe that by teaching decision-making skills, counselors are undermining parental authority, cultural traditions, and religious teachings (Lonborg & Bowen, 2004). Similarly, these groups challenge the appropriateness of interventions designed to increase self-esteem because they believe they reduce the level of obedience children show to those in authority. In such cases, the values of parents seem contradictory to central educational values in the mainstream of democratic societies (Kaplan, 1996). They are also inconsistent with the National Standards for School Counseling (ASCA, 1997; 1999), which define central roles for the school counseling in promoting the educational, career, and personal/social development of students.

Kaplan (1996) also contends, however, that this movement raises some important questions for counselors to consider. Parents who want to make informed decisions about the counseling activities in which their children participate deserve that right. Similarly, because parents bear the primary responsibility for their children, they deserve to know a great deal about the disclosures those young people make to other adults. Kaplan suggests that school counselors have some accountability for this growing opposition to their profession. In her view some counselors have failed to acknowledge legitimate parental rights or have delved into personal and social problems of students that are beyond the limits of their competence to treat. They have tended to view parents as adversaries rather than allies in helping children. In these ways counselors have risked harm to clients and created resentment among family members. These problems have occurred even with well-intentioned counselors motivated solely by a desire to promote their students' development. Research by Ritchie and Partin (1994) suggests that less than 10% of school counselors in Ohio seek the consent of parents even when they are counseling students on a regular basis.

Kaplan (1996) recommends parental and community education about counseling programs as a partial remedy to such misunderstandings. Parents are often reassured to learn that counselors do not intend to work outside the scope of their practice, that they will honor the rights of parents to information about students, and that they will be respectful of family values that run contradictory to some counseling programs. A practical way to educate families about school counseling programs is to develop and distribute a handbook including the credentials of school counselors, the mission of the program, and its policies and procedures about interaction with parents.

Of course, none of these remedies is a panacea for opposition by political and parent groups who strongly oppose counseling in the schools. Counselors whose very jobs may be at stake in some communities need to demonstrate the value of their programs to the community, to collaborate with other professionals and professional associations to preserve such services for students, and to keep as their guiding principle the best interests of the students they serve. Counselors can avoid some of these problems by taking into account community values as they carry out their duties. This does not mean counselors ought to be slaves to community preferences. Rather, it means that with sensitivity to the prevailing community norms, counselors are better equipped to anticipate resistance to interventions and act to prevent its occurrence in the first place.

Sometimes communities hold values that are inherently contradictory to the values of the counseling profession (Davis & Ritchie, 1993). Communities in which there is strong opposition to discussing sexuality or drug abuse in the schools can pose a problem for counselors whose students raise these issues. If the community frowns on providing contraceptive information, should a counselor refuse to provide a referral for contraceptive information to a student who seeks it? Should a counselor disclose to parents all student comments about drug experimentation in a community that expects such disclosures? In a community that has little tolerance or understanding of gay, lesbian, or bisexual orientations, should counselors help students who have questions about sexual identity? These are complicated questions, and the answers depend on a number of factors: the age and maturity of the student, the student's willingness to involve parents, the likelihood that the parents' response will not harm the child, the school policy on such matters, and the applicable laws and professional standards. No one benefits if counselors enrage a community and arouse its opposition to the whole counseling program. However, counselors cannot ignore the needs of adolescents who seek information and service about sensitive issues. Indeed, students who are gay, lesbian, or bisexual are at substantial risk for suicide, conflicts with family, and violence from others (McFarland, 1998; Remafedi, 1999). Strong parental and community values against sexual intimacy before marriage or drug experimentation will not guarantee that every student will act in accordance with those values. Ultimately, school counselors must make such decisions with the best interests of their students as the main priority and the Preamble of the ASCA *Ethical Guidelines* as the professional standard.

In some situations, state and federal laws protect the rights of counselors to advise adolescents about sensitive issues. Anderson (1996), Fischer and Sorenson (1996), and Stone (2002) all suggest that counselors who give adolescents competent advice and referrals to appropriate resources for birth control information are not likely to be successfully sued for malpractice. The critical consideration is competence of the counselor to discuss the topic. State laws often do not give counselors the same freedom about discussions of abortion, although there is great variability in state statutes on this matter. Counselors need to be cautious and alert to legal limitations on their comments when a student who is pregnant wants to discuss abortion. Anderson (1996) advises counselors to be especially circumspect about sharing their personal views on this highly controversial matter. Stone (2002) also recommends attention to school board policy on discussing this issue. Once again, the ideal resolution is to help the teenager involve her parents in the decision making. The law is silent or unclear on other sensitive matters that do not involve abuse, neglect, or clear and imminent danger. The ASCA code recognizes the rights of both students and parents, but it also affirms the appropriateness of a wide focus for school counseling on educational, personal, and social dimensions of development.

ASCA *Ethical Standards,* Preamble

- Each person has the right to be respected, be treated with dignity and have access to a comprehensive school counseling program that advocates for and affirms all students from diverse populations regardless of ethnic/racial status, age, economic status, special needs, English as a second language or other language group, immigration status, sexual orientation, gender, gender identity/expression, family type, religious/spiritual identity and appearance.

- Each person has the right to receive the information and support needed to move toward self-direction and self-development and affirmation within one's group identities, with special care being given to students who have historically not received adequate educational services: students of color, low socio-economic students, students with disabilities and students with nondominant language backgrounds.

- Each person has the right to understand the full magnitude and meaning of his/her educational choices and how those choices will affect future opportunities.

A.1. Responsibilities to Students

The professional school counselor:

a. Has a primary obligation to the student, who is to be treated with respect as a unique individual.

b. Is concerned with the educational, academic, career, personal and social needs and encourages the maximum development of every student.

c. Respects the student's values and beliefs and does not impose the counselor's personal values.

d. Is knowledgeable of laws, regulations and policies relating to students and strives to protect and inform students regarding their rights.

B. Responsibilities to Parents/Guardians

B.1. Parent Rights and Responsibilities

The professional school counselor:

a. Respects the rights and responsibilities of parents/guardians for their children and endeavors to establish, as appropriate, a collaborative relationship with parents/guardians to facilitate the student's maximum development.

b. Adheres to laws, local guidelines and ethical standards of practice when assisting parents/guardians experiencing family difficulties that interfere with the student's effectiveness and welfare.

c. Respects the confidentiality of parents/guardians.

d. Is sensitive to diversity among families and recognizes that all parents/guardians, custodial and noncustodial, are vested with certain rights and responsibilities for the welfare of their children by virtue of their role and according to law.

The Ethics of Peer Helping Programs

Peer support programs exist under many names—peer counseling, peer support, peer intervention, peer facilitation, peer mediation, and peer conflict resolution. Their central feature involves training students to act as support people for other students who have problems or are at risk for developing problems. Peer helper programs have become more common over the last two decades as schools try to increase student access to support services without increasing costs (Ehly & Vazquez, 1998; Morey, Millton, Fulton, Rosen, & Daly, 1989). Low cost has not been the only factor in their expansion, however. They have been viewed as valuable gateways to attract reluctant students to counseling services they need. Adolescents in particular are often hesitant to reveal their problems to adults. Peer mediation programs have also been used as a form of prevention for school violence. In fact, conflict resolution and peer mediation programs as a deterrent to school violence have been growing faster than any other method of prevention of such violence (Smith, Daunic, Miller, & Robinson, 2002).

The original peer helping concept was construed as limited to developmental concerns and peer tutoring (Anderson, 1976). According to Lewis and Lewis (1996), many peer helping programs have been initiated as a response to serious mental health issues—suicide, drug and alcohol abuse, eating disorders, and depression. Peer intervention programs for such problems have expanded beyond the high school level. Herring (1990) advocates peer helping programs for suicide prevention at the middle school as well, and many peer helping programs have been developed in elementary and middle schools (Myrick, Highland, & Sabella, 1995). For example, Bell, Coleman, Anderson, Whelan, and Wilder (2000) report on a peer mediation program for sixth through eighth graders that taught students conflict resolution and mediation skills and was successful in reducing aggressive behavior among participants. Smith et al. (2002) show similar decreases in verbal aggression when peer mediation programs were used in their research.

Are all peer helping programs as effective in meeting their goals as the programs studied by Bell and Smith, and what ethical problems arise from their use? According to Lewis and Lewis (1996), much of the evidence about the effectiveness and outcomes of peer helping programs that deal with substantive mental health issues is anecdotal rather than empirical. (Research supporting the positive effects of peer mediation programs and programs that aim at improving school performance and attitudes is more prevalent [for example, Tobias & Myrick, 1999], but no truly rigorous research demonstrates their efficacy [Smith et al., 2002]). Lewis and Lewis urge more research and evaluation on mental health interventions to better assess the power of such programs. They also question the merit of using peer helping models for serious mental health problems in the absence of such outcome data. They state, "[T]here is not yet a body of evidence documenting the effectiveness, or the safety, of using peer helping programs to address problems beyond the basic academic and developmental issues they were initially intended to address" (p. 312). To the degree, then, that counselors cannot demonstrate either the merit or the safety of such programs, there is serious question about the ethics of their use.

In addition, peer helping programs require high levels of supervision, both at initiation and throughout the program. Helpers must be carefully chosen, well trained, and continuously monitored to ensure that they are skilled enough to provide support services and that they do not exceed the limits of their competence. In their research Lewis and Lewis (1996) found a disturbing pattern. Many of the educators responsible for peer helping programs were not trained counselors. Thus, in those cases, there were no professionals with the requisite training and experience to accomplish important supervisory tasks. In those circumstances, neither the helpers nor the supervisors have the competence to assess the seriousness of a student's emotional problem or to decide on appropriate treatment. Needless to say, given the risks of peer counseling, supervision by trained counselors knowledgeable in supervision of volunteers appears to be a minimal requirement for an ethical program. The ASCA *Ethical Standards* (2004) speak directly to this issue.

ASCA *Ethical Standards,* Section A.11: Student Peer Support Programs

The professional school counselor:

Has unique responsibilities when working with student-assistance programs. The school counselor is responsible for the welfare of students participating in peer-to-peer programs under his/her direction.

Noncounselor supervisors are unlikely to understand guidelines for confidentiality, dual relationships, informed consent, and the myriad other professional guidelines for responsible helping services. School counselors therefore ought not to support the use of noncounselors in overseeing peer helping programs.

The role demands on students who volunteer to be peer helpers are substantial. Professionals responsible for such programs see benefits to those volunteers, but some wonder whether they are overburdened for their developmental level when they are asked to cope with serious mental health issues (Lewis & Lewis, 1996; Morey et al., 1989). In Lewis and Lewis's study of 263 peer programs in Washington state, they found two completed suicides by peer helpers. Two incidents is not a sufficient basis for a sweeping conclusion about the risks of the helper role, but these events illustrate the need to screen candidates carefully, monitor stress, and supervise closely. Regardless of the precautions, there is still reason to question whether adolescents or preadolescents ought to be put at risk for such stress under any circumstances. Burnout and secondary posttraumatic stress are real dangers even for trained professionals (Ackerley, Burnell, Holder, & Kurdek, 1988; Figley, 1995; Raquepaw & Miller, 1989). There is no evidence that young people are any less vulnerable to these problems.

Even peer counseling programs that limit their focus to conflict resolution or developmental and educational issues must cope with potential ethical issues regarding confidentiality of student disclosures. Adolescent volunteers must, of course, be oriented to the importance of confidentiality and reminded periodically about it, but their immaturity suggests that those precautions may still not prevent violations of confidentiality. Students using peer counseling services ought to understand the limits of confidentiality when they use such services, and supervisors should be prepared to respond when trust is broken. Volunteers should be ready to share student disclosures with supervisors, and users should be informed about such consultation. In addition, guidelines ought to be established to avoid dual-relationship problems and to explain to volunteers the rules for assisting friends.

In short, when school counselors initiate or take responsibility for existing peer counseling programs they must be prepared to devote extensive time and energy to the task of administering and supervising these programs. Moreover, they ought to systematically evaluate program impact on both those helped and volunteers and modify ineffective or harmful aspects of the program.

Legal Issues for School Counselors: State and Federal Statutes

The legal issues that concern school counselors derive from the laws passed by Congress and state legislatures and from case law, especially in the area of negligence and malpractice. One of the most important of these laws is the Family Education Rights and Privacy Act (FERPA) enacted in 1974 (previously referred to as the Buckley Amendment). This act contains four major sections, all of which are designed to ensure that parent's rights to information about their children's education are honored. Part 1 ties the availability of federal funding to parental access to school records. Because federal money is crucial to the operation of most school districts, virtually all allow parents to inspect school records. Students who are 18 or older also have the same rights as parents of younger children. Part 2 requires parental consent for medical, psychiatric, or psychological evaluations of a minor or for participation in "any school program designed to affect or change the personal behavior or values of a student" (Baker, 2000, p. 283). Part 3 prevents unauthorized people from viewing the educational records of children. Only school officials directly involved in the education of students may have access to their records. Parental consent is required for release unless exempted in the regulations, and release of information for special education students requires *written authorization* from parents (Sealander, 1999). Directory information is excepted from this policy, and schools can release it without parental consent under certain conditions (McCarthy & Sorenson, 1993). Moreover, if a child is transferring from one school to another, schools can also transfer records without express parental consent, as long as they notify parents about the transfer. The No Child

Left Behind Act of 2002 builds on this stipulation by including the provision that schools must allow military recruiters the same access to students and student data that college admissions staff are offered. Finally, if subpoenaed by a court, schools may produce educational records if they are germane to the issue before the court. The final section empowers the U.S. Secretary of Education to develop regulations relevant to student privacy.

FERPA implies that students and/or their parents own the information in official school records, ought to have free access to that information, and have the right to control access to educational records. This law does not alter the confidentiality of communications otherwise protected by law and does not cover private records of school counselors or teachers, provided those private records are not shared with others. FERPA stipulates that the records must be in the sole possession of the counselor or a substitute for the counselor. This allows some leeway for school counselors to have confidential communications with students and to keep separate records of such communications. In fact, given the provisions of FERPA and related laws, school counselors would be well advised to keep all records of counseling completely separate from the official educational record of the student (Anderson, 1996). However, they should note that if records of counseling are not truly private and are shared with other counselors or teachers, then those documents are considered educational records and should be available to parents (Fischer & Sorenson, 1996). According to Sorenson and Chapman (1985), noncompliance with this provision is high—66% of school counselors did not grant parents access to files that were shared with other school personnel. In another study, Davis and Mickelson (1994) found that most school counselors did not understand parental rights to records.

In this age of blended families and noncustodial parents, it is important to note that FERPA gives the same rights to noncustodial parents that it extends to custodial parents (Anderson, 1996). A parent becomes noncustodial when the court awards the rights to decision making about the children to the other parent in a sole custody arrangement, usually as a result of divorce (Wilcoxin & Magnuson, 1999). In a joint custody arrangement, both parents retain custody rights regardless of the place of residence of the child. Perhaps because the FERPA language is an exception to the exclusivity of the rights of custodial parents, Sorenson and Chapman (1985) found that 72% of school counselors they surveyed reported school policies that denied noncustodial parents equal access to school records. If a counselor is dealing with sensitive information that may negatively affect a child if disclosed to either parent, the counselor needs to make a judgment about disclosure based on the best interests of the child. Careful consultation and supervision are in order under such circumstances. FERPA and other laws should not be interpreted to supersede the health and welfare of any child. It is interesting that, according to Stone (2005), stepparents may also have some rights under FERPA provided that the stepparent is present on a daily basis with one natural parent and the other natural parent is not in the home with the child. (However, this right of stepparents does not deny the noncustodial parent his or her FERPA rights.)

The Individuals with Disabilities Education Act (1997) also mandates parental access to student files. That law stipulates that if parents are disabled, the school must provide information in the records in a form they can understand. If parents do not speak or read English, the school must provide information in a language they can understand.

The No Child Left Behind legislation mandates extensive assessment of academic achievement of elementary and secondary students. Many states have also enacted their own laws to set graduation standards and standards for promotion to higher educational levels for all students (Yen & Henderson, 2002). These statutes have significant effects both on school districts and individual students. As a result, great economic and political pressure exists for districts to achieve high passage rates on these large-scale educational assessments, for teachers and administrators to assist students in succeeding, and for individual students to obtain acceptable scores to graduate or advance to the next educational level. Although this legislation was enacted with the purpose of ensuring that all students received the education they needed to succeed, its implementation has led to several significant ethical dilemmas. Such high stakes tests must be as valid and reliable as possible if they are to be used as a single criterion for educational advancement according to the *Standards for Educational and Psychological Testing* (AERA/APA/NCME, 1999). Critics have pointed out that high stakes testing does not necessarily meet this high standard for reliability and validity (for example, Yen & Henderson, 2002). Evidence also suggests that success on these large-scale assessments is associated with ethnicity of students, their socioeconomic status, financial resources of the districts, and quality of teachers (Turek, 2005). Media reports also show that some administrators and teachers have even resorted to cheating by providing students with answers to test questions in a misguided effort to achieve higher passage rates for their students. School counselors have found that they are burdened with one more major administrative responsibility in overseeing such testing that compromises their ability to attend to other job duties. How do school counselors deal responsibly with these ethical challenges? They have several paths to ethical action. The first is to be advocates for their profession and students (Stone, 2005) by becoming active with professional associations that lobby state and federal legislatures to enact laws that truly assist all students in achieving their educational goals. Second, they need to assist teachers and principals in finding effective test preparation strategies that do not compromise the validity of test results. They also can consult with educators about managing the high stress associated with large scale educational assessments—stress that is felt by students, parents, and professionals alike. Third, they need to be particularly sensitive to the dilemmas that No Child Left Behind causes for students with limited proficiency in English and for special education students who are not likely to be exempted from such testing under this legislation.

Two other federal laws are relevant to the responsible practice of school counselors. They are the Grassley Amendment (1994) to the Goals 2000: Educate America Act of 1994 and the Drug Abuse Office and Treatment Act (1976). The Grassley Amendment mandates that schools require parental consent prior to including their children in any survey, research, or evaluation of information relative to the personal and family lives of students. Examples of research that requires consent include studies of political affiliations, income, illegal or antisocial behavior, and evaluations of mental or psychological problems of students or other individuals connected to the student.

The Drug Abuse Office and Treatment Act (1976) guarantees the privacy of all records related to evaluation and treatment for substance abuse for any entity receiving federal funding. This law establishes strict guidelines for the release of such records and stipulates that minors receiving such treatment have privacy rights and must consent to release of their records, even to their parents. Exceptions include emergency treatment, court orders, and research that does not include any individually identifiable data on the student.

Liability for School Counselors: An Emerging Reality

Not long ago, the folklore of the profession suggested that school counselors were insulated from most kinds of malpractice liability. The belief was that their peers in community agencies, hospitals, and private practice were targets for such actions but that they were immune, either because of legal protections for educators or because of the relative invisibility of their counseling activities. Such beliefs are, unfortunately, inconsistent with current realities. School counselors can and do get sued (Fischer & Sorenson, 1996). Claims of malpractice are still less common for school counselors than for mental health counselors, but they are increasing. Fischer and Sorenson (1996) identify six activities that make school personnel vulnerable to malpractice claims. These include (a) administering drugs, (b) giving birth control advice, (c) giving abortion-related advice, (d) making statements that might be defamatory, (e) assisting in searches of student lockers, and (f) violating confidentiality and privacy of records. As already mentioned, counselors who stay informed about federal and state laws regarding contraceptive and abortion discussions with minors and who act competently are not likely to be successfully sued for their activities in this domain. Similarly, close allegiance to confidentiality and privilege obligations dramatically reduces potential liability for defamation or other violations of privacy. When school counselors are involved in searches of student lockers, cars, or other possessions, they must take care that they abide by current policies and laws affecting such searches and that the privacy of the student is limited only to the degree necessary.

Liability for Student Suicides

One of the emerging sources of malpractice claims stems from student suicides. Until 1991, claims against school counselors related to student suicides resulted in little liability for counselors (Fischer & Sorenson, 1996). In that era, the courts generally ruled that a duty of care could not be imposed on school personnel who did not have sufficient training in diagnosing mental disorders. A Maryland court reversed that trend, finding that a school counselor could be held liable for a student suicide (*Eisel v. Board of Education,* 1991) in some circumstances. In that case, a 13-year-old girl's suicidal comments to her friends were reported by those friends to a school counselor. That counselor, in turn, informed the counselor assigned to the girl to whom the statements had been attributed. The two counselors called the girl into their office and asked her about the matter. The girl denied making those statements. The counselors did nothing further, and later that day the girl was shot in a suicide pact with another student. The court ruled that the school counselor did indeed have a special relationship with the student and a duty of care to act to prevent this suicide. Specifically, they faulted the counselor for not notifying the parents of the information the counselor had received about their daughter's suicidal comments. The court recognized that school counselors may not be able to control students to the same degree as professionals in hospitals and other restricted settings, but they asserted that counselors still have a duty to intervene to reduce foreseeable risks by informing the parents (Pate, 1992). Had the counselor in this case told the parents about the suicide threat, her liability probably would have ended at that point (Remley & Sparkman, 1993), unless the counselor had reason to expect that the parents would not respond appropriately. Sometimes adults deny the risk of suicide among young people (Wellman, 1984). In such circumstances, the counselor may need to act more energetically to ensure that the parents act to protect the child.

In the Eisel case, the central issue was the foreseeability of the risk to the student and the counselors' very limited response to a life-threatening problem (Hermann & Remley, 2000). It is important to note that in this case Ms. Eisel was not an ongoing client of the school counselor; she was a member of the student body assigned to that counselor. Once the counselor sought out Ms. Eisel to question her about her suicidal intentions, a special relationship was created. If future courts rule in similar ways, this suggests that school counselors cannot ignore risks to those with whom they do not have administratively assigned responsibility. The obligation of the counselor is to take reasonable steps to prevent suicide among all students for whom they have responsibility. This case also underscores the value of attending to comments of other students. Counselors need to evaluate the veracity of remarks of other youngsters and to follow up when they believe the information conveyed may be true.

These events should not cause school counselors to overreact to potentially suicidal situations, however. Not every case subsequent to the *Eisel* ruling has resulted in the decision that a negligence lawsuit could go forward, but several such cases now exist (Stone, 2005). Remley and Sparkman (1993) caution counselors not to make hasty, emotional judgments about suicidal risk. Physical restraint of students or calls to emergency personnel are rarely called for. Instead, school counselors ought to make careful, reasoned assessments of risk and act in an expeditious but not rash way when they judge risk to be high.

Because suicide mortality increases significantly over the adolescent years (Diekstra, 1995; Capuzzi, 2002), Sheeley and Herlihy (1989) and King (2000) suggest that school counselors consider implementing suicide prevention programs at their schools. Such programs alert adults and youngsters in the school to the warning signs for suicide and give them guidelines for responding. Prevention activities are helpful in reducing risk and in responding to serious mental health problems among adolescents. As King (2000) notes, a teacher with a typical high school class is likely to have at least one male and two female students who have attempted suicide in the last year. Currently, no legal obligation to have such a program exists, but Hermann and Remley (2000) caution that recent court rulings suggest that programs to help staff identify behaviors that place students at risk for suicide and to prevent the development of such behaviors in students may become necessary to avoid liability. Nevertheless, Remley and Sparkman (1993) argue that liability fears should not be the primary basis for their creation. The principle of beneficence, not self-protective impulses, should drive all such programs.

When suicide does occur, counselors should provide support services for the student body to help them grieve and come to grips with the loss. The suggestion that adolescents are sometimes at risk for "copycat" suicides also adds merit to this recommendation (Sheeley & Herlihy, 1989). Many schools have relationships with community mental health centers, and professionals from both settings work together to provide crisis intervention. Such interventions are consistent with the ethical and legal obligations of the profession. Capuzzi's writings (2002, 2004) are excellent guides to responsible practice in preventing and responding to student suicides. D. H. Henderson (1987) reminds school counselors that the duty of care is not limited to issues of suicide or injury to others. School counselors bear a legal and ethical obligation to act in other types of foreseeable risks. For example, he suggests that counselors ought to refer students to appropriate care when they display evidence of severe mental and emotional dysfunction. Usually the best way to implement this duty is to get the youngster to agree to the parents' involvement. In the absence of that agreement, counselors must make their judgment on the basis of the child's best interests. Here is the language in the ASCA standards regarding danger to self or others.

ASCA *Ethical Standards,* Section A.7: Danger to Self or Others

The professional school counselor:

a. Informs parents/guardians or appropriate authorities when the student's condition indicates a clear and imminent danger to the student or others. This is to be done after careful deliberation and, where possible, after consultation with other counseling professionals.

b. Will attempt to minimize threat to a student and may choose to 1) inform the student of actions to be taken, 2) involve the student in a three-way communication with parents/guardians when breaching confidentiality or 3) allow the student to have input as to how and to whom the breach will be made.

Liability for Academic Negligence In 2001 for the first time, a state supreme court allowed a charge of negligence related to the academic advice of a school counselor to go to trial. Prior to this time, virtually all state courts had rejected lawsuits against school counselors related to academic matters, largely because of the difficulties school counselors face in advising the large number of students in their caseloads about rapidly changing academic requirements (Stone, 2002). The case was *Sain v. Cedar Rapids Community School District* (2001).

In this case a student sought out the advice of his school counselor about the English courses that would satisfy the NCAA (National Collegiate Athletic Association) academic requirements to maintain his eligibility for an athletic scholarship. The counselor misinformed the boy, relying on his memory of requirements instead of checking the current list of approved courses, resulting in the revocation of the 5-year basketball scholarship he had been awarded from Northern Illinois University. In other words, the counselor's negligence in checking the facts, in exercising due care, cost the young man's family thousands of dollars. The high court found that the case could be tried as an issue of negligent *misrepresentation,* the type of error for which individuals in other professions such as accounting, law, and business have regularly been held accountable in civil court. By this ruling the Iowa Supreme Court allowed the case to be considered—it did not rule on the outcome, but it set forth the notion that this kind of case of educational negligence for a counselor could have merit.

This ruling sparked much comment in the counseling and educational literature, with some predicting disastrous effects on the willingness of school counselors to participate in academic advising (Reid, 2001). Calmer voices point to several unique factors about this case that make future lawsuits related to academic advising unlikely (Stone, 2002). First, most academic misinformation does not cause the level of personal and financial harm caused in the Iowa case. Second, the standard for a successful malpractice suit remains high and difficult for claimants to meet. Third, *Sain* represents a single case in one state and cannot necessarily be viewed as a portend of actions of other state courts. Finally, in my view, in an ironic way *Sain* represents progress in the public view of the profession of school counseling. School counselors are now seen as accountable, as professionals who have sufficient training, experience, and credentials to be expected to act competently and not provide misinformation at risk of injuring students if it is avoidable. All other professions can be subject to lawsuits when they commit major errors—how can school counseling expect to be treated any differently and still be considered a legitimate profession?

Not all recent cases for educational negligence have met the same fate as the Iowa case. Two cases in California and Wisconsin, both dealing with inaccurate advice that affected a student's eligibility for an NCAA scholarship, were thrown out of court (Stone, 2005). Thus counselors should not hesitate to participate fully in academic advising—their liability risks for such actions are infinitesimally small, and their potential to help students meet their educational goals from competent advice is great. School counselors simply need to be diligent in certifying the accuracy of the information they have access to and informing students when information is uncertain or likely to change.

Ethical and Legal Dimensions of School Violence and Sexual Harassment

In recent years tragic episodes of school violence have raised public awareness of the need for schools and communities to intervene to prevent students with destructive impulses from acting on them (Sandhu & Aspy, 2000; Hermann & Finn, 2002). Incidents in which the newborn infants of pregnant teenagers died soon after birth because of the neglect or other life-ending actions of their adolescent mothers have also caused a public outcry and demand for better support for girls facing unplanned pregnancies. In response to these events some school districts have initiated policies that mandate that disclosures to counselors related to either destructive impulses or pregnancy be immediately reported to school authorities and parents. Such directives are motivated by a desire to save others from harm and to protect the students in trouble and are consistent with the long-term goals of any school counselor. They are also consistent with ethical standards when the danger is clear and imminent.

At the same time, mandates clearly compromise the limited level of confidentiality that adolescents can be afforded when no imminent danger is anticipated. In that circumstance, such directives place school counselors and psychologists in a difficult position. They can make clear to students this limit of confidentiality (in addition to the others) and risk that the students will decide not to reveal that kind of information to them—clearly the more ethical option. Or, they can explain it only after the disclosure has been made, in which case the individual student feels betrayed and other students who learn of this disclosure to school authorities will quickly decide not to share such matters with anyone at school. In either case, the ultimate goal of the school officials—to prevent harm to students and their babies and get help for them—is thwarted. Counselors cannot be of assistance to students whose problems never get reported to them. Because such policies make students less likely to seek help, school counselors have an obligation to discuss the implications of these directives with administrators and to try to devise alternative approaches that do not impose a barrier to student access to counseling for those with such serious problems. Clearly, in the great majority of circumstances the disclosure of nonimminent aggressive or illegal actions or pregnancies to family members and school authorities is a desirable outcome, but unless adolescents have some sense of control of that disclosure and some sense of trust in adults at school they will not reveal such feelings and will try to manage these situations on their own or with the help of peers. In that event, the opportunity to reduce the risk of violence is missed. Therefore, professional associations and school personnel need to take an active role to educate parents and school administrators about the gains and losses inherent in the confidentiality policies they enact. They must also work with administrators and school boards to draft policies that are more balanced and do not cut off student willingness to discuss their personal and social problems with school counselors.

School counselors also have an ethical responsibility to act to prevent the day-to-day level of violence in schools that occurs when students are bullied and harassed. Physical intimidation and bullying are serious problems that affect substantial numbers of school-age children and can result in suicidal thinking for victims, violent forms of retaliation against bullies, and trauma responses (Carney, 2000; Hazler, 1996; Ross, 2003). Gender violence and sexual harassment directed at female students begins in elementary school, peaks in the middle and early high school years, and continues into college experiences (Ponton, 1996; Young & Mendez, 2003). Few girls escape it. Responses by school administrators have been uneven despite legal requirements that schools respond to claims of sexual harassment. For example, in their analysis of 27 sexual harassment cases, Sullivan and Zirkel (1999) found a consistent pattern in which the victims had notified multiple staff of the harassment with no satisfactory resolution despite repeated efforts to tell authorities about the problem.

Violence aimed at gay, lesbian, bisexual, and transgendered (LGBT) students is also disturbingly common—more common and more invisible than other crimes against students (McFarland & Dupuis, 2001). Approximately 25% of students who are LGBT are crime victims compared to 9% of the general population (Comstock, 1991), and they experience high levels of verbal and physical assault. According to Pilkington and D'Augelli (1995), 80% of the gay and lesbian youth they surveyed experienced verbal insults, 44% were threatened with violence, 33% had objects thrown at them, 31% were followed or chased, and 17% were physically assaulted. Youth who are LGBT are also five times more likely than students who are heterosexual to skip school out of fears for their safety (Massachusetts Department of Education, 1995). Even recent data suggest that two-thirds of youth who are LGBT feel unsafe at school (Parents of Lesbians and Gays, Safe Schools Initiative, 2004, www.pflag.org/fileadmin/Assessment_Report_2004.pdf).

Some evidence suggests that school officials contribute to this problem. In a Massachusetts study, 97% of students reported homophobic comments from students and 53% heard such comments from school staff (Massachusetts Governor's Commission on Gay and Lesbian Youth, 1993). A similar study in Iowa showed that teachers failed to respond to homophobic comments 97% of the time (Carter, 1997). Research on the attitudes of school counselors toward students who are LGBT suggests that they recognize that these students are an underserved and invisible minority but also indicates that many counselors may not be interested in working with such students. Price and Teljohann (1991) reported that only 20% of the counselors they surveyed would not find working with students who were gay or lesbian "gratifying." Students who are LGBT feel this lack of connection—80% of those surveyed in a report for the *Washington Post* say that they did not know a single supportive adult at school (Stepp, 2001).

Not only are such attitudes and behaviors inconsistent with the mandates in the codes of ethics to promote the welfare and dignity of clients and to act in nondiscriminatory ways, they may also be legally problematic. In 1999 the U.S. Supreme Court ruled that school officials who ignore student-on-student harassment may be held liable for violating Title IX when harassment is "so severe, pervasive, and objectively offensive that it denies the victim equal access to education" (*Davis v. Monroe County Board of Education*, 1999, p. 650). The literature on the experiences of sexual minority youth in school suggests that the harassment they experience often meets that criterion. Other civil and federal cases that deal more directly with violence and intimidation based on sexual orientation have also held that schools are responsible when they fail to act to protect the safety and rights of students who are gay or lesbian. See McFarland and Dupois (2001) for a detailed discussion of these cases.

Consequently, school counselors have both an ethical and legal responsibility to act to reduce the risk of harassment, intimidation, and violence against students. They need to use inclusive language themselves, challenge anti-gay and anti-female comments, make resources on homosexuality and gender bias visible to staff and students, take a leadership role in educating other staff about the relationship between harassment and school violence, and have appropriate referral sources available for students and parents who need them. The need for referral sources is especially crucial for students who are LGBT whose invisibility in society make it difficult for them to locate appropriate services on their own.

Both ACA (1998) and the American Psychological Association (APA, 1999) have produced materials to help school counselors and psychologists intervene to make schools safer. These materials clearly delineate the extent of the problem and offer strategies for helping, both in crisis situations and in the normal course of events. See the recommended readings for information on obtaining these materials. APA also has a Website entitled "Healthy Gay, Lesbian, and Bisexual Students" that includes many helpful resources and links (www.apa.org/ed/hlgb) for educators. When school counselors use such materials and take conspicuous action to make school a place where youth who are LGBT can thrive and not just survive, they will be implementing their full ethical responsibility to promote the welfare and dignity of students (Stone, 2003).

Ethical Issues in Postsecondary Planning

One important responsibility of secondary counselors is to advise and assist students in making the transition from high school to postsecondary education or training. The era in which a high school diploma was sufficient to obtain a stable and rewarding job has long passed, and so counselors play a crucial role in helping students and parents make decisions about what type of postsecondary education is best for them. Many colleges, for example, give considerable weight to the letter of recommendation from an applicant's school counselor in deciding admissibility of a candidate—the pressure on a counselor to support a student can lead to either inflated praise for the student's skills or disclosure of sensitive personal information about a student. Consider the following situation in light of that fact.

Mr. Bellasandro's Letter of Reference

Mr. Bellasandro has been the counselor for Maria her entire high school career. She has been an exceptional student, earning high grades, athletic honors, and awards for her participation in debate and chorus. Maria struggled the first semester of her junior year, a period in which she was sexually assaulted as she walked home from her part-time job one evening. She fought off her attacker but suffered a broken collarbone and other injuries. Maria also felt traumatized by the attack and had difficulty focusing on her school assignments for a few months. Her grades suffered that semester. Now that Maria is applying to highly competitive colleges, Mr. Bellasandro is worried that the weak semester will prevent her from being accepted in those colleges. To be sure that she is given full consideration, he discusses the sexual assault and its physical and emotional consequences for Maria in his letter of recommendation. Because Maria has signed a waiver for access to the letter, she has no idea that her counselor included information about the attack in his comments.

Mr. Bellasandro had both good intentions and a legal waiver supporting his decision to describe the reasons that Maria's grades were depressed that semester. His motives were altruistic, and the waiver Maria signed was virtually unconditional. However, his actions were still not entirely consistent with his ethical responsibilities to Maria. Why not? First, she had no reason to expect that the details of this violation would be included in his counselor's letter of reference—her counselor did not discuss this issue with her or her parents prior to the submission of the letter. Second, because no professional can guarantee that the confidentiality of personal information will be maintained when released, students should be able to decide for themselves whether they wish to proceed with the release of such personal content. Maria may be at risk for additional emotional distress should she learn after she arrives at college that the admissions committee knew the details of the assault. Third, Mr. Bellasandro had no need to offer details of the attack to explain that medical problems detracted from Maria's ability to maintain her high academic performance that one semester. He could still provide adequate information about the exceptional nature of this applicant without disclosure of such sensitive information. Because high schools often publicize the acceptances of students into elite colleges as evidence of their own excellence, the question also arises about whether even a small degree of self-interest entered into this counselor's decision or his haste to act without consultation. Getting accepted at an Ivy League school not only advances Maria's future, it advances the school's reputation as well. For all these reasons, Mr. Bellasandro's actions serve as a caution for high school counselors to be sensitive to the implications of the comments they write in letters of recommendation. A study by Stone (2005) shows that the overwhelming majority of school counselors would not take the action Mr. Bellasandro did and would protect such sensitive information from disclosure without explicit permission.

As the *New York Times* (Winter, 2004) noted, another ethical issue has emerged for high school counselors in recent years as many students and parents become focused on admission to elite colleges and universities. Second- and third-tier institutions without such reputations must work hard to attract the most qualified applicants, and they look to school counselors to inform students about the quality of the education they too offer. Such schools have begun to invite high school counselors to their campuses for more than the typical facility tour, sometimes offering counselors free tickets to sporting events and concerts, free skiing at major resorts, and complimentary meals at noteworthy local restaurants. They have been housed at the college's expense in deluxe hotels as well. Such perks are intended to help the counselors have a good experience during their campus visit and to pass along their good experiences at these lesser known colleges to students and parents when they advise them about college applications. Can counselors ethically accept such lavish treatment? The answer depends on the effect that accepting such perks would have on students and parents who are relying on the objectivity of counselors in their recommendations of colleges. It is difficult to imagine that students and parents would not question the motives of the counselors and view their actions as conflicts of interest. It would also be difficult to imagine that school counselors whose salaries are modest would be completely immune to the effects of such lavish treatment during their college visits. Therefore, counselors must decline these extra benefits, although they certainly may participate in campus tours that better acquaint them with the merits of these colleges.

Ethics of Group Counseling in Schools

According to Greenberg (2003), groups have been demonstrated to be an effective tool to help young people change and benefit from their education. Many of the problems that detract from young people's development relate to social skills and interpersonal relationships, two issues especially amenable to group work. They are also an efficient method for school counselors to reach many more students than they can work with individually. Psychoeducational and support groups that deal with the development of social skills, the management of emotions such as anger, and the response to losses such as divorce or death of a sibling are most common. School counselors are well advised to refrain from offering groups that deal with clinical issues such as eating disorders or bipolar disorder (Kaffenberger & Seligman, 2003).

Because groups that take place in schools derive from a closed system—that is, only young people who attend the school are eligible to participate—confidentiality can be a concern. First, students who are uninvolved in group may learn who attends, simply by virtue of their absence from class or by viewing them arriving at the counselor's office at group time. Second, helping young group members maintain the confidentiality of disclosures when they are likely to see other students outside of group and know them well can be difficult. The temptation to tell a friend is greater than if the group takes place in a location separate from school with individuals whose only contact with them is during group time. As mentioned in Chapters 4 and 8, clear informed consent procedures and extensive discussion of the importance of confidentiality assist in limiting the risk of violations, but they do not erase the possibility entirely. School counselors should also obtain the assent of children to participate and explain to them the extent to which their parents may be informed about their disclosures in group. School counselors should also be careful not to exceed the boundaries of their competence in conducting groups, taking care to focus on the issues for which the group was established and refraining from making the psychoeducational or support group a psychotherapy experience. School counselors should also be aware of a student's concurrent participation in counseling outside of school and should communicate with all involved (including the community counselor) about the advisability of inclusion in a group concurrent with individual treatment. With these precautions in place, group counseling can be a valuable tool for increasing the effectiveness of the school counselor.

SUMMARY

The ethical and legal issues confronting school counselors overlap significantly with those facing community counselors. Standards for competence to practice, informed consent, confidentiality, dual relationships, and fair assessment practices are applicable across all settings. However, five unique ethical challenges face school counselors. The first is the clash between the open communication patterns among educators and the limits of communication among professionals imposed by confidentiality standards and privilege laws. Counselors who understand such limits themselves and work to educate other school personnel about the impact of confidentiality on peer relationships

are more likely to serve students, the school, and the profession effectively. On occasion, the open pattern of communication in school includes gossip and informal communications among educators. The ethics of school counseling clearly prohibit participation in such conversation. In fact, gossiping about students may leave counselors vulnerable to legal charges of defamation of character. Second, counselors must be prepared to work with parents and communities whose values differ from the fundamental values of the counseling profession. They must be respectful of parental rights but also sensitive to the needs of the child. In many states, the right of school counselors to help children with matters relating to contraception, abortion, and other sensitive issues is legally protected, provided counselors work within the boundaries of their competence and do not insert their personal views into the counseling interaction. An active program of community education about counseling programs, coupled with evidence of program effectiveness, can reduce resistance and suspicion of counselors. Third, counselors who develop and oversee peer counseling programs must ensure that the programs are helpful to student volunteers and to those they serve. Peer helping programs should be supervised by counselors and should be limited to developmental and educational concerns because there is no clear evidence that such programs can responsibly assist young people with more serious mental health concerns.

Ethical school counselors should be familiar with the provisions of the Family Education Rights and Privacy Act of 1974 and related laws dealing with special education and the rights of those with disabilities. Because state and federal laws affecting education change so rapidly, school counselors bear a responsibility to keep current with those changes and to ensure that school policies are consistent with statutes. Finally, school counselors are not immune to malpractice claims, although such claims occur somewhat less frequently for them than for other mental health professionals. Courts in recent years have tended to view school counselors as having a duty of care to prevent foreseeable danger to students by involving parents or other adults to help keep the student safe and secure the needed care. Legal rulings have also highlighted the duty of school counselors and other officials to be proactive in preventing harassment and intimidation of students that prevents them from equal participation in the educational activities of the school. Much of this harassment has been aimed at female students and at students who are gay, lesbian, or bisexual.

Counselors also need to be sensitive to the ethical dimensions of advising students about postsecondary planning, being accurate in their statements to colleges about a given student's talents, and being sensitive to the impact of the content of their disclosures about a student's personal life. They must also act in ways that do not jeopardize their objectivity or parents' and students' perceptions of their objectivity in accepting college tour activities. When conducting groups in the school, counselors who are aware of the complications of doing groups in a closed system and who stay within the boundaries of their own competence are likely to be most successful.

CASES FOR DISCUSSION

Tito is a 16-year-old junior who has been in counseling with the school counselor, Miranda, intermittently since he began high school. Although he seems happy and easygoing most of the time at school, Tito has endured a great deal of family stress and disruption. Each of his parents has been married multiple times, and Tito has lived in 10 different houses during his life. He has had great difficulty getting along with his current stepfather with whom he resides. They argue constantly, and Tito is punished severely each time he raises his voice. The counselor has been monitoring the situation and observed no signs of abuse, although she clearly sees a mismatch between Tito's psychosocial needs at this time and his stepfather's style of parenting. One morning when Miranda enters her office she has a voicemail message from Tito with a pager number to call as soon as possible. When she contacts Tito she learns that he ran away yesterday after a huge argument with his stepfather that frightened him because he thought he was in danger of hitting the man. He also tells Miranda that he is safe and off the streets. He then asks her if he should tell her where he is. Miranda replies that if he gives her that information he must understand that she may need to disclose it to his mother and stepfather. Tito pauses and decides not to reveal his location. Miranda then devises a plan for Tito that includes contacting his biological father to see if he can help mediate the situation. Tito agrees to call back before the end of school. Two hours later Tito's stepfather calls Miranda and asks her if she knows where Tito is. When she says she does not, the stepfather remarks that he will call the police if he does not hear from the boy by dinnertime. Their conversation ends. Miranda plans to tell Tito of the stepfather's call when she hears from him and to ask him to contact his mother or stepfather immediately. Are Miranda's actions consistent with the ethical standards of the profession? Should she have maintained confidentiality about her telephone contact with Tito? What if the principal asked her if she knew where Tito was? Should she divulge what she knows to the principal?

Nellie, a high school counselor, meets regularly with a sophomore named Michelle who is struggling academically despite good test scores and good grades in middle school. The parents have been informed about the counseling sessions and have encouraged Nellie to discuss with their daughter any issues that will help her do better in school. As spring arrives and temperatures climb in the school Nellie notices that Michelle still wears long sleeves. When asked about this, Michelle begins to cry and reveals to Nellie that she makes small cuts on her arms to help her numb the psychological pain she feels. Michelle shows Nellie the cuts, which are very small, superficial, and few in number. She makes a contract with Michelle to stop cutting until they meet again. She also gets Michelle to agree to show the cuts to her pediatrician when she has her next appointment in 2 weeks. In light of these events, the minor nature of the physical harm, and her worry about destroying the girl's trust in her, Nellie decides not to inform the parents.

Justin, a high school counselor, receives many reference forms for students applying for college, jobs, or other postsecondary experiences. Frequently these forms ask the counselor to rank the student in comparison to other students. Justin is uncomfortable with such forms, believing that they do not allow him much opportunity to describe the talents of individual students. However, he knows that refusing to complete the specified document may not be wise, so he regularly places students in the top 20% of rankings even when he knows that ranking is inflated. He justifies his actions by attending to the inherent limitations of such ranking systems.

DISCUSSION QUESTIONS

1. Schools often have policies that all drug use information that comes to the attention of staff must be reported to administrators. Thinking of potential scenarios with students, at what point do you think it advisable for counselors to report drug use and at what point should they honor confidentiality?

2. School counseling has endured substantial criticism in recent years for many of its activities. For example, self-esteem programs have been labeled as too humanistic, and drug and alcohol support groups have been called too intrusive into family matters. When such criticisms are made about school counseling, what do you see as the ethical obligations of the school counselor?

3. Do the confidentiality requirements for school counselors make it difficult for them to establish strong professional ties with other school personnel? Do those requirements make personal friendships with other staff more difficult?

4. How would you respond to the criticism that peer helping programs place helpers and those helped at risk when they attempt to deal with issues such as depression, suicide, drug use, and related problems? How would you balance the risks of such programs against their potential value to students?

5. What do you see as the ethical issues involved in suicide prevention and crisis intervention programs?

6. Should school counselors be immune from liability claims?

RECOMMENDED READINGS

American Counseling Association. (1998). *Early warning, timely response: A guide to safe schools.* Alexandria, VA: Author. Retrieved August 1, 2005, from http://cecp.air.org/guide/guide.pdf

American Psychological Association. (1999). *Warning signs; A youth anti-violence initiative.* Washington, DC: Author.

American School Counselor Association. (2004). *Ethical standards for school counselors.* Retrieved August 17, 2004, from http://www.schoolcounselor.org/content.asp?contentid=173

Fischer, L., & Sorenson, G. P. (1996). *School law for counselors, psychologists, and social workers* (3rd ed.). White Plains, NY: Longman.

Glosoff, H. L., & Pate, R. H. (2002). Privacy and confidentiality in school counseling. *Professional School Counseling, 6,* 20–27.

Kaplan, L. S. (1996). Outrageous or legitimate concerns: What some parents are saying about school counseling. *The School Counselor, 43,* 165–170.

Lewis, M. W., & Lewis, A. C. (1996). Peer helping programs: Helper role, supervisor training and suicidal behavior. *Journal of Counseling and Development, 74,* 307–313.

McFarland, W. P., & Dupuis, M. (2001). The legal duty to protect gay and lesbian students from violence in school. *Professional School Counseling, 4,* 171–179.

Pedersen, P. B., & Carey, J. C. (Eds.). (2003). *Multicultural counseling in schools: A practical handbook.* Needham Heights, MA: Allyn & Bacon.

Remley, T. P., Jr., & Sparkman, L. B. (1993). Student suicides: The counselor's limited legal liability. *The School Counselor, 40,* 164–169.

Stone, C. B. (2005). *School counseling principles: Ethics and law.* Alexandria, VA: American School Counselor Association.

Chapter 13

The Ethics of Supervision
Modeling Responsible Behavior

A common misperception about supervision is that it is an activity that occupies a small and rather insignificant proportion of a professional's time and priorities. The reality is that it is an integral part of effective practice for many professionals. According to Osipow and Fitzgerald (1986), 64% of counseling psychologists regularly spend time supervising other professionals. Knapp and VandeCreek (1997) suggest that similar levels of supervisory involvement are common among clinical psychologists. Moreover, the scholarly literature emphasizes the crucial importance of supervision in developing and maintaining professional competence (for example, see Bernard & Goodyear, 2004; Bradley & Ladany, 2001; Falender, & Shafranske, 2004). Ethical and legal guidelines view supervised clinical experience as a prerequisite for competence and credentialing.

Nevertheless, little objective evidence is available about the quality or effectiveness of most supervision. The meager evidence that has been accumulated is not especially encouraging. For example, ethics complaints and malpractice claims relating to supervision are rather common. In 1985, VanHoose and Kottler concluded that negligent supervision was a leading cause in many malpractice suits. More than a decade later Keith-Spiegel and Koocher (1998) noted that supervisor failure to identify and act on supervisee inadequacies remains the most common cause of ethics complaints against supervisors. In addition, some of the most famous malpractice cases in the history of mental health have stemmed at least partly from inadequacies in supervision (for example, Tarasoff, 1974, 1976). In a fascinating argument Slovenko (1980) proposes that had the supervising mental health professional in the *Tarasoff* case handled his supervisory duties responsibly, the plaintiffs might not have been able to show negligence.

Research also shows that some supervisors exploit their supervisees, disregard their responsibilities to clients, and show disdain for the rights of the supervisee (for example, see Allen, Szollos, & Williams, 1986; Anderson, Schlossberg, & Rigazio-DiGilio, 2000; Greer, 2002). One study showed that one-third of counseling psychology trainees experienced supervisors who violated one or more guidelines in the standards of the Association for Counselor Education and Supervision (1993). One-third of these supervisors failed to honor standards for evaluating and monitoring trainee competence and activities, and nearly one-fifth (17.9%) violated guidelines related to confidentiality, session boundaries, respectful treatment of trainees, and openness to alternative perspectives (Ladany, Lehman-Waterman, Molinaro, & Wolgart, 1999). Overall, more than half of the supervisors in this study failed to uphold at least one of the ethical standards during the time period examined. Using a qualitative research design to explore what they bluntly termed "lousy supervision" Magnuson, Wilcoxin, and Norem (2000) identified three broad forms of incompetent supervision. One stems from poor management and organization of supervision, the next from technical and cognitive deficits, and the last from relational or affective deficits. The specific lapses the participants identified ranged from humiliation and intimidation during supervisory sessions to boundary violations with other supervisees and clinical incompetence. In their evaluation of "hindering experiences" during group supervision Enyedy, Arcinue, Puri, Carter, Goodyear, and Getzelman (2003) found that predoctoral interns in counseling identified similar problems, including supervisor distraction from their responsibilities, demeaning behaviors toward supervisees, and other behaviors that detracted from the ability of the interns to learn from the group or help each other.

Three factors may explain the discrepancy between the desired and actual state of supervision. The first factor is the rather common practice of equating competence as a practitioner with competence as a supervisor. Both the ethics codes and the literature on supervision strongly belie this assumption (Bernard & Goodyear, 2004; Vasquez, 1992). They view skill and experience as a practitioner as a necessary but not sufficient condition for competence in supervision. This chapter examines the components of supervisor competency presented in the codes and the literature.

Supervision is a process that involves multiple roles (Bernard & Goodyear, 2004; Falvey, 2002a; Overhosler, 2004; Sherry, Teschendorf, Anderson, & Guzman, 1991). The supervisor is a teacher, mentor, adviser, consultant, and evaluator to the supervisee as well as a counselor (from a distance) to the clients of the supervisee. Successfully managing these diverse roles requires knowledge, self-awareness, and experience. Thus, the second factor that helps explain some lapses in responsible supervision is a professional's inability to handle these varied roles simultaneously. The following pages elaborate on this issue and provide recommendations for success in this task.

The third and final factor that relates to improper supervision is the inability of the supervisor to place the welfare of the supervisee or the supervisee's clients ahead of his or her own interests. When this happens, supervisees get exploited. The form of such misbehavior varies substantially, from the imposition of personal values to sexual harassment and financial exploitation. Whatever its particular form, such misbehavior depreciates the effectiveness of the supervisory experience, compromises the value of the counseling experience to the clients, and sometimes traumatizes the supervisee (Allen et al., 1986; Slimp & Burian, 1994). The following pages examine in more detail the forms such exploitation takes and ways to minimize that risk. The content of this chapter is drawn from scholarly writings and the codes of ethics of the professions.

Competence to Supervise

To understand the ethical and legal dimensions of competence in supervision, we must retrace our steps to the components of competent practice. Competence requires knowledge, skill, and diligence in work with real clients. Novice counselors are deemed competent after they demonstrate to supervisors sufficient levels of these qualities in work with a variety of clients. Clinical supervisors, then, are the final gatekeepers of the profession, who act as the last checkpoint against the admission of unskilled or untherapeutic people into the professional community. The process of determining which novices are competent demands careful and sustained attention to the activities of the supervisee. Untrained supervisors are unlikely to meet those demands. When they fail in this ethical duty, they damage the profession, the public, and probably the person inappropriately admitted to the profession.

The Association for Counselor Education and Supervision (ACES) Standards for Counseling Supervisors (1990) elaborate in great detail the characteristics and competencies of effective supervisors. In this way they provide a road map for professionals who want to assess their supervisory competence. The characteristics identified by these standards are summarized as follows:

- Competence as counselors themselves, including skills in assessment and intervention, case conceptualization and case management, recordkeeping, and evaluation of counseling outcomes
- Attitudes and traits consistent with the role, such as sensitivity to individual differences, motivation and commitment to supervision, and comfort with the authority accompanying that role
- Familiarity with the ethical, legal, and regulatory dimensions of supervision
- Knowledge of the professional and personal facets of the supervisory relationship and the impact of supervision on the supervisee
- Understanding of the methods and techniques of supervision
- Appreciation of the process of counselor development and its unfolding in supervision
- Capacity to evaluate a supervisee's counseling performance fairly and accurately and to provide constructive feedback
- Grasp of the rapidly expanding body of theory and research on counselor supervision

Both the length and complexity of this list demonstrate that competence as a practitioner is but a small part of responsible supervision. In light of these standards, the notion that supervisory skills are acquired through "on-the-job-training" or by osmosis is clearly incorrect. When researchers (Navin, Beamish, & Johanson, 1995) used this document to ascertain the competence of counselors currently in the supervisory role, many fell short, especially of the standard relating to training in supervision. Other research also supports this conclusion (Hess & Hess, 1983). Even supervisees seem unsure of the supervisory training of those who oversee their work. A survey of psychologists by McCarthy, Kulakowski, and Kenfield (1994) found that 72% of the sample were uncertain about whether their supervisors had training in supervision. The Association of State and Provincial Psychology Boards (ASPPB) published similar guidelines for supervision in 1998, partly because they, too, were concerned to provide psychologists with better direction to avoid incompetent or impaired supervision.

Of course, ethical standards deal with more than objective knowledge and observable skill. They also place considerable emphasis on the attitudes and values of the supervisor, requiring the same kind of diligence in supervisory responsibilities that is expected in direct service. Also embedded in the standards and the other literature on supervision (for example, Ancis & Ladany, 2001; Leong & Wagner, 1994) is a mandate for sensitivity to individual differences and multicultural competence in supervision (Falendar & Shafranske, 2004; Locke & Faubert, 2003). Research suggests that many counseling supervisors do not appear sensitive to multicultural issues in their interactions with supervisees (Fukuyama, 1994; Ladany et al., 1999) and tend to have less training in multicultural issues than their supervisees (Constantine, 1997).

The American Counseling Association (ACA) ethics code addresses the topic, in these terms:

ACA *Code of Ethics,* Section F: Teaching, Training, and Supervision

Introduction: Counselors aspire to foster meaningful and respectful professional relationships and to maintain appropriate boundaries with supervisees and students. Counselors have theoretical and pedagogical foundations for their work and aim to be fair, accurate, and honest in their assessments of counselors-in-training.

F.2. Counselor Supervision Competence

a. Supervision Preparation. Prior to offering clinical supervision services, counselors are trained in supervision methods and techniques. Counselors who offer clinical supervision services regularly pursue continuing education activities, including both counseling and supervision topics and skills.

The American Psychological Association (APA) code focuses its comments on the need for the professional to assign responsibilities to supervisees in appropriate ways and to provide them with proper oversight.

APA *Ethical Principles,* Section 2.05: Delegation of Work to Others

Psychologists who delegate work to employees, supervisees, or research or teaching assistants or who use the services of others, such as interpreters, take reasonable steps to (1) avoid delegating such work to persons who have a multiple relationship with those being served that would likely lead to exploitation or loss of objectivity; (2) authorize only those responsibilities that such persons can be expected to perform competently on the basis of their education, training, or experience, either independently or with the level of supervision being provided; and (3) see that such persons perform these services competently.

Responsible Use of Supervisory Power

Supervision is often an emotionally intense experience for supervisees. They are coping with the heavy emotional demands of clinical work and are in the midst of making important decisions about their professional futures (Slimp & Burian, 1994; Watkins, 1997). Moreover, supervisees have limited ability to protect themselves when their supervisors act inappropriately. The supervisory relationship also involves a strong emotional connection between those involved, and it parallels therapy in some regards. Reactions similar to transference and countertransference happen frequently, and supervisors often become aware of the ways in which the personal problems of supervisees affect their functioning with clients (Bernard & Goodyear, 2004; Muratori, 2001). Supervisees also look to their supervisors as models of professional behavior (Ladany, 2004; Vasquez, 1992). Therefore supervisors who act unethically may be "teaching" those under their influence to engage in those behaviors. At the very least, however, supervisors who misuse their influence are losing an opportunity to show less experienced colleagues the proper behavior of a professional. For all these reasons, the person in the supervisory role has substantial power and can use it to help or harm supervisees.

The codes of ethics and guidelines address issues of power and exploitation in broad terms, grouping together many classes of people over whom professionals may have authority. The codes' most specific comments deal with sexual exploitation.

ACA *Code of Ethics,* Section C.6: Public Responsibility

d. Exploitation of Others. Counselors do not harmfully exploit others in their professional relationships.

F.3. Supervisory Relationships

a. Relationship Boundaries With Supervisees. Counseling supervisors clearly define and maintain ethical professional, personal, and social relationships with their supervisees. Counseling supervisors avoid nonprofessional relationships with current supervisees. If supervisors must assume other professional roles (e.g., clinical and administrative supervisor, instructor) with supervisees, they work to minimize potential conflicts and explain to supervisees the expectations and responsibilities associated with each role. They do not engage in any form of nonprofessional interaction that may compromise the supervisory relationship.

b. Sexual Relationships. Sexual or romantic interactions or relationships with current supervisees are prohibited.

c. Sexual Harassment. Counseling supervisors do not condone or subject supervisees to sexual harassment.

d. Close Relatives and Friends. Counseling supervisors avoid accepting close relatives, romantic partners, or friends as supervisees.

e. Potentially Beneficial Relationships. Counseling supervisors are aware of the power differential in their relationships with supervisees. If they believe nonprofessional relationships with a supervisee may be potentially beneficial to the supervisee, they take precautions similar to those taken by counselors when working with clients. Examples of potentially beneficial interactions or relationships include attending a formal ceremony; hospital visits; providing support during a stressful event; or mutual membership in a professional association, organization, or community. Counseling supervisors engage in open discussions with supervisees when they consider entering into relationships with them outside of their roles as clinical and/or administrative supervisors. Before engaging in nonprofessional relationships, supervisors discuss with supervisees and document the rationale for such interactions, potential benefits or drawbacks, and anticipated consequences for the supervisee. Supervisors clarify the specific nature and limitations of the additional role(s) they will have with the supervisee.

APA *Ethical Principles,* Section 3.04: Avoiding Harm

Psychologists take reasonable steps to avoid harming their clients/patients, students, supervisees, research participants, organizational clients, and others with whom they work, and to minimize harm where it is foreseeable and unavoidable.

3.08 Exploitative Relationships

Psychologists do not exploit persons over whom they have supervisory, evaluative, or other authority such as clients/patients, students, supervisees, research participants, and employees.

7.07 Sexual Relationships With Students and Supervisees

Psychologists do not engage in sexual relationships with students or supervisees who are in their department, agency, or training center or over whom psychologists have or are likely to have evaluative authority.

Legal prohibitions against sexual exploitation of supervisees are also common. According to Avery & Gressard (2000), 18 states have regulations that prohibit sexual contact between supervisors and trainees.

Avoiding Unhealthy Dependency

Kurpius, Gibson, Lewis, and Corbet (1991) assert that supervisors who foster an unhealthy dependency on them are also misusing their power. The goal of supervision is not to have the supervisee deferring all judgment to the supervisor; it is to help the supervisee develop the skills, judgment, and confidence to accurately discriminate when to work independently and when to seek assistance. At first, of course, novice counselors are rather dependent on their supervisors for guidance, reassurance, and practical strategies. This kind of dependence at this stage of development is not problematic. What is problematic is a supervisory style that fails to encourage independence, or worse, actively encourages dependency. Magnuson et al. (2000) found that supervisors who acted in rigid, authoritarian ways and demanded obedience and deference from trainees were often cited as examples of lousy supervisors. Supervisors who are uncertain whether their behavior meets this standard should evaluate it in light of the "clean, well-lit room" standard (Haas & Malouf, 2005) and seek consultation. Enyedy et al. (2003) also reported that supervisees felt that domineering and controlling behaviors hindered their professional development.

Limiting the Number of Supervisees

Responsible use of power in supervision encompasses more than avoiding exploitive behaviors. Four other dimensions exist. One is the responsibility to limit the number of supervisees to a manageable level so that the needs of supervisees and their clients are met. The ACA standard F.1 addresses this issue when it mandates that supervisors carefully monitor the actions of supervisees with clients.

ACA *Code of Ethics,* Section F.1: Counselor Supervision and Client Welfare

a. Client Welfare. A primary obligation of counseling supervisors is to monitor the services provided by other counselors or counselors-in-training. Counseling supervisors monitor client welfare and supervisee clinical performance and professional development. To fulfill this obligation, supervisors meet regularly with supervisees to review case notes, samples of clinical work, or live observations. Supervisees have a responsibility to understand and follow the ACA *Code of Ethics.*

What number of supervisees is manageable? The answer depends on several factors:

- The clinical and supervisory experience and competence of the supervisor
- The experience and competence of the supervisee
- The time available for supervision activities
- The nature of the client population served
- The existence of any state law/regulations stipulating a maximum number of supervisees

In general, when the demands of the population served and the needs of the supervisee are high, and the experience or time availability of the supervisor is low, fewer people should be supervised. Regulatory bodies often set a maximum of three to five supervisees per licensed professional. The ASPPB recommends no more than three supervisees per psychologist (ASPPB, 2003). These limits are sensible, given the often intense demands of the supervisory process and the legal dimensions of supervision. (The latter will be discussed in subsequent sections of this chapter.) However, that regulation does not imply that it is ethical for all licensed professionals to take on that number of supervisees. Such a judgment should be based on the criteria listed earlier. In some cases, there is no ethical justification for even a single supervisee. Professionals who tend to accept many supervisees need to examine their motivation. If supervision is being used as a method of increasing income or professional reputation, then the practice is misguided. The only supportable justification for multiple supervisees is public need, commitment to training, and interest in the development of the people being supervised.

Three other aspects of supervision are important to address. First, at least some portion of supervision should be a face-to-face activity, and the supervisor should be able to have face-to-face interaction with clients if necessary. They cannot meet their responsibilities to promote the welfare of the client if interaction with a client is logistically impossible. Supervision by memo or telephone is not a substitute for person-to-person contact, except in rare circumstances. Nor is "review of case notes" a viable alternative, although the research by Navin et al. (1995) shows that such a practice is common. The need to arrange in-person meetings puts a practical limit on the number of supervisees. Second, not all states stipulate a maximum number of supervisees for all professions. When such regulatory gaps exist, the determination of a prudent and responsible number of supervisees is left to the individual practitioner. Third, a supervisee cannot shift all the responsibility for decision making about this matter to the supervisor. A supervisee is also responsible for knowing and abiding by the ethical and legal standards governing practice. Thus, any professional is obliged to refuse to accept supervision from someone who has an excessive load of supervisees. In this situation, the trainee needs to make alternative arrangements and, if possible, to tactfully inform the supervisor about the reason for that decision.

Informed Consent to Supervision

The second aspect of responsible use of power to consider is that of respecting the supervisee's autonomy. One important way to honor this autonomy is through developing informed consent to supervision. It is the responsibility of the supervisor to ensure that the supervisee understands and freely consents to the conditions of supervision. Clients who are seen by trainees under supervision also have a right to consent or refuse to consent to service by a trainee. McCarthy, Kulakowski, and Kenfield (1994) identify seven specific topics that the supervisor ought to address in the informed consent process with trainees. Supervisees should be instructed, first, about the *purposes of supervision*—that is, to foster their development as competent professionals and to protect the welfare of their clients. Second, they also have a right to know the *qualifications, credentials, style, and theoretical orientation of the supervisor* as consumers of a professional service. Third, they should be briefed about the *logistics* of supervision—times, frequency, emergency procedures, paperwork, and other demands imposed by licensing boards or internship requirements. Supervisors should also provide the name of at least one other professional whom the supervisee might contact in the event that the supervisor was unreachable in a crisis. Fourth, supervisees have a right to understand the *process and procedures* for supervision, including the roles, expectations, and responsibilities of each person. For example, if a supervisor expects a supervisee to prepare for their meetings in a particular way, such an expectation should be communicated. Frequently, supervision involves reviewing tape recordings of sessions with clients. In this event, developing informed consent with the client would include explanation of taping procedures and the ways the tapes or other forms of electronic recording will be used in supervision. (Section E.4.a of the ACA code details this responsibility.)

The fifth, and perhaps the most crucial of all the guidelines suggested by McCarthy and her colleagues states that supervisees should be instructed about the *procedures for evaluating their performance*. This recommendation is supported by the ethics codes (APA, Section 7.06, and ACA, Section F.5). Evaluation procedures must include provisions for frequent, objective feedback sessions about performance and specific recommendations for remedying deficiencies. Supervisors' evaluation procedures should also aim at building the supervisees' skills in accurate self-evaluation (Disney & Stephens, 1994). Supervisees in danger of failing must be informed about this risk immediately (Falvey, 2002a). They should also be briefed about the particular areas of deficiency and the level of improvement necessary to remain in good standing (Bernard & Goodyear, 2004). To avoid confusion, written evaluations are essential. As discussed in the opening paragraph of this chapter, many ethics complaints regarding supervision involve violations of these evaluation guidelines. Too often supervisees misunderstand the role of the supervisor or misjudge their progress in supervision. Supervisees have much at stake in the process and have often had little prior experience with individual supervision as a method of evaluation. Consequently, comprehensive attention to this issue is crucial. Allen et al. (1986) found that supervisors judged by psychology interns to be ideal were clear, thorough, and respectful in their evaluation procedures. Robiner, Fuhrman, and Bobbitt (1990) have proposed an instrument called the Minnesota Supervisory Inventory (MSI) that supervisors may use to ensure objective and comprehensive feedback. Falvey (2002b) also offers guidance about procedures and forms for appropriately documenting supervisory activities.

The sixth component of informed supervision, according to McCarthy et al., is *instruction in the ethical and legal issues in supervision and practice*. Ethics education in graduate programs tends to focus more on direct service issues than on teaching and supervision concerns (Hill, 2004a; Urofsky & Sowa, 2004), so that supervisors cannot be confident that their supervisees are educated about these topics. Even if the material was discussed in ethics courses, prudent supervisors remind supervisees about relevant ethical and legal standards, providing copies of the codes and guidelines for supervisees to refer to as needed. See Section F.4.c of the ACA code for the specific wording on this responsibility. As mentioned, the ACA code specifically charges supervisors with the duty to instruct supervisees about the boundaries of their relationship.

Finally (seventh), McCarthy et al. recommend that supervisors use a *written informed consent document* that contains information relevant to each of the six areas just described, for each person to sign as a contract for their work together. This practice protects the legal rights of both parties and also symbolizes the dignity and autonomy of each. It formalizes their mutual commitment to the learning process and the welfare of the clients. McCarthy et al. include a sample contract in the appendix to their article that can serve as a model for others to use; Sutter, McPherson, & Geeseman, (2002) offer an alternative format.

The ACA code mandates that an informed consent process occur but does not specify that the consent be written.

ACA *Code of Ethics,* Section F.4: Supervisor Responsibilities

a. Informed Consent for Supervision. Supervisors are responsible for incorporating into their supervision the principles of informed consent and participation. Supervisors inform supervisees of the policies and procedures to which they are to adhere and the mechanisms for due process appeal of individual supervisory actions.

Other scholars recommend documenting each supervisory session, both to improve evaluation of supervisees and to monitor the care given to clients (Falendar & Shafranske, 2004; Falvey, 2002b; Harrar, VandeCreek, & Knapp, 1990). The content of these documents should include five items:

1. Date and time for the meeting
2. A listing of cases discussed
3. Notes about client progress
4. Recommendations to the supervisee
5. Issues for follow-up in future meetings

If the supervisee is having significant difficulty in meeting client needs or learning required concepts, documentation of the meeting should also contain a plan for remedying those deficiencies. These records should be kept in a confidential file, accessible to supervisor and supervisee. Bridge and Bascue (1988) have published a one-page form that efficiently meets these requirements.

Occasionally licensing boards and ethics committees mandate that professionals obtain supervision if they wish to maintain their license after a disciplinary action. This is a form of practice oversight that is designed both to assist the disciplined professional to learn more responsible behavior and to monitor his or her work with clients to ensure that no further violations occur (Cobia & Pipes, 2002). The potential benefit to such an arrangement is the rehabilitation of the professional and the protection of the public. The professional who agrees to provide the mandated supervision can be providing a valuable professional and public service, but there are risks involved. One risk is that the degree of oversight needed is beyond the capacity of the supervisor to provide. Another is that the supervisor may find it difficult to maintain objectivity about the quality and effectiveness of the service provided by the supervisee who is still a professional colleague. The supervisor may be at some liability risk as well (Cobia & Pipes, 2002). For all these reasons, professionals who agree to provide this service should be clear about what the disciplinary body is asking them to do, should undertake a thorough informed consent with the supervisee, and should contact their liability insurers to verify that their policies cover such activities.

Sensitivity to Issues of Diversity

The third aspect of responsible use of power relates to the sensitivity of the supervisor to issues of diversity. In particular, the supervisor is obligated to avoid actions that reflect gender, ethnic, age, religious, or sexual orientation bias. The ACA code addresses this standard as follows.

ACA *Code of Ethics,* Section F.2.b: Multicultural Issues/Diversity in Supervision

Counseling supervisors are aware of and will address the role of multiculturalism/diversity play in the supervisory relationship.

Unfortunately, research shows that insensitivity about these issues persists. In the Allen et al. (1986) study, such behaviors were a major factor in earning counselors the designation "worst supervisor." Even well-intentioned supervisors can exhibit inappropriate behaviors. Williams and Halgin (1995) point out that in the hope of fostering congenial relationships, European-American supervisors of African-American supervisees often avoid discussing their racial difference. That avoidance is likely to have the opposite impact. Similarly, these scholars suggest that supervisors sometimes show insensitivity to the impact of their power over African-American supervisees. They fail to understand the supervisees' level of discomfort with the one-down position in a society that has so often discriminated against their race. It is interesting to note that in one of the few empirical studies of cross-cultural supervision, Vander Kolk (1974) found that at the start of the supervision experience, African-American students anticipated less acceptance and empathy from their supervisors than did their European-American counterparts. The research of Cook and Helms (1988) and of McRoy, Freeman, Logan, and Blackmon (1986) offers similar findings, suggesting that ethnically and culturally diverse supervisees begin the supervisory relationship with a more guarded and distant attitude toward European-American supervisors.

In parallel fashion, supervisors can hold different objectives or behaviors unfairly based on the age, gender, religion, sexual orientation, or cultural background of supervisees. They may even discriminate on the basis of these factors in accepting students to supervise. Again, Allen et al. (1986) found that students who encountered supervisors who acted in these ways labeled those professionals as bad supervisors.

Bernard and Goodyear (2004) offer some suggestions for minimizing these problems. First, supervisors must reject the "myth of sameness" and acknowledge the reality and contributions of cultural diversity. Second, they must understand that their own views of the world may not be shared by their supervisees and that this difference does not represent a deficiency in anyone. Third, they encourage supervisors to devote the same energy to appreciating cultural diversity in supervision as they may use in understanding how cultural diversity affects therapy relationships. They must also be committed to self-monitoring their own behavior and to developing the knowledge and skills required for effective cross-cultural supervision. Vasquez (1992) offers another valuable recommendation: Supervisors of culturally diverse professionals ought to become familiar with the special challenges inherent in integrating ethnic identity with professional identity.

Other Personal Values and Beliefs

Supervisors also need to be aware of the ways in which other personal beliefs and values may affect the supervisory process. This responsibility closely parallels the counselor's duty with clients; hence, the following sections of the ethics codes are relevant.

ACA *Code of Ethics,* Section A.4: Avoiding Harm and Imposing Values

b. Personal Values. Counselors are aware of their own values, attitudes, beliefs, and behaviors and avoid imposing values that are inconsistent with counseling goals. Counselors respect the diversity of clients, trainees, and research participants.

APA *Ethical Principles,* Principle A: Beneficence and Nonmaleficence

Psychologists strive to benefit those with whom they work and take care to do no harm. In their professional actions, psychologists seek to safeguard the welfare and rights of those with whom they interact professionally and other affected persons, and the welfare of animal subjects of research. When conflicts occur among psychologists' obligations or concerns, they attempt to resolve these conflicts in a responsible fashion that avoids or minimizes harm. Because psychologists' scientific and professional judgments and actions may affect the lives of others, they are alert to and guard against personal, financial, social, organizational, or political factors that might lead to misuse of their influence. Psychologists strive to be aware of the possible effect of their own physical and mental health on their ability to help those with whom they work.

Because of the limited power of the supervisee, the person in authority must be able to separate professional from personal beliefs and values and to use only the former in teaching and evaluating the supervisee. Consider the following situation.

Dr. Ziblinksy and the Intern

Dr. Ziblinsky supervises two predoctoral interns at a college counseling center. She also serves on the board of directors of the Planned Parenthood agency in her community. One of her interns, Mr. Appleton, is an active participant in the local Right-to-Life group. Dr. Ziblinsky learns of Mr. Appleton's involvement in that organization a few months into the internship. Soon thereafter she begins assigning female clients to the other intern, in the belief that Mr. Appleton's personal values would prevent him from effectively counseling female students about reproductive issues. Dr. Ziblinsky also finds herself being more businesslike and task oriented with Mr. Appleton than with the other intern. When Mr. Appleton realizes what is happening, he asks for a private meeting with her to discuss the matter. In that meeting, Dr. Ziblinsky defends her decision, arguing that it is in the best interests of the students who seek counseling at the center.

In this scenario, Dr. Ziblinsky has failed to distinguish personal from professional belief. She has allowed her own strong beliefs about reproductive issues to inappropriately influence her professional judgment about a supervisee. She is preventing Mr. Appleton from seeing female clients based on speculation rather than on any evidence that he intends to impose his beliefs on clients. Thus, this supervisor acted unethically. First, the frequency with which female clients seek counseling about an unexpected pregnancy is rather low. It certainly happens, but most female clients have other issues. To eliminate all female clients from his calendar is an overreaction to a relatively low-probability event. Second, even if a client does present with an unexpected pregnancy, Dr. Ziblinsky has no evidence that her intern will attempt to impose his personal beliefs on that client. Mr. Appleton may have already thought through this issue and decided on a strategy to refer the client to another counselor under this circumstance. In addition, Dr. Ziblinsky is violating professional standards insofar as she is allowing her disdain for this intern's personal beliefs to affect her behavior in supervision. She has begun a pattern of treating Mr. Appleton differently from the other intern. This is discrimination based on a characteristic that has not shown any relevance to his competence as a professional. The intern also needs to have broad training. Preventing him from counseling women limits his training and his competence. Such limits should be imposed only when justified by evidence of incompetence or misconduct. Then she further complicates her ethical error by failing to recognize the problem when her intern speaks to her about it. The supervisor has thereby missed an opportunity to change her behavior to comply with her duty to this student. In short, in the name of doing what she believes to be the right thing for women with unexpected pregnancies, she has failed to act responsibly. Her initial motivation was not self-interested because she did not personally profit in any way from her decision, but it was self-absorbed and inattentive to her duties to the intern. If she continues her current behavior, Dr. Ziblinsky will violate all five ethical principles—beneficence, nonmaleficence, justice, fidelity, and respect for autonomy.

When faced with such issues in supervision, supervisors ought to ask themselves the following questions:

- Is this belief or value truly relevant to professional behavior?
- Am I treating supervisees or their clients unfairly by my actions?
- Am I fostering the growth of the supervisee by this action?
- Would objective colleagues be likely to come to the same conclusion?
- What alternatives to the course of action under consideration may better comply with professional standards?
- Will supervision or therapy assist me in meeting my obligations to the supervisee?
- If I have already acted in inappropriate ways, how can I undo or minimize the harm that has already been done?

Supervisors are also obliged to respect differences in theoretical orientation. Failure to respect theoretical differences implies that one already has "the truth" about effective therapy. Such an attitude is not only disrespectful of the autonomy of others, it is also inconsistent with scientific evidence. No research shows that one theoretical approach to counseling is superior to all the others. Thus supervisors ought not criticize supervisees for using alternative approaches as long as the intern is competent and can show the relevance of the approach to a client's problem. If a supervisor has a strong investment in a particular theory or method, that investment should be made known to the supervisee before the relationship begins, so that he or she can make an informed decision about whether to engage in this supervisory relationship. Of course, if a supervisee is using an approach that one believes will be counterproductive or ineffective, then the supervisor is obligated to suggest alternatives. The encouragement of alternative strategies should be based on objective analysis rather than on personal preferences or overidentification with a theory.

Responsibilities for Client Welfare

Supervisors have ultimate legal and ethical responsibility for the welfare of their supervisees' clients. When counseling supervisors have competent, diligent supervisees who foster the welfare of their clients, there is little conflict between their obligations to both parties. However, when supervisees act in ways that do not positively affect the well-being of clients, supervisors feel conflicting obligations. On the one hand, they must help supervisees overcome problems so that they can continue to develop as professionals. If a supervisor intervened with every mistake, supervisees would not be able to improve their skills, and if high levels of competence were established for novice professionals to work with clients, very few would attain the standard. On the other hand, supervisors must protect the welfare of the client from inept care. How can a supervisor meet both these obligations? The ACA code is explicit in this regard. It establishes that both are important duties, but that the supervisor's first responsibility is to the client. The duty to the supervisee's development as a professional is secondary.

ACA *Code of Ethics,* Section F.1: Counselor Supervision and Client Welfare

a. Client Welfare. A primary obligation of counseling supervisors is to monitor the services provided by other counselors or counselors-in-training. Counseling supervisors monitor client welfare and supervisee clinical performance and professional development. To fulfill this obligation, supervisors meet regularly with supervisees to review case notes, samples of clinical work, or live observationss.

The best remedy for the problem, of course, is prevention. Supervisors must thoroughly assess the skills of the supervisee at the beginning of the experience and must assiduously monitor changes. Novice counselors should be carefully supervised so that errors can be prevented or minimized when they occur. The complexity of cases they are given should match their prior training and experience, and the clients they serve should understand the nature of the counseling they are receiving and the recourse they have if dissatisfied. None of these responsibilities can be met with a laissez-faire style of supervision. Supervisors should be guided by the goal of maximizing student learning without risking client welfare.

Vasquez (1992) and Forrest, Elman, Gizara, and Vacha-Hasse (1999) note that interns and others under supervision sometimes suffer distress that impairs their functioning in the professional role. They are not immune from the problems that can afflict other professionals—substance abuse, major mental illness, grief, loneliness, or marital dissatisfaction. Thus she recommends that supervisors be alert for such difficulties and intervene as soon as such problems begin to compromise a supervisee's work. The ACA *Code of Ethics* and the ACES document (1993) support this recommendation (ACA, Section F.5.b; ACES, Section 2.12). Lamb, Cochran, and Jackson (1991) have defined impairment more broadly, to encompass two other characteristics. One is an unwillingness to comply with professional ethical standards, and the second is an inability to meet minimum criteria for competence. Regardless of the scope of an individual supervisor's definition of distress that impairs performance, it is clear that supervisors are obliged to monitor supervisee progress and intervene when meaningful deficits occur to protect client welfare and to facilitate supervisee development. Lamb et al. have offered a comprehensive set of guidelines to aid in identifying and remedying intern impairment. These guidelines emphasize the importance of frequent communication among supervisors, regular feedback meetings with supervisees, and formal procedures for responding to severe distress when other efforts are insufficient. When such interventions are unsuccessful, probation or dismissal may become necessary. (See Kerl, Garcia, McCullough, and Maxwell [2002] for a discussion of legal and ethical issues in dismissing students from academic programs for other than academic reasons.)

The responsibility of the supervisor to the client extends to two other areas. First, the supervisor is bound to oversee the confidentiality of client disclosures and records. This duty behooves supervisors to educate and monitor those they oversee regarding confidentiality standards and procedures. It also means that they make sure clients have been informed about and consented to the supervisee's communications with the supervisor. Second, when sessions are to be recorded or observed, supervisors should ascertain that clients have agreed to the practice and understand how the recordings will be used. They also monitor the care supervisees take over the confidentiality of those tapes. If a client refuses consent for taping, the supervisor must judge whether the supervisee is capable of providing competent service in the absence of such monitoring. If the supervisor concludes that recording is essential for competent service or is a requirement for the supervisee, he or she must help the supervisee communicate that to clients and obtain alternate care. Prudent supervisors guard the client's right to autonomy about recording and recognize the obligation of the institution to provide competent, beneficial service to that client.

Boundary Violations in Supervision

Sexual exploitation is not the only form of boundary violation to which supervisors are vulnerable. Because of the close, collegial nature of supervisory relationships, those in authority can lose track of the evaluative aspect of those relationships and begin to see supervisees as friends or fully qualified colleagues. If you recall the case of Yolanda from Chapter 2, she was at risk for entering a dual relationship with her supervisee when she wanted to invite her supervisee to join her in social and community activities. Because the boundaries between supervisee and supervisor can get blurred even more easily than boundaries in other professional relationships, counselors must be vigilant about monitoring their behavior and should set clear limits. The codes do not absolutely forbid social or business relationships with supervisees, but they strongly caution against them. The responsibility to place client welfare ahead of the supervisee's experience means that the supervisor must be able to clearly see what is happening with the client and have the energy to intervene when needed. Social or business relationships compromise that capacity. In a dual relationship, counselors can come to prize their friendship or financial connection to the supervisee more than they value a client's welfare. When a counselor is in doubt about the ethics of a particular relationship, he or she should consult with colleagues for guidance. Research suggests that boundary violations occur rather frequently. For instance, Navin et al. (1995) reported that 25% of their sample of field supervisors were aware of social interactions between supervisors and trainees that they viewed as incompatible with the supervisors' duties.

Supervisors are sometimes tempted to serve as counselors for those they supervise. In a survey of mental health professionals at college counseling centers, Sherry et al. (1991) found that 48% of respondents admitted such behavior at least on rare occasions. Of these, 3% acknowledged treating supervisees at least fairly often. The therapylike nature of supervision makes this role slippage understandable but rarely ethical. Whiston and Emerson (1989) identify several specific problems with this practice. First, it can compromise a supervisor's objectivity about both the supervisee and the client and thereby interfere with one's duty to both. In addition, it diminishes the capacity of supervisors to carry out their responsibility to the profession and the public to act as gatekeeper against admitting ineffective individuals into the profession. Second, the client/supervisee is more vulnerable to a supervisor's misuse of power and is likely to be confused about which rules apply when. A supervisee might be reluctant to reveal personal information in counseling, fearing its impact on supervision. Moreover, they point out that when such a boundary violation is occurring, another violation must have preceded it—a failure of informed consent. Consent probably has not been properly obtained. Finally, if there are any group supervision activities occurring, a dual relationship with one supervisee complicates the process of group supervision. If other group members know of the counseling activity, they may be uncomfortable and fail to take full advantage of the experience. Similarly, the supervisee in the dual relationship may have worries about the confidentiality of counseling information and about the way he or she will be evaluated in the supervision.

The wording of the ACA code on this issue suggests that the profession finds that reasoning cogent.

ACA *Code of Ethics,* Section F.5.c: Counseling for Supervisees

If supervisees request counseling, supervisors provide them with acceptable referrals. Counselors do not provide counseling services to supervisees. Supervisors address interpersonal competencies in terms of the impact of these issues on clients, the supervisory relationship, and professional functioning.

Unfortunately, many practitioners seem oblivious to the ethical implications of counseling supervisees. In 1987, 13% of psychologists labeled this practice as ethical (Pope et al., 1987). Four years later, Gibson and Pope (1993) found that 44% of the counselors participating in their survey endorsed this view.

At first glance, avoiding an intense counseling component of supervision seems inconsistent with the recommendation to monitor the effect of supervisees' personal problems on their work. However, ethics scholars provide a reasonable resolution of the dilemma. The bedrock of their scholarship is a recognition of the limits on the depth and breadth of exploration of personal issues in supervision. Whiston and Emerson (1989) offer guidelines for distinguishing supervision from counseling. First, as the ACES *Guidelines* also advise, any discussion of personal issues should focus on their relationship to professional development. Personal issues that appear irrelevant to professional functioning have no place in a supervisory discussion. Second, the function of the supervisor is to *identify* personal problems that may be inhibiting the supervisee's performance, not to *resolve* those issues. The latter is the task of a counselor with no conflicting role obligations, to whom the supervisor may refer the supervisee. Third, when supervisees reveal personal matters in connection with a case discussion, supervisors should respond with basic empathy and understanding of the issue but should refrain from interpretations or comments that would make deep exploration of personal matters more likely. Supervisors ought not to act in a cold and unfeeling way in response to such supervisee disclosures, however. Supervisor warmth is a highly valued quality among interns and facilitates their development (Allen et al., 1986). Thus, supervisors should show compassion and concern but refrain from moving into deeper therapeutic territory. Moreover, supervisees who are informed about the distinction between therapy and supervision are better able to respect the boundaries between those two activities and to understand the meaning of supervisors' responses to personal issues. For example, if a supervisee reveals that he is distracted by news that his parent has been diagnosed with advanced cancer, a supervisor may discuss the matter with him, show sympathy, and ask whether there is any way in which she can be of assistance. None of those actions involves deep probing into personal issues. (See Neufeldt and Nelson [1999]) for a fuller discussion of this issue.)

What if students do not request counseling or seem unaware of the need for it? Wise, Lowery, and Silverglade (1989) suggest that students' capacity to respond to a supervisor's recommendation to seek counseling may be related to their stage of professional development and trust of the supervisor. They suggest that students who have moved beyond their initial fears of incompetence and focus on specific counseling techniques are more likely to be receptive to such advice.

Layered Supervision

To become a competent supervisor, one must have supervised experience in supervision (along with knowledge and diligence, of course). Graduate programs often provide clinical experience in supervision to advanced students by having them oversee the work of beginning students (Scott, Ingram, Vitanza, & Smith, 2000). Doctoral students commonly supervise master's-level students, for example. In the long run, this practice benefits the profession, the public, and the supervisees. However, it also raises difficulties. For example, when there are several layers of supervision the professionals who have the ultimate responsibility for the client find more distance between them and the client. Their sense of the client's progress is obscured. They must develop careful and consistent data-gathering methods to overcome this weakness. Second, they have responsibilities for the learning of not one, but two supervisees, whose needs, skills, and attitudes may vary significantly. Third, supervisors must be especially alert for compromised confidentiality of client disclosures and violations of client autonomy rights. The more people who hold confidential information, the more likely that inadvertent breaches will occur. Fourth, when supervision is layered, the responsibility for client welfare may be diffused and problems may be missed because each professional assumes another was responsible. The supervisor at the top layer must guard against such a diffusion of responsibility. Finally, as Herlihy and Corey (1996) note, even when layered supervision is carried out within the boundaries of the ethical standards, the experience of being supervised by other students can be uncomfortable. Thus supervisors need to appreciate this discomfort and keep discussion lines open so that those who are ill at ease with the arrangement feel they may voice their concerns and get them resolved.

Distance Supervision

Consider the following situation.

Marsha's Supervision Dilemma

Marsha is a doctoral student in counseling who hopes to complete an internship in a shelter for survivors of domestic violence. This agency has no professional there with the proper credential to supervise her, although there are several highly competent professionals from other disciplines who work at the shelter. Because she is committed to this population and site, Marsha devises an arrangement that she believes will allow her to complete her internship at the agency she wants and still meet all training and licensing requirement. She has set up a distance supervision contract with a highly competent supervisor in her field who lives 100 miles away. Marsha will send audiotapes and videotapes to him weekly, and they will conduct supervision by telephone and by email communication at regular times each week. In all the supervisor has agreed to spend a minimum of 2 hours per week in supervision activities, for which Marsha will reimburse him $50 weekly. The director of the domestic violence shelter has been made aware of this arrangement, has accepted it, and has agreed to allow the supervisor to call her to discuss any clients that he feels Marsha is not serving competently. The state licensing board has also agreed to this arrangement as long as the agency and the supervisor put their arrangement in writing and send them a copy.

In this era of electronic communication and increased disciplinary emphasis on specific supervisor qualifications, such arrangements are likely to become more common. They certainly have advantages. They make a much larger potential pool of qualified supervisors available; they help students obtain the kinds of internship experiences they most desire; and they allow more training experiences in small agencies and underserved areas. But are they advisable from an ethical and legal perspective? They appear to carry several ethical risks, although distance supervision is not prohibited by either the ACA or APA standards. One risk is that the supervisor in this circumstance has no immediate access to Marsha's clients or their records (unless they are stored in computer files that can be transmitted safely), and his capacity to intervene in an emergency is limited. Second, his capacity to evaluate the student's personal or professional limitations that might impede future professional performance is restricted. Marsha can hide from her supervisor information about clients or her behaviors with them that she finds embarrassing or unflattering more easily than she could with an on-site supervisor. Also, as mentioned in Chapter 4, whenever communications via computer are involved, risks to client confidentiality increase, as do the risks of miscommunications in exclusively text-based interactions. Finally, the payment for training supervision could be seen as a multiple relationship that impairs the objectivity of the supervisor and compromises his ability to carry out his gatekeeping responsibilities if Marsha proved to be an incompetent counselor. In short, distance supervision is inadvisable in general and especially at risk for problems when it involves payment for supervision of a trainee. (See Clingerman and Bernard [2004] and Kanz [2001] for a detailed discussion of the perils and promise of supervision via the Internet.)

Legal Aspects of Supervision

Two kinds of legal issues are of special concern to mental health professionals involved in supervision: (a) the liability of supervisors for both their own actions and the actions of supervisees and (b) the legal rights of professionals under supervision.

Liability Issues

The most important legal issue in supervision relates to the degree of liability a supervisor bears for the actions of supervisees. To understand the liability issues, one must begin with the nature of the service a client has a right to expect when working with a supervisee. As Harrar et al. (1990) point out so perceptively, when a client agrees to such counseling, he or she is *not* consenting to substandard or harmful care. The contract implicit in that consent is for the service providers to give competent, helpful service. When that does not occur, clients have been wronged and it is their right to seek redress. Thus, supervisors are liable for their own actions and for the negligent acts of those they supervise. Harrar et al. define the first kind of liability as *direct liability.* It parallels the liability any practicing mental health professional would have in relation to negligence in his or her work. In other words, this form of liability holds when the harm to the client occurred at least partly because the supervisor failed to conduct supervision in accordance with ethical and legal standards. Supervisors may be directly liable under a variety of circumstances, including, but not limited to, the following: failing to meet with supervisees, neglecting important client information that supervisees share with them, or assigning clients to supervisees who are inadequately trained to deal with the clients' concerns.

Vicarious liability also exists for supervisors. The Latin term associated with this concept is *respondeat superior,* and it means "Let the master respond." It means that supervisors may be held liable for the actions of their supervisees even when the supervisors have not been negligent in carrying out their supervisory duties. The term *imputed liability* has the same meaning. The rationale behind this principle is based on the profit supervisors gain from their supervisees and on their power over them. (The term *profit* is defined broadly and need not be monetary.) Because supervisors choose who they will accept as supervisees, regularly decide whether supervisees will be allowed to continue in a professional capacity, and benefit when supervisees perform admirably, the law has reasoned that supervisors ought to share the financial burdens for the misconduct of subordinates (Disney & Stephens, 1994; Harrar et al., 1990). Vicarious liability applies only to actions "within the course and scope of the supervisory relationship" (Disney & Stephens, 1994, p. 15) and is tempered by other factors such as the extent of the supervisor's power over the subordinate, the aspect of the counseling in which the negligence occurred, the particular circumstances of the actions, the motivation of the supervisee, and the likelihood that the supervisor could have reasonably predicted the supervisee's action. Vicarious liability also assumes that the subordinate has voluntarily chosen to be under the supervisor's guidance and direction (Harrar et al., 1990). In short, even exemplary supervisory behavior does not eliminate the risk of vicarious liability. Vicarious liability might occur if a supervisee provides incompetent service to a client but has withheld relevant information about the course of treatment from the supervisor. A supervisor might also be held liable, for example, if a supervisee disclosed confidential information to someone outside the workplace. The Insurance Trust of the National Association of Social Workers (2003) has produced a useful document on reducing the liability risks in supervision.

Given these facts, one may wonder why mental health professionals agree to take on the responsibilities of supervision in the first place. Are they ignorant of the liability issues? Do they value supervision so much that they willingly accept the risk? Do they act grudgingly, feeling there is little alternative? Based on the available evidence, ignorance of this legal standard probably is the most significant factor, but no definitive research exists on that issue. Regardless, supervision is vital to the future of the profession and the provision of quality services is vital to the public. Competent professionals, then, must find ways to minimize their risk. Bernard and Goodyear (2004) recommend that supervisors establish an open, trusting relationship with supervisees so that supervisees are willing to discuss all aspects of their work with clients in supervisory sessions. I would add to that a requirement that supervisees record counseling sessions so that supervisors can hear or see exactly what has transpired in session. Although supervisors may not have the time to review a complete recording of every supervisee session, as long as a tape exists the option is available if needed. Moreover, tapes encourage supervisees to share more fully with supervisors in their discussions, as they recognize that supervisors may learn about the events in counseling through the tape anyway. A comprehensive orientation to the supervision experience that focuses on ethical and legal issues and allows the supervisor to carefully assess supervisee strengths and weaknesses may also reduce the likelihood of subordinate misconduct or client disservice. Finally, Bernard and Goodyear encourage professionals to stay current with legal developments that may affect them and to take special care in documenting supervision when supervisees are acting incompetently. A good record of supervision will at least minimize direct liability. Liability insurance for supervisors is also in order. It does not prevent problems, but it may reassure professionals that their financial resources are not vulnerable to a lawsuit.

Due Process Rights

When working in public institutions, supervisees have the same due process rights against unfair government action as do other citizens. These rights derive from the Fourteenth Amendment to the U.S. Constitution and prevent states from taking actions against individuals without giving them notice and opportunity to oppose such action. Those who work for private organizations have due process rights if the policies and procedures of the organization stipulate them. Many private universities, hospitals, and community agencies recognize this right. Applied to supervision, this means that the supervisee has a legal right to supervisory feedback, periodic evaluations, and opportunities to file grievances about actions they think have been unfair. Bernard and Goodyear (2004) argue that some of the most egregious violations of trainees' due process rights occur when they receive negative final evaluations without any prior warning that their performance is significantly substandard. To avoid such violations, they advise professionals to periodically communicate negative performance evaluations in specific terms that include the changes that would be deemed adequate performance. Such an action prevents misunderstanding about how much improvement is sufficient for success. Due process rights are meant to protect supervisees from arbitrary action based on incomplete, irrelevant, or untrue evidence. Such rights do not mean that all supervisees have the right to a passing grade or a positive evaluation; the duty of the supervisor is also to protect the public from incompetent professionals. Instead, due process suggests that supervisors must be sensitive to the implications of negative findings on those they oversee and must ensure that negative judgments are fair and appropriate.

Guest and Dooley (1999) discuss the issue of whether supervisors can be held liable for actions toward supervisees that do not directly harm clients. Can they be sued for malpractice if they failed a student without prior warning, made disrespectful statements about a student, or insisted on doing therapy with a supervisee? These scholars argue that a duty of care probably exists and that a supervisee may be able to meet the other standards for a successful malpractice suit based on such actions. Bernard and Goodyear (2004) point out, however, that no such lawsuits have been brought to court to date.

Relations with Third-Party Payors

Frequently, clients of unlicensed supervisees are submitting the costs of their care for reimbursement by insurers, who before providing payment usually require evidence that the supervisee is supervised by a licensed mental health professional. Some unscrupulous but energetic supervisors have used this mechanism to increase their incomes. The most egregious cases have involved supervisors overseeing the work of dozens of supervisees and submitting the claims as though they themselves had provided the service (Harrar et al., 1990). As already mentioned, supervision under these conditions fails to meet the standard for competent oversight and thereby violates ethical rules. If it also deceives the third-party payor about the nature of the service provided, the practice is likely to be illegal, too, as a form of insurance fraud. Neither private insurers nor government agencies allow this behavior. In fact, they have aggressively pursued legal action against serious violators. For all these reasons, supervisors are cautioned to be exceedingly cautious about practices that may be inconsistent with guidelines and contracts and to educate those they oversee about the proper methods for submitting claims.

SUMMARY

When people take on supervisory responsibilities, they must keep in mind a number of ethical obligations and legal duties. Not only must they demonstrate competence to supervise as well as competence to practice, they must also guard the rights of the supervisee to a beneficial learning experience with fair and appropriate feedback about performance. Even more important than the progress of the trainee, however, is the welfare of the clients served by the trainee. A supervisor holds both ethical and legal responsibility for clients' welfare, and when the needs of the supervisee conflict with those of the clients, the codes mandate that clients' concerns take precedence. The legal requirement to care for the client stems from the client's right to competent service regardless of the counselor's level of training.

Supervisors are also ethically bound not to engage in activities that exploit their supervisees. They are especially cautioned to avoid sexual contact, insensitivity to issues of diversity, and introjection of personal values into the professional relationship. Supervisors who fail to act responsibly themselves, or who have supervisees who act unethically, are held liable for the consequences. The latter principle is called *vicarious liability*. Similarly, those who violate the due process rights of trainees or clients' rights to confidentiality can be held legally responsible for those failures. Finally, supervisors need to be attuned to their legal and ethical obligations when working with third-party payors and to be scrupulously accurate about reporting services rendered by supervisees.

CASES FOR DISCUSSION

Bart is widely regarded as the most talented supervisor and clinician in the community mental health center where he works. He usually supervises several interns who learn a great deal from him and express great satisfaction with the process and outcome of their experiences in supervision. Bart also has a part-time private practice. A number of former interns have sought Bart out for counseling when they needed support. In fact, former interns and their friends and loved ones have come to represent about 25% of Bart's caseload. He finds therapy with these clients a rewarding and productive endeavor. Consequently, after students successfully complete their internship Bart distributes his business card to

each intern in the event that they want to contact him in the future. Are any of Bart's actions here in violation of the code of ethics of ACA or the ACES guidelines? If you were in Bart's position, would you also distribute your cards to graduating interns? If not, what would you do if a former intern asked to see you in counseling?

Philip is a school counseling intern at a middle school. One of his clients has a number of bruises on her arms and legs. When asked, the girl cannot account for the bruises—she just shrugs her shoulders and says, "I don't know." Philip reports this client's injuries to Vivian, his supervisor, and he tells her he plans to call the child abuse hotline. Vivian suggests that no report is necessary because her case is already under investigation for a different injury that was reported to them by the child's teacher 2 weeks ago. At first, Philip is surprised by his supervisor's advice, but then he decides that she must be correct and does not report this new incident. Should Philip have made a report anyway? Did Vivian meet her ethical and legal responsibilities as a supervisor? If a complaint was filed against Philip for his inaction here, could he defend himself by saying that he was an intern following his supervisor's recommendation?

DISCUSSION QUESTIONS

1. Many current supervisors indicate that they have had little formal training in supervision. Given the standards you have read, how would you address this problem? Should such training be mandated? Should there be a test for supervision? What other ideas do you have?

2. A substantial minority of supervisors in one study referred to supervisees as "friends." Some strongly believed that their personal connection to the trainee enhanced rather than compromised their supervision. Is there any merit to that view? If you were consulting with them about this issue, how would you respond?

3. What do you believe is the ethically ideal way for a supervisor to respond to a sincere, well-motivated, but incompetent performance by an intern? How long should a supervisor allow an intern whose interactions with clients are unsatisfactory to continue to try to improve?

RECOMMENDED READINGS

Bernard, J. M., & Goodyear, R. K. (2004). *Fundamentals of clinical supervision* (3rd ed.). Boston: Allyn & Bacon.

Disney, M. J., & Stephens, A. M. (1994). Legal issues in clinical supervision. In T. P. Remley (Ed.)., *ACA Legal Series* (Vol. 8). Alexandria, VA: American Counseling Association.

Falender, C. A., & Shafranske, E. P. (2004). *Clinical supervision: A competency based approach.* Washington, DC: American Psychological Association.

Falvey, J. E. (2002a). *Managing clinical supervision: Ethical practice and legal risk management.* Pacific Grove, CA: Brooks/Cole.

Ladany, N. (2004). Psychotherapy supervision: What lies beneath. *Psychotherapy Research, 14,* 1–19.

Ladany, N., Lehman-Waterman, D., Molinaro, M., & Wolgart, B. (1999). Psychotherapy supervisor ethical practices, working alliance, and supervisee satisfaction. *The Counseling Psychologist, 27,* 443–475.

Chapter 14

Counselors as Teachers and Researchers
Integrity, Science, and Care

Many counselors and counseling psychologists are involved in training the next generation of professionals and in research to advance the science of the profession. The central ethical issues embedded in these activities mirror those of direct service: competence, responsible use of power, and promotion of the welfare of those in their care. This chapter discusses how each obligation is met when teaching and conducting research.

The Ethics of Teaching

Our society views teachers ambivalently. On the one hand, they are held in high regard: "What office is there which involves more responsibility, which requires more qualifications, and which ought, therefore, to be more honourable, than that of teaching?" (Martineau, 1837). On the other hand, they are viewed with disdain and distrust: "He who can, does. He who cannot, teaches" (Shaw, 1903). Even those who see some value in teaching are concerned about its potential for abuse: "A teacher should have maximal authority, and minimal power" (Szasz, 1973). This ambivalence stems partly from the high hopes that citizens have for education and partly from their frequent disappointments over unrealized hopes. The enterprise of teaching others to be effective counselors and therapists is also fraught with potential for good or ill. When good occurs, the next generation is entrusted with the wisdom of the past and provided the skills to extend it, and when bad happens, either incompetent people are admitted to the profession, or qualified people are discouraged from it. Szasz's wish to contain the power of the teacher cannot be realized, however. Instead, the task of the profession is to ensure that its teachers use their power responsibly.

Unfortunately, the literature on the ethics of training mental health professionals is not as abundant as the publications on ethics in counseling, but there are still valuable resources available. Several experts have addressed the issue, the recent versions of the ethics codes speak to this activity, and some empirical studies have been conducted. The central ethical issues in this body of literature deal with competence to teach; the responsible use of power; the management of multiple and sometimes conflicting role obligations; and the duties to the profession, the students, and the public.

Competence to Teach

Faculty who teach counselors and therapists ought first to be competent practitioners. In addition, they must be knowledgeable about their subject matter, prepared for their work, and committed to facilitating student learning. Nearly all psychology faculty acknowledge occasional incidences of inadequate preparation for classes, but the number who admit sometimes teaching material they have not mastered is also surprisingly high—38% (Tabachnick, Keith-Spiegel, & Pope, 1991). The percentage of counselor educators who report teaching material for which they are not competent is almost identical—36%, according to Schwab and Neukrug (1994). Faculty also have a responsibility to present information fairly and to distinguish between personal opinions and established theory and research. In the same survey, nearly 4% admitted bias in teaching is a frequent practice. The obligation to stay current in a rapidly changing discipline is especially important. Tabachnick et al. (1991) found uneven compliance with this standard. In that study, 36% of teaching psychologists admitted teaching a course without updating lecture notes.

When teaching content for which scientific support is scarce, that limitation needs to be clearly stated. Cutting-edge, speculative, or experimental material should be labeled as such. This recommendation does not mean that faculty must curtail their presentations to long-established constructs, but it does suggest that students should be informed about the distinction between concepts in the mainstream of professional thinking and those too new or speculative to be widely accepted. For example, in discussing innovative therapeutic techniques such as eye movement desensitization and reprocessing (EMDR) (Herbert & Mueser, 1992; Shapiro, 1995), faculty should give students a sense of both the promise and the limitations of the technique, including review of the research evidence and its limitations (for example, Hubert, Lillenfeld, Lohr, Montgomery, O'Donoghue, Rosen, & Tolin, 2000; Spector & Read, 1999). Professors who keep in mind the ultimate goal of teaching—to educate practitioners who will be capable of making objective, informed, independent judgments about the merits of innovations—will be better equipped to make wise decisions about such matters. If there is substantial debate about the merits of a particular theory or method, both sides of the argument should be presented. This guideline does not imply that faculty need to hide their own perspectives from students. Showing students the rationale for one's personal assessments about unsettled issues in the profession can help students develop appropriate criteria for making similar judgments themselves. However, neither demeaning others who hold different views nor dismissing the valid positions of others is consistent with ethical standards. Following is the American Psychological Association's (APA) statement on this subject.

APA *Ethical Principles,* Section 7.03: Accuracy in Teaching

(a) Psychologists take reasonable steps to ensure that course syllabi are accurate regarding the subject matter to be covered, bases for evaluating progress, and the nature of course experiences. This standard does not preclude an instructor from modifying course content or requirements when the instructor considers it pedagogically necessary or desirable, so long as students are made aware of these modifications in a manner that enables them to fulfill course requirements. (b) When engaged in teaching or training, psychologists present psychological information accurately.

The American Counseling Association (ACA) limits its attention to the responsibility of the counselor educator when discussing innovative methods:

ACA *Code of Ethics,* Section F.6.f: Innovative Theories and Techniques

When counselor educators teach counseling techniques/procedures that are innovative, without an empirical foundation, or without a well-grounded theoretical foundation, they define the counseling techniques/procedures as "unproven" or "developing" and explain to students the potential risks and ethical considerations of using such techniques/procedures.

In some universities faculty are asked to teach courses not directly related to their research and teaching expertise. When such requests are made, faculty must evaluate whether they can perform competently, just as practitioners need to judge whether a particular activity falls within their boundaries of competence. If a subject falls outside their areas of competence, they must decline to teach it unless they can obtain continuing education beforehand. The statement from the ethics codes on working within the boundaries of one's competence apply equally to teaching and therapy. (See Section C.2.a of the ACA code and Section 2.01 of the APA code.)

Frequently, graduate students in counseling and psychology serve as teaching assistants or instructors in undergraduate or master's-level courses (Branstetter & Handelsman, 2000). However, most had no formal instruction in teaching effectiveness and no coursework in professional ethics prior to teaching, but still less than half of the teaching assistants they surveyed had ever received any supervision for their teaching (Branstetter & Handelsman, 2000). Not surprisingly, then, in one survey 90% of undergraduates reported witnessing unethical behavior by psychology graduate assistants (Fly, van Bark, Weinman, Kitchener, & Long, 1997). The APA standards (Section 2.05) require professionals to train subordinates appropriately and oversee the work of those to whom they are delegating responsibility. Clearly, this evidence shows that compliance with these standards is low.

Responsible Use of Power

As discussed in relation to supervision and in Chapter 6, sexual harassment, sexual exploitation, and related abuse of the less powerful position of students happen rather frequently in graduate programs in counseling and psychology. In published research, the mean percentage of faculty who admit sexual contact with students is 8.8%. In one study, almost one-third of female psychology graduate students reported incidents of sexual harassment (Glaser & Thorpe, 1986). In another study, psychology internship directors singled out faculty–student sexual contact as a continuing blind spot for those who teach (Welfel, 1992), a finding echoed in a study of mental health counselors and social workers by Barnett-Queen and Larrabee (2000). These researchers reported that 1.8% of the sample had sexual contact with educators during their training. The attention sexual harassment has received in the media does not seem to have eliminated the problem because even recent researchers found 11.7% of students experiencing harassment (Mintz, Rideout, & Bartells, 1994) or sexual advances (6.8%) (Barnett-Queen & Larrabee, 2000). In the latter study, counseling students experienced sexual advances at approximately twice the rate of social work students—9.5% of counselors in comparison to 4% of social workers.

Blevins-Knabe (1992) offers some insights into the reasons sexual harassment occurs in higher education. She suggests that faculty are blind to the implications of their actions, a hypothesis supported by the findings of Kolbert, Morgan, and Brendel (2002), which show that students have more negative reactions to faculty-student multiple relationships than faculty have. Faculty tend to perceive their behavior as friendly and supportive and are reluctant to admit its sexual motivation, but students find it harassing. Sometimes both faculty and students are willing participants in sexual relationships. When sexual relationships are consensual, Blevins-Knabe believes that shared professional interests, personal insecurities in the students, unresolved personal issues in faculty, and sex role socialization factors all are influential. It is interesting, however, when viewed in retrospect, that neither faculty nor students perceive "consensual" relationships as freely chosen or beneficial to the personal or professional development of e ither party (Glaser & Thorpe, 1986; Miller & Larrabee, 1995; Pope, Levenson, & Schover, 1979; Robinson & Reid, 1985). There are also effects on other students who hear discussion of sexual advances by faculty to their peers. Adams, Kottke, and Padgit (1983) reported that 13% of female students and 3% of male students tried to avoid working with faculty known or rumored to have made sexual advances to other students. Rubin, Hampton, and McManus (1997) found that women students were especially uncomfortable with sexually harassing behaviors. Of course, some faculty prey on vulnerable students and are exclusively motivated by self-interest, but others initiate sexual contact because of personal dissatisfactions, life crises, or neurotic tendencies. None of these reasons justifies such involvement. The current ethics codes are the first to explicitly forbid sexual contact with current students (ACA, Section F.10.a; APA, Section 7.07). Thus, faculty need to set clear boundaries in their relationships with students and seek out professional assistance when tempted to make sexual advances. (The consideration of a sexual relationship with a student is rather common; Lamb, Catanzaro, and Moorman (2004) found that a majority of the psychologists they surveyed—54%—had entertained that thought.)

Sexual contact is not the only abuse of faculty power, nor is it probably the most common. Faculty sometimes exploit students' needs for professional success and clinical or research experience as well. They also abuse their power when they discriminate on the basis of characteristics unrelated to academic performance and when they fail to be sensitive to the implications of their decisions on students' or colleagues' futures. Following are some examples of such abuses.

Professor Yelter's Grading Procedures

Professor Yelter assigns research topics to students in her course according to the content areas she needs to include in her book in progress. The topics for some of these papers are only peripherally related to course content, and students have no option to change topics. When the papers are submitted, she attends only to the quality of the reference list, rather than the analysis of the topic. She grades according to the potential usefulness of the students' work to her book.

Dr. Marsher's Classroom Style

Dr. Marsher encourages discussion in his classes. When many students have raised their hands to respond to an issue he has offered for discussion, he almost always acknowledges male students first. In addition, he is more likely to give male students time to develop their thoughts and respond to differing perspectives. His typical interaction with female students is briefer and less patient.

Professor Pastione's Research Projects

Doctoral students assigned to Professor Pastione soon learn that if they wish to receive a positive letter of recommendation from her after they graduate, they should volunteer to help her with her research projects. If they are involved in other faculty research or do not have the time to volunteer for Professor Pastione, they ought to find another adviser because she will not support them, no matter what their other competencies or experiences.

In the first case, Professor Yelter is using students in the class as unpaid, unacknowledged research assistants. Moreover, she is placing her own interests ahead of their learning and providing them with no viable alternative to the plan she has established. Such an action is contrary to the ethical principles of beneficence and respect for autonomy. It is also inconsistent with the sections of the codes that require faculty to "conduct training programs in an ethical manner and serve as role models for professional behavior" (ACA, *Code of Ethics,* Section F.6.a), to give students credit for research contributions (ACA, *Code of Ethics,* Section G.5.d), and to avoid exploitive relationships (APA, *Ethical Principles,* Section 3.08). Dr. Yelter's ethical problems do not end there. Her behavior also violates the stipulations in the codes dealing with objectivity in assessment.

APA *Ethical Principles*, Section 7.06(b): Assessing Student and Supervisee Performance
Psychologists evaluate students and supervisees on the basis of their actual performance on relevant and established program requirements.

Needless to say, Professor Yelter ought to stop this practice, assign topics directly related to course content, and use fair and objective grading criteria. If she needs research assistance with her project, she should hire someone. If a student elects to volunteer for that job to gain experience, that arrangement would also be ethical provided the student's efforts were acknowledged and other forms of exploitation were avoided. She also could benefit from remedial education about the power she holds over students who may not feel free to challenge her requirements or question their grades. Her current actions stand in direct opposition to acting as an appropriate professional role model.

Dr. Marsher is engaging in gender bias. This behavior is inappropriate because it gives unfair advantage to some students on the basis of a characteristic irrelevant to professional competence or performance. It violates sections of the code that proscribe discrimination. Dr. Marsher may be unaware of this aspect of his behavior, but his ignorance does not excuse it. Students taking his courses may feel unable to communicate their experience to him for fear of retribution. Once grades are submitted, however, those who will not be participating in additional courses with Dr. Marsher are ideal candidates to address the matter, through course evaluations, conversations with the professor, or discussions with other faculty in the program. Needless to say, if other faculty learn of this behavior, they too have an obligation to address it with Dr. Marsher, assuming that the student involved does not object to such an approach.

The essence of Professor Pastione's ethical problem is the way in which she has transformed a basic obligation of her position, the writing of letters of recommendation, into a "service for sale" in exchange for labor on her projects. Students willing to work "earn" a positive evaluation, apparently without regard for their actual capacities as counselors. This practice not only exploits students' vulnerabilities, it also violates a professor's obligation to ensure that only competent students are admitted into the profession. The ACA code is quite explicit on this issue, although it substitutes the term *endorsement* for *recommendation*.

ACA *Code of Ethics*, Section F.5.d: Endorsement
Supervisors only endorse supervisees for certification, licensure, employment, or completion of an academic or training program only when they believe supervisees are qualified for the endorsement. Regardless of qualifications, supervisors do not endorse supervisees they believe to be impaired in any way that would interfere with the performance of the duties associated with the endorsement.

Professor Pastione has also violated her duty to respect autonomy and avoid harm to those she oversees. Unless assisting this faculty member with her research is an explicit condition of admission or continuation in the doctoral program that is fully disclosed in writing at the time of application, her demand violates students' rights to informed consent to educational procedures. However, as long as Professor Pastione uses research assistance as the "*quid pro quo*" of evaluation, no degree of informed consent could transform her behavior into an ethically acceptable practice.

ACA *Code of Ethics*, Section F.7: Student Welfare
a. Orientation. Counselor educators recognize that orientation is a developmental process that continues throughout the educational and clinical training of students. Counseling faculty provide prospective students with information about the counselor education program's expectations: (1) the type and level of skill and knowledge acquisition required for successful completion of the training; (2) program

training goals, objectives, and mission, and subject matter to be covered; (3) bases for evaluation; (4) training components that encourage self-growth or self-disclosure as part of the training process; (5) the type of supervision settings and requirements of the sites for required clinical field experiences; (6) student and supervisee evaluation and dismissal policies and procedures; and (7) up-to-date employment prospects for graduates.

APA's *Ethical Principles* communicate the same position in Section 7.02 but with greater economy of language. In addition, Professor Pastione harms students in several ways. Those who reject participation in her project, unaware of the consequences, are injured by the unexpected and unfair endorsement they receive. Other students may not have the luxury of working for free, needing to support themselves through graduate school. The professor's practice may even cause harm to those who get an undeserved positive reference. Students whose talents lie in another field are not necessarily better off for earning a credential they do not deserve. In the long run, these students may be better helped by learning at this stage that they are sufficiently competent in counseling. The pain in that event may be significantly less than the pain of a malpractice suit, lost positions, or other problems that stem from incompetence in professional service. Even more important, Professor Pastione may be harming the public served by these ineffective students. The solution? Obviously, Professor Pastione must stop this practice, recruit research assistants in a more appropriate fashion, and base comments in letters of evaluation on actual performance. She should also seek to redress the wrongs she has done in past letters of reference, sending revised copies to students for future use.

None of these faculty is adhering to the opening section of ACA's standards for counselor educators because none is acting as positive role models for students:

ACA *Code of Ethics,* Section F.6: Responsibilities of Counselor Educators

a. Counselor Educators. Counselor educators who are responsible for developing, implementing, and supervising educational programs are skilled as teachers and practitioners. They are knowledgeable regarding the ethical, legal, and regulatory aspects of the profession, are skilled in applying that knowledge, and make students and supervisees aware of their responsibilities. Counselor educators conduct counselor education and training programs in an ethical manner and serve as role models for professional behavior.

Neglect of Responsibilities: Another Form of Misuse of Power

Keith-Spiegel (1994) makes a point about psychology educators that applies to faculty in related professions. The mandate to avoid harm is more complex to interpret in the teacher role than in the role of counselor or therapist. Clearly, a teacher wishes not to cause harm to students, but when students' work is substandard or their attitude is irresponsible, a teacher's concern about harm to students must be balanced against his or her duty to the clients whom the student may serve and the reputation of the profession. As discussed in Chapter 3, admitting people who are unable or unwilling to abide by professional standards does not inspire public trust. Thus, faculty who fail to prevent unqualified people from practicing are overlooking one of their major responsibilities. The goal of faculty is, of course, to help all students meet the standards set for competence, but when that fails, they must not accept unqualified people. Again, the ACA code speaks to this issue directly, specifying procedures for dealing with student deficiencies.

ACA *Code of Ethics,* Section F.9.b: Limitations

Counselor educators, throughout ongoing evaluation and appraisal, are aware of and address the inability of some students to achieve counseling competencies that might impede performance.

Counselor educators: (1) assist students in securing remedial assistance when needed, (2) seek professional consultation and document their decision to dismiss or refer students for assistance and (3) ensure that students have recourse in a timely manner to address decisions made to require them to seek assistance or to dismiss them, and provide students with due process, according to institutional policies and procedures.

The following case exemplifies a common ethical failure to meet this standard.

Dr. Dorian's Dilemma

Dr. Dorian is an untenured faculty member who hopes to achieve tenure in a few years. In his university, competent teaching and good relationships with students figure prominently in tenure review. Dr. Dorian has a student in counseling practicum whose performance is unsatisfactory. His substantial efforts to help this student to improve his performance have been fruitless. Moreover, the student does not seem to understand the limits of his competence and tends to take on cases for which he is unqualified. Dr. Dorian believes this student ought not to pass practicum, but he also fears that this vocal and well-connected student will file a grievance over a failing grade and attempt to focus the attention of university administrators on his situation. In light of the complications a failing grade will cause for him, Dr. Dorian decides to pass this student.

To comply with the ethical standards, Dr. Dorian should record the grade he believes the student earned, despite the discomfort that may ensue. If Dr. Dorian has graded fairly, communicated the poor performance to the student, and documented his repeated interventions to help the student remediate his problems, responding to a grievance or other inquiry is not difficult. In most universities students must demonstrate that grading procedures were arbitrary or discriminatory—a rather difficult standard to meet. It seems that Dr. Dorian's anxiety about tenure is overriding his judgment. At a deeper level, Dr. Dorian may think ethical behavior is a matter of convenience. When standards are easy to follow, he may willingly comply, but when compliance causes him personal discomfort, he breaks the rules. Such behavior is unprofessional.

Other violations of this standard are not so blatant. Some derive from a good-hearted desire on the part of faculty to help all students reach their full potential. This aim is admirable and ought to be a guidepost for faculty behavior. It becomes problematic, however, when students who do not perform competently are allowed to progress. Faculty cannot lose sight of their obligations to such students' potential clients. In this situation, faculty ought to focus on helping students redirect their career goals if remediation efforts fail. At other times, overcrowded classes make careful assessment of each student's competencies difficult. Faculty overwhelmed by their teaching load, research responsibilities, and administrative demands may succumb to giving all students "the benefit of the doubt" rather than engage in the difficult task before them. Neither overwork nor compassion for an individual student are sufficient justifications for actions that defy a professional standard, although 10% of psychology faculty admitted that the likeability of a student had influenced their grading (Tabachnick et al., 1991).

In one study exploring why psychology faculty sometimes ignore cheating, Keith-Spiegel, Tabachnick, Whitley, and Washburn (1998) found that most often faculty feel the evidence is insufficient to confirm the dishonesty, but several less rational reasons also play a part. For example, faculty say that sometimes reporting feels too stressful, takes more courage than they have, involves more effort than they want to expend, and results in retaliation or legal challenges they want to avoid. Others rationalized that cheating students would probably fail the course anyway and that only the inexperienced cheaters not the chronic offenders are likely to get caught. None of these reasons justifies failing to confront incidences of academic dishonesty by students in mental health disciplines. Those who cut corners by cheating may be at risk for taking other unethical actions with clients and colleagues when they complete their degrees. In a more recent study, Vacha-Hasse, Davenport, and Kerewsky (2004) reported that most psychology training programs (52%) in their sample do dismiss at least one student every 3 years, but an almost equal percentage (54%) did not have written guidelines for intervening with problematic students.

The fear of a lawsuit challenging their judgment or right to fail or dismiss a student is a real concern of some faculty, and it appears as a real barrier to the initiation of dismissal procedures for students who are problematic (Vacha-Hasse, 1995; Vacha-Hasse et al., 2004). This anxiety has little rational basis. As long as faculty have clear evidence of unsatisfactory performance in academic or clinical courses, the courts have been supportive of their judgments (Remley & Herlihy, 2005). Approximately 80% of students who experience dismissal do not contest the program's actions (Vacha-Hasse et al., 2004). Many faculty prefer to counsel students who are unsuccessful in mastering the requisite content and skills into alternative careers (Forrest, Elman, Gizara, & Vacha-Haase, 1999). Such a course of action protects the student's privacy and saves him or her from embarrassment. When students are dismissed from a program they have all the due process rights to a fair hearing of their concerns that they have in internship (Kaplin & Lee, 1995; Kerl, Garcia, McCullough, & Maxwell, 2002). (See Chapter 13 for a discussion of trainee due process rights.)

Distinguishing Mentoring from Problematic Dual Relationships

Faculty and students often have several different kinds of professional contacts. A student may serve as research assistant, pupil in a class, collaborator on a manuscript, and supervisee in practicum seminar to the same faculty member simultaneously. Consecutive involvement in multiple roles is even more common with students and faculty. For example, one of my former research assistants was simultaneously a teaching intern under my supervision and a collaborator on a manuscript in preparation. Before that she had been enrolled in clinical practicum, academic courses, and independent studies with me. Were either of us acting unethically? Many would see no ethical dimension to our multiple types of interaction. In fact, multifaceted and prolonged connections between faculty and students, usually termed *mentoring relationships,* are often viewed as desirable, both by scholars and by the parties involved (Bowman, Bowman, & DeLucia, 1990; Bowman, Hatley, & Bowman, 1995; Schweibert, 2000). Some scholars associate mentoring with higher student achievement, satisfaction, and persistence in academic programs (for example, see Bean & Kuh, 1984). Mentoring relationships are very common in graduate study in psychology; research shows that 67% of graduate students in psychology report that they had mentors during their degree programs and the overwhelming majority (91%) were satisfied with them (Clark, Harden, & Johnson, 2000).

Still, some ethics scholars have expressed caution about multiple connections with students and their risks (Johnson & Nelson, 1999; Kitchener, 1992; Warren, 2005). Clark et al. (2000) reported that 2% of mentors had sexualized their relationships with students. Mentoring can blur the objectivity of the professional, incur jealousy or misunderstanding in other students (Bowman et al., 1995), and make other boundaries that ought to be observed harder to maintain. For instance, faculty working closely with students may begin to use students as confidants about personal matters, socialize extensively with those students, or otherwise forget the distinction between professional and personal relationships. When students become more like friends than students, faculty may have difficulty honoring their responsibilities as gatekeepers in the profession. The power imbalance in the relationship cannot be ignored either because it diminishes the reciprocity that characterizes ordinary friendships. In most cases, the faculty member probably feels freer than the student to express feelings, ask favors, or seek emotional support. At some level, the student is aware that the faculty member has tremendous influence over his or her future. For these reasons the codes caution professionals to honor boundaries (ACA, *Code of Ethics*, Sections F.10.d and F.10.f.; APA *Ethical Principles*, Section 3.05). The two criteria used in the APA code to evaluate the advisability of a particular multiple relationship are worth reviewing here. A multiple relationship is inappropriate when it would impair the professional's objectivity or might harm or exploit the other person. ACA allows for a multiple relationship when it appears to benefit the student.

ACA *Code of Ethics*, Section F.10.f: Potentially Beneficial Relationships

Counselor educators are aware of the power differential in the relationship between faculty and students. If they believe a nonprofessional relationship with a student may be potentially beneficial to the student, they take precautions similar to those taken by counselors when working with clients. Examples of potentially beneficial interactions or relationships include, but are not limited to, attending a formal ceremony; hospital visits; providing support during a stressful event; or mutual membership in a professional association, organization, or community. Counselor educators engage in open discussions with students when they consider entering into relationships with students outside of their roles as teachers and supervisors. They discuss with students the rationale for such interactions, the potential benefits and drawbacks, and the anticipated consequences for the student. Educators clarify the specific nature and limitations of the additional role(s) they will have with the student prior to engaging in a nonprofessional relationship. Nonprofessional relationships with students should be time-limited and initiated with student consent.

Honoring boundaries is a rather abstract term. In relation to faculty–student relationships, I believe it means:

- Refraining from using the student as a confidant about personal matters or about matters of frustration with colleagues.
- Ensuring that the bulk of the time spent together focuses on professional rather than personal issues. Friendly interactions are certainly not to be avoided, but a preponderance of talk about social events is inadvisable. (One should keep in mind that in virtually all interactions, the goal of the student is to learn from the faculty member.)
- Declining repeated one-on-one social engagements in favor of group events.
- Setting limits to exploration of personal stresses or dilemmas that the student is experiencing, or referring the student to another counselor, just as one ought to do as a clinical supervisor.
- Refusing a mentoring relationship with relatives or with students with whom one has had a prior or ongoing personal relationship.
- Clarifying the parameters of the relationship and the roles at the onset so that both student and faculty member understand the nature of the interaction and the relevant contents of the ethics codes.
- Making mentoring activities available to all qualified students, with awareness that students from culturally diverse populations may have less access to mentors than other students.
- Consulting with colleagues periodically about mentoring issues so that one can deal with minor problems and receive external feedback about the relationship.
- Allowing students who wish to withdraw from a mentoring relationship to do so with dignity and without retribution.

Using these criteria and the decision-making model from Chapter 2, consider the ethics of the following situations.

Faculty–Student Multiple Relationships

A graduate student runs a house-painting service in the summer. She uses the earnings from this business to fund her education for a doctoral degree. A faculty member who notices a flyer advertising her business on a bulletin board contracts with the student to have his house painted next summer. The student will be enrolling in his group therapy course the following fall.

A faculty member has a part-time psychotherapy practice. She asks an especially talented student, who has recently graduated, to join the practice.

A student's family has lost everything they owned in Hurricane Katrina. Because her parents had been funding her education and are no longer in a position to do so, she fears she will not be able to continue enrollment next quarter. She has applied for financial aid but is unlikely to receive the aid in time for registration. Her advisor, on hearing of her situation, writes her a check for next quarter's tuition, telling her she can repay the loan when her financial aid gets straightened out.

A professor's car is out of service. One of the students in his class lives nearby. The professor asks that student for a ride to campus the next day.

Bowman et al. (1995) surveyed students and faculty to ascertain their views on the ethics of several kinds of multiple relationships. They included vignettes dealing with social, monetary, mentoring, and sexual contacts. As expected, virtually all respondents found sexual contacts inappropriate, but there was little unanimity in other responses. No more than three-fourths of the sample came to agreement on the ethics of faculty who hire students to baby-sit, maintain a concurrent friendship with a student, or have students as primary social contacts, or keep silent from other faculty a student's slur against homosexuals made in a social setting. This disparity in response speaks to several issues, including the general lack of attention this topic has received in the professional literature, the abstractness of the codes on this matter, and the conflict in professional and personal obligations. In other words, both faculty and students seem to recognize the complexity of ethical decision making in this area and the degree to which a particular activity must be evaluated in its context. The survey by Tabachnick and her associates (1991) suggests similar uncertainty about the ethics of nonsexual faculty–student contacts. Nearly 49% labeled asking a student for a small favor (such as a ride home) as ethical under many or all circumstances, and 37% saw it as rarely or never ethical. Similarly, 29% of faculty viewed lending students money as ethical in most or all situations, but 50% held a contrary view.

Faculty who are tempted to take rigid stances in opposition to all forms of multiple connections with students are probably overreacting to the risks and sidestepping their ethical obligation to foster the development of their students. Lloyd (1992) has remarked that some faculty seem to have a "mentoring phobia." Although that characterization seems strongly worded (and inconsistent with research evidence), it does put a name to the discomfort and worry some faculty feel about their relationships with graduate students. Careful consideration of ethical guidelines, and the preceding criteria for managing multiple professional contacts, should reduce the risks of such relationships without compromising their potential benefits. (Those who seek examples of other hypothetic cases that have ethical dimensions should refer to Keith-Spiegel, Wittig, Perkins, Balogh, and Whitley, 1993.)

Personal Growth Experiences for Students

The emotional stability of the mental health professional is crucial to the success of counseling. Many ethics complaints result from character flaws, neurotic tendencies, or other deficiencies in coping with personal stresses. Many students that educators identify as impaired are emotionally unstable or unsuited for clinical work (Forrest et al., 1999). For these reasons counselor educators have a duty to ensure that students have the emotional stability and temperament for the profession and that the personal issues that may be impeding their effectiveness are identified and resolved. Accreditation standards also mandate that training programs ensure that graduates are emotionally stable enough to be competent to work with clients.

Experiences that increase empathy with clients, give students opportunities to "walk in clients' shoes," and involve students in experimental learning are all valued by mental health professions as crucial teaching tools in the training process. These same experiences also help students become aware of the ways in which their own emotions, defenses, and coping strategies affect their capacity to work effectively with clients. Thus many programs interweave personal growth experiences in the curriculum (Merta, Wolfgang, & McNeil, 1993). In counseling labs students frequently practice counseling skills on each other, in group classes they engage in group experiences, and in testing courses they often take the psychological tests they are studying. The inclusion of such personal growth experiences has been controversial, partly because it pits a student's right to privacy against the profession's responsibility to admit only competent professionals to the field (Corey, Corey, & Callanan, 2003). Counselor educators have divided views of the ethics of such experiences (Schwab & Neukrug, 1994). Students express both positive and negative attitudes toward such experiences, believing that they are important teaching tools but worrying that such experiences will push them into uncomfortable levels of personal disclosure or relationships with faculty (Anderson & Price, 2001). The ACA code has provided standards for such experiences so that professionals can adequately balance competing ethical values.

ACA *Code of Ethics,* Section F.7.b: Self-Growth Experiences

Counselor education programs delineate requirements for self-disclosure or self-growth experiences in their admission and program materials. Counselor educators use professional judgment when designing training experiences they conduct that require student and supervisee selfgrowth or self-disclosure. Students and supervisees are made aware of the ramifications their self-disclosure may have when counselors whose primary role as teacher, trainer, or supervisor requires acting on ethical obligations to the profession. Evaluative components of experiential training experiences explicitly delineate predetermined academic standards that are separate and do not depend on the student's level of selfdisclosure. Counselor educators may require trainees to seek professional help to address any personal concerns that may be affecting their competency.

In its 2002 revision of the APA *Ethical Principles,* the following language was used.

7.04 Student Disclosure of Personal Information

Psychologists do not require students or supervisees to disclose personal information in course- or program-related activities, either orally or in writing, regarding sexual history, history of abuse and neglect, psychological treatment, and relationships with parents, peers, and spouses or significant others except if (1) the program or training facility has clearly identified this requirement in its admissions and program materials or (2) the information is necessary to evaluate or obtain assistance for students whose personal problems could reasonably be judged to be preventing them from performing their training- or professionally related activities in a competent manner or posing a threat to the students or others.

7.05 Mandatory Individual or Group Therapy

(a) When individual or group therapy is a program or course requirement, psychologists responsible for that program allow students in undergraduate and graduate programs the option of selecting such therapy from practitioners unaffiliated with the program.

(b) Faculty who are or are likely to be responsible for evaluating students' academic performance do not themselves provide that therapy.

The appropriate use of such experiences depends on adequate informed consent, on a boundary between materials subject to grading and the type or quality of self-disclosure in the experience, and on an agreement that the faculty member acts in all possible ways to respect the dignity of the student. Because at times faculty are obligated to reveal or follow up on disclosures in growth experiences, students should clearly understand, prior to the experience, the circumstances that would require such action. For example, a student should be informed that comments about child abuse or neglect made in the presence of a mental health professional cannot be held in complete confidence. The counselor educator must take appropriate action to report that abuse. Similarly, if a student reveals a strong dislike for another racial group with whom she is likely to work, a faculty member must pursue that matter with the student. Because so much may be at stake for them, students ought to understand in advance the implications of disclosures. Faculty involved in growth experiences may find that written documents are helpful accompaniments to oral review of these issues with students.

When a course involves a significant amount of self-disclosure or involvement in personal growth activities, programs sometimes use part-time faculty. These faculty are less involved in other dimensions of the program and are less likely to have continuing contact with students, so both students and faculty may approach the experience more comfortably and confidently. If the part-time faculty member is competent in the task and if the student is more open to disclose and participate, student growth may occur at a faster rate than with a regular faculty member. This option is not essential or always feasible, but it eases the ethical complications for all involved. Patrick (1989) also recommends avoiding placing the student in the client role in peer counseling whenever possible, suggesting instead that students from other programs in the university are more appropriate.

Faculty overseeing such experiences have a demanding task. The codes provide guidance, but ultimately they must make difficult judgments. Student deficiencies are often on the border between competence and incompetence and between outrageous and simply undesirable. Following a systematic strategy for ethical decision making is crucial in such ambiguous situations, as is consultation with colleagues. Rigorous admissions standards help reduce the problem, but they do not eliminate it.

The 2002 revision of the APA standards made more explicit the limitations on student disclosure of personal information, explicitly requiring training programs to provide advance notice to students if such disclosure was a required part of the curriculum. That disclosure should be made in admission and catalog materials. The exception to this limitation applies when personal information is essential to the development of competence of the student or the protection of the safety of the student or others. A similar requirement appears in *ACA Code of Ethics,* Section F.7.a.

An Ethics of Care

Kitchener (1992) highlights a fundamental ethical issue for faculty in mental health. Commitment to teaching is not the only reason mental health professionals become educators. Many find research, consultation, and community involvement at least as important. Indeed, universities often make rewards for faculty contingent on activities outside the classroom. Inadequacies with students or in instructional approach are regularly overlooked by institutions when faculty bring in research grants or consulting contracts to the university. One can invest in other activities, of course, not only because they can reflect positively on the training program and advance knowledge but also because of personal enjoyment. However, counselors ought not sacrifice competent and caring teaching to attend to other responsibilities. Applying Nodding's concept of an ethics of care (1984), Kitchener points out that faculty who fail to care about the program, the courses, and the students are inadequate role models who are failing to promote the welfare of those they serve.

Such an uncaring attitude is not a minor ethical deviation; it runs contrary to the profession's deepest ethical values.

Obligations to Colleagues

Of course, faculty have obligations to colleagues as well as to students. The Preamble to the APA *Ethical Principles* captures these responsibilities well.

APA *Ethical Principles,* Principle B: Fidelity and Responsibility

Psychologists establish relationships of trust with those with whom they work. They are aware of their professional and scientific responsibilities to society and to the specific communities in which they work. Psychologists uphold professional standards of conduct, clarify their professional roles and obligations, accept appropriate responsibility for their behavior, and seek to manage conflicts of interest that could lead to exploitation or harm. Psychologists consult with, refer to, or cooperate with other professionals and institutions to the extent needed to serve the best interests of those with whom they work.

The next case illustrates misconduct toward colleagues.

Professor Caste's Letter of Reference

Professor Caste agrees to review the promotion file of a counselor educator at another university because he is an expert in the same field as the candidate. His two-paragraph letter of review arrives several weeks later. It shows very little attention to the file of materials submitted to him. Not only does Professor Caste's letter show no evidence of having read the most important materials submitted for review, but it miscounts the total number of publications, misinterprets others, and makes inferences not supported by the evidence. Professor Caste ends his letter with a negative recommendation for promotion.

This behavior is inconsistent with the provisions of the codes that deal with avoiding harm and acting competently. Universities regularly rely on external evaluations of scholarship, and professionals asked to undertake this duty must carry it out diligently. Professor Caste's negligence may have cost a worthy teacher a promotion, or even a job, if a tenure decision was involved. The best way for Professor Caste to remedy his mistake (in the event that he recognizes the error of his ways) is to send a retraction of his initial letter admitting the inadequacies in his first review, along with a replacement letter that fairly evaluates the candidate's work. If the promotion has been denied, he ought to encourage the university to reconsider its decision and share his communications with the candidate. He also owes an apology to the candidate. In the absence of such action or other attempt to undo the harm caused, the candidate for promotion would certainly be justified in filing an ethics complaint against him.

The Ethics of Research

Most counselors and psychologists do not identify themselves as researchers. Instead, they perceive research as an activity for those in academia or in specialized research settings. Although much attention has been given to developing graduate curricula to train competent scientist-practitioners, in reality most graduates fit that definition only insofar as they are consumers of research.

Economic and societal changes seem to be fueling a challenge to this distinction between researchers and mental health practitioners. The demand for accountability and outcome data in both mental health and educational settings suggests that over the next decade a much wider sampling of professionals will be involved in designing and implementing research and evaluation activities (Eisen & Dickey, 1996; Sexton, Whiston,

Bleuer, & Walz, 1997). For example, managed health care systems are seeking data on the effectiveness of given treatments with particular clients and information about the outcomes of a specific form of treatment or setting (Wedding, Topolski, & McGaha, 1995). Schools and community agencies are experiencing increased pressures for accountability. Consequently, the days may be passing when practicing professionals could relinquish involvement in research and evaluation. Third-party payors, especially, are seeking more evidence that treatments are effective and produce the outcomes that practitioners expect (Sexton & Liddle, 2001). The movement to use evidence-based practice has emerged as a major topic in the professional literature (for example, Stout & Hages, 2005). Practitioners must refurbish clinical research skills, and they also must also reacquaint themselves with ethical issues in research in clinical and educational settings. This section highlights the major ethical issues practitioners will confront and directs them to appropriate resources for future study. The essential ethical responsibilities of the researcher are (a) to develop scientifically acceptable research protocols that are worth participants' time and have a reasonable chance of yielding meaningful findings, (b) to protect the rights of participants (both human and animal) in the research process, (c) to report results fairly and accurately, and (d) to cooperate with colleagues and share research data. Students who seek more detailed information about planning research to conform to ethical standards may find Sieber (1992) and Sales and Folkman (2000) useful resources.

Good Science and Good Ethics

Most research in our field requires the participation of human beings; some research designs carry risks for those participants. A researcher who wants to examine the social and emotional effects on children whose parents have human immunodeficiency virus (HIV) disorders is exposing those children and their parents to a psychological risk. In revealing information that the researcher requests, participants may feel painful emotions or become aware of problems they had not yet recognized. The parents and children may encounter some difficulties in their interactions subsequent to the research interview. These risks are not insurmountable and may be worth enduring for the information gained. However, if the research design is not scientifically rigorous, the chance of making valid and meaningful conclusions is almost nonexistent. Substantial flaws in the design might even lead to results that contradict the actual state of affairs. In either event, it is unfair to subject people to the psychological risks of such research without the potential for scientific gain.

Rosenthal (1994) takes this analysis one step further. He contends that poorly designed and executed research is unethical even if the participants are not at risk for harm or discomfort. He argues that participants are donating valuable commodities, such as their time, attention, and cooperation. These commodities are no less valuable in low-risk research than in higher-risk research. In an interesting analogy, he encourages researchers to view participants as a kind of "granting source" to whom investigators have obligations. Poorly designed research wastes people's time and prevents them from engaging in other activities for that interval, and it also makes people more skeptical about the value of research participation and makes it more difficult for other researchers with more meritorious projects to recruit participants. In terms of the ethical principles, inadequate research designs violate the duty to beneficence and to fidelity even if they avoid risk of harm. Gelso (1985) frames this question as one of rigor and relevance. Meritorious research attends to both the rigor of the research design and the potential of the research to be relevant to practice.

Good science also assumes sensitivity to issues of diversity (Scott-Jones, 2000). Researchers, for example, who make generalizations to both genders on the basis of research with only one gender or who fail to acknowledge limitations of their samples in cultural or ethnic diversity are acting inappropriately. Their findings are vulnerable to misuse, particularly with populations not represented in their samples. The ACA *Code of Ethics* attends briefly to this issue as follows.

ACA *Code of Ethics*, Section G.1.g: Multicultural/Diversity Considerations in Research

When appropriate to research goals, counselors are sensitive to incorporating research procedures that take into account cultural considerations. They seek consultation when appropriate.

How can a practitioner ensure that a study is of sufficiently high quality to justify the risks? Obviously, good science requires researchers who are competent to conceptualize, design, and analyze data in their projects and are knowledgeable about recent research on the same topic. Practitioners with weaknesses in any of these domains should seek training and consultation before embarking on research that involves human or animal subjects.

Protecting the Rights of Research Participants

Ensuring that a project has scientific merit is only one component of ethical research. Scientific gains cannot be made at the cost of the health or well-being of participants. History has taught many lessons about the devastation blind devotion to science can inflict when the rights of participants are ignored. The Tuskegee experiments, the injection of live cancer cells into chronically ill patients in the 1960s, and the electronic surveillance of jury rooms without jurors' knowledge are just three of the most notorious of such examples of research harmful to people (Katz, 1972). The mental health professions have attempted to prevent the recurrence of such misconduct by giving this topic extensive coverage in the ethics codes. In fact, protecting the rights of participants receives more attention in the codes than any other issue in research ethics. In essence, these documents require the following:

- Fair and noncoercive recruiting of participants that honors their dignity.
- Responsibly and appropriately using incentives to participate, avoiding incentives that are practically impossible to refuse.
- Communicating informed consent procedures in ways participants can comprehend.
- Vigorously protecting the rights of those vulnerable to abuse (such as prisoners or institutionalized patients) or those incompetent to give consent.
- Providing for children to *assent* to research, although the formal consent for such participation must come from parents and guardians (Kodish, 2005; Powell & Vache-Hasse, 1994).
- Avoiding deception about particulars of the research unless deception is justified by the scientific merit of the study and no good alternatives exist (Lindsey, 1984; Pittinger, 2002).
- Describing the results of research to participants if they wish, as soon as the data are ready for dissemination (Fernandez, Kodish, & Weijer, 2003). (This process is also referred to as *debriefing.*)
- Protecting the anonymity of research participants and the confidentiality of their disclosures unless they explicitly consent to release of personal information.
- Overseeing others involved in the research, such as graduate students and technical staff, so that they do not violate participants' rights.

Many of the ethical mandates just listed have also been codified into laws or regulations. Federal rules are spelled out in Title 45 of the Code of Federal Regulations (Office for Protection from Research Risks, 1991). Thus penalties for their violation can extend beyond the discipline of a professional association. As part of regulations governing human research subjects, the federal government has mandated the creation of institutional review boards (IRBs) at research institutions to approve and oversee the conduct of any research that involves risk of harming human subjects. Much of the responsibility of institutional review boards is directed toward ensuring that researchers respect participants' rights and minimize risks. These committees have the power to approve, reject, or mandate changes in research proposals that come before them and to monitor ongoing research for compliance with legal mandates. A negative vote by an IRB prevents research from going forward, and an unfavorable review of research in progress can stop its continuance. In psychological or clinical research, IRB review panels are especially attentive to the completeness and comprehensibility of informed consent procedures, the voluntariness of participation, and the protection of the confidentiality of information received. They also examine research proposals to ensure that participants understand that they can withdraw from research at any point without penalty and that they can contact researchers with questions at any point in the process. All investigators connected with an institution must have their research approved by an IRB. This duty applies to students, faculty, volunteers, and other paid employees.

Mental health researchers rely on animal research less commonly than their counterparts in basic social science, but there have been important studies, particularly using primates, in which mental health researchers have been involved. In the last two decades, the animal rights movement has severely criticized the use of animals in psychological and medical research as inherently cruel (Galvin & Herzog, 1992; Keith-Spiegel & Koocher, 1998). The philosophical debate about the morality of animal research is not resolved, but this movement has caused several changes, including more federal regulation, clearer ethical standards, and the emergence of IRBs at organizations that conduct animal research (Bersoff, 2003). Therefore, it behooves mental health professionals to be aware of the ethical guidelines for research with animals. In 1993 the APA published the *Guidelines for Ethical Conduct in the Care and Use of Animals* (1993a), which explains the circumstances under which animal research is justified, the responsibilities of those who care for the animals, the conditions for humanely housing animals, the appropriate experimental and field research procedures, and the responsible use of animals for educational purposes. These standards were designed to help prevent the abuses of animal welfare that helped fuel the protests by animal rights activists and to ensure that meritorious research can continue.

Fair and Objective Reporting of Results

Once data are collected and analyzed, researchers have several more ethical obligations. The most basic of these obligations is not to misrepresent the results in any publication or communication of them to participants or colleagues. Unfortunately, this form of research misconduct has occurred on more than one occasion. Miller and Hersen (1992) cite several notorious examples of such misconduct. Investigators have fabricated data, changed findings, selectively reported only supportive results, and engaged in a variety of efforts to mislead the public about the nature of their findings. Sales and Lavin (2000) also note that pressure on researchers to maintain funding by grant sources sometimes tempts researchers to engage in misconduct. Research by Martinson, Anderson, and de Vries (2005) reveals that research misconduct is more common than ever believed. In their study of thousands of research scientists in the United States they found that one-third of the respondents had engaged in at least one type of research misconduct (aside from plagiarism or fabrication) in the previous 3 years. All such actions constitute research fraud and are highly unethical. The codes are quite explicit on this point.

APA *Ethical Principles,* Section 8.10: Reporting Research Results
(a) Psychologists do not fabricate data.

(b) If psychologists discover significant errors in their published data, they take reasonable steps to correct such errors in a correction, retraction, erratum, or other appropriate publication means.

8.11 Plagiarism

Psychologists do not present portions of another's work or data as their own, even if the other work or data source is cited occasionally.

ACA *Code of Ethics,* Section G.4: Reporting Results

a. Accurate Results. Counselors plan, conduct, and report research accurately. They provide thorough discussions of the limitations of their data and alternative hypotheses. Counselors do not engage in misleading or fraudulent research, distort data, misrepresent data, or deliberately bias their results. They explicitly mention all variables and conditions known to the investigator that may have affected the outcome of a study or the interpretation of data. They describe the extent to which results are applicable for diverse populations.

b. Obligation to Report Unfavorable Results. Counselors report the results of any research judged to be of professional value. Results that reflect unfavorably on institutions, programs, services, prevailing opinions, or vested interests are not withheld.

c. Reporting Errors. If counselors discover significant errors in their published research, they take reasonable steps to correct such errors in a correction erratum, or other appropriate publication means.

Violations of this kind seem to happen when researchers' self-interests overtake their judgment and when research environments push hard for productivity without regard for professional standards of conduct.

One other cause of trimming or altering research data must be acknowledged. In small, single-authored studies and qualitative research designs, the principal investigator is often the only person who has access to the raw data. Investigators conducting this kind of research tend to have little supervision and a relatively small chance of being caught if they alter the data. When researchers have much riding on the outcome of a study, they can be vulnerable to altering data to fit their expectations. Consequently, the ethics of research depend on the integrity of the individual researcher and the commitment of research centers to properly oversee all projects under way at their institutions. Researchers who are tempted to turn a blind eye to the ethical standards in this matter and who cannot be swayed by an appeal to the ethical values of the profession are well advised to remember two things: Even a small misrepresentation of the data can ruin a career and a reputation, and enforcement of standards in this arena is improving.

Sometimes researchers obtain findings that are contrary to their expectations or to their current theory. In this situation, an investigator may be tempted not to publish these results. However, not publishing such findings also runs counter to the duty to accurately communicate results and is inappropriate. Hiding such results may mean that other researchers pursue unproductive paths and that a more complete explanation of the phenomenon of interest is delayed. Once again, the professional's responsibility is to serve the greater good rather than his or her own personal preferences.

The emergence of qualitative methods of research has been met with both enthusiasm and skepticism in the field of mental health. The paradigm on which it operates is quite different from traditional quantitative methods, and it presents its own unique research challenges. The potential impact of the unconscious assumptions of the researcher on the results, the increased risks to participants who often reveal much more about themselves than they do in quantitative studies, and the issue of dual role relationships take on great importance in qualitative research. See Haverkamp (2005) and Rowan (2000) for a detailed discussion of these issues.

Cooperation with Research Colleagues

The ultimate goal of clinical research is to add to the profession's understanding of human behavior. Research serves a social good insofar as it informs professionals about matters that affect the efficacy of their work with clients. The aim of research is not to build the reputation of an investigator or to gain anyone job security or financial reward, although these outcomes may be secondary benefits of good research. Thus, research is by definition a cooperative endeavor in which research findings are shared with colleagues and peer criticism is conducted in an educative rather than punitive fashion. Withholding information from colleagues who are making good-faith requests for data is unethical precisely because it contradicts the fundamental purpose of research. Of course, it is important to acknowledge that researchers are often in competition with each other for funding, promotions, or public acclaim. To some degree this competition can motivate researchers to conduct more rigorous research, but it can also spark hostile and uncooperative attitudes among those working in the same field.

Researchers are also advised to retain raw data for a number of years so that other qualified researchers may have access to it if they wish to reanalyze the data. The code does not specify an exact interval for retaining such data, but it is prudent to keep data for at least 10 years. Now that a great deal of data can be stored on a portable computer disk, it may be feasible to keep raw data indefinitely. The only caution about such sharing of data relates to the rights of research participants.

Credit for Publication of Research Findings

The same pressures that sometimes influence the willingness of professionals to share data also affect their attitudes toward research publications and cause them to accept undue credit in publications (Jones, 1999). In a "publish or perish" environment, researchers may become overconcerned about the number of their publications and less attentive about their quality or their actual contribution to the study. Some have been known to "trade authorships" in exchange for favors. Both codes speak directly to this issue, and their messages are clear. They dictate that professionals accept authorship on work in which they have made a significant contribution. The order of authorship ought to reflect the level of contribution to the research and writing. Second, no counselors or psychologists may take credit for publications with which they were uninvolved. A role as director or department chair at the time a project was conducted, for example, does not constitute involvement. Third, when student theses or dissertations are published, students have first authorship if the adviser's name also appears on the publication. Generally, advisers should consider a second authorship only if they were substantially involved in the research (APA Ethics Committee, 1983). In other faculty–student research collaborations, faculty are obliged to respect the contributions of students and give them appropriate credit for their work (Fine & Kurdek, 1993; Goodyear, Crego, & Johnston, 1992). Finally, when submitting a manuscript for publication, it should be sent only to one journal at a time. Duplicate submissions are expressly prohibited. However, if one journal chooses not to publish the manuscript, of course the author may send the manuscript to another journal.

ACA *Code of Ethics*, Section G.5: Publication

a. Recognizing Contributions. When conducting and reporting research, counselors are familiar with and give recognition to previous work on the topic, observe copyright laws, and give full credit to those to whom credit is due.

d. Contributors. Counselors give credit through joint authorship, acknowledgment, footnote statements, or other appropriate means to those who have contributed significantly to research or concept development in accordance with such contributions. The principal contributor is listed first and minor technical or professional contributions are acknowledged in notes or introductory statements.

e. Agreement of Contributors. Counselors who conduct joint research with colleagues or students/supervisees establish agreements in advance regarding allocation of tasks, and types of acknowledgement, and any publication credit that will be received.

f. Student Research. For articles that are substantially based on students course papers, projects, dissertations or theses, and on which students have been the primary contributors, they are listed as principal authors.

Special Ethical Concerns for Counseling and Therapy Researchers

There are four special concerns of researchers in counseling and psychotherapy process and outcome. The first relates to experimental design. Research that explores the usefulness of counseling interventions usually employs comparison groups. One or more groups receive the experimental treatment, and another receives either a standard treatment or a placebo. Because all participants might benefit from the new treatment for their problems, one must question whether it is ethical to withhold the experimental treatment. Several factors should be considered when designing such research. First, there is no assurance that the experimental treatment will be helpful; it may have no effect or may even be counterproductive. Second, without comparison groups, no one can be sure of the effects of the new treatment in comparison to other approaches, and its real usefulness to practitioners cannot be determined with confidence. Third, usually experimental treatments are not truly withheld—they are delayed. When comparison groups are used, the standard of practice is to offer the new treatment to those groups once the initial round is complete. Researchers who are considering a research design that does not at least offer a delayed exposure to an experimental treatment found useful after a first round of experimentation are not acting consistently with current guidelines.

The second special concern deals with the impact of treatments on participants. Whenever research is being conducted on clinical populations, researchers have an obligation to be alert for deterioration effects on any participants and to intervene if the deterioration puts a participant at risk. In this situation, the scientific profit must be sacrificed to the well-being of the individual. An appropriate referral must be made. Those who volunteer for such research should also clearly understand this option at the time they give consent for participation.

The third special issue concerns the accessibility of written information about clients and the need for client consent to such activities. Research that reviews client records without the actual participation of the client is controversial. Because no one is put at risk or inconvenienced, in one sense no consent for this research seems necessary; however, a review of client records is probably not within the expectations clients had when they consented to counseling. A commitment by the researcher to honor the confidentiality of the documents lessens the ethical concerns somewhat, but the practice is still not fully consistent with respect to the client's dignity and privacy. Thus, when possible, it is best to obtain client consent before review of any records or to include a provision for that consent in the general consent obtained at the onset of counseling or therapy. HIPAA regulations should also be met, where applicable in regard to treatment research.

Ethical questions also arise when clinicians publish clinical case material. The APA code addresses this issue as follows.

APA *Ethical Principles,* Section 4.07: Use of Confidential Information for Didactic or Other Purposes

Psychologists do not disclose in their writings, lectures, or other public media, confidential, personally identifiable information concerning their clients/patients, students, research participants, organizational clients, or other recipients of their services that they obtained during the course of their work, unless (1) they take reasonable steps to disguise the person or organization, (2) the person or organization has consented in writing, or (3) there is legal authorization for doing so.

Stoller (1988) cites examples of clients who found case material about them published without their knowledge or consent. They felt sad and betrayed. Even when consent is sought for such publication, Garvey and Braun (1997) caution that mental health professionals must be alert for clients who acquiesce rather than consent for fear of alienating the professional. Because dissemination of knowledge from case studies is an important mechanism to teaching new professionals and exploring the effects of complex treatments, professionals ought not to be discouraged from using them. Rather, they should be scrupulous that the rights of the client to consent, confidentiality, and anonymity are protected.

The fourth special concern is the provision of feedback. The ethics codes mandate that participants be given feedback about the outcomes of research if they are interested in that information (ACA, Section G.2.h; APA, Section 8.08). Some research suggests that feedback to participants about the results of a study is frequently neglected, however. McConnell and Kerbs (1993) found that more than 30% of the researchers in their study failed to provide the feedback they had agreed to provide when people were asked to participate in their studies. According to the authors, this happened largely because researchers gave feedback a low priority. They seemed to know what they ought to do, but they could not put together the energy to accomplish it. To avoid this problem, researchers ought to realign their priorities and structure their time better to honor their duty to feedback. The failure to follow up may diminish participants' willingness to volunteer for future studies.

SUMMARY

The ethical issues of teaching closely parallel supervision. The faculty member has obligations not only to students, but also to the public those students will serve and to the profession. Faculty members violate ethical standards when they teach without proper knowledge, without proper sensitivity to individual differences, or with nonobjective techniques. They are also guilty of misconduct when they exploit their students' needs for positive evaluations, research experience, or clinical involvement. Faculty who act irresponsibly with colleagues are no less guilty of misconduct.

Because faculty are encouraged to act as mentors to students, they must be careful not to take mentoring past the boundary of an appropriate professional contact. Boundaries of faculty–student relationships need not be drawn as rigidly or as small as boundaries between clients and therapists, but they still exist. An ethics of care and respect for student autonomy is one useful guide to effective, responsible teaching and advising.

Researchers have several important ethical obligations, including conducting research studies that are of sufficient quality to contribute to knowledge, protecting the rights of human and animal participants, communicating and sharing research results with the professional community, avoiding fraudulent or misleading publication of results, and claiming authorship only when justified. Researchers must give priority to their responsibilities to honor the dignity of participants and help advance science over their personal interests.

CASES FOR DISCUSSION

Jefferson teaches methods of counseling to mental health counselors. In the course he illustrates concepts with examples from his own private practice and sometimes shows videotaped role-plays of techniques to the class. In one session he asks for a volunteer from the class who is willing to reveal a personal concern before the group so that he can do a live demonstration of a counseling session in class. He sees such demonstrations as crucial to effective teaching of counseling methods. In 18 years of teaching he has never been refused this request. The personal concerns students have discussed have ranged from test anxiety to suicidal depression. After the class he refers volunteers who need further counseling to the university counseling center. Is Jefferson's practice consistent with ethical guidelines for mental health educators? If not, what can he do to make it more ethical?

Kara is conducting research on the ethics of Internet counseling. She is most interested in the quality of the counseling Internet counselors provide. She poses as a client with depressive feelings and gets online counseling from 35 different Websites. She publishes her research in a major journal. One of the Internet counselors recognizes the question that Kara poses and files an ethics complaint against her. He charges that she violated the ethics code because she deceived him into believing she was a real client and that he did not consent to participate in research. If you were on the ethics committee, how would you respond to this complaint against Kara?

DISCUSSION QUESTIONS

1. Some counseling and psychotherapy training programs require students to obtain individual counseling during graduate school. Assuming counseling is not provided by the teaching faculty, what do you see as the ethical dimensions of this practice?

2. How should faculty members deal with insensitive and prejudiced comments they overhear students making outside the classroom?

3. Universities are strongly encouraging faculty to teach courses via distance learning and the Internet. Some entire programs in mental health are in a distance learning format. What do you see as the ethical implications of such approaches to clinical training in light of the gatekeeper responsibilities of faculty?

4. Some doctoral programs strongly encourage doctoral students to do their dissertations in the same areas as faculty research. They are not prohibited from choosing other options, but they get little support for such choices. Is this an ethical violation? Why or why not?

5. Much research in our field involves "convenient samples," such as college or graduate students, rather than other, less accessible groups in society. What ethical issues does such a practice engender?

6. Complete objectivity in research is impossible. Researchers naturally "hope" for particular outcomes for their studies. How can those involved in research deal effectively with the ethical implications of their disappointment when research findings contradict their expectations?

RECOMMENDED READINGS

American Psychological Association. (1982). *Ethical principles in the conduct of research with human participants.* Washington, DC: Author.

Fine, M. A., & Kurdek, L. A. (1993). Reflections on determining authorship credit and authorship order on faculty–student collaborations. *American Psychologist, 48,* 1141–1147.

Haverkamp, B. E. (2005). Ethical perspectives on qualitative research in applied psychology. *Journal of Counseling Psychology, 52,* 146–155.

Keith-Spiegel, P., Wittig, A. F., Perkins, D. V., Balogh, D. W., & Whitley, B. E., Jr. (1993). *The ethics of teaching: A casebook.* Muncie, IN: Ball State University.

Kodish, E. (2005). *Ethics and research with children: A case-based approach.* New York: Oxford.

Rosenthal, R. (1994). Science and ethics in conducting, analyzing, and reporting psychological research. *Psychological Science, 5,* 127–134.

Sales, B.D., & Folkman, S. (Eds.). (2000). *Ethics in research with human participants.* Washington, D.C.: American Psychological Association.

Sieber, J. E. (1992). *Planning ethically responsible research: A guide for students and internal review boards.* Newbury Park, CA: Sage.

Tabachnick, B. G., Keith-Spiegel, P. S., & Pope, K. S. (1991). Ethics of teaching: Beliefs and behaviors of psychologists as educators. *American Psychologist, 46,* 506–515.

PART FOUR

When Prevention Fails: Ethical Responses to Unethical Behavior

Chapter 15

Responsibilities for Self and Colleagues
Reporting, Recovery, and Rehabilitation of Misconduct

Consider the following situation.

Jack and Martina

A 20-year-old college student named Martina makes an appointment at the university counseling center. Martina tells her counselor Dominic that she has been feeling anxious and depressed for a long time but that lately these feelings have worsened. She goes on to say that she tried counseling at home last summer but had "a bad experience" and did not want to see that counselor again. She says the other counselor (Jack) kept suggesting that she ought to have a more active social life and repeatedly volunteered to take her to the movies to distract her from her anxiety. She refused Jack's offers and kept attending sessions until he suggested that maybe they could start dating once counseling was over. At this session he also commented on her attractiveness. Martina's best friend told her that Jack was acting unprofessionally, that most counselors did not do such things. Martina now wants to take some action against Jack so that "he cannot keep using his practice as a dating service." She asks Dominic for guidance in figuring out how to report Jack's behavior.

Although the particular facts presented in this case are fictional, research suggests that clients frequently tell their counselors about unethical behaviors by other mental health professionals. According to Pope (1994), approximately half of all American therapists have had at least one client who revealed sexual involvement with a prior therapist. The percentage for British psychologists is 22.7% (Garrett, 1998). Sometimes clients are not as aware as Martina of the inherent problems in sexual exploitation and other ethical violations, but they do mention them in subsequent counseling experiences with sufficient frequency to require that counselors be prepared for such eventualities. When this happens, the new counselors have an opportunity to model ethical behavior and to counteract some of the damage done to the client and the profession by the prior counselor.

Information about ethics violations also may come from co-workers and from one's own observations of others' behavior in the workplace. Reports from practicing professionals show that between 15% and 28% of practicing psychologists had personal knowledge of an incompetent or unethical colleague (Floyd, Myszka, & Orr, 1999; Schwebel, Skorina, & Schoener, 1994; Wood, Klein, Cross, Lammers, & Elliott, 1985). In one study that used a looser definition of personal knowledge (Golden & Schmidt, 1998) the percentage was much higher—69% of the counselors and therapists surveyed reported knowing of at least one unethical action by a professional in the prior 2 years. Golden and

Schmidt found four types of misconduct predominated: financial exploitation (39%), practice by unqualified personnel (25%), sexual exploitation (19%), and breach of confidentiality (17%). Training directors in professional psychology programs also express personal knowledge of misconduct by faculty colleagues. Barich and Dimperio (2002) report that 53% of the training directors they surveyed had worked with colleagues exhibiting unethical behavior at least occasionally. These data suggest that counselors should prepare themselves to respond to a violation by another counselor and should be aware of the practical and emotional aspects of filing ethics complaints to help clients like Martina.

This chapter describes complaint procedures used by professional associations and licensing boards and identifies the criteria for filing a complaint. Next, this chapter discusses counseling interventions to help the client who wants to take action against an unethical mental health professional. Finally, the chapter discusses an often neglected aspect of professional ethics, accountability for self, and examines how counselors ought to respond when they recognize that they have violated ethical guidelines for professional practice.

Accountability of Counselors and Therapists

When counselors act unethically, they may be disciplined by their employers, the state or provincial licensing board, and all the national and state professional associations to which they belong. Conceivably, complaints for the same set of actions may be filed in each organization. Professional associations commonly forward complaints against their members to licensing boards in the states where the member holds a license. Interstate communication among licensing boards and professional associations also occurs through the Disciplinary Data System for psychologists so that disciplined professionals cannot fraudulently obtain licenses in other states as easily as they once were able to (Kirkland, Kirkland, & Reaves, 2004). A parallel system of reporting exists for counselors and social workers through the Association of Social Work Boards who then convey disciplinary information to the National Practitioner Data Bank (Department of Health and Human Services, 1999). As discussed repeatedly in this book, counselors and therapists who violate standards are accountable to the courts in civil lawsuits for negligence, malpractice, or breach of contract or in criminal court for serious violations. In 15 states, sexual contact with a client carries criminal penalties for psychologists (Haspel, Jorgenson, Wincze, & Parsons, 1997). Three other states (Alabama, Michigan, and Ohio) criminalize sexual misconduct if it occurs through therapeutic deception—that is, if the therapist represents that sexual contact has a therapeutic purpose for the client. Multiple accountability also means multiple choices for those who wish to seek redress against professional misconduct. Clients often profit by assistance from their new counselors in sorting through their options.

Procedures for Filing Ethics Complaints

The procedures for making an ethics complaint vary according to the seriousness of the misconduct, with formal complaints generally reserved for more egregious violations.

Informal Remedies through Professional Associations The ethics codes of the American Psychological Association (APA) and American Counseling Association (ACA) both recommend informal remedies as a first step in addressing misconduct. Their rationale for this strategy is not explicitly stated, but it is reasonable to surmise that it is based on loyalty to colleagues; an interest in a speedy, nonbureaucratic resolution of problems; and minimization of negative publicity damaging to the mental health professions and the practitioner. The wording is as follows.

ACA *Code of Ethics,* Section H.2.b: Informal Resolution

When counselors have reason to believe that another counselor is violating or has violated an ethical standard, they attempt first to resolve the issue informally with the other counselor if feasible, providing such action does not violate confidentiality rights that may be involved.

APA *Ethical Principles,* Section 1.04: Informal Resolution of Ethical Violations

When psychologists believe that there may have been an ethical violation by another psychologist, they attempt to resolve the issue by bringing it to the attention of that individual, if an informal resolution appears appropriate and the intervention does not violate any confidentiality rights that may be involved.

Formal Remedies When an informal resolution is not appropriate or feasible, counselors, on reasonable cause, take action such as reporting the suspected ethics violation to the state or national ethics committees, unless this action conflicts with confidentiality rights that cannot be resolved.

APA *Ethical Principles,* Section 1.05: Reporting Ethical Violations

If an apparent ethical violation has substantially harmed or is likely to substantially harm a person or organization and is not appropriate for informal resolution under Standard 1.04, Informal Resolution of Ethical Violations, or is not resolved properly in that fashion, psychologists take further action appropriate to the situation. Such action might include referral to state or national committees on professional ethics, to state licensing boards, or to the appropriate institutional authorities. This standard does not apply when an intervention would violate confidentiality rights or when psychologists have been retained to review the work of another psychologist whose professional conduct is in question.

If an apparent ethical violation is not appropriate for informal resolutions under Standard 1.05, or is not resolved properly in that fashion, psychologists take further action appropriate to the situation, unless such action conflicts with confidentiality rights in a way that cannot be resolved. Such action might include referral to state or national committees on professional ethics or to state licensing boards. Section H.2.c of the ACA Standards uses similar language.

A careful reading shows that neither code mandates that an ethics complaint be made; they say only *some action* must be taken if an informal approach to the problem is unsuccessful. The APA statement also suggests avenues for the professional to pursue to address the suspected violation and uses the seriousness of the suspected offense and its harm or potential to harm consumers as the major criteria for deciding whether to file a formal complaint.

Minor violations seem amenable to private interventions such as a one-on-one conversation between the offending and the concerned counselor. Consider the counselor who does not obtain a complete informed consent to counseling as advised in the ethics code. Instead, she discusses only the limits of confidentiality very briefly. If there is no known harm to clients thus far and she seems to be acting from ignorance of the codes rather than disdain for them, informal confrontation seems a prudent choice. In this conversation, she can be educated about the ethics of informed consent and placed on notice that further noncompliance will be taken more seriously. This approach lets the colleague retain some dignity and probably achieves as much behavior change as would be gained from a full ethics committee investigation. In addition, there is a practical argument in favor of an informal approach—it's speedier. A formal complaint can take months, even years, to resolve. An intervention for a minor infraction can take place immediately and the harm can be remedied almost as quickly.

Using the employing institution to help change practitioner behavior before moving into association or licensing board channels also makes sense, especially in minor or moderate offenses. An employer with policies for adjudicating complaints can respond in a reasonable time frame and with consideration for the rights of all involved. The employer has clout over the counselor and is in the position to monitor future behavior. The disadvantages of complaining to employers are variability in enforcement procedures and lack of influence over the counselor if he or she takes employment elsewhere. In addition, personal relationships among employees often hinder objective processing of a complaint. Consequently, reporting a problem to an employer is more likely to be beneficial if it is mildly or moderately serious and needs an objective investigation, if monitoring the counselor's future behavior is desirable, and if the employee is not likely to change jobs in the immediate future.

Using the seriousness of the offense as a criterion to determine the level of intervention, let us return to Martina's case. Clearly, her former counselor (Jack) did not comply with the ethical standards of either ACA or APA regarding multiple relationships. In addition, Jack's invitation to begin dating immediately after counseling was terminated showed he was probably interested in a physical relationship with Martina. The latter is even more emphatically prohibited by the codes.

The harm from such behavior is also important to examine, to ascertain whether this offense was serious enough for a formal complaint. Research evidence suggests significant harm to clients whose counselors engage in sexual contact with them (for example, Bouhoutsos, Holroyd, Lerman, Forer, & Greenberg, 1983; Luepker, 1999; Wohlberg, 1999). Martina herself reports feeling even worse after her encounter with Jack. Although no sexual contact took place, Martina's functioning deteriorated after Jack expressed romantic interest in her. That is probably sufficient to constitute psychological injury to Martina. Is there also harm that extends beyond Martina? The research evidence also suggests that counselors who engage in sexual contact with one client are more likely to have had sex with other clients (Pope, 1994). The possibility exists, then, that Martina is not the first client who has suffered Jack's advances. In any case, unless something changes Jack's behavior, Martina may not be the last client injured by this man's irresponsibility. Taken together, then, the evidence suggests that a formal complaint to the licensing board and the professional association are warranted. This man hurt Martina, may have hurt other clients in the past, and may do so again.

The ability of Dominic, the current counselor, to help rehabilitate Jack comes into play in the decision about using a formal resolution in serious cases such as Martina's. Because Dominic does not work at the same agency and has no supervisory relationship with the offender he has no effective way to monitor Jack's behavior on an ongoing basis. Moreover, Dominic probably does not have time to fully investigate the incident and objectively evaluate the evidence presented by both parties. If no wrongdoing occurred, a counselor accused of a serious violation by a client also deserves the opportunity to have his or her name cleared. An informal resolution does not really allow such an outcome. Thus, from several perspectives, it is wiser to report a potentially serious violation to a body empowered to carefully investigate and to assert authority over future behavior than to use a private intervention. It offers better protection both to the professional who may be falsely accused and to the client who may have been victimized.

Another option that has been recommended and used with clients who have been sexually exploited by their therapists is mediation. Its primary advantage is its speed and moderate structure. It is processed faster than a formal complaint and has more structure than a one-on-one intervention. Its disadvantage is that a formal complaint to an association or licensing board may not be forthcoming, which is a substantial limitation for a serious offense. Mediation may also function to favor the counselor, who is usually the more powerful party in the dispute. See Bouhoutsos and Brodsky (1985) for a more detailed examination of the use of mediation for professional misconduct.

One caution is in order about reporting violations. The language in the codes about resolving ethical violations also establishes the priority of the client's right to confidentiality over the counselor's duty to intervene when another professional acts irresponsibly (Fisher, 2003). One can approach a colleague or file a complaint to a board or committee that involves a client *only* if the client has consented and waived his or her preexisting right to confidentiality. The only exceptions are situations in which there may be a legal mandate to act otherwise. (For example, a few states mandate reporting of sexual misconduct by therapists regardless of client consent. See Haspel et al. [1997] and Nugent [1996]). Therefore if Martina wanted to do nothing about her former therapist and wanted no information disclosed, professional ethics demand honoring her decision. When an adult client makes this choice, mental health professionals may worry about future clients of this man, but the duty to the current client takes precedence. Of course, with time and good care the client may change her mind about making a complaint against the former professional.

American Counseling Association Complaint Procedures

The functions and goals of the ACA Ethics Committee are to educate members about ethical standards and deal with ethics questions and complaints (ACA, 2003). The committee has nine members, all of whom are professional counselors who serve 3-year terms. This body aims to protect the rights of the person who originated the action and the rights of the counselor to a fair hearing.

Complaints against ACA members can come from the public, other members, or the committee itself, acting *sua sponte*. A *sua sponte* action means that if the Ethics Committee has information suggesting a member violated the standards, the committee itself can initiate the complaint. The committee has established and periodically revises its rules and procedures for handling ethics complaints. The most recent version went into effect in October 2003.

The Ethics Office's first contact with a person considering an ethics complaint usually comes by telephone, although the ACA Website also has information on the steps in the ethics complaint process at www.counseling.org/ethics. The first step is to verify the membership of the individual in question, usually done by a faxed or mailed request. Once membership is verified, the person making the complaint is sent an official ethics complaint form to complete. Only signed, written complaints are processed. Once that form is received, if sufficient reason exists to explore the matter further, the person named in the complaint is notified of the charges being made and is given copies of the complaint and all related materials. He or she is asked to respond in writing within 60 days. Accused members have the option of asking for a face-to-face hearing before the committee. When all material has been obtained within the stated time limits, the committee deliberates about the case. The committee has several options in its ruling. It can determine that no ethics violation took place, that there isn't enough information to determine whether a violation took place, or that the person accused is guilty of the ethics violation. If misconduct is found, the committee then determines the appropriate sanction. The sanctions can range from remedial requirements to permanent expulsion from the organization. The latter is a rare occurrence—only two counselors were expelled from ACA for ethics violations in the period from 2001 to 2004 (Hubert & Freeman, 2004; Kocet & Freeman, 2005; Sanders & Freeman, 2003). Detailed procedures are outlined so that members can appeal unfavorable decisions. The appeal committee is composed of six members appointed by the President-Elect, subject to confirmation by the ACA Governing Council.

American Psychological Association Complaint Procedures

The APA Ethics Committee also has both educational and enforcement mandates from the association (APA, Ethics Committee, 2001). Currently eight people serve on the committee as regular members for 3-year terms. One is a public, nonpsychologist member, and the rest are psychologists. There are also four associate members who do not vote and who act as fact finders. APA also hires professional and support staff to assist the committee. All procedures for handling ethics complaints are published (APA, 2003 and at www.apa.org) and are designed to balance the rights of the person complaining against the rights of the psychologist, respecting the dignity of each party in the process. Their goal is to prevent harm to the public and to prevent harm to members from malicious or frivolous claims. The approach usually taken by both APA's and ACA's ethics committees is rehabilitative, with as much emphasis on interventions that can rehabilitate the counselor as on sanctions against him or her.

A complaint may come before the APA committee in one of three ways. A consumer or other citizen can file a complaint; another mental health professional can make a complaint; or the Ethics Committee can initiate action against a member, *sua sponte*. Usually the initial inquiry about a potential violation comes by telephone to the Ethics Office. In this contact the person learns that all complaints must be written and is sent an official complaint form. This form requests identifying information from the person accusing as well as the accused, along with a detailed description of the situation. When the APA Ethics Committee receives a complaint, it conducts a preliminary review focused on three areas. The first review determines whether the complaint is within the committee's jurisdiction, which usually means whether the person named in the complaint is an APA member. If the person named is not a member, the case is immediately closed and that information is forwarded to the person who originated the complaint. Information is usually provided so that the person can file a complaint with a state licensing board or other professional association if appropriate. The second review examines whether the complaint has been filed within the appropriate time limits. If the time limit is exceeded, the person who complains is given an opportunity to ask for a waiver of the time limit. The third focus is on the sufficiency of the information furnished. In other words, the committee assesses whether there is adequate evidence to warrant further investigation. APA Ethics Committee reports (for example, APA, 2004) indicate that many complaints fail to progress beyond the preliminary investigation. Most cases are closed for one of these three reasons.

When a claim remains open, the next step is an evaluation by the chair of the Ethics Committee and the director of the Ethics Office. This involves a determination of whether a *cause for action* exists. According to APA, a "cause for action shall exist when the respondent's alleged actions and/or omissions, if proved, would in the judgment of the decision maker constitute a breach of ethics" (APA, Ethics Committee, 2001, Rules and Procedure, Section 5.1). If a cause for action has been found, the person named in the complaint is notified of the filing and that person receives copies of the complaint. The member is required to respond in writing to the complaint within 60 days and may submit additional information about the matter for the committee to consider. The committee may also seek information from other sources that it deems potentially relevant. Once this information is gathered the committee decides if there is enough information to show a cause for action. If there is not, the case is closed at this point, but if there is reason to suspect an ethics violation, a formal case is opened.

The psychologist involved is then formally charged with an ethics violation. The member receives written notification of the nature of the charges and the section(s) of the ethics code he or she is alleged to have violated. As in the preliminary step, the psychologist is now required to respond in writing within 30 days. In some cases, the psychologist is asked to appear in person before the committee. The person filing the claim is also notified of the formal charge and can submit additional information relevant to the charges in the allotted time period. When the investigation is complete, the committee deliberates and issues its ruling. It may dismiss the charges, recommend a sanction less than formal charges, or issue formal charges against the member. A lesser sanction is recommended when the committee believes that the violation occurred but would be better resolved without formal charges. In this respect, the committee is given a good deal of discretion. Formal charges are issued when the misconduct represented a substantial harm to another person or the profession. In this event, the committee recommends to the board of directors that the individual be dropped from membership in the organization. Here, too, the committee has a good measure of flexibility because it can let a member resign instead of being dropped if it believes the severity of the misconduct does not warrant the full action. Between 2001 and 2003, 39 members either resigned or were dropped from APA membership subsequent to an ethics investigation (APA Ethics Committee, 2004). The board of directors may accept or reject the recommendations of the Ethics Committee. Of course, a member may appeal a decision of the Ethics Committee, and a rather elaborate description of the appeal process is presented in the published rules.

Licensing Board Procedures

The procedures for complaining about the activities of a licensed professional vary from state to state and profession to profession. Generally, licensing boards are authorized to discipline professionals who violate the written regulations. The type of discipline ranges from reprimands and limitations placed on one's practice to loss of license. For some offenses, criminal sanctions may also exist, and the board will turn evidence over to the legal system. A person seeking to give information about an ethics violation to a licensing board begins the process with a telephone call or letter to the appropriate state agency. Some state licensing boards provide information about initiating complaints on their Websites. Because licensing boards have more authority and power to regulate the future actions of a professional, some scholars advocate that aggrieved clients should file first with a licensing board (for example, Siegel, 1991). Interstate reporting has also begun so that a licensing board in one state can know if an applicant has been judged guilty of an offense in another state. Such reporting is also an argument for including a state board in any ethics complaint.

Some licensing boards do not offer professionals the option of informal resolutions of minor violations. The Ohio Counselor, Social Worker, and Marriage and Family Therapy Board, for example, mandates that these professionals report all suspected violations of other professionals unless such reporting would violate client confidentiality. Therefore practicing professionals should be aware of licensing board regulations. Both ACA and APA codes state that professionals should follow state and provincial law even if it contradicts the provisions of these codes (ACA *Code of Ethics,* H.1.b, and APA *Ethical Principles,* 1.02).

Complaints to Employers

As already mentioned, people who believe a mental health professional has acted inappropriately may also notify employers or supervisors about the problem. If a practitioner has partners in a group practice, any or all partners can be contacted. Large employers, such as community mental health centers and psychiatric hospitals, are more likely to have procedures in place for investigating such complaints. Smaller employers and colleagues in a practice are more prone to handle matters on a case-by-case basis. Again, people who complain need to identify themselves and provide specific information and documentation, if possible, about the events they believe are problematic. Employers who know that such information is also being forwarded to the licensing board or professional association may give the matter more serious attention, although they may postpone a decision about the matter until the other bodies have ruled. Obviously, counselors in individual private practices are self-employed, so complaints against them must be referred to a professional association, licensing board, or both.

Supporting the Client Through the Complaint Process

When a client such as Martina wants to complain to an authority about a mental health professional, the current counselor can play an important role in helping a client make sound judgments based on accurate information about the practical and emotional aspects of the process. Most clients have very little knowledge of professional rules and regulations, and professionals provide a valuable service when they give clients such information. They can also help clients sort out their emotions about the prior experience and about the complaint process. Clients should understand that their identity will be known to the committee and that the accused professional will have access to all materials they submit to the committee. The client is also likely to feel victimized by the former counselor and may not easily understand the committee's responsibility to protect the rights of the accused as well as the victim's. It may reduce the client's frustration to explain that the principle of "innocent until proven guilty" holds in this arena.

Clients need full autonomy in deciding whether to proceed with the complaint, especially because only a minority of complaints submitted to professional associations result in formal charges against the member. So far, there is very limited empirical evidence that complaining will help the person heal from the wound (Vinson, 1987). Clients should appreciate that the most realistic benefit for them is the knowledge that if the action is successful, future clients are at less risk for harm.

Some counselors and therapists may have difficulty acknowledging that fellow professionals behave irresponsibly. They may take a "head in the sand" approach and minimize client accounts of counselor misconduct or attribute such accounts to negative transference or psychopathology. They may feel uncomfortable helping a client take action against a colleague for whom they feel empathy (Floyd et al., 1999; Levenson, 1986). Despite these entirely human feelings, professionals are bound to explore evidence of unethical practice by colleagues when clients mention them. If additional discussion clarifies a potentially serious unethical practice, the new counselor has a duty to inform the client about ethical standards for professionals and his or her options for action. The professional's goal in such discussion is to keep an open mind, respect the dignity of all involved, and help the client determine his or her next step.

False claims against counselors are relatively rare. Pope and Vetter (1991) report that about 4% of claims of sexual contact between therapists and clients were not true. The elaborate, time-consuming, and often uncomfortable process of filing a complaint militates against the filing of large numbers of false complaints. A counselor who believes a client is falsely accusing a prior therapist of misconduct should explore the matter extensively in counseling. Counselors who worry about such false claims can also take comfort in the careful analysis by the committees and boards involved that also militates against a false finding against an innocent professional. In a controversial article on false claims using anecdotal evidence, based on anecdotal evidence, Williams (2000) hypothesizes that there are six major antecedents that motivate false claims. These are malingering and fraud, revenge, psychopathology, recovered memory, advice from a subsequent therapist, and escape from unwanted treatment.

The client needs extra support at several other crucial points in the counseling process. First, putting the information in writing to the committee may cause the client to revisit the pain of the experience itself. Counseling time devoted to those feelings is wisely spent, focusing on the reality of the pain and attributing responsibility to the mental health professional (not the client) for the misconduct. The second point at which support is crucial arises if the committee decides not to pursue the complaint and issue formal charges (an event that occurs in a substantial proportion of cases). According to California enforcement data for January 2000 through April 2005, for example, only 703 of 2,635 complaints received were judged appropriate for investigation. Of those investigated only 213 resulted in penalties to the professional (California Board of Psychology, 2005). Professionals should be prepared to help clients process feelings of anger and sadness and brainstorm about alternatives when this happens. A third crucial point comes if the committee issues a ruling against the member. The outcome may be less than the client hoped for and may evoke feelings of betrayal. However, even if the outcome seems to fit the offense, the client may feel guilty about the negative consequences for the violator. Again, the client may take on the responsibility for the professional's behavior, blaming himself or herself for the outcome. Clarifying the professional's duty to honor the profession's standards in all situations may help the client think more accurately about whose behavior was problematic. Finally, no matter what the outcome of the complaint, the counselor must help the client find ways to bring closure to this episode.

Responding If an Ethics Complaint Is Filed Against You

As discussed in Chapter 1, the risk of an ethics complaint happening to an individual counselor is extremely low (Van Horne, 2004). Even when a complaint is filed, 74% of psychologists in one state found that it was resolved to their satisfaction (Montgomery, Cupit, & Wimberley, 1999). Counselors and therapists who worry excessively about a complaint are misdirecting their energies. However, realistic concern is appropriate because as much as 11% of claims in a given jurisdiction can result in disciplinary action (Montgomery et al., 1999; Schoenfeld, Hatch, & Gonzalez, 2001; Thomas, 2002; Van Horne, 2004). If you are informed that an ethics complaint has been leveled against you, the ethics codes contain guidelines for your response.

ACA *Code of Ethics,* Section H.3: Cooperation with Ethics Committees

Counselors assist in the process of enforcing the ACA *Code of Ethics.* Counselors cooperate with investigations, proceedings, and requirements of the ACA Ethics Committee or ethics committees of other duly constituted associations or boards having jurisdiction over those charged with a violation. Counselors are familiar with the ACA *Policies and Procedures for Processing Complaints of Ethical Violations* and use it as a reference in assisting the enforcement of the *Code of Ethics.*

APA *Ethics Principles,* Section 1.06: Cooperating with Ethics Committees

Psychologists cooperate in ethics investigations, proceedings, and resulting requirements of the APA or any affiliated state psychological association to which they belong. In doing so, they address any confidentiality issues. Failure to cooperate is itself an ethics violation. However, making a request for deferment of adjudication of an ethics complaint pending the outcome of litigation does not alone constitute noncooperation.

The central message is that ignoring an inquiry by an ethics committee or licensing board is the worst possible response because failing to cooperate is an ethics violation in itself. The counselor may be especially tempted to ignore a inquiry that appears groundless, but even frivolous and false claims require a response (Anderson & Swanson, 1994). Cooperation entails providing all relevant information in a timely fashion. Each professional organization has somewhat different timelines, so it is important to refer to the rules governing the process in the organization in which the claim is made. Cooperation also means that you do not try to resign from the organization to avoid an ethics inquiry. Once a proceeding has begun, a member is not allowed to resign until the investigation is complete. Even then, a resignation may be accepted only under certain conditions. Many people wisely hire attorneys to assist them in this process and ensure that their rights are protected.

Learning of an ethics claim arouses strong emotions (Schoenfeld, et al., 2001; Thomas, 2002). (See Peterson, 2001 for an example of the reaction of a professional who believes he was wrongly accused and convicted.) A wise professional seeks appropriate emotional support in this situation (Chauvin & Remley, 1996). If you believe that you have been falsely accused, these emotions can be truly overwhelming. In that situation, some reality testing is in order. History shows that most claims are dismissed before formal charges are issued, so likely there is no need to panic about a preliminary investigation.

If you have committed the unethical action with which you are charged but believe there are relevant extenuating circumstances, you should document the particulars to the committee or licensing board. Extenuating circumstances do not excuse such behaviors (and members who try to make excuses hardly ever win the favor of the committee), but they can put the misconduct in context. If you have subsequently taken steps on your own to prevent such actions in the future, your case may be strengthened by providing such information to the committee. Such an approach is consistent with the committee's interest in rehabilitating professionals rather than punishing them. Professionals who take responsibility for their mistakes and demonstrate a sincere commitment to rehabilitation go a long way in helping to save their careers.

Thomas (2002) recommends that the accused professional refrain from making any contact with the client who has filed the complaint. The only exception to this advice occurs when the professional's attorney advises such contact. She also agrees with the advice of Chauvin and Remley (1996) to refrain from disclosing detailed information about the complaint to family and friends. This is an understandable but misguided effort to relieve the stress of a complaint that represents a violation of confidentiality in itself. The client filing the complaint released information to the Board or Ethics Committee, not others.

Self-Monitoring: Taking Responsibility in the Absence of a Complaint

The typical mental health professional probably spends 30 to 40 years in practice. Even those who undertake this profession as a second career are likely to work for two decades. In that span of time ethical mistakes of varying seriousness will almost certainly occur. As discussed in Chapter 1, many mental health practitioners admit both intentional and unintentional violations of ethical standards (Pope, Tabachnick, & Keith-Spiegel, 1987; Sherry, Teschendorf, Anderson, & Guzman, 1991; Tubbs & Pomerantz, 2001), but few of those violations are reported to any disciplinary body (Pope & Vasquez, 1998; Williams, 2000). Inadvertent disclosures of confidential information are especially common examples of these missteps (Pope et al., 1987). Counselors who fail to acknowledge their vulnerability to misconduct are naive at best and frightening at worst. The novelist D. H. Lawrence speaks with conviction on the subject: "This is the very worst wickedness, that we refuse to acknowledge the passionate evil that is in all of us. That makes us secret and rotten" (1915, reprinted in Zytaruk & Boulton, 1981). In its essence, ethical practice is not about expecting perfection; rather, it is about taking responsibility for one's actions (whether ethical or unethical) and keeping the improvement of one's clients as the central aim. In some ways, one of the truest tests of a professional's commitment to ethical practice is the way that person reacts when he or she deviates from that path and disciplinary bodies are not likely to discover that deviation. This capacity to acknowledge one's failings and act to ameliorate their negative effects in the absence of external reprimands is closely related to the virtue ethics about which Meara, Schmidt, and Day (1996) write so eloquently. Virtuous professionals believe so strongly in the ethical values of the profession that they hold themselves accountable even when others do not. The ethical principles underlying this personal accountability are beneficence and fidelity. The very definition of a profession includes the notion that members of a profession are self-regulating individuals who have internalized the ethical values of the profession they have voluntarily joined and who are committed to acting in the best interest of the communities they serve (Pryzwansky & Wendt, 1999).

Unfortunately, the ethics codes do not address this issue directly. Instead, they deal with the professional's responsibility to know the codes, act in accordance with them, and consult with others when in doubt (ACA, Section H; APA, Section 1). In the same sections, the codes also describe strategies for handling the questionable behaviors of colleagues, but they are largely silent on one's duty after recognizing one's own ethical misconduct as a professional. The ethics literature also addresses the issue of colleague misconduct (for example, Levenson, 1986) and response to others' accusations (Chauvin & Remley, 1996; Thomas, 2002) but contains little reference to recovery from one's own misconduct. Principle B of the APA *Ethical Principles* (2002) touches on the matter in its statement: "Psychologists uphold professional standards of conduct, clarify their professional roles and obligations, accept appropriate responsibility for their behavior, and seek to manage conflicts of interest that could lead to exploitation or harm." Similarly, the following section of the ACA *Code of Ethics* seems relevant.

ACA *Code of Ethics,* Section C.2.d: Monitor Effectiveness

Counselors continually monitor their effectiveness as professionals and take steps to improve when necessary. Counselors in private practice take reasonable steps to seek out peer supervision as needed to evaluate their efficacy as counselors.

The ethics codes emphasize prevention of misconduct, and this emphasis is both understandable and noble, but any discussion of professional ethics that attends only to prevention is ultimately insufficient, in the light of human nature, research evidence about misconduct, and the limitations of current reporting mechanisms. Not discussing remediation leads to the mistaken impression that mistakes are rare or avoidable or always egregious. In this context, practitioners are more likely to view their less serious ethical violations as problems that ought to be kept secret and hidden away. The focus of this section, then, is on frank and open attention to ethical violations and on recommendations for coping responsibly with one's own mistakes. Because these recommendations are not codified in any official document, they are advisory, not enforceable. Their aim is to encourage mental health professionals to understand accountability at its most fundamental level. The foundation for these recommendations derives partly from the literature on the rehabilitation of offending counselors and psychotherapists (Brown, 1997; Gonsiorek, 1997; Layman & McNamara, 1997; Schoener & Gonsiorek, 1988; Welfel, 2005). The three essential questions that professionals need to answer when confronting their own mistakes are as follows:

- Have I really acknowledged that I have violated professional standards?
- What damage have I done, and how can I undo or ameliorate that damage?
- What steps should I take to ensure that I do not repeat this mistake?

Acknowledging the Violation

As professionals in human service professions we like to think of ourselves as honorable people, motivated by altruism rather than self-interest. Even when abundant evidence of serious misconduct exists, we seem to want to minimize or rationalize our actions (Pope & Vasquez,

1998). The tendency to minimize violations that do not cause substantial harm or that are hidden from public view is likely to be even greater. The first task in self-monitoring is to fully acknowledge the ethical lapse and understand its nature and scope without catastrophizing about it. This task requires careful reflection and tolerance for the emotional discomfort that accompanies such reflection. Allowing awareness of the emotional distress can act as a motivator to address the negative effects and work toward prevention of a recurrence. It is important here to focus on the ethical dimensions of the conduct, not its legal ramifications. The legal standard for malpractice, for example, is evidence of harm to the client, but the ethical standard is *risk or threat of harm to the client,* derived from the ethical principle of nonmaleficence.

Assessing and Responding to the Damage

Once a professional has become aware of a problematic behavior, the next step is to determine how much harm has been caused. Assessing harm to the client is the top priority, followed by damage to colleagues, to others in the community, and to the reputation of the profession. Consulting with a trusted colleague who is objective, knowledgeable, and able to identify biases of which the individual is unaware is often helpful. Colleagues can sometimes act as intermediaries with disaffected clients or colleagues who resist additional contacts with the offending counselor because of their negative experience. For example, a colleague might telephone a client to explore ways in which the client's needs can be met, assuming, of course, that such a contact would not breach confidentiality obligations to the client. Perhaps a client would be willing to make an appointment with a different professional or participate in a meeting with the counselor with other professionals present to find an acceptable solution to the difficulty.

Once the level of damage is determined, the third step is to develop a strategy that will ameliorate that harm. The more serious the infraction, the more complicated the remediation is likely to be. A counselor who has for several weeks provided incompetent service because of alcohol abuse has a much greater task in this regard than a therapist who acted incompetently on a single day because of illness or personal crisis. In the latter case, providing a day's worth of sessions without cost to compensate for the day of poor service is probably all that is required as long as the incompetent sessions did not inflict significant damage on clients.

The therapist seeking to compensate for weeks of incompetent service faces a more difficult task. The length of the incompetent service also increases the likelihood of meaningful negative effects for clients. A client who is depressed who receives inadequate therapy for 3 weeks will probably suffer more than one who gets a single bungled session. Clients may have terminated counseling prematurely and may be unwilling to engage in counseling again because of their bad experience. The ill effects may extend not only to clients but also to the client's family members and friends, to whom the counselor has little or no access. Colleagues may have experienced some negative fallout during the period of impairment. Some attention to remedying negative impact on them is also in order. Obviously, in this kind of situation the counselor's capacity to remedy the harm is limited. If the original victims of the misconduct are inaccessible, then professionals may perform the equivalent of the "community service" penalty that criminal courts often impose for minor offenses. The point of such actions is to act to compensate the community for misbehaviors. Community service activities serve two purposes. They balance the scales in a small way, and they remind those involved of their responsibilities to the broader community.

One cautionary note is in order here. Ethical ideals do not require a Herculean effort to ameliorate all ill effects. The crucial feature of all such efforts is one's good-faith commitment to help those he or she has harmed and to address the damage to the profession's reputation in the community. Brown (1997) uses the term *amends* in this regard, and it seems quite fitting to express the notion that some sort of compensation is in order. Consultation can assist here, too, in sorting out reasonable from unreasonable efforts and in devising a workable plan to remedy damage.

The impact of remedies on those who suffered the original ill effects must also be assessed. Put plainly, if the cure is worse than the disease, it's no cure at all. Because the most important ethical standard is the welfare of the client, remediation efforts that jeopardize that welfare have no place in recovery from an ethical misstep. For example, if a counselor reveals a client name to a close friend in a lunchtime chat, that counselor has violated the ethics code. The purpose of the discussion with the colleague was not professional, it was not in the client's best interest, and there was no client authorization for the disclosure. When the counselor recognizes the blunder, he or she needs to carefully examine the best way to remedy that mistake. Speaking with the friend again to acknowledge the error and asking that person to honor confidentiality is one remedy that injures no one. Whether the violation is best disclosed to the client depends on its effects on the client, especially because it is a minor infraction with little likelihood of negative consequences for that client. If an objective assessment of a remedy reveals that it risks additional harm to a client, the counselor should seek alternative remedies. Because the task of implementing a remedy is emotionally stressful, however, particularly when it involves disclosure to a client, counselors may be tempted to rationalize that all such disclosures will be harmful and should not be done. The criterion for judging the appropriateness of a remedy is the long-term welfare of the client rather than the immediate self-interest of the counselor. Consultation is essential here, too, in sorting out reasonable and helpful interventions from unreasonable or self-serving ones.

Rehabilitating the Professional

A counselor who has erred begins the process of recovery with an honest self-evaluation that unflinchingly recognizes the mistakes made and seeks out the causes so that they will be less likely to recur. The goal here is not to engender guilt or shame; the goal is to gather energy for the process of change. The nature of the rehabilitative activities will vary significantly with the violation. For minor infractions, one may need simply to reread the ethics code and consult with colleagues for a period to verify that one is interpreting the code in an acceptable way. For more serious matters, a formal plan for rehabilitation is in order. That plan may include the following:

- Therapy for the counselor if personal problems or character flaws are at the root of the misconduct, although this is no panacea for the problem.
- Reduction in the scope of one's practice to reduce risk. (A person who has violated multiple relationship prohibitions, for instance, may wish to refrain from accepting clients similar to the client with whom the violation was committed to reduce the risk of a recurrence.)
- A temporary moratorium on therapeutic work until stability is regained.
- An arrangement with another counselor to closely supervise one's practice so that any problematic behaviors can be quickly identified and stopped.
- A program of self-education or formal ethics education to gain a better understanding of the codes and the ethical values of the profession.
- Enrollment in training experiences that improve clinical competency.

This list is not comprehensive. Rehabilitation activities should be tailored to the individual violation and to the violator's characteristics. Similarly, the period of time devoted to rehabilitation will vary widely. Approaches to subsequent offenses in the same domain ought to be treated more aggressively than first offenses, but even first offenses ought not to be ignored. Finally, even when the rehabilitation period seems complete, because of human frailty the professional ought to periodically engage in supervision activities that ensure that no slippage has occurred. Unfortunately, there is no convincing evidence that rehabilitation efforts are effective when they have been imposed by licensing boards and ethics committees (Gonsiorek, 1997; Layman & McNamara, 1997).

Compassion and Empathy

There is one additional value in personal accountability: compassion. It reminds professionals that we are all vulnerable to ethical missteps and deters us from adopting an attitude of moral superiority toward professionals who have been accused of misconduct. By recognizing our own mistakes, we gain compassion and empathy for others. As Jerome (1889) wrote more than a hundred years ago, "It is in our faults and failings, not in our virtues, that we touch each other and find sympathy. . . . It is in our follies that we are one." Thus, when others seek us out for consultation after an infraction, we are more likely to take an approach of seeking rehabilitation rather than punishment, of giving sympathy rather than harsh personal judgment. This compassion is not incompatible with full accountability for behavior; it is the fullest application of ethical ideals.

CASES FOR DISCUSSION

The following cases are representative examples of ethical missteps that others are unlikely to file complaints about (or even know about). They highlight both the need for remedies for misconduct and the difficulty in implementing it on occasion. They also raise interesting questions about rehabilitation. Reflect on each case, come to a conclusion about the ideal ethical remedy, and plan for rehabilitation.

Dr. Portrain and Hypnosis

Dr. Portrain, a psychologist, attended a 1-day seminar on the use of clinical hypnosis for posttraumatic stress. This seminar was his first exposure to hypnosis and was taught by an expert in hypnosis who has received high ratings for the quality of her presentation. Since that seminar, Dr. Portrain has spent several hours reading about hypnosis and has discussed that material with his colleagues. A few days later a man who had barely escaped a serious fire in his apartment building came for counseling. An assessment indicated a moderate level of posttraumatic stress. Dr. Portrain recommended hypnosis as the treatment of choice, omitting any mention of other approaches that might help this client. The psychologist was eager and excited about the ability to use this new treatment tool so soon after the workshop. The man

agreed to hypnosis, and Dr. Portrain conducted three sessions using hypnosis. At the end of those sessions, the man showed no improvement in his symptoms. While watching the man weep over his disappointment about not improving, Dr. Portrain then realized that he had been practicing beyond the boundaries of his competence and had unfairly pushed his client into an experimental treatment without explaining other options.

Dr. MacDuff's Funny Story

Dr. MacDuff's client, Mr. Betts, reveals to him a very embarrassing event that occurred on his recent honeymoon. The client was relieved to be able to discuss the issue with his therapist and by the end of the session, the client began to appreciate the humor as well as the pain in the situation. The next weekend, Dr. MacDuff was at a party at a neighbor's home. During that party, the host initiated a "Tell us your most embarrassing moment" game, and the partygoers agreed to participate. When Dr. MacDuff's turn came, he had difficulty thinking of anything that would spark real laughter in the group, so he told of Mr. Bett's incident without identifying his client. In fact, he simply referred to the person as an acquaintance. The group enjoyed the anecdote immensely; it was the highlight of the party. The next day he encountered a partygoer in the supermarket who again expressed his enjoyment of Dr. MacDuff's anecdote. At this point, the doctor began to feel uneasy about his behavior and to regret it.

Ms. Spend's Creative Problemsolving

Ms. Spend, a licensed clinical counselor in private practice, has become increasingly frustrated with the demands of third-party payors. Recently, when treating a woman with major depression, the insurance company authorized only five sessions and would not raise that limit. The client decided to pay out-of-pocket for the rest of her sessions, but this represented a hardship to the client, even at reduced fees. The next time Ms. Spend encountered a client insured by the same company, she entered a diagnosis more severe than the client's true symptoms so as to obtain more reimbursement. In this case, the insurer agreed to 10 sessions, a number both the counselor and the client judged adequate for the problem. Two weeks after that client terminated, Ms. Spend attended a seminar on ethical and legal issues in counseling and realized that her behavior with this client was not only unethical but also probably illegal.

The Case of Ms. Monderly

Ms. Monderly is a licensed clinical social worker who has been in practice for 10 years. She has recently moved to a new community and feels lonely. One day she encountered a client who seemed to have all the characteristics she values in a friend. The client seemed to be experiencing the same feelings about Ms. Monderly. Ms. Monderly decided to refer this client to another therapist after three sessions. The other therapist is an expert in the problem the client was experiencing, but Ms. Monderly's motivation was based primarily on her desire to begin a friendship with this client. Two months after the termination, Ms. Monderly telephoned the client to invite her to a museum opening. They began to attend cultural activities regularly. At one activity a few months later, Ms. Monderly saw a colleague from the practice. The colleague seemed surprised when he recognized the client. His expression of surprise changed to disapproval when the client revealed in their brief conversation that she and Ms. Monderly had become very close friends. Ms. Monderly wondered whether she should have resisted her personal interest in this client and made other efforts to find friends in her new community.

The Case of Bob and Ted

Bob is a licensed clinical counselor who has operated a small group practice in a suburban office building for 20 years. He is well recognized for his expertise in working with clients with complex problems who require long-term counseling. One day he receives a telephone call from another counselor (Ted) working in the same neighborhood. Bob does not know Ted. Ted tells Bob that he is currently in the office with a woman named Nancy who has come to see him to discuss her depression. Ted proceeds to tell Bob that Nancy has just accused him of sexual misconduct and that Ted wants him to explain what happened when Nancy came to see Bob. Ted tells Bob that nothing he can say will dissuade him from reporting Bob to the licensing board but that he still wants to hear what he has to say. Ted goes on to tell Bob that his actions have been totally unprofessional and that he has traumatized this woman. Bob is shocked and first tries to ascertain that this is not a crank call and to clarify that Ted is indeed a licensed professional. The information Ted shares clarifies that he is a licensed clinical social worker and that he has Nancy's permission to make this phone call. As he listens to Ted describe Nancy and the comments she has made to Ted, Bob realizes that he does not even recognize the woman to whom Ted is referring. Bob asks Nancy to describe his physical appearance, but her description could fit many men and is not very helpful. Next Bob asks if Nancy would be willing to speak with him on the phone because he still has no memory of seeing Nancy. As soon as they begin the conversation Nancy realizes that she does not recognize Bob's voice. After a few more exchanges Nancy comes to seriously doubt whether she has identified the right counselor. Ted mumbles a few words about getting more information and calling back later and hangs up. Bob is so upset by this conversation that he cannot sleep that night and immediately consults with a colleague. Bob then tries to figure out how to follow up with Ted who falsely accused him of a serious violation. (Bob later learns that Nancy had seen another counselor in a nearby building with the first name of Robert.) Discuss the ethical issues involved in the actions of both Ted and Bob. Should Bob just forget the whole matter at this point?

SUMMARY

Counselors learn of ethics violations by other professionals in several ways—from clients, from colleagues, and through their own experience. Hearing of colleagues' misbehavior from clients is not uncommon. Counselors are obliged to address these violations themselves, or they must help clients who choose to address them to do so. However, when the desire to confront a colleague about an ethics violation conflicts with a client's right to confidentiality, confidentiality takes precedence.

The ethics codes recommend beginning with an attempt at an informal resolution of the problem. Usually, this starts with a conversation between the concerned and the offending counselor. If the concerned counselor is convinced that the offense did not occur or that rehabilitation efforts will be effective, no further action is necessary. If the counselor doubts whether the public will be protected from further misconduct, a formal complaint is the next step. Individuals may submit ethics complaints to a variety of bodies, including licensing boards, professional associations, and employers. Procedures for handling such complaints are laid out in state regulations, ethics committee rules and procedures, or employee policy manuals. The central issue for the committees hearing such complaints is balancing the rights of the person making the complaint against the rights of the person accused. As in all other aspects of U.S. society, a professional is assumed innocent until proven guilty.

If a client has experienced unethical behavior by a former counselor, the current counselor should explain the client's options about reporting and help the client deal with the emotions during the process. The client should be free to decide autonomously about pursuing a complaint because the complaint process is long and demanding and can result in some reexperiencing of the initial pain. If the client decides to proceed, he or she needs to recognize that its primary benefit will be to future clients of that therapist, although it's possible the client will find the experience a healing one.

No mental health professional is immune to unethical practice. Survey data suggest that violations of confidentiality, informed consent, and dual relationships are rather common. Those studies also show that professionals express concern about their past misbehaviors and worry about future missteps. In this context, counselors and therapists ought to recognize their own vulnerability to ethical violations and take personal responsibility for acting to remedy them even if outside disciplinary bodies fail to catch their misconduct. This obligation is not codified in any professional ethical standards and thus is not enforceable, but it is consistent with the ethical ideals of mental health professions to promote the welfare of others and place clients' needs ahead of one's own. Specifically, professionals ought to assess the damage their misconduct has caused, develop a plan for intervening to reduce or compensate for that damage, and then turn their attention to rehabilitation so that they are less vulnerable to that violation in the future.

DISCUSSION QUESTIONS

1. Do you agree with the author's resolution of the case of Martina? Would you argue for an informal resolution? Why or why not?

2. Reporting an unethical behavior to an employer has both benefits and disadvantages. Discuss the strengths and weaknesses of this strategy.

3. Should the ethics codes contain more explicit references to remedies and rehabilitation? If so, what wording would you find acceptable? If not, why not?

4. Is commitment to the ethical ideal of minimizing damage to clients and others naive and unrealistic in a world of malpractice litigation and disciplinary action by licensing boards?

5. What feelings may affect a counselor trying to support a client who is filing an ethics complaint against another counselor?

6. Do you think the findings of ethics committees should be made known to the public? Currently, many organizations provide information about members who have been disciplined for ethics breaches. What might be gained or lost by more widespread communication of such findings?

7. Under what circumstances do you think implementing a remedy for a misstep might be as harmful as the misstep itself? If clients are ignorant of ethical violations, should they be informed?

8. What are the ethical dilemmas for the colleague who acts as a consultant to a professional who discloses a serious ethical violation?

RECOMMENDED READINGS

American Counseling Association. (2003). *Policies and procedures for processing complaints of ethical violations.* Alexandria, VA: Author.

American Psychological Association Ethics Committee. (2001). *Rules and procedures.* Washington, DC: Author.

Chauvin, J. C., & Remley, T. P., Jr. (1996). Responding to allegations of unethical conduct. *Journal of Counseling and Development, 74,* 563–568.

Levenson, J. L. (1986). When a colleague acts unethically: Guidelines for intervention. *Journal of Counseling and Development, 64,* 315–317.

Meara, N. M., Schmidt, L. D., & Day, J. D. (1996). Principles and virtues: A foundation for ethical decisions, policies and character. *The Counseling Psychologist, 24,* 4–77.

Thomas, J. T. (2002, August). *Facing a board complaint: The impact on the psychologist's objectivity.* Paper presented at the annual meeting of the American Psychological Association, Chicago.

Van Horne, B. A. (2004). Psychology licensing board disciplinary actions: The realities. *Professional Psychology: Research and Practice, 35,* 170–178.

References

Ackerley, G. D., Burnell, J., Holder, D. C., & Kurdek, L. A. (1988). Burnout among licensed psychologists. *Professional Psychology: Research and Practice, 19,* 424–431.

Acuff, C., Bennett, B. E., Bricklin, P. M., Canter, M. B., Knapp, L. J., Moldawsky, S., et al. (1998). Considerations for ethical practice in managed care. *Professional Psychology: Research and Practice, 30,* 563–575.

Adams, J., Kottke, J. L., & Padgit, J. S. (1983). Sexual harassment of university students. *Journal of College Student Personnel, 24,* 484–490.

Adelman, J., & Barrett, S. E. (1990). Overlapping relationships: Importance of a feminist ethical perspective. In H. Lerman & N. Porter (Eds.), *Feminist ethics in psychotherapy* (pp. 87–91). New York: Springer.

AdvocateWeb (2005). *Sexual exploitation laws:* Retrieved July 14, 2005, from http://www.advocateweb.org/hope/laws.asp

Ahia, C. E., & Martin, D. (1993). The danger-to-self-or-others exception to confidentiality. In T. P. Remley (Ed.), *ACA legal series* (Vol. 9). Alexandria, VA: American Counseling Association.

Alexander, K., & Alexander, M. D. (2005). *American public school law* (6th ed). Belmont, CA: Thomson West.

Alstrand, K. R., Crumlin, J., Korinek, L. L., Lasky, G. B., & Kitchener, K. S. (2003, August). *Sexual contact between students and educators: Issues and ethics.* Paper presented at the annual meeting of the American Psychological Association, Toronto, CAN.

Akamatsu, T. J. (1988). Intimate relationships with former clients: National survey of attitudes and behavior among practitioners. *Professional Psychology: Research and Practice, 19,* 454–458.

Alleman, J. R. (2002). Online counseling: The Internet and mental health treatment. *Psychotherapy: Theory/Research/Practice/Training, 39,* 199–215.

Allen, G. J., Szollos, S. J., & Williams, B. E. (1986). Doctoral students' comparative evaluations of best and worst psychotherapy supervision. *Professional Psychology: Research and Practice, 17,* 91–99.

Alyn, J. H. (1988). The politics of touch in therapy: A response to Willison and Masson. *Journal of Counseling and Development, 66,* 432–433.

Amada, G. (1993). Some ethical considerations: A commentary on "Between Cordelia and Guido: The consultant's role in urgent situations." *Journal of College Student Psychotherapy, 7,* 23–34.

American Association for Marriage and Family Therapy. (2001). *Code of ethics.* Retrieved March 9, 2005, from http://www.aamft.org/resources/LRMPlan/Ethics/ethicscode2001.asp

American Association of State Psychology Boards. (1979). *Guidelines for the employment and supervision of uncredentialed persons providing psychological services.* Montgomery, AL: Author.

American Counseling Association. (1994). *Policies and procedures for processing complaints of ethical violations.* Alexandria, VA: Author.

American Counseling Association. (1995). *Code of ethics and standards of practice.* Alexandria, VA: Author.

American Counseling Association. (1998). *Early warning, timely response: A guide to safe schools.* Alexandria, VA: Author.

American Counseling Association. (1999). *Ethical standards for Internet online counseling.* Alexandria, VA: Author. Retrieved August 5, 2005, from http://www.counseling.org/Content/NavigationMenu/RESOURCES/ETHICS/EthicalStandardsforInternetOnlineCounseling/Ethical_Stand_Online.htm

American Counseling Association. (2003). *Policies and procedures for processing complaints of ethical violations.* Alexandria, VA: Author.

American Counseling Association. (2005). *Code of ethics and standards of practice.* Alexandria, VA: Author.

American Educational Research Association, American Psychological Association, & National Council on Measurement in Education. (1999). *Standards for Educational and Psychological Tests.* Washington, DC: Author.

American Psychiatric Association. (2000). *Diagnostic and statistical manual for mental and emotional disorders* (4th ed., text revision). Washington, DC: Author.

American Psychiatric Association. (2001). *Principles of medical ethics with annotations especially applicable to psychiatry.* Washington, DC: Author.

American Psychological Association. (1973). *Guidelines for psychologists conducting growth groups.* Washington, DC: Author.

American Psychological Association. (1978). Guidelines for therapy with women. *American Psychologist, 33,* 1122–1123.

American Psychological Association. (1981). *Ethical principles.* Washington, DC: Author.

American Psychological Association. (1991). *Legal liability related to confidentiality and the prevention of HIV transmission.* Washington, DC: Author.

American Psychological Association. (1992). *Ethical principles of psychologists and code of conduct.* Washington, DC: Author.

American Psychological Association. (1993a). *Guidelines for ethical conduct in the care and use of animals.* Washington, DC: Author.

American Psychological Association. (1993b). *Guidelines for providers of psychological services to ethnic, linguistic and culturally diverse populations.* Washington, DC: Author.

American Psychological Association. (1993c). *Record keeping guidelines.* Washington, DC: Author.

American Psychological Association. (1994). Guidelines for child custody evaluations in divorce proceedings. *American Psychologist, 49,* 677–680.

American Psychological Association. (1997). *Mental health patient's bill of rights.* Retrieved August 5, 2005, from http://www.apa.org/pubinfo/rights/rights.html

American Psychological Association. (1999a). Guidelines for psychological evaluations in child protection matters. *American Psychologist, 54,* 586–593.

American Psychological Association. (1999b). *Warning signs: A youth anti-violence initiative.* Washington, DC: Author.

American Psychological Association. (2001). *Council resolution on assisted suicide.* Retrieved May 5, 2005, from http://www.apa.org/ppo/issues/asreolu.html

American Psychological Association. (2001). Rules and procedures. *American Psychologist, 51,* 529–548.

American Psychological Association. (2002). Ethical principles of psychologists and code of conduct. *American Psychologist, 57,* 1060–1075.

American Psychological Association. (2003a). Guidelines on multicultural education, training, research, practice, and organizational change for psychologists. *American Psychologist, 58,* 377–402.

American Psychological Association. (2003b). Guidelines for providers of psychological services to older adults. *American Psychologist, 59,* 236–260.

American Psychological Association. (2004). Report of the Ethics Committee, 2003. *American Psychologist, 59,* 434–441.

American Psychological Association. (2005a). *Policy statement on evidence-based practice in psychology.* Retrieved August 25, 2005 from http://www.apa.org/practice/ebpstatement.pdf.

American Psychological Association. (2005b). *Statement on the use of secure psychological tests in the education of graduate and undergraduate psychology students.* Washington, DC: Author.

American Psychological Association, Committee on Legal Issues. (1996). Strategies for private practitioners coping with subpoenas or compelled testimony for client records or test data. *Professional Psychology: Research and Practice, 27,* 245–251.

American Psychological Association, Committee on Professional Practice and Standards. (1995). Twenty-four questions (and answers) about professional practice in the area of child abuse. *Professional Psychology: Research and Practice, 26,* 377–383.

American Psychological Association, Committee on Professional Practice and Standards. (2003). Legal issues in the professional practice of psychology. *Professional Psychology: Research and Practice, 34,* 595–600.

American Psychological Association, Committee on Women in Psychology. (1989). If sex enters into the psychotherapy relationship. *Professional Psychology: Research and Practice, 20,* 112–115.

American Psychological Association, Education Directorate. (2003). *Survey of state and provincial mandatory continuing education requirements.* Retrieved October 20, 2004, from http://www.apa.org/ce/mcesurvey03.html

American Psychological Association, Ethics Committee. (1983). *Authorship guidelines for dissertation supervision.* Washington, DC: Author.

American Psychological Association, Ethics Committee. (2001). *Rules and procedures.* Washington, DC: Author.

American Psychological Association, Ethics Committee. (2004). Report of the Ethics Committee, 2003. *American Psychologist, 59,* 434–441.

American Psychological Association, Insurance Trust. (1990). *Bulletin: Sexual misconduct and professional liability claims.* Washington, DC: Author.

American Psychological Association, Task Force. (1975). Report of the task force on sex bias and sex role stereotyping in psychotherapeutic practice. *American Psychologist, 30,* 1169–1175.

American Psychological Association, Working Group on Assisted Suicide and End-of-Life Decisions. (2000). *Report to the Board of Trustees.* Retrieved May 5, 2005, from http://www.apa.org/pi/aseolf.html

American School Counselor Association. (1996). *Developing and informed consent brochure for secondary students.* Washington, DC: Author.

American School Counselor Association. (1997). *Executive summary: The national standards for school counseling programs.* Alexandria, VA: Author.

American School Counselor Association. (1999a). *ASCA role statement: The role of the professional school counselor.* Alexandria, VA: Author.

American School Counselor Association. (1999b). *Sharing information with the school principal.* Alexandria, VA: Author.

American School Counselor Association. (2004). *Ethical standards for school counselors.* Retrieved August 17, 2004, from http://www.schoolcounselor.org/content.asp?contentid=173

Americans with Disabilities Act of 1990, 42 U. S. Code B12101–213.

Anastasi, A. (1992). What counselors should know about the use and interpretation of psychological tests. *Journal of Counseling and Development, 70,* 610–615.

Anastasi, A., & Urbana, S. (1997). *Psychological testing* (7th ed.). New York: Macmillan.

Ancis, J. R., & Ladany, N. (2001). A multicultural framework for counselor supervision. In L. J. Bradley & N. Ladany (Eds.). *Counselor supervision: Principles process and practice* (3rd ed., pp. 63–90). Philadelphia: Brunner-Routledge.

Anderson, B. S. (1996). *The counselor and the law* (4th ed.). Alexandria, VA: American Counseling Association.

Anderson, D., & Swanson, C. D. (1994). *Legal issues in licensure.* Alexandria, VA: American Counseling Association.

Anderson, J. R., & Barret, R. L. (Eds.). (2001). *Ethics in HIV-related psychotherapy: Clinical decision making in complex cases.* Washington, DC: American Psychological Association.

Anderson, R. (1976). Peer facilitation: History and issues. *Elementary School Guidance and Counseling, 11,* 16–25.

Anderson, R. D., & Price, G. E. (2001). Experiential groups in counselor education: Student attitudes and instructor participation. *Counselor Education and Supervision, 41,* 111–119.

Anderson, S. A., Schlossberg, M., & Rigazio-DiGilio, S. (2000). Family therapy trainees' evaluations of their best and worst supervisors. *Journal of Marital and Family Therapy, 26,* 79–91.

Anderson, S. K., & Kitchener, K. S. (1996). Nonromantic, nonsexual posttherapy relationships between psychologists and former clients: An exploratory student of critical incidents. *Professional Psychology: Research and Practice, 27,* 59–66.

Anderson, S. K., & Kitchener, K. S. (1998). Nonsexual posttherapy relationships: A conceptual framework to assess ethical risks. *Professional Psychology: Research and Practice, 29,* 91–99.

Anderton, P., Staulcup, V., & Grisso, T. (1980). On being ethical in legal places. *Professional Psychology: Research and Practice, 11,* 764–773.

Anonymous. (1991). Sexual harassment: A female counseling student's experience. *Journal of Counseling and Development, 69,* 502–506.

Appelbaum, P. S. (1993). Legal liability in managed care. *American Psychologist, 48,* 251–257.

Appelbaum, P. S. (1998). Managed care's responsibility for decisions to deny benefits: The ERISA obstacle. *Psychiatric Services, 49,* 461–462, 471.

Appelbaum, P. S., & Greer, A. (1993). Confidentiality in group therapy. *Hospital and Community Psychology, 44,* 311–313.

Appelbaum, P. S., & Gutheil, T. G. (1991). *Clinical handbook of psychiatry and the law* (2nd ed.). Baltimore: Williams & Wilkins.

Appelbaum P. S., Lidz, C. W., & Meisel, A. (1987). *Informed consent: Legal theory and clinical practice.* New York: Oxford University Press.

Arrendondo, P., Toporek, R., Brown, S. P., Jones, J., Locke, D., Sanchez, J., et al. (1996). Operationalization of the multicultural counseling competencies. *Journal of Multicultural Counseling and Development, 24,* 42–78.

Arthur, G. L., Jr., & Swanson, C. D. (1993). Confidentiality and privileged communication. In T. P. Remley (Ed.), *ACA legal series* (Vol. 6). Alexandria, VA: American Counseling Association.

Arthur, W., Woehr, D. J., & Graziano, W. G. (2001). Personality testing in employment settings: Problems and issues in the application of typical selection practices. *Personnel Review, 30,* 657–676.

Association for Counselor Education and Supervision. (1990). Standards for counseling supervisors. *Journal of Counseling and Development, 69,* 30–32.

Association for Counselor Education and Supervision. (1993). Ethical guidelines for counseling supervisors. *Counselor Education and Supervision, 34,* 270–276.

Association for Specialists in Group Work, Executive Board. (1989). *Ethical guidelines for group counselors.* Alexandria, VA: American Counseling Association.

Association for Specialists in Group Work. (1998). *Best practice guidelines.* Retrieved August 5, 2005, from http://www.asgw.org/best.htm

Association of State and Provincial Psychology Boards. (2003). *ASPPB supervision guidelines.* Retrieved July 11, 2005, from http://asppb.org/publications/pdf/SupervisionGuidelines.pdf

Association of Trial Lawyers of America. (2001). Psychotherapy records are discoverable in cases involving emotional distress. *Trial, 37,* 106.

Aubrey, M., & Dougher, M. J. (1990). Ethical issues in outpatient group therapy with sex offenders. *Journal for Specialists in Group Work, 15,* 75–82.

Avery, L. D., & Gressard, C. F. (2000). Counseling regulations regarding sexual misconduct: A comparison across states. *Counseling and Values, 45,* 67–78.

Bacorn, D., & Dixon, D. (1984). The effects of touch on depressed and vocationally undecided clients. *Journal of Counseling Psychology, 31,* 488–496.

Baer, B. E., & Murdock, N. L. (1995). Nonerotic multiple relationships between therapists and clients: The effects of sex, theoretical orientation and interpersonal boundaries. *Ethics and Behavior, 5,* 131–145.

Bailey, S. M. (1996). Shortchanging girls and boys. *Educational Leadership, 53,* 75–79.

Baird, K. A., & Rupert, P. A. (1987). Clinical management of confidentiality: A survey of psychologists in seven states. *Professional Psychology: Research and Practice, 18,* 347–352.

Bajt, T. R., & Pope, K. S. (1989). Therapist–patient sexual intimacy involving children and adolescents. *American Psychologist, 44,* 455.

Baker, E. K. (2003). *Caring for ourselves: A therapist's guide to personal and professional well being.* Washington, DC: American Psychological Association.

Baker, L. C., & Patterson, J. E. (1990). The first to know: A systematic analysis of confidentiality and the therapist's family. *American Journal of Family Therapy, 18,* 295–300.

Baker, S. B. (2000). *School counseling for the twenty-first century* (3rd ed.). Englewood Cliffs, NJ: Prentice Hall.

Barich, A. W., & Dimperio, K. B. (2002, August). *Ethical dilemmas of graduate training directors.* Paper presented at the annual meeting of the American Psychological Association, Chicago.

Barlow, D. H. (2004). Psychological treatments. *American Psychologist, 59,* 869–878.

Barnett, J. E. (1994). Documentation guidelines and ethical practice in psychotherapy. *Psychotherapy, 31,* 35–39.

Barnett, J. E., & Hillard, D. (2001). Psychologist distress and impairment: The availability, nature, and use of colleague assistance programs for psychologists. *Professional Psychology: Research and Practice, 32,* 205–210.

Barnett-Queen, T., & Larrabee, M. J. (2000). Sexually oriented relationships between educators and students in mental health education programs. *Journal of Mental Health Counseling, 22,* 68–84.

Bates, C. M., & Brodsky, A. M. (1989). *Sex in the therapy hour: A case of professional incest.* New York: Guilford.

Baumoel, J. (1992). The beginning of the end for the psychotherapist–patient privilege. *Cincinnati Law Review, 60,* 797–826.

Beahrs, J. O., & Gutheil, T. G. (2001). Informed consent in psychotherapy. *American Journal of Psychotherapy, 158,* 4–8.

Bean, J. P., & Kuh, G. (1984). The reciprocity between student-faculty informal contact and academic performance. *Research in Higher Education, 21,* 461–477.

Beauchamp, T. L., & Childress, J. F. (1983). *Principles of biomedical ethics.* Oxford, England: Oxford University Press.

Beauchamp, T. L., & Childress, J. F. (2001). *Principles of biomedical ethics* (5th ed.). Oxford, England: Oxford University Press.

Becvar, D. S., & Becvar, R. J. (1996). *Family therapy: A systemic integration.* Boston: Allyn & Bacon.

Bednar, R. L., Bednar, S. C., Lambert, M. J., & Waite, D. R. (1991). *Psychotherapy with high-risk clients: Legal and professional standards.* Pacific Grove, CA: Brooks/Cole.

Beeman, D. G., & Scott, N. A. (1991). Therapists' attitudes toward psychotherapy informed consent with adolescents. *Professional Psychology: Research and Practice, 22,* 230–234.

Behnke, S. (2003). Release of test data and APA's new ethics code, *APA Monitor, 34,* 70–71.

Behnke, S. (2004). Release of test data and the new ethics code. *APA Monitor, 35,* 90–91.

Behnke, S. (2005). Diagnoses, record reviews, and the new Ethics Code. *APA Monitor, 36,* 80–82.

Bell, S. K., Coleman, J. K., Anderson, A., Whelan, J. P., & Wilder, C. (2000). The effectiveness of peer mediation in a low-SES rural community school. *Psychology in the Schools, 37,* 505–516.

Benjamin, G., Andrew, H., & Gollan, J. K. (2003). *Family evaluation in custody litigation: Reducing risks of ethical infractions and malpractice.* Washington, DC: American Psychological Association.

Bennett, B., Bryant, B., VanderBos, G., & Greenwood, A. (1990). *Professional liability and risk management.* Washington, DC: American Psychological Association.

Benson, E. (2004, June). Beyond 'urbancentrism'. *APA Monitor, 35,* 54–57.

Berg, M. (1986). Toward a diagnostic alliance between psychiatrist and psychologist. *American Psychologist, 41,* 52–59.

Bernard, J. M., & Goodyear, R. K. (2004). *Fundamentals of clinical supervision* (3rd ed.). Boston: Allyn & Bacon.

Bernard, J. L., & Jara, C. S. (1986). The failure of clinical psychology graduate students to apply understood ethical principles. *Professional Psychology: Research and Practice, 17,* 313–315.

Bernard, J. L., Murphy, M., & Little, M. (1987). The failure of clinical psychologists to apply understood ethical principles. *Professional Psychology: Research and Practice, 18,* 489–491.

Berndt, D. J. (1983). Ethical and professional considerations in psychological assessment. *Professional Psychology: Research and Practice, 14,* 580–587.

Bernsen, A., Tabachnick, B. G., & Pope, K. S. (1994). National survey of social workers' sexual attraction to their clients: Results, implications and comparison to psychologists. *Ethics and Behavior, 4,* 369–388.

Bernstein, B. E., & Hartsell, T. L., Jr. (1998). *The portable lawyer for mental health professionals.* New York: Wiley.

Bernstein, R. (2005). Hispanic population passes 40 million. *U. S. Census Bureau.* Retrieved June 9, 2005, from http://www.census.gov/Press-Release/www/releases/archives/population/005164.html

Bersoff, D. N. (Ed.). (2003). *Ethical conflicts in psychology* (3rd ed.). Washington, DC: American Psychological Association.

Bersoff, D. N., & Hofer, P. J. (1991). *Legal issues in computerized psychological testing.* Hillsdale, NJ: Erlbaum.

Bersoff, D. N., & Koeppl, P. M. (1993). The relationship between ethics codes and moral principles. *Ethics and Behavior, 3,* 345–357.

Betan, E. J., & Stanton, A. L. (1999). Fostering ethical willingness: Integrating emotional and contextual awareness with rational analysis. *Professional Psychology: Research and Practice, 30,* 295–301.

Biaggio, M., Duffy, R., & Staffelbach, D. F. (1998). Obstacles to addressing professional misconduct. *Clinical Psychology Review, 18,* 273–285.

Bisbing, S. B., Jorgenson, L. B., & Sutherland, P. K. (1995). *Sexual abuse by professionals: A legal guide.* Charlottesville, VA: Mitchie.

Bissell, L., & Haberman, P. (1984). *Alcoholism in the professions.* New York: Oxford University Press.

Bittner, S., Bialek, E., Nathiel, S., Ringwalld, J., & Tupper, M., (1999). An alternative to managed care: A "guild" model for the independent practice of psychotherapy. *Journal of Marriage and Family Therapy, 25,* 99–111.

Blanchard, C. A., & Lichtenberg, J. L. (1998). Counseling psychologists' training to deal with their sexual feelings in therapy. *Counseling Psychologist, 26,* 624–639.

Bleiberg, J. R., & Baron, J. (2004). Entanglement in multiple relationships in a university counseling center. *Journal of College Student Psychotherapy, 19,* 21–34.

Blevins-Knabe, B. (1992). The ethics of dual relationships in higher education. *Ethics and Behavior, 2,* 151–163.

Bloom, J. W., & Walz, G. R. (Eds.). (2000). *Cybercounseling and cyberlearning: Strategies and resources for the millennium.* Alexandria, VA: American Counseling Association.

Bok, S. (1989). *Secrets: On the ethics of concealment and revelation.* New York: Vintage Books.

Bollas, C., & Sundelson, D. (1995). *The new informants: The betrayal of confidentiality in psychoanalysis and psychotherapy.* Northvale, NJ: Aronson.

Bombara, M. J. (2002). Relationships among school counselors' level of moral reasoning, demographic characteristics, and their use of ethical decision making resources. *Dissertation Abstracts International, 62*(11), 3687B.

Bongar, B. (1988). Clinicians, microcomputers and confidentiality. *Professional Psychology: Research and Practice, 19,* 286–289.

Bongar, B. (2002). *The suicidal patient: Clinical and legal standards of care* (2nd ed.). Washington, DC: American Psychological Association.

Borum, R. (1996). Improving the clinical practice of violence risk assessment: Technology, guidelines and training. *American Psychologist, 51,* 945–956.

Borum, R., & Reddy, M. (2001). Assessing violence risk in *Tarasoff-*situations: A fact-based model of inquiry. *Behavioral Sciences and the Law, 19,* 375–385.

Borys, D. S., & Pope, K. S. (1989). Dual relationships between therapist and client: A national study of psychologists, psychiatrists and social workers. *Professional Psychology: Research and Practice, 20,* 283–293.

Boudreaux, C. T. (2001). Psychologist disclosures of client information to significant others. *Dissertation Abstracts International, 62,* 1566B.

Bouhoutsos, J. C. (1984). Sexual intimacy between psychotherapists and clients. In L. Walker (Ed.), *Women and mental health policy* (pp. 207–227). Beverly Hills, CA: Sage.

Bouhoutsos, J. C. (1985). Therapist-client sexual involvement: A challenge for mental health professionals and educators. *American Journal of Orthopsychiatry, 55,* 177–182.

Bouhoutsos, J. C., & Brodsky, A. M. (1985). Mediation in therapist–client sex: A model. *Psychotherapy: Research and Practice, 22,* 189–193.

Bouhoutsos, J. C., Holroyd, J., Lerman, J., Forer, B., & Greenberg, M. (1983). Sexual intimacy between psychotherapists and patients. *Professional Psychology: Research and Practice, 14,* 185–196.

Bowlby, J. (1951). *Maternal care and mental health.* Geneva: World Health Organization.

Bowman, R. L., Bowman, V. E., & DeLucia, J. L. (1990). Mentoring in a graduate counseling program: Students helping students. *Counselor Education and Supervision, 30,* 58–65.

Bowman, V. E., Hatley, L. D., & Bowman, R. L. (1995). Faculty–student relationships: The dual role controversy. *Counselor Education and Supervision, 34,* 232–242.

Braaten, E. B., Otto, S., & Handelsman, M. M. (1993). What do people want to know about psychotherapy? *Psychotherapy, 30,* 565–570.

Brabeck, M. M., Walsh, M., F., Kinney, M., & Comilang, K. (1997). Interprofessional collaboration for children and families: Opportunities for counseling psychology in the 21st century. *The Counseling Psychologist, 21,* 257–277.

Bradley, L. J., & Ladany, N. (2001). *Counselor supervision: Principles, process and practice* (3rd ed.). Philadelphia: Brunner-Routledge.

Brady, J. L., Guy, J. D., Poelstra, P. L., & Brokaw, B. F. (1997). Vicarious traumatization, spirituality, and the treatment of adult and child survivors of sexual abuse. In B. H. Stamm (Ed.). *Secondary traumatic stress: Self care for clinicians, researchers, and educators* (pp. 29–36). Luthersville, MD: Sidran.

Bram, A. D. (1995). The physically ill or dying psychotherapist: A review of ethical and clinical considerations. *Psychotherapy, 32,* 568–580.

Branstetter, S. A., & Handelsman, M. M. (2000). Graduate teaching assistants: Ethical training, beliefs, and practices. *Ethics and Behavior, 10,* 27–50.

Bray, J. H., Shepherd, J. N., & Hays, J. R. (1985). Legal and ethical issues in informed consent to psychotherapy. *American Journal of Family Therapy, 13,* 50–60.

Brems, C. (2000). *Dealing with challenges in psychotherapy and counseling.* Pacific Grove, CA: Brooks/Cole.

Bricklin, P. (2001). Being ethical: More than obeying the law and avoiding harm. *Journal of Personality Assessment, 77,* 195–202.

Bridge, P., & Bascue, L. (1988). A record form for psychotherapy supervision. In P. Keller & S. Heyman (Eds.), *Innovations in clinical practice* (Vol. 7, pp. 331–336). Sarasota, FL: Professional Resource Exchange.

Brodie, R. E. (2004). Race, sex, and class bias in the diagnosis of DSM-IV disorders. *Dissertation Abstracts International, 64*(11), 5774B.

Brosig, C. L., & Kalichman, S. C. (1992). Clinicians' reporting of suspected child abuse: A review of the empirical literature. *Clinical Psychology Review, 12,* 155–168.

Broverman, I. K., Broverman, D., Clarkson, F. E., Rosencrantz, P., & Vogel, S. (1970). Sex role stereotypes and clinical judgments of mental health. *Journal of Consulting and Clinical Psychology, 34,* 1–7.

Brown, D., Pryzwansky, W. B., & Schulte, A. C. (1991). *Psychological consultations: Introduction to theory and practice.* Boston: Allyn & Bacon.

Brown, L. (1988). Harmful effects of posttermination sexual and romantic relationships between therapists and their former clients. *Psychotherapy, 25,* 249–255.

Brown, L. S. (1997). Remediation, amends, or denial? *Professional Psychology: Research and Practice, 28,* 297–299.

Buchanan, T. (2002). Online assessment: Desirable or dangerous? *Professional Psychology: Research and Practice, 33,* 148–154.

Burke, C. A. (1995). Until death do us part: An exploration into confidentiality following the death of a client. *Professional Psychology: Research and Practice, 26,* 278–280.

Butcher, J. N., Dahlstrom, W. G., Graham, J. R., Tellegen, A., & Kaemmer, B. (1989). *Minnesota Multiphasic Personality Inventory-2 (MMPI-2): Manual for administration and scoring.* Minneapolis, MN: University of Minnesota Press.

Caldwell, L. W. (2003). Sexual relationships between supervisors and supervisees during psychology graduate training. *Dissertation Abstracts International, 63*(10), 4879B.

California Board of Psychology. (2005). *Enforcement statistics, 2000–2005.* Retrieved July 10, 2005, from http://www .psychboard.ca.gov/enforce/stats.pdf

California Department of Consumer Affairs. (1997). *Professional therapy never includes sex.* (Available from the Board of Psychology, 1426 Howe Avenue, Sacramento, CA 95825)

Callanan, K., & O'Connor, T. (1988). *Staff comments and recommendations regarding the Senate Task Force on Psychotherapist and Patient Sexual Relations.* Sacramento, CA: Board of Behavioral Science Examiners and Psychology Licensing Committee.

Camera, W. J., & Schneider, D. L. (1994). Integrity tests: Facts and unresolved issues. *American Psychologist, 49,* 112–119.

Campbell, C. D., & Gordon, M. C. (2003). Acknowledging the inevitable: Understanding multiple relationships in rural practice. *Professional Psychology: Research and Practice, 34,* 430–434.

Campbell, T. W. (1999). Challenging the evidentiary reliability of the DSM-IV. *American Journal of Forensic Psychology, 17,* 47–68.

Canter, M. B., Bennett, B. E., Jones, S. E., & Nagy, T. E. (1994). *Ethics for psychologists: A commentary on the 1992 APA ethics code.* Washington, DC: American Psychological Association.

Canterbury v. Spence, 464 F.2d 772 (D.C. Cir. 1972).

Capuzzi, D. C. (2002). Legal and ethical challenges in counseling suicidal students. *Professional School Counseling, 6,* 36–45.

Capuzzi, D. C. (Ed.). (2004). *Suicide across the lifespan.* Washington, DC: American Counseling Association.

Carney, J. V. (2000). Bullied to death: Perceptions of peer abuse and suicidal behavior during adolescence? *School Psychology International, 21,* 44–54.

Carter, K. (1997, March 7). Gay slurs abound. *Des Moines Register,* p. 3.

Cassileth, B. R., Zupkis, R. V., Sutton-Smith, K., & March, V. (1980). Informed consent? Why are its goals imperfectly realized? *New England Journal of Medicine, 323,* 896–900.

Cates, J. A. (1999). The art of assessment in psychology: Ethics, expertise, and validity. *Journal of Clinical Psychology, 55,* 631–641.

Chauvin, J. C., & Remley, T. P., Jr. (1996). Responding to allegations of unethical conduct. *Journal of Counseling and Development, 74,* 563–568.

Chenneville, T. (2000). HIV, confidentiality and duty to protect: A decision-making model. *Professional Psychology: Research and Practice, 31,* 661–670.

Childress, C. (1998). *Potential risks and benefits of online therapeutic interventions.* Retrieved August 5, 2005, from http://www.ismho.org/issues/9801.htm

Christiansen, J. R. (2000). *Electronic health information: Privacy and security compliance under HIPAA.* Washington, DC: American Health Lawyers Association.

Claiborn, C. D., Berberoglu, L. S., Nerison, R. M., & Somberg, D. R. (1994). The client's perspective: Ethical judgments and perceptions of therapist's practices. *Professional Psychology: Research and Practice, 25,* 268–274.

Clark, R. A., Harden, S. L., & Johnson, B. W. (2000). Mentor relationships in clinical psychology doctoral programs: Results of a national survey. *Teaching of Psychology, 27,* 262–268.

Clayton, S., & Bongar, B. (1994). The use of consultation in psychological practice: Ethical, legal and clinical considerations. *Ethics and Behavior, 4,* 43–57.

Clingerman, T. L., & Bernard, J. M. (2004). An investigation of the use of e-mail as a supplemental modality for clinical supervision. *Counselor Education and Supervision, 44,* 82–95.

Cobia, D. C., & Pipes, R. B. (2002). Mandated supervision: An intervention for disciplined professionals. *Journal of Counseling and Development, 80,* 140–144.

Cohen, E. D., & Cohen, G. S. (1999). *The virtuous therapist: Ethical practice of counseling and psychotherapy.* Pacific Grove, CA: Brooks/Cole.

Collins, N., & Knowles, A. D. (1995). Adolescents' attitudes towards confidentiality between the school counselor and the adolescent client. *Australian Psychologist, 30,* 179–182.

Committee on Ethical Guidelines for Forensic Psychologists. (1991). Specialty guidelines for forensic psychologists. *Law and Human Behavior, 15,* 655–665.

Comer, R. J. (1996). *Fundamentals of abnormal psychology.* New York: W. H. Freeman.

Comstock, G. D. (1991). *Violence against lesbians and gay men.* New York: Columbia University.

Constantine, M. G. (1997). Facilitating multicultural competency in counseling supervision. In D. B. Pope-Davis & H. L. K. Coleman (Eds.), *Multicultural counseling competencies: Assessment, education and training, and supervision* (pp. 310–324). Thousand Oaks, CA: Sage.

Constantine, M. G., & Sue, D. W. (Eds). (2005). *Strategies for building multicultural competence in mental health and educational settings.* New York: Wiley.

Cook, D. A., & Helms, J. E. (1988). Visible racial/ethnic group supervisees' satisfaction with cross-cultural supervision as predicted by relationship characteristics. *Journal of Counseling Psychology, 35,* 268–273.

Cooney, J. (1985). An ethical approach to teacher referral of children for individual counseling. *Elementary School Guidance and Counseling, 19,* 198–201.

Cooper, C. C., & Gottlieb, M. C. (2000). Ethical issues with managed care: Challenges facing counseling psychology. *Counseling Psychologist, 28,* 179–236.

Corcoran, K., & Winslade, W. J. (1994). Eavesdropping on the 50-minute hour: Managed mental health care and confidentiality. *Behavioral Sciences and the Law, 12,* 351–365.

Corey, G., Corey, M., & Callanan, P. (2002). *Issues and ethics in the helping professions* (6th ed.). Pacific Grove, CA: Brooks/Cole.

Corey, G., Williams, G. T., & Moline, M. E. (1995). Ethical and legal issues in group counseling. *Ethics and Behavior, 5,* 161–183.

Corey, M. S., & Corey, G. (2003). *Groups: Process and practice* (7th ed.). Pacific Grove, CA: Brooks/Cole.

Costa, L., & Altekruse, M. (1994). Duty-to-warn guidelines for mental health counselors. *Journal of Counseling and Development, 72,* 346–350.

Coster, J. S., & Schwebel, M. (1997). Well-functioning in professional psychologists. *Professional Psychology: Research and Practice, 28,* 5–13.

Cottone, R. R. (2001). A social constructivism model of ethical decision making in counseling. *Journal of Counseling and Development, 79,* 39–45.

Cottone, R. R. (2004). Displacing the psychology of the individual in ethical decision-making: The social constructivism model. *Canadian Journal of Counseling, 38,* 1–13.

Cottone, R. R. (2005). Detrimental therapist-client relationships—beyond thinking of multiple or multiple roles: Reflections on the 2001 AAMFT Code of Ethics. *American Journal of Family Therapy, 33,* 1–17.

Cottone, R. R., & Claus, R. E. (2000). Ethical decision making models: A review of the literature. *Journal of Counseling and Development, 78,* 275–283.

Cottone, R. R., Tarvdas, V., & House, G. (1994). The effect of number and type of consulted relationships on the ethical decision making of graduate students in counseling. *Counseling and Values, 39,* 56–68.

Cowen, E. L., Weissberg, R. P., & Lotyczewski, B. S. (1983). Physical contact in interactions between clinicians and young children. *Journal of Consulting and Clinical Psychology, 51,* 132–138.

Coyle, B. E. (1999). Practical tools for rural psychiatric practice. *Bulletin of the Menninger Clinic, 63,* 202–222.

Crawford, I., Humfleet, G., Ribordy, S., Ho, F., & Vickers, V. (1991). Stigmatization of AIDS patients by mental health professionals. *Professional Psychology: Research and Practice, 22,* 357–361.

Crawford, R. L. (1994). Avoiding counselor malpractice. In T. P. Remley (Ed.), *ACA legal series* (Vol. 10). Alexandria, VA: American Counseling Association.

Crego, C. A. (1985). Ethics: The need for improved consultation training. *The Counseling Psychologist, 13,* 473–476.

Croarkin, P., Berg, J., Spira, J. (2003). Informed consent to psychotherapy: A look at therapists' understanding, opinions, and practices. *American Journal of Psychotherapy, 57,* 384–401.

Cronbach, L. (1984) *Essentials of psychological testing* (4th ed.). New York: Harper & Row.

Cummings, N. A. (1995). Unconscious fiscal convenience. *Psychotherapy in Private Practice, 14,* 23–28.

Cunningham, S. (1984). Genovese: 20 years later, few heed a stranger's cries. *Social Action and the Law, 10,* 24–25.

Dahlberg, C. C. (1970). Sexual contact between patient and therapist. *Contemporary Psychoanalysis, 5,* 107–124.

Danzinger, P. R., & Welfel, E. R. (2000). Age, gender and health bias in counselors: An empirical analysis. *Journal of Mental Health Counseling, 22,* 135–149.

Danzinger, P. R., & Welfel, E. R. (2001). The impact of managed care on mental health counselors: A survey of perceptions, practices and compliance with ethical standards. *Journal of Mental Health Counseling, 23,* 137–150.

Danzinger, P. R., & Welfel, E. R. (2001, March). *The impact of managed care on the work of community counselors: A survey of perceptions and practices.* Paper presented at the annual meeting of the American Counseling Association, San Antonio, TX.

Davis, J. L., & Mickelson, D. J. (1994). School counselors: Are you aware of ethical and legal aspects of counseling? *The School Counselor, 42,* 5–13.

Davis, K. L. (1980). Is confidentiality in group counseling realistic? *Personnel and Guidance Journal, 58,* 197–201.

Davis, T., & Ritchie, M. (1993). Confidentiality and the school counselor: A challenge for the 1990s. *The School Counselor, 41,* 23–29.

DeKraai, M. B., Sales, B. D., & Hall, S. R. (1998). Informed consent, confidentiality, and duty to report laws in the conduct of child therapy. In R. J. Morris & T. R. Kratochwill (Eds.). *The practice of child therapy* (3rd ed., pp. 540–560). Boston: Allyn & Bacon.

DeLucia, J. L., Coleman, V. D., & Jenson-Scott, R. L. (1992). Cultural diversity in group counseling. *Journal for Specialists in Group Work, 17,* 194–195.

Department of Health and Human Services. (1999). *National practitioner data base.* Retrieved July 10, 2005, from http://www.npdb-hipdb.com/pubs/fs/Fact_SheetNational_Practitioner_Data_Bank.pdf

Department of Health and Human Services. (2003, February 20). Health insurance reform: Security standards final rule [rules and regulations]. *Federal Register, 68* (34), 8333–8381.

DeTrude, J. (2001). Counselors dealing with the media. In E. R. Welfel & R. E. Ingersoll (Eds.), *The mental health desk reference: A practice-based guide to diagnosis, treatment, and professional ethics* (pp. 398–403). New York: Wiley.

Deutsch, C. J. (1984). Self-reported sources of stress among psychotherapists. *Professional Psychology: Research and Practice, 15,* 833–845.

Deutsch, C. J. (1985). A survey of therapists' personal problems and treatment. *Professional Psychology: Research and Practice, 16,* 305–315.

Diekstra, R. F. W. (1995). Depression and suicidal behavior in adolescence: Sociocultural time trends. In M. Rutter (Ed.), *Psychosocial disturbances in young people: Challenges for prevention* (pp. 212–243). New York: Cambridge University Press.

Dinger, T. J. (1997). The relationship between two ethical decision making models and counselor trainees' responses to an ethical discrimination task and their perceptions of ethical therapeutic behavior. *Dissertation Abstracts International, 58*(03), *750B.*

Dishion, T. J., McCord, J., & Poulin, F. (1999). When interventions harm: Peer groups and problem behavior. *American Psychologist, 54,* 755–764.

Disney, M. J., & Stephens, A. M. (1994). *Legal issues in clinical supervision.* In T. P. Remley (Ed.), *ACA legal series* (Vol. 9). Alexandria, VA: American Counseling Association.

Doromal, Q. S., & Creamer, D. G. (1988). An evaluation of the Ethical Judgment Scale. *Journal of College Student Development, 29,* 151–158.

Dorr, D. (1981). Conjoint psychological testing in marriage therapy: New wine in old skins. *Professional Psychology: Research and Practice, 12,* 549–555.

Dougherty, A. M. (1990). *Consultation: Practice and perspectives.* Pacific Grove, CA: Brooks/Cole.

Drane, J. F. (1982). Ethics and psychotherapy: A philosophical perspective. In M. Rosenbaum (Ed.), *Ethics and values in psychotherapy* (pp. 15–50). New York: Free Press.

Driscoll, J. M. (1992). Keeping covenants and confidences sacred: One point of view. *Journal of Counseling and Development, 70,* 704–708.

Drexler, L. P. (1996). Does money matter? The effect of fee structure on psychotherapy effort and outcome variables. *Dissertation Abstracts International, 56B,* 7042.

Drug Abuse Office and Treatment Act of 1976, 42 U.S.C. § 3, 42 C.F.R. Part 2.

Dubin, S. S. (1972). Obsolescence or lifelong education: A choice for the professional. *American Psychologist, 27,* 486–496.

Dudley, E. (1988, October). *Ethical complaints against family therapists submitted to the AAMFT ethics committee.* Paper presented at the National Meeting of the Association of Marriage and Family Therapists, New Orleans, LA.

Duke, D. L. (2004). The role and influence of ethics consultation in psychology. *Dissertation Abstracts International, 65*(06), 3153B.

Durana, C. (1998). The use of touch in psychotherapy: Ethical and clinical guidelines. *Psychotherapy: Theory, research, practice, training, 35,* 269–280.

Eberlein, L. (1987). Introducing ethics to beginning psychologists: A problem-solving approach. *Professional Psychology: Research and Practice, 18,* 353–359.

Ebert, B. W. (1997). Multiple relationship prohibitions: A concept whose time never should have come. *Applied and Preventive Psychology, 6,* 137–156.

Eckholm, E. (2001, February 18). China's crackdown on sect stirs alarm over psychiatric abuse. *New York Times*, pp. 1, 6.

Education for All Handicapped Children Act of 1975, 20 U.S.C. § 1400 *et seq.*

Ehly, S. W., & Vazquez, E. G. (1998). Peer counseling. In K. Topping & S. W. Ehly (Eds.). *Peer-assisted learning* (pp. 219–233). Mahwah, NJ: Lawrence Erlbaum.

Eisel v. Board of Education, 597 A.2d 447 (Md. Ct. App. 1991).

Eisen, S. V., & Dickey, B. (1996). Mental health outcome assessment: The new agenda. *Psychotherapy, 33,* 181–189.

Eliot, D. M., & Guy. J. D. (1993). Mental health professionals versus non mental health professionals: Childhood trauma and adult functioning. *Professional Psychology: Research and Practice, 24,* 83–90.

Ellis, J. W. (1996). Voluntary admission and involuntary hospitalization of minors. In B. D. Sales & D. W. Shuman (Eds.), *Law, mental health, and mental disorder* (pp. 487–502). Pacific Grove, CA: Brooks/Cole.

Enyedy, K. C., Arcinue, F., Puri, N. N., Carter, J. W., Goodyear, R. K., & Getzelman, M. A. (2003). Hindering phenomena in group supervision: Implications for practice. *Professional Psychology: Research and Practice, 34,* 312–317.

Epstein, R. S., & Simon, R. I. (1990). The Exploitation Index: An early warning indicator of boundary violations in psychotherapy. *Bulletin of the Menninger Clinic, 54,* 450–465.

Erard. R. E. (2004). Release of test data under the 2002 Ethics Code and the HIPAA privacy rule: A raw deal or just a half-baked idea? *Journal of Personality Assessment, 82,* 23–30.

Everett, C. A. (1990). The field of marriage and family therapy. *Journal of Counseling and Development, 68,* 498–502.

Ewing, C. P. (2005). Tarasoff Reconsidered. *APA Monitor, 36,* 112.

Eyde, L. D., Moreland, K. I., & Robertson, G. J. (1988). *Test-user qualifications: A data-based approach to promoting good test use.* Washington, DC: American Psychological Association.

Eyde, L. D., Robertson, G. J., Krug, S. E., Moreland, K. L., Robertson, A. G., Shewan, C. M., et al. (1993). *Responsible test use: Case studies for assessing human behavior.* Washington, DC: American Psychological Association.

Falender, C. A., & Shafranske, E. P. (2004). *Clinical supervision: A competency based approach.* Washington, DC: American Psychological Association.

Falvey, J. E. (2002a). *Managing clinical supervision: Ethical practice and legal risk management.* Pacific Grove, CA: Brooks/Cole.

Falvey, J. E. (2002b). *Documentation in supervision: The focused risk-management supervisions system.* Pacific Grove, CA: Brooks/Cole.

Family Educational Rights and Privacy Act of 1974, 20 U.S.C.A. § 1232g, 34 C.F.R. Part 99 (West 1997).

Farber, E. W., & McDaniel, J. S. (1999). Assessment and psychotherapy: Practice implications of the new combination antiviral therapies for HIV disease. *Professional Psychology: Research and Practice, 30,* 173–179.

Federal Child Abuse Prevention and Treatment Act, 42. U.S.C. 1510 (Supp. 1987).

Feldman, S. R., Vanarthos, J., & Fleisher, A. B., Jr. (1994). The readability of patient education materials designed for patients with psoriasis. *Journal of the American Academy of Dermatology, 30,* 284–286.

Feldman-Summers, S., & Jones, G. (1984). Psychological impacts of sexual contacts between therapists or other health care professionals and their clients. *Journal of Consulting and Clinical Psychology, 52,* 1054–1061.

Fernandez, C. V., Kodish, E., & Weijer, C. (2003). Informing study participants of research results: An ethical imperative. *IRB: A Review of Human Subjects Research, 25,* 12–19.

Ferris, P. A., & Linville, M. E. (1985). The child's rights: Whose responsibility? *Elementary School Guidance and Counseling, 19,* 172–180.

Figley, C. R. (1995). *Compassion fatigue: Coping with secondary traumatic stress disorder in those who treat the traumatized.* New York: Bruner/Mazel.

Filaccio, M. (2005). Discovery, confidentiality, and in camera review: Is it possible to serve two masters? *The Family Journal: Counseling and Therapy for Couples and Families, 13,* 68–70.

Fine, M. A., & Kurdek, L. A. (1993). Reflections on determining authorship credit and authorship order on faculty–student collaborations. *American Psychologist, 48,* 1141–1147.

Finn, S. E., & Butcher, J. N. (1991). Clinical objective personality assessment. In M. Hersen, A. E. Kazdin, & A. S. Bellack (Eds.), *The clinical psychology handbook* (2nd ed., pp. 362–373). New York: Pergamon.

Finn, S. E., & Tonsager, M. E. (1992). Therapeutic effects of providing MMPI-2 test feedback to college students awaiting therapy. *Psychological Assessment, 4,* 278–287.

Fischer, A. R., Jome, L. M., & Atkinson, D. R. (1998). Reconceptualizing multicultural counseling: Universal healing conditions in a culturally specific context. *Counseling Psychologist, 26,* 525–588.

Fischer, C. T. (1986). *Individualizing psychological assessment.* Pacific Grove, CA: Brooks/Cole.

Fischer, L., & Sorenson, G. P. (1996). *School law for counselors, psychologists, and social workers* (3rd ed.). White Plains, NY: Longman.

Fisher, C. B. (2003). *Decoding the ethics code: A practical guide for psychologists.* Thousand Oaks, CA: Sage.

Fisher, C. D. (2004). Ethical issues in therapy: Therapist self-disclosure of sexual feelings. *Ethics and Behavior, 14,* 105–121.

Fitzgerald, B. (1999). Children of lesbian and gay parents: A review of the literature. *Marriage and Family Review, 29,* 57–75.

Fitzgerald, L. F., & Nutt, R. (1986). Division 17 principles concerning the counseling/psychotherapy of women: Rationale and implementation. *Counseling Psychologist, 14,* 180–216.

Fleck-Hendersen, A. (1995). Ethical sensitivity: A theoretical and empirical study. *Dissertation Abstracts International, 56,* 2862B.

Flower, J. T. (1992). A comparative study of how psychologist gender relates to moral sensitivity. *Dissertation Abstracts International, 53*(05), 2527B.

Floyd, M., Myszka, M. T., & Orr, P. (1999). Licensed psychologists' knowledge and utilization of a state association colleague assistance committee. *Professional Psychology: Research and Practice, 29,* 594–598.

Fly, B. J., van Bark, W. P., Weinman, L., Kitchener, K. S., & Long, P. R. (1997). Ethical transgressions of psychology graduate students: Critical incidents with implications for training. *Professional Psychology: Research and Training, 28,* 492–495.

Foreman, T., & Bernet, W. (2000). A misunderstanding regarding the duty to report suspected child abuse. *Child Maltreatment, 5,* 190–196.

Forester-Miller, H. (2002). Group counseling: Ethical considerations. In D. Capuzzi & D. R. Gross (Eds.), *Introduction to group counseling* (3rd ed., pp. 185–204). Denver: Love Publishing.

Forrest, L., Elman, N., Gizara, S., & Vacha-Haase, T. (1999). Trainee impairment: A review of identification, remediation, dismissal and legal issues. *Counseling Psychologist, 27,* 627–686.

Fortener, R. G. (2000). The relationship between work setting, client progress, suicide ideation, and burnout in psychologists and counselors. *Dissertation Abstracts International, 60*(12), 6404B.

Foster, S. (1996, April). Taking the stand as an expert witness. *Counseling Today,* pp. 2, 26.

Fowers, B. J., & Richardson, F. C. (1996). Why is multiculturalism good? *American Psychologist, 51,* 609–621.

Fox, P. J. (2003, August). *Walking the walk: Does moral judgment equal ethical behavior?* Paper presented at the annual meeting of the American Psychological Association, Toronto, CA.

Fox, R. E. (1995). The rape of psychotherapy. *Professional Psychology: Research and Practice, 26,* 147–155.

Frager, S. (2000). *Managing managed care: Secrets of a former case manager.* New York: Wiley.

Frauenhoffer, D., Ross, M. J., Gfeller, J., Searight, H. R., Piotrowski, C. (1998). Psychological test usage among licensed mental health practitioners: A multidisciplinary survey. *Journal of Psychological Practice, 4,* 28–33.

Freeman, S. J. (2000). *Ethics: An introduction to philosophy and practice.* Belmont, CA: Wadsworth.

Freud, S. (1954). *The origins of psychoanalysis: Letters to Wilhelm Fliess, drafts and notes (1887–1902).* New York: Basic Books.

Fukuyama, M. A. (1994). Critical incidents in multicultural counseling supervision: A phenomenological approach in supervision research. *Counselor Education and Supervision, 34,* 142–151.

Fundudis, T. (2003). Current issues in medico-legal procedures: How competent are children to make their own decisions? *Child and Adolescent Mental Health, 8,* 18–22.

Gabbard, G. O. (Ed.). (1989). *Sexual exploitation in professional relationships.* Washington, DC: American Psychiatric Press.

Gabbard, G. O. (1994a). Reconsidering the American Psychological Association's policy on sex with former patients: Is it justifiable? *Professional Psychology: Research and Practice, 25,* 329–335.

Gabbard, G.O. (1994b). Teetering on precipice: A commentary on Lazarus's "How certain boundaries and ethics diminish therapeutic effectiveness." *Ethics and Behavior, 4,* 283–286.

Gabbard, G. O. (2002). Post-termination sexual boundary violations. *Psychiatric Clinics of North America, 25,* 593–603.

Galley, M., & Walsh, M. (2002, February 27). Statements to school counselors not protected Michigan court rule. *Education Week, 21,* 9.

Galvin, S. L., & Herzog, H. A. (1992). The ethical judgment of animal research. *Ethics and Behavior, 2,* 263–286.

Gantrell, N., Herman, J., Olarte, S., Feldstein, M., & Localio, R. (1989). Prevalence of psychiatrist–patient sexual contact. In G. O. Gabbard (Ed.), *Sexual exploitation in professional relationships* (pp. 27–38). Washington, DC: American Psychiatric Press.

Garb, H. N. (1997). Race bias, social class bias, and gender bias in clinical judgment. *Clinical Psychology: Science and Practice, 4,* 99–120.

Garb, H. N. (2000). Introduction to the special section on the use of computers for making psychological judgments and decisions. *Psychological Assessment, 12,* 3–5.

Garcia, J. G., Cartwright, B., Winston, S. M., & Borzuchowska, B. (2003). A transcultural integrative model for ethical decision making in counseling. *Journal of Counseling and Development, 81,* 268–277.

Garrett, T. (1998). Sexual contact between patients and psychologists. *Psychologist, 11,* 227–230.

Garvey, N., & Braun, V. (1997). Ethics and the publication of clinical case material. *Professional Psychology: Research and Practice, 28,* 399–404.

Gates, K. P., & Speare, K. H. (1990). Overlapping relationships in rural communities. In H. Lerman & N. Porter (Eds.), *Feminist ethics in psychotherapy* (pp. 97–101). New York: Springer.

Gechtman, L. (1989). Sexual contact between social workers and their clients. In G. O. Gabbard (Ed.), *Sexual exploitation in professional relationships* (pp. 27–38). Washington, DC: American Psychiatric Press.

Geib, P. G. (1982). The experience of nonerotic physical contacts in traditional psychotherapy: A critical investigation of the taboo against touch. *Dissertation Abstracts International, 43,* 0248A. (University Microfilms No. 82-13, 453).

Gelso, C. J. (1985). Rigor, relevance, and counseling research: On the need to maintain our course between Scylla and Charybdis. *Journal of Counseling and Development, 63,* 551–553.

Gergen, K. J., Hoffman, L., & Anderson, H. (1996). Is diagnosis a disaster? A constructionist trailogue. In F. W. Kaslow (Ed), *Handbook of relational diagnosis* (pp. 102–118). New York: Wiley.

Ghadban, R. (1995). Paradoxical intention. In M. Ballou (Ed.). *Psychological interventions: A guide to strategies* (pp. 1–19). Westport, CT: Praeger.

Gibb, J. J. (2005). Patients' experience of friendship with their therapists: A phenomenological study of non-sexual dual relationships. *Dissertation Abstracts International, 65*(1), 3707B.

Gibson, W. T., & Pope, K. S. (1993). The ethics of counseling: A national survey of certified counselors. *Journal of Counseling and Development, 71,* 330–336.

Gilligan, C. (1982). *In a different voice: Psychological theory and women's development.* Cambridge, MA: Harvard University Press.

Giovazolias, T., & Davis, P. (2001). How common is sexual attraction to clients? The experiences of sexual attraction of counseling psychologists toward their clients and the impact on the therapeutic process. *Counseling Psychology Quarterly, 14,* 281–286.

Givelber, D. J., Bowers, W. J., & Blitch, C. L. (1984). *Tarasoff,* myth and reality: An empirical study of private law in action. *Wisconsin Law Review, 84,* 443–497.

Gizara, S. S., & Forrest, L. (2004). Supervisors' experiences of trainee impairment and incompetence at APA-accredited internship sites. *Professional Psychology: Research and Practice, 35,* 131–140.

Gladding, S. T. (2002). *Group work: A counseling specialty* (4th ed.). Englewood Cliffs, NJ: Prentice Hall.

Gladding, S. T. (2003). *Counseling: A comprehensive profession* (5th ed.). New York: Macmillan.

Gladding, S. T., Remley, T. P., Jr., & Huber, C. H. (2000). *Ethical, legal, and professional issues in the practice of marriage and family therapy* (3rd ed.). Englewood Cliffs, NJ: Prentice Hall.

Glaser, R., & Thorpe, J. (1986). Unethical intimacy: A survey of sexual contact and advances between psychology educators and female graduate students. *American Psychologist, 41,* 43–51.

Glickhauf-Hughes, C., & Mehlman, E. (1996). Narcissistic issues in therapists: Diagnostic and treatment considerations. *Psychotherapy, 32,* 213–221.

Glosoff, H. L. (1997). Multiple relationships in private practice. In B. Herlihy & G. Corey, *Boundary issues in counseling* (pp. 114–120). Alexandria, VA: American Counseling Association.

Glosoff, H. L. (2001). Ethical issues related to interprofessional communication. In E. R. Welfel & R. E. Ingersoll (Eds.), *Mental health desk reference: A sourcebook for counselors and therapists* (pp. 419–425). New York: Wiley.

Glosoff, H. L., Garcia, J., Herlihy, B., & Remley, T. P., Jr. (1999). Managed care: Ethical considerations for counselors. *Counseling and Values, 44,* 8–16.

Glosoff, H. L., Herlihy, B., & Spence, E. B. (2000). Privileged communication in the counselor-client relationship. *Journal of Counseling and Development, 78,* 454–462.

Glosoff, H. L., & Pate, R. H. (2002). Privacy and confidentiality in school counseling. *Professional School Counseling, 6,* 20–27.

Golden, L., & Schmidt, S. J. (1998). Unethical practice as perceived by mental health professionals: The next generation. *Counseling and Values, 42,* 166–170.

Goldenberg, I., & Goldenberg, H. (2004). *Family therapy: An overview* (6th ed.). Belmont, CA: Wadsworth.

Gonsiorek, J. C. (1997). Suggested remediations to "Remediation." *Professional Psychology: Research and Practice, 28,* 300–303.

Gonsiorek, J. C., & Brown, L. S. (1989). Post-therapy sexual relationships with clients. In G. R. Schoener, J. H. Milgron, J. C. Gonsiorek, E. T. Luepker, & R. M. Conroe (Eds.), *Psychotherapists' sexual involvement with clients* (pp. 289–301). Minneapolis, MN: Walk-in Counseling Center.

Goodyear, R. K., Coleman, T., & Brunson, B. I. (1986, August). *Informed consent for clients: Effects in two counseling settings.* Paper presented at the annual meeting of the American Psychological Association, Washington, DC.

Goodyear, R. K., Crego, C. A., & Johnston, M. W. (1992). Ethical issues in the supervision of student research: A study of critical incidents. *Professional Psychology: Research and Practice, 23,* 203–210.

Goodyear, R. K., & Shumate, J. L. (1996). Perceived effects of therapist self-disclosure of attraction to clients. *Professional Psychology: Research and Practice, 27,* 613–616.

Gorkin, M. (1987). *The uses of countertransference.* London: Aronson.

Gottlieb, M. C. (1993). Avoiding exploitive dual relationships: A decision-making model. *Psychotherapy, 30,* 41–48.

Gottlieb, M. C., Sell, J. M., & Schoenfeld, L. S. (1988). Social/romantic relationships with present and former clients: State licensing board actions. *Professional Psychology: Research and Practice, 19,* 459–462.

Grassley Amendment. (1994). Sec. 1017 of GOALS 2000: The Educate America Act under the heading "Protection of Pupils": 20 U.S.C. Section 1232h.

Gray-Little, B., & Kaplan, D. A. (1998). Interpretation of psychological tests in clinical and forensic evaluations. In J. Sundoval, C. L. Frisby, K. L. Geisinger, J. D. Scheuneman, & J. R. Grenier (Eds.). *Test interpretation and diversity* (pp. 141–178). Washington, DC: American Psychological Association.

Greenberg, K. R. (2003). *Group counseling in K-12 schools: A handbook for counselors.* Needham Heights, MA: Allyn & Bacon.

Greenberg, S. A., & Shuman, D. W. (1997). Irreconcilable conflict between therapeutic and forensic roles. *Professional Psychology: Research and Practice, 28,* 50–57.

Greer, J. A. (2002). Where to turn for help: Responses to inadequate clinical supervision. *Clinical Supervisor, 21,* 135–143.

Greer, M. (2005, February). Expansion of the duty to warn in California. *APA Monitor, 36,* 45.

Gregory, J. C., & McConnell, S. C. (1986). Ethical issues with psychotherapy in group contexts. *Psychotherapy in Private Practice, 4,* 51–62.

Grohol, J. M. (1999). *Best practices in e-therapy: Confidentiality and privacy.* Retrieved August 8, 2005, from http://www.psychcentral.com/best/best2.htm

Gudeman, R. (2003). Federal privacy protection for substance abuse treatment records: Protecting adolescents. *Youth Law News.* Retrieved January 17, 2005, from http://www.youthlaw.org/downloads/YLN_No3_2003.pdf

Guest, C. L., Jr., & Dooley, K. (1999). Supervisor malpractice: Liability to the supervisee in clinical supervision. *Counselor Education and Supervision, 38,* 269–279.

Guntheil, T., & Gabbard, G. (1993). The concept of boundaries in a clinical practice: Theoretical and risk management dimensions. *American Journal of Psychiatry, 150,* 188–196.

Gurman, A. (1985). On saving marriages. *Family Therapy Networker, 9,* 17–18.

Gustafson, K. E., & McNamara, J. R. (1987). Confidentiality with minor clients: Issues and guidelines for therapists. *Professional Psychology: Research and Practice, 18,* 503–508.

Guterman, M. (1991). Working couples: Finding a balance between family and career. In J. M. Kummerow (Ed.), *New directions in career planning and the workplace* (pp. 167–193). Palo Alto, CA: Consulting Psychologists Press.

Guttman, V. (2005). Ethical reasoning and mental health services with deaf clients. *Journal of Deaf Studies and Deaf Education, 10,* 171–183.

Guy, J. D., Poelstra, P. L., & Stark, M. J. (1989). Personal distress and therapeutic effectiveness: National survey of psychologists practicing psychotherapy. *Professional Psychology: Research and Practice, 20,* 48–50.

Haas, L. J., & Malouf, J. L. (2005). *Keeping up the good work: A practitioner's guide to mental health ethics* (4th ed.). Sarasota, FL: Professional Resource Exchange.

Haas, L. J., Malouf, J. L., & Mayerson, N. H. (1988). Personal and professional characteristics as factors in psychologists' ethical decision making. *Professional Psychology: Research and Practice, 19,* 35–42.

Haley, J. (1976). *Problem solving therapy.* San Francisco: Jossey-Bass.

Hamilton, J. C., & Spruill, J. (1999). Identifying and reducing risk factors related to trainee-client sexual misconduct. *Professional Psychology: Research and Practice, 30,* 318–327.

Hammel, G. A., Olkin, R., & Taube, D. O. (1996). Student–educator sex in clinical and counseling psychology doctoral training. *Professional Psychology: Research and Practice, 27,* 93–97.

Hampton, B. R., & Hulgus, Y. F. (1993). The efficacy of paradoxical strategies: A quantitative review of the research. *Psychotherapy in Private Practice, 12,* 53–71.

Handelsman, M. M. (2001). Accurate and effective informed consent. In E. R. Welfel & R. E. Ingersoll (Eds.), *The mental health desk reference: A sourcebook for counselors and therapists* (pp. 453–458). New York: Wiley.

Handelsman, M. M, Gottlieb, M. C., & Knapp. S. (2005). Training ethical psychologists: An acculturation model. *Professional Psychology: Research and Practice, 26,* 59–65.

Handelsman, M. M., & Galvin, M. D. (1988). Facilitating informed consent for outpatient psychotherapy: A suggested written format. *Professional Psychology: Research and Practice, 19,* 223–225.

Handelsman, M. M., Kemper, M. B., Kesson-Craig, P., McLain, J., & Johnsrud, C. (1986). Use, content and readability of written informed consent forms for treatment. *Professional Psychology: Research and Practice, 17,* 514–518.

Handelsman, M. M., & Martin, W. L., Jr. (1992). The effects of readability on the impact and recall of written consent material. *Professional Psychology: Research and Practice, 23,* 500–503.

Handelsman, M. M., Martinez, A., Geisendorfer, S., Jordan, L., Wagner, L., Daniel, P., et al. (1995). Does legally mandated consent to psychotherapy ensure ethical appropriateness? The Colorado experience. *Ethics and Behavior, 5,* 119–129.

Hansen, N. D., & Goldberg, S. G. (1999). Navigating the nuances: A matrix of considerations for ethical-legal dilemmas. *Professional Psychology: Research and Practice, 30,* 495–503.

Hardin, E. E., & Leong, F. T. L. (2004). Decision-making theories and career assessment: A psychometric evaluation of the Decision Making Inventory. *Journal of Career Assessment, 12,* 51–64.

Harding, A., Gray, L., & Neal, M. (1993). Confidentiality limits with clients who have HIV: A review of ethical and legal guidelines and professional policies. *Journal of Counseling and Development, 71,* 297–305.

Hare-Mustin, R. T. (1980). Family therapy may be dangerous to your health. *Professional Psychology: Research and Practice, 11,* 935–938.

Hare-Mustin, R. T., Marecek, J., Kaplan, A. G., & Liss-Levinson, N. (1979). Rights of clients, responsibilities of therapists. *American Psychologist, 34,* 3–16.

Hargrove, D. S. (1982). An overview of professional considerations in the rural community. In P. A. Kelly & J. D. Murray (Eds.), *Handbook of rural community mental health* (pp. 169–182). New York: Human Sciences Press.

Hargrove, D. S. (1986). Ethical issues in rural mental health practice. *Professional Psychology: Research and Practice, 17,* 20–23.

Harlow, H. F. (1971). *Learning to love.* New York: Albion.

Harper, F. D., & McFadden, J. (Eds.). *Culture and counseling: New approaches.* Needham Heights, MA: Allyn & Bacon.

Harrar, W. R., VandeCreek, L., & Knapp, S. (1990). Ethical and legal aspects of clinical supervision. *Professional Psychology: Research and Practice, 21,* 37–41.

Hartlaub, G. H., Martin, G. C., & Rhine, M. W. (1986). Recontact with the analyst following termination: A survey of 71 cases. *Journal of the American Psychoanalytic Association, 34,* 895–910.

Haspel, K. C., Jorgenson, L. M., Wincze, J. P., & Parsons, J. P. (1997). Legislative intervention regarding therapist sexual misconduct: An overview. *Professional Psychology: Research and Practice, 28,* 63–72.

Haverkamp, B. E. (2005). Ethical perspectives on qualitative research in applied psychology. *Journal of Counseling Psychology, 52,* 146–155.

Hayman, P. M., & Covert, J. A. (1986). Ethical dilemmas in college counseling centers. *Journal of Counseling and Development, 64,* 318–319.

Hazler, R. J. (1996). *Breaking the cycle of violence: Interventions for bullies and victims.* Bristol, PA: Accelerated Development.

Heinlen, K. T., Welfel, E. R., Richmond, E. N., & O'Donnell, M. S. (2003). The nature, scope and ethics of psychologists' E-therapy Websites: What consumers find when surfing the Web. *Psychotherapy: Theory/Research/Practice/Training, 40,* 112–124.

Heinlen, K. T., Welfel, E. R., Richmond, E. N., & Rak, C. F. (2001, March). *Cybercounseling: Best and worst practices and future directions.* Paper presented at the annual meeting of the American Counseling Association, San Antonio, TX.

Heinlen, K. T., Welfel, E. R., Richmond, E. N., & Rak, C. F. (2003). The scope of WebCounseling: A survey of services and compliance with NBCC's guidelines for Internet counseling. *Journal of Counseling and Development, 81,* 61–69.

Heitler, S. (2001). Combined individual/marital therapy: A conflict resolution framework and ethical considerations. *Journal of Psychotherapy Integration, 11,* 349–383.

Helbok, C. M. (2003). The practice of psychology in rural communities: Potential ethical dilemmas. *Ethics and Behavior, 13,* 367–384.

Helms, J. E. (2003). A pragmatic view of social justice. *Counseling Psychologist, 31,* 305–313.

Helms, J. L. (2003). Barriers to help seeking among 12th graders. *Journal of Educational and Psychological Consultation, 14,* 27–40.

Henderson, D. H. (1987). Negligent liability and the foreseeability factor: A critical issue for school counselors. *Journal of Counseling and Development, 66,* 86–89.

Henderson, M. C. (1987). Paradoxical processes and ethical considerations. *Family Therapy, 14,* 187–193.

Hendin, H., Lipschitz, A., Maltsberger, J. T., Haas, A. P., & Wynecoop, W. (2000). Therapists' reactions to patients' suicides. *American Journal of Psychiatry, 157,* 2022–2027.

Hendrick, S. S. (1988). Counselor self-disclosure. *Journal of Counseling and Development, 66,* 419–424.

Heppner, P. P. (Ed.). (1990). *Pioneers in counseling and development: Personal and professional perspectives.* Alexandria, VA: American Counseling Association.

Herbert, J. D., & Mueser, K. T. (1992). Eye movement desensitization: A critique of the evidence. *Journal of Behavior Therapy and Experimental Psychiatry, 23,* 169–174.

Herbert, P. B. (2003). The duty to warn: A reconsideration and critique. *Journal of the American Academy of Psychiatry and the Law, 30,* 417–424.

Herlihy, B., & Corey, G. (1992). *Dual relationships in counseling.* Alexandria, VA: American Association for Counseling and Development.

Herlihy, B., & Corey, G. (1996). *ACA ethical standards casebook* (5th ed.). Alexandria, VA: American Counseling Association.

Herlihy, B., & Corey, G. (1997). *Boundary issues in counseling.* Alexandria, VA: American Counseling Association.

Herlihy, B., & Watson, Z. E. (2003). Ethical issues and multicultural competencies in counseling. In F. D. Harper & J. McFadden (Eds.), *Culture and counseling: New approaches* (pp. 363–378). Needham Heights, MA: Allyn & Bacon.

Herman, J. L., Gantrell, N., Olarte, S., Feldstein, M., & Localio, R. (1987). Psychiatrist-patient sexual contact. Results of a national survey. *American Journal of Psychiatry, 144,* 164–169.

Hermann, M. (2002). A study of legal issues encountered by school counselors and perceptions of their preparedness to respond to legal challenges. *Professional School Counseling, 6,* 12–19.

Hermann, M. A., & Finn, A. (2002). An ethical and legal perspective on the role of school counselors in preventing violence in schools. *Professional School Counseling, 6,* 46–54.

Hermann, M. A., & Remley, T. P., Jr. (2000). Guns, violence and schools: The results of school violence—litigation against educators and students shredding more constitutional rights at the school house gate. *Loyola Law Review, 46,* 386–439.

Herring, R. (1990). Suicide in the middle school: Who said kids will not? *Elementary School Guidance and Counseling, 25,* 129–137.

Herrington, R. (1979). The impaired physician—Recognition, diagnosis and treatment. *Wisconsin Medical Journal, 78,* 21–23.

Hess, A. K. (1998). Accepting forensic case referrals: Ethical and professional considerations. *Professional Psychology: Research and Practice, 29,* 109–114.

Hess, A. K., & Hess, K. A. (1983). Psychotherapy supervision: A survey of internship training practices. *Professional Psychology: Research and Practice, 14,* 504–513.

Hess, A. K., & Weiner, I. B (1999). *Handbook of forensic psychology.* New York: Wiley.

Hetrick, E. S., & Martin, A. D. (1987). Developmental issues and their resolutions for gay and lesbian adolescents. *Journal of Homosexuality, 14,* 25–43.

Hill, A. L. (2004a). Ethics education: Recommendations for an evolving discipline. *Counseling and Values, 48,* 183–203.

Hill, A. L. (2004b). Ethical analysis in counseling: A case for narrative ethics, moral visions, and virtue ethics. *Counseling and Values, 48,* 131–148.

Hill, C. E. (2004). *Helping skills: Facilitating exploration, insight, and action* (2nd ed.). Washington, DC: American Psychological Association.

Hill, C. L., & Ridley, C. R. (2001). Diagnostic decision making: DO counselors delay final judgments? *Journal of Counseling and Development, 79,* 98–104.

Hill, M., Glaser, K., & Harden, J. (1998). A feminist model for ethical decision making. *Women & Therapy, 21,* 101–121.

Hobson, S. M., & Kanitz, H. M. (1996). Multicultural counseling: An ethical issue for school counselors. *The School Counselor, 43,* 245–255.

Hogan, R., Hogan, J., & Roberts, B. W. (1996). Personality measurement and employment decisions: Questions and answers. *American Psychologist, 51,* 469–477.

Hohenshil, T. H. (1996). Editorial: The role of assessment and diagnosis in counseling. *Journal of Counseling and Development, 75,* 64–67.

Holcomb-McCoy, C. C., & Myers, J. E. (1999). Multicultural competence and counselor training A national survey. *Journal of Counseling and Development, 77,* 294–302.

Holland, T. P., & Kilpatrick, A. C. (1991). Ethical issues in social work: Toward a grounded theory of professional ethics. *Social Work, 36,* 138–144.

Holloway, J. D. (2003, February). More protections for patients and psychologists under HIPAA. *APA Monitor, 34,* 22.

Holroyd, J., & Brodsky, A. (1977). Psychologists' attitudes and practices regarding erotic and nonerotic physical contact with clients. *American Psychologist, 32,* 843–849.

Holub, E. A., & Lee, S. S. (1990). Therapists' use of nonerotic physical contact: Ethical concerns. *Professional Psychology: Research and Practice, 21,* 115–117.

Horst, E. A. (1989). Multiple relationships between psychologists and clients in rural and urban areas. *Journal of Rural Community Psychology, 10,* 15–24.

Horton, J. A., Clance, P. R., Sterk-Elifson, C., Emshoff, J. (1995). Touch in psychotherapy: A survey of patients' experiences. *Psychotherapy, 32,* 443–457.

Houskamp, B. (1994). Assessing and treating battered women: A clinical review of issues and approaches. *New Directions for Mental Health Services, 64,* 79–89.

Housman, L. M., & Stake, J. E. (1998). The current state of sexual ethics training in clinical psychology: Issues of quantity, quality, and effectiveness. *Professional Psychology: Research and Practice, 30,* 302–311.

Hsiung, R. C. (Ed.). (2002). *E-therapy: Case studies, guiding principles, and the clinical potential of the Internet.* New York: Norton.

Hubble, M. A., Duncan, B. L., & Miller, S. D. (1999). *The heart and soul of change: What works in therapy.* Washington, DC: American Psychological Association.

Huber, C. H., & Baruth, L. G. (1987). *Ethical, legal and professional issues in the practice of marriage and family therapy.* Columbus, OH: Merrill.

Huber, P. W. (1991). *Galileo's revenge: Junk science in the courtroom.* New York: Basic Books.

Hubert, J. D., Lillenfeld, S. O., Lohr, J. M., Montgomery, R. W., O'Donoghue, W. T., Rosen, G. M., et al. (2000). Science and pseudoscience in the development of eye movement desensitization and reprocessing: Implications for clinical psychology. *Clinical Psychology Review, 20,* 945–971.

Hubert, R. M., & Freeman, L. T. (2004). Report of the ACA Ethics Committee, 2002-2003. *Journal of Counseling and Development, 82,* 248–251.

Humphreys, K., Winzelberg, A., & Klaw, E. (2000). Psychologists' ethical responsibilities in Internet-based groups: Issues, strategies, and a call for dialogue. *Professional Psychology: Research and Practice, 31,* 493–496.

Humphreys, K. L. (2000). Influences on ethical decision making among practicing school psychologists. *Dissertation Abstracts International, 60*(07), 2370A.

Ibrahim, F. A., & Arrendondo, P. M. (1986). Ethical standards for cross-cultural counseling. *Journal of Counseling and Development, 64,* 349–352.

In re Gault, 387 U.S.I. (1967).

Individuals with Disabilities Education Act. Pub. L. No 105–17, 34 CFR 300–574 (1997).

Ingram, J. (1998). *Cybertherapy: Pariah or promise.* Retrieved August 8, 2005, from http://www.cybertowers.com/selfhelp/ppc/viewpoint/cybpaper.html

Isaacs, M. L., & Stone, C. B. (1999). School counselors and confidentiality: Factors affecting professional choices. *Professional School Counseling, 2,* 258–266.

Ivey, A. E., & Ivey, M. B. (1998). Reframing the DSM: Positive strategies from developmental counseling and therapy. *Journal of Counseling and Development, 76,* 334–350.

Jacob, S., & Hartshorne, T. S. (2003). *Ethics and law for school psychologists* (4th ed.). New York: Wiley.

Jacob-Timm, S. (1999). Ethically challenging situations encountered by school psychologists. *Psychology in the Schools, 36,* 205–217.

Jaffee v. Redmond, 1996 WL 315841 (U.S. June 13, 1996).

James, S. H., & DeVaney, S. B. (1995). Preparing to testify: The school counselor as court witness. *The School Counselor, 43,* 97–102.

Janson, G. R. (2002). Family counseling and referral with gay, lesbian, bisexual, and transgendered clients: Ethical considerations. *The Family Journal, 10,* 328–333.

Janson, G. R., & Steigerwald, F. J. (2002). Family counseling and ethical challenges with gay, lesbian, bisexual, and transgendered (GLBT) clients: More questions than answers. *The Family Journal, 10,* 415–418.

Jeffords, J. M. (1999). Confidentiality of medical information: Protecting privacy in an electronic age. *Professional Psychology: Research and Practice, 30,* 115–116.

Jennings, F. L. (1992). Ethics of rural practice. *Psychotherapy in Private Practice, 10,* 85–104.

Jensen, J. A., McNamara, J. R., & Gustafson, K. E. (1991). Parents' and clinicians' attitudes toward the risks and benefits of child psychotherapy: A study of informed consent content. *Professional Psychology: Research and Practice, 22,* 161–170.

Jensen, R. E. (1979). Competent professional service in psychology: The real issue behind continuing education. *Professional Psychology: Research and Practice, 10,* 381–389.

Jerome, J. K. (1889). *Idle thoughts of an idle fellow.* New York: Dutton.

Jevne, P., & Williams, D. R. (1998). *When dreams don't work: Professionals caregivers and burnout.* Amityville, NY: Baywood.

Johnson, B. W., & Nelson, N. (1999). Mentor-protégé relationships in graduate training: Some ethical concerns. *Ethics and Behavior, 9,* 189–210.

Johnson, C. E., Stewart, A. L., Brabeck, M. M., Huber, V. S., & Rubin, H. (2004). Interprofessional collaboration: Implications for combined-integral doctoral training in professional psychology. *Journal of Clinical Psychology, 60,* 995–1010.

Johnson, I. H., Santos-Torres, J., Coleman, V. D., & Smith, M. C. (1995). Issues and strategies in leading culturally diverse counseling groups. *Journal for Specialists in Group Work, 20,* 143–150.

Johnson, W. B., Ralph, J., & Johnson, S. J. (2005). Managing multiple relationships in embedded environments: The case of aircraft carrier psychology. *Professional Psychology: Research and Practice, 36,* 73–81.

Joint Committee on Testing Practices. (1988). *Code of fair testing practices in education.* Washington, DC: Author.

Jones, J. H. (1981). *Bad blood: The Tuskegee syphilis experiment—A tragedy of race and medicine.* New York: Free Press.

Jones, K. D. (1999). Ethics in publication. *Counseling and Values, 43,* 99–105.

Jones, N. A., & Smith, A. S. (2001). Census 2000 brief: Two or more races. *U.S. Census Bureau.* Retrieved June 8, 2005, from http://www.census.gov/prod/2001pubs/c2kbr01-6.pdf

Jordan, A. E., & Meara, N. M. (1990). Ethics and the professional practice of psychologists: The role of virtues and principles. *Professional Psychology: Research and Practice, 21,* 107–114.

Kachgian, C., & Felthous, A. R. (2004). Court responses to *Tarasoff* statues. *Journal of the American Academy of Psychiatry and Law, 32,* 263–273.

Kaffenberger, C., & Seligman, L. (2003). Helping students with mental and emotional disorders. In B. T. Erford (Ed.) *Transforming the school counseling profession.* (pp. 221–240). Upper Saddle River, NJ: Merrill Prentice-Hall.

Kalichman, S. C. (1998). *Understanding AIDS: Advances in research and treatment* (2nd ed.). Washington, DC: American Psychological Association.

Kalichman, S. C. (1999). *Mandated reporting of suspected child abuse: Ethics, law and policy* (2nd ed.). Washington, DC: American Psychological Association.

Kalichman, S. C. (2003). *The inside story on AIDS.* Washington, DC: American Psychological Association.

Kant, I. (1964). *Groundwork of the metaphysics of morals* (H. J. Paton, Trans.). New York: Harper & Row. (Original work published 1785)

Kanz, J. E. (2001). Clinical-supervision.com: Issues in the provision of online supervision. *Professional Psychology: Research and Practice, 32,* 415–420.

Kaplan, L. S. (1996). Outrageous or legitimate concerns: What some parents are saying about school counseling. *The School Counselor, 43,* 165–170.

Kaplan, M. (1983). A woman's view of the DSM-III. *American Psychologist, 38,* 786–792.

Kaplin, W. A., & Lee, B. A. (1995). *The law of higher education* (3rd ed.). San Francisco: Jossey-Bass.

Kaser-Boyd, N., Adelman, H. S., & Taylor, L. (1985). Minors' ability to identify risks and benefits of therapy. *Professional Psychology: Research and Practice, 16,* 411–417.

Kaslow, F. W. (Ed.). (1996). *Handbook of relational diagnosis.* New York: Wiley.

Katz, J. (1972). *Experimentation with human beings.* New York: Russell Sage Foundation.

Keaton, B., & Yamatani, H. (1993). Benefits of mandatory EAP participation: A study of employees with last-chance contracts. *Employee Assistance Quarterly, 9,* 67–77.

Keeling, R. P. (1993). HIV disease: Current concepts. *Journal of Counseling and Development, 71,* 261–274.

Keffala, V. J., & Stone, G. L. (1999). Role of HIV serostatus, relationship status of the patient, homophobia, and social desirability of the psychologist on decisions regarding confidentiality. *Psychology and Health, 14,* 567–584.

Keith-Spiegel, P. (1994). Teaching psychologists and the new APA ethics code: Do we fit in? *Professional Psychology: Research and Practice, 25,* 362–368.

Keith-Spiegel, P., & Koocher, G. P. (1998). *Ethics in psychology: Professional standards and cases* (2nd ed.). New York: Oxford.

Keith-Spiegel, P., Tabachnick, B. G., Whitley, B. E., Jr., & Washburn, J. (1998). Why professors ignore cheating: Opinions of a national sample of psychology instructors. *Ethics and Behavior, 8,* 215–227.

Keith-Spiegel, P., Wittig, A. F., Perkins, D. V., Balogh, D. W., & Whitley, B. E., Jr. (1993). *The ethics of teaching: A casebook.* Muncie, IN: Ball State University.

Kennel, R. G., & Agresti, A. A. (1995). Effects of gender and age on psychologists' reporting of child sexual abuse. *Professional Psychology: Research and Practice, 26,* 612–615.

Kerl, S. B., Garcia, J. L., McCullough, S., & Maxwell, M. W. (2002). Systematic evaluation of professional performance: Legally supported procedure and process. *Counselor Education and Supervision, 41,* 321–334.

Kertay, L., & Reviere, S. L. (1993). The use of touch in psychotherapy: Theoretical and ethical considerations. *Psychotherapy, 30,* 32–40.

Kessler, L. E., & Waehler, C. A. (2005). Addressing multiple relationships between clients and therapists in lesbian, gay, bisexual and transgender communities. *Professional Psychology: Research and Practice, 36,* 66–72.

Kielbasa, A. M., Pomerantz, A. M., Krohn, E. J., & Sullivan, B. F. (2004). How does clients' method of payment influence psychologists' diagnostic decisions? *Ethics and Behavior, 14,* 187–195.

Kier, F. J., & Molinari, V. (2004). Do-it-yourself testing for mental illness: Ethical issues, concerns, and recommendations. *Professional Psychology: Research and Practice, 35,* 261–267.

Kiesler, C. A. (2000). The next wave of change for psychology and mental health in the health care revolution. *American Psychologist, 55,* 481–487.

Kilburg, R. R. (2000). *Executive coaching: Developing managerial wisdom in a world of chaos.* Washington, DC: American Psychological Association.

Kilburg, R. R., Nathan, P. E., & Thoreson, R. W. (Eds.). (1986). *Professionals in distress: Issues, syndromes and solutions in psychology.* Washington, DC: American Psychological Association.

King, K. A., (2000). Preventing adolescent suicide: Do counselors know the risk factors? *Professional School Counseling, 3,* 255–263.

Kirk, S. A., & Kutchins, H. (1992). *The selling of DSM: The rhetoric of science in psychiatry.* New York: Aldine DeGruyter.

Kirtland, K., & Kirtland, K. L. (2001). Frequency of child custody evaluation complaints and related disciplinary action: A survey of the Association of State and Provincial Psychology Boards. *Professional Psychology: Research and Practice, 32,* 171–174.

Kirtland, K., Kirtland, K. L., & Reaves, R. P. (2004). On the professional use of disciplinary data. *Professional Psychology: Research and Practice, 35,* 179–184.

Kitchener, K. S. (1984). Intuition, critical evaluation and ethical principles: The foundation for ethical decisions in counseling psychology. *Counseling Psychologist, 12,* 43–55.

Kitchener, K. S. (1988). Multiple role relationships? What makes them so problematic? *Journal of Counseling and Development, 67,* 217–221.

Kitchener, K. S. (1992). Psychologist as teacher and mentor: Affirming ethical values throughout the curriculum. *Professional Psychology: Research and Practice, 23,* 190–195.

Kitchener, K.S. (2000). *Foundations of ethical practice, research and teaching in psychology.* Mahwah, NJ: Lawrence Erlbaum.

Kitchener, K. S., & Harding, S. S. (1990). Dual role relationships. In B. Herlihy & L. B. Golden (Eds.), *Ethical Standards Casebook.* Alexandria, VA: American Counseling Association.

Klerman, G. L. (1990). The psychiatric patient's right to effective treatment: Implications of Osheroff v. Chestnut Lodge. *American Journal of Psychiatry, 147,* 419–427.

Klontz, B. T. (2004). Ethical practice of group experiential psychotherapy. *Psychotherapy: Theory, Research, Practice and Training, 41,* 172–179.

Kluft, R. P. (1990). Incest and subsequent revictiminaztion: The case of therapist-patient sexual exploitation with a description of the sitting duck syndrome. In R.P. Kluft (Ed.), *Incest related syndromes of adult psychopathology.* Washington, DC: American Psychiatric Press.

Knapp, S., Bowers, T. G., & Metzler, B. (1992). A survey of Pennsylvania psychologists. *Psychotherapy in Private Practice, 11,* 83–99.

Knapp, S., & VandeCreek, L. (1986). Privileged communication for psychotherapists: An overview. *Psychotherapy in Private Practice, 4,* 13–22.

Knapp, S., & VandeCreek, L. (1993). Legal and ethical issues in billing patients and collecting fees. *Psychotherapy, 30,* 25–31.

Knapp, S., & VandeCreek, L. (1997). Ethical and legal aspects of clinical supervision. In C. E. Watkins (Ed.), *Handbook of psychotherapy supervision* (pp. 589–599). New York: Wiley.

Knapp. S., & VandeCreek, L. (2003). *A guide to the 2002 revision of the American Psychological Association's Ethics Code.* Sarasota, FL: Professional Resource Press.

Knutsen, E. (1977). On the emotional well-being of psychiatrists: Overview and rationale. *American Journal of Psychoanalysis, 40,* 84–96.

Kocet, M. M., & Freeman, L. T. (2005). Report of the ACA Ethics Committee 2003–2004. *Journal of Counseling and Development, 83,* 249–252.

Kodish, E. (2005). *Ethics and research with children: A case-based approach.* New York: Oxford.

Kohlberg, L. (1984). *The psychology of moral development: The nature and validation of moral stages.* San Francisco: Harper & Row.

Kolbert, J. B., Morgan, B., Brendel, B., & Johnston, M. (2002). Faculty and student perceptions of dual relationships within counselor education: A qualitative analysis. *Counselor Education and Supervision, 41,* 193–206.

Koocher, G. P. (1979). Credentialing in psychology: Close encounters with competence? *American Psychologist, 34,* 696–702.

Koocher, G. P. (1994a). APA and the FTC: New adventures in consumer protection. *American Psychologist, 49,* 322–328.

Koocher, G. P. (1994b). The commerce of professional psychology and the new ethics code. *Professional Psychology: Research and Practice, 25,* 355–361.

Koocher, G., & Keith-Spiegel, P. S. (1990). *Children, ethics and the law.* Lincoln, NE: University of Nebraska Press.

Kottler, J. A. (1982). Unethical behaviors we all do and pretend we do not. *Journal for Specialists in Group Work, 7,* 182–186.

Kottler, J. A. (1994). *Advanced group leadership.* Pacific Grove, CA: Brooks/Cole.

Kozlowski, N.F. (2004). Management of confidentiality with HIV-positive male and female psychotherapy clients. *Dissertation Abstracts International, 64,* 4045B.

Kraus, R., Zack, J., & Stricker, G. (2004). *Online counseling: A handbook for mental health professionals.* New York: Academic Press.

Kress, V. E., Eriksen, K. P., Rayle, A. D., & Ford, S. J. W. (2005). The DSM-IV-TR and culture: Considerations for counselors. *Journal of Counseling and Development, 83,* 97–104.

Kurpius, D., Gibson, G., Lewis, J., & Corbet, M. (1991). Ethical issues in supervising counseling practitioners. *Counselor Education and Supervision, 31,* 48–57.

Kutchins, H., & Kirk, S. A. (1997). *Making us crazy: DSM: The psychiatric bible and the creation of mental disorders.* New York: The Free Press.

Kuther, T.L. (2003). Promoting positive ethics: An interview with Mitchell M. Handelsman. *Teaching of Psychology, 30,* 339–343.

Ladany, N. (2004). Psychotherapy supervision: What lies beneath. *Psychotherapy Research, 14,* 1–18.

Ladany, N., Lehman-Waterman, D., Molinaro, M., & Wolgart, B. (1999). Psychotherapy supervisor ethical practices, working alliance and supervisee satisfaction. *Counseling Psychologist, 27,* 443–475.

Ladany, N., O'Brien, K. M., Hill, C. E., Melincoff, D. S., Knox, S., & Peterson, D. A. (1997). Sexual attraction toward clients, use of supervision, and prior training: A qualitative study of predoctoral psychology interns. *Journal of Counseling Psychology, 44,* 413–424.

Ladd, J. (1991). The quest for a code of professional ethics: An intellectual and moral confusion. In D. G. Johnson (Ed.), *Ethical issues in engineering* (pp. 130–136). Englewood Cliffs, NJ: Prentice Hall.

LaFromboise, T. D., Foster, S., & James, A. (1996). Ethics in multicultural counseling. In P. B. Pedersen, J. G. Draguns, W. J. Lonner, & J. E. Trimble (Eds.), *Counseling across cultures* (4th ed., pp 47–72). Thousand Oaks, CA: Sage.

Lakin, M. (1994). Morality in group and family therapies: Multiperson therapies and the 1992 ethics code. *Professional Psychology: Research and Practice, 25,* 344–348.

Laliotis, D. A., & Grayson, J. H. (1985). Psychologist heal thyself. *American Psychologist, 40,* 84–96.

Lamb, D. H., & Catanzaro, S. J. (1998). Sexual and nonsexual boundary violations involving psychologists, clients, supervisees and students: Implications for professional practice. *Professional Psychology: Research and Practice, 29,* 498–503.

Lamb, D. H., & Catanzaro, S. J., & Moorman, A. S. (2003). Psychologists reflect on their sexual relationships with clients, supervisees, and students: Occurrence, impact, rationales, and collegial interventions, *Professional Psychology: Research and Practice, 34,* 102–107.

Lamb, D. H., Catanzaro, S. J., & Moorman, A. S. (2004). A preliminary look at how psychologists identify, evaluate, and proceed when faced with possible multiple relationship dilemmas. *Professional Psychology: Research and Practice, 35,* 248–254.

Lamb, D. H., Cochran, D. J., & Jackson, V. R. (1991). Training and organizational issues associated with identifying and responding to intern impairment. *Professional Psychology: Research and Practice, 22,* 291–296.

Lamb, D. H., Strand, K. K., Woodburn, J. R., Buchko, K. J., Lewis, J. T., & Kang, J. B. (1994). Sexual and business relationships between therapists and former clients. *Psychotherapy: Theory/Research/Practice/Training, 31,* 270–278.

Lambert, M. J. (Ed.). (2003). *Bergin and Garfield's Handbook of psychotherapy and behavior change.* New York: Wiley.

Langer, E. J., & Abelson, R. P. (1974). A patient by any other name . . . : Clinician group differences and labeling bias. *Journal of Consulting and Clinical Psychology, 42,* 4–9.

LaRoche, M. J., & Maxie, A. (2003). Ten considerations in addressing cultural differences in psychotherapy. *Professional Psychology: Research and Practice, 34,* 180–186.

Larry P. v. Riles, 495 F. Supp. 971 (1979).

Lawrence, G., & Kurpius, S. E. R. (2000). Legal and ethical issues involved when counseling minors in nonschool settings. *Journal of Counseling and Development, 78,* 130–136.

Layman, M. J., & McNamara, R. (1997). Remediation for ethics violations: Focus on psychotherapists' sexual contact with clients. *Professional Psychology: Research and Practice, 28,* 281–292.

Lazarus, A., & Zur, O. (2002). *Multiple relationships and psychotherapy.* New York: Springer.

Lear, C. M. (1997). Nonsexual multiple relationships: How do therapists decide? *Dissertation Abstracts International, 58A,* 3320.

Leong, F. T. L., & Wagner, N. S. (1994). Cross-cultural counseling supervision: What do we know? What do we want to know? *Counselor Education and Supervision, 34,* 117–131.

Leong, G. B., Eth, S., & Silva, J. A. (1992). The psychotherapist as witness for the prosecution: The criminalization of *Tarasoff*. *American Journal of Psychiatry, 149,* 1011–1015.

Lerman, H., & Porter, N. (1990). *Feminist ethics in psychotherapy.* New York: Springer.

Levenson, J. L. (1986). When a colleague acts unethically: Guidelines for intervention. *Journal of Counseling and Development, 64,* 315–317.

Levine, M., Anderson, E., Terreti, L., Sharma, A., Steinberg, K. L., & Wallach, L. (1991, August). *Mandated reports and therapy in the context of the child protection system.* Paper presented at the annual meeting of the American Psychological Association, San Francisco.

Levine, M., & Doueck, H. J. (1995). *The impact of mandated reporting on the therapeutic process: Picking up the pieces.* Thousand Oaks, CA: Sage.

Levy, C. (1974). On the development of a code of ethics. *Social Work, 19,* 207–216.

Levy, R. B. (1973). *I can only touch you now.* Englewood Cliffs, NJ: Prentice Hall.

Lewis, J. A., & Mellman, S. (1999). Ethics and family therapy: Issues of gender. In P. Stevens (Ed.), *Ethical casebook for the practice of marriage and family counseling* (pp. 93–102). Alexandria, VA: American Counseling Association.

Lewis, M. W., & Lewis, A. C. (1996). Peer helping programs: Helper role, supervisor training and suicidal behavior. *Journal of Counseling and Development, 74,* 307–313.

Lewis, N. A. (2005, July 6). Psychologists warned on role in detentions. *New York Times,* p. 6.

Lien, C. (1993). The ethics of the sliding fee scale. *Journal of Mental Health Counseling, 15,* 334–341.

Lindsey, C. R., & Kalafat, J. (1998). Adolescents' view of preferred helper characteristics and barriers to seeking help from school-based adults. *Journal of Educational and Psychological Consultation, 19,* 171–193.

Lindsay, G., & Clarkson, P. (1999). *Ethical dilemmas of psychotherapists.* New York: Oxford.

Lindsey, R. T. (1984). Informed consent and deception in psychotherapy research: An ethical analysis. *The Counseling Psychologist, 12,* 79–86.

Lindsey, R. T. (1985, August). *Moral sensitivity: The relationship between training and experience.* Paper presented at the annual meeting of the American Psychological Association, Los Angeles.

Lloyd, A. (1992). Dual relationship problems in counselor education. In B. Herlihy & G. Corey (Eds.), *Dual relationships in counseling* (pp. 59–64). Alexandria, VA: American Counseling Association.

Locke, D. C., & Faubert, M. (2003). Cultural considerations in counselor training and supervision. In F. D. Harper & J. McFadden (Eds.), *Culture and counseling: New approaches* (pp. 324–338). Boston: Allyn & Bacon.

Lockyer, B., & Duncan, S. D. (2004). California Attorney General Opinion 04-112.

Lonborg, S. D., & Bowen, N. (2004). Counselors, communities, and spirituality: Ethical and multicultural considerations. *Professional School Counseling, 7,* 318–325.

Lonner, W. J., & Ibrahim, F. A. (1996). Appraisal and assessment in cross-cultural counseling. In P. B. Pedersen, J. G. Draguns, W. J. Lonner, & J. E. Trimble (Eds.), *Counseling across cultures* (4th ed., pp. 293–322). Thousand Oaks, CA: Sage.

Lopez, S. R., & Guarnaccia, P. J. (2005). Cultural dimensions of psychopathology: The social world's impact on mental illness. In J. E. Maddux & B. A. Winstead (Eds.), *Psychopathology: Foundations for a contemporary understanding* (pp. 19–38). Mahwah, NJ: Lawrence Erlbaum.

Lowman, R. L. (1985). Ethical practice of psychological consultation: Not an impossible dream. *The Counseling Psychologist, 13,* 466–472.

Lowman, R. L. (Ed.). (1998). *The ethical practice of psychology in organizations.* Washington, DC: American Psychological Association.

Luepker, E. T. (1999). Effects of practitioners' sexual misconduct: A follow-up study. *Journal of the American Academy of Psychiatry and Law, 27,* 51–63.

Lum, D. (1992). *Social work practice with people of color: A process-stage approach* (2nd ed.). Pacific Grove, CA: Brooks/Cole.

Mabe, A. R., & Rollin, S. A. (1986). The role of a code of ethical standards in counseling. *Journal of Counseling and Development, 64,* 294–297.

MacCluskie, K. M., & Ingersoll, R. E. (2000). *Becoming a 21st century agency counselor.* Pacific Grove, CA: Brooks/Cole.

Maddux, J. E., & Winstead, B. A. (Eds), *Psychopathology: Foundations for a contemporary understanding.* Mahwah, NJ: Lawrence Erlbaum.

Magnuson, S., Wilcoxin, S. A., & Norem, K. (2000). A profile of lousy supervisors: Experienced counselors' perspectives. *Counselor Education and Supervision, 39,* 189–202.

Maheu, M. M., & Gordon, B. I. (2000). Counseling and therapy on the Internet. *Professional Psychology: Research and Practice, 31,* 484–489.

Maheu, M. M., Whitten, P., & Allen, A. (2001). *E-health, telehealth, and telemedicine: A guide to start-up and success.* San Francisco: Jossey-Bass.

Mahoney, M. (1997). Psychotherapists' personal problems and self-care patterns. *Professional Psychology: Research and Practice, 28,* 14–16.

Malley, P., Gallagher, R., & Brown, S. (1992). Ethical problems in university and college counseling centers: A Delphi study. *Journal of College Student Development, 33,* 238–244.

Manderscheid, R., & Barrett, S. (Eds.). (1991). *Mental health in the United States, 1987* (National Institute of Mental Health, DHHS Publication No. ADM-87-1518). Washington, DC: U.S. Government Printing Office.

Manese, J. E., Wu, J. T., Nepomuceno, C. A. (2001). The effect of multicultural counseling competencies: An exploratory study over a ten-year period. *Journal of Multicultural Counseling and Development, 29,* 31–40.

Mann, L., Harmoni, R., & Power, C. (1989). Adolescent decision making: The development of competence. *Journal of Adolescence, 12,* 265–278.

Mannheim, C. L., Sancillio, M., Phipps-Yonas, S., Brunnquell, D., Somers, P., Farseth, G., et al. (2002). Ethical ambiguities in the practice of clinical child psychology. *Professional Psychology: Research and Practice, 33,* 24–29.

Marcan, S., & Shapiro, D. (1998). The role of personal therapy for therapists: A review. *British Journal of Medical Psychology, 71,* 13–25.

Marcan, S., Stiles, W. B., & Smith, J. A. (1999). How does personal therapy affect therapists' practice? *Journal of Counseling Psychology, 46,* 419–431.

Marecek, J. (1993). Disappearance, silences, and anxious rhetoric: Gender in abnormal psychology textbooks. *Journal of Theoretical and Philosophical Psychology, 13,* 115–123.

Margolin, G. (1982). Ethical and legal considerations in marital and family therapy. *American Psychologist, 37,* 788–801.

Marino, T. W. (1995, December). Battle for testing rights continues. *Counseling Today,* p. 6.

Marsella, A. J., & Kaplan, A. (2002). Cultural considerations for understanding, assessing and treating depressive experience. In M. A. Reinecke & M. R. Davison (Eds.), *Comparative treatment of depression* (pp. 47–78). New York: Springer.

Marsh, J. E. (2003). Empirical support for the United States Supreme Court's protection of the psychotherapist-patient privilege. *Ethics and Behavior, 13,* 385–400.

Martineau, H. (1837). *Society in America* (Vol. 3). New York: Saunders & Otley.

Martinson, B. C., Anderson, M. S., & de Vries, R. (2005). Scientists behaving badly. *Nature, 435,* 737–738.

Maslach, C., & Jackson, S. E. (1986). *Maslach Burnout Inventory: Manual* (2nd ed.). Palo Alto, CA: Consulting Psychologists Press.

Massachusetts Department of Education. (1995). *Youth risk behavior study.* Boston: Author.

Massachusetts Governor's Commission on Gay and Lesbian Youth. (1993). *Breaking the silence in schools and families.* Boston: Author.

Matarazzo, J. D. (1986). Computerized clinical psychological test interpretations: Unvalidated plus all mean and no sigma. *American Psychologist, 41,* 14–24.

May, W. F. (1984). The virtues in a professional setting. *Soundings, 67,* 245–266.

McAdams, C. R., III, & Foster, V. A. (2000). Client suicide: Its frequency and impact on counselors. *Journal of Mental Health Counseling, 22,* 107–121.

McCann, I. L., & Pearlman, L. A. (1990). Vicarious traumatization: A framework for the psychological effects of working with victims. *Journal of Traumatic Stress, 3,* 131–149.

McCarthy, M. M., & Sorenson, G. P. (1993). School counselors and consultants: Legal duties and liabilities. *Journal of Counseling and Development, 72,* 159–167.

McCarthy, P., Kulakowski, D., & Kenfield, J. (1994). Clinical supervision practices of licensed psychologists. *Professional Psychology: Research and Practice, 25,* 177–181.

McCarthy, P., Sugden, S., Koker, M., Lamendola, F., Maurer, S., & Renninger, S. (1995). A practical guide to informed consent in clinical supervision. *Counselor Education and Supervision, 35,* 130–138.

McCarthy, R. (1998, August). Behavioral health: Don't ignore, integrate. *Business and Health,* pp. 46, 51.

McCartney, J. (1966). Overt transference. *Journal of Sex Research, 2,* 227–237.

McConnell, W. A., & Kerbs, J. J. (1993). Providing feedback in research with human subjects. *Professional Psychology: Research and Practice, 24,* 266–270.

McDivitt, K. L. (2001). Ethics in group work with children and adolescents. *Dissertation Abstracts International, 61*(12), 4673A.

McFarland, W. P. (1998). Gay, lesbian, and bisexual student suicide. *Professional School Counseling, 1,* 26–29.

McFarland, W. P., & Dupuis, M. (2001). The legal duty to protect gay and lesbian students from violence in school. *Professional School Counseling, 4,* 171–179.

McGuire, J., Nieri, D., Abbott, D., Sheridan, K., & Fisher, R. (1995). Do *Tarasoff* principles apply in AIDS-related psychotherapy? Ethical decision making and the role of therapist homophobia and perceived client dangerousness. *Professional Psychology: Research and Practice, 26,* 608–611.

McLaughlin, J. E. (2002). Reducing diagnostic bias. *Journal of Mental Health Counseling, 24,* 256–269.

McLean, S., Wade, T. D., & Encel, J. S. (2003). The contribution of therapist beliefs to psychological distress in therapists: An investigation of vicarious traumatization, burnout and symptoms of avoidance and intrusion. *Behavioral and Cognitive Psychotherapy, 31,* 417–428.

McMinn, M. R., Ellens, B. M., Soref, E. (1999). Ethical perspectives and practice behaviors involving computer-based test interpretation. *Assessment, 9,* 71–77.

McNeil-Haber, F. M. (2004). Ethical considerations in the use of nonerotic touch in psychotherapy with children. *Ethics and Behavior, 14,* 123–140.

McRoy, R. G., Freeman, E. M., Logan, S. L., & Blackmon, B. (1986). Cross-cultural field supervision: Implications for social work education. *Journal of Social Work Education, 22,* 50–56.

Meara, N. M., Schmidt, L. D., & Day, J. D. (1996). Principles and virtues: A foundation for ethical decisions, policies and character. *Counseling Psychologist, 24,* 4–77.

Meehl, P. E. (1960). The cognitive activity of the clinician. *American Psychologist, 15,* 19–27.

Meer, D., & VandeCreek, L. (2002). Cultural considerations in release of information. *Ethics and Behavior, 12,* 143–156.

Melchert, T. P., & Patterson, M. M. (1999). Duty to warn and interventions with HIV-positive clients. *Professional Psychology: Research and Practice, 30,* 180–186.

Melito, R. (2003). Values in the role of the family therapist: Self determination and justice. *Journal of Marital and Family Therapy, 29,* 3–11.

Melton, G. B. (1981). Children's participation in treatment planning: Psychological and legal issues. *Professional Psychology: Research and Practice, 12,* 246–252.

Melton, G. B. (1983). Towards "personhood" for adolescents: Autonomy and privacy as values in public policy. *American Psychologist, 38,* 99–103.

Melton, G. B. (1994). Expert opinions: Not for cosmic understanding. In B. D. Sales & G. B. Vandenbos (Eds.), *Psychology in litigation and legislation* (pp. 55–100). Washington, DC: American Psychological Association.

Melton, G. B., Goodman, G. S., Kalichman, S. C., Levine, M., Saywitz, K. J., & Koocher, G. P. (1995). Empirical research on child maltreatment and the law. *Journal of Clinical Child Psychology, 24* (Supp.), 47–77.

Menninger, K. (1958). *Theory of psychoanalytic technique.* New York: Basic Books.

Merta, R. J. (1995). Group work: Multicultural perspectives. In J. G. Ponterotto, J. M. Casas, L. A. Suzuki, & C. M. Alexander (Eds.), *Handbook of multicultural counseling* (pp. 567–585). Newbury Park, CA: Sage.

Merta, R. J., & Sisson, J. A. (1991). The experiential group: An ethical and professional dilemma. *The Journal for Specialists in Group Work, 16,* 236–245.

Merta, R. J., Wolfgang, L., & McNeil, K. (1993). Five models for using the experiential group in the preparation of group counselors. *Journal for Specialists in Group Work, 18,* 200–207.

Meyers, C. J. (1991). Where the protective privilege ends: California changes the rules for dangerous psychotherapy patients. *Journal of Psychiatry and the Law, 19,* 5–31.

Miller, D. J., & Hersen, M. (1992). *Research fraud in the behavioral and biomedical sciences.* New York: Wiley.

Miller, D. J., & Thelen, M. H. (1986). Knowledge and beliefs about confidentiality in psychotherapy. *Professional Psychology: Research and Practice, 17,* 15–19.

Miller, G. M., & Larrabee, M. J. (1995). Sexual intimacy in counselor education and supervision: A national survey. *Counselor Education and Supervision, 34,* 332–343.

Miller, I. J. (1995). Managed care is harmful to outpatient mental health services: A call for accountability. *Professional Psychology: Research and Practice, 27,* 349–363.

Miller, I. J. (1996). Ethical and liability issues concerning invisible rationing. *Professional Psychology: Research and Practice, 27,* 583–587.

Miller, T. R., Scott, R., & Searight, H. R. (1990). Ethics for marital and family therapy and subsequent training issues. *Family Therapy, 17,* 163–171.

Minter, M., & Struve, J. (1998). *The ethical use of touch in psychotherapy.* Thousand Oaks, CA: Sage.

Mintz, L. B., Rideout, C. A., & Bartells, K. M. (1994). A national survey of interns' perceptions of their preparation for counseling women and of the atmosphere of their graduate education. *Professional Psychology: Research and Practice, 25,* 221–227.

Minuchin, S. (1974). *Families and family therapy.* Cambridge, MA: Harvard University Press.

Mitchell, C. W., Disque, J. G., & Robertson, P. (2002). When parents want to know: Responding to parental requests for confidential information. *Professional School Counseling, 6,* 156–161.

Mitchell, R. W. (1991). *Documentation in counseling records.* In T. P. Remley (Ed.), *ACA Legal Series* (Vol. 2). Alexandria, VA: American Counseling Association.

Moleski, S. M., & Kiselica, M. S. (2005). Multiple relationships: A continuum ranging from the destructive to the therapeutic. *Journal of Counseling and Development, 83,* 3–11.

Moline, M. E., Williams, G. T., & Austin, K. M. (1998). *Documenting psychotherapy: Essentials for mental health practitioners.* Thousand Oaks, CA: Sage.

Monahan, J. (1981). *Preventing violent behavior: An assessment of clinical techniques.* Beverly Hills, CA: Sage.

Monahan, J. (1993). Limiting therapist exposure to *Tarasoff* liability: Guidelines for risk management. *American Psychologist, 48,* 242–250.

Montgomery, B. (1996). Ohio Attorney General's Opinion 96-029.

Montgomery, L. M., Cupit, B. E., & Wimberley, T. K. (1999). Complaints, malpractice, and risk management: Professional issues and personal experiences. *Professional Psychology: Research and Practice, 30,* 402–410.

Morey, R., Millton, C., Fulton, R., Rosen, L., & Daly, J. (1989). Peer counseling: Students served, problems discussed, overall satisfaction, and perceived helpfulness. *The School Counselor, 37,* 137–143.

Morran, D., Stockton, R., & Bond, L. (1991). Delivery of positive and corrective feedback in counseling groups. *Journal of Counseling Psychology, 38,* 410–414.

Morrow-Bradley, C., & Elliott, R. (1986). Utilization of psychotherapy research by practicing psychotherapists. *American Psychologist, 41,* 188–197.

Mossman, D. (1994). Assessing predictions of violence: Being accurate about accuracy. *Journal of Consulting and Clinical Psychology, 62,* 783–792.

Muratori, M. C. (2001). Examining supervisor impairment from the counselor trainee's perspective. *Counselor Education and Supervision, 41,* 41–56.

Murphy, M. J., DeBernardo, C. R., & Shoemaker, W. E. (1998). Impact of managed care on independent practice and professional ethics: A survey of independent practitioners. *Professional Psychology: Research and Practice, 29,* 43–51.

Myers, J. E. B. (1991). When the parents are at war: How to get the child's side of the story. *Family Advocate, 14,* 36–48.

Myrick, R. D., Highland, W. H., & Sabella, R. A. (1995). Peer helpers and perceived effectiveness. *Elementary School Guidance and Counseling, 29,* 278–288.

Naglieri, J. A., Drasgow, F., Schmit, M., Handler, L., Prifitera, A., Margolis, A., et al. (2004). Psychological testing on the Internet: New problems, old issues. *American Psychologist, 59,* 150–162.

Nagy, T. F. (2000). *Ethics in plain English: An illustrative casebook for psychologists.* Washington, DC: American Psychological Association.

Napier, A., & Whitaker, C. (1978). *The family crucible.* New York: Harper & Row.

Natanson v. Kline, 186 Kans. 393, 406, 350P. 2d 1093 (1960).

National Association of Social Workers. (1999). *Code of ethics.* Silver Spring, MD: Author.

National Association of Social Workers Insurance Trust. (2003). *Supervisor beware: Reducing your exposure to vicarious liability.* Retrieved July 5, 2005, from http://www.naswinsurancetrust.org/understanding_risk_management/pointers/PP%20Vicarious%20Liability.pdf

National Board of Certified Counselors. (2001). *The practice of internet counseling.* Greensboro, NC: Author. Retrieved March 21, 2005, from http://www.nbcc.org/ethics/webethics.htm

National Clearinghouse on Child Abuse and Neglect. (2002). *Child maltreatment 2002: Summary of key findings.* Retrieved

March 9, 2005, from http://nccanch.acf.hhs.gov/pubs/fact-sheets/canstats.cfm

National Institute of Mental Health. (1980). *Hispanic Americans and mental health services: A comparison of Hispanic, Black and White admissions to selected mental health facilities, 1975* (DHHS Publication No. ADM 80-1006). Washington, DC: U.S. Government Printing Office.

Navin, S., Beamish, P., & Johanson, G. (1995). Ethical practices of field-based mental health counselor supervisors. *Journal of Mental Health Counseling, 17,* 243–253.

Nerison, R. M. (1992). Dual client-therapist relationships: Incidence and consequences to clients. *Dissertation Abstracts International, 54,* 1107B. (University Microfilms No. 93-18, 479)

Nessman, A., & Herndon, P. (2000, December). New Jersey settlement offers strong protections for psychologists. *APA Monitor, 31,* 20–21.

Neufeldt, S. A., & Nelson, M. L. (1999). When is counseling an appropriate and ethical supervision function? *Clinical Supervisor, 18,* 125–135.

Neukrug, E. S., Milliken, T., & Walden, S. (2001). Ethics complaints against credentials counselors: An updated survey of state licensing boards. *Counselor Education and Supervision, 41,* 57–70.

Nevas, D. B., & Farber, B. A. (2001). Parents' attitudes toward their child's therapist and therapy. *Professional Psychology: Research and Practice, 32,* 165–170.

Neville, H. A., & Mobley, M. (2001). An ecological model of multicultural counseling psychology processes. *Counseling Psychologist, 29,* 471–486.

Newman, J. L. (1993). Ethical issues in consultation. *Journal of Counseling and Development, 72,* 148–156.

Newman, J. L., Robinson-Kurpius, S. E., & Fuqua, D. R. (2002). Issues in the ethical practice of consulting psychology. In R. L. Lowman (Ed.), *The California School of Organizational Studies: Handbook of organizational consulting psychology: A comprehensive guide to theory, skills, and techniques* (pp. 733–758). San Francisco: Jossey-Bass.

Newman, M. L., & Greenway, P. (1997). Therapeutic effects of providing MMPI-2 test feedback to clients at a university counseling service: A collaborative approach. *Psychological Assessment, 9,* 122–131.

Newman, R., & Bricklin, P. M. (1991). Parameters of managed mental health care: Legal, ethical and professional guidelines. *Professional Psychology: Research and Practice, 22,* 26–35.

Newton, L. (1989). *Ethics in America study guide.* Englewood Cliffs, NJ: Prentice Hall.

Nichols, L. H. (2003). Ethical decision-making in therapists with HIV-positive patients in duty-to-protect situations. *Dissertation Abstracts International, 64,* 971B.

Nickell, N. J., Hecker, L. L., Ray, R. E., & Bercik, J. (1995). Marriage and family therapists' sexual attraction to clients: An exploratory study. *American Journal of Family Therapy, 23,* 315–327.

Nigro, T. (2004a). Multiple relationships in counseling: A survey of British Columbian counselors. *Canadian Journal of Counseling, 38,* 36–53.

Nigro, T. (2004b). Counselors' experiences with problematic multiple relationships. *Ethics and Behavior, 14,* 51–64.

Nodding, N. (1984). *Caring.* Berkeley, CA: University of California.

Noel, B., & Watterson, K. (1992). *You must be dreaming.* New York: Poseidon.

Norcross, J. C. (2000). Psychotherapist self-care: Practitioner-tested, research-informed strategies. *Professional Psychology: Research and Practice, 31,* 710–713.

Norman, G. (1985). Defining competence: A methodological review. In V. Neufeld & G. Norman (Eds.), *Assessing clinical competence.* New York: Springer.

Nowell, D., & Spruill, J. (1993). If it's not absolutely confidential, will information be disclosed? *Professional Psychology: Research and Practice, 24,* 367–369.

Nugent, C. (1996). *Report of the Maryland Task Force to study health-professional-client sexual exploitation.* Retrieved July 9, 2005, from http://www.advocateweb.org/hope/maryland/tfreport.asp #TOP

O'Leary, K. D. (2002). Conjoint therapy for partners who engage in physically aggressive behavior: Rationale and research. *Journal of Aggression, Maltreatment, & Trauma, 5,* 145–164.

Oberlander, L. B. (1995). Ethical responsibilities in child custody evaluations: Implications for evaluation methodology. *Ethics and Behavior, 5,* 311–332.

Office for Protection from Research Risks, Protection of Human Subjects. (1991, June 18). Protection of human subjects: Title 45, Code of Federal Regulations, Part 46 (GPO 1992 O-307-551). *OPOR Reports,* 4–17.

Ohio Board of Psychology. (2003). *When clients are in domestic relations litigation psychologists must proceed with caution.* Retrieved May 25, 2005, from http://psychology.ohio.gov/pdfs/ALERT2003revised.pdf

Ohio Revised Code § 3701.74.

Orme, D. R., & Doerman, A. L. (2001). Ethical dilemmas and U. S. Air Force clinical psychologists: A survey. *Professional Psychology: Research and Practice, 32,* 305–311.

Orr, T. J. (2000). Psychologists' perceptions of managed mental health care practice: Implications for burnout. *Dissertation Abstracts International, 61*(06), 3287B.

Osipow, S., & Fitzgerald, L. F. (1986). An occupational analysis of counseling psychology: How special is the specialty? *American Psychologist, 41,* 535–545.

Otto, R. (1992). The prediction of dangerous behavior: A review and analysis of "second generation" research. *Forensic Reports, 5,* 103–133.

Otto, R. (2000). Assessing and managing violence risk in outpatient settings. *Journal of Clinical Psychology, 56,* 1239–1262.

Overholser, J. C. (2004). The four pillars of psychotherapy supervision. *Clinical Supervisor, 23,* 1–14.

Overholser, J. C., & Fine, M. A. (1990). Defining the boundaries of professional competence: Managing subtle cases of clinical incompetence. *Professional Psychology: Research and Practice, 21,* 462–469.

Packman, W. L., & Harris, E. A. (1998). Legal issues and risk management in suicidal patients. In B. Bongar, A. L. Berman, R. W. Maris, E. A. Harris, W. L. Packman, (Eds.). *Risk management with suicidal patients* (pp. 150–186). New York: Guilford.

Pais, S., Piercy, F., & Miller, J. (1998). Factors related to family therapists' breaking confidence when clients disclose high-risks to HIV/AIDS sexual behaviors. *Journal of Marriage and Family Therapy, 24,* 457–472.

Palma, T. V., & Iannelli, R. J. (2002). Therapeutic reactivity to confidentiality with HIV positive clients: Bias or epidemiology? *Ethics and Behavior, 12,* 353–370.

Paradise, L. V., & Kirby, P. C. (1990). Some perspectives on the legal liability of group counseling in private practice. *Journal for Specialists in Group Work, 15,* 114–118.

Parents of Lesbians and Gays. (2004). *Safe Schools Initiative 2004.* Retrieved June 30, 2005, from http://www.pflag.org/fileadmin/Assessment_Report_2004.pdf

Parker, J., Clevenger, J. E., & Sherman, J. (1997). The psychotherapist-patient privilege in group therapy. *Journal of Group Psychotherapy, Psychodrama & Sociometry, 49,* 157–160.

Pate, R. H., Jr. (1992). Are you liable? *The American Counselor, 1,* 14–19

Patrick, K. D. (1989). Unique ethical dilemmas in counselor training. *Counselor Education and Supervision, 28,* 337–341.

Patten, C., Barnett, T., & Houlihan, D. (1991). Ethics in marital and family therapy: A review of the literature. *Professional Psychology: Research and Practice, 22,* 171–175.

Pavkov, T. W., Lewis, D. A., & Lyons, J. S. (1989). Psychiatric diagnosis and racial bias: An empirical investigation. *Professional Psychology: Research and Practice, 20,* 364–368.

Pearson, B., & Piazza, N. (1997). Classification of multiple relationships in the helping professions. *Counselor Education and Supervision, 37,* 89–99.

Pedersen, P. B. (1991a). The multicultural perspective as a fourth force in counseling. *Journal of Mental Health Counseling, 12,* 93–95.

Pedersen, P. B. (1991b). Multiculturalism as a generic approach to counseling. *Journal of Counseling and Development, 70,* 3–14.

Pedersen, P. B. (1995). Cross cultural ethical guidelines. In J. B. Ponterotto, J. M. Casas, L. A. Suzuki, & C. M. Alexander (Eds.), *Handbook of multicultural counseling* (pp. 34–50). Thousand Oaks, CA: Sage.

Pedersen, P. B. (1997). The cultural context of the American Counseling Association code of ethics. *Journal of Counseling and Development, 76,* 23–28.

Pedersen, P. B. (2000). *A handbook for developing multicultural awareness* (3rd ed.). Alexandria, VA: American Counseling Association.

Pedersen, P. B. (2001). Cross cultural ethical guidelines. In J. B. Ponterotto, J. M. Casas, L. A. Suzuki, & C. M. Alexander (Eds.), *Handbook of multicultural counseling* (2nd ed., pp. 34–50). Thousand Oaks, CA: Sage.

Pedersen, P. B., & Carey, J. C. (Eds). (2003). *Multicultural counseling in schools: A practical handbook.* Needham Heights, MA: Allyn & Bacon.

Pedersen, P. B., Draguns, J. G., Lonner, W. J., & Trimble, J. E. (1996). *Counseling across cultures* (4th ed.). Thousand Oaks, CA: Sage.

Pepper, R. S. (2003). Confidentiality and dual relationships in group psychotherapy. *International Journal of Group Psychotherapy, 54,* 103–114.

Perrin, G. I., & Sales, B. D. (1994). Forensic standards in the American Psychological Association's new Ethics Code. *Professional Psychology: Research and Practice, 25,* 376–381.

Peters, R. H., & Murrin, M. R. (2000). Effectiveness of treatment-based drug courts in reducing criminal recidivism. *Criminal Justice and Behavior, 27,* 72–96.

Peterson, C. (1996). Common problem areas and their causes resulting in disciplinary action. In L. J. Bass, S. T. DeMers, J. R. P. Ogloff, C. Peterson, J. L. Pettifor, R. P. Reaves, et al (Eds.). *Professional conduct and discipline in psychology* (pp. 71–89). Washington, DC: American Psychological Association.

Peterson, M. B. (2001). Recognizing concerns about how some psychology boards are treating psychologists. *Professional Psychology: Research and Practice, 32,* 339–340.

Pettifor, J. J. (2004). Professional ethics across national boundaries. *European Psychologist, 9,* 264–272.

Phelps, R., Eisman, E. J., & Kohut, J. (1998). Psychological practice and managed care: Results of the CAPP practitioner survey. *Professional Psychology: Research and Practice, 29,* 31–36.

Piazza, N. J., & Baruth, N. E. (1990). Client record guidelines. *Journal of Counseling and Development, 68,* 313–316.

Pilkington, N. W., & D'Augelli, A. R. (1995). Victimization of lesbian, gay, and bisexual youth in community settings. *Journal of Community Psychology, 23,* 34–56.

Pittinger, D. A. (2002). Deception in research: Distinctions and solutions from the perspective of utilitarianism. *Ethics and Behavior, 12,* 117–142.

Podbelski, J., & Weisgerber, K. (1988, August). *Differences in moral sensitivity of master's level counselors.* Paper presented at the annual meeting of the American Psychological Association, Atlanta, GA.

Pomerantz, A. M., & Handelsman, M. M. (2004). Informed consent revisited: An updated written question format. *Professional Psychology: Research and Practice, 35,* 201–205.

Ponterotto, J. G., Casas, J. M., Suzuki, L. A., & Alexander, C. M. (Eds.). (2001). *Handbook of multicultural counseling* (2nd ed.). Thousand Oaks, CA: Sage.

Ponterotto, J. G., Gretchen, D., & Chauhan, R. V. (2001). Cultural identity and multicultural assessment: Quantitative and qualitative tools for the clinician. In L. A. Suzuki, J. G. Ponterotto, & P. J. Meller (Eds.), *Handbook of multicultural assessment: Clinical, psychological, and educational practice* (2nd ed., pp. 66–99). San Francisco: Jossey-Bass.

Ponton, L. (1996). Sexual harassment of children and girls. In D. K. Shier (Ed.), *Sexual harassment in the workplace and academia: Psychiatric issues* (pp. 181–201). Washington, DC: American Psychiatric Association.

Pope, K. S. (1988a). How clients are harmed by sexual contact with mental health professionals. *Journal of Counseling and Development, 67,* 222–226.

Pope, K. S. (1988b. Fees, policies and procedures: Causes of malpractice suits and ethics complaints. *Independent Practitioner, 8,* 24–29.

Pope, K. S. (1990a). Therapist–patient sex as sex abuse: Six scientific, professional and practical dilemmas in addressing victimization and rehabilitation. *Professional Psychology: Research and Practice, 21,* 227–239.

Pope, K. S. (1990b). Therapist–patient sexual involvement: A review of the research. *Clinical Psychology Review, 10,* 477–490.

Pope, K. S. (1992). Responsibilities in providing psychological test feedback to clients. *Psychological Assessment, 4,* 268–271.

Pope, K. S. (1994). *Sexual involvement with therapists: Patient assessment, subsequent therapy, forensics.* Washington, DC: American Psychological Association.

Pope, K. S. (2000). Therapists' sexual feelings and behaviors: Research, trends, and quandaries. In L. T. Szuchman & F. Muscarella (Eds.). *Psychological perspectives on human sexuality* (pp. 603–658). New York: Wiley.

Pope, K. S., & Bajt, T. R. (1988). When laws and values conflict: A dilemma for psychologists. *American Psychologist, 43,* 828.

Pope, K. S., & Bouhoutsos, J. C. (1986). *Sexual intimacies between therapists and patients.* New York: Praeger.

Pope, K. S., Keith-Spiegel, P. S., & Tabachnick, B. G. (1986). Sexual attraction to clients: The human therapist and the (sometimes) inhuman training system. *American Psychologist, 41,* 147–158.

Pope, K. S., Levenson, H., & Schover, L. R. (1979). Sexual intimacy in psychology training: Results and implications of a national survey. *American Psychologist, 34,* 682–689.

Pope, K. S., Sonne, J. L., & Holroyd, J. (1993). *Sexual feelings in psychotherapy: Explorations for therapists and therapists-in-training.* Washington, DC: American Psychological Association.

Pope, K. S., & Tabachnick, B. G. (1993). Therapists' anger, hate, fear, and sexual feelings: National survey of therapist responses, client characteristics, critical events, formal complaints, and training. *Professional Psychology: Research and Practice, 24,* 142–152.

Pope, K. S., Tabachnick, B. G., & Keith-Spiegel, P. S. (1987). Ethics of practice: The beliefs and behaviors of psychologists as therapists. *American Psychologist, 42,* 993–1006.

Pope, K. S., & Vasquez, M. J. T. (1998). *Ethics in psychotherapy and counseling* (2nd ed.). San Francisco: Jossey-Bass.

Pope, K. S., & Vasquez, M. J. T. (2005). *How to survive and thrive as a therapist.* Washington, DC: American Psychological Association.

Pope, K. S., & Vetter, V. A. (1991). Prior therapist–patient sexual involvement among patients seen by psychologists. *Psychotherapy: Theory/Research/Practice/Training, 28,* 429–438.

Pope, K. S., & Vetter, V. A. (1992). Ethical dilemmas encountered by members of the American Psychological Association. *American Psychologist, 47,* 397–411.

Pope-Davis, D. B., & Coleman, H. L. K. (Eds.). (1998) *Multicultural counseling competencies: Assessment, education, training, and supervision.* Thousand Oaks, CA: Sage.

Powell, M. P., & Vacha-Haase, T. (1994). Issues related to research with children: What counseling psychologists need to know. *The Counseling Psychologist, 22,* 444–453.

Price, J. H., & Teljohann, S. K. (1991). School counselor perceptions of adolescent homosexuals. *Journal of School Health, 61,* 433–438.

Procidano, M. E., Busch-Rossnagel, N. A., Reznikoff, M., & Geisinger, K. F. (1995). Responding to graduate students' pro-

fessional deficiencies: A national survey. *Journal of Clinical Psychology, 51,* 426–233.

Pryzwansky, W. B., & Wendt, R. N. (1999). *Professional and ethical issues in psychology: Foundations of practice.* New York: W. W. Norton.

Pulakos, J. (1994). Incidental encounters between therapists and clients: The client's perspective. *Professional Psychology: Research and Practice, 25,* 300–303.

Quattrocchi, M. R., & Schopp, R. F. (2005). Tarasaurus Rex: A standard of care that could not adapt. *Psychology, Public Policy and Law, 11,* 109–137.

Rabasca, L. (2000, April). Taking telehealth the next step. *APA Monitor, 31,* 36–37.

Rabinowitz, J., & Efron, N. J. (1997). Diagnosis, dogmatism, and rationality. *Journal of Mental Health Counseling, 19,* 40–56.

Radeke, J. T., & Mahoney, M. J. (2000). Comparing the personal lives of psychotherapists and research psychologists. *Professional Psychology: Research and Practice, 31,* 284–292.

Rae, W. A., & Worchel, F. F. (1991). Ethical beliefs and behaviors of pediatric psychologists: A survey. *Journal of Pediatric Psychology, 16,* 727–745.

Raimy, V. (1975). *Misunderstandings of the self.* San Francisco: Jossey-Bass.

Raquepaw, J., & Miller, R. S. (1989). Psychotherapist burnout: A componential analysis. *Professional Psychology: Research and Practice, 20,* 32–36.

Reamer, F. G. (1995). Malpractice claims against social workers: First facts. *Social Work, 40,* 595–601.

Reaves, R. P., & Ogloff, J. R. P. (1996). Liability for professional misconduct. In L. J. Bass, S. T. DeMers, J. R. P. Ogloff, C. Peterson, J. L. Pettifor, R. P. Reaves, et al (Eds.). *Professional conduct and discipline in psychology* (pp. 117–142). Washington, DC: American Psychological Association.

Regehr, C., & Glancy, G. (1995). Sexual exploitation of patients: Issues for colleagues. *American Journal of Orthopsychiatry, 65,* 194–202.

Reid, K. (2001). Iowa's high court holds counselors liable. *Education Week.* Retrieved June 30, 2005, from http://secure.edweek.org/ew/ew_printstory.cfm?slug=33guide.h20

Remafedi, G. (1999). Sexual orientation and youth suicide. *Journal of the American Medical Association, 282,* 1291–1292.

Remley, T. P., Jr., & Herlihy, B. (2005). *Ethical, legal and professional issues in counseling* (2nd ed.). Upper Saddle River, NJ: Pearson.

Remley, T. P., Jr., Herlihy, B., & Herlihy, S. B. (1997). The U.S. Supreme Court decision in *Jaffee v. Redmond:* Implications for counselors. *Journal of Counseling and Development, 75,* 213–218.

Remley, T. P., Jr., & Sparkman, L. B. (1993). Student suicides: The counselor's limited legal liability. *The School Counselor, 40,* 164–169.

Rest, J. R. (1983). Morality. In J. Flavell & E. Markman (Eds.), *Cognitive development.* In P. Mussen (General Ed.), *Manual of child psychology* (Vol. 4, pp. 550–629). New York: Wiley.

Rest, J. R. (1984). Research on moral development: Implications for training counseling psychologists. *The Counseling Psychologist, 12,* 19–29.

Rest, J. R. (1994). Background: Theory and research. In J. R. Rest & D. Navarez (Eds.). *Moral development in the professions: Psychology and applied ethics* (pp. 1–26). Hillsdale, NJ: Lawrence Erlbaum.

Ridley, C. R. (1995). *Overcoming unintentional racism in counseling: A practitioner's guide to intentional intervention.* Thousand Oaks, CA: Sage.

Ridley, C. R., & Tan, S.Y. (1986). Unintentional paradoxes and potential pitfalls in paradoxical psychotherapy. *The Counseling Psychologist, 14,* 303–308.

Ridley, C. R., Baker, D. M., & Hill, C. L. (2001). Critical issues concerning cultural competence. *The Counseling Psychologist, 29,* 822–832.

Ridley, C. R., Hill, C. L., Thompson, C. E., & Ormerod, A. J. (2001). Clinical practice guidelines in assessment: Toward an idiographic perspective. In D. Pope-Davis & H. Coleman (Eds.), *The intersection of race, class, and gender in multicultural counseling* (pp. 191–211). Thousand Oaks, CA: Sage.

Ridley, C. R., Li, L., & Hill, C. L. (1998). Multicultural assessment: Reexamination, reconceptualization, and practical application. *Counseling Psychologist, 26,* 827–910.

Ridley, C. R., Liddle, M. C., Hill, C. L., & Li, L. C. (2001). Ethical decision making in multicultural counseling. In J. G. Ponterotto, J. M. Casas, L. A. Suzuki, & C. M. Alexander (Eds.), *Handbook of multicultural counseling* (pp. 165–188). Newbury Park, CA: Sage.

Riester, A. E. (2002). Group counseling in the American high school. In S. Aronson & S. Scheidlinger (Eds.), *Group treatment of adolescents in context: Outpatient, inpatient, and school* (pp. 191–203). Madison, CT: International Universities Press.

Ritchie, M. H., & Huss, S. N. (2000). Recruitment and screening of minors for group counseling. *Journal for Specialists in Group Work, 25,* 145–156.

Ritchie, M. H., & Partin, R. L. (1994). Parent education and consultation about activities of school counselors. *The School Counselor, 41,* 165–170.

Ritter, K. Y., & Terndrup, A. I. (2002). *Handbook of affirmative psychotherapy with lesbians and gay men.* New York: Guilford.

Roback, H. B., Ochoa, E., Bloch, F., & Purdon, S. (1992). Guarding confidentiality in clinical groups: The therapist's dilemma. *International Journal of Group Psychotherapy, 42,* 81–103.

Roberts, L. W., Battaglia, J., & Epstein, R. S. (1999). Frontier ethics: Mental health care needs and ethical dilemmas in rural communities. *Psychiatric Services, 50,* 497–503.

Robertson, J., & Fitzgerald, L. F. (1990). The (mis)treatment of men: Effects of client gender role and life style on diagnosis and attribution of pathology. *Journal of Counseling Psychology, 37,* 3–9.

Robiner, W. N., Fuhrman, M. J., & Bobbitt, B. J. L. (1990). Supervision in the practice of psychology: Toward the development of a supervisory instrument. *Psychotherapy in Private Practice, 8,* 87–98.

Robinson, W. L., & Reid, P. T. (1985). Sexual intimacies in psychology revisited. *Professional Psychology: Research and Practice, 16,* 512–520.

Rodolfo, E., Bent, R., Eisman, E., Rehm, L., & Ritchie, P. (2005). A cube model for competency development: Implications for psychology educators and regulators. *Professional Psychology: Research and Practice, 36,* 347–354.

Rodolfa, E., Hall, T., Holms, V., Davena, A., Komatz, D., Antunez, M., et al. (1994). The management of sexual feelings in therapy. *Professional Psychology: Research and Practice, 25,* 168–172.

Roeske, N. (1986). Risk factors: Predictable hazards of a health care career. In C. Scott & J. Hawk (Eds.), *Heal thyself: The health of health care professionals.* New York: Brunner/Mazel.

Rogers, J. R., Gueulette, C. M., Abbey-Hines, J., Carney, J.V., & Werth, J. L. (2001). Rational suicide: An empirical investigation of counselor attitudes. *Journal of Counseling and Development, 80,* 493–502.

Rogers, W. H., Wells, K. B., Meredith, L. S., Sturm, R., & Burman, A. (1993). Outcomes for adult outpatients with depression under pre-paid or fee-for-service financing. *Archives for General Psychiatry, 50,* 517–525.

Rohrbaugh, J. B. (1992). Lesbian families: Clinical issues and theoretical implications. *Professional Psychology: Research and Practice, 23,* 467–473.

Rokop, J. J. (2003). The effects of cps mandated reporting on the therapeutic relationship: The client's perspective. *Dissertation Abstracts International, 64* (5-B), 135.

Rooney, R. (2001). Guidelines for counseling mandated and non-voluntary clients. In E. R. Welfel & R. E. Ingersoll (Eds.). *The mental health desk reference: A sourcebook for counselors and therapists* (pp. 94–98). New York: Wiley.

Rorschach, H. (1951). *Psychodiagnostics.* New York: Grune & Stratton.

Rosen, L. D., & Weil, M. M. (1996). Psychologists and technology: A look at the future. *Professional Psychology: Research and Practice, 27,* 635–637.

Rosenhan, D. L. (1973). On being sane in insane places. *Science, 179,* 250–258.

Rosenthal, R. (1994). Science and ethics in conducting, analyzing, and reporting psychological research. *Psychological Science, 5,* 127–133.

Ross, D. M. (2003). *Childhood bullying, teasing, and violence: What school personnel, other professionals, and parents can do.* Alexandria, VA: American Counseling Association.

Rovero, M.V. (2004). A study of burnout in elementary, middle and secondary school counselors. *Dissertation Abstracts International, 64*(09), 3204A.

Rowan, J. (2000). Research ethics. *International Journal of Psychotherapy, 5,* 103–111.

Rowley, W. J., & MacDonald, D. (2001). Counseling and the law: A cross-cultural perspective. *Journal of Counseling and Development, 79,* 422–429.

Roy v. Hartogs, 366 NY, S2d 297 (1975).

Royer, R. I. (1985). *Ethical orientation of mental health practitioners: A comparative study.* Paper presented at the annual meeting of the American Psychological Association, Los Angeles.

Roysircar, G. (2005). Culturally sensitive assessment, diagnosis, and guidelines. In M. G. Constantine & D. W. Sue (Eds.). *Strategies for building multicultural competence in mental health and educational settings* (pp. 19–38). New York: Wiley.

Rozovsky, F. A. (2000). *Consent to treatment: A practical guide* (3rd ed.). Boston: Little Brown.

Rubin, L. J., Hampton, B. R., & McManus, P. W. (1997). Sexual harassment of students by professional psychology educators: A national survey. *Sex Roles, 37,* 753–771.

Rubinson, E., Asnis, G. M., Harkavy, S., & Friedman, J. M. (1988). Knowledge of the diagnostic criteria for major depression: A survey of mental health professionals. *Journal of Nervous and Mental Disease, 176,* 480–484.

Rupert, P. A., & Baird, K. A. (2004). Managed care and the independent practice of psychology. *Professional Psychology: Research and Practice, 35,* 185–191.

Rutter, P. (1989). *Sex in the forbidden zone: When men in power—therapists, doctors, clergy, teachers and others—betray women's trust.* Los Angeles: Tarcher.

Sain v. Cedar Rapids Community School District, 626 N. W. 2d 115 (Iowa, 2001).

Sales, B. D., & Folkman, S. (Eds.). (2000). *Ethics in research with human participants.* Washington, DC: American Psychological Association.

Sales, B. D., & Lavin, M. Identifying conflicts of interest and resolving ethical dilemmas. In B. D. Sales & S. Folkman (Eds.), *Ethics in research with human participants* (pp. 109–128). Washington, DC: American Psychological Association.

Salisbury, W. A., & Kinnier, R. T. (1996). Posttermination friendship between counselors and clients. *Journal of Counseling and Development, 74,* 495–500.

Sampson, J. P., Kolodinsky, R. W., & Greeno, B. P. (1997). Counseling on the information highway: Future possibilities and potential problems. *Journal of Counseling and Development, 75,* 203–212.

Sampson, K. (1993). The use and misuse of expert evidence in courts. *Judicature, 77,* 68–76.

Sanders, J. L. (2003). Report of the ACA Ethics Committee 2002–2003. *Journal of Counseling and Development, 81,* 251–254.

Sandhi, D. S., & Aspy, C. B. (2000). *Violence in American schools: A practical guide for counselors.* Alexandria, VA: American Counseling Association.

Sank, L. I. (1997). Taking on managed care: One reviewer at a time. *Professional Psychology: Research and Practice, 28,* 548–554.

Scarf, M. (1996, June 16). Keeping secrets. *New York Times,* pp. 38–42, 50, 54.

Schank, J. A. (1998). Ethical issues in rural counseling practice. *Canadian Journal of Counseling, 32,* 270–283.

Schank, J. A., & Skovholt, T. M. (1997). Multiple-relationship dilemmas of rural and small community psychologists. *Professional Psychology: Research and Practice, 28,* 44–49.

Schoener, G. R., & Gonsiorek, J. (1988). Assessment and development of rehabilitation plans for counselors who have sexually exploited their clients. *Journal of Counseling and Development, 67,* 227–232.

Schoener, G. R., Milgrom, J., & Gonsiorek, J. (1989). Therapeutic responses to clients who have been sexually abused by psychotherapists. In G. Schoener & J. Milgrom (Eds.), *Psychotherapists' sexual involvement with clients: Intervention and prevention* (pp. 95–112). Minneapolis, MN: Walk-in Counseling Center.

Schoenfeld, L. S., Hatch, J. P., & Gonzalez, J. M. (2001). Responses of psychologists to complaints filed against them with a state licensing board. *Professional Psychology: Research and Practice, 32,* 491–495.

Schulenberg, S. E., & Yutrzenka, B. A. (2004). Ethical issues in the use of computerized assessment. *Computers in Human Behavior, 20,* 477–490.

Schulte, J. M., & Cochrane, D. B. (1995). *Ethics of school counseling.* New York: Teachers College Press.

Schultz, B. M. (1982). *Legal liability in psychotherapy.* San Francisco: Jossey-Bass.

Schwab, R., & Neukrug, E. (1994). A survey of counselor educators' ethical concerns. *Counseling and Values, 39,* 42–55.

Schwartz, L. L. (Ed.). (1999). *Psychologists and the media: A second look.* Washington, DC: American Psychological Association.

Schwebel, M., Schoener, G., & Skorina, J. K. (1994). *Assisting impaired psychologists* (Rev. ed.). Washington, DC: American Psychological Association.

Schweibert, V. L. (2000). *Mentoring: Creating connected, empowered relationships.* Alexandria, VA: American Counseling Association.

Scott, K. J., Ingram. K. M., Vitanza, S. A., & Smith, N. G. (2000). Training in supervision: A survey of current practices. *Counseling Psychologist, 28,* 403–422.

Scott-Jones, D. (2000). Recruitment of research participants. In B. D. Sales & S. Folkman (Eds.), *Ethics in research with human participants* (pp. 27–34). Washington, DC: American Psychological Association.

Scrivner, R. (1997). Ethical and legal issues in lesbian, gay, and bisexual family therapy. In D. Marsh & R. D. Magee (Eds.), *Ethical and legal issues in professional practice with families* (pp. 140–160). New York: Wiley.

Sealander, K. A. (1999). Confidentiality and the law. *Professional School Counseling, 3,* 122–127.

Sekaran, U. (1986). *Dual career families.* San Francisco: Jossey-Bass.

Seligman, M. E. P. (1995). The effectiveness of psychotherapy: The Consumer Reports study. *American Psychologist, 50,* 965–974.

Sell, J. M., Gottlieb, M. C., & Schoenfeld, L. S. (1986). Ethical considerations of social/romantic relationships with present and former clients. *Professional Psychology: Research and Practice, 17,* 504–508.

Sexton, T. L., & Liddle, M. C. (2001). Practicing evidence-based mental health: Using research and measuring outcomes. In E. R. Welfel & R. E. Ingersoll (Eds.), *Mental health desk reference: A sourcebook for counselors and therapists* (pp. 387–392). New York: Wiley.

Sexton, T. L., & Montgomery, D. (1994). Ethical and therapeutic acceptability: A study of paradoxical techniques. *The Family Journal, 2,* 215–228.

Sexton, T. L., Montgomery, D., Goff, K., & Nugent, W. (1993). Ethical, therapeutic, and legal considerations in the use of paradoxical techniques: The emerging debate. *Journal of Mental Health Counseling, 15,* 260–277.

Sexton, T. L., & Whiston, S. C. (1994). The status of the counseling relationship: An empirical review, theoretical implications, and research directions. *Counseling Psychologist, 22,* 6–78.

Sexton, T. L., Whiston, S. C., Bleuer, J. C., & Walz, G. R. (1997). *Integrating outcome research into counseling practice and training.* Alexandria, VA: American Counseling Association.

Shapiro, F. (1995). *Eye movement desensitization and reprocessing: Basic principles, protocols, and procedures.* New York: Guilford Press.

Sharkin, B. S., & Plageman, P. M. (2003). What do psychologists think about mandatory continuing education? A survey of Pennsylvania practitioners. *Professional Psychology: Research and Practice, 34,* 318–323.

Shaw, G. B. (1903). *Man and Superman.* London: Constable.

Shaw, L. R., Chan, F., Lam, C. S., & McDougall, A. G. (2004). Professional disclosure practices of rehabilitation counselors. *Rehabilitation Counseling Bulletin, 48,* 38–50.

Shead, N. W., & Dobson, K. S. (2004). Psychology for sale: The ethics of advertising professional services. *Canadian Psychology, 45,* 126–136.

Shearer, R. A. (2003). Court ordered counseling: An ethical minefield for psychotherapists. *Annals of the American Psychotherapy Association, 6,* 8–11.

Shechtman, A. (2002). Child group psychotherapy in the school at the threshold of a millennium. *Journal of Counseling and Development, 80,* 293–299.

Shechtman, A., & Yanuv, H. (2001). Interpretive interventions: Feedback, confrontation, and interpretation. *Group Dynamics, 5,* 124–135.

Sheeley, V. L., & Herlihy, B. (1989). Counseling suicidal teens: A duty to warn and protect. *The School Counselor, 37,* 89–97.

Shepard, M. (1972). *The love treatment.* New York: Paperback Library.

Sherman, M. D., & Thelen, M. H. (1998). Distress and professional impairment among psychologists in clinical practice. *Professional Psychology: Research and Practice, 29,* 79–85.

Sherry, P. (1991). Ethical issues in the conduct of supervision. *Counseling Psychologist, 19,* 566–584.

Sherry, P., Teschendorf, R., Anderson, S., & Guzman, F. (1991). Ethical beliefs and behaviors of counseling center professionals. *Journal of College Student Development, 32,* 350–358.

Shuman, D. W., & Foote, W. (1999). Jaffee v. Redmond's impact: Life after the Supreme Court's recognition of a psychotherapist-patient privilege. *Professional Psychology: Research and Practice, 30,* 479–487.

Shumate, S., & Espina, M. R. (1999). Report of the ACA ethics committee. *Journal of Counseling and Development, 77,* 243–245.

Sieber, J. E. (1992). *Planning ethically responsible research: A guide for students and internal review boards.* Newbury Park, CA: Sage.

Siegel, S. J. (1991). *What to do when psychotherapy goes wrong.* Las Vegas, NV: Priority One Consultants.

Simon, R. I. (1991). Psychological injury caused by boundary violation precursors to therapist–patient sex. *Psychiatric Annals, 21,* 614–619.

Simon, R. I. (1992). Treatment of boundary violations: Clinical, ethical and legal considerations. *Bulletin of the American Academy of Psychiatry and the Law, 20,* 269–288.

Simpson case: Confidences survive clients. (1994, September). *National Association of Social Workers Newsletter,* p. 8.

Skovholt, T. M. (2001). *The resilient practitioner: Burnout prevention and self care strategies for counselors, therapists, teachers and health professionals.* Boston: Allyn & Bacon.

Sleek, S. (1994, December). Ethical dilemmas plague rural practice. *APA Monitor, 25,* 26–27.

Slimp, P. A. O., & Burian, B. K. (1994). Multiple role relationships during internship: Consequences and recommendations. *Professional Psychology: Research and Practice, 25,* 39–45.

Slovenko, R. (1980). Legal issues in psychotherapy supervision. In A. K. Hess (Ed.), *Psychotherapy supervision: Theory, research and practice* (pp. 453–473). New York: Wiley.

Slovenko, R. (2000). Psychiatric opinion without examination. *Journal of Psychiatry & Law, 28,* 103–143.

Smith, D., & Dumont, F. (1995). A cautionary study: Unwarranted interpretations of the Draw-A-Person Test. *Professional Psychology: Research and Practice, 26,* 298–303.

Smith, D., & Fitzpatrick, M. (1995). Patient–therapist boundary issues: An integrative review of theory and research. *Professional Psychology: Research and Practice, 26,* 499–506.

Smith, E. W. L., Clance, P. R., & Imes, S. (Eds.). (1998). *Touch in psychotherapy: Theory, research and practice.* New York: Guilford.

Smith, R. L. (1999). Client confidentiality in marriage and family counseling. In P. Stevens (Ed.), *Ethical casebook for the practice of marriage and family counseling* (pp. 83–92). Alexandria, VA: American Counseling Association.

Smith, S. R., & Meyer, R. G. (1987). *Law, behavior and mental health policy and practice.* New York: New York University Press.

Smith, S. W., Daunic, A. P., Miller, M. D., & Robinson, T. R. (2002). Conflict resolution and peer mediation in middle schools: Extending the process and knowledge outcome base. *Journal of School Psychology, 14,* 567–586.

Smith, T. S., McGuire, J. M., Abbott, D. W., & Blau, B. I. (1991). Clinical ethical decision making: An investigation of the rationales used to justify doing less than one believes one should. *Professional Psychology: Research and Practice, 22,* 235–239.

Snyder, D. K. (2000). Computer-assisted judgment: defining strengths and weaknesses. *Psychological Assessment, 12,* 52–60.

Sobel, S. B. (1992). Small town practice of psychotherapy: Ethical and personal dilemmas. *Psychotherapy in Private Practice, 10,* 61–69.

Sodowsky, G. R., Taffe, R. C., Gutlin, T. B., & Wise, S. L. (1994). Development of the Multicultural Counseling Inventory: A self-report measure of multicultural competencies. *Journal of Counseling Psychology, 41,* 137–148.

Soisson, E. L., VandeCreek, L., & Knapp, S. (1987). Thorough record keeping: A good defense in a litigious era. *Professional Psychology: Research and Practice, 18,* 498–502.

Solovey, A. D., & Duncan, B. L. (1992). Ethics and strategic therapy: A proposed ethical direction. *Journal of Marital and Family Therapy, 18,* 53–61.

Somberg, D. R. (1995). The influence of narcissism on psychologists' moral sensitivity. *Dissertation Abstracts International, 55*(12), 5577B.

Somberg, D. R., Stone, G. L., & Claiborn, C. D. (1993). Informed consent: Therapists' beliefs and practices. *Professional Psychology: Research and Practice, 24,* 153–159.

Somer, E., & Nachmani, I. (2005). Constructions of therapist–client sex: A comparative analysis of reconstructive victim reports. *Sexual Abuse: A Journal of Research and Treatment, 17,* 47–62.

Somer, E., & Saadon, M. (1999). Therapist–client sex: Clients' retrospective reports. *Professional Psychology: Research and Practice, 30,* 504–509

Sommers-Flanagan, R., Elliott, D., & Sommers-Flanagan, J. (1998). Exploring the edges: Boundaries and breaks. *Ethics and Behavior, 8,* 37–48.

Sonne, J. L. (1987). Proscribed sex: Counseling the patient subjected to sexual intimacy by a therapist. *Medical Aspects of Human Sexuality, 16,* 18–23.

Sonne, J. L. (1994). Multiple relationships: Does the new ethics code answer the right questions? *Professional Psychology: Research and Practice, 25,* 336–343.

Sonne, J. L., Meyer, C., Borys, D., & Marshall, V. (1985). Clients' reactions to sexual intimacy in therapy. *American Journal of Orthopsychiatry, 55,* 183–189.

Sonne, J. L., & Pope, K. S. (1991). Treating victims of therapist–patient sexual involvement. *Psychotherapy, 28,* 174–187.

Sorensen, J. L., Masson, C. L., Clark, W. W., & Morin, S. F. (1998). Providing public testimony: A guide for psychologists. *Professional Psychology: Research and Practice, 29,* 588–593.

Sorenson, G., & Chapman, D. W. (1985). School compliance with federal law concerning the release of student records. *Educational Evaluation & Policy Analysis, 7,* 9–18.

Spengler, P. (2000). Does vocational overshadowing even exist? A test of the robustness of the vocational overshadowing bias. *Journal of Counseling Psychology, 47,* 342–351.

Spector, J., & Read, J. (1999). The current status of eye movement desensitization and reprocessing (EMDR). *Clinical Psychology and Psychotherapy, 6,* 165–174.

Spitzer, R. L. (1975). On pseudoscience in science, logic in remission and psychiatric diagnosis: A critique of Rosenhan's "On being sane in insane places." *Journal of Abnormal Psychology, 84,* 442–452.

Sporakowski, M. J., Prouty, A. M., & Habben, C. (2001). Assessment in couple and family counseling. In E. R. Welfel & R. E. Ingersoll (Eds.), *Mental health desk reference: A practice-based guide to diagnosis, treatment, and professional ethics* (pp. 372–378). New York: Wiley.

Spruill, J., Rozensky, R. H., Stigall, T. T., Vasquez, M. J. T., Bingham, R. P., & Olvey, C. D. (2004). Becoming a competent clinician: Basic competencies in intervention. *Journal of Clinical Psychology, 60,* 741–754.

St. Germaine, J. (1997). Ethical practices of certified addiction counselors: A national survey of state certification boards. *Alcoholism Treatment Quarterly, 15,* 63–72.

Stadler, H. A. (1990). Counselor impairment. In B. Herlihy & L. Golden (Eds.), *Ethical standards casebook.* Alexandria, VA: American Association for Counseling and Development.

Stadler, H. A. (2001). Impairment in the mental health professions. In E. R. Welfel & R. E. Ingersoll (Eds.), *Mental health desk reference: A practice-based guide to diagnosis, treatment, and professional ethics* (pp. 413–418). New York: Wiley.

Stadler, H. A., Willing, K. L., Eberhage, M. G., & Ward, W. H. (1988). Impairment: Implications for the counseling profession. *Journal of Counseling and Development, 66,* 258–260.

Stahl, P. M. (1994). *Conducting child custody evaluations: A comprehensive guide.* Thousand Oaks, CA: Sage

Stahl, P. M. (1999). *Complex issues in child custody evaluations.* Thousand Oaks, CA: Sage.

Stake, J. E., & Oliver, J. (1991). Sexual contact and touching between therapist and client: A survey of psychologists' attitudes and behavior. *Professional Psychology: Research and Practice, 22,* 297–307.

Stanard, R., & Hazler, R. (1995). Legal and ethical implications of HIV and duty to warn for counselors: Does *Tarasoff* apply? *Journal of Counseling and Development, 73,* 397–400.

Steinberg, K. L. (1994). In the service of two masters: Psychotherapists struggle with child maltreatment reporting laws. *Dissertation Abstracts International, 55,* 2412B. (University Microfilms No. AAI8213453)

Stenzel, C. L., & Rupert, P. A. (2004). Psychologists' use of touch in individual psychotherapy. *Psychotherapy: Theory, Research, Practice and Training, 41,* 332–347.

Stepp, L. S. (2001, June 19). A lesson in cruelty: Anti-gay slurs common at school: Some say insults increase as gays' visibility rises. *The Washington Post,* p. A01.

Stern, L. (2004). Executive coaching: A working definition. *Consulting Psychology Journal, 56,* 154–162.

Stevanovic, P., & Rupert, P. A. (2004). Career-sustaining behaviors, satisfactions, and stresses of professional psychologists. *Psychotherapy: Theory, Research, Practice and Training, 41,* 301–309.

Stevens-Smith, P., & Hughes, M. M. (1993). Legal issues in marriage and family counseling. In T. P. Remley (Ed.), *ACA legal series* (Vol. 7). Alexandria, VA: American Counseling Association.

Stith, S. M., Rosen, K. H., & McCollum, E. E. (2003). Effectiveness of couples treatment for spouse abuse. *Journal of Marital and Family Therapy, 29,* 407–426.

Stokes, L. S., & Remley, T. P., Jr., (2001). Counselors in forensic settings. In E. R. Welfel & R. E. Ingersoll (Eds.), *Mental health desk reference: A practice-based guide to diagnosis, treatment, and professional ethics* (pp. 404–411). New York: Wiley.

Stokes, L. S., & Remley, T. P., Jr. (2001). Counselors as expert witnesses. In E. R. Welfel & R. E. Ingersoll (Eds.), *Mental health desk reference: A practice-based guide to diagnosis, treatment, and professional ethics* (pp. 404–411). New York: Wiley.

Stokes, T. J. (1999). Sexual orientation and clinical decisions. *Dissertation Abstracts International, 59,* 4488B. (University Microfilms No. 95004-063)

Stoller, R. J. (1988). Patients' responses to their own case reports. *Journal of the American Psychoanalytic Association, 36,* 371–391.

Stone, A. A. (1978, March 19). Mentally ill: To commit or not, that is the question. *New York Times,* p. 10E.

Stone, C., & Isaacs, M. I. (2003). Confidentiality with minors: The need for policy to promote and protect. *Journal of Educational Research, 96,* 140–147.

Stone, C. B. (2002). Negligence in academic advising and abortion counseling: Courts rulings and implications. *Professional School Counseling, 6,* 28–35.

Stone, C. B. (2003). Counselors as advocates for gay, lesbian and bisexual youth: A call for equity and action. *Journal of Multicultural Counseling and Development, 31,* 143–155.

Stone, C. B. (2005). *School counseling principles: Ethics and law.* Alexandria, VA: American School Counselor Association.

Stout, C. E., & Hayes R. A. (Eds.), *The evidence-based practice: Methods, models, and tools for mental health professionals.* New York: Wiley.

Strom-Gottfried, K. (1999). Professional boundaries: An analysis of violations by social workers. *Families in Society, 80,* 439–449.

Sturdivant, S. (1993). The ethics of marketing a private practice. *Psychotherapy in Private Practice, 12,* 23–28.

Sue, D. W. (1995). Ethical issues in multicultural counseling. In B. Herlihy & G. Corey (Eds.), *ACA ethical standards casebook* (5th ed., pp. 193–204). Alexandria, VA: American Counseling Association.

Sue, D. W., Arrendondo, P., & McDavis, R. J. (1992). Multicultural competencies and standards: A call to the profession. *Journal of Counseling and Development, 70,* 477–486.

Sue, D. W., Carter, R. T., Casas, J. M., Fouad, N. A., Ivey, A. E., Jensen, M., et al. (1998). *Multicultural counseling competencies: Individual and organizational development.* Thousand Oaks, CA: Sage.

Sue, D. W., Ivey, A. E., & Pedersen, P. B. (1996). *A theory of multicultural counseling and therapy.* Pacific Grove, CA: Brooks/Cole.

Sue, D. W., & Sue, D. (2003). *Counseling the culturally different: Theory and practice* (4th ed.). New York: Wiley.

Sullivan, J. R., Ramirez, E., Rae, W. A., Razo, N. P., & George, C. A. (2002). Factors contributing to breaking confidentiality with adolescent clients: A survey of pediatric psychologists. *Professional Psychology: Research and Practice, 33,* 396–401.

Sullivan, K., & Zirkel, P. L. (1999). Student to student sexual harassment: Which tack will the Supreme Court take in a sea of analyses? *West Education Law Reporter, 132,* 609–628.

Sullivan, T., Martin, W. L., & Handelsman, M. M. (1993). Practical benefits of an informed-consent procedure: An empirical investigation. *Professional Psychology: Research and Practice, 24,* 160–163.

Sutter, E., McPherson, R. H., & Geeseman, R. (2002). Contracting for supervision. *Professional Psychology: Research and Practice, 33,* 495–498.

Suzuki, L. A., & Kugler, J. F (2001). Multicultural assessment. In E. R. Welfel & R. E. Ingersoll (Eds.), *Mental health desk reference: A practice-based guide to diagnosis, treatment, and professional ethics* (pp. 279–285). New York: Wiley.

Suzuki, L. A., Ponterotto, J. G., & Meller, P. J., (2001). *Handbook of multicultural assessment* (2nd ed.). San Francisco: Jossey-Bass.

Swenson, L. C. (1997). *Psychology and law for the helping professions* (2nd ed.). Pacific Grove, CA: Brooks/Cole.

Szasz T. S. (1971). The sane slave: An historical note on the use of medical diagnosis as justificatory rhetoric. *American Journal of Psychotherapy, 25,* 228–239.

Szasz, T. S. (1973). *The second sin.* Garden City, NJ: Anchor.

Tabachnick, B. G., Keith-Spiegel, P. S., & Pope, K. S. (1991). Ethics of teaching: Beliefs and behaviors of psychologists as educators. *American Psychologist, 46,* 506–515.

Talbert, F. S., & Pipes, R. B. (1988). Informed consent for psychotherapy: Content analysis of selected forms. *Professional Psychology: Research and Practice, 19,* 131–132.

Tarasoff v. Regents of the University of California, 118 Cal. Rptr. 129, 529 P. 2d 533 (1974).

Tarasoff v. Regents of the University of California, 131 Cal. Rptr. 14, 551 P. 2d 334 (1976).

Taylor, L., & Adelman, H. S. (1998). Confidentiality: Competing principles, inevitable dilemmas. *Journal of Educational and Psychological Consultation, 9,* 267–275.

Taylor, L., & Adelman, H. S. (1989). Reframing the confidentiality dilemma to work in children's best interests. *Professional Psychology: Research and Practice, 20,* 79–83.

Taylor, L., & Adelman, H. S. (2001). Enlisting appropriate parental cooperation and involvement in children's mental health treatment. In E. R. Welfel & R. E. Ingersoll (Eds.), *Mental health desk reference: A practice-based guide to diagnosis, treatment, and professional ethics* (pp. 219–224). New York: Wiley.

Taylor, L., Adelman, H. S., & Kaser-Boyd, N. (1984). Attitudes towards involving minors in decisions. *Professional Psychology: Research and Practice, 15,* 436–449.

Taylor, R. E., & Gazda, G. M. (1991). Concurrent individual and group therapy: The ethical issues. *Journal of Group Psychotherapy, Psychodrama, & Sociometry, 44,* 51–59.

Teisman, M. (1980). Convening strategies in family therapy. *Family Process, 19,* 393–400.

Thomas, J. T. (2002, August). *Facing a board complaint: The impact on the psychologist's objectivity.* Paper presented at the annual meeting of the American Psychological Association, Chicago.

Thompson, T. L. (1999). Managed care: Views, practices, and burnout of psychologists. *Dissertation Abstracts International, 60,* 1318B. (University Microfilms No. 91–14, 449)

Thoreson, R. W., Miller, M., & Krauskopf, C. J. (1989). The distressed psychologist: Prevalence and treatment considerations. *Professional Psychology: Research and Practice, 20,* 153–158.

Thoreson, R. W., Nathan, P., Skorina, J., & Kilburg, R. (1983). The alcoholic psychologist: Issues, problems, implications for the profession. *Professional Psychology: Research and Practice, 14,* 670–684.

Thoreson, R. W., Shaughnessy, P., & Frazier, P. A. (1995). Sexual contact during and after professional relationships: Practices and attitudes of female counselors. *Journal of Counseling and Development, 74,* 84–89.

Thoreson, R. W., Shaughnessy, P., Heppner, P. P., & Cook, S. W. (1993). Sexual contact during and after the professional relationships: Attitudes and practices of male counselors. *Journal of Counseling and Development, 71,* 429–434.

Thorn, B. E., Shealy, R. C., & Briggs, S. D. (1993). Sexual misconduct in psychotherapy: Reactions to a consumer-oriented brochure. *Professional Psychology: Research and Practice, 24,* 75–82.

Tjeltveit, A. C. (1999). *Ethics and values in psychotherapy.* New York: Routledge.

Tobias, A. K., & Myrick, R. D. (1999). A peer facilitator-led intervention with middle school problem behavior students. *Professional School Counseling, 3,* 27–33.

Tompkins, L., & Mehring, T. (1993). Client privacy and the school counselor: Privilege, ethics and employer policies. *The School Counselor, 40,* 335–342.

Toporek, R. L., & Reza, J. V. (2001). Context as a critical dimension of multicultural counseling: Articulating personal, professionals, and institutional competence. *Journal of Multicultural Counseling and Development, 29,* 13–30.

Tori, C., & Ducker, D. G. (2004). Sustaining the commitment to multiculturalism: A longitudinal study in a graduate psychology program. *Professional Psychology: Research and Practice, 35,* 649–657.

Treppa, J. A. (1998). A practitioner's guide to ethical decision making. In R. M. Anderson, T. L. Needels, & H. V. Hall (Eds.). *Avoiding ethical misconduct in psychology specialty areas* (pp. 26–41). Springfield, IL: Charles C. Thomas.

Trippany, R. L., Kress, V. E. W, & Wilcoxon, S. A. (2004). Preventing vicarious trauma: What counselors should know when working with trauma survivors. *Journal of Counseling and Development, 82,* 31–37.

Trippany, R. L., Wilcoxon, S. A., & Satcher, J. F. (2003). Factors influencing vicarious trauma for therapists of survivors of sexual victimization. *Journal of Trauma Practice, 2,* 47–60.

Truman v. Thomas, 611 P.2d 902, 27 Cal. 3d 285 (1980).

Truscott, D., & Evans, J. (2001). Responding to dangerous clients. In E. R. Welfel & R. E. Ingersoll (Eds.), *Mental health desk reference: A practice-based guide to diagnosis, treatment, and professional ethics* (pp. 271–276). New York: Wiley.

Tubbs, P., & Pomerantz, A. M. (2001). Ethical behavior of psychologists: Changes since 1987. *Journal of Clinical Psychology, 57,* 395–399.

Turek, P. W. (2005). Research in the high stakes era: Achievement, resources, and No Child Left Behind. *Psychological Science, 16,* 419–425.

Turner, S. M., DeMers, S. T., Fox, H. R., & Reed, G. M. (2001). APA's guidelines for test user qualifications: An executive summary. *American Psychologist, 56,* 1099–1112.

Ukens, C. (1995). The tragic truth. *Drug Topics, 139,* 66–74.

Urofsky, R. I., & Engels, D. W. (2003). Philosophy, moral philosophy, and counseling ethics: Not an abstraction. *Counseling and Values, 47,* 118–130.

Urofsky, R. L., & Sowa, C. (2004). Ethics education in CACREP-accredited counselor education programs. *Counseling and Values, 49,* 37–47.

Uthe-Burow, C. M. (2002). An exploratory study of ethical training as a factor of moral development. *Dissertation Abstracts International, 63* (4-A), AA13048768.

Vacha-Haase, T. (1995). Impaired graduate students in APA-accredited clinical, counseling, and school psychology programs. Unpublished doctoral dissertation, Texas A&M University, College Station, Texas.

Vacha-Hasse, T., Davenport, D. S., & Kerewsky, S. D. (2004). Problematic students: Gatekeeping practices of academic professional psychology programs. *Professional Psychology: Research and Practice, 35,* 115–122.

Valliant, G. E. (1984). The disadvantages of DSM-III outweigh its advantages. *American Journal of Psychiatry, 141,* 542–545.

Van Horne, B. A. (2004). Psychology licensing board disciplinary actions: The realities. *Professional Psychology: Research and Practice, 35,* 170–178.

VandeCreek, L, & Jackson, T. L. (Eds.). (2000). *Innovations in clinical practice: A sourcebook* (pp. 441–453). Sarasota, FL: Professional Resource Press.

VandeCreek, L., Knapp, S., & Brace, K. (1990). Mandatory continuing education for licensed psychologists: Its rationale and current implementation. *Professional Psychology: Research and Practice, 21,* 135–140.

VandeCreek, L., Miars, R., & Herzog, C. (1987). Client anticipations and preferences for confidentiality of records. *Journal of Counseling Psychology, 34,* 62–67.

Vander Kolk, C. J. (1974). The relationship of personality, values and race to anticipation of the supervisory relationship. *Rehabilitation Counseling Bulletin, 18,* 41–46.

Vanek, C. A. (1990). Survey of ethics education in clinical and counseling psychology. *Dissertation Abstracts International, 52,* 5797B. (University Microfilms No. 91–14, 449)

VanHoose, W. H., & Kottler, J. A. (1985). *Ethical and legal issues in counseling and psychotherapy* (2nd ed.). San Francisco: Jossey-Bass.

VanHorne, B. A. (2004). Psychology licensing board disciplinary actions: The realities. *Professional Psychology: Research and Practice, 35,* 170–178.

Vansandt, C. V. (2002). An examination of the relationship between ethical work climate and moral awareness. *Dissertation Abstracts International, 62* (7-A), 2486.

Vasquez, M. J. T. (1988). Counselor client sexual contact: Implications for ethics training. *Journal of Counseling and Development, 67,* 238–241.

Vasquez, M. J. T. (1992). Psychologist as clinical supervisor: Promoting ethical practice. *Professional Psychology: Research and Practice, 23,* 196–202.

Vera, E. M., & Speight, S. L. (2993). Multicultural competence, social justice, and counseling psychology. *Counseling Psychologist, 31,* 253–272.

Vetere, A, & Cooper, J. (2001). Working systemically with family violence: Risk, responsibility and collaboration. *Journal of Family Therapy, 23,* 378–396.

Vinson, J. S. (1987). Use of complaint procedures in cases of therapist–patient sexual contact. *Professional Psychology: Research and Practice, 18,* 159–164.

Volker, J. M. (1983, August). *Counseling experience, moral judgment, awareness of consequences and moral sensitivity in counseling practice.* Paper presented at the annual meeting of the American Psychological Association, Toronto, CAN.

Wagner, C. (1978). Elementary school counselors' perceptions of confidentiality with children. *The School Counselor, 25,* 240–248.

Wagner, C. (1981). Confidentiality and the school counselor. *The Personnel and Guidance Journal, 59,* 305–310.

Wagner, L., Davis, S., & Handelsman, M. M. (1998). In search of the abominable consent form: The impact of readability and personalization. *Journal of Clinical Psychology, 54,* 115–120.

Wakefield, J. C. (1992). The concept of mental disorder: On the boundary between biological facts and social values. *American Psychologist, 47,* 373–388.

Walsh, W. B., & Betz, N. E. (1995). *Tests and assessment* (3rd ed.). Englewood Cliffs, NJ: Prentice Hall.

Walter, M. I., & Handelsman, M. M. (1996). Informed consent for mental health counseling: Effects of information specificity on clients' ratings of counselors. *Journal of Mental Health Counseling, 18,* 253–262.

Wampold, B. E. (2001). *The great psychotherapy debate.* Mahwah, NJ: Lawrence Erlbaum.

Warren, E. S. (2005). Future colleague or convenient friend: The ethics of mentorship. *Counseling and Values, 49,* 141–146.

Warwick, D., & Kelman, H. (1973). Ethical issues in social intervention. In G. Zaltman (Ed.), *Processes and phenomena of social change* (pp. 377–417). New York: Wiley Interscience.

Watkins, C. E. (Ed) (1997). *Handbook of psychotherapy supervision.* New York: Wiley.

Watson, C. H. (1990). Gossip and the guidance counselor: An ethical dilemma. *The School Counselor, 38,* 34–39.

Watson, H., & Levine, M. (1989). Psychotherapy and mandated reporting of child abuse. *American Journal of Psychiatry, 59,* 246–256.

Wechsler, D. (1999). *Wechsler adult intelligence scale III.* San Antonio, TX: Psychological Corporation.

Wedding, D., Topolski, J., & McGaha, A. (1995). Maintaining the confidentiality of computerized mental health outcome data. *Journal of Mental Health Administration, 22,* 237–244.

Weikel, W. J., & Hughes, P. R. (1993). *The counselor as expert witness.* In T. P. Remley (Ed.), *ACA legal series* (Vol. 5). Alexandria, VA: American Counseling Association.

Weiner, I. B. (1989). On competence and ethicality in psychodiagnostic assessment. *Journal of Personality Assessment, 53,* 827–831.

Weiner, M. F. (1983). *Therapist disclosure: The use of self in psychotherapy* (2nd ed.). Baltimore: University Park Press.

Weithorn, L. A. (1983). Involving children in decisions affecting their own welfare: Guidelines for professionals. In G. B. Melton, G. P. Koocher, & M. J. Saks (Eds.), *Children's competence to consent* (pp. 235–260). New York: Plenum.

Welfel, E. R. (1992). Psychologists as ethics educators: Successes, failures, and unanswered questions. *Professional Psychology: Research and Practice, 23,* 182–189.

Welfel, E. R. (2001). Responsible interactions with managed care organizations. In E . R. Welfel & R. E. Ingersoll (Eds.), *The mental health desk reference: A practice-based guide to diagnosis, treatment, and professional ethics* (pp. 496–502). New York: Wiley.

Welfel, E. R. (2005). Accepting fallibility: A model for personal responsibility for nonegregious ethics violations. *Counseling and Values, 49,* 120–131.

Welfel, E. R., & Bunce, R. (2003, August). *How psychotherapists use electronic communication with current clients.* Presented at the annual meeting of the American Psychological Association, Toronto, CA.

Welfel, E. R., Danzinger, P. R., & Santoro, S. (2000). Mandated reporting of abuse/maltreatment of older adults: A primer for counselors. *Journal of Counseling and Development, 78,* 284–292.

Welfel, E. R., & Heinlen, K. T. (2001). The responsible use of technology in mental health practice. In E. R. Welfel & R. E. Ingersoll (Eds.), *Mental health desk reference: A practice-based guide to diagnosis, treatment, and professional ethics* (pp. 484–489). New York: Wiley.

Welfel, E. R., & Lipsitz, N. E. (1983). Ethical orientation of counselors: Its relationship to moral reasoning and level of training. *Counselor Education and Supervision, 22,* 35–45.

Welfel, E. R., & Patterson, L. E (2004). *The counseling process* (6th ed.). Pacific Grove, CA: Brooks/Cole.

Wellman, M. M. (1984). The school counselor's role in the communication of suicidal ideation by adolescents. *The School Counselor, 32,* 104–109.

Wells, K. B., Hays, R. D., Burman, A., Rogers, W., Greenfield, S., & Ware, J. E., Jr. (1989). Detection of depressive disorder for patients receiving prepaid or fee-for-service care: Results for the medical outcomes study. *Journal of the American Medical Association, 262,* 3298–3302.

Wendorf, D. J., & Wendorf, R. J. (1985). A systemic view of family therapy ethics. *Family Process, 24,* 443–453.

Werth, J. L., & Gordon, J. R. (2002). Amicus curiae brief for the United States Supreme Court on mental health issues associated with "physician-assisted suicide." *Journal of Counseling and Development, 80,* 160–172.

Werth, J. L., Jr., Burke, C., Bardash, R. J. (2002). Confidentiality in end-of-life and after-death situations. *Ethics and Behavior, 12,* 205–222.

Whiston, S. C., & Emerson, S. (1989). Ethical implications for supervisors in counseling of trainees. *Counselor Education and Supervision, 28,* 318–325

Whiteley, J. M. (1984). A historical perspective on the development of counseling psychology as a profession. In S. D. Brown & R. W. Lent (Eds.), *Handbook of counseling psychology* (pp. 3–55). New York: Wiley.

Whittinghill, K. (2002). Ethical considerations for the use of family therapy in substance abuse treatment. *The Family Journal, 10,* 75–78.

Wilbert, J. R., & Fulero, S. M. (1988). Impact of malpractice litigation on professional psychology: Survey of practitioners. *Professional Psychology: Research and Practice, 19,* 379–382.

Wilcoxin, A., & Fennel, D. (1983). Engaging non-attending spouse in marital therapy through the use of therapist-initiated written communication. *Journal of Marital and Family Therapy, 9,* 199–203.

Wilcoxin, S. A., & Magnuson, S. (1999). Considerations for school counselors serving noncustodial parents: Premises and suggestions. *Professional School Counseling, 2,* 275–279.

Wilkins, M., McGuire, J. M., Abbott, D. W., & Blau, B. I. (1990). Willingness to apply understood ethical principles. *Journal of Clinical Psychology, 46,* 539–547.

Williams, G. T. (1996). A group leader's risky interventions. In B. Herlihy & G. Corey (Eds.), *ACA ethical standards casebook* (pp. 237–240). Alexandria, VA: American Counseling Association.

Williams, M. H. (1992). Exploitation and interference: Mapping the damage from patient–therapist sexual involvement. *American Psychologist, 47,* 412–421.

Williams, M. H. (2000). Victimized by "victims": A taxonomy of antecedents of false complaints against psychotherapists. *Professional Psychology: Research and Practice, 31,* 75–81.

Williams, S., & Halgin, R. P. (1995). Issues in psychotherapy supervision between the white supervisor and the black supervisee. *The Clinical Supervisor, 13,* 39–61.

Willison, B. G., & Masson, R. L. (1986). The role of touch in therapy: An adjunct to communication. *Journal of Counseling and Development, 64,* 497–500.

Wilson, L. S., & Ranft, V. A. (1993). The state of ethical training for counseling psychology doctoral students. *Counseling Psychologist, 21,* 445–456.

Wincze, J. P., Richards, J., Parsons, J., & Bailey, S. (1996). A comparative survey of therapist sexual misconduct between an American state and an Australian state. *Professional Psychology: Research and Practice, 27,* 289–294.

Winter, G. (2004, July 8). Wooing of school counselors in raising profiles and eyebrows. *New York Times,* p. A1.

Wise, P. S., Lowery, S., & Silverglade, L. (1989). Personal counseling for counselors in training: Guidelines for supervisors. *Counselor Education and Supervision, 28,* 326–336.

Witmer, J. M., & Davis, T. E. (1996). A question of informed consent. In B. Herlihy & G. Corey (Eds.), *ACA ethical standards casebook* (5th ed., pp. 187–191). Alexandria, VA: American Counseling Association.

Wohlberg, J. W. (1999). Treatment subsequent to abuse by a mental health professional: The victim's perspective of what works and what doesn't. *Journal of Sex Education and Therapy, 24,* 252–261.

Wolberg, L. R. (1967). *The technique of psychotherapy* (2nd ed.). New York: Grune & Stratton.

Wood, B., Klein, S., Cross, H., Lammers, C., & Elliott, J. (1985). Impaired practitioners: Psychologists' opinions about prevalence and prognosis for intervention. *Professional Psychology: Research and Practice, 16,* 843–850.

Woody, R. H. (1988). *Fifty ways to avoid malpractice: A guide for mental health professionals.* Sarasota, FL: Professional Resource Exchange.

Woody, R. H. (1997). Dubious and bogus credentials in mental health practice. *Ethics and Behavior, 7,* 337345.

Woody, R. H. (1999). Domestic violations of confidentiality. *Professional Psychology: Research and Practice, 30,* 607–610.

Woody, R. H. (2000). *Child custody: Practice standards, ethical issues, and legal safeguards for mental health professionals.* Sarasota, FL: Professional Resource Exchange.

Wrenn, C. G. (1962). The culturally encapsulated counselor. *Harvard Educational Review, 32,* 444–449.

Wrenn, C. G. (1985). Afterword: The culturally encapsulated counselor revisited. In P. Pedersen (Ed.), *Handbook of cross-cultural counseling and therapy* (pp. 323–329). Westport, CT: Greenwood.

Wrich, J. T. (1995, March–April). Who's at risk? *EAP Digest, 25,* 19–25.

Wrightsman, L. S. (2000). *Forensic psychology.* Belmont, CA: Wadsworth.

Wylie, C. L. (2003). An investigation into burnout in the field of school psychology. *Dissertation Abstracts International, 64*(02), 401A.

Yen, W. M., & Henderson, D. L. (2002). Professional standards related to using large-scale sate assessments in decisions for individual students. *Measurements and Evaluation in Counseling and Development, 35,* 132–143.

Young, E. L., & Mendez, L. M. R. (2003). The mental health professional's role in understanding, preventing, and responding to student sexual harassment. *Journal of Applied School Psychology, 19,* 7–23.

Younggren, J. N., & Gottlieb, M. C. (2004). Managing risk when contemplating multiple relationships. *Professional Psychology: Research and Practice, 35,* 255–260.

Zane, M. (1990, January 27). $1.5 million verdict against doctor who seduced patient. *San Francisco Chronicle,* p. 4.

Zayas, H. H., Torres, L. R., Malcolm, J., & DesRosiers, F. S. (1996). Clinicians' definitions of ethnically sensitive therapy. *Professional Psychology: Research and Practice, 27,* 78–82.

Ziebert, J., Engels, D. W., Kern, C. W., & Durodoye, B. A. (1998). Ethical knowledge of counselors. *Counseling and Values, 43,* 34–39.

Zimmerman, J. K., & Asnis, G. M. (Eds.). (1995). *Treatment approaches with suicidal adolescents.* New York: Wiley.

Zuckerman, E. L. (2003). *The paper office: Forms, guidelines, resources* (3rd ed.). New York: Guilford.

Zytaruk, G. J., & Boulton, J. T. (Eds.). (1981). *The letters of D.H. Lawrence* (Vol. 2). New York: Cambridge University Press.

American Counseling Association, Code of Ethics and Standards of Practice

ACA Code of Ethics Preamble

The American Counseling Association is an educational, scientific, and professional organization whose members work in a variety of settings and serve in multiple capacities. ACA members are dedicated to the enhancement of human development throughout the life span. Association members recognize diversity and embrace a cross-cultural approach in support of the worth, dignity, potential, and uniqueness of people within their social and cultural contexts.

Professional values are an important way of living out an ethical commitment. Values inform principles. Inherently held values that guide our behaviors or exceed prescribed behaviors are deeply ingrained in the counselor and developed out of personal dedication, rather than the mandatory requirement of an external organization.

ACA Code of Ethics Purpose

The *ACA Code of Ethics* serves five main purposes:

1. The *Code* enables the association to clarify to current and future members, and to those served by members, the nature of the ethical responsibilities held in common by its members.
2. The *Code* helps support the mission of the association.
3. The *Code* establishes principles that define ethical behavior and best practices of association members.
4. The *Code* serves as an ethical guide designed to assist members in constructing a professional course of action that best serves those utilizing counseling services and best promotes the values of the counseling profession.
5. The *Code* serves as the basis for processing of ethical complaints and inquiries initiated against members of the association.

The *ACA Code of Ethics* contains eight main sections that address the following areas:

Section A: The Counseling Relationship
Section B: Confidentiality, Privileged Communication, and Privacy
Section C: Professional Responsibility
Section D: Relationships With Other Professionals
Section E: Evaluation, Assessment, and Interpretation
Section F: Supervision, Training, and Teaching
Section G: Research and Publication
Section H: Resolving Ethical Issues

Each section of the *ACA Code of Ethics* begins with an Introduction. The introductions to each section discuss what counselors should aspire to with regard to ethical behavior and responsibility. The Introduction helps set the tone for that particular section and provides a starting point that invites reflection on the ethical mandates contained in each part of the *ACA Code of Ethics.*

When counselors are faced with ethical dilemmas that are difficult to resolve, they are expected to engage in a carefully considered ethical decision-making process. Reasonable differences of opinion can and do exist among counselors with respect to the ways in which values, ethical principles, and ethical standards would be applied when they conflict. While there is no specific ethical decision-making model that is most effective, counselors are expected to be familiar with a credible model of decision making that can bear public scrutiny and its application.

Through a chosen ethical decision-making process and evaluation of the context of the situation, counselors are empowered to make decisions that help expand the capacity of people to grow and develop. A brief glossary is given to provide readers with a concise description of some of the terms used in the *ACA Code of Ethics.*

Section A: The Counseling Relationship

Introduction
Counselors encourage client growth and development in ways that foster the interest and welfare of clients and promote formation of healthy relationships. Counselors actively attempt to understand the diverse cultural backgrounds of the clients they serve. Counselors also explore their own cultural identities

and how these affect their values and beliefs about the counseling process.

Counselors are encouraged to contribute to society by devoting a portion of their professional activity to services for which there is little or no financial return (pro bono publico).

A.1. Welfare of Those Served by Counselors

A.1.a. Primary Responsibility
The primary responsibility of counselors is to respect the dignity and to promote the welfare of clients.

A.1.b. Records
Counselors maintain records necessary for rendering professional services to their clients and as required by laws, regulations, or agency or institution procedures. Counselors include sufficient and timely documentation in their client records to facilitate the delivery and continuity of needed services. Counselors take reasonable steps to ensure that documentation in records accurately reflects client progress and services provided. If errors are made in client records, counselors take steps to properly note the correction of such errors according to agency or institutional policies. *(See A.12.g.7., B.6., B.6.g., G.2.j.)*

A.1.c. Counseling Plans
Counselors and their clients work jointly in devising integrated counseling plans that offer reasonable promise of success and are consistent with abilities and circumstances of clients. Counselors and clients regularly review counseling plans to assess their continued viability and effectiveness, respecting the freedom of choice of clients. *(See A.2.a., A.2.d., A.12.g.)*

A.1.d. Support Network Involvement
Counselors recognize that support networks hold various meanings in the lives of clients and consider enlisting the support, understanding, and involvement of others (e.g., religious/spiritual/community leaders, family members, friends) as positive resources, when appropriate, with client consent.

A.1.e. Employment Needs
Counselors work with their clients considering employment in jobs that are consistent with the overall abilities, vocational limitations, physical restrictions, general temperament, interest and aptitude patterns, social skills, education, general qualifications, and other relevant characteristics and needs of clients. When appropriate, counselors appropriately trained in career development will assist in the placement of clients in positions that are consistent with the interest, culture, and the welfare of clients, employers, and/or the public.

A.2. Informed Consent in the Counseling Relationship
(See A.12.g., B.5., B.6.b., E.3., E.13.b., F.1.c., G.2.a.)

A.2.a. Informed Consent
Clients have the freedom to choose whether to enter into or remain in a counseling relationship and need adequate information about the counseling process and the counselor. Counselors have an obligation to review in writing and verbally with clients the rights and responsibilities of both the counselor and the client. Informed consent is an ongoing part of the counseling process, and counselors appropriately document discussions of informed consent throughout the counseling relationship.

A.2.b. Types of Information Needed
Counselors explicitly explain to clients the nature of all services provided. They inform clients about issues such as, but not limited to, the following: the purposes, goals, techniques, procedures, limitations, potential risks, and benefits of services; the counselor's qualifications, credentials, and relevant experience; continuation of services upon the incapacitation or death of a counselor; and other pertinent information. Counselors take steps to ensure that clients understand the implications of diagnosis, the intended use of tests and reports, fees, and billing arrangements. Clients have the right to confidentiality and to be provided with an explanation of its limitations (including how supervisors and/or treatment team professionals are involved); to obtain clear information about their records; to participate in the ongoing counseling plans; and to refuse any services or modality change and to be advised of the consequences of such refusal.

A.2.c. Developmental and Cultural Sensitivity
Counselors communicate information in ways that are both developmentally and culturally appropriate. Counselors use clear and understandable language when discussing issues related to informed consent. When clients have difficulty understanding the language used by counselors, they provide necessary services (e.g., arranging for a qualified interpreter or translator) to ensure comprehension by clients. In collaboration with clients, counselors consider cul-

tural implications of informed consent procedures and, where possible, counselors adjust their practices accordingly.

A.2.d. Inability to Give Consent

When counseling minors or persons unable to give voluntary consent, counselors seek the assent of clients to services, and include them in decision making as appropriate. Counselors recognize the need to balance the ethical rights of clients to make choices, their capacity to give consent or assent to receive services, and parental or familial legal rights and responsibilities to protect these clients and make decisions on their behalf.

A.3. Clients Served by Others

When counselors learn that their clients are in a professional relationship with another mental health professional, they request release from clients to inform the other professionals and strive to establish positive and collaborative professional relationships.

A.4. Avoiding Harm and Imposing Values

A.4.a. Avoiding Harm

Counselors act to avoid harming their clients, trainees, and research participants and to minimize or to remedy unavoidable or unanticipated harm.

A.4.b. Personal Values

Counselors are aware of their own values, attitudes, beliefs, and behaviors and avoid imposing values that are inconsistent with counseling goals. Counselors respect the diversity of clients, trainees, and research participants.

A.5. Roles and Relationships With Clients

(See F.3., F.10., G.3.)

A.5.a. Current Clients

Sexual or romantic counselor–client interactions or relationships with current clients, their romantic partners, or their family members are prohibited.

A.5.b. Former Clients

Sexual or romantic counselor–client interactions or relationships with former clients, their romantic partners, or their family members are prohibited for a period of 5 years following the last professional contact. Counselors, before engaging in sexual or romantic interactions or relationships with clients, their romantic partners, or client family members after 5 years following the last professional contact, demonstrate forethought and document (in written form) whether the interactions or relationship can be viewed as exploitive in some way and/or whether there is still potential to harm the former client; in cases of potential exploitation and/or harm, the counselor avoids entering such an interaction or relationship.

A.5.c. Nonprofessional Interactions or Relationships (Other Than Sexual or Romantic Interactions or Relationships)

Counselor–client nonprofessional relationships with clients, former clients, their romantic partners, or their family members should be avoided, except when the interaction is potentially beneficial to the client. *(See A.5.d.)*

A.5.d. Potentially Beneficial Interactions

When a counselor–client nonprofessional interaction with a client or former client may be potentially beneficial to the client or former client, the counselor must document in case records, prior to the interaction (when feasible), the rationale for such an interaction, the potential benefit, and anticipated consequences for the client or former client and other individuals significantly involved with the client or former client. Such interactions should be initiated with appropriate client consent. Where unintentional harm occurs to the client or former client, or to an individual significantly involved with the client or former client, due to the nonprofessional interaction, the counselor must show evidence of an attempt to remedy such harm. Examples of potentially beneficial interactions include, but are not limited to, attending a formal ceremony (e.g., a wedding/commitment ceremony or graduation); purchasing a service or product provided by a client or former client (excepting unrestricted bartering); hospital visits to an ill family member; mutual membership in a professional association, organization, or community. *(See A.5.c.)*

A.5.e. Role Changes in the Professional Relationship

When a counselor changes a role from the original or most recent contracted relationship, he or she obtains informed consent from the client and explains the right of the client to refuse services related to the change. Examples of role changes include

1. changing from individual to relationship or family counseling, or vice versa;
2. changing from a nonforensic evaluative role to a therapeutic role, or vice versa;

3. changing from a counselor to a researcher role (i.e., enlisting clients as research participants), or vice versa; and

4. changing from a counselor to a mediator role, or vice versa. Clients must be fully informed of any anticipated consequences (e.g., financial, legal, personal, or therapeutic) of counselor role changes.

A.6. Roles and Relationships at Individual, Group, Institutional, and Societal Levels

A.6.a. Advocacy
When appropriate, counselors advocate at individual, group, institutional, and societal levels to examine potential barriers and obstacles that inhibit access and/or the growth and development of clients.

A.6.b. Confidentiality and Advocacy
Counselors obtain client consent prior to engaging in advocacy efforts on behalf of an identifiable client to improve the provision of services and to work toward removal of systemic barriers or obstacles that inhibit client access, growth, and development.

A.7. Multiple Clients
When a counselor agrees to provide counseling services to two or more persons who have a relationship, the counselor clarifies at the outset which person or persons are clients and the nature of the relationships the counselor will have with each involved person. If it becomes apparent that the counselor may be called upon to perform potentially conflicting roles, the counselor will clarify, adjust, or withdraw from roles appropriately. *(See A.8.a., B.4.)*

A.8. Group Work
(See B.4.a.)

A.8.a. Screening
Counselors screen prospective group counseling/therapy participants. To the extent possible, counselors select members whose needs and goals are compatible with goals of the group, who will not impede the group process, and whose well-being will not be jeopardized by the group experience.

A.8.b. Protecting Clients
In a group setting, counselors take reasonable precautions to protect clients from physical, emotional, or psychological trauma.

A.9. End-of-Life Care for Terminally Ill Clients

A.9.a. Quality of Care
Counselors strive to take measures that enable clients

1. to obtain high quality end-of-life care for their physical, emotional, social, and spiritual needs;
2. to exercise the highest degree of self-determination possible;
3. to be given every opportunity possible to engage in informed decision making regarding their end-of-life care; and
4. to receive complete and adequate assessment regarding their ability to make competent, rational decisions on their own behalf from a mental health professional who is experienced in end-of-life care practice.

A.9.b. Counselor Competence, Choice, and Referral
Recognizing the personal, moral, and competence issues related to end-of-life decisions, counselors may choose to work or not work with terminally ill clients who wish to explore their end-of-life options. Counselors provide appropriate referral information to ensure that clients receive the necessary help.

A.9.c. Confidentiality
Counselors who provide services to terminally ill individuals who are considering hastening their own deaths have the option of breaking or not breaking confidentiality, depending on applicable laws and the specific circumstances of the situation and after seeking consultation or supervision from appropriate professional and legal parties. *(See B.5.c., B.7.c.)*

A.10. Fees and Bartering

A.10.a. Accepting Fees From Agency Clients
Counselors refuse a private fee or other remuneration for rendering services to persons who are entitled to such services through the counselor's employing agency or institution. The policies of a particular agency may make explicit provisions for agency clients to receive counseling services from members of its staff in private practice. In such instances, the clients must be informed of other options open to them should they seek private counseling services.

A.10.b. Establishing Fees
In establishing fees for professional counseling services, counselors consider the financial status of clients and locality. In the event that the established fee structure is inappropriate for a client, counselors assist

clients in attempting to find comparable services of acceptable cost.

A.10.c. Nonpayment of Fees

If counselors intend to use collection agencies or take legal measures to collect fees from clients who do not pay for services as agreed upon, they first inform clients of intended actions and offer clients the opportunity to make payment.

A.10.d. Bartering

Counselors may barter only if the relationship is not exploitive or harmful and does not place the counselor in an unfair advantage, if the client requests it, and if such arrangements are an accepted practice among professionals in the community. Counselors consider the cultural implications of bartering and discuss relevant concerns with clients and document such agreements in a clear written contract.

A.10.e. Receiving Gifts

Counselors understand the challenges of accepting gifts from clients and recognize that in some cultures, small gifts are a token of respect and showing gratitude. When determining whether or not to accept a gift from clients, counselors take into account the therapeutic relationship, the monetary value of the gift, a client's motivation for giving the gift, and the counselor's motivation for wanting or declining the gift.

A.11. Termination and Referral

A.11.a. Abandonment Prohibited

Counselors do not abandon or neglect clients in counseling. Counselors assist in making appropriate arrangements for the continuation of treatment, when necessary, during interruptions such as vacations, illness, and following termination.

A.11.b. Inability to Assist Clients

If counselors determine an inability to be of professional assistance to clients, they avoid entering or continuing counseling relationships. Counselors are knowledgeable about culturally and clinically appropriate referral resources and suggest these alternatives. If clients decline the suggested referrals, counselors should discontinue the relationship.

A.11.c. Appropriate Termination

Counselors terminate a counseling relationship when it becomes reasonably apparent that the client no longer needs assistance, is not likely to benefit, or is being harmed by continued counseling. Counselors

may terminate counseling when in jeopardy of harm by the client, or another person with whom the client has a relationship, or when clients do not pay fees as agreed upon. Counselors provide pretermination counseling and recommend other service providers when necessary.

A.11.d. Appropriate Transfer of Services

When counselors transfer or refer clients to other practitioners, they ensure that appropriate clinical and administrative processes are completed and open communication is maintained with both clients and practitioners.

A.12. Technology Applications

A.12.a. Benefits and Limitations

Counselors inform clients of the benefits and limitations of using information technology applications in the counseling process and in business/ billing procedures. Such technologies include but are not limited to computer hardware and software, telephones, the World Wide Web, the Internet, online assessment instruments and other communication devices.

A.12.b. Technology-Assisted Services

When providing technology-assisted distance counseling services, counselors determine that clients are intellectually, emotionally, and physically capable of using the application and that the application is appropriate for the needs of clients.

A.12.c. Inappropriate Services

When technology-assisted distance counseling services are deemed inappropriate by the counselor or client, counselors consider delivering services face to face.

A.12.d. Access

Counselors provide reasonable access to computer applications when providing technology-assisted distance counseling services.

A.12.e. Laws and Statutes

Counselors ensure that the use of technology does not violate the laws of any local, state, national, or international entity and observe all relevant statutes.

A.12.f. Assistance

Counselors seek business, legal, and technical assistance when using technology applications, particularly when the use of such applications crosses state or national boundaries.

A.12.g. Technology and Informed Consent

As part of the process of establishing informed consent, counselors do the following:

1. Address issues related to the difficulty of maintaining the confidentiality of electronically transmitted communications.
2. Inform clients of all colleagues, supervisors, and employees, such as Informational Technology (IT) administrators, who might have authorized or unauthorized access to electronic transmissions.
3. Urge clients to be aware of all authorized or unauthorized users including family members and fellow employees who have access to any technology clients may use in the counseling process.
4. Inform clients of pertinent legal rights and limitations governing the practice of a profession over state lines or international boundaries.
5. Use encrypted Web sites and e-mail communications to help ensure confidentiality when possible.
6. When the use of encryption is not possible, counselors notify clients of this fact and limit electronic transmissions to general communications that are not client specific.
7. Inform clients if and for how long archival storage of transaction records are maintained.
8. Discuss the possibility of technology failure and alternate methods of service delivery.
9. Inform clients of emergency procedures, such as calling 911 or a local crisis hotline, when the counselor is not available.
10. Discuss time zone differences, local customs, and cultural or language differences that might impact service delivery.
11. Inform clients when technology-assisted distance counseling services are not covered by insurance. *(See A.2.)*

A.12.h. Sites on the World Wide Web

Counselors maintaining sites on the World Wide Web (the Internet) do the following:

1. Regularly check that electronic links are working and professionally appropriate.
2. Establish ways clients can contact the counselor in case of technology failure.
3. Provide electronic links to relevant state licensure and professional certification boards to protect consumer rights and facilitate addressing ethical concerns.
4. Establish a method for verifying client identity.
5. Obtain the written consent of the legal guardian or other authorized legal representative prior to rendering services in the event the client is a minor child, an adult who is legally incompetent, or an adult incapable of giving informed consent.
6. Strive to provide a site that is accessible to persons with disabilities.
7. Strive to provide translation capabilities for clients who have a different primary language while also addressing the imperfect nature of such translations.
8. Assist clients in determining the validity and reliability of information found on the World Wide Web and other technology applications.

Section B: Confidentiality, Privileged Communication, and Privacy

Introduction

Counselors recognize that trust is a cornerstone of the counseling relationship. Counselors aspire to earn the trust of clients by creating an ongoing partnership, establishing and upholding appropriate boundaries, and maintaining confidentiality. Counselors communicate the parameters of confidentiality in a culturally competent manner.

B.1. Respecting Client Rights

B.1.a. Multicultural/Diversity Considerations

Counselors maintain awareness and sensitivity regarding cultural meanings of confidentiality and privacy. Counselors respect differing views toward disclosure of information. Counselors hold ongoing discussions with clients as to how, when, and with whom information is to be shared.

B.1.b. Respect for Privacy

Counselors respect client rights to privacy. Counselors solicit private information from clients only when it is beneficial to the counseling process.

B.1.c. Respect for Confidentiality

Counselors do not share confidential information without client consent or without sound legal or ethical justification.

B.1.d. Explanation of Limitations

At initiation and throughout the counseling process, counselors inform clients of the limitations of confidentiality and seek to identify foreseeable situations in which confidentiality must be breached. *(See A.2.b.)*

B.2. Exceptions

B.2.a. Danger and Legal Requirements

The general requirement that counselors keep information confidential does not apply when disclosure is required to protect clients or identified others from serious and foreseeable harm or when legal requirements demand that confidential information must be revealed. Counselors consult with other professionals when in doubt as to the validity of an exception. Additional considerations apply when addressing end-of-life issues. *(See A.9.c.)*

B.2.b. Contagious, Life-Threatening Diseases

When clients disclose that they have a disease commonly known to be both communicable and life threatening, counselors may be justified in disclosing information to identifiable third parties, if they are known to be at demonstrable and high risk of contracting the disease. Prior to making a disclosure, counselors confirm that there is such a diagnosis and assess the intent of clients to inform the third parties about their disease or to engage in any behaviors that may be harmful to an identifiable third party.

B.2.c. Court-Ordered Disclosure

When subpoenaed to release confidential or privileged information without a client's permission, counselors obtain written, informed consent from the client or take steps to prohibit the disclosure or have it limited as narrowly as possible due to potential harm to the client or counseling relationship.

B.2.d. Minimal Disclosure

To the extent possible, clients are informed before confidential information is disclosed and are involved in the disclosure decision-making process. When circumstances require the disclosure of confidential information, only essential information is revealed.

B.3. Information Shared With Others

B.3.a. Subordinates

Counselors make every effort to ensure that privacy and confidentiality of clients are maintained by subordinates, including employees, supervisees, students, clerical assistants, and volunteers. *(See F.1.c.)*

B.3.b. Treatment Teams

When client treatment involves a continued review or participation by a treatment team, the client will be informed of the team's existence and composition, information being shared, and the purposes of sharing such information.

B.3.c. Confidential Settings

Counselors discuss confidential information only in settings in which they can reasonably ensure client privacy.

B.3.d. Third-Party Payers

Counselors disclose information to third-party payers only when clients have authorized such disclosure.

B.3.e. Transmitting Confidential Information

Counselors take precautions to ensure the confidentiality of information transmitted through the use of computers, electronic mail, facsimile machines, telephones, voicemail, answering machines, and other electronic or computer technology. *(See A.12.g.)*

B.3.f. Deceased Clients

Counselors protect the confidentiality of deceased clients, consistent with legal requirements and agency or setting policies.

B.4. Groups and Families

B.4.a. Group Work

In group work, counselors clearly explain the importance and parameters of confidentiality for the specific group being entered.

B.4.b. Couples and Family Counseling

In couples and family counseling, counselors clearly define who is considered "the client" and discuss expectations and limitations of confidentiality. Counselors seek agreement and document in writing such agreement among all involved parties having capacity to give consent concerning each individual's right to confidentiality and any obligation to preserve the confidentiality of information known.

B.5. Clients Lacking Capacity to Give Informed Consent

B.5.a. Responsibility to Clients

When counseling minor clients or adult clients who lack the capacity to give voluntary, informed consent, counselors protect the confidentiality of information received in the counseling relationship as specified by federal and state laws, written policies, and applicable ethical standards.

B.5.b. Responsibility to Parents and Legal Guardians

Counselors inform parents and legal guardians about the role of counselors and the confidential nature of the counseling relationship. Counselors are sensitive to the cultural diversity of families and respect the inherent rights and responsibilities of parents/guardians over the welfare of their children/charges according to law. Counselors work to establish, as appropriate, collaborative relationships with parents/guardians to best serve clients.

B.5.c. Release of Confidential Information

When counseling minor clients or adult clients who lack the capacity to give voluntary consent to release confidential information, counselors seek permission from an appropriate third party to disclose information. In such instances, counselors inform clients consistent with their level of understanding and take culturally appropriate measures to safeguard client confidentiality.

B.6. Records

B.6.a. Confidentiality of Records

Counselors ensure that records are kept in a secure location and that only authorized persons have access to records.

B.6.b. Permission to Record

Counselors obtain permission from clients prior to recording sessions through electronic or other means.

B.6.c. Permission to Observe

Counselors obtain permission from clients prior to observing counseling sessions, reviewing session transcripts, or viewing recordings of sessions with supervisors, faculty, peers, or others within the training environment.

B.6.d. Client Access

Counselors provide reasonable access to records and copies of records when requested by competent clients. Counselors limit the access of clients to their records, or portions of their records, only when there is compelling evidence that such access would cause harm to the client. Counselors document the request of clients and the rationale for withholding some or all of the record in the files of clients. In situations involving multiple clients, counselors provide individual clients with only those parts of records that related directly to them and do not include confidential information related to any other client.

B.6.e. Assistance With Records

When clients request access to their records, counselors provide assistance and consultation in interpreting counseling records.

B.6.f. Disclosure or Transfer

Unless exceptions to confidentiality exist, counselors obtain written permission from clients to disclose or transfer records to legitimate third parties. Steps are taken to ensure that receivers of counseling records are sensitive to their confidential nature. *(See A.3., E.4.)*

B.6.g. Storage and Disposal After Termination

Counselors store records following termination of services to ensure reasonable future access, maintain records in accordance with state and federal statutes governing records, and dispose of client records and other sensitive materials in a manner that protects client confidentiality. When records are of an artistic nature, counselors obtain client (or guardian) consent with regards to handling of such records or documents. *(See A.1.b.)*

B.6.h. Reasonable Precautions

Counselors take reasonable precautions to protect client confidentiality in the event of the counselor's termination of practice, incapacity, or death. *(See C.2.h.)*

B.7. Research and Training

B.7.a. Institutional Approval

When institutional approval is required, counselors provide accurate information about their research proposals and obtain approval prior to conducting their research. They conduct research in accordance with the approved research protocol.

B.7.b. Adherence to Guidelines

Counselors are responsible for understanding and adhering to state, federal, agency, or institutional policies or applicable guidelines regarding confidentiality in their research practices.

B.7.c. Confidentiality of Information Obtained in Research

Violations of participant privacy and confidentiality are risks of participation in research involving human participants. Investigators maintain all research records in a secure manner. They explain to participants the risks of violations of privacy and confidentiality and disclose to participants any limits of confidentiality that reasonably can be expected. Regardless of the degree to which confidentiality will be maintained, investigators must disclose to participants any limits of confidentiality that reasonably can be expected. *(See G.2.e.)*

B.7.d. Disclosure of Research Information

Counselors do not disclose confidential information that reasonably could lead to the identification of a research participant unless they have obtained the prior consent of the person. Use of data derived from counseling relationships for purposes of training, research, or publication is confined to content that is disguised to ensure the anonymity of the individuals involved. *(See G.2.a., G.2.d.)*

B.7.e. Agreement for Identification

Identification of clients, students, or supervisees in a presentation or publication is permissible only when they have reviewed the material and agreed to its presentation or publication. *(See G.4.d.)*

B.8. Consultation

B.8.a. Agreements

When acting as consultants, counselors seek agreements among all parties involved concerning each individual's rights to confidentiality, the obligation of each individual to preserve confidential information, and the limits of confidentiality of information shared by others.

B.8.b. Respect for Privacy

Information obtained in a consulting relationship is discussed for professional purposes only with persons directly involved with the case. Written and oral reports present only data germane to the purposes of the consultation, and every effort is made to protect client identity and to avoid undue invasion of privacy.

B.8.c. Disclosure of Confidential Information

When consulting with colleagues, counselors do not disclose confidential information that reasonably could lead to the identification of a client or other person or organization with whom they have a confidential relationship unless they have obtained the prior consent of the person or organization or the disclo sure cannot be avoided. They disclose information only to the extent necessary to achieve the purposes of the consultation. *(See D.2.d.)*

Section C: Professional Responsibility

Introduction

Counselors aspire to open, honest, and accurate communication in dealing with the public and other professionals. They practice in a nondiscriminatory manner within the boundaries of professional and personal competence and have a responsibility to abide by the *ACA Code of Ethics.* Counselors actively participate in local, state, and national associations that foster the development and improvement of counseling. Counselors advocate to promote change at the individual, group, institutional, and societal levels that improve the quality of life for individuals and groups and remove potential barriers to the provision or access of appropriate services be-

ing offered. Counselors have a responsibility to the public to engage in counseling practices that are based on rigorous research methodologies. In addition, counselors engage in self-care activities to maintain and promote their emotional, physical, mental, and spiritual well-being to best meet their professional responsibilities.

C.1. Knowledge of Standards

Counselors have a responsibility to read, understand, and follow the *ACA Code of Ethics* and adhere to applicable laws and regulations.

C.2. Professional Competence

C.2.a. Boundaries of Competence

Counselors practice only within the boundaries of their competence, based on their education, training, supervised experience, state and national professional credentials, and appropriate professional experience. Counselors gain knowledge, personal awareness, sensitivity, and skills pertinent to working with a diverse client population. *(See A.9.b., C.4.e., E.2., F.2., F.11.b.)*

C.2.b. New Specialty Areas of Practice

Counselors practice in specialty areas new to them only after appropriate education, training, and supervised experience. While developing skills in new specialty areas, counselors take steps to ensure the competence of their work and to protect others from possible harm. *(See F.6.f.)*

C.2.c. Qualified for Employment

Counselors accept employment only for positions for which they are qualified by education, training, supervised experience, state and national professional credentials, and appropriate professional experience. Counselors hire for professional counseling positions only individuals who are qualified and competent for those positions.

C.2.d. Monitor Effectiveness

Counselors continually monitor their effectiveness as professionals and take steps to improve when necessary. Counselors in private practice take reasonable steps to seek peer supervision as needed to evaluate their efficacy as counselors.

C.2.e. Consultation on Ethical Obligations

Counselors take reasonable steps to consult with other counselors or related professionals when they have questions regarding their ethical obligations or professional practice.

C.2.f. Continuing Education

Counselors recognize the need for continuing education to acquire and maintain a reasonable level of awareness of current scientific and professional information in their fields of activity. They take steps to maintain competence in the skills they use, are open to new procedures, and keep current with the diverse populations and specific populations with whom they work.

C.2.g. Impairment

Counselors are alert to the signs of impairment from their own physical, mental, or emotional problems and refrain from offering or providing professional services when such impairment is likely to harm a client or others. They seek assistance for problems that reach the level of professional impairment, and, if necessary, they limit, suspend, or terminate their professional responsibilities until such time it is determined that they may safely resume their work. Counselors assist colleagues or supervisors in recognizing their own professional impairment and provide consultation and assistance when warranted with colleagues or supervisors showing signs of impairment and intervene as appropriate to prevent imminent harm to clients. *(See A.11.b., F.8.b.)*

C.2.h. Counselor Incapacitation or Termination of Practice

When counselors leave a practice, they follow a prepared plan for transfer of clients and files. Counselors prepare and disseminate to an identified colleague or "records custodian" a plan for the transfer of clients and files in the case of their incapacitation, death, or termination of practice.

C.3. Advertising and Soliciting Clients

C.3.a. Accurate Advertising

When advertising or otherwise representing their services to the public, counselors identify their credentials in an accurate manner that is not false, misleading, deceptive, or fraudulent.

C.3.b. Testimonials

Counselors who use testimonials do not solicit them from current clients nor former clients nor any other persons who may be vulnerable to undue influence.

C.3.c. Statements by Others

Counselors make reasonable efforts to ensure that statements made by others about them or the profession of counseling are accurate.

C.3.d. Recruiting Through Employment

Counselors do not use their places of employment or institutional affiliation to recruit or gain clients, supervisees, or consultees for their private practices.

C.3.e. Products and Training Advertisements

Counselors who develop products related to their profession or conduct workshops or training events ensure that the advertisements concerning these products or events are accurate and disclose adequate information for consumers to make informed choices. *(See C.6.d.)*

C.3.f. Promoting to Those Served

Counselors do not use counseling, teaching, training, or supervisory relationships to promote their products or training events in a manner that is deceptive or would exert undue influence on individuals who may be vulnerable. However, counselor educators may adopt textbooks they have authored for instructional purposes.

C.4. Professional Qualifications

C.4.a. Accurate Representation

Counselors claim or imply only professional qualifications actually completed and correct any known misrepresentations of their qualifications by others. Counselors truthfully represent the qualifications of their professional colleagues. Counselors clearly distinguish between paid and volunteer work experience and accurately describe their continuing education and specialized training. *(See C.2.a.)*

C.4.b. Credentials

Counselors claim only licenses or certifications that are current and in good standing.

C.4.c. Educational Degrees

Counselors clearly differentiate between earned and honorary degrees.

C.4.d. Implying Doctoral-Level Competence

Counselors clearly state their highest earned degree in counseling or closely related field. Counselors do not imply doctoral-level competence when only possessing a master's degree in counseling or a related field by referring to themselves as "Dr." in a counseling context when their doctorate is not in counseling or related field.

C.4.e. Program Accreditation Status

Counselors clearly state the accreditation status of their degree programs at the time the degree was earned.

C.4.f. Professional Membership

Counselors clearly differentiate between current, active memberships and former memberships in associations. Members of the American Counseling

Association must clearly differentiate between professional membership, which implies the possession of at least a master's degree in counseling, and regular membership, which is open to individuals whose interests and activities are consistent with those of ACA but are not qualified for professional membership.

C.5. Nondiscrimination

Counselors do not condone or engage in discrimination based on age, culture, disability, ethnicity, race, religion/spirituality, gender, gender identity, sexual orientation, marital status/partnership, language preference, socioeconomic status, or any basis proscribed by law. Counselors do not discriminate against clients, students, employees, supervisees, or research participants in a manner that has a negative impact on these persons.

C.6. Public Responsibility

C.6.a. Sexual Harassment

Counselors do not engage in or condone sexual harassment. Sexual harassment is defined as sexual solicitation, physical advances, or verbal or nonverbal conduct that is sexual in nature, that occurs in connection with professional activities or roles, and that either

1. is unwelcome, is offensive, or creates a hostile workplace or learning environment, and counselors know or are told this; or
2. is sufficiently severe or intense to be perceived as harassment to a reasonable person in the context in which the behavior occurred. Sexual harassment can consist of a single intense or severe act or multiple persistent or pervasive acts.

C.6.b. Reports to Third Parties

Counselors are accurate, honest, and objective in reporting their professional activities and judgments to appropriate third parties, including courts, health insurance companies, those who are the recipients of evaluation reports, and others. *(See B.3., E.4.)*

C.6.c. Media Presentations

When counselors provide advice or comment by means of public lectures, demonstrations, radio or television programs, prerecorded tapes, technology-based applications, printed articles, mailed material, or other media, they take reasonable precautions to ensure that

1. the statements are based on appropriate professional counseling literature and practice,
2. the statements are otherwise consistent with the *ACA Code of Ethics,* and

3. the recipients of the information are not encouraged to infer that a professional counseling relationship has been established.

C.6.d. Exploitation of Others

Counselors do not exploit others in their professional relationships. *(See C.3.e.)*

C.6.e. Scientific Bases for Treatment Modalities

Counselors use techniques/procedures/modalities that are grounded in theory and/or have an empirical or scientific foundation. Counselors who do not must define the techniques/procedures as "unproven" or "developing" and explain the potential risks and ethical considerations of using such techniques/procedures and take steps to protect clients from possible harm. *(See A.4.a., E.5.c., E.5.d.)*

C.7. Responsibility to Other Professionals

C.7.a. Personal Public Statements

When making personal statements in a public context, counselors clarify that they are speaking from their personal perspectives and that they are not speaking on behalf of all counselors or the profession.

Section D: Relationships With Other Professionals

Introduction

Professional counselors recognize that the quality of their interactions with colleagues can influence the quality of services provided to clients. They work to become knowledgeable about colleagues within and outside the field of counseling. Counselors develop positive working relationships and systems of communication with colleagues to enhance services to clients.

D.1. Relationships With Colleagues, Employers, and Employees

D.1.a. Different Approaches

Counselors are respectful of approaches to counseling services that differ from their own. Counselors are respectful of traditions and practices of other professional groups with which they work.

D.1.b. Forming Relationships

Counselors work to develop and strengthen interdisciplinary relations with colleagues from other disciplines to best serve clients.

D.1.c. Interdisciplinary Teamwork

Counselors who are members of interdisciplinary teams delivering multifaceted services to clients, keep the focus on how to best serve the clients. They participate in and contribute to decisions that affect the well-being of clients by drawing on the perspectives, values, and experiences of the counseling profession and those of colleagues from other disciplines. *(See A.1.a.)*

D.1.d. Confidentiality

When counselors are required by law, institutional policy, or extraordinary circumstances to serve in more than one role in judicial or administrative proceedings, they clarify role expectations and the parameters of confidentiality with their colleagues. *(See B.1.c., B.1.d., B.2.c., B.2.d., B.3.b.)*

D.1.e. Establishing Professional and Ethical Obligations

Counselors who are members of interdisciplinary teams clarify professional and ethical obligations of the team as a whole and of its individual members. When a team decision raises ethical concerns, counselors first attempt to resolve the concern within the team. If they cannot reach resolution among team members, counselors pursue other avenues to address their concerns consistent with client well-being.

D.1.f. Personnel Selection and Assignment

Counselors select competent staff and assign responsibilities compatible with their skills and experiences.

D.1.g. Employer Policies

The acceptance of employment in an agency or institution implies that counselors are in agreement with its general policies and principles. Counselors strive to reach agreement with employers as to acceptable standards of conduct that allow for changes in institutional policy conducive to the growth and development of clients.

D.1.h. Negative Conditions

Counselors alert their employers of inappropriate policies and practices. They attempt to effect changes in such policies or procedures through constructive action within the organization. When such policies are potentially disruptive or damaging to clients or may limit the effectiveness of services provided and change cannot be effected, counselors take appropriate further action. Such action may include referral to appropriate certification, accreditation, or state licensure organizations, or voluntary termination of employment.

D.1.i. Protection From Punitive Action

Counselors take care not to harass or dismiss an employee who has acted in a responsible and ethical manner to expose inappropriate employer policies or practices.

D.2. Consultation

D.2.a. Consultant Competency

Counselors take reasonable steps to ensure that they have the appropriate resources and competencies when providing consultation services. Counselors provide appropriate referral resources when requested or needed. *(See C.2.a.)*

D.2.b. Understanding Consultees

When providing consultation, counselors attempt to develop with their consultees a clear understanding of problem definition, goals for change, and predicted consequences of interventions selected.

D.2.c. Consultant Goals

The consulting relationship is one in which consultee adaptability and growth toward self-direction are consistently encouraged and cultivated.

D.2.d. Informed Consent in Consultation

When providing consultation, counselors have an obligation to review, in writing and verbally, the rights and responsibilities of both counselors and consultees. Counselors use clear and understandable language to inform all parties involved about the purpose of the services to be provided, relevant costs, potential risks and benefits, and the limits of confidentiality. Working in conjunction with the consultee, counselors attempt to develop a clear definition of the problem, goals for change, and predicted consequences of interventions that are culturally responsive and appropriate to the needs of consultees. *(See A.2.a., A.2.b.)*

Section E: Evaluation, Assessment, and Interpretation

Introduction

Counselors use assessment instruments as one component of the counseling process, taking into account the client personal and cultural context. Counselors promote the well-being of individual clients or groups of clients by developing and using appropriate educational, psychological, and career assessment instruments.

E.1. General

E.1.a. Assessment

The primary purpose of educational, psychological, and career assessment is to provide measurements that are valid and reliable in either comparative or absolute terms. These include, but are not limited to, measurements of ability, personality, interest, intelligence, achievement, and performance. Counselors recognize the need to interpret the statements in this section as applying to both quantitative and qualitative assessments.

E.1.b. Client Welfare

Counselors do not misuse assessment results and interpretations, and they take reasonable steps to prevent others from misusing the information these techniques provide. They respect the client's right to know the results, the interpretations made, and the bases for counselors' conclusions and recommendations.

E.2. Competence to Use and Interpret Assessment Instruments

E.2.a. Limits of Competence

Counselors utilize only those testing and assessment services for which they have been trained and are competent. Counselors using technology assisted test interpretations are trained in the construct being measured and the specific instrument being used prior to using its technology based application. Counselors take reasonable measures to ensure the proper use of psychological and career assessment techniques by persons under their supervision. *(See A.12.)*

E.2.b. Appropriate Use

Counselors are responsible for the appropriate application, scoring, interpretation, and use of assessment instruments relevant to the needs of the client, whether they score and interpret such assessments themselves or use technology or other services.

E.2.c. Decisions Based on Results

Counselors responsible for decisions involving individuals or policies that are based on assessment results have a thorough understanding of educational, psychological, and career measurement, including validation criteria, assessment research, and guidelines for assessment development and use.

E.3. Informed Consent in Assessment

E.3.a. Explanation to Clients

Prior to assessment, counselors explain the nature and purposes of assessment and the specific use of results by potential recipients. The explanation will be given in the language of the client (or other legally authorized person on behalf of the client), unless an explicit exception has been agreed upon in advance. Counselors consider the client's personal or cultural context, the level of the client's understanding of the results, and the impact of the results on the client. *(See A.2., A.12.g., F.1.c.)*

E.3.b. Recipients of Results

Counselors consider the examinee's welfare, explicit understandings, and prior agreements in determining who receives the assessment results. Counselors include accurate and appropriate interpretations with any release of individual or group assessment results. *(See B.2.c., B.5.)*

E.4. Release of Data to Qualified Professionals

Counselors release assessment data in which the client is identified only with the consent of the client or the client's legal representative. Such data are released only to persons recognized by counselors as qualified to interpret the data. *(See B.1., B.3., B.6.b.)*

E.5. Diagnosis of Mental Disorders

E.5.a. Proper Diagnosis

Counselors take special care to provide proper diagnosis of mental disorders. Assessment techniques (including personal interview) used to determine client care (e.g., locus of treatment, type of treatment, or recommended follow-up) are carefully selected and appropriately used.

E.5.b. Cultural Sensitivity

Counselors recognize that culture affects the manner in which clients' problems are defined. Clients' socioeconomic and cultural experiences are considered when diagnosing mental disorders. *(See A.2.c.)*

E.5.c. Historical and Social Prejudices in the Diagnosis of Pathology

Counselors recognize historical and social prejudices in the misdiagnosis and pathologizing of certain individuals and groups and the role of mental health professionals in perpetuating these prejudices through diagnosis and treatment.

E.5.d. Refraining From Diagnosis

Counselors may refrain from making and/or reporting a diagnosis if they believe it would cause harm to the client or others.

E.6. Instrument Selection

E.6.a. Appropriateness of Instruments

Counselors carefully consider the validity, reliability, psychometric limitations, and appropriateness of instruments when selecting assessments.

E.6.b. Referral Information

If a client is referred to a third party for assessment, the counselor provides specific referral questions and sufficient objective data about the client to ensure that appropriate assessment instruments are utilized. *(See A.9.b., B.3.)*

E.6.c. Culturally Diverse Populations

Counselors are cautious when selecting assessments for culturally diverse populations to avoid the use of instruments that lack appropriate psychometric properties for the client population. *(See A.2.c., E.5.b.)*

E.7. Conditions of Assessment Administration
(See A.12.b., A.12.d.)

E.7.a. Administration Conditions

Counselors administer assessments under the same conditions that were established in their standardization. When assessments are not administered under standard conditions, as may be necessary to accommodate clients with disabilities, or when unusual behavior or irregularities occur during the administration, those conditions are noted in interpretation, and the results may be designated as invalid or of questionable validity.

E.7.b. Technological Administration

Counselors ensure that administration programs function properly and provide clients with accurate results when technological or other electronic methods are used for assessment administration.

E.7.c. Unsupervised Assessments

Unless the assessment instrument is designed, intended, and validated for self-administration and/or scoring, counselors do not permit inadequately supervised use.

E.7.d. Disclosure of Favorable Conditions

Prior to administration of assessments, conditions that produce most favorable assessment results are made known to the examinee.

E.8. Multicultural Issues/Diversity in Assessment

Counselors use with caution assessment techniques that were normed on populations other than that of the client. Counselors recognize the effects of age, color, culture, disability, ethnic group, gender, race, language preference, religion, spirituality, sexual orientation, and socioeconomic status on test administration and interpretation, and place test results in proper perspective with other relevant factors. *(See A.2.c., E.5.b.)*

E.9. Scoring and Interpretation of Assessments

E.9.a. Reporting

In reporting assessment results, counselors indicate reservations that exist regarding validity or reliability due to circumstances of the assessment or the inappropriateness of the norms for the person tested.

E.9.b. Research Instruments

Counselors exercise caution when interpreting the results of research instruments not having sufficient technical data to support respondent results. The specific purposes for the use of such instruments are stated explicitly to the examinee.

E.9.c. Assessment Services

Counselors who provide assessment scoring and interpretation services to support the assessment process confirm the validity of such interpretations. They accurately describe the purpose, norms, validity, reliability, and applications of the procedures and any special qualifications applicable to their use. The public offering of an automated test interpretations service is considered a professional-to-professional consultation. The formal responsibility of the consultant is to the consultee, but the ultimate and overriding responsibility is to the client. *(See D.2.)*

E.10. Assessment Security

Counselors maintain the integrity and security of tests and other assessment techniques consistent with legal and contractual obligations. Counselors do not appropriate, reproduce, or modify published assessments or parts thereof without acknowledgment and permission from the publisher.

E.11. Obsolete Assessments and Outdated Results

Counselors do not use data or results from assessments that are obsolete or outdated for the current purpose. Counselors make every effort to prevent the misuse of obsolete measures and assessment data by others.

E.12. Assessment Construction

Counselors use established scientific procedures, relevant standards, and current professional knowledge for assessment design in the development, publication, and utilization of educational and psychological assessment techniques.

E.13. Forensic Evaluation: Evaluation for Legal Proceedings

E.13.a. Primary Obligations
When providing forensic evaluations, the primary obligation of counselors is to produce objective findings that can be substantiated based on information and techniques appropriate to the evaluation, which may include examination of the individual and/or review of records. Counselors are entitled to form professional opinions based on their professional knowledge and expertise that can be supported by the data gathered in evaluations. Counselors will define the limits of their reports or testimony, especially when an examination of the individual has not been conducted.

E.13.b. Consent for Evaluation
Individuals being evaluated are informed in writing that the relationship is for the purposes of an evaluation and is not counseling in nature, and entities or individuals who will receive the evaluation report are identified. Written consent to be evaluated is obtained from those being evaluated unless a court orders evaluations to be conducted without the written consent of individuals being evaluated. When children or vulnerable adults are being evaluated, informed written consent is obtained from a parent or guardian.

E.13.c. Client Evaluation Prohibited
Counselors do not evaluate individuals for forensic purposes they currently counsel or individuals they have counseled in the past. Counselors do not accept as counseling clients individuals they are evaluating or individuals they have evaluated in the past for forensic purposes.

E.13.d. Avoid Potentially Harmful Relationships
Counselors who provide forensic evaluations avoid potentially harmful professional or personal relationships with family members, romantic partners, and close friends of individuals they are evaluating or have evaluated in the past.

Section F: Supervision, Training, and Teaching

Introduction
Counselors aspire to foster meaningful and respectful professional relationships and to maintain appropriate boundaries with supervisees and students. Counselors have theoretical and pedagogical foundations for their work and aim to be fair, accurate, and honest in their assessments of counselors-in-training.

F.1. Counselor Supervision and Client Welfare

F.1.a. Client Welfare
A primary obligation of counseling supervisors is to monitor the services provided by other counselors or counselors-in-training. Counseling supervisors monitor client welfare and supervisee clinical performance and professional development. To fulfill these obligations, supervisors meet regularly with supervisees to review case notes, samples of clinical work, or live observations. Supervisees have a responsibility to understand and follow the *ACA Code of Ethics.*

F.1.b. Counselor Credentials
Counseling supervisors work to ensure that clients are aware of the qualifications of the supervisees who render services to the clients. *(See A.2.b.)*

F.1.c. Informed Consent and Client Rights
Supervisors make supervisees aware of client rights including the protection of client privacy and confidentiality in the counseling relationship. Supervisees provide clients with professional disclosure information and inform them of how the supervision process influences the limits of confidentiality. Supervisees make clients aware of who will have access to records of the counseling relationship and how these records will be used. *(See A.2.b., B.1.d.)*

F.2. Counselor Supervision Competence

F.2.a. Supervisor Preparation
Prior to offering clinical supervision services, counselors are trained in supervision methods and techniques. Counselors who offer clinical supervision services regularly pursue continuing education activities including both counseling and supervision topics and skills. *(See C.2.a., C.2.f.)*

F.2.b. Multicultural Issues/Diversity in Supervision
Counseling supervisors are aware of and address the role of multiculturalism/diversity in the supervisory relationship.

F.3. Supervisory Relationships

F.3.a. Relationship Boundaries With Supervisees
Counseling supervisors clearly define and maintain ethical professional, personal, and social relationships

with their supervisees. Counseling supervisors avoid nonprofessional relationships with current supervisees. If supervisors must assume other professional roles (e.g., clinical and administrative supervisor, instructor) with supervisees, they work to minimize potential conflicts and explain to supervisees the expectations and responsibilities associated with each role. They do not engage in any form of nonprofessional interaction that may compromise the supervisory relationship.

F.3.b. Sexual Relationships

Sexual or romantic interactions or relationships with current supervisees are prohibited.

F.3.c. Sexual Harassment

Counseling supervisors do not condone or subject supervisees to sexual harassment. *(See C.6.a.)*

F.3.d. Close Relatives and Friends

Counseling supervisors avoid accepting close relatives, romantic partners, or friends as supervisees.

F.3.e. Potentially Beneficial Relationships

Counseling supervisors are aware of the power differential in their relationships with supervisees. If they believe nonprofessional relationships with a supervisee may be potentially beneficial to the supervisee, they take precautions similar to those taken by counselors when working with clients. Examples of potentially beneficial interactions or relationships include attending a formal ceremony; hospital visits; providing support during a stressful event; or mutual membership in a professional association, organization, or community. Counseling supervisors engage in open discussions with supervisees when they consider entering into relationships with them outside of their roles as clinical and/or administrative supervisors. Before engaging in nonprofessional relationships, supervisors discuss with supervisees and document the rationale for such interactions, potential benefits or drawbacks, and anticipated consequences for the supervisee. Supervisors clarify the specific nature and limitations of the additional role(s) they will have with the supervisee.

F.4. Supervisor Responsibilities

F.4.a. Informed Consent for Supervision

Supervisors are responsible for incorporating into their supervision the principles of informed consent and participation. Supervisors inform supervisees of the policies and procedures to which they are to adhere and the mechanisms for due process appeal of individual supervisory actions.

F.4.b. Emergencies and Absences

Supervisors establish and communicate to supervisees procedures for contacting them or, in their absence, alternative on-call supervisors to assist in handling crises.

F.4.c. Standards for Supervisees

Supervisors make their supervisees aware of professional and ethical standards and legal responsibilities. Supervisors of postdegree counselors encourage these counselors to adhere to professional standards of practice. *(See C.1.)*

F.4.d. Termination of the Supervisory Relationship

Supervisors or supervisees have the right to terminate the supervisory relationship with adequate notice. Reasons for withdrawal are provided to the other party. When cultural, clinical, or professional issues are crucial to the viability of the supervisory relationship, both parties make efforts to resolve differences. When termination is warranted, supervisors make appropriate referrals to possible alternative supervisors.

F.5. Counseling Supervision Evaluation, Remediation, and Endorsement

F.5.a. Evaluation

Supervisors document and provide supervisees with ongoing performance appraisal and evaluation feedback and schedule periodic formal evaluative sessions throughout the supervisory relationship.

F.5.b. Limitations

Through ongoing evaluation and appraisal, supervisors are aware of the limitations of supervisees that might impede performance. Supervisors assist supervisees in securing remedial assistance when needed. They recommend dismissal from training programs, applied counseling settings, or state or voluntary professional credentialing processes when those supervisees are unable to provide competent professional services. Supervisors seek consultation and document their decisions to dismiss or refer supervisees for assistance. They ensure that supervisees are aware of options available to them to address such decisions. *(See C.2.g.)*

F.5.c. Counseling for Supervisees

If supervisees request counseling, supervisors provide them with acceptable referrals. Counselors do not provide counseling services to supervisees. Supervisors address interpersonal competencies in terms of the impact of these issues on clients, the supervisory relationship, and professional functioning. *(See F.3.a.)*

F.5.d. Endorsement

Supervisors endorse supervisees for certification, licensure, employment, or completion of an academic or training program only when they believe supervisees are qualified for the endorsement. Regardless of qualifications, supervisors do not endorse supervisees whom they believe to be impaired in any way that would interfere with the performance of the duties associated with the endorsement.

F.6. Responsibilities of Counselor Educators

F.6.a. Counselor Educators

Counselor educators who are responsible for developing, implementing, and supervising educational programs are skilled as teachers and practitioners. They are knowledgeable regarding the ethical, legal, and regulatory aspects of the profession, are skilled in applying that knowledge, and make students and supervisees aware of their responsibilities. Counselor educators conduct counselor education and training programs in an ethical manner and serve as role models for professional behavior. *(See C.1., C.2.a., C.2.c.)*

F.6.b. Infusing Multicultural Issues/ Diversity

Counselor educators infuse material related to multiculturalism/diversity into all courses and workshops for the development of professional counselors.

F.6.c. Integration of Study and Practice

Counselor educators establish education and training programs that integrate academic study and supervised practice.

F.6.d. Teaching Ethics

Counselor educators make students and supervisees aware of the ethical responsibilities and standards of the profession and the ethical responsibilities of students to the profession. Counselor educators infuse ethical considerations throughout the curriculum. *(See C.1.)*

F.6.e. Peer Relationships

Counselor educators make every effort to ensure that the rights of peers are not compromised when students or supervisees lead counseling groups or provide clinical supervision. Counselor educators take steps to ensure that students and supervisees understand they have the same ethical obligations as counselor educators, trainers, and supervisors.

F.6.f. Innovative Theories and Techniques

When counselor educators teach counseling techniques/procedures that are innovative, without an empirical foundation, or without a well-grounded theoretical foundation, they define the counseling techniques/procedures as "unproven" or "developing" and explain to students the potential risks and ethical considerations of using such techniques/procedures.

F.6.g. Field Placements

Counselor educators develop clear policies within their training programs regarding field placement and other clinical experiences. Counselor educators provide clearly stated roles and responsibilities for the student or supervisee, the site supervisor, and the program supervisor. They confirm that site supervisors are qualified to provide supervision and inform site supervisors of their professional and ethical responsibilities in this role.

F.6.h. Professional Disclosure

Before initiating counseling services, counselors-in-training disclose their status as students and explain how this status affects the limits of confidentiality. Counselor educators ensure that the clients at field placements are aware of the services rendered and the qualifications of the students and supervisees rendering those services. Students and supervisees obtain client permission before they use any information concerning the counseling relationship in the training process. *(See A.2.b.)*

F.7. Student Welfare

F.7.a. Orientation

Counselor educators recognize that orientation is a developmental process that continues throughout the educational and clinical training of students. Counseling faculty provide prospective students with information about the counselor education program's expectations:

1. the type and level of skill and knowledge acquisition required for successful completion of the training;
2. program training goals, objectives, and mission, and subject matter to be covered;
3. bases for evaluation;
4. training components that encourage self-growth or self-disclosure as part of the training process;

5. the type of supervision settings and requirements of the sites for required clinical field experiences;
6. student and supervisee evaluation and dismissal policies and procedures; and
7. up-to-date employment prospects for graduates.

F.7.b. Self-Growth Experiences
Counselor education programs delineate requirements for self-disclosure or self-growth experiences in their admission and program materials. Counselor educators use professional judgment when designing training experiences they conduct that require student and supervisee self-growth or self-disclosure. Students and supervisees are made aware of the ramifications their self-disclosure may have when counselors whose primary role as teacher, trainer, or supervisor requires acting on ethical obligations to the profession. Evaluative components of experiential training experiences explicitly delineate predetermined academic standards that are separate and do not depend on the student's level of self-disclosure. Counselor educators may require trainees to seek professional help to address any personal concerns that may be affecting their competency.

F.8. Student Responsibilities

F.8.a. Standards for Students
Counselors-in-training have a responsibility to understand and follow the *ACA Code of Ethics* and adhere to applicable laws, regulatory policies, and rules and policies governing professional staff behavior at the agency or placement setting. Students have the same obligation to clients as those required of professional counselors. *(See C.1., H.1.)*

F.8.b. Impairment
Counselors-in-training refrain from offering or providing counseling services when their physical, mental, or emotional problems are likely to harm a client or others. They are alert to the signs of impairment, seek assistance for problems, and notify their program supervisors when they are aware that they are unable to effectively provide services. In addition, they seek appropriate professional services for themselves to remediate the problems that are interfering with their ability to provide services to others. *(See A.1., C.2.d., C.2.g.)*

F.9. Evaluation and Remediation of Students

F.9.a. Evaluation
Counselors clearly state to students, prior to and throughout the training program, the levels of competency expected, appraisal methods, and timing of evaluations for both didactic and clinical competencies. Counselor educators provide students with ongoing performance appraisal and evaluation feedback throughout the training program.

F.9.b. Limitations
Counselor educators, throughout ongoing evaluation and appraisal, are aware of and address the inability of some students to achieve counseling competencies that might impede performance. Counselor educators

1. assist students in securing remedial assistance when needed,
2. seek professional consultation and document their decision to dismiss or refer students for assistance, and
3. ensure that students have recourse in a timely manner to address decisions to require them to seek assistance or to dismiss them and provide students with due process according to institutional policies and procedures. *(See C.2.g.)*

F.9.c. Counseling for Students
If students request counseling or if counseling services are required as part of a remediation process, counselor educators provide acceptable referrals.

F.10. Roles and Relationships Between Counselor Educators and Students

F.10.a. Sexual or Romantic Relationships
Sexual or romantic interactions or relationships with current students are prohibited.

F.10.b. Sexual Harassment
Counselor educators do not condone or subject students to sexual harassment. *(See C.6.a.)*

F.10.c. Relationships With Former Students
Counselor educators are aware of the power differential in the relationship between faculty and students. Faculty members foster open discussions with former students when considering engaging in a social, sexual, or other intimate relationship. Faculty members discuss with the former student how their former relationship may affect the change in relationship.

F.10.d. Nonprofessional Relationships
Counselor educators avoid nonprofessional or ongoing professional relationships with students in which there is a risk of potential harm to the student or that may compromise the training experience or grades assigned. In addition, counselor educators do not accept any form of professional services, fees, commissions, reimbursement, or remuneration from a site for student or supervisee placement.

F.10.e. Counseling Services

Counselor educators do not serve as counselors to current students unless this is a brief role associated with a training experience.

F.10.f. Potentially Beneficial Relationships

Counselor educators are aware of the power differential in the relationship between faculty and students. If they believe a nonprofessional relationship with a student may be potentially beneficial to the student, they take precautions similar to those taken by counselors when working with clients. Examples of potentially beneficial interactions or relationships include, but are not limited to, attending a formal ceremony; hospital visits; providing support during a stressful event; or mutual membership in a professional association, organization, or community. Counselor educators engage in open discussions with students when they consider entering into relationships with students outside of their roles as teachers and supervisors. They discuss with students the rationale for such interactions, the potential benefits and drawbacks, and the anticipated consequences for the student. Educators clarify the specific nature and limitations of the additional role(s) they will have with the student prior to engaging in a nonprofessional relationship. Nonprofessional relationships with students should be time-limited and initiated with student consent.

F.11. Multicultural/Diversity Competence in Counselor Education and Training Programs

F.11.a. Faculty Diversity

Counselor educators are committed to recruiting and retaining a diverse faculty.

F.11.b. Student Diversity

Counselor educators actively attempt to recruit and retain a diverse student body. Counselor educators demonstrate commitment to multicultural/diversity competence by recognizing and valuing diverse cultures and types of abilities students bring to the training experience. Counselor educators provide appropriate accommodations that enhance and support diverse student well-being and academic performance.

F.11.c. Multicultural/Diversity Competence

Counselor educators actively infuse multicultural/diversity competency in their training and supervision practices. They actively train students to gain awareness, knowledge, and skills in the competencies of multicultural practice. Counselor educators include case examples, role-plays, discussion questions, and other classroom activities that promote and represent various cultural perspectives.

Section G: Research and Publication

Introduction

Counselors who conduct research are encouraged to contribute to the knowledge base of the profession and promote a clearer understanding of the conditions that lead to a healthy and more just society. Counselors support efforts of researchers by participating fully and willingly whenever possible. Counselors minimize bias and respect diversity in designing and implementing research programs.

G.1. Research Responsibilities

G.1.a. Use of Human Research Participants

Counselors plan, design, conduct, and report research in a manner that is consistent with pertinent ethical principles, federal and state laws, host institutional regulations, and scientific standards governing research with human research participants.

G.1.b. Deviation From Standard Practice

Counselors seek consultation and observe stringent safeguards to protect the rights of research participants when a research problem suggests a deviation from standard or acceptable practices.

G.1.c. Independent Researchers

When independent researchers do not have access to an Institutional Review Board (IRB), they should consult with researchers who are familiar with IRB procedures to provide appropriate safeguards.

G.1.d. Precautions to Avoid Injury

Counselors who conduct research with human participants are responsible for the welfare of participants throughout the research process and should take reasonable precautions to avoid causing injurious psychological, emotional, physical, or social effects to participants.

G.1.e. Principal Researcher Responsibility

The ultimate responsibility for ethical research practice lies with the principal researcher. All others involved in the research activities share ethical obligations and responsibility for their own actions.

G.1.f. Minimal Interference

Counselors take reasonable precautions to avoid causing disruptions in the lives of research participants that could be caused by their involvement in research.

G.1.g. Multicultural/Diversity Considerations in Research

When appropriate to research goals, counselors are sensitive to incorporating research procedures that take into account cultural considerations. They seek consultation when appropriate.

G.2. Rights of Research Participants

(See A.2, A.7.)

G.2.a. Informed Consent in Research

Individuals have the right to consent to become research participants. In seeking consent, counselors use language that

1. accurately explains the purpose and procedures to be followed,
2. identifies any procedures that are experimental or relatively untried,
3. describes any attendant discomforts and risks,
4. describes any benefits or changes in individuals or organizations that might be reasonably expected,
5. discloses appropriate alternative procedures that would be advantageous for participants,
6. offers to answer any inquiries concerning the procedures,
7. describes any limitations on confidentiality,
8. describes the format and potential target audiences for the dissemination of research findings, and
9. instructs participants that they are free to withdraw their consent and to discontinue participation in the project at any time without penalty.

G.2.b. Deception

Counselors do not conduct research involving deception unless alternative procedures are not feasible and the prospective value of the research justifies the deception. If such deception has the potential to cause physical or emotional harm to research participants, the research is not conducted, regardless of prospective value. When the methodological requirements of a study necessitate concealment or deception, the investigator explains the reasons for this action as soon as possible during the debriefing.

G.2.c. Student/Supervisee Participation

Researchers who involve students or supervisees in research make clear to them that the decision regarding whether or not to participate in research activities does not affect one's academic standing or supervisory relationship. Students or supervisees who choose not to participate in educational research are provided with an appropriate alternative to fulfill their academic or clinical requirements.

G.2.d. Client Participation

Counselors conducting research involving clients make clear in the informed consent process that clients are free to choose whether or not to participate in research activities. Counselors take necessary precautions to protect clients from adverse consequences of declining or withdrawing from participation.

G.2.e. Confidentiality of Information

Information obtained about research participants during the course of an investigation is confidential. When the possibility exists that others may obtain access to such information, ethical research practice requires that the possibility, together with the plans for protecting confidentiality, be explained to participants as a part of the procedure for obtaining informed consent.

G.2.f. Persons Not Capable of Giving Informed Consent

When a person is not capable of giving informed consent, counselors provide an appropriate explanation to, obtain agreement for participation from, and obtain the appropriate consent of a legally authorized person.

G.2.g. Commitments to Participants

Counselors take reasonable measures to honor all commitments to research participants. *(See A.2.c.)*

G.2.h. Explanations After Data Collection

After data are collected, counselors provide participants with full clarification of the nature of the study to remove any misconceptions participants might have regarding the research. Where scientific or human values justify delaying or withholding information, counselors take reasonable measures to avoid causing harm.

G.2.i. Informing Sponsors

Counselors inform sponsors, institutions, and publication channels regarding research procedures and outcomes. Counselors ensure that appropriate bodies and authorities are given pertinent information and acknowledgement.

G.2.j. Disposal of Research Documents and Records

Within a reasonable period of time following the completion of a research project or study, counselors take steps to destroy records or documents (audio, video, digital, and written) containing confidential data or information that identifies research participants. When records are of an artistic nature, researchers obtain participant consent with regard to handling of such records or documents. *(See B.4.a, B.4.g.)*

G.3. Relationships With Research Participants (When Research Involves Intensive or Extended Interactions)

G.3.a. Nonprofessional Relationships
Nonprofessional relationships with research participants should be avoided.

G.3.b. Relationships With Research Participants
Sexual or romantic counselor–research participant interactions or relationships with current research participants are prohibited.

G.3.c. Sexual Harassment and Research Participants
Researchers do not condone or subject research participants to sexual harassment.

G.3.d. Potentially Beneficial Interactions
When a nonprofessional interaction between the researcher and the research participant may be potentially beneficial, the researcher must document, prior to the interaction (when feasible), the rationale for such an interaction, the potential benefit, and anticipated consequences for the research participant. Such interactions should be initiated with appropriate consent of the research participant. Where unintentional harm occurs to the research participant due to the nonprofessional interaction, the researcher must show evidence of an attempt to remedy such harm.

G.4. Reporting Results

G.4.a. Accurate Results
Counselors plan, conduct, and report research accurately. They provide thorough discussions of the limitations of their data and alternative hypotheses. Counselors do not engage in misleading or fraudulent research, distort data, misrepresent data, or deliberately bias their results. They explicitly mention all variables and conditions known to the investigator that may have affected the outcome of a study or the interpretation of data. They describe the extent to which results are applicable for diverse populations.

G.4.b. Obligation to Report Unfavorable Results
Counselors report the results of any research of professional value. Results that reflect unfavorably on institutions, programs, services, prevailing opinions, or vested interests are not withheld.

G.4.c. Reporting Errors
If counselors discover significant errors in their published research, they take reasonable steps to correct such errors in a correction erratum, or through other appropriate publication means.

G.4.d. Identity of Participants
Counselors who supply data, aid in the research of another person, report research results, or make original data available take due care to disguise the identity of respective participants in the absence of specific authorization from the participants to do otherwise. In situations where participants self-identify their involvement in research studies, researchers take active steps to ensure that data is adapted/changed to protect the identity and welfare of all parties and that discussion of results does not cause harm to participants.

G.4.e. Replication Studies
Counselors are obligated to make available sufficient original research data to qualified professionals who may wish to replicate the study.

G.5. Publication

G.5.a. Recognizing Contributions
When conducting and reporting research, counselors are familiar with and give recognition to previous work on the topic, observe copyright laws, and give full credit to those to whom credit is due.

G.5.b. Plagiarism
Counselors do not plagiarize, that is, they do not present another person's work as their own work.

G.5.c. Review/Republication of Data or Ideas
Counselors fully acknowledge and make editorial reviewers aware of prior publication of ideas or data where such ideas or data are submitted for review or publication.

G.5.d. Contributors
Counselors give credit through joint authorship, acknowledgment, footnote statements, or other appropriate means to those who have contributed significantly to research or concept development in accordance with such contributions. The principal contributor is listed first and minor technical or professional contributions are acknowledged in notes or introductory statements.

G.5.e. Agreement of Contributors
Counselors who conduct joint research with colleagues or students/supervisees establish agreements in advance regarding allocation of tasks, publication credit, and types of acknowledgement that will be received.

G.5.f. Student Research
For articles that are substantially based on students course papers, projects, dissertations or theses, and on

which students have been the primary contributors, they are listed as principal authors.

G.5.g. Duplicate Submission

Counselors submit manuscripts for consideration to only one journal at a time. Manuscripts that are published in whole or in substantial part in another journal or published work are not submitted for publication without acknowledgment and permission from the previous publication.

G.5.h. Professional Review

Counselors who review material submitted for publication, research, or other scholarly purposes respect the confidentiality and proprietary rights of those who submitted it. Counselors use care to make publication decisions based on valid and defensible standards. Counselors review article submissions in a timely manner and based on their scope and competency in research methodologies. Counselors who serve as reviewers at the request of editors or publishers make every effort to only review materials that are within their scope of competency and use care to avoid personal biases.

Section H: Resolving Ethical Issues

Introduction

Counselors behave in a legal, ethical, and moral manner in the conduct of their professional work. They are aware that client protection and trust in the profession depend on a high level of professional conduct. They hold other counselors to the same standards and are willing to take appropriate action to ensure that these standards are upheld. Counselors strive to resolve ethical dilemmas with direct and open communication among all parties involved and seek consultation with colleagues and supervisors when necessary. Counselors incorporate ethical practice into their daily professional work. They engage in ongoing professional development regarding current topics in ethical and legal issues in counseling.

H.1. Standards and the Law
(See F.9.a.)

H.1.a. Knowledge

Counselors understand the *ACA Code of Ethics* and other applicable ethics codes from other profes-

sional organizations or from certification and licensure bodies of which they are members. Lack of knowledge or misunderstanding of an ethical responsibility is not a defense against a charge of unethical conduct.

H.1.b. Conflicts Between Ethics and Laws

If ethical responsibilities conflict with law, regulations, or other governing legal authority, counselors make known their commitment to the *ACA Code of Ethics* and take steps to resolve the conflict. If the conflict cannot be resolved by such means, counselors may adhere to the requirements of law, regulations, or other governing legal authority.

H.2. Suspected Violations

H.2.a. Ethical Behavior Expected

Counselors expect colleagues to adhere to the *ACA Code of Ethics.* When counselors possess knowledge that raises doubts as to whether another counselor is acting in an ethical manner, they take appropriate action. *(See H.2.b., H.2.c.)*

H.2.b. Informal Resolution

When counselors have reason to believe that another counselor is violating or has violated an ethical standard, they attempt first to resolve the issue informally with the other counselor if feasible, provided such action does not violate confidentiality rights that may be involved.

H.2.c. Reporting Ethical Violations

If an apparent violation has substantially harmed, or is likely to substantially harm a person or organization and is not appropriate for informal resolution or is not resolved properly, counselors take further action appropriate to the situation. Such action might include referral to state or national committees on professional ethics, voluntary national certification bodies, state licensing boards, or to the appropriate institutional authorities. This standard does not apply when an intervention would violate confidentiality rights or when counselors have been retained to review the work of another counselor whose professional conduct is in question.

H.2.d. Consultation

When uncertain as to whether a particular situation or course of action may be in violation of the *ACA*

Code of Ethics, counselors consult with other counselors who are knowledgeable about ethics and the *ACA Code of Ethics,* with colleagues, or with appropriate authorities

H.2.e. Organizational Conflicts

If the demands of an organization with which counselors are affiliated pose a conflict with the *ACA Code of Ethics,* counselors specify the nature of such conflicts and express to their supervisors or other responsible officials their commitment to the *ACA Code of Ethics.* When possible, counselors work toward change within the organization to allow full adherence to the *ACA Code of Ethics.* In doing so, they address any confidentiality issues.

H.2.f. Unwarranted Complaints

Counselors do not initiate, participate in, or encourage the filing of ethics complaints that are made with reckless disregard or willful ignorance of facts that would disprove the allegation.

H.2.g. Unfair Discrimination Against Complainants and Respondents

Counselors do not deny persons employment, advancement, admission to academic or other programs, tenure, or promotion based solely upon their having made or their being the subject of an ethics complaint. This does not preclude taking action based upon the outcome of such proceedings or considering other appropriate information.

H.3. Cooperation With Ethics Committees

Counselors assist in the process of enforcing the *ACA Code of Ethics.* Counselors cooperate with investigations, proceedings, and requirements of the ACA Ethics Committee or ethics committees of other duly constituted associations or boards having jurisdiction over those charged with a violation. Counselors are familiar with the *ACA Policy and Procedures for Processing Complains of Ethical Violations* and use it as a reference for assisting in the enforcement of the *ACA Code of Ethics.*

American Psychological Association, Ethical Principles of Psychologists and Code of Conduct

INTRODUCTION AND APPLICABILITY

The American Psychological Association's (APA's) Ethical Principles of Psychologists and Code of Conduct (hereinafter referred to as the Ethics Code) consists of an Introduction, a Preamble, five General Principles (A–E), and specific Ethical Standards. The Introduction discusses the intent, organization, procedural considerations, and scope of application of the Ethics Code. The Preamble and General Principles are aspirational goals to guide psychologists toward the highest ideals of psychology. Although the Preamble and General Principles are not themselves enforceable rules, they should be considered by psychologists in arriving at an ethical course of action. The Ethical Standards set forth enforceable rules for conduct as psychologists. Most of the Ethical Standards are written broadly, in order to apply to psychologists in varied roles, although the application of an Ethical Standard may vary depending on the context. The Ethical Standards are not exhaustive. The fact that a given conduct is not specifically addressed by an Ethical Standard does not mean that it is necessarily either ethical or unethical.

This Ethics Code applies only to psychologists' activities that are part of their scientific, educational, or professional roles as psychologists. Areas covered include but are not limited to the clinical, counseling, and school practice of psychology; research; teaching; supervision of trainees; public service; policy development; social intervention; development of assessment instruments; conducting assessments; educational counseling; organizational consulting; forensic activities; program design and evaluation; and administration. This Ethics Code applies to these activities across a variety of contexts, such as in person, postal, telephone, internet, and other electronic transmissions. These activities shall be distinguished from the purely private conduct of psychologists, which is not within the purview of the Ethics Code.

Membership in the APA commits members and student affiliates to comply with the standards of the APA Ethics Code and to the rules and procedures used to enforce them. Lack of awareness or misunderstanding of an Ethical Standard is not itself a defense to a charge of unethical conduct.

The procedures for filing, investigating, and resolving complaints of unethical conduct are described in the current Rules and Procedures of the APA Ethics Committee. APA may impose sanctions on its members for violations of the standards of the Ethics Code, including termination of APA membership, and may notify other bodies and individuals of its actions. Actions that violate the standards of the Ethics Code may also lead to the imposition of sanctions on psychologists or students whether or not they are APA members by bodies other than APA, including state psychological associations, other professional groups, psychology boards, other state or federal agencies, and payors for health services. In addition, APA may take action against a member after his or her conviction of a felony, expulsion or suspension from an affiliated state psychological association, or suspension or loss of licensure. When the sanction to be imposed by APA is less than expulsion, the 2001 Rules and Procedures do not guarantee an opportunity for an in-person hearing, but generally provide that complaints will be resolved only on the basis of a submitted record.

The Ethics Code is intended to provide guidance for psychologists and standards of professional conduct that can be applied by the APA and by other bodies that choose to adopt them. The Ethics Code is not intended to be a basis of civil liability. Whether a psychologist has violated the Ethics Code standards does not by itself determine whether the psychologist is legally liable in a court action, whether a contract is enforceable, or whether other legal consequences occur.

The modifiers used in some of the standards of this Ethics Code (e.g., reasonably, appropriate, potentially) are included in the standards when they would (1) allow professional judgment on the part of psychologists, (2) eliminate injustice or inequality that would occur without the modifier, (3) ensure applicability across the broad range of activities conducted by psychologists, or (4) guard against a set of rigid rules that might be quickly outdated. As used in this Ethics Code, the term reasonable means the prevailing professional judgment of psychologists engaged in similar activities in similar circumstances, given the knowledge the psychologist had or should have had at the time.

In the process of making decisions regarding their professional behavior, psychologists must consider this Ethics Code in addition to applicable laws and psychology board regulations. In applying the Ethics Code to their professional work, psychologists may consider other materials and guidelines that have been adopted or endorsed by scientific and professional psychological organizations and the dictates of their own conscience, as well as consult with others within the field. If this Ethics Code establishes a higher standard of conduct than is required by law, psychologists must meet the higher ethical standard. If psychologists' ethical responsibilities conflict with law, regulations, or other governing legal authority, psychologists make known their commitment to this Ethics Code and take steps to resolve the conflict in a responsible manner. If the conflict is unresolvable via such means, psychologists may adhere to the requirements of the law, regulations, or other governing authority in keeping with basic principles of human rights.

PREAMBLE

Psychologists are committed to increasing scientific and professional knowledge of behavior and people's understanding of themselves and others and to the use of such knowledge to improve the condition of individuals, organizations, and society. Psychologists respect and protect civil and human rights and the central importance of freedom of inquiry and expression in research, teaching, and publication. They strive to help the public in developing informed judgments and choices concerning human behavior. In doing so, they perform many roles, such as researcher, educator, diagnostician, therapist, supervisor, consultant, administrator, social interventionist, and expert witness. This Ethics Code provides a common set of principles and standards upon which psychologists build their professional and scientific work.

This Ethics Code is intended to provide specific standards to cover most situations encountered by psychologists. It has as its goals the welfare and protection of the individuals and groups with whom psychologists work and the education of members, students, and the public regarding ethical standards of the discipline.

The development of a dynamic set of ethical standards for psychologists' work-related conduct requires a personal commitment and lifelong effort to act ethically; to encourage ethical behavior by students, supervisees, employees, and colleagues; and to consult with others concerning ethical problems.

GENERAL PRINCIPLES

This section consists of General Principles. General Principles, as opposed to Ethical Standards, are aspirational in nature. Their intent is to guide and inspire psychologists toward the very highest ethical ideals of the profession. General Principles, in contrast to Ethical Standards, do not represent obligations and should not form the basis for imposing sanctions. Relying upon General Principles for either of these reasons distorts both their meaning and purpose.

Principle A: Beneficence and Nonmaleficence

Psychologists strive to benefit those with whom they work and take care to do no harm. In their professional actions, psychologists seek to safeguard the welfare and rights of those with whom they interact professionally and other affected persons, and the welfare of animal subjects of research. When conflicts occur among psychologists' obligations or concerns, they attempt to resolve these conflicts in a responsible fashion that avoids or minimizes harm. Because psychologists' scientific and professional judgments and actions may affect the lives of others, they are alert to and guard against personal, financial, social, organizational, or political factors that might lead to misuse of their influence. Psychologists strive to be aware of the possible effect of their own physical and mental health on their ability to help those with whom they work.

Principle B: Fidelity and Responsibility

Psychologists establish relationships of trust with those with whom they work. They are aware of their professional and scientific responsibilities to society and to the specific communities in which they work. Psychologists uphold professional standards of conduct, clarify their professional roles and obligations, accept appropriate responsibility for their behavior, and seek to manage conflicts of interest that could lead to exploitation or harm. Psychologists consult with, refer to, or cooperate with other professionals and institutions to the extent needed to serve the best interests of those with whom they work. They are concerned about the ethical compliance of their colleagues' scientific and professional conduct. Psychologists strive to contribute a portion of their professional time for little or no compensation or personal advantage.

Principle C: Integrity

Psychologists seek to promote accuracy, honesty, and truthfulness in the science, teaching, and practice of psychology. In these activities psychologists do not steal, cheat, or engage in fraud, subterfuge, or intentional misrepresentation of fact. Psychologists strive to keep their promises and to avoid unwise or unclear commitments. In situations in which deception may be ethically justifiable to maximize benefits and minimize harm, psychologists have a serious obligation to consider the need for, the possible consequences of, and their responsibility to correct any resulting mistrust or other harmful effects that arise from the use of such techniques.

Principle D: Justice

Psychologists recognize that fairness and justice entitle all persons to access to and benefit from the contributions of psychology and to equal quality in the processes, procedures, and services being conducted by psychologists. Psychologists exercise reasonable judgment and take precautions to ensure that their potential biases, the boundaries of their competence, and the limitations of their expertise do not lead to or condone unjust practices.

Principle E: Respect for People's Rights and Dignity

Psychologists respect the dignity and worth of all people, and the rights of individuals to privacy, confidentiality, and self-determination. Psychologists are aware that special safeguards may be necessary to protect the rights and welfare of persons or communities whose vulnerabilities impair autonomous decision making. Psychologists are aware of and respect cultural, individual, and role differences, including those based on age, gender, gender identity, race, ethnicity, culture, national origin, religion, sexual orientation, disability, language, and socioeconomic status and consider these factors when working with members of such groups. Psychologists try to eliminate the effect on their work of biases based on those factors, and they do not knowingly participate in or condone activities of others based upon such prejudices.

ETHICAL STANDARDS

1. Resolving Ethical Issues

1.01 Misuse of Psychologists' Work
If psychologists learn of misuse or misrepresentation of their work, they take reasonable steps to correct or minimize the misuse or misrepresentation.

1.02 Conflicts Between Ethics and Law, Regulations, or Other Governing Legal Authority
If psychologists' ethical responsibilities conflict with law, regulations, or other governing legal authority, psychologists make known their commitment to the Ethics Code and take steps to resolve the conflict. If the conflict is unresolvable via such means, psychologists may adhere to the requirements of the law, regulations, or other governing legal authority.

1.03 Conflicts Between Ethics and Organizational Demands
If the demands of an organization with which psychologists are affiliated or for whom they are working conflict with this Ethics Code, psychologists clarify the nature of the conflict, make known their commitment to the Ethics Code, and to the extent feasible, resolve the conflict in a way that permits adherence to the Ethics Code.

1.04 Informal Resolution of Ethical Violations
When psychologists believe that there may have been an ethical violation by another psychologist, they attempt to resolve the issue by bringing it to the attention of that individual, if an informal resolution appears appropriate and the intervention does not violate any confidentiality rights that may be involved. (See also Standards 1.02, Conflicts Between Ethics and Law, Regulations, or Other Governing Legal Authority, and 1.03, Conflicts Between Ethics and Organizational Demands.)

1.05 Reporting Ethical Violations

If an apparent ethical violation has substantially harmed or is likely to substantially harm a person or organization and is not appropriate for informal resolution under Standard 1.04, Informal Resolution of Ethical Violations, or is not resolved properly in that fashion, psychologists take further action appropriate to the situation. Such action might include referral to state or national committees on professional ethics, to state licensing boards, or to the appropriate institutional authorities. This standard does not apply when an intervention would violate confidentiality rights or when psychologists have been retained to review the work of another psychologist whose professional conduct is in question. (See also Standard 1.02, Conflicts Between Ethics and Law, Regulations, or Other Governing Legal Authority.)

1.06 Cooperating With Ethics Committees

Psychologists cooperate in ethics investigations, proceedings, and resulting requirements of the APA or any affiliated state psychological association to which they belong. In doing so, they address any confidentiality issues. Failure to cooperate is itself an ethics violation. However, making a request for deferment of adjudication of an ethics complaint pending the outcome of litigation does not alone constitute noncooperation.

1.07 Improper Complaints

Psychologists do not file or encourage the filing of ethics complaints that are made with reckless disregard for or willful ignorance of facts that would disprove the allegation.

1.08 Unfair Discrimination Against Complainants and Respondents

Psychologists do not deny persons employment, advancement, admissions to academic or other programs, tenure, or promotion, based solely upon their having made or their being the subject of an ethics complaint. This does not preclude taking action based upon the outcome of such proceedings or considering other appropriate information.

2. Competence

2.01 Boundaries of Competence

(a) Psychologists provide services, teach, and conduct research with populations and in areas only within the boundaries of their competence, based on their education, training, supervised experience, consultation, study, or professional experience.

(b) Where scientific or professional knowledge in the discipline of psychology establishes that an understanding of factors associated with age, gender, gender identity, race, ethnicity, culture, national origin, religion, sexual orientation, disability, language, or socioeconomic status is essential for effective implementation of their services or research, psychologists have or obtain the training, experience, consultation, or supervision necessary to ensure the competence of their services, or they make appropriate referrals, except as provided in Standard 2.02, Providing Services in Emergencies.

(c) Psychologists planning to provide services, teach, or conduct research involving populations, areas, techniques, or technologies new to them undertake relevant education, training, supervised experience, consultation, or study.

(d) When psychologists are asked to provide services to individuals for whom appropriate mental health services are not available and for which psychologists have not obtained the competence necessary, psychologists with closely related prior training or experience may provide such services in order to ensure that services are not denied if they make a reasonable effort to obtain the competence required by using relevant research, training, consultation, or study.

(e) In those emerging areas in which generally recognized standards for preparatory training do not yet exist, psychologists nevertheless take reasonable steps to ensure the competence of their work and to protect clients/patients, students, supervisees, research participants, organizational clients, and others from harm.

(f) When assuming forensic roles, psychologists are or become reasonably familiar with the judicial or administrative rules governing their roles.

2.02 Providing Services in Emergencies

In emergencies, when psychologists provide services to individuals for whom other mental health services are not available and for which psychologists have not obtained the necessary training, psychologists may provide such services in order to ensure that services are not denied. The services are discontinued as soon as the emergency has ended or appropriate services are available.

2.03 Maintaining Competence

Psychologists undertake ongoing efforts to develop and maintain their competence.

2.04 Bases for Scientific and Professional Judgments
Psychologists' work is based upon established scientific and professional knowledge of the discipline. (See also Standards 2.01e, Boundaries of Competence, and 10.01b, Informed Consent to Therapy.)

2.05 Delegation of Work to Others
Psychologists who delegate work to employees, supervisees, or research or teaching assistants or who use the services of others, such as interpreters, take reasonable steps to (1) avoid delegating such work to persons who have a multiple relationship with those being served that would likely lead to exploitation or loss of objectivity; (2) authorize only those responsibilities that such persons can be expected to perform competently on the basis of their education, training, or experience, either independently or with the level of supervision being provided; and (3) see that such persons perform these services competently. (See also Standards 2.02, Providing Services in Emergencies; 3.05, Multiple Relationships; 4.01, Maintaining Confidentiality; 9.01, Bases for Assessments; 9.02, Use of Assessments; 9.03, Informed Consent in Assessments; and 9.07, Assessment by Unqualified Persons.)

2.06 Personal Problems and Conflicts
(a) Psychologists refrain from initiating an activity when they know or should know that there is a substantial likelihood that their personal problems will prevent them from performing their work-related activities in a competent manner.

(b) When psychologists become aware of personal problems that may interfere with their performing work-related duties adequately, they take appropriate measures, such as obtaining professional consultation or assistance, and determine whether they should limit, suspend, or terminate their work-related duties. (See also Standard 10.10, Terminating Therapy.)

3. Human Relations

3.01 Unfair Discrimination
In their work-related activities, psychologists do not engage in unfair discrimination based on age, gender, gender identity, race, ethnicity, culture, national origin, religion, sexual orientation, disability, socioeconomic status, or any basis proscribed by law.

3.02 Sexual Harassment
Psychologists do not engage in sexual harassment. Sexual harassment is sexual solicitation, physical advances, or verbal or nonverbal conduct that is sexual in nature, that occurs in connection with the psychologist's activities or roles as a psychologist, and that either (1) is unwelcome, is offensive, or creates a hostile workplace or educational environment, and the psychologist knows or is told this or (2) is sufficiently severe or intense to be abusive to a reasonable person in the context. Sexual harassment can consist of a single intense or severe act or of multiple persistent or pervasive acts. (See also Standard 1.08, Unfair Discrimination Against Complainants and Respondents.)

3.03 Other Harassment
Psychologists do not knowingly engage in behavior that is harassing or demeaning to persons with whom they interact in their work based on factors such as those persons' age, gender, gender identity, race, ethnicity, culture, national origin, religion, sexual orientation, disability, language, or socioeconomic status.

3.04 Avoiding Harm
Psychologists take reasonable steps to avoid harming their clients/patients, students, supervisees, research participants, organizational clients, and others with whom they work, and to minimize harm where it is foreseeable and unavoidable.

3.05 Multiple Relationships
(a) A multiple relationship occurs when a psychologist is in a professional role with a person and (1) at the same time is in another role with the same person, (2) at the same time is in a relationship with a person closely associated with or related to the person with whom the psychologist has the professional relationship, or (3) promises to enter into another relationship in the future with the person or a person closely associated with or related to the person.

A psychologist refrains from entering into a multiple relationship if the multiple relationship could reasonably be expected to impair the psychologist's objectivity, competence, or effectiveness in performing his or her functions as a psychologist, or otherwise risks exploitation or harm to the person with whom the professional relationship exists.

Multiple relationships that would not reasonably be expected to cause impairment or risk exploitation or harm are not unethical.

(b) If a psychologist finds that, due to unforeseen factors, a potentially harmful multiple relationship has arisen, the psychologist takes reasonable steps to resolve it with due regard for the best interests of the affected person and maximal compliance with the Ethics Code.

(c) When psychologists are required by law, institutional policy, or extraordinary circumstances to serve in more than one role in judicial or administrative proceedings, at the outset they clarify role expectations and the extent of confidentiality and thereafter as changes occur. (See also Standards 3.04, Avoiding Harm, and 3.07, Third-Party Requests for Services.)

3.06 Conflict of Interest
Psychologists refrain from taking on a professional role when personal, scientific, professional, legal, financial, or other interests or relationships could reasonably be expected to (1) impair their objectivity, competence, or effectiveness in performing their functions as psychologists or (2) expose the person or organization with whom the professional relationship exists to harm or exploitation.

3.07 Third-Party Requests for Services
When psychologists agree to provide services to a person or entity at the request of a third party, psychologists attempt to clarify at the outset of the service the nature of the relationship with all individuals or organizations involved. This clarification includes the role of the psychologist (e.g., therapist, consultant, diagnostician, or expert witness), an identification of who is the client, the probable uses of the services provided or the information obtained, and the fact that there may be limits to confidentiality. (See also Standards 3.05, Multiple Relationships, and 4.02, Discussing the Limits of Confidentiality.)

3.08 Exploitative Relationships
Psychologists do not exploit persons over whom they have supervisory, evaluative, or other authority such as clients/patients, students, supervisees, research participants, and employees. (See also Standards 3.05, Multiple Relationships; 6.04, Fees and Financial Arrangements; 6.05, Barter With Clients/Patients; 7.07, Sexual Relationships With Students and Supervisees; 10.05, Sexual Intimacies With Current Therapy Clients/Patients; 10.06, Sexual Intimacies With Relatives or Significant Others of Current Therapy Clients/Patients; 10.07, Therapy With Former Sexual Partners; and 10.08, Sexual Intimacies With Former Therapy Clients/Patients.)

3.09 Cooperation With Other Professionals
When indicated and professionally appropriate, psychologists cooperate with other professionals in order to serve their clients/patients effectively and appropriately. (See also Standard 4.05, Disclosures.)

3.10 Informed Consent
(a) When psychologists conduct research or provide assessment, therapy, counseling, or consulting services in person or via electronic transmission or other forms of communication, they obtain the informed consent of the individual or individuals using language that is reasonably understandable to that person or persons except when conducting such activities without consent is mandated by law or governmental regulation or as otherwise provided in this Ethics Code. (See also Standards 8.02, Informed Consent to Research; 9.03, Informed Consent in Assessments; and 10.01, Informed Consent to Therapy.)

(b) For persons who are legally incapable of giving informed consent, psychologists nevertheless (1) provide an appropriate explanation, (2) seek the individual's assent, (3) consider such persons' preferences and best interests, and (4) obtain appropriate permission from a legally authorized person, if such substitute consent is permitted or required by law. When consent by a legally authorized person is not permitted or required by law, psychologists take reasonable steps to protect the individual's rights and welfare.

(c) When psychological services are court ordered or otherwise mandated, psychologists inform the individual of the nature of the anticipated services, including whether the services are court ordered or mandated and any limits of confidentiality, before proceeding.

(d) Psychologists appropriately document written or oral consent, permission, and assent. (See also Standards 8.02, Informed Consent to Research; 9.03, Informed Consent in Assessments; and 10.01, Informed Consent to Therapy.)

3.11 Psychological Services Delivered To or Through Organizations
(a) Psychologists delivering services to or through organizations provide information beforehand to clients and when appropriate those directly affected by the services about (1) the nature and objectives of the services, (2) the intended recipients, (3) which of the individuals are clients, (4) the relationship the psychologist will have with each person and the organization, (5) the probable uses of services provided and information obtained, (6) who will have access to the information, and (7) limits of confidentiality. As soon as

feasible, they provide information about the results and conclusions of such services to appropriate persons.

(b) If psychologists will be precluded by law or by organizational roles from providing such information to particular individuals or groups, they so inform those individuals or groups at the outset of the service.

3.12 Interruption of Psychological Services

Unless otherwise covered by contract, psychologists make reasonable efforts to plan for facilitating services in the event that psychological services are interrupted by factors such as the psychologist's illness, death, unavailability, relocation, or retirement or by the client's/patient's relocation or financial limitations. (See also Standard 6.02c, Maintenance, Dissemination, and Disposal of Confidential Records of Professional and Scientific Work.)

4. Privacy And Confidentiality

4.01 Maintaining Confidentiality

Psychologists have a primary obligation and take reasonable precautions to protect confidential information obtained through or stored in any medium, recognizing that the extent and limits of confidentiality may be regulated by law or established by institutional rules or professional or scientific relationship. (See also Standard 2.05, Delegation of Work to Others.)

4.02 Discussing the Limits of Confidentiality

(a) Psychologists discuss with persons (including, to the extent feasible, persons who are legally incapable of giving informed consent and their legal representatives) and organizations with whom they establish a scientific or professional relationship (1) the relevant limits of confidentiality and (2) the foreseeable uses of the information generated through their psychological activities. (See also Standard 3.10, Informed Consent.)

(b) Unless it is not feasible or is contraindicated, the discussion of confidentiality occurs at the outset of the relationship and thereafter as new circumstances may warrant.

(c) Psychologists who offer services, products, or information via electronic transmission inform clients/patients of the risks to privacy and limits of confidentiality.

4.03 Recording

Before recording the voices or images of individuals to whom they provide services, psychologists obtain permission from all such persons or their legal representatives. (See also Standards 8.03, Informed Consent for Recording Voices and Images in Research; 8.05, Dispensing With Informed Consent for Research; and 8.07, Deception in Research.)

4.04 Minimizing Intrusions on Privacy

(a) Psychologists include in written and oral reports and consultations, only information germane to the purpose for which the communication is made.

(b) Psychologists discuss confidential information obtained in their work only for appropriate scientific or professional purposes and only with persons clearly concerned with such matters.

4.05 Disclosures

(a) Psychologists may disclose confidential information with the appropriate consent of the organizational client, the individual client/patient, or another legally authorized person on behalf of the client/patient unless prohibited by law.

(b) Psychologists disclose confidential information without the consent of the individual only as mandated by law, or where permitted by law for a valid purpose such as to (1) provide needed professional services; (2) obtain appropriate professional consultations; (3) protect the client/patient, psychologist, or others from harm; or (4) obtain payment for services from a client/patient, in which instance disclosure is limited to the minimum that is necessary to achieve the purpose. (See also Standard 6.04e, Fees and Financial Arrangements.)

4.06 Consultations

When consulting with colleagues, (1) psychologists do not disclose confidential information that reasonably could lead to the identification of a client/patient, research participant, or other person or organization with whom they have a confidential relationship unless they have obtained the prior consent of the person or organization or the disclosure cannot be avoided, and (2) they disclose information only to the extent necessary to achieve the purposes of the consultation. (See also Standard 4.01, Maintaining Confidentiality.)

4.07 Use of Confidential Information for Didactic or Other Purposes

Psychologists do not disclose in their writings, lectures, or other public media, confidential, personally identifiable information concerning their clients/patients, students, research participants, organizational clients, or other recipients of their services that they obtained during the course of their work, unless (1) they take reasonable steps to disguise the person or organization, (2) the person or organization has consented in writing, or (3) there is legal authorization for doing so.

5. Advertising and Other Public Statements

5.01 Avoidance of False or Deceptive Statements
(a) Public statements include but are not limited to paid or unpaid advertising, product endorsements, grant applications, licensing applications, other credentialing applications, brochures, printed matter, directory listings, personal resumes or curricula vitae, or comments for use in media such as print or electronic transmission, statements in legal proceedings, lectures and public oral presentations, and published materials. Psychologists do not knowingly make public statements that are false, deceptive, or fraudulent concerning their research, practice, or other work activities or those of persons or organizations with which they are affiliated.

(b) Psychologists do not make false, deceptive, or fraudulent statements concerning (1) their training, experience, or competence; (2) their academic degrees; (3) their credentials; (4) their institutional or association affiliations; (5) their services; (6) the scientific or clinical basis for, or results or degree of success of, their services; (7) their fees; or (8) their publications or research findings.

(c) Psychologists claim degrees as credentials for their health services only if those degrees (1) were earned from a regionally accredited educational institution or (2) were the basis for psychology licensure by the state in which they practice.

5.02 Statements by Others
(a) Psychologists who engage others to create or place public statements that promote their professional practice, products, or activities retain professional responsibility for such statements.

(b) Psychologists do not compensate employees of press, radio, television, or other communication media in return for publicity in a news item. (See also Standard 1.01, Misuse of Psychologists' Work.)

(c) A paid advertisement relating to psychologists' activities must be identified or clearly recognizable as such.

5.03 Descriptions of Workshops and Non-Degree-Granting Educational Programs
To the degree to which they exercise control, psychologists responsible for announcements, catalogs, brochures, or advertisements describing workshops, seminars, or other non-degree-granting educational programs ensure that they accurately describe the audience for which the program is intended, the educational objectives, the presenters, and the fees involved.

5.04 Media Presentations
When psychologists provide public advice or comment via print, internet, or other electronic transmission, they take precautions to ensure that statements (1) are based on their professional knowledge, training, or experience in accord with appropriate psychological literature and practice; (2) are otherwise consistent with this Ethics Code; and (3) do not indicate that a professional relationship has been established with the recipient. (See also Standard 2.04, Bases for Scientific and Professional Judgments.)

5.05 Testimonials
Psychologists do not solicit testimonials from current therapy clients/patients or other persons who because of their particular circumstances are vulnerable to undue influence.

5.06 In-Person Solicitation
Psychologists do not engage, directly or through agents, in uninvited in-person solicitation of business from actual or potential therapy clients/patients or other persons who because of their particular circumstances are vulnerable to undue influence. However, this prohibition does not preclude (1) attempting to implement appropriate collateral contacts for the purpose of benefiting an already engaged therapy client/patient or (2) providing disaster or community outreach services.

6. Record Keeping and Fees

6.01 Documentation of Professional and Scientific Work and Maintenance of Records
Psychologists create, and to the extent the records are under their control, maintain, disseminate, store, retain, and dispose of records and data relating to their professional and scientific work in order to (1) facilitate provision of services later by them or by other professionals, (2) allow for replication of research design and analyses, (3) meet institutional requirements, (4) ensure accuracy of billing and payments, and (5) ensure compliance with law. (See also Standard 4.01, Maintaining Confidentiality.)

6.02 Maintenance, Dissemination, and Disposal of Confidential Records of Professional and Scientific Work
(a) Psychologists maintain confidentiality in creating, storing, accessing, transferring, and disposing of records

under their control, whether these are written, automated, or in any other medium. (See also Standards 4.01, Maintaining Confidentiality, and 6.01, Documentation of Professional and Scientific Work and Maintenance of Records.)

(b) If confidential information concerning recipients of psychological services is entered into databases or systems of records available to persons whose access has not been consented to by the recipient, psychologists use coding or other techniques to avoid the inclusion of personal identifiers.

(c) Psychologists make plans in advance to facilitate the appropriate transfer and to protect the confidentiality of records and data in the event of psychologists' withdrawal from positions or practice. (See also Standards 3.12, Interruption of Psychological Services, and 10.09, Interruption of Therapy.)

6.03 Withholding Records for Nonpayment
Psychologists may not withhold records under their control that are requested and needed for a client's/patient's emergency treatment solely because payment has not been received.

6.04 Fees and Financial Arrangements
(a) As early as is feasible in a professional or scientific relationship, psychologists and recipients of psychological services reach an agreement specifying compensation and billing arrangements.

(b) Psychologists' fee practices are consistent with law.

(c) Psychologists do not misrepresent their fees.

(d) If limitations to services can be anticipated because of limitations in financing, this is discussed with the recipient of services as early as is feasible. (See also Standards 10.09, Interruption of Therapy, and 10.10, Terminating Therapy.)

(e) If the recipient of services does not pay for services as agreed, and if psychologists intend to use collection agencies or legal measures to collect the fees, psychologists first inform the person that such measures will be taken and provide that person an opportunity to make prompt payment. (See also Standards 4.05, Disclosures; 6.03, Withholding Records for Nonpayment; and 10.01, Informed Consent to Therapy.)

6.05 Barter With Clients/Patients
Barter is the acceptance of goods, services, or other nonmonetary remuneration from clients/patients in return for psychological services. Psychologists may barter only if (1) it is not clinically contraindicated,

and (2) the resulting arrangement is not exploitative. (See also Standards 3.05, Multiple Relationships, and 6.04, Fees and Financial Arrangements.)

6.06 Accuracy in Reports to Payors and Funding Sources
In their reports to payors for services or sources of research funding, psychologists take reasonable steps to ensure the accurate reporting of the nature of the service provided or research conducted, the fees, charges, or payments, and where applicable, the identity of the provider, the findings, and the diagnosis. (See also Standards 4.01, Maintaining Confidentiality; 4.04, Minimizing Intrusions on Privacy; and 4.05, Disclosures.)

6.07 Referrals and Fees
When psychologists pay, receive payment from, or divide fees with another professional, other than in an employer-employee relationship, the payment to each is based on the services provided (clinical, consultative, administrative, or other) and is not based on the referral itself. (See also Standard 3.09, Cooperation With Other Professionals.)

7. Education and Training

7.01 Design of Education and Training Programs
Psychologists responsible for education and training programs take reasonable steps to ensure that the programs are designed to provide the appropriate knowledge and proper experiences, and to meet the requirements for licensure, certification, or other goals for which claims are made by the program. (See also Standard 5.03, Descriptions of Workshops and Non-Degree-Granting Educational Programs.)

7.02 Descriptions of Education and Training Programs
Psychologists responsible for education and training programs take reasonable steps to ensure that there is a current and accurate description of the program content (including participation in required course- or program-related counseling, psychotherapy, experiential groups, consulting projects, or community service), training goals and objectives, stipends and benefits, and requirements that must be met for satisfactory completion of the program. This information must be made readily available to all interested parties.

7.03 Accuracy in Teaching
(a) Psychologists take reasonable steps to ensure that course syllabi are accurate regarding the subject matter to be covered, bases for evaluating progress, and

the nature of course experiences. This standard does not preclude an instructor from modifying course content or requirements when the instructor considers it pedagogically necessary or desirable, so long as students are made aware of these modifications in a manner that enables them to fulfill course requirements. (See also Standard 5.01, Avoidance of False or Deceptive Statements.)

(b) When engaged in teaching or training, psychologists present psychological information accurately. (See also Standard 2.03, Maintaining Competence.)

7.04 Student Disclosure of Personal Information
Psychologists do not require students or supervisees to disclose personal information in course- or program-related activities, either orally or in writing, regarding sexual history, history of abuse and neglect, psychological treatment, and relationships with parents, peers, and spouses or significant others except if (1) the program or training facility has clearly identified this requirement in its admissions and program materials or (2) the information is necessary to evaluate or obtain assistance for students whose personal problems could reasonably be judged to be preventing them from performing their training- or professionally related activities in a competent manner or posing a threat to the students or others.

7.05 Mandatory Individual or Group Therapy
(a) When individual or group therapy is a program or course requirement, psychologists responsible for that program allow students in undergraduate and graduate programs the option of selecting such therapy from practitioners unaffiliated with the program. (See also Standard 7.02, Descriptions of Education and Training Programs.)

(b) Faculty who are or are likely to be responsible for evaluating students' academic performance do not themselves provide that therapy. (See also Standard 3.05, Multiple Relationships.)

7.06 Assessing Student and Supervisee Performance
(a) In academic and supervisory relationships, psychologists establish a timely and specific process for providing feedback to students and supervisees. Information regarding the process is provided to the student at the beginning of supervision.

(b) Psychologists evaluate students and supervisees on the basis of their actual performance on relevant and established program requirements.

7.07 Sexual Relationships With Students and Supervisees
Psychologists do not engage in sexual relationships with students or supervisees who are in their department, agency, or training center or over whom psychologists have or are likely to have evaluative authority. (See also Standard 3.05, Multiple Relationships.)

8. Research and Publication

8.01 Institutional Approval
When institutional approval is required, psychologists provide accurate information about their research proposals and obtain approval prior to conducting the research. They conduct the research in accordance with the approved research protocol.

8.02 Informed Consent to Research
(a) When obtaining informed consent as required in Standard 3.10, Informed Consent, psychologists inform participants about (1) the purpose of the research, expected duration, and procedures; (2) their right to decline to participate and to withdraw from the research once participation has begun; (3) the foreseeable consequences of declining or withdrawing; (4) reasonably foreseeable factors that may be expected to influence their willingness to participate such as potential risks, discomfort, or adverse effects; (5) any prospective research benefits; (6) limits of confidentiality; (7) incentives for participation; and (8) whom to contact for questions about the research and research participants' rights. They provide opportunity for the prospective participants to ask questions and receive answers. (See also Standards 8.03, Informed Consent for Recording Voices and Images in Research; 8.05, Dispensing With Informed Consent for Research; and 8.07, Deception in Research.)

(b) Psychologists conducting intervention research involving the use of experimental treatments clarify to participants at the outset of the research (1) the experimental nature of the treatment; (2) the services that will or will not be available to the control group(s) if appropriate; (3) the means by which assignment to treatment and control groups will be made; (4) available treatment alternatives if an individual does not wish to participate in the research or wishes to withdraw once a study has begun; and (5) compensation for or monetary costs of participating including, if appropriate, whether reimbursement from the participant or a third-party payor will be sought. (See also Standard 8.02a, Informed Consent to Research.)

8.03 Informed Consent for Recording Voices and Images in Research

Psychologists obtain informed consent from research participants prior to recording their voices or images for data collection unless (1) the research consists solely of naturalistic observations in public places, and it is not anticipated that the recording will be used in a manner that could cause personal identification or harm, or (2) the research design includes deception, and consent for the use of the recording is obtained during debriefing. (See also Standard 8.07, Deception in Research.)

8.04 Client/Patient, Student, and Subordinate Research Participants

(a) When psychologists conduct research with clients/patients, students, or subordinates as participants, psychologists take steps to protect the prospective participants from adverse consequences of declining or withdrawing from participation.

(b) When research participation is a course requirement or an opportunity for extra credit, the prospective participant is given the choice of equitable alternative activities.

8.05 Dispensing With Informed Consent for Research

Psychologists may dispense with informed consent only (1) where research would not reasonably be assumed to create distress or harm and involves (a) the study of normal educational practices, curricula, or classroom management methods conducted in educational settings; (b) only anonymous questionnaires, naturalistic observations, or archival research for which disclosure of responses would not place participants at risk of criminal or civil liability or damage their financial standing, employability, or reputation, and confidentiality is protected; or (c) the study of factors related to job or organization effectiveness conducted in organizational settings for which there is no risk to participants' employability, and confidentiality is protected or (2) where otherwise permitted by law or federal or institutional regulations.

8.06 Offering Inducements for Research Participation

(a) Psychologists make reasonable efforts to avoid offering excessive or inappropriate financial or other inducements for research participation when such inducements are likely to coerce participation.

(b) When offering professional services as an inducement for research participation, psychologists clarify the nature of the services, as well as the risks, obligations, and limitations. (See also Standard 6.05, Barter With Clients/Patients.)

8.07 Deception in Research

(a) Psychologists do not conduct a study involving deception unless they have determined that the use of deceptive techniques is justified by the study's significant prospective scientific, educational, or applied value and that effective nondeceptive alternative procedures are not feasible.

(b) Psychologists do not deceive prospective participants about research that is reasonably expected to cause physical pain or severe emotional distress.

(c) Psychologists explain any deception that is an integral feature of the design and conduct of an experiment to participants as early as is feasible, preferably at the conclusion of their participation, but no later than at the conclusion of the data collection, and permit participants to withdraw their data. (See also Standard 8.08, Debriefing.)

8.08 Debriefing

(a) Psychologists provide a prompt opportunity for participants to obtain appropriate information about the nature, results, and conclusions of the research, and they take reasonable steps to correct any misconceptions that participants may have of which the psychologists are aware.

(b) If scientific or humane values justify delaying or withholding this information, psychologists take reasonable measures to reduce the risk of harm.

(c) When psychologists become aware that research procedures have harmed a participant, they take reasonable steps to minimize the harm.

8.09 Humane Care and Use of Animals in Research

(a) Psychologists acquire, care for, use, and dispose of animals in compliance with current federal, state, and local laws and regulations, and with professional standards.

(b) Psychologists trained in research methods and experienced in the care of laboratory animals supervise all procedures involving animals and are responsible for ensuring appropriate consideration of their comfort, health, and humane treatment.

(c) Psychologists ensure that all individuals under their supervision who are using animals have received instruction in research methods and in the care, maintenance, and handling of the species being used, to the extent appropriate to their role. (See also Standard 2.05, Delegation of Work to Others.)

(d) Psychologists make reasonable efforts to minimize the discomfort, infection, illness, and pain of animal subjects.

(e) Psychologists use a procedure subjecting animals to pain, stress, or privation only when an alternative procedure is unavailable and the goal is justified by its prospective scientific, educational, or applied value.

(f) Psychologists perform surgical procedures under appropriate anesthesia and follow techniques to avoid infection and minimize pain during and after surgery.

(g) When it is appropriate that an animal's life be terminated, psychologists proceed rapidly, with an effort to minimize pain and in accordance with accepted procedures.

8.10 Reporting Research Results

(a) Psychologists do not fabricate data. (See also Standard 5.01a, Avoidance of False or Deceptive Statements.)

(b) If psychologists discover significant errors in their published data, they take reasonable steps to correct such errors in a correction, retraction, erratum, or other appropriate publication means.

8.11 Plagiarism

Psychologists do not present portions of another's work or data as their own, even if the other work or data source is cited occasionally.

8.12 Publication Credit

(a) Psychologists take responsibility and credit, including authorship credit, only for work they have actually performed or to which they have substantially contributed. (See also Standard 8.12b, Publication Credit.)

(b) Principal authorship and other publication credits accurately reflect the relative scientific or professional contributions of the individuals involved, regardless of their relative status. Mere possession of an institutional position, such as department chair, does not justify authorship credit. Minor contributions to the research or to the writing for publications are acknowledged appropriately, such as in footnotes or in an introductory statement.

(c) Except under exceptional circumstances, a student is listed as principal author on any multiple-authored article that is substantially based on the student's doctoral dissertation. Faculty advisors discuss publication credit with students as early as feasible and throughout the research and publication process as appropriate. (See also Standard 8.12b, Publication Credit.)

8.13 Duplicate Publication of Data

Psychologists do not publish, as original data, data that have been previously published. This does not preclude republishing data when they are accompanied by proper acknowledgment.

8.14 Sharing Research Data for Verification

(a) After research results are published, psychologists do not withhold the data on which their conclusions are based from other competent professionals who seek to verify the substantive claims through reanalysis and who intend to use such data only for that purpose, provided that the confidentiality of the participants can be protected and unless legal rights concerning proprietary data preclude their release. This does not preclude psychologists from requiring that such individuals or groups be responsible for costs associated with the provision of such information.

(b) Psychologists who request data from other psychologists to verify the substantive claims through re-analysis may use shared data only for the declared purpose. Requesting psychologists obtain prior written agreement for all other uses of the data.

8.15 Reviewers

Psychologists who review material submitted for presentation, publication, grant, or research proposal review respect the confidentiality of and the proprietary rights in such information of those who submitted it.

9. Assessment

9.01 Bases for Assessments

(a) Psychologists base the opinions contained in their recommendations, reports, and diagnostic or evaluative statements, including forensic testimony, on information and techniques sufficient to substantiate their findings. (See also Standard 2.04, Bases for Scientific and Professional Judgments.)

(b) Except as noted in 9.01c, psychologists provide opinions of the psychological characteristics of individuals only after they have conducted an examination of the individuals adequate to support their statements or conclusions. When, despite reasonable efforts, such an examination is not practical, psychologists document the efforts they made and the result of those efforts, clarify the probable impact of their limited information on the reliability and validity of their opinions, and appropriately limit the nature and extent of their conclusions or recommendations. (See also Standards 2.01, Boundaries of Competence, and 9.06, Interpreting Assessment Results.)

(c) When psychologists conduct a record review or provide consultation or supervision and an individual examination is not warranted or necessary for the opinion, psychologists explain this and the sources of information on which they based their conclusions and recommendations.

9.02 Use of Assessments

(a) Psychologists administer, adapt, score, interpret, or use assessment techniques, interviews, tests, or instruments in a manner and for purposes that are appropriate in light of the research on or evidence of the usefulness and proper application of the techniques.

(b) Psychologists use assessment instruments whose validity and reliability have been established for use with members of the population tested. When such validity or reliability has not been established, psychologists describe the strengths and limitations of test results and interpretation.

(c) Psychologists use assessment methods that are appropriate to an individual's language preference and competence, unless the use of an alternative language is relevant to the assessment issues.

9.03 Informed Consent in Assessments

(a) Psychologists obtain informed consent for assessments, evaluations, or diagnostic services, as described in Standard 3.10, Informed Consent, except when (1) testing is mandated by law or governmental regulations; (2) informed consent is implied because testing is conducted as a routine educational, institutional, or organizational activity (e.g., when participants voluntarily agree to assessment when applying for a job); or (3) one purpose of the testing is to evaluate decisional capacity. Informed consent includes an explanation of the nature and purpose of the assessment, fees, involvement of third parties, and limits of confidentiality and sufficient opportunity for the client/patient to ask questions and receive answers.

(b) Psychologists inform persons with questionable capacity to consent or for whom testing is mandated by law or governmental regulations about the nature and purpose of the proposed assessment services, using language that is reasonably understandable to the person being assessed.

(c) Psychologists using the services of an interpreter obtain informed consent from the client/patient to use that interpreter, ensure that confidentiality of test results and test security are maintained, and include in their recommendations, reports, and diagnostic or evaluative statements, including forensic testimony, discussion of any limitations on the data obtained. (See also Standards 2.05, Delegation of Work to Others; 4.01, Maintaining Confidentiality; 9.01, Bases for Assessments; 9.06, Interpreting Assessment Results; and 9.07, Assessment by Unqualified Persons.)

9.04 Release of Test Data

(a) The term test data refers to raw and scaled scores, client/patient responses to test questions or stimuli, and psychologists' notes and recordings concerning client/patient statements and behavior during an examination. Those portions of test materials that include client/patient responses are included in the definition of test data. Pursuant to a client/patient release, psychologists provide test data to the client/patient or other persons identified in the release. Psychologists may refrain from releasing test data to protect a client/patient or others from substantial harm or misuse or misrepresentation of the data or the test, recognizing that in many instances release of confidential information under these circumstances is regulated by law. (See also Standard 9.11, Maintaining Test Security.)

(b) In the absence of a client/patient release, psychologists provide test data only as required by law or court order.

9.05 Test Construction

Psychologists who develop tests and other assessment techniques use appropriate psychometric procedures and current scientific or professional knowledge for test design, standardization, validation, reduction or elimination of bias, and recommendations for use.

9.06 Interpreting Assessment Results

When interpreting assessment results, including automated interpretations, psychologists take into account the purpose of the assessment as well as the various test factors, test-taking abilities, and other characteristics of the person being assessed, such as situational, personal, linguistic, and cultural differences, that might affect psychologists' judgments or reduce the accuracy of their interpretations. They indicate any significant limitations of their interpretations. (See also Standards 2.01b and c, Boundaries of Competence, and 3.01, Unfair Discrimination.)

9.07 Assessment by Unqualified Persons

Psychologists do not promote the use of psychological assessment techniques by unqualified persons, except when such use is conducted for training purposes with appropriate supervision. (See also Standard 2.05, Delegation of Work to Others.)

9.08 Obsolete Tests and Outdated Test Results

(a) Psychologists do not base their assessment or intervention decisions or recommendations on data or test results that are outdated for the current purpose.

(b) Psychologists do not base such decisions or recommendations on tests and measures that are obsolete and not useful for the current purpose.

9.09 Test Scoring and Interpretation Services

(a) Psychologists who offer assessment or scoring services to other professionals accurately describe the purpose, norms, validity, reliability, and applications of the procedures and any special qualifications applicable to their use.

(b) Psychologists select scoring and interpretation services (including automated services) on the basis of evidence of the validity of the program and procedures as well as on other appropriate considerations. (See also Standard 2.01b and c, Boundaries of Competence.)

(c) Psychologists retain responsibility for the appropriate application, interpretation, and use of assessment instruments, whether they score and interpret such tests themselves or use automated or other services.

9.10 Explaining Assessment Results

Regardless of whether the scoring and interpretation are done by psychologists, by employees or assistants, or by automated or other outside services, psychologists take reasonable steps to ensure that explanations of results are given to the individual or designated representative unless the nature of the relationship precludes provision of an explanation of results (such as in some organizational consulting, preemployment

or security screenings, and forensic evaluations), and this fact has been clearly explained to the person being assessed in advance.

9.11. Maintaining Test Security

The term test materials refers to manuals, instruments, protocols, and test questions or stimuli and does not include test data as defined in Standard 9.04, Release of Test Data. Psychologists make reasonable efforts to maintain the integrity and security of test materials and other assessment techniques consistent with law and contractual obligations, and in a manner that permits adherence to this Ethics Code.

10. Therapy

10.01 Informed Consent to Therapy

(a) When obtaining informed consent to therapy as required in Standard 3.10, Informed Consent, psychologists inform clients/patients as early as is feasible in the therapeutic relationship about the nature and anticipated course of therapy, fees, involvement of third parties, and limits of confidentiality and provide sufficient opportunity for the client/patient to ask questions and receive answers. (See also Standards 4.02, Discussing the Limits of Confidentiality, and 6.04, Fees and Financial Arrangements.)

(b) When obtaining informed consent for treatment for which generally recognized techniques and procedures have not been established, psychologists inform their clients/patients of the developing nature of the treatment, the potential risks involved, alternative treatments that may be available, and the voluntary nature of their participation. (See also Standards 2.01e, Boundaries of Competence, and 3.10, Informed Consent.)

(c) When the therapist is a trainee and the legal responsibility for the treatment provided resides with the supervisor, the client/patient, as part of the informed consent procedure, is informed that the therapist is in training and is being supervised and is given the name of the supervisor.

10.02 Therapy Involving Couples or Families

(a) When psychologists agree to provide services to several persons who have a relationship (such as spouses, significant others, or parents and children), they take reasonable steps to clarify at the outset (1) which of the individuals are clients/patients and (2) the relationship the psychologist will have with each person. This clarification includes the psychologist's role and the probable uses of the services provided or the information obtained. (See also Standard 4.02, Discussing the Limits of Confidentiality.)

(b) If it becomes apparent that psychologists may be called on to perform potentially conflicting roles (such as family therapist and then witness for one party in divorce proceedings), psychologists take reasonable steps to clarify and modify, or withdraw from, roles appropriately. (See also Standard 3.05c, Multiple Relationships.)

10.03 Group Therapy

When psychologists provide services to several persons in a group setting, they describe at the outset the roles and responsibilities of all parties and the limits of confidentiality.

10.04 Providing Therapy to Those Served by Others

In deciding whether to offer or provide services to those already receiving mental health services elsewhere, psychologists carefully consider the treatment issues and the potential client's/patient's welfare. Psychologists discuss these issues with the client/patient or another legally authorized person on behalf of the client/patient in order to minimize the risk of confusion and conflict, consult with the other service providers when appropriate, and proceed with caution and sensitivity to the therapeutic issues.

10.05 Sexual Intimacies With Current Therapy Clients/Patients

Psychologists do not engage in sexual intimacies with current therapy clients/patients.

10.06 Sexual Intimacies With Relatives or Significant Others of Current Therapy Clients/Patients

Psychologists do not engage in sexual intimacies with individuals they know to be close relatives, guardians, or significant others of current clients/patients. Psychologists do not terminate therapy to circumvent this standard.

10.07 Therapy With Former Sexual Partners

Psychologists do not accept as therapy clients/patients persons with whom they have engaged in sexual intimacies.

10.08 Sexual Intimacies With Former Therapy Clients/Patients

(a) Psychologists do not engage in sexual intimacies with former clients/patients for at least two years after cessation or termination of therapy.

(b) Psychologists do not engage in sexual intimacies with former clients/patients even after a two-year interval except in the most unusual circumstances. Psychologists who engage in such activity after the two years following cessation or termination of therapy and of having no sexual contact with the former client/patient bear the burden of demonstrating that there has been no exploitation, in light of all relevant factors, including (1) the amount of time that has passed since therapy terminated; (2) the nature, duration, and intensity of the therapy; (3) the circumstances of termination; (4) the client's/patient's personal history; (5) the client's/patient's current mental status; (6) the likelihood of adverse impact on the client/patient; and (7) any statements or actions made by the therapist during the course of therapy suggesting or inviting the possibility of a posttermination sexual or romantic relationship with the client/patient. (See also Standard 3.05, Multiple Relationships.)

10.09 Interruption of Therapy

When entering into employment or contractual relationships, psychologists make reasonable efforts to provide for orderly and appropriate resolution of responsibility for client/patient care in the event that the employment or contractual relationship ends, with paramount consideration given to the welfare of the client/patient. (See also Standard 3.12, Interruption of Psychological Services.)

10.10 Terminating Therapy

(a) Psychologists terminate therapy when it becomes reasonably clear that the client/patient no longer needs the service, is not likely to benefit, or is being harmed by continued service.

(b) Psychologists may terminate therapy when threatened or otherwise endangered by the client/patient or another person with whom the client/patient has a relationship.

(c) Except where precluded by the actions of clients/patients or third-party payors, prior to termination psychologists provide pretermination counseling and suggest alternative service providers as appropriate.

List of Specialized Ethics Codes and Guidelines in Mental Health Disciplines

American Association for Marriage and Family Therapy. (2001). *Code of ethics.* Washington, DC: Author. Retrieved March 9, 2005, from http://www.aamft.org/resources/LRMPlan/Ethics/ethicscode2001.asp

American Association of Sex Educators, Counselors and Therapists. (2004). *Code of ethics of sex educators, counselors and therapists.* Chicago: Author. Retrieved August 1, 2005, from http://www.aasect.org/codeofethics.asp

American College Personnel Association. (1992). *Statement of ethical principles and standards.* Retrieved July 11, 2005, from http://www.myacpa.org/au/au_ethical1.cfm

American Counseling Association. (1999a). *Ethical standards for Internet on-line counseling.* Alexandria, VA: Author. Retrieved August 1, 2005, from http://www.counseling.org/gc/cybertx.htm

American Counseling Association. (1999b). *The layperson's guide to counselor ethics: What you should know about the ethical practice of professional counselors.* Alexandria, VA: Author.

American Group Psychotherapy Association. (2002). *AGPA and NRCGP guidelines for ethics.* Retrieved July 11, 2005, from http://www.groupsinc.org/group/ethicalguide.html

American Mental Health Counselors Association. (2000). *Code of ethics for mental health counselors.* Alexandria, VA: Author. Retrieved August 2, 2005, from http://www.amhca.org/about2.html#

American Psychiatric Association. (1999). *Statement on psychotherapy and managed care.* Retrieved July 11, 2005, from http://www.psych.org/edu/other_res/lib_archives/archives/199902.pdf

American Psychiatric Association. (2001). *Principles of medical ethics with annotations especially applicable to psychiatry.* Washington, DC: Author. Retrieved July 11, 2005, from http://www.psych.org/psych_pract/ethics/ppaethics.cfm

American Psychological Association. (1981). *Specialty guidelines for the delivery of services: Clinical psychologists, counseling psychologists, organizational/industrial psychologists, school psychologists.* Washington, DC: Author.

American Psychological Association. (1986). *Guidelines for computer-based tests and interpretations.* Washington, DC: Author.

American Psychological Association. (1993a). *Guidelines for ethical conduct in the care and use of animals.* Washington, DC: Author. Retrieved August 2, 2005, from http://www.apa.org/science/anguide.html

American Psychological Association. (1993b). *Guidelines for providers of psychological services to ethnic, linguistic and culturally diverse populations.* Washington, DC: Author.

American Psychological Association. (1993c). *Record keeping guidelines.* Washington, DC: Author.

American Psychological Association. (1994). Guidelines for child custody evaluations in divorce proceedings. *American Psychologist, 49,* 677–680.

American Psychological Association. (1997). *Mental health patient's bill of rights.* Retrieved September 18, 2005, from http://www.apa.org/pubinfo/rights/rights.html

American Psychological Association. (1997). *Resolution on appropriate therapeutic responses to sexual orientation.* Retrieved July 11, 2005, from http://www.apa.org/pi/sexual.html

American Psychological Association. (1997). *What practitioners should know about working with older adults.* Retrieved July 11, 2005, from http://www.apa.org/pi/aging/practitioners.pdf

American Psychological Association. (1999). *Suggestions for psychologists working with the media.* Washington, DC: Author.

American Psychological Association. (2003). *Guidelines for psychotherapy with lesbian, gay, and bisexual clients.* Retrieved July 11, 2005, from http://www.apa.orb/pi/lgbc/guidelines.html

American Psychological Association. (2004). Guidelines for psychological practice with older adults. *American Psychologist, 59,* 236–260.

American Psychological Association Board of Professional Affairs. (1999). Guidelines for psychological evaluations in child protection matters. *American Psychologist, 54,* 586–593.

American Psychological Association, Committee on Legal Issues. (1996). Strategies for private practitioners coping with subpoenas or compelled testimony for client records or test data. *Professional Psychology: Research and Practice, 27,* 245–251.

American Psychological Association, Committee on Professional Practice and Standards. (1995). Twenty-four questions (and answers) about professional practice in the area of child abuse. *Professional Psychology: Research and Practice, 26,* 377–383.

American Psychological Association, Committee on Professional Practice and Standards. (1994). Guidelines for child custody evaluations in divorce proceedings. *American Psychologist, 49,* 677–680.

American Psychological Association, Committee on Psychological Testing and Assessment. (1996). Statement on the disclosure of test data. *American Psychologist, 51,* 644–648.

American Psychological Association, Committee on Women in Psychology. (1989). If sex enters into the psychotherapy relationship. *Professional Psychology: Research and Practice, 20,* 112–115.

American Psychological Association, Division 44/Committee on Lesbian, Gay and Bisexual Concerns Joint Task Force. (2001). Guidelines for psychotherapy with lesbian, gay and bisexual clients. *American Psychologist, 55,* 1440–1451.

American School Counselor Association. (2004). *Ethical standards for school counselors.* Alexandria, VA: Author. Retrieved August 1, 2005, from http://www.schoolcounselor.org/content.asp?contentid=173

Association for Counselor Education and Supervision. (1990). Standards for counseling supervisors. *Journal of Counseling and Development, 69,* 30–32.

Association for Counselor Education and Supervision. (1993). Ethical guidelines for counseling supervisors. *Counselor Education and Supervision, 34,* 270–276.

Association for Counselor Education and Supervision. (1999). *Guidelines for online instruction in counselor education.* Alexandria, VA: Author.

Association for Specialists in Group Work. (1998a). *Best practice guidelines.* Retrieved September 18, 2005, from http://www.asgw.educ.kent/diversity.htm

Association for Specialists in Group Work. (1998b). *Principles for diversity-competent group workers.* Retrieved September 18, 2005, from http://www. asgw.educ. kent/diversity.htm

Association for Specialists in Group Work. (2000). *Professional standards for the training of group workers.* Retrieved September 18, 2005, from http://www. asgw.educ.kent/diversity.htm

Association of State and Provincial Psychology Boards. (2003). *ASPPB supervision guidelines.* Retrieved July 11, 2005, from http://asppb.org/publications/pdf/SupervisionGuidelines.pdf

Association of State and Provincial Psychology Boards. (2005). *ASPPB code of conduct.* Retrieved July 11, 2005, from http://asppb.org/publications/model/conduct.aspx

British Association for Counselling and Psychotherapy. (2001). *Ethical framework for good practice in counselling and psychotherapy.* Retrieved July 11, 2005, from http://www.bacp.co.uk/ethical_framework/

Canadian Psychological Association. (2000). *Canadian code of ethics for psychologists. Revised.* Ottawa, ON: Author. Retrieved August 2, 2005, from http://www.cpa.ca/ethics2000.html

Commission on Rehabilitation Counselor Certification. (2001). *Code of professional ethics for rehabilitation counselors.* Retrieved August 1, 2005, from http://www.crccertification.com/Code_0102_Updated_Format_0105.htm

Committee on Ethical Guidelines for Forensic Psychologists. (1991). Specialty guidelines for forensic psychologists. *Law and Human Behavior, 15,* 655–665.

International Association of Marriage and Family Counselors. (1993). *Ethical code for the International Association for Marriage and Family Counselors.* Alexandria, VA: Author. Retrieved August 2, 2005, from http://www.iamfc.com/ethical_codes.html

National Academy of Neuropsychology (1999). *Official position statement on test security.* Washington, DC: Author.

National Association of School Psychologists. (2000). *Principles for professional ethics.* Silver Spring, MD: Author. Retrieved July 11, 2005, from http://www.nasponline.org/pdf/ProfessionalCond.pdf

National Association of Social Workers. (1999). *Code of ethics.* Silver Spring, MD: Author. Retrieved July 11, 2005, from http://www.socialworkers.org/pubs/code/code.asp

National Board for Certified Counselors. (2001). *The practice of Internet counseling.* Washington, DC: Author. Retrieved July 11, 2005, from http://www.nbcc.org/webethics2

National Board for Certified Counselors. (2005). *National Board for Certified Counselors: Code of ethics.* Alexandria, VA: Author. Retrieved July 11, 2005, from http://www.nbcc.org/extras/pdfs/ethics/NBCC-CodeofEthics.pdf

National Career Development Association. (1997). *Career development competencies.* Retrieved July 11, 2005, from http://www.ncda.org/pdf/counselingcompetencies.pdf

National Career Development Association. (2003). *National Career Development Association ethical standards.* Alexandria, VA: Author. Retrieved July 11, 2005, from http://www.ncda.org/pdf/EthicalStandards.pdf

Author Index

Abbey-Hines, J., 85
Abbott, D. W., 7, 86
Abelson, R. P., 198
Ackerley, G. D., 58, 281
Acuff, C., 258
Adams, J. 314
Adelman, H. S., 13, 31, 90, 91, 116
Adelman, J., 166
Agresti, A. A., 79
Ahia, C. E., 66, 82, 84
Ahlstrand, K. R., 137, 138
Akamatsu, T. J., 131, 132
Alexander, C. M., 233
Alexander, K., 274
Alexander, M. D., 274
Allen, A., 96
Allen, G. J., 293, 294, 299, 301, 306
Altekruse, M., 83
Alyn, J. H., 142
Amada, G., 257
American Association of Marriage and Family Therapists, 49, 93, 124, 190, 192, 194, 195, 197, 200, 247
American Counseling Association, 6, 8, 9, 10, 11, 14, 15, 16, 17, 18, 28, 30, 49, 51, 54, 61, 70, 71, 75, 76, 77, 80, 81, 82, 87, 88, 90, 92, 108, 109, 111, 112, 117, 124, 131, 134, 135, 136, 139, 141, 158, 159, 172, 174, 189, 192, 193, 200, 202 203, 204, 205, 210, 211, 213, 215, 216, 223, 224, 225, 226, 241, 242, 246, 248, 249, 254, 255, 257, 260, 271, 288, 295, 296, 297, 298, 300, 301, 302, 304, 305, 313, 315, 316, 317, 318, 320, 322, 326, 328, 329, 330, 336, 337, 339, 341, 343, 345
American Educational Research Association (AERA), 202, 203, 212, 214
American Psychiatric Association, 123, 196, 202
American Psychological Association, 6, 8, 9, 10, 11, 13, 14, 17, 28, 30, 49, 51, 54, 61, 70, 71, 75, 76, 77, 80, 81, 82, 87, 88, 90, 92, 108, 109, 111, 112, 117, 124, 131, 134, 135, 136, 139, 141, 158, 159, 172, 174, 189, 192, 193, 200, 202, 203, 205, 206, 207, 208, 210, 212, 215, 223, 225, 226, 227, 240, 246, 247, 248, 249, 250, 254, 255, 257, 260, 263, 266, 267, 289, 296, 297, 302, 313, 315, 316, 317, 320, 322, 323, 324, 327, 329, 330, 336, 337, 340, 341, 343
American School Counselor Association, 27, 28, 182, 271, 273, 275, 276, 277, 279, 280, 285
Anastasi, A., 198, 200, 207, 209, 213, 214, 216
Ancis, J. R., 295
Anderson, A., 280
Anderson, B. S., 82, 251, 252, 278, 280, 282
Anderson, D. 343
Anderson, H. 197
Anderson, J. R., 85
Anderson, M. A., 327
Anderson, R., 291
Anderson, R. D., 322
Anderson, S., 119, 344
Anderson, S. A., 293, 294, 305
Anderson, S. K., 161, 162
Anderton, P., 265
Anonymous, 137
Antunez, M. 130
Appelbaum, P. S., 111, 180, 251, 260, 261
Arcinue, F., 294, 297
Arrendondo, P. M., 55, 209, 224, 226
Arthur, G. L., Jr., 180
Arthur, W., 217
Asnis, G. M. 198
Aspy, C. B., 286
Association for Counselor Education and Supervision, 226, 293, 295
Association for Multicultural Counseling and Development, 226
Association for Specialists in Group Work, 93, 176, 180, 181, 182, 184, 185, 188, 189, 194
Association of State and Provincial Psychology Boards, 295, 298
Association of Trial Lawyers of America, 78
Atkinson, D. R., 229

Subject Index